Institutional and Policy Dynamics of EU Migration Law

IMMIGRATION AND ASYLUM LAW AND POLICY IN EUROPE

Volume 10

Editors

Elspeth Guild
Kingsley Napley Solicitors, London,
Centre for Migration Law, Radboud University Nijmegen

Jan Niessen
Migration Policy Group, Brussels

The series is a venue for books on European immigration and asylum law and policies where academics, policy makers, law practitioners and others look to find detailed analysis of this dynamic field. Works in the series will start from a European perspective. The incresed co-operation within the European Union and the Council of Europe on matters related to immigration and asylum requires the publication of theoretical and empirical research. The series will contribute to well-informed policy debates by analysing and interpreting the evolving European legislation and its effects on national law and policies. The series brings together the various stakeholders in these policy debates: the legal profession, researchers, employers, trade unions, human rights and other civil society organisations.

The titles published in this series are listed at the end of this volume.

Institutional and Policy Dynamics of EU Migration Law

Georgia Papagianni

Martinus Nijhoff Publishers
Leiden • Boston

A C.I.P. Catalogue record for this book is available from the Library of Congress.

Printed on acid-free paper.

ISBN 10 90 04 15279 2

Koninklijke Brill NV incorporates the imprints Brill Academic Publishers, Martinus Nijhoff Publishers and VSP.

http://www.brill.nl

Printed and bound in The Netherlands.

Στους γονείς μου

Table of Contents

Preface

The tourist visiting Luxembourg – which together with Brussels and Strasbourg is one of the capitals of Europe – will, on his exploration of the town, have the occasion to come across the "spirit" of Robert Schuman, the founding father of Europe, born in the city of Luxembourg.

Besides the house where he was born, now occupied by a European institute, the visitor can find a monument built in memory of this French politician who stands, together with Jean Monnet, as one of the founders of the European idea. Between Robert Schuman Square and the bridge leading to the Kirchberg area, where all the European Institutions are located (Court of Justice, European Investment Bank, Commission Services, European Parliament and the meeting facilities for the Council of the European Union), our tourist will find a steel monument with the famous sentence taken from his speech of 9th May 1950: "*L'Europe ne se fera pas d'un coup, ni dans une construction d'ensemble, mais dans des réalisations concrètes créant des solidarités de fait.*"

In a French newspaper (Le Figaro, 09.03.2006), some days before drafting these introductory words, I read in an article entitled "European countries close their doors to immigration" that several Member States are on their way to introducing new trends in their policy concerning both legal immigration and the fight against illegal immigration.

Some, like Spain, have introduced quota systems, others, like Germany, concentrate on highly qualified workers and introduce measures to facilitate expulsions, whereas the Netherlands starts with its new policy concerning the integration of third country nationals (obligation to speak the language and to prove knowledge about the culture and the way of life in the country of destination). The need to fight terrorism has, on the other hand, increased the measures in favour of better security (at the borders, or by means of biometric passports, identity cards and visas). Nevertheless, illegal immigrants continue to move towards the European Union, and their increasing numbers create problems, especially for the first countries of entry into the European Union.

From time to time, a single Member State decides to "regularize" thousands and thousands of illegal immigrants living on its territory who are mainly black market workers; no coordination takes place at European level in view of such a decision.

It is my view that Robert Schuman's words apply perfectly to the situation concerning Europe's policy and achievements in the field of migration.

There are many reasons that would explain why the achievements in this field have been rather slow and to some extent modest.

First, one needs to explore the treaties and the way in which they have evolved. Neither the Rome Treaty nor the Single Act mentioned Justice and Home Affairs. It is only under the 1991 Maastricht Treaty that asylum, immigration and border security were put on the European agenda, as matters of common interest under the so-called "third pillar."

Much has been said and written about the weaknesses of the third pillar instruments. This book describes, in detail, the main problems arising from this situation. But those who criticize the mechanisms of the third pillar should bear in mind that in the Maastricht negotiations on the asylum / immigration issue, the choice was not between a first pillar and a third pillar solution but between a third pillar and a "no Union competence" solution. Let us also bear in mind that at this time – 1991 – the two Schengen instruments had already been adopted and that the "no Union competence" solution would have probably closed the European doors for a very long period.

It seems clear to me that the Maastricht rules on asylum and immigration paved the way for major improvements that were achieved under the Amsterdam Treaty which entered into force in 1999 and which was the beginning of a new area.

Very concrete objectives, a clear-cut timetable, a first move towards first pillar instruments, improved third pillar instruments and a better use of the Council structures allowed for substantial progress, even if the unanimity rule remained a serious handicap. In my view however, the most remarkable achievement was the Schengen integration into the framework of the Council.

Among the different possible solutions to harmonize the work between the Schengen area and the European Union, the Dutch Presidency insisted on the most difficult: the integration of the Schengen cooperation at the time of the entry into force of the Amsterdam Treaty. It was hard work to solve all the problems linked to this integration. However, thanks to the work of the Council Legal Service, solutions were found to solve all the problems, including those of developing the Schengen *acquis* as well as the relations with the Schengen – but not EU – Member States, Norway and Iceland.

I spent ten years at the head of the Directorate "Justice and Home Affairs" in the Council Secretariat starting early in 1994, in the aftermath of the entry of the Maastricht Treaty, and leaving in 2004. In my opinion, 1999 was the most successful year in that period as far as developments in Justice and Home Affairs are concerned.

I touched above on the improvements of the Amsterdam Treaty, which entered into force in May 1999. The second major event was the very successful European Council held under the Finnish Presidency in Tampere in October 1999. The Conclusions of this summit, known as the Tampere Milestones, indicated, in detail, the way forward and contained clear commitments from Heads of State and Governments, including in the field of migration policy. In reality, practice often shows that Heads of State are more dynamic than their "technical" ministers, not to mention the experts in all or some of the Member States.

Georgia Papagianni's book shows all this in a brilliant manner. It is not a frequent occurrence to meet an academic researcher who has actually experienced the day-to-day workings of the "European business". This is what makes this book so interesting.

It starts with a well-developed historical background, of which I particularly appreciated the in-depth information on the work of Schengen: in my experience so far no academic work has highlighted, so correctly, the major role played by the Schengen cooperation, especially in the field of immigration / frontiers.

This personal experience, especially during the Greek Presidency in 2003 where the author was a key player in the strong team led by Ambassador Mara Marinaki and chaired a very active Council working party on migration, makes it possible for the author to have a very keen knowledge of the decision-making process and the different actors involved in it. The very interesting Chapter 5 of the book opens the door wide and gives an insightful view into the work of the European Institutions: the Presidency, the Council Secretariat, the Commission and the European Parliament, who are the main actors of this game; their performances are not only described but also analysed without fear or favour.

How to evaluate the work done so far on migration matters? This brings us back to our starting point and to Robert Schuman's famous sentence. The results achieved may appear as poor, the work may be considered as piecemeal, and the fact that some Member States have specific opt-out type possibilities may appear as a weakness, but this seems to be the price to pay in order to make progress, step by step. Let us not forget that the Schengen experience started with five Member States, and that finally all of them will participate – with some exceptions – to this experience first described as a "*laboratoire d'essai.*"

Georgia Papagianni's first draft of this work was completed in July 2004, just after agreement had been reached under the Irish Presidency on the Constitutional Treaty. She comments briefly on the very important improvements which this Constitutional Treaty would provide. We now know that there might be a long way to go before this objective is reached.

Fortunately, some of the problems that stem from this "stand still" situation have been overcome thanks to a Council decision dated 22.12.04, making use of a possibility introduced by the Amsterdam Treaty under Article 67(2), second indent TEC. According to that decision, as from 1 May 2005, the co-decision procedure applies to most of the areas in the field of asylum and migration. This is a small but important step towards complete communitarisation and another element to confirm using the author's terms that the Rubicon line between intergovernmentalism and Community migration policy has been definitely crossed and that the unanimity rule, which is the biggest handicap for progress, has been abandoned.

There is no place for complacency. In the final concluding remarks Georgia Papagianni indicates briefly that the next steps could consist of the new exhaustive programme that was adopted at the European Council in Brussels on 4/5 November 2004 under the title "The Hague Programme: Strengthening freedom, security and justice in the European Union."

This Programme, later complemented by a detailed action plan, contains *inter alia* a request by the European Council to the Commission to present, before the end of 2005, an action plan on legal immigration. Such a plan was presented by the Commission on 23 December 2005.

Even if the European Council makes it clear that the volume of migrant workers is a competence of the Member States, there is nevertheless room for action. Let us hope that, in accordance with Robert Schuman's statement, the Council will make progress, step by step, with concrete achievements thus creating solidarity between the Member States.

Charles Elsen
Director General Honorary of the Council

Acknowledgements

The present book is the outcome of several years of both academic research and work experience in the area of Justice and Home Affairs under quite diverse capacities. My main objective has been to provide an overall account, which is up to date with extensive historical references and combines both an academic and practical perspective to the legal and political issues involved, in order to contribute to a new understanding of the main aspects of EU migration law and its policy ramifications.

A previous draft of this book has been submitted to the European University Institute (Florence, Italy) with a view to obtaining the degree of Doctor of Laws. I would like to express my sincere and deep gratitude first and foremost to my supervisor, Prof. Bruno de Witte, who has never ceased to encourage, guide and support me. I would also like to thank Prof. Gráinne de Búrca (EUI), Mr Charles Elsen (former Director of DG-H, CGS) and Prof. Takis Tridimas (Queen Mary/College of Europe) for the great honour of having them as members of my jury. And, last but not least, my sincere thanks to the EUI for granting me the possibility of conducting the present research under what should be considered as the ideal circumstances for completing a PhD.

The completion of the present research would not have been possible without the help and advice of certain persons. Though it is impossible to mention all those to whom I feel indebted individually, certain persons who were particularly helpful need to be named. First of all, Mr Jan de Ceuster (Head of Unit, Commission, DG-JHA) for sharing with me his Schengen expertise as well as for all his comments, ideas and advice during our long discussions all these years and Mr Martino Cossu (DG-H, Council Secretariat) who, apart from being an excellent colleague and great friend has devoted endless time to discuss with me most of the parts of this book. Many thanks go also to Prof. Steve Peers (University of Essex), Mr Gilbert El Kaim (JHA Counselor, French Permanent Representation) and Mr Friedrich Loeper (JHA Counselor, German Permanent Representation) for reading and commenting on parts of my work. I am further indebted to my colleagues in the C4 JHA Directorate of the Greek

MFA – in particular Amb. Mara Marinaki – and in the JHA Unit of the Greek Permanent Representation as well as to all the Commission, Council Secretariat and national delegates with whom I have had extensive discussions for all their time and help. It goes without saying that all errors and omissions are my sole responsibility.

On a more personal basis I would like to express my gratitude to my family for their endless and unconditional love and support as well as to my friends for standing by me.

General Introduction

Even if the formation of a common migration policy *per se* had not been initially included among the main objectives of European integration, the increasing salience of migration related matters within the framework of national politics as well as the linkages with other European objectives have progressively brought migration policy issues to the forefront of European politics. Over the course of the last three decades the European Union (EU) has taken a series of initiatives in this area, whereas migration related issues have also been among the main issues examined both at the Maastricht and Amsterdam Intergovernmental Conferences (IGC) as well as in the course of the last IGC.

The legislative and policy developments over the course of the last two decades have been spectacular. A Community competence, albeit not unlimited and still contested, has been established. The EU agenda was considerably amplified and the EU now aspires not only to regulate the mere entry and movement of third country nationals – as was the case within the Schengen framework, under the Single European Act or even up to the Maastricht era – but also to further establish a migration agenda in the classic sense of the term. Rules on the admission of third country nationals for long-stays, their rights and integration into host societies, the conditions concerning their residence in another Member State, external relations aspects and issues such as return policy and co-development are currently on the agenda.

Most likely, the globalisation of the migration phenomenon, the inevitable need to reinforce co-operation at the EU level as well as the direct impact on people's everyday lives will keep the issue at the top of the European agenda in the years to come. However, forging a migration policy at the EU level has proved, and still proves, to be a rather complex issue. The problems faced during the last decades have been numerous, while the number of obstacles to the formation of a common and comprehensive policy remain considerable.

The main objective of this book is to present this on-going process via a comprehensive analysis of the institutional dynamics of, and politics linked with, the emerging migration law and policy of the EU. It endeavours to provide a comprehensive study of the institutional framework, the substantive EC/EU law as well as the EU policy-making procedure regarding the formation of a common migration policy. More specifically it will present the historical evolution, the main legislative and policy steps, the position of, and interactions among, the different actors and the factors impeding the formation of a common policy. On this basis a critical analysis is provided of the main institutional problems, the current policy framework, the overarching rationale and the content and quality of the nascent EU migration law.

Given the fragmented character of the current legal framework as well as the vast number of issues that could fall under the scope of the concept of 'migration law' it is necessary for reasons of clarity to define the personal and material scope of the present work. The concept of 'migrant' *de jure* includes, and in the early stages of Community integration primarily referred to EU nationals and their family members moving to another Member State or to third country nationals falling within the scope of agreements between the Community and third States or moving as posted workers within the framework of an EU company providing services in another Member State. However, this book does not examine these categories because they are in principle regulated by special, and usually more favourable, arrangements. The present work will focus exclusively on the policy of the EU with regard to third country nationals that do not have any special links with the Community. Despite the deep and mainly practical linkages between asylum and migration policy, the case of refugees is also not examined in this work. The legal framework, the philosophy and the politics of these two categories are very different. Whereas the entry of immigrants is considered a sovereign right of the State, seeking asylum is a human right and the examination of an asylum application is an obligation for every State on the basis of international agreements. Moreover, while the approach with regard to asylum is mainly humanitarian, the emphasis in migration matters is put on economic considerations.

As far as the material scope is concerned this book will endeavour to present in a comprehensive manner the main aspects of EU migration policy. This includes the policy and legislative framework regarding the admission, movement and return of third country nationals as well as some issues of a more general, and mainly horizontal, character, such as operational co-operation, external relations and financing. Migration policy at the EU level is essentially based on a two-track approach. On the one hand, a sort of migration *stricto sensu* based on the Schengen rationale regulating issues of entry, movement and expulsion of third country nationals entering on a short-term basis. And, on the other hand, migration policy in the classic sense of the term concerning the admission, residence and return of third country nationals entering for long-term stays. Accordingly the analysis herein will cover both these sets of issues. It will examine both issues regarding border controls and visa policy as well as issues linked with the nascent and more general EU migration agenda. Moreover, considering that the impact of the Schengen heritage has been, and still remains, strong on European affairs – since the Schengen co-operation's scope and rationale coincides with that of what can be defined as migration *stricto sensu* – special emphasis will be placed on the Schengen *acquis*, its content and impact on the process of forging an EU migration policy.

The book is divided into three parts each of which contains two chapters. The first two parts will provide an analysis of the institutional structure and a brief presentation of the main legislative developments respectively. The third and final part will provide a more general analysis of the policy-making process. Since the major achievements in the field of migration are recent, the book will focus to a greater extent on the post-Amsterdam era. However for reasons of coherence and in order to better evaluate recent developments it is essential to have a clear picture of the origins of this policy. Accordingly the first chapter in parts one and two, chapters one and three respectively, will survey developments prior to the Amsterdam Treaty. The justification for choosing the Treaty of Amsterdam as the border line lies mainly in the fact that it constitutes in many respects a major dividing line between two different stages of policy-making.

The first part of the book is devoted to the *institutional* aspects governing the formation of a European migration policy. There, via a detailed presentation of the various Treaty and intergovernmental legal bases and the numerous competence skirmishes, it will be demonstrated that EU migration policy has traditionally been characterised by two interlinked phenomena: an intense competence debate and a situation which could be characterised as a legal 'limbo' between intergovernamentalism and the Community method. Special emphasis will be placed on the partial character of the communitarisation brought about by the Amsterdam Treaty. More specifically, a detailed analysis will be provided of the legal problems stemming from the opt-out Protocols of the UK, Ireland and Denmark and the special institutional characteristics of Title IV TEC, since these inevitably render the formation of a comprehensive policy an obstacle race.

The second part of the book will provide an overview of the implementation of the different Treaty provisions as well as a preliminary analysis of *substantive* migration law until now. In a first chapter, chapter three, devoted to the developments in the pre-Amsterdam era emphasis will be placed on the Schengen *acquis*. The reason is two-fold: first, because this is undoubtedly the most vital part of the pre-Amsterdam *acquis*, and second, because its importance remains focal, since following its incorporation into the EU framework it constitutes the main EU *acquis* with regard to visas, border and security issues. Indeed, the mark left by the Schengen regime on European affairs in this area is unquestionable. Even though the Schengen *acquis* has been 'renamed' and redefined as EU law in the post-Amsterdam era its influence on EU policy had been evident at a much earlier stage. It will be argued that the Maastricht era *acquis* had been deeply influenced by the Schengen approach and that the measures adopted therein to a large extent literally 'copied' Schengen measures.

Subsequently, chapter four will examine the implementation of the Amsterdam agenda, in which migration related issues were placed under the more general policy framework of an "area of freedom, security and justice". Following the structure of the policy proposals made by the European Council at the Tampere Summit, the so-called 'Tampere milestones', the chapter is subdivided into three separate sections in which the relevant legislative measures are presented. Firstly, 'management of migration flows', i.e. measures regarding visa policy, border controls and return policy. Secondly, 'fair treatment of third country nationals', i.e. measures regarding the admission of third country nationals and integration policy. And, thirdly, issues regarding more general aspects of migration policy, such as external relations, operational co-operation and financing. Developments under the Hague Programme are also briefly reviewed.

Building on the first two parts of the book, the third part will provide a comprehensive presentation of the negotiation process and an overall critical analysis of EU migration law and policy. The fifth chapter will attempt to highlight the interests, goals and weaknesses as well as the negotiating weight of the various policy actors involved. It seeks to provide a comprehensive analysis, employing some of the insights of a political sociological approach, of the everyday institutional practice and the negotiation process, emphasizing a series of informal and, in principle, deliberately un-codified factors and practices. The chapter is divided into four main sections, which examine respectively the role of the four institutions that are at present implicated in the migration policy-making process, namely the Council, the Commission, the Parliament and the Court.

The sixth and concluding chapter provides an overall critical analysis of Europe's nascent migration law and policy. The analysis will centre around two main axes: first, an overview of the general features and framework of policy-making with regard to migration; and, second, a critical analysis of the content and quality of EC migration law particularly in the post-Amsterdam era. The first section highlights the factors directly affecting the evolution of this policy as well as the reasons impeding its development and provides a more contextual evaluation of the Amsterdam *acquis*. A second concluding section examines, on the one hand, the extent to which migration law lives up to the Tampere milestones, which call for a common, comprehensive and balanced policy, and on the other hand, the quality of this policy in terms of transparency and human rights protection.

Even though migration policy as such could be considered a rather recent policy area, there is an extensive literature covering several aspects of migration that have been examined within the framework of the present research. The piecemeal and step-by-step development of the area is also reflected in the relevant literature. For instance, aspects of migration policy were initially principally examined within the framework of more general research dealing with aspects of the internal market and in particular the free movement of persons. There the academic debate reached somewhat of a crescendo in the early 1990s as a result of the lapse of the 1992 deadline. This focused, *inter alia*, on competence issues. Subsequently, in the Maastricht era migration related issues were examined in books or collections of essays on Justice and Home Affairs (JHA) a section of which addressed specifically asylum and migration issues. There one can find contributions examining both more general institutional, and substantive law, aspects of the Maastricht *acquis*. At the same time, academics examined the existing and developing case law on the association agreements notably as they pertained to the free movement of persons. The same period is characterized by an extensive literature on the evolution and institutional framework of Schengen. The eve of the Amsterdam IGC saw the launching of a critical debate on the need to reform the third pillar.

The Treaty of Amsterdam seems to have constituted a major point in the migration policy literature as well. At first the academic focus was mainly on the institutional framework and in particular on the issue of closer co-operation. Subsequently the emphasis was also placed on more horizontal and central issues such as the substance and limits of the new legal bases; the EU approach to migration policy; the policy dynamics for its development, more recently focusing on terrorism; a more general discussion on the impact of migration and the links between migration and other related policies i.e. employment policy and external relations. Excellent contributions have been forthcoming from both academics (lawyers and political scientists) and practitioners. Migration related academic contributions are also included in more general collections of essays regarding issues of a more horizontal character such as transparency, enlargement, IGCs and human rights. However, the role of the institutional dynamics has not been given much detailed consideration. There are excellent general contributions to the policy-making process but very limited attention has been devoted to JHA, much less migration, issues. It should be of little surprise that there are not yet many major contributions on the substantive law in the post-Amsterdam era, the major developments being very recent.

The present book clearly builds upon the existing literature. However, its scope is both narrower and wider. It is narrower in the sense that major categories of third country nationals have been excluded, i.e. family members of EU nationals and third country nationals falling under the scope of bilateral agreements. It purports to be wider by bringing under the same roof issues that have been examined in different frameworks and many only partially – i.e. the competence debate; analysis of the institutional framework and dynamics; security issues and in particular developments within the Schengen co-operation; and policy dynamics. In this manner it puts together a more comprehensive and up to date analysis of EU migration law and policy.

It attempts to enrich the current debate through a detailed examination of the following issues. Firstly, the institutional framework and the competence debate during the last three decades. In parallel and in addition to the presentation of this debate, it provides a detailed and systematic analysis of the role and interactions of the policy actors involved. Moreover, even in the tried and tested terrain of the Amsterdam Protocols and the Amsterdam legal bases it offers a different perspective by bringing to light the practice in relation to these provisions. Specifically, it gives an updated analysis of how and also why these provisions have been employed in a particular fashion. Secondly, in relation to Schengen's institutional framework which has also been exhaustively commented upon in the literature the contribution herein adopts a different approach. It places special emphasis on Schengen's substantive law and its interactions with EU policy-making and its influence therein. Thirdly, it provides a comprehensive presentation of the EU *acquis* in particular in the post-Amsterdam era while emphasizing the evolution and interactions among the different policy-making eras. Fourthly, much consideration is given to the practicalities and intricacies of policy-making and the decision-making process in the migration field. In this sense it attempts to be more contextual than some of the existing literature in this field. Lastly, the research is based extensively on primary sources, Council and other EU institutional documents as well as on extensive interviews with EU officials.

Overall the attempt has been to provide an account, which is up to date with extensive historical references and combines both an academic and practical perspective to the legal and political issues involved. It is to be hoped that the approach based on the above elements will contribute to a new understanding of the main aspects of EU migration law and its policy ramifications and that it will be of use to both academics and practitioners alike.

List of Abbreviations

CCI	Common Consular Instructions
CDE	Cahiers de Droit Européen
CFSP	Common Foreign and Security Policy
CIA	Committee on Immigration and Asylum
CIREFI	Center for Information, Discussion and Exchange on the crossing of Frontiers and Immigration
CISA	Convention Implementing the Schengen Agreement
CMLRev	Common Market Law Review
EC	European Community
EEC	European Economic Community
EIPA	European Institute of Public Administration
EJML	European Journal of Migration and Law
ELJ	European Law Journal
ELRev	European Law Review
EMN	European Migration Network
EU	European Union

DG	Directorate General
IGC	Intergovernmental Conference
JHA	Justice and Home Affairs
MEP	Member of the European Parliament
RMC	Revue du Marché Commun et de l'Union européenne
RMUE	Revue du Marché Unique européen
RTDE	Revue Trimestrielle de Droit européen
SCH/Com-ex	Schengen Executive Committee
SCIFA	Strategic Committee for Immigration, Frontiers and Asylum
YEL	Yearbook of European Law

PART I: The Institutional Framework

Chapter 1: The Institutional Framework *Ante*-Amsterdam

Introduction

Locating the exact moment in time in which a European migration policy began to emerge is a difficult exercise given that, until recently, there had been a lack of any clear legal bases regulating migration policy within the framework of the EC and/or EU Treaties. Indeed, the term "immigration" did not make its first appearance in the EU and EC Treaties until 1991 and 1997 respectively.[1] That said, one of the fundamental objectives of European integration has been the free movement of persons which clearly constitutes an aspect of migration policy. However its personal scope remained unclear and has been heavily debated for several decades.

EU policy on the migration related issues has been traditionally characterised by an intense competence debate. Member States have constantly questioned Community competence on the matter and showed a clear preference for cooperation at the intergovernmental level. As a result, the attempts to regulate migration policy were usually found in a 'limbo' situation between intergovernmentalism and the Community method thus inevitably reinforcing the existing competence skirmishes.

Through an analysis of the relevant EC and EU legal bases up to Amsterdam, this Chapter seeks to trace and present the origins of a Community competence on migration. The Treaty of Rome, the Single European Act and the Treaty of Maastricht will be examined in turn. Particular attention will be given to the Schengen Agreements and the importance of their impact on the formation of a Community migration policy. The reasons for the birth of this parallel track will be explored and an account of the institutional characteristics of this project will be provided.

---

1 Within the framework of the so-called "third pillar" of the Maastricht Treaty and Title IV TEC of the Amsterdam Treaty respectively. More specifically see former Article K.1 (3) TEU and Article 63 (3) TEC.

This chapter is thus structured around the two aforementioned themes. Firstly, the competence debate and, secondly, the arduous process of searching for a proper institutional framework during this first stage of migration policy-making.

1.1 The First Segments of a Community Competence

1.1.1 The Treaty of Rome: Migration in the Margins

The provisions regarding migration policy in the Treaty of Rome were not only few but the vast majority of them were also 'hidden'. They were in principle either linked with other EEC objectives or had been developed via external relations instruments. Furthermore, their scope was also heavily contested. They could be classified under three main separate categories.

First of all, certain aspects of migration policy have been examined within the framework of the provisions on the free movement of persons. In fact, the abolition of obstacles to the freedom of movement of persons as between Member States appeared within the major objectives of the Community,[2] and was closely linked with the task of establishing a "common market" during a transitional period of twelve years.[3] In that respect, the Treaty also included a legal basis for the adoption of Directives for the approximation of national provisions directly affecting the establishment or functioning of the common market.[4]

The Treaty included express provisions for the movement of certain categories of individuals, i.e. workers, self-employed persons and providers of services. Article 52 EEC, regarding the right of establishment, and Article 59 EEC, concerning the provision of services, clarified that the respective persons should be "nationals of a Member State" moving in the territory of another Member State. However, the scope of Article 48 concerning the free movement of workers was debated since it was not clear whether the concept of "workers" included also third country nationals. Secondary legislation and subsequent Treaty amendments have confirmed that third country nationals were not intended to benefit

2 Article 3 (c) EEC.

3 Article 2 in conjunction with Article 8 (1) EEC.

4 Article 100 EEC.

from this provision.[5] Moreover, the issue has been further clarified by the Court of Justice.[6]

Secondary legislation and the Treaty itself did establish a right of movement for two specific categories of third country nationals, whose circulation was linked with that of Community nationals and firms. On the one hand, all the relevant secondary law instruments implementing the Treaty provisions on the free movement of workers, the right of establishment and the provision of services contained provisions regarding the free movement of family members, irrespective of their nationality.[7] And, on the other hand, Article 59 (2) EEC stated clearly that, "the Council may, acting unanimously on a proposal from the Commission, extend the provisions of this Chapter to nationals of a third country who provide services and who are established within the Community". This provision was initially given effect on the basis of case law of the Court of Justice,[8] but it was not until 1999 that the Commission presented proposals for Directives in that regard.[9] However, it is worth stressing that the visa obli-

---

5 See Article 1 of Regulation (EEC) No 1612/68 of the Council of 15 October 1968 on freedom of movement for workers within the Community, OJ L 257/2, 19.10.1968. Moreover, the establishment of relevant legal bases both in the framework of the Treaties of Maastricht and Amsterdam prove that third country nationals were not covered by the said provision. For further discussion on this point see De Ceuster J., "De Europese Unie En De Verblyfsreglemententering", in De Feyter K. (ed.), *Migratie- En Migrantenrecht: Recente Ontwikkelingen,* Die Keure, Brugge, 1995, p. 147-237.

6 Case C-228/83 *Caisse d' Allocations Familiales v Meade*, [1987] ECR I-2631, at para. 7, and more recently, Case C-230/97 *Awoyemi* [1998] ECR I-6781. On this point see Wouters J., "European citizenship and the case-law of the Court of Justice of the European Communities on the free movement of persons", in Marias E. A. (ed.), *European Citizenship,* EIPA, Maastricht, 1994, p. 25-61, at p. 29, and Guild E., *Immigration Law in the European Community,* Kluwer, The Hague, 2001, at p. 22-23 and 69-70.

7 See Article 10 of Regulation 1612/68, *op. cit.*, and Council Directive 73/148/EEC of 21 May 1973 on the abolition of restrictions on movement and residence within the Community for nationals of Members States with regard to establishment and the provision of services, OJ L 172/14, 28.6.1973.

8 Case C-113/89 *Rush Portuguesa* [1990] ECR I-1417 and Case C-43/93 *Van der Elst* [1994] ECR I–3803. For a discussion of the *Van der Elst* case law see Castillo de la Torre F., "La libre circulation des services et les ressortissants des pays tiers: quelques réflexions au sujet de l'arrêt Vander Elst", *RMUE*, Vol. 2, 1995, p. 405-433.

9 Proposal for a Directive of the European Parliament and of the Council on the posting of workers who are third-country nationals for the provision of cross-border services and Proposal for a Council Directive extending the freedom to provide cross-border services to third-country nationals established within the Community, COM (1999) 3 final, 26.2.1999. See also Amended proposal for a Directive of the European Parliament and of the Council on the posting of workers who are third

gation and controls at frontiers for the entry and movement within EU territory remained unaffected both for family members as well as for third country nationals moving within the framework of a Community company.

The second set of provisions granting rights to third country nationals stems from international agreements that the Community has signed with third States. These can be divided into three different eras: first, the agreements with Greece and Turkey; second, the agreements with the Maghreb countries; and third, the agreements with Central and Eastern European countries. These agreements establish in principle only post-entry rights, meaning rights that could only be exercised once the third country national had entered the territory of a Member State in accordance with the latter's national legislation on admission of foreigners.[10] Moreover, their scope varies depending on the time of their conclusion, the countries concerned and the EU interests at stake.[11]

The third basis for Community competence in the migration sphere, admittedly rather tenuous, was established via the Treaty provisions on social policy, Articles 117 and 118 EEC. According to these provisions the Commission had the task of promoting close cooperation between Member State in the social field, particularly in matters relating to employment, labour law and working conditions and other related areas. Despite the rather weak link between these provisions and migration policy, they have given rise to a major competence debate between the Member States and the Commission.

1.1.2 Competence Skirmishes (Part I)

The Commission on the basis of Articles 117 and 118 adopted a Decision setting up a prior communication and consultation procedure in order to promote cooperation between Member States in the field of migration policy in relation to non-member countries.[12] According to the Decision, Member States would have to inform the Commission and other Member States on draft measures and agreements regarding workers from non-countries in the areas of entry, residence and employment and also to communicate the relevant texts.[13] The

---

country nationals for the provision of cross-border services, COM (2000) 271 final, 8.5.2000.

10 The sole exception consists in the possibility of access into the territory for the purpose of provision of services that was granted to the beneficiaries of the agreements with Central and Eastern European countries, mainly because EU countries wanted to make sure that their nationals would benefit from the same advantage.

11 For an extensive analysis of the relevant agreements see Guild E., *Immigration Law in the European Community, op.cit.*, Chapters 3 to 6.

12 Commission Decision 85/381/EEC setting up a prior communication and consultation procedure on migration policies in relation to non-member countries, OJ L 217/25, 14.8.1985.

13 Article 1 of Decision 85/381/EEC, *op.cit.*

Commission, following receipt of such information, could set in motion a consultation procedure that would facilitate the adoption of common position, in order to ensure that the referred measures were in conformity with Community policies and actions. Finally, the Commission would also examine the advisability of measures, which might be taken with the aim of achieving harmonisation of national legislation.[14]

Five Member States, led by Germany, challenged the Decision before the Court of Justice.[15] The main plea of the Member States was lack of competence.[16] Their basic argument was two-fold. First, according to the five Member States the Commission extended the powers that Article 118 EEC conferred on it, since this Article did not entail the adoption of binding measures. And, second, the contested decision dealt with fields that fell outside Article 118 EEC, namely migration policy which, they argued, fell under their exclusive competence. One of the arguments that the Member States sought to run in support of exclusive competence was premised on the public security ramifications of the matter in question.[17]

Despite the fact that the contested decision was finally declared partially void, it is worth stressing that the main argument of the Member States –i.e. lack of Community competence on migration- was dismissed by the Court. First of all, the Court rejected the Member States' argument that migration policy falls entirely outside the social field on the grounds that the employment situation is liable to be affected by the policy pursued by the Member States with regard to workers from non-member countries.[18] Ironically enough the Court based its decision on previous Council Resolutions, which recognised the link between migration policies pursued by the Member States and the Community's social

14 Articles 2 and 3 of Decision 85/381/EEC, *op.cit.*

15 Joined cases C-281, 283 to 285 and 287/85, *Germany and Others v Commission of the European Communities* [1987] ECR 3203 (hereinafter 'migration policy case'). For a detailed discussion of the case see Guild E., *Immigration Law in the European Community, op.cit.*, at p. 234-240.

16 There was a second plea regarding infringement of essential procedural requirements in failing to consult the Economic and Social Committee. But this will not be discussed due to its tenuous link with the subject matter in question, i.e. Community competence on migration. For the record it needs to be noted that the Court rejected the relevant plea. See Joined cases C-281, 283 to 285 and 287/85, *op.cit.* paras. 39 to 40.

17 More specifically the French Republic argued that the whole area of policy on foreign nationals fell outside the social field inasmuch as it involved questions of public security for which the Member States alone were responsible. Joined cases C-281, 283 to 285 and 287/85, *op.cit.*, para. 25.

18 Joined cases C-281, 283 to 285 and 287/85, *op.cit.*, paras. 16 to 18.

policy.[19] Furthermore, whilst recognising Member States' exclusive competence on public security issues, the Court refused to accept that the whole area of policy on foreign nationals necessarily falls within the scope of public security.[20] Nonetheless, the Court considered that the issue of cultural integration fell outside the scope of Article 118 EEC.[21]

Inasmuch as the Commission's ability to adopt binding measures on the matter was concerned, the Court recognised that the relevant provisions conferred on the Commission *per se* the powers, which were indispensable to carry out its tasks. However, it considered that the objective of ensuring conformity between, on the one hand, national draft measures and agreements, and on the other, Community policies and actions exceeded the scope of the Commission's powers under Article 118 EEC.[22]

It is worth highlighting the analysis of Advocate General Mancini on the reasons behind these proceedings. After providing an excellent review of the historical background of the case, Advocate General Mancini concluded that the opposition of the Member States was due to three factors: firstly, "the irritation aroused by unexpected and displeasing events", since Member States "must have been greatly surprised when they were faced with a measure and a full bodied one....and great must have been their desire to bring the institution responsible for that measure back into line with a good judicial rap over the knuckles"; secondly, the fact that "Member States are genuinely – or better vitally – interested in preserving full control over the admission to their territory of workers from non-member countries, *inter alia*, because of the obvious political and public-policy ramifications"; and, thirdly, the Commission's errors, since according to Mancini "it is permissible to conjecture that if the Commission had put its emphasis on the *Community's* labour market ... it would perhaps have avoided the actions...yet without renouncing the objectives that it had in view."[23]

Following the European Court of Justice's judgment, the Commission adopted a new Decision and accordingly sought to initiate a consultation procedure.[24] For their part, however, the Member States were unwilling to cooperate.[25]

---

19 For the exact references and a brief analysis on the relevant Council Resolutions, see *infra* at 3.1.

20 Joined cases C-281, 283 to 285 and 287/85, *op.cit.*, para. 25.

21 *Idem,* para. 24.

22 *Idem,* paras 28 and 35 to 36.

23 Opinion of Mr Advocate General Mancini, ECR [1987] at p. 3228 and 3229.

24 Commission Decision 88/384/EEC of 8 June 1988 setting up a prior communication and consultation procedure on migration policies in relation to non-member countries, OJ L 183/35, 14.7.1988.

25 Guild E. and Niessen J., *The Developing Immigration and Asylum Policies of the European Union Adopted Convention, Resolutions, Recommendations, Decisions and*

1.2. The Single European Act: A Nascent Migration Debate

1.2.1 Establishing an "Area without Internal Frontiers"

The Single European Act was linked with the re-launching of the common market project, which was renamed the "internal market".[26] A series of new provisions were inserted into the Treaty, which not only provided a definition of the Community's strategic objectives for the 1980s and established a series of new legal bases for the adoption of the relevant measures, but also set a specific deadline for the completion of this project, the 31 December 1992.[27]

In legal terms, and as pertains to this study, the developments signified by the Single European Act were somewhat limited. A new Article 8a clarified that "the internal market shall comprise an area without internal frontiers in which the free movement of ... persons ... is ensured in accordance with the provisions of this Treaty". Nevertheless, the new legal basis of Article 100A regarding the adoption of measures for the approximation of national legislation having as their object the establishment and functioning of the internal market expressly excluded from its scope provisions relating to the free movement of persons.[28] The only positive legal development concerns the extension of the qualified majority voting procedure to Article 59 (2) EEC regarding the extension of the right of provision of services to third country nationals.[29]

However, despite the lack of any new legal bases relating to migration, the existence of a great number of Declarations attached to Articles 13 to 19 of the SEA – most likely the product of the intense competence debate initiated by the 'migration policy case'- brought the migration question to the fore and considerably reinforced the existing debate. The contradictory character of the relevant Declarations is clear testimony to the lack of consensus on the matter. Whereas the Member States declared their will to cooperate "in order to promote the free movement of persons...without prejudice to the powers of the Community, in particular as regards the entry, movement and residence of nationals of third countries",[30] at the same time they underlined the fact that nothing in the relevant provisions shall affect the "right of Member States to take such measures as they consider necessary for the purpose of controlling immigration from third countries ...".[31] And whilst they reaffirmed their political will for the completion

---

Conclusions, Kluwer, The Hague, 1996, at p. 24.

26 Single European Act (SEA), OJ L 169/1, 29.6.1987.

27 Articles 13 to 19 of the SEA.

28 See Article 100A (2), inserted to the EEC by Article 18 of the SEA.

29 Article 16 (3) of the SEA amending the voting procedure applied in the framework of Article 59 (2) EEC.

30 Political declaration (No 2) by the Governments of the Member States on the free movement of persons.

31 General Declaration (No 6) on Articles 13 to 19 of the Single European Act.

of the internal market within the set deadlines and subscribed to the implementation of the Commission White Paper, they felt the need to "clarify that the date of 31 December 1992 does not create an automatic legal effect".[32] A major part of the debate in the post-Single European Act era was to centre on the effect of this deadline, in conjunction with the value of the relevant Declaration.

It is also important to note that following the entry into force of the Single European Act, cooperation on migration policy issues was for the first time institutionalised.[33] First of all, in October 1986, under the British Presidency, an Ad Hoc Immigration Group was formed and meetings of Interior Ministers became semi-regular.[34] The very creation of the Group was considered to constitute a statement on the part of the Member States that the question of compensatory measures was not a Community competence but rather fell under their own competence.[35] However, despite its purely intergovernmental character, the Community institutions, which is to say the Commission and the General Secretariat of the Council, were given a place in this Group.[36] Moreover, in December 1988 the Rhodes European Council having noticed that there were too many groups dealing with the free movement of persons without any overall coordination, decided to set up a specific body to provide the necessary coordination, the so-called "Free Movement Coordinators" Group.[37]

1.2.2 Competence Skirmishes (Part II)

The existence of the 1992 deadline for the creation of an area without internal frontiers reinforced the already vivid debate on migration related issues. The core of this debate was two-fold and concerned: first, the scope of the concept of "persons", and second, the eventual direct effect of Article 8a EEC. The former was primarily dealt with in the framework of the Council, however, the latter

32 Declaration (No 3) on Article 8a of the EEC Treaty.

33 However, since 1975 justice and interior officials had been working on an *ad hoc* basis mainly with regard to security issues. See *infra* at 3.1.

34 For a brief presentation of the group, its structure and mandate see Papademetriou D., *Coming together or pulling apart? The European Union's struggle with immigration and asylum*, Carnegie Endowment for International Peace, Washington, 1996, at p. 28, and Guild and Niessen, *op.cit.*, at p. 31-32.

35 De Ceuster, *op.cit.* Moreover, as it has been rightly highlighted, the fact that the creation of the Group stems from a British initiative is not without relevance. More specifically, it was convincingly argued that it constitutes a British effort to keep cooperation at intergovernmental level and ensure the application of unanimity. See De Lobkowicz W., *L'Europe et la sécurité intérieure Une élaboration par étapes,* La documentation Française, Paris, 2002, at p. 29.

36 Nonetheless, it is worth highlighting the fact that the Commission did obviously not enjoy its privileges under Community law, which is to say the right of initiative.

37 Rhodes European Council, 2 and 3 December 1988, Bull. EC 12-1988.

was examined mostly in academic discussion though there have also been a few Court cases as well.

With respect to the scope of the concept of persons, there was a clear division at Community level. Certain Member States insisted that the abolition of controls at internal frontiers did not include the removal of controls for third country nationals.[38] However, the vast majority of the Member States and the Commission, did not share this view.[39] The position of both sides was intimately linked with the security ramifications of the relevant objective but it cashed out in very different approaches. The former group completely rejected the idea of abolishing border controls for third country nationals due to their security concerns, whereas the latter group in principle accepted the idea, while setting a series of conditions in order to guarantee internal security.[40]

Inasmuch as the second aspect of the debate was concerned the main question was whether Article 8a had a direct effect that would ensure its applicability after the lapse of the 31 December 1992 deadline. Though the argument for direct effect was not without support, it was likewise acknowledged that the adoption of further measures was indeed required prior to the full implementation of the principle of free movement established by Article 8a.[41] In contrast to the academic debate, the judicial position was much clearer. Both British Courts[42] and the European Court itself refused to recognise direct effect to the said provision.[43]

38 According to the Commission it was mainly the UK that considered that a move to dismantle controls applied only to Community nationals whereas the Commission and eleven Member States considered that the abolition of internal border controls related to all persons, regardless of their nationality. See Answer given by Commissioner V. d' Archirafi to Written question E-2692/92 by Dieter Rogalla, OJ C 349/2, 9.12.1994. See also Guild E., *Immigration Law in the European Community, op.cit.*, at p. 225. One commentator has however observed that the UK position was also supported by Ireland, Denmark and Greece. See Guild and Niessen, *op.cit.*, at p. 40.

39 *Idem.*

40 Guild and Niessen, *op.cit.*, at p. 40.

41 For further discussion and references on this point see Guild E., *Immigration Law in the European Community, op.cit.*, at p. 222-225. For a concise presentation of all the arguments for and against direct effect as well as of the various issues linked with the abolition of border controls see Ayral M., "La suppression des contrôles aux frontières intra-communautaires", *RMUE*, Issue 1, 1993, p. 59-90.

42 *R v Secretary of State for the Home Department ex p Flynn* [1995] Imm AR 594, CA. For a brief discussion of the case see Guild E., *Immigration Law in the European Community, op.cit.*, at p. 224.

43 The issue was for the first time examined –even if the specific case of border controls was not discussed- in Case C-297/92 *Baglieri* [1993] ECR I-5211. For a commentary see Handoll J., *Free Movement of Persons in the EU,* John Wiley & sons, Chichester, 1995, at p. 34. The Court came back to this point several years later and clarified the

Another issue, closely linked with the direct effect question and the subject of extensive academic debate, was the impact of the Declaration attached to Article 8a. On the basis of an international law analysis, certain authors came to the conclusion that the Declaration had "no legal effect" and could not "in any way restrict, exclude, qualify or amend the clear provisions of Article 8a".[44] More cautiously others concluded that the Declaration did not deprive the date of all legal effects whilst at the same time recognising that it should be seen as the authentic interpretation of the use of the 31 December 1992 date, which means that the date as such had "no automatic legal effect".[45] A robust position was also taken by the Commission, which even threatened to take legal action against those Member States that would continue to carry out internal frontier checks on persons after 1993.[46] The Council, being unable to reach consensus on the objective and scope of the provision itself, does not appear to have seriously examined this issue.

In connection with this point and through an analysis of previous case law of the Court, one learned commentator reached the conclusion that the obligation described in Article 8a was "sufficiently well-defined for disregard of it to be subject of a finding of a failure to act pursuant to Article 175".[47] And, indeed, a mere few months after the lapse of the 1993 deadline the Parliament did bring an action for failure to act against the Commission, though it did not result in a decision as it was removed from the register without being examined by the Court.[48]

---

matter despite the fact that the question had in practice become obsolete due to the integration of the Schengen *acquis* within the EU framework. See Case C-378/97 *Wijsenbeek* [1999] ECR I-6207. For a discussion on this second case see Martin D., "Comments on *Florus Ariël Wijsenbeek* (Case C-378/97 of 21 September 1999) and *Arblade* (Joined Cases C-369/96 and C-376/96 of 23 November 1999), *EJML*, Vol. 2, 2000, p. 101-107, Guild E., *Immigration Law in the European Community, op.cit.*, at p. 231-233, and Papagianni G., "La circulation des citoyens de l'Union: de Maastricht à Amsterdam et au délà", *Actualités de droit*, Vol. 4, 1999, p. 625-665.

44 Toth A. G., "The legal status of the declarations annexed to the Single European Act", *CMLRev*, Vol. 23, 1986, p. 803-812.

45 See Schermers H.G., "The effect of the date 31 December 1992", *CMLRev,* Vol. 28, 1991, p. 275-289 and Mattera A., "Un espace sans frontières intérieures: le défi de l'Europe 1993", *RMUE,* Issue 1, 1992, p. 5-10.

46 See Commission Communication to the Council and the Parliament on Abolition of Border Controls, SEC (92) 877/5 final, 5.5.1992 and the Commission Statement to the European Council in Copenhagen on the implementation of Article 8a of the Treaty of Rome with regard to the movement of persons. See also Guild and Niessen, *op.cit.*, at p. 41.

47 Schermers H.G., 'The effect of the date 31 December 1992, *op.cit.*

48 Case C-445/93 *European Parliament v Commission*, removed from the register by Order of 11 July 1996.

In parallel to all this intense academic, judicial, inter-State and inter-institutional debate, it soon became clear that the privilege of moving freely within the "area without internal frontiers" could not be limited to Community citizens, but should be extended to *all* persons. It also became clear that the abolition of internal border controls should be accompanied by the adoption of a series of "flanking" or "compensatory" measures, such as stricter, and mainly common, standards for external border controls, a common visa policy, coordination of asylum and admission policies, judicial cooperation and police cooperation. Indeed, it has been correctly argued that although Article 8a did not itself constitute a legal basis it had set goals that could not be achieved without EC wide policies on migration.[49] Ironically enough, and despite the Community character of the free movement of persons objective, most of the initiatives that have been launched and measures adopted in this respect have been purely intergovernmental.[50]

1.3 Schengen: The Parallel Track

The patent lack of consensus within the Community framework as to the very scope of the free movement objective and the means for attaining it, led some of the Member States to take a parallel track. Prompted by, *inter alia*, the practical problems caused by long queues at their common borders, President Mitterand and Chancellor Kohl decided to conclude a bilateral agreement on abolishing frontier controls. This was signed on 13 July 1984 at Saarbrücken. The Benelux countries having a long-standing experience on the matter immediately associated themselves with this project, via a Memorandum of the Benelux Economic Union of 12 December 1984 forwarded to the Governments of the Federal Republic of Germany and the French Republic. The five Member States signed a first agreement on 14 June 1985 in Schengen, setting the general principles of their cooperation and providing a list of the measures to be adopted in the short and in the longer term. This was followed by a second more detailed Implementing Convention signed on the 19 June 1990 also at Schengen.[51] Consequently, the

49 Papademetriou, *op.cit.*, at p. 22.

50 The irony of this juxtaposition is observed by O' Keeffe. See O' Keeffe D., "The emergence of a European Immigration Policy", *ELRev*, Vol. 20, 1995, p. 20-36, at p. 21.

51 Both the 1985 Schengen Agreement and the 1990 Convention Implementing the Schengen Agreement (CISA) have been following the incorporation of the Schengen *acquis* within the framework of the EU published in the Official Journal, OJ L 239, 22.9.2000. For a brief historical review on the conclusion of the Schengen Agreements and a brief presentation, see Louette J.-S., *Les Etats Benelux et la France face aux accords de Schengen*, Courrier Hebdomadaire, No 1586-1587, CRISP, 1998, and Papademetriou, *op.cit.*, at p. 26-27. For a detailed analysis of the Schengen system see Meijers et al., *Schengen Internationalisation of central chapters of the law*

first major case of closer cooperation among Member States eager to go further without being willing to wait for the rest of their companions was established.

Right from its very birth, Schengen was intended to be complementary to Community action.[52] Already in the 1985 Agreement, the Schengen Contracting Parties had expressed their attachment to the European Communities. Within the preamble of the 1985 Agreement one can find references to the objective of abolishing border checks on the movement of nationals of the Member States of the European Communities and to the Fontainebleau European Council Conclusions on the abolition of police and customs formalities for people crossing intra-Community frontiers. Subsequently, specific provisions ensuring the compatibility between Schengen and Community law have been introduced within the 1990 Convention Implementing the Schengen Agreement (CISA).[53] And since 1988 the Schengen Contracting Parties had also accorded observer status to a representative of the European Communities. That being said, one should not lose sight of the fact that Schengen was established and functioned under a substantially different legal regime from that of the Community framework. Both its creation and further development was on a completely pragmatic basis. Moreover, Schengen's institutional structure and the scope of the cooperation differed in many respects from that of the Community.

Schengen as a 'public international law product' was endowed with an institutional framework, which could generally be characterised as 'loose'.[54] The institutional provisions included in the Schengen Implementing Convention were not only limited in nature but also drafted in a quite general way. Schengen had an Executive Committee, composed of one Minister from every Contracting Party, which was Schengen's higher body and which could "set

---

on aliens, refugees, privacy, security and the police, Stichting NJCM-Boekerij, The Netherlands, 1992 and Hreblay V., *Les accords de Schengen: origine, fonctionnement, avenir*, Bruyland, Bruxelles, 1999.

52 It is rather revealing that in 1995 Nanz not only sustained that Schengen did not have an end to itself but was also arguing for the integration of the Schengen within the EU framework. Nanz K. P., "The Schengen Agreement: preparing the free movement of persons in the European Union", in Bieber R. and Monar J. (eds.), *Justice and Home Affairs in the European Union The Development of the Third Pillar*, European Interuniversity Press, Brussels, 1995, p. 29-48.

53 See Articles 134, 140 and 142 CISA.

54 For a detailed presentation of the Schengen system and institutional structure apart from the literature cited above see also Van de Rijt W., "Le fonctionnement des institutions Schengen: 'Pragmatisme toujours'", in Den Boer M. (ed.), *Schengen's Final Days? The Incorporation of Schengen into the New TEU, External Borders and Information Systems*, EIPA, Maastricht, 1998, p. 59-66; De Zwaan W.J., "Schengen and its Incorporation into the New Treaty: The Negotiating Process", in Den Boer M. (ed.), *Schengen's Final Days? The Incorporation of Schengen into the New TEU, External Borders and Information Systems*, EIPA, Maastricht, 1998, p. 13-24.

up working parties composed of representatives of the administrations of the Contracting Parties in order to prepare decisions or to carry out other tasks".[55] The basic decision-making rule was unanimity. There were no other provisions regarding the rules of procedure of the Executive Committee, no list of types of legal instruments to be adopted, no provisions regarding the competence of the working parties, no linguistic provisions, no specific confidentiality rules, nor of course any provisions with regard to judicial control.

But despite this lack of any express institutional rules, Schengen, in the course of the fourteen years of its life, developed its own 'ritual', 'off the record' and mainly flexible set of institutional rules. Another level of decision-making – known as the "Schengen Central Group" and composed of highly ranked officials- was created in order to coordinate the work of the working parties and to prepare the Ministerial meetings. At the beginning meetings were rather random and the Presidency order was set in a pragmatic way, however, in 1988 the Schengen Contracting Parties decided to follow the Community semester rotation rule. Meetings were held in national languages though certain permanent working groups used a 'common language'.[56] The adopted legal acts were not officially published and the confidential character of a document was based either on a Decision of the Executive Committee,[57] or on a Decision of the Schengen Central Group.[58] Schengen also developed the tendency to proceed to innovative and mainly flexible solutions such as the association of Norway and Iceland, two non-Community States, on the basis of a cooperation agreement.[59]

To be sure, the remit of the Schengen cooperation was much more limited than that of the Community. The Community addresses migration within the framework of a much wider spectrum of issues linked not exclusively with the

55 Articles 131 to 133 CISA.

56 Hreblay, *op.cit.*

57 See for example SCH/Com-ex (93) 22 Rev, 14.12.1993 and SCH/Com-ex (98) 17, 23.6.1998, both published in OJ L 239, 22.9.2000.

58 See the House of Lords Report, *Incorporating the Schengen acquis into the EU*, Select Committee on European Union Thirty-First Report, Session 1997-98, London, 28 July 1998, pt. 118.

59 However, according to Article 140 of the Schengen Convention it seems that only Community Member States could adhere to Schengen. For further information regarding the provisions of the 1996 Cooperation Agreement and the problems arising from its transposition into the EU framework see "Norway joins Schengen", *Statewatch*, Vol. 9, No 2, March-April 1999, p. 7-8; Piçarra N., "La mise en oeuvre du protocole intégrant l'*acquis* de Schengen dans le cadre de l'Union europeéenne: règles et procedures", in Den Boer M. (ed) *Schengen's Final Days? The Incorporation of Schengen into the New TEU, External Borders and Information Systems*, EIPA, Maastricht, 1998, p. 25-58, and De Zwaan J. W., "Opting in and opting out of rules concerning the free movement of persons: problems and practical arrangements", *Cambridge Yearbook of European Legal Studies*, Vol. 1, 1998, p. 107-124.

freedom of movement but also with other policy aspects such as social policy, employment matters and external relations. The Schengen cooperation, however, focuses exclusively on the objective of internal border controls, whilst migration policy is seen exclusively as a security issue. The Schengen Convention does not contain any legal bases on legal migration. There are only provisions regarding the flanking measures, that is security oriented measures that would compensate for any eventual risks stemming from the abolition of internal border controls. Given the fact that this approach is explored and tested for the first time in practice, it becomes obvious why Schengen was initially referred to as a *laboratoire d'essai*.[60]

Schengen also had its own 'logic' as has already been alluded to. Within the Schengen framework no transfer of competence from the part of its Contracting Parties took place.[61] Moreover, due to the abolition of internal border controls and their replacement with controls at the external borders of the 'Schengenland' the question of mutual trust among the partners, regarding the safeguarding of these common external frontiers, was crucial.[62] The Schengen Convention, based on a rather pragmatic approach, has established a special double-check adhesion mechanism. There is a clear distinction between, on the one hand, the entry into force of the Convention, which takes place following the deposit of the final instrument of ratification, and, on the other hand, the full implementation of the Convention, which does not take place "until the preconditions for its implementation have been fulfilled in the Signatory States and checks at external borders were effective".[63] Thus, two of the core principles of Schengen cooperation have been security and sovereignty.

1.4 The Maastricht Treaty: Forging an Institutional Framework

1.4.1 The New Institutional Framework: Putting an End to the **Clandestinité Institutionnelle**

The Maastricht Treaty should definitely be considered one of the major legal steps in the formation of an EU migration policy. The 1991 IGC was initially

60 The expression "*laboratoire d'essai*" was first used by Edith Cresson, French Minister of European Affairs, in the course of the signature of the Schengen Implementing Convention, on 19 June 1990, See De Lobkowicz W., *L'Europe et la sécurité intérieure Une élaboration par étapes, op.cit.*, at p. 114.

61 De Zwaan J.W., "Schengen and its Incorporation into the New Treaty: The Negotiating Process", *op. cit.*

62 The term 'Schengenland' refers to the territory where the Schengen Agreements are applicable. It is used in order to emphasise the fact that it is considered a single territory with common external borders.

63 See Article 139 CISA as well as the first Joint Declaration attached to the Convention Implementing the Schengen Agreement.

conceived as the Economic and Monetary Union (EMU) IGC,[64] but following a rather unanticipated German proposal for communitarising migration and asylum policies during the course of the Luxembourg EU Council in June 1991,[65] a third pillar providing for cooperation in Justice and Home Affairs (JHA) issues was inserted in the Treaties framework at Maastricht.[66] The 1993 Maastricht Treaty was the first attempt to provide some answers to the problems that had stalled Community action for decades. The progress achieved at Maastricht was two-fold: firstly, proper legal bases – which tried to clarify the competence debate and render the adoption of legal measures for the accomplishment of the internal market possible – were created; and, secondly, a certain institutional structure within the wider EU framework which consisted mainly in the institutionalisation of a series of pre-existing informal forums was established.[67]

64 A decision for an IGC for EMU was taken at the European Council of Strasbourg – Strasbourg European Council, 8 and 9 December 1989, Bull. EC 12-1989 – followed some months later by the decision of the Dublin European Council – Dublin European Council, 25 and 26 June 1990, Bull. EC 6-1990 – to convene a second parallel Conference on Political Union. It was within the framework of the latter that migration issues would be examined. See Guild and Niessen, *op.cit.,* at p. 41.

65 Without really having forewarned his partners Chancellor Kohl made a proposal at the European Council of Luxembourg to communitarise asylum and immigration policies, and to put forward a work programme on these questions, which would no longer concern merely the crossing of internal borders. For the text of the German proposal see Annex I of the Presidency Conclusions of the Luxembourg European Council, 28 and 29 June 1991, Bull. EC 6-1991. The German proposal for communitarisation was only supported by Belgium. For more details see De Lobkowicz W., "Intergovernmental cooperation in the field of migration – From the Single European Act to Maastricht", in Monar J. and Morgan R. (eds.), *The Third Pillar of the European Union – Cooperation in the fields of Justice and Home Affairs*, European Interuniversity Press, Brussels, 1994, p. 99-122, and De Lobkowicz W., *L'Europe et la sécurité intérieure Une élaboration par étapes, op.cit.*, at p. 44.

66 Title VI TEU. Articles K to K.9 TEU.

67 For a detailed presentation of the new legal bases see Müller-Graff P.-C., "The legal bases of the Third Pillar and its position in the framework of the Union Treaty", *CMLRev*, Vol. 31, 1994. p. 493-510; D'Oliveira J., "Expanding External and Shrinking Internal Borders: Europe's Defence Mechanisms in the Areas of Free Movement, Immigration and Asylum", in Twomey P. M. (ed.), *Legal issues of the Maastricht Treaty* , Wiley, Chichester, 1994, p. 261-278; Fernhout R., "Justice and Home Affairs: Immigration and Asylum Policy: From JHA cooperation to communitarisation", in Winter J., Curtin D., Kellerman A. and de Witte B. (eds.), *Reforming the Treaty on European Union – The Legal Debate*, T.M.C. Asser Instituut, Kluwer Law International, The Hague, 1996, p. 377-399; Hailbronner K., "Migration Law and Policy within the Third Pillar of the Union Treaty", in Bieber R. and Monar J. (eds.), *Justice and Home Affairs in the European Union The Development of*

Firstly, and as regards the competence debate, the Maastricht Treaty drew up a catalogue of measures to be adopted at Community and/or Union level and also attempted to draw a line between the competence of the Community and that of the Member States. The answer to the problem was as many would have expected a hybrid one. The final compromise was to take the form of an artificial split between two pillars and a promise to look into the matter in the coming years. Certain aspects of visa policy were placed within the framework of the EC Treaty (Article 100C TEC) but the vast majority of legal bases concerning related policy aspects were placed in a new separate pillar that guaranteed a safe distance from the European institutions and the Community procedures. The Heads of State did, however, include a *passerelle clause* to the third pillar.[68] And in an attempt to create a link between the third pillar and the Community structure, a special provision expressly made twenty-two clauses of the EC Treaty applicable to the third pillar.[69]

The influence of the intergovernmental era was quite strong in both pillars. First, the role of Community institutions was rather limited. Though the Commission maintained its right of initiative with regard to visa policy it was also bound to examine Member State initiatives.[70] Moreover, a clear clause functioning as a sort of safety net was introduced in order to safeguard Member States competence with regard to public order and internal security and to keep the Court at an acceptable distance.[71] Insofar as the third pillar was concerned, the right of initiative was, in most cases, shared between the Commission and the Member States.[72] The European Parliament was merely to be "informed"[73] and

the Third Pillar, European Interuniversity Press, Brussels, 1995, p. 95-126; O'Keeffe D., "A Critical View of the Third Pillar", in Pauly A., Best E., Guggenbuhl A. and Marinho C. (eds.), *De Schengen à Maastricht: voie royale et course d'obstacles,* EIPA, Maastricht, 1996, p. 1-16 and Lepoivre M., "Le domaine de la Justice et des Affaires Intérieures dans la perspective de la Conférence Intergouvernementale de 1996", *CDE*, Issues 3-4, 1995, p. 323-349.

68 Article K.9 TEU.

69 Article K.8 (1) TEU. These clauses dealt with the structure of the Council, the Commission and the European Parliament as well as the rules on the EC's official languages. In fact Article C TEU provided that the EU had a unique institutional framework. On this point see Jacqué J.-P., "Affaires intérieures et justice Quelques reflections", in Mattera A. (sous la direction de), *Le La Conférence Intergouvernementale sur l'UE – Répondre aux défis du XXI siècle,* Clément Juglar, Paris, 1996, p. 337-343.

70 Article 100 C (4) TEC.

71 Article 100 C (5) TEC. An identical provision was included in the third pillar. See Article K.2 (2) TEU.

72 Member States had exclusive right of initiative regarding judicial, police and customs cooperation. See Article K.3 (2) TEU.

73 Article K.6 TEU.

the attribution of competence to the Court was optional and concerned exclusively Conventions.[74] And, furthermore, the relevant matters were considered simply as "matters of common interest".[75] In addition, the Council remained wedded to its secretive attitude for quite some time. In fact, most of the documents adopted within the framework of the third pillar were only published in 1996 following a special Council Decision.[76]

All this being said the third pillar approach was dynamic and gave hope for further rapprochement with the Community system in the future. For example, it was clearly stated that after 1 January 1996 the Council would apply the qualified majority voting rule with regard to visa policy.[77] And the aforementioned *passerelle clause* was inserted into the Treaty providing for the passage from the third to the first pillar.[78] According to this provision the transfer to the first pillar would be possible on the basis of a unanimous decision of the Council, which would, at the same time, determine the relevant voting procedures to be applied in the communitarised area. It is interesting to underline the existence of transitory law provisions in that respect. In particular, the Treaty specified that the effects of Conventions would be maintained until their content has been replaced by Directives or measures adopted pursuant to this Article.[79] One should nonetheless keep in mind that any eventual recourse to this clause was politically problematic.[80]

74 Article K.3 (2) TEU.

75 Introductory phrase of Article K.1 TEU.

76 Council Decision of 23 November 1995 on publication in the Official Journal of the European Communities of acts and other texts adopted by the Council in the field of asylum and immigration, OJ C 274/1, 19.9.1996.

77 Article 100 C (3) TEC. It should be noted that as regards the uniform format of visas, the qualified majority voting rule applied immediately after the entry into force of the Treaty.

78 Article K.9 TEU.

79 Article 100C (7) TEC. Most probably the Heads of State and Government had in mind the External Frontiers Convention, which was never adopted. See *infra* at 3.4.1.2.

80 See Unilateral Declaration of Denmark on cooperation in the fields of Justice and Home Affairs, to be associated to the Danish Act of Ratification of the Treaty on European Union and of which the 11 other Member States will take cognisance, Edinburgh European Council, 11 and 12 December 1992, Bull. EC 12-1992. According to this Declaration any decision on the basis of Article K.9 would have to be adopted in accordance with the constitutional requirements of each Member State before entering into force. In Denmark such adoption would require either a majority of 5/6 of members of the Folketing or both majority of the members of the Folketing and a majority of voters in a referendum. See Mc Mahon R., "Maastricht's Third Pillar: Load bearing or purely decorative?", *Legal Issues of European Integration,* Vol. 1, 1995, p. 51-64, at p. 61.

The second important contribution of the Maastricht Treaty was the creation of legal bases for the formation of a European migration policy albeit as part of a wider catalogue of flanking measures related to the free movement of persons. So, for example, Article 100C TEC provided for the adoption of a common list of countries whose nationals would be under a visa obligation and a uniform format for visas and Article K.1 (2) TEU provided for the adoption of rules governing the crossing of external borders. More importantly, Article K.1 (3) TEU provided for the adoption of measures on both legal and illegal migration. The legal instruments envisaged were as far as the first pillar was concerned the classic Community instruments. The objectives of the third pillar were, however, to be accomplished via the adoption of the classic international law instrument of Conventions as well as through certain new types of measures whose value was not clear, notably Joint Positions and Joint Actions.[81]

Following the establishment of an EU migration competence, an institutional framework for the cooperation among Member States was also *de facto* created. Nonetheless, as it has been rightly argued the Maastricht Treaty's third pillar was much more of a coordination of the work of all the pre-existing groups, rather than a genuinely new framework.[82] The newly formed JHA Council took over the work of the Ad Hoc Group for Immigration and a newly established Committee, the so-called "K.4 Committee", took over the work of the Group of Coordinators. Considering that the matters in question were rather vast and that further coordination was needed, three separate Steering Groups were also created in order to coordinate and supervise the work of the respective working parties.[83]

It is useful to also highlight another series of legal bases. Firstly, migration policy was brought within the EC budget. Whilst administrative expenditure would be under the EC budget, the Council would have to decide whether the operational expenditure to which the implementation of the relevant provisions gives rise would be charged to the EC budget or to the Member States.[84] Secondly, a residual and quite general provision on external relations calling Member States to defend "common positions" adopted under Title VI "within

81 Article K.3 (2) TEU.

82 See Monar J., 'European Union – Justice and Home Affairs: a balance sheet and an agenda for reform', in Edwards G. and Pijpers A. (eds.), *The Politics of European Treaty Reform – The 1996 Intergovernmental Conference and beyond*, Printer, London, 1997, p. 326-339. For a scheme see De Lobkowicz W., *L'Europe et la sécurité intérieure Une élaboration par étapes, op.cit.*, p. 58.

83 For a detailed presentation of the institutional actors in the Maastricht era and the interaction among them see Den Boer M., *Taming the Third Pillar: Improving the Management of Justice and Home Affairs Cooperation in the EU*, EIPA, Maastricht, 1998.

84 Article K.8 (2) TEU.

international organizations and at international conferences" was created.[85] And, thirdly, the new Treaty also included a provision allowing for collaboration between the relevant departments of the Member States administrations.[86]

As a final point it is worth underlining the insertion of express provisions legitimising the actions taken outside the Treaty framework, the Heads of State clearly recognising the limits of the existing legal bases and aware that certain Member States had already expressed their will to go further.[87]

1.4.2 Cross-pillar Skirmishes (Part I)

The artificial split between the two pillars, instead of clarifying and resolving competence matters, has further fuelled the competence debate and led to cross-pillar skirmishes. First of all, the border line between those aspects of visa policy falling under the first and those falling under the third pillar was, from a substantive point of view, far from clear. It is revealing that even the Commission itself seemed to be rather confused. Interestingly, a provision regarding mutual recognition of visas was inserted both in the first pillar proposal for a Regulation on a visa list and the third pillar proposal for a Convention for the crossing of the external frontiers. This undoubtedly attests to the legal difficulties in drawing the line between the two pillars.[88] The matter became much more acute in view of the express precedence of the Community pillar over the intergovernmental third pillar.[89]

85 Article K.5 TEU.

86 Article K.3 (1) TEU.

87 See Article K.7 TEU, the so-called "Schengen clause". Relevant provisions were also included into the framework of the legal acts adopted on the basis of both Article 100C TEC and the third pillar. See Article 6 of Council Regulation (EC) No 574/1999 of 12 March 1999 determining the third countries whose nationals must be in possession of visas when crossing the external borders of the Member States, OJ L 72/2, 18.3.1999 and Article 9 of Joint Action 96/197/JHA of 4 March 1996 adopted by the Council on the basis of Article K.3 of the Treaty on the European Union on airport transit arrangements, OJ L 63/8, 13.3.1996.

88 De Lobkowicz W., *L'Europe et la sécurité intérieure Une élaboration par étapes, op.cit.*, at p. 54. See also Articles 8 (1) and 18 of the Proposal for a Decision, based on Article K.3 of the Treaty on European Union establishing the Convention on the crossing of the external frontiers of the Member States, in conjunction with Article 2 of the Proposal for a Regulation, based on Article 100 C of the Treaty establishing the European Community, determining the third countries whose nationals must be in possession of visas when crossing the external borders of the Member States, COM (93) 684 final, 10.12.1993.

89 Article K.1 TEU stated clearly that the matters of common interest and the relevant cooperation among Member States would be "without prejudice to the powers of the European Community" and Article M TEU further clarified the point by stat-

Once again the competence issue was to reach the Court. Two separate actions were brought by Community institutions against the Council concerning the line between the communitarised part of JHA, Article 100C TEC, and the third pillar. The first was an action by the Parliament regarding the Visa Regulation,[90] and the second was a Commission action for annulment of the Airport Transit Visas Joint Action.[91] Both cases were triggered by the fact that the Council had shown an inclination towards the third pillar which the relevant institutions considered to encroach on the Community competence. The issue was not tackled directly in the first case, since the Court focused mainly on the question of whether the Council's amendments were substantive thus violating the Parliament's prerogatives. But it was addressed much more clearly in the second judgement.

In the first case, the European Parliament had called for the annulment of the Visa Regulation on the basis of a lack of re-consultation following a series of substantive amendments to the Commission's proposal. So whilst the Commission proposal provided, after the lapse of the 30 June deadline, only for one common list designating the third countries whose nationals had to be in possession of a visa when crossing the Member States' external frontiers, the Regulation adopted by the Council allowed Member States to maintain for an indefinite period their lists of countries not appearing on the common list whose nationals are subject to visa requirements.[92] The Commission proposal also provided for a mutual recognition of visas issued by Member States which was deleted by the Council which also underlined in the preamble that this and other aspects of visa policy came under the third pillar.[93] Finally, the list of countries appearing in the Annex was considerably limited in the Regulation.[94] Unfortunately, the Court did not take a clear position on any of these matters. It mainly focused on whether the changes were substantive. Of course, under the Maastricht Treaty the Parliament could only challenge a measure for procedural reasons and not the very substance of the measure. Having decided that the first change was substantive, the Court did not consider it necessary to examine the

---

ing that "nothing in this Treaty shall affect the Treaties establishing the European Communities".

90 Case C-392/95, *European Parliament v Council,* [1998] ECR I-3213.

91 Case C-170/96, *European Commission v Council* [1998] ECR I-2763.

92 See Article 1 (2) of the Commission proposal, *op.cit.* in conjunction with Article 2 of Council Regulation (EC) No 2317/95 of 25 September 1995 determining the third countries whose nationals must be in possession of visas when crossing the external borders of the Member States, OJ L 234/1, 3.10.1995.

93 See Article 2 of the Commission proposal, *op.cit.,* in conjunction with the second and fourth recital of the Regulation 2317/95, *op.cit.*

94 Whereas in the Commission proposal 126 countries appeared, in the Regulation there were only 98.

rest of the arguments advanced by the Parliament, but confined itself to applying the classic case law on the need for re-consulting the Parliament in the case of substantive changes.

The second case is a great deal more interesting from an institutional point of view. The Commission, supported by the Parliament, had challenged the fact that the Council adopted the legal act establishing an Airport Transit Visa on the basis of a third pillar legal basis instead of Article 100C TEC.[95] It is worth highlighting the fact that the Commission had included the Airport Transit Visa case in its initial proposal for the visa list Regulation.[96] Thus, in accordance with the Commission's opinion the Council had clearly acted in breach of Article 100C TEC and infringed the Community competence on visa policy. The judgement is interesting on a series of grounds. First, on the basis of a joint reading of Articles L and M TEU the Court established its jurisdiction over the control of the borderline between the first and the third pillar.[97] Second, inasmuch as the substance is concerned, the Court decided in favour of the Council. The decisive arguments were two-fold. On the one hand, on the basis of a joint reading of Articles 3 (d) and 100C TEC, the Court considered that Article 100C TEC applied to measures concerning the crossing of the external borders only insofar as they relate to the entry into, and movement within, the internal market.[98] And, on the other hand, it considered that the airport transit visa did not constitute entry into the territory. Thus, given that the concept of visas in the light of Article 100C TEC entailed entry and movement into the territory of the Member State, airport transit visas were excluded from its scope.[99]

Concluding Remarks

This brief overview of the institutional framework and the consequent skirmishes preceding Amsterdam enables one to draw some preliminary conclusions. First, despite the apparent lack of any Community competence on migration up to the Treaty of Maastricht, there were unquestionably some traces of competence, albeit strongly contested, since the very beginning of the Communities' history. Second, Member States have initially preferred to deal with migration related issues almost exclusively at the intergovernmental level, mainly due to discord among themselves as to the final objective and the sovereignty implications of the matters in question.

95 See Joint Action 96/197/JHA, *op.cit.*

96 For a discussion on transit visas as well as the present case law see Guild E., *Immigration Law in the European Community, op.cit.*, at p. 285-290.

97 Case C-170/96, *op.cit.*, paras 15 to 17. Actually the only party that had questioned the competence of the Court was the UK.

98 Case C-170/96, *op.cit.,* paras 21 and 22.

99 Case C-170/96, *op.cit.*, paras 28 to 32.

However, over the course of the years, European Heads of State and Government realised that intergovernmental cooperation could not take them far. Indeed, both the Maastricht third pillar and Schengen cooperation have been heavily criticised; the former for its ineffectiveness, and, the latter, for its secretive character, its duplicative role and the absence of any democratic or judicial control.[100] Thus, during the 1996 IGC, justice and home affairs issues were on the agenda once more.

100 Regarding the third pillar see O'Keeffe D., "Recasting the Third Pillar", *CMLRev*, Vol. 32, 1995, p. 893-920; O' Keeffe D., "Reforming the Third Pillar: Transparency and structural reform in the long term perspective", in Bieber R. and Monar J. (eds.), *Justice and Home Affairs in the European Union The Development of the Third Pillar,* European Interuniversity Press, Brussels, 1995, p. 397-421; Dehousse F. and Van den Hende L., "Plaidoyer pour la réforme du troisième pilier", *RMC*, No 403, décembre 1996, p. 714-718 and Vignes D., "Plaidoyer pour le IIIème Pilier", *RMC*, No 397, avril 1996, p. 273-281. Regarding Schengen see Mazzi-Zissis S., 'Les Accords de Schengen et la libre circulation des personnes dans l'Union européenne: exemple à suivre ou dangereux précédent?', in Ehlermann C. D. (ed.), *Multi-Speed Europe – the Legal Framework of Variable Geometry in the European Union,* Bundesanzeiger, Bonn, 1999, p. 47-66; O'Keeffe D., "The Schengen Convention : A Suitable Model for European Integration?", *YEL*, Vol. 11, 1991, p. 185-219 and Curtin D. and Meijers H., "The principle of open government in Schengen and the European Union: democratic retrogression?, *CMLRev,* Vol. 32, 1995, p. 391-442.

Chapter 2: The Institutional Framework *Post*-Amsterdam

Introduction

The communitarisation of migration and other policies related to the free movement of persons has been one of the most widely debated issues during the 1996 IGC and the concluding Amsterdam Summit.[1] In contrast to previous attempts, the Amsterdam Treaty endeavoured to provide a coherent and comprehensive solution, for the first time, *within* the EC framework. Most of the provisions that are relevant to migration policy were communitarised and were gathered under a new Title IV inserted into the EC Treaty. This communitarisation was the result of two contemporaneous operations: on the one hand, most of the provisions of the former third pillar have been transferred to Title IV TEC,[2] whereas, on the other, these new Community legal bases would also host the Schengen *acquis*, which has been integrated into the EU framework via a Protocol annexed to the Amsterdam Treaty.[3] At long last, a *Community* migration policy was supposed to take shape in principle within the five years following the entry into force of the Amsterdam Treaty.[4]

---

1 Some of the material in this chapter has appeared in an earlier form in the *Yearbook of European Law.* See Papagianni G. "Free Movement of Persons in the light of the new Title IV TEC: from intergovernmentalism towards a Community policy", *YEL*, 2002, p. 107-162.

2 Articles 61-69 TEC. While in principle the provisions of Title IV TEC reproduce the wording of Articles K.1 to K.6 of the former third pillar, there have been a few amendments, which in some cases might be indicative of the will of Heads of State with regard to certain issues. See *infra* at 6.1.2.

3 Protocol integrating the Schengen *acquis* into the framework of the European Union.

4 The existence of a five-year transitory period is provided by Articles 61 (1) and 67 (1) TEC. The legal bases regarding the central issues linked with the formation of an immigration policy are excluded from this deadline. The last paragraph of Article 63 TEC provides that "measures to be adopted pursuant to points … 3 (a) and 4 shall not be subject to the five year period".

The divorce from intergovernmentalism was, however, neither abrupt nor smooth. Indeed, the concessions that the Heads of State and Government had to make in order to arrive at these developments were so numerous, and their impact on the evolution of this area, so important that one could convincingly argue that the achievement was merely a Pyrrhic victory. Moreover, the partial character of this communitarisation as well as the innovative legal solutions that the negotiators had to find in order to achieve political consensus are set to render the establishment of a Community policy a long and evolving process, which especially in the initial phases might appear to be an obstacle race.

The purpose of this chapter is to provide a comprehensive analysis of the institutional aspects associated with the establishment of a Community migration policy within the framework of Title IV TEC. In the course of this chapter, the passage from intergovernmentalism towards a Community policy will be sketched out as clearly as possible. Bearing in mind that the communitarisation of migration policy is still an evolving process, it will attempt to trace the remnants of the intergovernmental era and to analyse their causes as well as their impact on this ambitious on-going operation.

The chapter is divided into three sections. The first section provides a comprehensive overview of the institutional imbroglio of Title IV TEC. Emphasis will be placed on the effect of the 'partial communitarisation' of the relevant policies. The term 'partial communitarisation' is mainly used in the literature in order to stress the fact that only a part of the former third pillar issues are transferred to the first pillar.[5] Certain other issues, mainly regarding judicial cooperation in penal matters and police cooperation, have remained under the intergovernmental third pillar.[6] However, seeing this term *au sens large*, the partial character of this communitarisation concerns two other aspects as well. The first being that the communitarisation is partial since the number of Member States involved is variable. Two Member States are *de facto* 'out' and another one is bound exclusively on an international law basis. Thus, the number of Member States bound by a legal act depends quite often on the specific issue to be regulated and/or the wishes of the Member State concerned. In fact an innovative and rather complicated system of predetermined flexibility on the basis of Protocols was established in order to accommodate all national interests. The other aspect is that communitarisation is also partial since the newly communitarised former third pillar provisions have preserved many of their intergovernmental characteristics, placing the Title IV institutional framework in a 'limbo' situation between intergovernmentalism and the Community method.

The second section of this chapter will be devoted to a preliminary presentation of the problems stemming from this complicated institutional framework.

5 Which is to say within the framework of the new Title IV TEC (Articles 61-69 TEC), Article 135 TEC and Article 280 TEC.

6 Articles 29-32 TEU.

There, the problems arising from both the Protocols and the newly communitarised legal bases of Title IV, as well as the pragmatic solutions that have been found in order to cut the various Gordian knots, will be explored. Moreover, while emphasising the evolutionary but irreversible character of the changes wrought at Amsterdam with regard to the establishment of a Community, even if not common, policy regarding the entry and residence of third country nationals, it will be clearly shown that the competence debate is still going strong.

A third and final section presents the recent developments that took place at Nice and within the framework of the Draft Constitutional Treaty process, while trying to draw some preliminary conclusions regarding the prospects for the future.

2.1 The Institutional Framework: Partial Communitarisation

2.1.1 Predetermined Flexibility

Before discussing in detail the form and impact of predetermined flexibility in this area it is worth highlighting the reasons for which its use was deemed necessary. Despite the existence of the former Article K.9 *passerelle* clause, which permitted the communitarisation of areas falling under the third pillar, it was made clear that any decision to do so should be taken at the level of Heads of State and Government.[7] Moreover, in political terms, the use of former Article K. 9 TEU could not possibly have justified the extent of the concessions that were indispensable for such a communitarisation.[8] In fact, the communitarisation question proved to be a profound puzzle even for the IGC itself.[9] The dif-

7 As already mentioned Denmark had via a Unilateral Declaration expressed its concerns with regard to an eventual application of the clause. Moreover, given the negative results to the first Danish referendum regarding the ratification of the Treaty of Maastricht, the use of the *passerelle* clause could prove rather risky. Another reason that undoubtedly contributed in excluding *de facto* the application of the said clause was the delay of the entry into force of the Treaty and the pre-set date for a new IGC in 1996, leading *inter alia* the Commission to take a pragmatic approach on the matter. Thus, in 1993 it suggested that the transfer was premature, whereas in 1995 that it should be better dealt with in the framework of the IGC. See respectively SEC (93) 1687/4 final, 3.11.1993 and COM (95) 566 final, 22.11.1995. For further discussion on this point see Peers S., *EU Justice and Home Affairs Law*, Longman, London, 2000, at p. 32-33.

8 Adam R., "La cooperazione in materiae di justizia e affari interni tra communitariszazione e metodo intergovernativo", *Il Dirittto dell'Unione Europea,* Vol. 2-3, 1998, p. 481-509, at p. 505.

9 For a detailed analysis of all the relevant phases and proposals examined during the course of the 1996 IGC regarding the communitarisation of policies related to free movement of persons see Labayle H., "La coopération européenne en matière de justice et d'affaires intérieures et la Conférence intergouvernementale", *RTDE,* Vol. 33, Issue 1, janv.-mars 1997, p. 1-35; Labayle H., "Un espace de liberté, de

ferences among the Member States were insurmountable.[10] Things became even more complicated when the question of integrating the Schengen *acquis* into the EU framework was also put on the agenda.[11] As political differences over the trajectory of integration in this area threatened to crystallise divisions between Member States and to lead to eternal stagnation,[12] recourse to a type of predetermined flexible model, given also the extant wide-ranging discussion over flexibility,[13] was considered an excellent and, most importantly, a very convenient idea.

Nevertheless, despite the common origins and logic behind the introduction of the general and the predetermined flexibility clauses, it should be underlined that the two regimes are profoundly distinct.[14] On the one hand, the general clauses seem quite promising, less divisive and threatening to the concept of

sécurité et de justice", *RTDE*, Vol. 33, No 4, oct.-déc. 1997, p. 813-881; Montaut I., "La Communautarisation du Second et du Troisième Piliers du Traité de l'Union européenne, dans la perspective de la Réforme Institutionnelle de la CIG de 1996", *RMC*, No 408, mai 1997, p. 335-348, and, Trotta R., "La dimension extérieure de la circulation des personnes après Amsterdam", in Dony M. (ed.), *L'Union européenne et le monde après Amsterdam,* Université de Bruxelles, Bruxelles, 1999, p. 107-141.

10 For a brief overview of the Member States positions see Kölliker A. and Milner F., *How to make use of Closer Cooperation? The Amsterdam clauses and the dynamics of European Integration,* European Commission, Forward Studies Unit, 1999. A definitive version of this paper is available at <http://www.europa.eu.int/comm/cdp/working-paper/index_en.htm>.

11 It should be underlined that this question was not put on the agenda until the very late stages of the negotiations. However, the Dutch Presidency was determined to incorporate Schengen into the Treaty in order to prevent the development of two separate systems for the same subject. See De Zwaan J., "Schengen and its Incorporation into the New Treaty: The Negotiating Process", *op.cit.* See also Petite M., "The Treaty of Amsterdam", *Harvard Working Papers,* 5 October 1997, available at <http://www.jeanmonnetprogram.org/papers/98/98-2-.html>. It is very probable that the negotiators were concerned about the implications of this process.

12 At least as far as the Community framework was concerned.

13 One should recall that one of the issues that prevailed during the 1996 IGC was the establishment of flexibility clauses within the EU framework. Regarding the general discourse concerning the legitimacy of flexibility, see Metcalfe L., "Flexible integration in and after the Amsterdam Treaty", in Den Boer M., Guggenbuhl A. and Van Hoonacker S. (eds.), *Coping with flexibility after Amsterdam,* EIPA, Maastricht, 1998, p. 11-30.

14 By the term 'general' I refer to the Treaty provisions that institutionalise the establishment of closer cooperation. See Articles 43-45 TEU, Article 11 TEC and Article 40 TEU. Whereas the term 'predetermined' flexibility refers to the relevant Protocols annexed to Title IV TEC. The common reason that justifies the introduction of all these clauses lies in the fact that progress should not be prevented for those willing to go further in a certain area within the EC/EU framework.

uniformity and are respectful of the EC core and the concept of the *acquis communautaire*.[15] Whereas on the other, the Title IV flexibility mechanisms appear to be no more than a quasi-legitimate way of accommodating diverging interests associated with the communitarisation of policies related to the free movement of persons. They clearly allow for an indefinite 'pick and choose' in areas closely linked to the EC core, while they also seem to place in danger even the traditional idea of Community solidarity.[16]

The flexibility mechanisms governing Title IV TEC neither correspond to the theoretical categorisation of the various flexibility models, nor respect the general rules governing flexibility in the European framework, as these were introduced in Amsterdam.[17] Their distinction from the general closer cooperation regime seems to be codified even by the Treaty itself.[18] Moreover, the Treaty makes clear that there is not one but many forms of closer cooperation, which will all be based on various cross-references among the Protocols.[19] Each of these closer cooperations functions basically with its own rules,[20] and contrary

---

15 According to Article 43 (1) (e) TEU, any closer cooperation should not affect the EU *acquis*.

16 These comments are made, mainly, with regard to the position of the United Kingdom and Ireland.

17 For a general overview regarding flexibility models, see Ehlermann C.D., 'Différentiation accrue ou uniformité renforcée', *RMUE,* Issue 3, 1995, p. 191-208 and Ehlermann C.D., 'Différentiation, flexibilité, coopération renforcée: les nouvelles dispositions du traité d'Amsterdam', *RMUE*, Issue 3, 1997, p. 53-90. For a presentation of the Amsterdam general clauses on closer cooperation, see Gaja G., 'How flexible is flexibility under the Amsterdam Treaty?', *CMLRev,* Vol. 35, 1998, p. 855-870 and Kortenberg H., 'Closer Cooperation in the Treaty of Amsterdam', *CMLRev*, Vol. 35, 1998, p. 833-854.

18 It needs to be underlined that the Title IV flexibility clauses are established on primary law bases. See Article 69 Title IV TEC and the relevant Protocols.

19 For example, whereas the UK and Ireland are clearly 'out' as far as the borders question is concerned – mainly due to the safety net function of the Protocol on Article 14 – they might be involved in numerous initiatives concerning immigration and asylum policy, given their flexible opt-in rights. For a detailed presentation of the various cases of differentiated integration that might be formed see Monar J., 'Schengen and Flexibility in the Treaty of Amsterdam: Opportunities and Risks of Differentiated Integration in the EU Justice and Home Affairs' in M. Den Boer (ed.), *Schengen, Judicial Cooperation and Policy Coordination,* EIPA, Maastricht, 1997, p. 9-28.

20 For a detailed analysis on this point as well as for arguments supporting the conclusions that are drawn with regard to the special characteristics of the flexibility mechanisms of Title IV TEC, see Papagianni G., "Flexibility in Justice and Home Affairs: an old phenomenon taking new forms", in De Witte B., Hanf D. and Vos E. (eds.), *The Many Faces of Differentiation in EU Law*, Intersentia, Antwerpen, 2001, p. 101-128.

to the general rules regarding closer cooperation, they do affect parts of the *acquis communautaire* that already existed in that area.[21] Finally, the measures adopted within their framework, as opposed to the *acquis* developed within the framework of the other forms of closer cooperation, will form part of the Union *acquis*.[22]

Thus, the flexibility clauses introduced within the framework of Title IV should be regarded less as closer cooperation, and more as a communitarisation *à la carte*. The Member States who mounted strong objections to any sort of communitarisation – either with regard to former third pillar issues or to Schengen matters – were given the possibility of participating to the extent and in the way that they preferred.

Predetermined flexibility in this area takes the form of two main sorts of Protocols attached to the Treaty of Amsterdam: first, a series of national protocols with regard to Title IV, and second, a protocol integrating the Schengen *acquis* within the EU framework.

2.1.1.1 National Protocols

The Member States benefiting from a special status are, on the one hand, those having expressed intense concerns in the past, namely the UK and Denmark, and on the other, Ireland. The Irish position was, in fact, based on different reasons, since Ireland had chosen to opt-out mainly due to its specific relations with the UK.[23] On the basis of the specific concerns and wishes of the outsiders two main sets of arrangements could be distinguished: one arrangement regarding the UK and Ireland and another regarding Denmark. In contrast to the British/Irish objections, which concerned the very objective of the measures to be adopted, the Danish objections concerned their legal status. Whereas Denmark, a Schengen contracting party, was willing to participate in a cooperation concerning the establishment of an "area without internal frontiers", it contested, mainly for internal political reasons, the transfer of such a competence to the

21 Meaning the existing Community visa *acquis* and the former third pillar *acquis*, both developed at the course of the Maastricht era.

22 See new Article 44 in conjunction with Article 43 (i) TEU as amended by the Treaty of Nice, OJ C 80/1, 10.3.2001. See also Article 8 of the Schengen Protocol.

23 Ireland had already abolished border controls with the UK since 1920 within the framework of a Common Travel Area. Considering on the one hand that the movement of persons between the UK and Ireland represents 80% of the entire movement of persons to Ireland, whereas on the other an Irish participation to Schengen would inevitably lead to the reintroduction of border controls with the UK, Ireland opted to associate its position to that of the UK for pragmatic reasons. De Lobkowicz W., *L'Europe et la sécurité intérieure Une élaboration par étapes, op.cit.*, at p. 113.

EC level. It opted instead for the maintenance of such cooperation within the intergovernmental sphere.[24]

The United Kingdom was allowed to maintain its traditional position on former Article 7a TEC (now 14 TEC), as well as the right not to be bound either by the Schengen *acquis* that would be integrated into the EU framework or by any measures that would be adopted on the basis of Title IV TEC.[25] This special British status was safeguarded, first, by a special Protocol on Article 14,[26] secondly, by the introduction of a national Protocol with regard to Title IV TEC,[27] and thirdly, by the introduction of special provisions into the Schengen Protocol to the extent that Schengen relevant issues were concerned.[28] An analogous status was granted to Ireland.[29] Both the United Kingdom and Ireland were granted the possibility to opt-in on a 'pick and choose' basis both as to the Schengen *acquis* and to Title IV measures, albeit with different opting in proce-

24 It is likely that Denmark found itself unable to back down from the position that it had adopted at the time of the Edinburgh Council with regard to justice and home affairs issues and which enabled it to ratify the Maastricht Treaty. See Petite, *op.cit.*

25 The United Kingdom had traditionally sustained that this provision concerned exclusively the free movement of EU nationals. Moreover, it should be recalled that the United Kingdom and Ireland were the only EC Member States that were not Schengen contracting parties. For a detailed presentation of the UK position see O' Keeffe D., " Non-Accession to the Schengen Convention : The cases of the United Kingdom and Ireland ", in Pauly A. (ed.), *Schengen en panne,* EIPA, Maastricht, 1994, p. 43-53; Wiener A., "Forging Flexibility – The British 'No' to Schengen", Arena Working Paper, No 1, January 2000 and Schutte J., "The Incorporation of the Schengen *Acquis* in the European Union", in Cullen P. and Gilmore W. (eds.) *Crime Sans Frontières: International and European Legal Approaches*, Edinburgh University Press, Edinburgh, 1998, p. 124-132. See also House of Lords, *Schengen and the United Kingdom's Border Controls,* European Communities Select Committee Seventh Report, Session 1998-99, London, 10 March 1999.

26 Granting the United Kingdom the possibility to exercise border controls at its national frontiers. See Protocol on the application of certain aspects of Article 14 (ex Article 7a) of the Treaty establishing the European Community to the United Kingdom and Ireland.

27 Granting the United Kingdom an 'out' status regarding Title IV TEC. See Protocol on the position of the United Kingdom and Ireland.

28 Declaring expressly that the United Kingdom will not be bound by this new *acquis.* See Article 4 of the Schengen Protocol.

29 The Irish position is safeguarded by the same legal instruments that were drafted with regard to the UK. See *supra.* However, given that the Irish opt-out was much more of a practical necessity than a political desire, Ireland was further granted the possibility of waiving the national Protocol at any time. See Article 8 of the British/ Irish Protocol. See also Declaration (No 55) by Ireland on Article 3 of the Protocol on the position of the United Kingdom and Ireland.

dures.[30] And, as it turns out, they have both exercised their opt-in possibilities regarding both areas.[31]

Furthermore, as already mentioned the introduction of special arrangements was also deemed necessary in order to attain Danish accord regarding both the transfer of certain areas of the former third pillar to the first pillar and the integration of a part of the Schengen *acquis* into the EC framework. The Danish position as far as Title IV TEC is concerned is regulated by a national Protocol,[32] whereas the Danish special position as a Schengen contracting party is regulated by a series of express provisions that were inserted into both the

30 See Articles 3 and 4 of the British/Irish Protocol and Article 5 of the Schengen Protocol. It needs to be highlighted that the Council decision with regard to opting into Schengen relevant measures needs to be unanimous. Moreover, despite the lack of any express legal constraints regarding the opting-in possibility of the United Kingdom and Ireland one should not lose sight of certain practical limitations imposed by the logic of the Schengen system, given that certain issues are considered as closely inter-linked with the proper functioning of the system. The exercise of the opting-in possibility in a coherent manner is also stressed by the Commission in its opinions regarding the relevant British and Irish requests. See respectively SEC (1999) 1198 final and SEC (2000) 1439 final.

31 See Council Decision 2000/365/EC of 29 May 2000 concerning the request of the United Kingdom to take part in some of the provisions of the Schengen *acquis* OJ L 131/43, 1.6.2000. For the text of the UK request and a brief presentation see Pallett L., "The United Kingdom Position: Implementing the Schengen Protocol", in Marinho C. (ed), *Asylum, Immigration and Schengen Post-Amsterdam – A First Assessment,* EIPA, Maastricht, 2001, p. 91-105. For further details regarding the British request, see House of Lords, *UK Participation in the Schengen acquis*, Select Committee on European Union Fifth Report, Session 2000, London, 15 February 2000. An almost identical request was also submitted by Ireland. Council Decision 2002/192/EC of 28 February 2002 concerning Ireland's request to take part in some of the provisions of the Schengen *acquis,* OJ L 64/20, 7.3.2002. However, Ireland has decided not to opt in to the Schengen provision for cross border surveillance (Article 40 of the Schengen Implementing Convention), most probably for political reasons. See 'Schengen: Ireland follows UK opt-in', *Statewatch,* June-August 2000, Vol. 10, No 3/4, p. 3. As a final note it needs to be mentioned that the Council has also already adopted the Decision regarding the full implementation of the Schengen *acquis* and its application to the UK. See Council Decision 2004/926/EC of 22 December 2004 on the putting into effect of parts of the Schengen *acquis* by the United Kingdom of Great Britain and the Northern Ireland, OJ L 395/70, 31.12.2004. An analogous Decision for Ireland is still awaited. Moreover, both the UK and Ireland have already opted into a series of Title IV measures on the basis of their general Title IV opt-out Protocols.

32 Protocol on the position of Denmark.

Danish national Protocol and the Schengen Protocol safeguarding the Danish rights and obligations towards its Schengen partners.[33]

More specifically, Denmark will not be bound by any of the measures adopted on the basis of Title IV TEC. The only exceptions to this rule concern certain aspects of visa policy, since Denmark has expressly declared its will to remain bound on a Community law basis by the objectives described in former Article 100C TEC.[34] Insofar as measures 'building upon the Schengen *acquis*' are concerned, Denmark will have to decide within a six-month period after the Council has decided on such a proposal whether to implement the decision.[35] If it decides to do so, it will be bound exclusively on an international law basis.[36] As to the rest of the measures adopted on the basis of Title IV TEC, Denmark will have the sole option of waiving its Protocol.[37] It needs to be underlined that an opting-in possibility analogous to the one offered to the United Kingdom and Ireland was neither preferable nor appropriate for the Danish case, given that due to national constitutional considerations Denmark might have had to organise a referendum every time it opted into a measure adopted on the basis of Title IV TEC.[38]

A special status was also recognized to the two Nordic outsiders, namely Norway and Iceland. This was mainly due to the Danish interest in preserving its association with the Nordic Passport Union. In fact both Norway and Iceland had been associated with Schengen since 1996. A clause providing for the conclusion of an association agreement with Norway and Iceland was thus inserted into the Schengen Protocol. On the basis of this clause Norway and Iceland have already signed an Association Agreement with the Community.[39]

33 See Article 3 of the Schengen Protocol and Article 5 of the Danish Protocol.

34 Now Article 62 (2) (b) (i) and (iii) TEC. See Article 4 of the Danish Protocol. However, things have not been simple even in that case given that the scope of the new Article 62 (2) (b) (ii) TEC is wider than that of former Article 100C TEC. See *infra* at 2.2.1.3.

35 In fact the Danish Permanent Representative periodically informs the Council General Secretariat on the implementation of Schengen relevant acts in Danish law. See for example the following Council documents: 5096/04, 14822/03, 14588/03, 14807/03, 9963/02, 14261/01 and 14241/01.

36 It needs to be underlined that should Denmark decide not to implement the relevant measures, it will have to face the "penalties" that might eventually be adopted by its Schengen partners which would most probably be the re-introduction of border controls at the frontiers with Denmark. See Article 5 (2) of the Schengen Protocol.

37 See Article 7 of the Danish Protocol.

38 See Declaration (No 53) by Denmark on Article 42 of the Treaty on European Union.

39 Article 6 of the Schengen Protocol. See also the Agreement concluded by the Council of the European Union and the Republic of Iceland and the Kingdom of

Finally, given the practical implications that JHA cooperation and especially the Schengen agreement has on Switzerland due to its geographical position, the latter has also expressed the wish to be associated with the Schengen *acquis*.[40] After three years of negotiations political agreement was reached during the first-ever EU-Switzerland Summit held in Brussels on the 19 May 2004.[41] An

---

Norway concerning the latters' association with the implementation, application and development of the Schengen *acquis* OJ C 176/36, 10.7.1999, as well as the Council Decision 1999/437/EC of 17 May 1999 on certain arrangements for the application of the Agreement concluded by the Council of the European Union and the Republic of Iceland and the Kingdom of Norway concerning the association of those two States with the implementation, application and development of the Schengen *acquis*, OJ C 176/31, 10.7.1999. Moreover, in view of an eventual British/ Irish opt-in to Schengen, a second agreement has been concluded. See Agreement concluded by the Council of the European Union and the Republic of Iceland and the Kingdom of Norway on the establishment of rights and obligations between Ireland and the United Kingdom of Great Britain and Northern Ireland, on the one hand, and the Republic of Iceland and the Kingdom of Norway, on the other, in areas of the Schengen *acquis* which apply to these States, OJ L 15/2, 20.1.2000. Given the subsidiary character of this second agreement, the discussion will focus on the 'main' association agreement.

40 For a detailed discussion on the implications of Schengen on Switzerland see Bieber R., Lyon A.-C., Monar J. (eds), *Justice et Affaires Intérieures – L'Union européenne et la Suisse,* Staempfli Editions SA, Berne, 1997. For the text of the Swiss request see Council doc. 9524/01 AELE 13 JAI 62 FISC 116 AGRI 137, 18.6.2001 where the relevant Swiss request is annexed [Annex 3]. The EC had already signed an Agreement on the free movement of persons with Switzerland. See Peers S., "The EC-Switzerland Agreement on Free Movement of Persons : Overview and Analysis", *EJML,* Vol. 2, 2000, p. 127-142. Moreover, the Schengen Contracting Parties had signed numerous bilateral agreements with Switzerland. See "Switzerland: Treaties with Schengen countries", *Statewatch*, Vol. 9, No 3 & 4, May-August 1999, p. 29-30; "Switzerland: Into Schengen by back door?", *Statewatch*, Vol. 8, No 1, January-February 1998, p. 4.

41 See Council Decision 2004/860/EC of 25 October 2004 on the signing, on behalf of the European Community, and on the provisional application of certain provisions of the Agreement between the European Union, the European Community and the Swiss Confederation's association with the implementation, application and development of the Schengen *acquis*, OJ L 370/78, 17.12.2004; Council Decision 2004/849/EC of 25 October 2004 on the signing, on behalf of the European Union, and on the provisional application of certain provisions of the Agreement between the European Union, the European Community and the Swiss Confederation's association with the implementation, application and development of the Schengen *acquis*, OJ L 368/26, 15.12.2004, and Council Decision No 1/2004 of the EU/Switzerland Mixed Committee established by the Agreement concluded by the European Union, the European Community and the Swiss Confederation concerning the latter's association in the implementation, application and development of the

analogous request for association with the Schengen *acquis* has been submitted by Liechtenstein.[42]

2.1.1.2 Incorporation of the Schengen *Acquis* into the EC Framework: The Return of the 'Prodigal Son'

The second major development within the framework of the Amsterdam Treaty, which is also the second aspect of predetermined flexibility in this area, concerns the integration of the Schengen *acquis* within the EU framework. Schengen cooperation has undoubtedly been the traditional competitor to EU action in the area of JHA. The Schengen contracting parties have managed to achieve what the fifteen have failed to do both within the EC and EU framework. However, Schengen has also been traditionally seen as a '*laboratoire d'essai*', something that was not supposed to last forever.[43] Therefore, its integration into the EU framework could be viewed as the return of the 'prodigal son'.

The political and practical reasons for which the Heads of State and Government have decided to integrate the Schengen *acquis* into the EU framework are numerous: the need for coherence, the need to prevent the development of two parallel systems, the need to legitimise the Schengen 'black-market', as well as the need to provide the Union with a solid *acquis* in this area in light of the

Schengen *acquis* of 26 October 2004 adopting its Rules of Procedure, OJ C 308/2, 14.12.2004. See also "EU-Switzerland reach number of agreements at first joint summit", Irish Presidency Press Release of 19 May 2004, <www.eu2004.ie> and "Switzerland inches closer to EU as President hails a 'new era", www.euobserver.com, 19.5.2004. For an overview of the discussions within the Council see Council doc. 14637/01 AELE 22 JAI 157 JUR 357, 28.11.2001, Council doc. 10240/03 AELE 23,6.6.2003 and Council doc. 9544/04 AELE 12, 17.5.2004. Lastly, for an exhaustive presentation of the state of relations and the negotiations between Switzerland and the EU on the three closely linked files of taxation of savings, fight against fraud and cooperation on Schengen related issues with a series of useful references to official Federal Council documents see Filliez F., "Le rapprochement de la Suisse à l'Espace penal européen à l'exemple des negotiations en cours avec l'Union européenne" in De Kerchove G. and Weyembergh A. (eds.), *Sécurité et justice: enjeu de la politique extérieure de l'Union européenne*, Institut d'Etudes Européennes, Editions de l'Université de Bruxelles, Bruxelles, 2003, p. 231-246.

42 See Council doc. 10024/02 AELE 14 JAI 145, 13.6.2002.

43 See O'Keeffe D., 'The free movement of persons and the Single Market', *ELRev*, Vol. 2, 1992, p. 3-19; Elsen C., "Schengen et la coopération dans les domaines de la justice et des affaires intérieures. Besoins actuels et options futures", in Den Boer M. (ed.), *The Implementation of Schengen: First the Widening, Now the Deepening,* EIPA, Maastricht, 1997, p. 3-9 and Schutte J., "Schengen: Its meaning for the free movement of persons in Europe", *CMLRev*, 1991, Vol. 28, p. 549-570.

forthcoming enlargement.[44] There is no doubt that by integrating the Schengen *acquis,* the EU has instantly acquired a wide-ranging *acquis* in JHA as well as an "area without internal frontiers" to which the Union has always aspired.[45] Moreover, one needs to further underscore the fact that the only Member States that were not Schengen contracting parties – the United Kingdom and Ireland- were not in any case willing to participate in a cooperation with regard to these matters within the EC framework.

The integration of Schengen took the form of a Protocol attached to the Treaty of Amsterdam. The objective of the Protocol was two-fold. Firstly, to clarify and set the rules regarding the position of the Member States not participating in the Schengen closer cooperation and also the position of Denmark which was not willing to be bound on a Community law legal basis. Secondly, to provide a series of legal bases, successfully characterised as "*ordres de législation adressés au Conseil*",[46] in order to enable the Council to take the necessary legal steps for the incorporation of the Schengen *acquis*, since this was far too complicated to be completed by the IGC itself.[47] Indeed, the integration of Schengen

---

44 The term 'black market' is used in order to underline the parallel development of the Schengen *acquis* as well as the secrecy prevailing in it. The term was used by Steve Peers, see Peers S. *EU Justice and Home Affairs Law, op.cit.*, at p. 2. For a detailed analysis on the reasons for the integration of the Schengen *acquis,* see De Kerchove G., 'Un espace de liberté, de sécurité et de justice aux dimensions incertaines: Quelques réflexions sur le recours aux coopérations renforcées en matière de justice et d'affaires intérieures', in Den Boer M., Guggenbuhl A. and Van Hoonacker S. (eds.), *Coping with Flexibility and Legitimacy after Amsterdam,* EIPA, Maastricht, 1998, p. 197-204.

45 See Article 8a EEC. See *supra* at 1.2 and *infra* at 3.2.

46 Piçarra, *op.cit.*

47 On the basis of these specific 'legislation orders' the Council has adopted, among others, the following Decisions: Council Decision 1999/435/EC of 20 May 1999 concerning the definition of the Schengen *acquis* for the purpose of determining, in conformity with the relevant provisions of the Treaty establishing the European Community and the Treaty on European Union, the legal basis for each of the provisions or decisions which constitute the *acquis*, OJ L 176/1, 10.7.1999; Council Decision 1999/436/EC of 20 May 1999 determining, in conformity with the relevant provisions of the Treaty establishing the European Community and the Treaty on European Union, the legal basis for each of the provisions or decisions which constitute the Schengen *acquis,* OJ L 176/17, 10.7.1999; Council Decision 1999/307/EC of 1 May 1999 laying down the detailed arrangements for the integration of the Schengen Secretariat into the General Secretariat of the Council, OJ 117/49, 7.5.1999; Council Decision 1999/438/EC concerning the Joint Supervisory Authority set up under Article 115 of the Convention applying the Schengen Agreement of 14 June 1985, on the gradual abolition of checks at common borders, signed on 19 June 1990, OJ L 176/34, 10.7.1999. Moreover, a part of the Schengen *acquis* – the elements of the *acquis* for which a legal basis has been determined, either in the EC

proved to be a long process posing a series of legal problems that led the Council to a series of 'off the record' actions in order to address them.[48]

The first step with regard to the incorporation of the Schengen *acquis* into the EU framework consisted in defining the Schengen *acquis* and attributing an EC or EU legal basis to every Schengen provision. Given the ritual development of the Schengen *acquis* within a purely intergovernmental framework, as well as the inevitable overlaps with certain elements of the EC/EU JHA *acquis*, this proved far from an easy process. At a first stage, the Schengen contracting parties were attributed the task of performing a sort of *nettoyage* in order to incorporate into the EU framework only the parts of their *acquis* that were still operative and/or the parts that had not been superseded by Schengen or Union acts.[49] Inasmuch as the definition of the EC/EU legal bases is concerned a series of elements of the Schengen *acquis* were not attributed any specific Treaty legal basis, since they were not entirely compatible, or indispensable, or simply did not fit into the EU framework.[50] Thus, it is only a part of the Schengen *acquis* that

or in the EU Treaty, and which at the time of the adoption of the Decision were not classified as 'confidential' by the Schengen Executive Committee – has been published in a special edition of the *Official Journal*, OJ L 239, 22.9.2000.

48 The term 'off the record' is coined by Den Boer and Corrado. For a detailed analysis regarding the integration of the Schengen *acquis* see Den Boer M. and Corrado L., "For the Record or Off the Record: Comments About the Incorporation of Schengen into the EU", *EJML*, 2000, p. 397-418; Peers S., "*Caveat emptor*? Integrating the Schengen *acquis* into the European Union legal order", *Cambridge Yearbook of European Legal Studies*, Vol. 2, 1999, p. 87-123; Wagner E., "The integration of Schengen into the framework of the European Union", *Legal Issues of European Integration*, Vol. 2, 1998, p. 1-60.

49 It was estimated that by the time of its integration about forty Articles of the Schengen Implementing Convention had already been superseded by Community or Union acts. See Schutte J., "The Incorporation of the Schengen *Acquis* in the European Union", *op.cit.* Given that within the Schengen system the possibility of replacing or repealing previous acts was not provided for or at least not exercised in practice, this *nettoyage* was considered indispensable. The legal basis that has been used is Article 2 (1) second sub-paragraph, first sentence of the Schengen Protocol, according to which the Council, under its Schengen composition, is authorised to take "any measure necessary" for the integration of the Schengen *acquis* into the EU framework. It needs to be noted that this provision has functioned as a "blank cheque" that helped the Council to face part of the problems that have arisen following the decision for the integration of the Schengen *acquis* into the EU framework. See *infra* at 2.2.1.

50 i.e. Schengen institutional provisions, declarations that were not binding, financial provisions, visa waiver agreements. See Council Decisions 1999/435/EC and 1999/436/EC, *op.cit.*

has actually been integrated. Still it is worth stressing that the legal validity of the rest of the Schengen *acquis* was expressly maintained.[51]

Moreover, due to time constraints[52] and major deadlocks in the negotiations,[53] the Council has proceeded to take only those steps that were absolutely indispensable to the incorporation of the Schengen *acquis*, leaving a great number of other issues to fester. The examples are numerous. First of all, the provisions regarding the Schengen Information System, a large part of the Schengen *acquis*, were not attributed a legal basis.[54] Second, it has not been possible to 'commu-

---

51 See the fifth recital of Council Decision 1999/435/EC, *op. cit.*

52 According to a Declaration attached to the Treaty of Amsterdam, the Council would have to adopt all the relevant measures upon the date of entry into force of the Amsterdam Treaty. See Declaration (No 44) on Article 2 of the Protocol integrating the Schengen *acquis* into the framework of the European Union.

53 Given the political sensitivity of some issues as well as certain special Member States' interests, the procedure was often blocked by national vetoes. Spain was probably the country that most used its veto possibility. Some of the major Spanish objections with regard to the Gibraltar question have been finally surmounted thanks to a dynamic initiative for a trilateral meeting organised by the German Presidency, which finally gave rise to a British/Spanish agreement on Gibraltar. See "Gibraltar: status resolved", *Statewatch*, Vol. 10, No 2, March-May 2000, p. 23.

54 Due to the lack of consensus on the choice of the EC/EU appropriate legal bases that would host it, the entire SIS *acquis* has been integrated provisionally in the third pillar in accordance with the default mechanism provided by Article 2 (1) fourth sub-paragraph of the Schengen Protocol. The core difficulty in allocating the SIS provisions lies in the fact that SIS is partly in the first pillar (Article 96 SISA provides for SIS entries regarding immigration and asylum matters) and partly in the third pillar (for police and judicial cooperation related data). It is interesting to note that in 1998 around 80% of the SIS person-related data were Article 96 entries (i.e. aliens to be rejected at the borders or reported). Unfortunately, the attribution of parts of the SIS *acquis* to Title IV TEC legal bases, the position sustained by the Commission and certain delegations (i.e. Netherlands and Belgium) is not supported by all the Member States. See the Statement made by the Netherlands delegation, which is annexed to Council Decision 1999/436/EC determining the legal bases for the Schengen *acquis*, *op.cit.*. For a comprehensive analysis regarding the SIS integration negotiating process, see Den Boer and Corrado, *op. cit.* Two supplementary problems regarding SIS are: first, the question of data protection, especially in view of the absence of any specific relevant provisions within the third pillar, and, second, the question regarding the management of SIS from an operational point of view. With regard to the data protection question, see the interesting documentation file of the European Parliament's Hearing: "The European Union and Data Protection", available at <http://www.europarl.ep.ec/dg2/hearings/20000222/libe/subject/en/default.htm> It is worth noting that the Commission has recently announced its intention to present a comprehensive proposal for data protection in the third pillar. See House of Lords, *Evidence by Commissioner Franco Frattini, Commissioner for Justice, Freedom and Security on Justice and Home Affairs Matters,* EU Committee

nitarise' certain Schengen procedural aspects that were not entirely compatible with the Community system. The Schengen contracting parties, working within an 'off the record' legal framework based on secrecy, mutual trust and solidarity, had adopted institutional rules and developed practices that would be difficult to reconcile with the *esprit communautaire*, i.e. the Schengen confidentiality rules; the attribution of all the implementing powers to the Executive Committee; the tolerance of the abusive use of the possibility for unilateral reintroduction of border controls;[55] the attribution of considerable rights to associated third States,[56] and the absence of any judicial or democratic control. Moreover, certain Schengen measures such as the possibility of including family members of EU citizens in the Schengen Information System most probably needed to be revisited or at least further clarified.[57] Thirdly, the legal value of the Schengen

---

1st Report, 2005-6 Session, London, 13 June 2005, at p. 2. As far as the question of the SIS management is concerned, the Parliament, the Commission as well as certain academics have proposed the creation of an independent Agency. See European Parliament Report on the initiative of the Kingdom of Belgium and of the Kingdom of Sweden with a view to the adoption of a Council Regulation on the development of the second generation Schengen information system (SIS II), and on the initiative of the Kingdom of Belgium and of the Kingdom of Sweden with a view to the adoption of a Council Decision on the development of the second generation Schengen information system (SIS II), A5-0333/2001, 11.10.2001; Communication from the Commission to the Council and the European Parliament on the Development of the Schengen Information System II and possible synergies with a future Visa Information System, COM (2003) 771 final, 11.12.2003 and Anderson M., "Border Regimes and Security in an Enlarged European Community: Implications of the entry into force of the Amsterdam Treaty", EUI Working Papers, RSC No 2000/8, at p. 13.

55 See Article 2 (2) SISA. One could mention the abusive use of this right by France, which for several years refused to lift the controls at its borders with Belgium and Luxembourg due to its objections to the Dutch drug policy. See Louette J.-L., *Les Etats Benelux et la France face aux accords de Schengen*, *op.cit.* and Groenendijk K., "Reinstatement of Controls at the Internal Borders of Europe : Why and Against Whom", *ELJ*, Vol. 10, Issue 2, March 2004, p. 150-170.

56 Namely Norway and Iceland. Unfortunately the text of the 1996 Cooperation Agreement between Norway and Iceland and the Schengen countries does not form part of the *acquis* that has been integrated and, consequently, it has not been published. However, it is generally accepted that the rights, that were recognized to the two outsiders within the Schengen framework could not possibly have been transposed to the EU framework. See Kuijper P.J., "Some legal problems associated with the communitarisation of policy on visas, asylum and immigration under the Amsterdam Treaty and incorporation of the Schengen *acquis*", *CMLRev*, Vol. 37, 2000, p. 345-366.

57 According to an Executive Committee Declaration whereas EU citizens should not be listed in the SIS, their third country national family members could be. See

rules, which were adopted in a legal environment that was quite different from that of the Community, was, and remains, unclear.[58] One of the main sources of legal uncertainty has been the Schengen Common Manual whose legal value was rather blurred due to its hybrid nature.[59]

Declaration of the Executive Committee of 18 April 1996 defining the concept of alien (SCH/Com-ex (96) decl. 5) OJ L 23/458, 22.9.2000. A Commission statement included in the minutes of the Executive Committee asserts that inclusion of a beneficiary of Community law in the SIS list will only be compatible with EU law if the data concerns a person who presents an actual, genuine and serious threat to public policy and public security in each Schengen State. See the Commission Communication to the Council and the European Parliament on the special measures concerning the movement and residence of citizens of the Union which are justified on grounds of public policy public security or public health, COM (1999) 372 final, 19.7.1999, at p. 19, footnote 43. See also Peers S., *EU Justice and Home Affairs Law*, *op.cit.*, at p. 68. However, bearing in mind the soft law legal value of the Commission statement, the practice of certain Member States to proceed to SIS listing following rejection of an asylum application which inevitably leads to the rejection of subsequent visa applications due to SIS listing – see *infra* at 6.4 – and the difficulties regarding the judicial protection of individuals, the need to revisit or at least clarify further the relevant rules remains relevant. Moreover, it needs to be recalled that according to the *MRAX* judgement the lack of identity papers, and if a visa obligation exists the lack of a visa, cannot justify sending a family member back to the borders if he/she can prove his identity, the family relationship with an EU citizen and there is no evidence that he/she constitutes a threat. See Case C-459/99 *Mouvement contre le racism, l'antisémitisme et la xénophobie ASBL (MRAX) v Belgian State* [2002] ECR I-6591. As a final point, it is worth underlining that the issue has already reached the Court. See Opinion of Advocate General Mrs Kokott of 10 March 2005 in Case C-503/03 *Commission of the European Communities v. Kindgom of Spain*. Advocate General Kokott, underlining the primacy of EC law over the Schengen *acquis,* concludes for the condemnation of Spain for having violated the provisions of Directive 64/221. It remains to be seen what will be the Court's final judgment on the matter. See also *infra* at 2.2.1.1.

58 See Den Boer M. and Corrado L., *op.cit.*; Peers S., "*Caveat emptor*? Integrating the Schengen *acquis* into the European Union legal order", *op.cit.*

59 The Common Manual contained both legal and operational measures being at the same time the basic legal document on the crossing of internal borders and a practical guide for border guards. The Common Manual contained at least three types of provisions: first, regulatory provisions; second, implementing provisions; and, third, a list or compilations of authorities, documents or national rules. For further discussion see Commission Staff Working Document on the Recasting of the Common Manual: towards a "Community Borders Code as regards Movement of Persons?", SEC (2003) 736, 20.6.2003. In 2004 the Commission presented a legislative proposal for the recasting of the Common Manual, on which the Council and the European Parliament have reached political agreement at the first reading in July 2005. For the Commission proposal see Proposal for a Council Regulation

Despite the practical reasons making the above choices inevitable, one is bound to question the secrecy with which this whole exercise has been conducted as well as the lack of legal certainty characterizing the final result.[60] One could thus convincingly argue about the existence of an imperative need for communitarisation of Schengen.[61] Indeed, it has been rightly sustained that, 'l'*acquis* de Schengen ne sera pleinement assimilé au droit dérivé de la Communauté et de l'Union qu'à la 'deuxième génération''.[62]

Further, one should not lose sight of all the legal and practical problems arising from the innovative compromise solutions in order to achieve the Danish, British and Irish consensus with regard to the integration of Schengen, as well as the need to associate Norway and Iceland. The famous Schengen relevance test, in fact, became one of the major problems imported by Schengen into the EU framework.[63]

It becomes clear then that the return of the prodigal son is not only a source of joy, but also a source of serious problems, leaving Schengen resembling a Trojan horse. The negative impact of all these open wounds on the evolution of this area should not be neglected for it has virtually been rendered an obstacle race.

---

establishing a Community Code on the rules governing the movement of persons across borders, COM (2004) 391 final, 26.5.2004. For the final text agreed see European Parliament and Council Regulation establishing a Community Code on the rules governing the movement of persons across borders (Schengen Borders code), Council doc. PE-CONS 3643/05 FRONT 129 COMIX 495 CODEC 649 OC 566, 28.11.2005. For a discussion see *infra* at 4.1.1.

60 In fact, certain parts of the *acquis*, not always identifiable, have remained in the international law sphere. See Den Boer and Corrado, *op. cit.*

61 The need for a reappraisal of the substantial Schengen law in case it would be incorporated into the EU framework was stressed quite early on by some academics. See O'Keeffe D., "The Schengen Convention: A Suitable Model for European Integration?", *op.cit.* Moreover, the need for communitarisation of Schengen seems to have been recognised by the Commission as well. Indeed, the 'communitarisation' or 'conversion' of the Schengen *acquis* has been one of the objectives set by the Commission in its "Biannual update of the Scoreboard to review progress on the creation of an Area of "Freedom, Security and Justice" in the EU. For more information and references regarding the Scoreboard mechanism see *infra* at 5.1.1.4.

62 Piçarra, *op. cit.*

63 Meaning whether these proposals constitute or not a development of the Schengen *acquis*. See *infra* at 2.2.1.1.

2.1.2 The Title IV Institutional Framework: A 'Limbo' between Intergovernmentalism and the Community Method

2.1.2.1 An Institutional Legal 'Ghetto' within the EC Framework

A close examination of the institutional provisions of Title IV TEC reveals a series of institutional exceptions or deviations from the classic Community legal order, thereby justifying its description as a 'ghetto'.[64] Moreover, the similarities between Title IV TEC and the revised third pillar were remarkable. However, such a rapprochement should not be seen exclusively as a positive evolution of intergovernmental mechanisms, but also as a regression to those of the Community.[65]

The first compromise regards the decision-making process. The restrictions are two-fold. Firstly, one observes a certain re-weighting of the inter-institutional balance, with the role of the Member States being considerably reinforced. More specifically, for an initial five-year transitory period the right of initiative has been shared between the Commission and the Member States.[66] After the lapse of this period on 1 May 2004 the Commission reacquired its exclusive right of initiative, although it is still obliged to examine any request made by a Member State.[67] Furthermore, during the five-year transitory period, the role of the European Parliament was, and in certain areas is still, limited to simple consultation rights though its role has been reinforced after the passage to the co-decision procedure. Though this passage has not been automatic. A Decision providing for the passage of all the areas covered by Title IV TEC to the co-decision procedure had to be taken by the Council unanimously after the lapse of the five-year transitory period, with the exception of Article 62 (2) (b) (ii) and (iv) TEC, for which the co-decision procedure applies automatically since the lapse of the five year period.[68] Secondly, there have been major restrictions regarding the voting rules. Unanimity was the rule for the five-year transitory period with the sole exception of those aspects of visa policy that were included in former Article 100C TEC, to which the qualified majority voting rule applied immediately after

64 The term 'ghetto' was coined by Peers. See Peers S., "Justice and Home Affairs: decision-making after Amsterdam", *CMLRev* Vol. 25, 2000, p. 183-191.

65 Adam, *op.cit.*, at p. 508.

66 Article 67 (1) TEC. An analogous provision exists in the third pillar. See Article 34 (2) TEU.

67 Article 67 (2) first intent TEC. An analogous provision existed also in former Article 100C TEC.

68 See Council Decision 2004/927/EC of 22 December 2004 providing for certain areas covered by Title IV of Part Three of the Treaty establishing the European Community to be governed by the procedure laid down in Article 251 of that Treaty, OJ L 396/45, 31.12.2004. See also Article 67 (2) second intent and Article 67 (4) TEC. For the changes brought by the Treaty of Nice in that respect as well as for a discussion on the passage to qualified majority voting see *infra* at 2.3.1 and 2.3.2.

the entry into force of the Amsterdam Treaty.[69] This still remains so with regard to measures in the field of legal migration.[70]

A second series of institutional limitations concerns the role of the Court within the framework of Title IV TEC. First of all, it needs to be stressed that taking into account the impact of the Amsterdam Protocols, Title IV TEC becomes *de facto* an area where it will be extremely difficult for the Court to establish a uniform regime.[71] Despite these intrinsic difficulties, Member States have introduced a series of other limitations with regard to the role of the Court. Article 68 (1) TEC constitutes a clear limitation of the preliminary ruling mechanism, given that only national "courts or tribunals against whose decisions there is no judicial remedy under national law" are allowed to request a preliminary ruling from the Court. The reason for the exclusion of the traditional right of national courts of every level of jurisdiction was two-fold: on the one hand, the fear of an eventual judicial overload, and, on the other, the recognition of the need for quick judicial decisions.[72] Though these reasons may be well founded,[73] one cannot but underline the risk of diverging interpretations, which

69 See Article 62 (2) b (i) and (iii) TEC in conjunction with Article 67 (3) TEC. It needs to be stressed that the qualified majority voting rule already applied to these areas under the Maastricht Treaty as well. See former Article 100C TEC.
There is also a second exception, albeit not linked to the subject matter of this book, regarding temporary protection measures. See Article 64 (2) TEC.

70 See Recital No 7 of Council Decision 2004/927/EC, *op.cit.*

71 Since the decisions of the Court of Justice will not have uniform force throughout the Community. Moreover, different standards of judicial protection will apply to nationals of different Member States. See Albors-Llorens A., "Changes in the jurisdiction of the European Court of Justice under the Treaty of Amsterdam", *CMLRev,* Vol. 35, 1998, p. 1273-1294, at p. 1291.

72 See Fennelly N., "Where power now lies – Institutional reform", *Irish Journal of European Law,* 1998, Issue 7, No 1, p. 10-20. Despite the validity of these reasons one should not lose sight of the Member States' implicit preference for a limitation of the role of the Court. In fact, according to several observers a more unofficial reason for the limitation of the role of the Court was that Germany, in particular, was against references in this sensitive policy area given the Court's past record in social policy. Beach D., *Between Law and Politics – The relationship between the European Court of Justice and EU Member States,* DJØF Publishing, Copenhagen, 2001, at p. 105. The limitations on the role of the Court have been heavily criticised by Guild and Peers, who sustain that even a significant number of references would not justify the restrictions, see Guild E. and Peers S., "Deference or Defiance? The Courts of Justice's Jurisdiction over Immigration and Asylum", in Guild E. and Harlow C. (eds.), *Implementing Amsterdam: immigration and asylum rights in EC law*, Hart Publishing, Oxford, 2001, p. 267-289.

73 Nonetheless, it needs to be mentioned that the number of cases brought before the Court until now have been limited. The only existing case law for the moment are cases of a mainly institutional character, i.e. the staff cases concerning the integration

might inevitably diminish the prospects of the system achieving uniformity and reduce the possibility of consolidating the *acquis* in this area.[74] In view of the integration of the Schengen *acquis* into the EU framework, the negative impact of this limitation with regard to the preliminary ruling mechanism appears even more dangerous and the risk of a lack of uniformity more palpable. Indeed, the lack of an overriding judicial interpretation of the Schengen *acquis,* as well as the lack of communication between the national judges, has been considered to constitute a major deficiency regarding the uniform application of the Schengen *acquis*.[75]

The very insertion of this limitation, as well as the way that it is drafted prompts certain additional questions. Basing their considerations on the fact that the authors of the Treaty have not opted for the reproduction of the third

---

of the Schengen Secretariat into the Secretariat of the Council – see Case T-166/99, *Luis Fernando Andres de Dios v. Council* [2001] ECR II-1857; and Joint Cases T-164/99, T-37/00 and T-38/00, *Leroy, Chevalier-Delanoue and Matos v. Council* [2001] ECR II-1819 – a Commission action against the Council regarding the reservation of implementing powers with regard to visas and frontiers issues – Case C-257/01 *Commission v Council* –; two actions of the UK against the Council for rejection of opt-in requests –Cases C-77/05 and C-137/05 (pending)- as well as Commission actions against Member States for non implementation of Directives – see Cases C-449/04 *Commission v. Luxembourg*, C-514/04 *Commission v. Belgium*, C-460/04 *Commission v. Netherlands*, C-450/04 *Commission v. France*, C-448/04 *Commission v. Luxembourg*, C-462/04 *Commission v. Italy*, C-474/04 *Commission v. Greece* –. More recently there has also been a European Parliament action against the Council for the annulment of the family reunification Directive – Case C-540/03 *European Parliament v Council* (pending) – as well as a preliminary ruling concerning the concept of first entry within the Schengen framework – Case C-241/05 *Bot v. Préfecture du Val-de-Marne* (pending). One should, however, also take into consideration the fact that apart from the Schengen *acquis*, which has now become secondary EC/EU law, there is not yet any substantial law fully implemented by the Member States in this area after the entry into force of the Treaty of Amsterdam. In addition, lower courts under the current legal framework cannot request preliminary rulings.

74 Monar J., "Justice and Home Affairs in the Treaty of Amsterdam: Reform at the Price of Fragmentation", *ELRev*, Vol. 23, 1998, p. 320-335, at p. 330 and Albors-Llorens, *op.cit.,* at p. 1288.

75 For an overview of the national case law regarding the implementation of the Schengen agreements see Aubin E., "Le juge administratif français face à l'application de la Convention de Schengen dans ses positions sur le droit d'asile. Bilan juridictionnel de l'application en France des Accords de Schengen", *Revue du Droit Public et de la Science Politique en France et à l'étranger*, No 3, 2000, p. 829-862; Guild E., "Adjudicating Schengen: National Judicial control in France", *EJML*, Vol. 2, 2000, p. 419-439; Hurwitz A., "The 'Schengen' practice and case law in Belgium", *EJML*, Vol. 2, 2000, p. 37-48; Staples H., "Adjudicating the Schengen Agreements in the Netherlands", *EJML*, Vol. 2, 2000, p. 49-83.

sub-paragraph of Article 234 TEC, whereas they have further added the phrase "if it considers that a decision on the question is necessary to enable it to give a judgment", certain academics have considered that this implies a possibility rather than an obligation on the part of the higher courts to refer a preliminary question.[76] However, a comparative examination of the two provisions,[77] as well as the relevant case law of the Court, makes it clear that it is in fact an obligation.[78]

Another question concerned the continuous validity of the case law of the Court with regard to preliminary rulings in the light of Article 68 (1) TEC. Special emphasis has been placed on the validity of the *Foto Frost* case law.[79] Two questions can be posed in this regard. First, given the impossibility of referring a preliminary question, can national courts whose decisions can be challenged under national law declare an EC act, or a national act that has been adopted on the basis of an EC act, invalid? And, second, if they are not allowed to declare such an act invalid, can a preliminary request from such a court be declared admissible for this reason? A positive response to the first question would obviously constitute a major threat to the uniform application of EC law. However, accepting a preliminary request from a national court whose decisions can be challenged on that basis would also be difficult to reconcile with the express

---

76 For an overview of the relevant literature see Girend P., "L'article 68 CE: un renvoi préjudiciel d'interpétation et d'application incertaines", *RTDE,* Vol. 4-6, 1999, p. 239-260, at p. 242-243. See also Hailbronner K., *Immigration and Asylum Law and Policy of the European Union*, Kluwer, The Hague, 2000, at p. 94-95.

77 The use of the verb "shall" is significant. See also Article 234 second sub-paragraph TEC, where the authors of the Treaty use the verb "may".

78 This position is sustained by Gialdino C., "Schengen et le troisième pilier: Le contrôle juridictionnel organisé par le traité d'Amsterdam, *RMUE,* Vol. 2, 1998, p. 89-124; Girend and others. For more details see Girend, *op.cit.*

79 See Case C-314/85 *Foto Frost* [1987] ECR I-4199. According to this case law, national courts are not competent to nullify Community legislation.

exclusion of such a possibility by the Treaty.[80] In fact, the Court has already declared that it is not competent and dismissed relevant cases.[81]

Putting aside the thorny question regarding *Foto Frost*, the largest part of the case law of the Court will most probably remain valid and might be invoked with regard to preliminary requests concerning Title IV TEC provisions.[82] And, further, one should not neglect the fact that the limitation of the possibility to request a preliminary ruling to the higher courts is an *exception*. Consequently, it should be interpreted strictly and in any case should not lead to further restrictions that do not derive from the text of Article 68 (1) TEC itself. For all of the above reasons one could argue that the relevant case law of the Court should be applied *mutatis mutandis* to preliminary ruling requests regarding issues related to Title IV TEC.[83]

Another question that has become a source of diverging interpretations is Article 68 (2) TEC, according to which the Court "shall have no jurisdiction to rule on any measure or decision taken pursuant to Article 62 (1) relating to the

80 For a detailed analysis concerning the validity of the *Foto Frost* case law with regard to Title IV TEC as well as regarding the consequences of the eventual end of *Foto Frost*, see Peers S., "Who's Judging the Watchmen? The Judicial System of the 'Area of Freedom Security and Justice'", *YEL*, Vol. 18, 1998, p. 337-413, at p. 353-357; Hailbronner K., *Immigration and Asylum Law and Policy of the European Union*, *op.cit,* at p. 94-95; Wagner, *op.cit*, at p. 24-25. It is interesting to note that according to Peers an eventual solution could be based on the *Zuckerfabrik* and *Atlanta* case law on interim relief. Finally, in view of the devastating consequences of the eventual end of *Foto Frost*, it has been argued that the invalidation of an EC act by a lower national court might even be useful, given that it might constitute implicit pressure for the review of Article 68 (1) TEC. This view was expressed by a *Référendaire* of the Court at a Conference on "La création d'un espace de liberté sécurité et justice" that was organised by the Association of the *Référendaires* and the EUI, in Florence, on 25 and 26 May 2001.

81 See Case C-45/03 *Dem'Yanenko*, dismissed by Order of 18 March 2004 (not published) and Case C-555/03 *Warbecq et Ryanair Ltd*, dismissed by Order of 10 June 2004.

82 For an overview of the case law of the Court on Article 234 TEC see Simon D., *Le système juridique* communautaire, puf, Paris, 1997, at p. 455-491; Craig P. and de Búrca G., *EU Law Text, Cases & Materials,* Third edition, Oxford University Press, Oxford, 2003, Chapter 11. For an extensive analysis of the application of the case law of the Court with regard to Title IV TEC, see Peers S., "Who's Judging the Watchmen? The Judicial System of the 'Area of Freedom Security and Justice", *op.cit.*, at p. 353-357. According to Peers the Court might need to revisit its *CILFIT* case law. However, he argues that there is no valid legal justification defending the non-application of the case law of the Court for example regarding the concept of "court or tribunal" or the theory of "acte clair".

83 Peers S., "Who's Judging the Watchmen? The Judicial System of the 'Area of Freedom Security and Justice", *op.cit.*

maintenance of law and order and the safeguarding of internal security". The reference to Article 62 (1) TEC was initially considered to be an error, given that a reference to Article 64 (1) seemed much more logical.[84] However, an overview of the negotiating background makes it clear that the introduction of this specific clause was the result of French pressure[85] and is closely linked to Article 2(2) of the Schengen Convention, according to which a Member State can reintroduce border controls for public policy or national security reasons. Bearing in mind the special French interest with regard to this provision,[86] as well as the preference of all the Member States to maintain their freedom of action in this area, and to minimise the possibilities of being attacked before the Court, this reference to Article 62 (1) TEC seems to be justified. Even so, as has been rightly argued, it is, to a certain extent, up to the Court to set the limits of its jurisdiction, even if an analogous application of the case law of the Court with regard to the concept of public order seems rather difficult.[87] As an exemption the provision should, of course, be interpreted strictly. Finally, it needs to be stressed once more that apart from these two limitations all the other classic provisions regarding the competence of the Court remain intact.[88]

However, the role of the Court is not only limited but there are also certain new tasks attributed to it. In an effort to counterbalance the limitation of the preliminary ruling mechanism and to diminish the danger of diverging interpretations, the Treaty grants to the Member States, the Council and the Commission the possibility of requesting the Court to give a "ruling on a question of interpretation" on Title IV TEC or on Community acts based on this Title (Article 67 (3) TEC). This provision is drafted in the light of Article 4 of the Brussels Convention and is expected to compensate for the loss of the preliminary ruling request possibility by the national courts whose decisions can be challenged.[89]

84 Fennelly N., "The Area of "Freedom, Security and Justice" and the European Court of Justice-A Personal View", *International and Comparative Law Quarterly*, Vol. 49, 2000, p. 1-14.

85 See Monar, "Justice and Home Affairs in the Treaty of Amsterdam: Reform at the Price of Fragmentation", *op.cit.*

86 Given the fact that France had been applying this specific provision for years. See *supra* at 2.1.1.2.

87 In contrast to Articles 39 (3) etc, here, the limitation does not concern the *exercise* of a right conferred by the Treaty but the very competence of the Court. On that point see Hailbronner K., *Immigration and Asylum Law and Policy of the European Union, op.cit,* at p. 96-99, and Fennelly, "The Area of "Freedom, Security and Justice" and the European Court of Justice – A Personal View", *op.cit.*, at p. 6-7.

88 Namely Articles 226, 230, 232, 239 etc. See Fennelly, "The Area of "Freedom, Security and Justice" and the European Court of Justice – A Personal View", *op.cit.*

89 See Fennelly N., "Preserving the Legal Coherence within the New Treaty", in Den Boer M., Guggenbuhl A. and Van Hoonacker S. (eds.), *op.cit.*, p. 69-84.

As a final comment, it should be noted that, according to Article 67 (2) TEC, the provisions relating to the role of the Court would be revised by a unanimous decision of the Council after the lapse of the five-year transitory period. And, according to a Declaration attached to the Treaty of Amsterdam, the Conference had agreed that the Council would examine the elements of the Decision referred to in Article 67 (2) before the end of the five year period.[90] Nonetheless, neither the Commission nor the Council have yet examined the issue and thus far no decision has been taken on the matter. However, it is worth noting that in view of the entry into force of the Constitutional Treaty, the European Council has invited the Commission to submit a proposal on means to enable the Court to handle requests for preliminary rulings concerning the area of freedom, security and justice.[91]

2.1.2.2 Legal 'Safety Nets' and Cross-Title/Cross-Pillar Skirmishes (Part II)

Apart from the introduction of the aforementioned restrictions regarding the application of the Community decision-making and judicial mechanisms leading to a limitation of the role of the Community institutions, Member States have tried to further control this passage from intergovernmentalism to the Community sphere as well as to defend their turf from potential Community intrusion by inserting a series of safeguard clauses.

First of all, one observes an intense effort to safeguard national sovereignty, especially with regard to issues related to internal security. The implications of Article 68 (2) TEC regarding the role of the Court have already been discussed. Member States have also introduced a general safeguard clause expressly stating that Title IV TEC "shall not affect the exercise of the responsibilities incumbent upon Member States with regard to the maintenance of law and order and the safeguarding of internal security" (Article 64 (1) TEC).[92] At first sight, this clause seems somewhat strange, since in any case issues of policing have remained under the framework of the third pillar. Bearing in mind that this provision is linked with Articles 62 (1) and 62 (2) (a) TEC and Articles 2 (2), 4 and 5 of the Schengen Convention, all of which concern the question of the crossing of frontiers,[93] one might surmise that the ultimate goal of this provision

90 Declaration (No 21) on Article 67 of the Treaty establishing the European Community.

91 On this point see the Hague Programme as well the relevant Action Plan. See Section 3.1 of the The Hague Programme strengthening Freedom, Security and Justice in the European Union, OJ C 53/1, 3.3.2005 and Section 1.3 of the Council and Commission Action Plan implementing the Hague Programme strengthening Freedom, Security and Justice in the European Union, OJ C 198/1, 12.8.2005.

92 An analogous clause was provided by former Article 100C (5) TEC.

93 See Council Decision 1999/436/EC regarding the EC legal bases to which the Schengen *acquis* is attributed, *op.cit.*

is two-fold. On the one hand, Member States wanted to safeguard both their right to reintroduce controls at their frontiers at any time they might judge it to be necessary as well as their sovereign rights regarding politically sensitive questions such as the conditions for admission of aliens. On the other hand, this provision constitutes a way to keep the Court at an acceptable distance as far as these issues are concerned. Also of particular importance is Article 2 (1) third sub-paragraph, second sentence of the Schengen Protocol, which functions as a 'catch-all clause'. It negates any sort of jurisdiction by the Court over "measures or decisions relating to the maintenance of law and order and the safeguarding of national security" with regard to the existing Schengen *acquis* that has been integrated within the EC/EU framework.[94]

A second set of safety nets is established by a series of Protocols and Declarations that have been annexed to the Amsterdam Treaty, whose implicit purpose is undoubtedly the will to maintain a sort of control over the implementation of Title IV TEC provisions as well as in safeguarding national competences or preferences on specific issues. Thus, for example, with the objective of ensuring the unwritten principle of mutual trust and the predominant role of security issues within the Schengen framework, the Heads of State and Government declared that any measures taken to replace the Schengen *acquis* should maintain the same level of security assured by Schengen.[95] And, through a series of Declarations they made sure that their foreign policy considerations would be taken into account in the application of Title IV TEC.[96] Furthermore, the penultimate paragraph of Article 63 TEC, expressly allows Member States to maintain or introduce national provisions regarding immigration, provided that they are compatible with the Treaty and thus clearly reflects a concession to those Member States who were reluctant to give up part of their sovereignty in immigration policy.[97] Finally, the communitarisation of provisions regarding asylum has offered the possibility to resolve certain political differences between

94 Nonetheless, according to the first sentence of the third sub-paragraph of the same provision, following its integration into the EU framework, the Schengen *acquis* will be subject to the relevant provisions regarding the powers of the Court.

95 See Declaration (No 15) on the preservation of the level of protection and security provided by the Schengen *acquis*.

96 See Declaration (No 16) on Article 62 (2) (b) of the Treaty establishing the European Community as well as Declaration (No 19) on Article 64 (1) of the Treaty establishing the European Community.

97 The German interpretation of this provision is rather interesting. According to a letter submitted to the British Presidency, Germany interprets this provision as not impeding it from maintaining its national immigration policy and further denying third country nationals a right of residence. See Hailbronner, "European immigration and asylum law under the Amsterdam Treaty", *CMLRev,* Vol. 35, 1998, p. 1047-1067, at p. 1052. On this point see also the analysis and position of Advocate General Kokkot in her Opinion in Case C-540/03. See paras 34 to 42 of the Opinion

the Member States, such as, for example, the Belgian-Spanish diplomatic crisis regarding the refusal of Belgium to extradite to Spain two ETA members who had claimed asylum in Belgium.[98]

Also of importance have been the various cross-pillar and cross-title skirmishes arising from the partial character of the communitarisation of the relevant provisions.[99] Firstly, it is worth recalling that certain aspects of migration policy have been maintained under the third pillar, albeit the limits between Title IV TEC and Title VI TEU have not always been clear.[100] Certain policy areas are undoubtedly placed in the borderline between the first and the third pillar.[101] Secondly, the fact that certain aspects of the policies regarding the free movement of persons fall within the framework of the first pillar, but outside the scope of Title IV TEC, suggests that one could eventually also talk about

---

of Advocate General Kokott of 8 September 2005 in Case C-540/03, *European Parliament v. Council*.

98 In order to avoid relevant diplomatic crises in the future, and, mainly, in order to facilitate their cooperation in extradition issues, Member States adopted a Protocol according to which Member States shall be regarded as constituting safe countries of origin and any application for asylum made by an EU citizen may be taken into consideration or declared admissible for processing by another Member State only under exceptional circumstances. In case a Member State should declare unilaterally to examine such an application, it should be dealt with on the basis of the presumption that it is manifestly unfounded. See Protocol on asylum for nationals of Member States of the European Union. The Protocol was accompanied by a Belgian Declaration clarifying the Belgian position on this issue. Declaration (No 56) by Belgium on the Protocol on asylum for nationals of Member States of the European Union. The asylum Protocol has been considered an unacceptable limitation of the geographical scope of the Geneva Convention. See Pollet K., "The Amsterdam Treaty and Asylum and Immigration Policies: A Legal Analysis", *Revue des Affaires Européennes,* Vol. 1-2, April 2000, p. 57-80. Moreover, it has been convincingly argued that this Protocol should be seen, mainly, as an extradition measure in disguise. See Peers S., *EU Justice and Home Affairs Law*, *op.cit.*, at p. 129. See also Maresceau M., "Editorial: L'Union européenne et l'immigration au début du nouveau millénaire", *Revue des Affaires Européennes,* Vol. 1-2, April 2000, p. 3-6.

99 For a list of the eventual overlaps see Peers S., "Who's Judging the Watchmen? The Judicial System of the 'Area of Freedom Security and Justice'", *op.cit*.

100 See also express reference to Article 31 (e) TEU in Article 61 TEC, which is the provision that enumerates the list of the flanking measures that are necessary in order to achieve the abolition of internal border controls.

101 One example being the case of illegal immigrants sneaked into the Community territory by professional traffickers of human beings, which involves both illegal immigration and organised crime. The question of penal sanctions also proves to be quite problematic. The problem regarding the choice of the legal basis is frequently solved by the adoption of two separate parallel instruments. See *infra* at 2.2.2.

cross-title conflicts.[102] Given the differences between the two pillars, as well as the special characteristics of Title IV TEC in comparison with the rest of the first pillar, this confusion regarding their boundaries inevitably creates considerable legal problems.[103] All these difficulties are exacerbated due to the existence of the Title IV TEC Protocols, which create further divisions and conflicts.[104]

2.2 Problems Incurred in Implementation

2.2.1 Problems Arising from Title IV Protocols

The brief presentation of the predetermined flexibility system inserted within the framework of Title IV TEC has clearly proved that the Protocols annexed to Title IV TEC have formed a rather complicated and unique *status quo*. Aside from the theoretical interest in this phenomenon, this complex new regime also generates practical legal problems.

First of all, it undoubtedly complicates enormously the decision-making process, since the number of actors involved and the procedure to be followed is not always clear.[105] Second, a series of difficult political problems, which nevertheless require legal solutions, are imported within the EC framework. One might literally refer to Gordian knots, which the Community would have to face and seek to untie. Given the deep political and practical implications of these problems and the imperative need to find legal solutions that accommodate the political interests of all the involved parties, the Council usually adopts a purely pragmatic approach. The solutions found have, unfortunately, not always been legally correct or easy for an EC lawyer to predict or to evaluate. On certain occasions, one might even talk about authorised distortions of EC law.

2.2.1.1 Schengen Relevance

The vast majority of legal problems stemming from flexibility in this area are linked with the integration of Schengen, since despite its incorporation, Schen-

102 See Articles 14, 18, 39, 49 and 137 TEC. One could mention, for example, the case of third country nationals that are members of a European citizen's family, or that of third country nationals that are employed by an EC company.

103 Two of the major problems that might raise concerns are, on the one hand, the scope of the Court's jurisdiction, and, on the other hand, the decision-making process to be followed.

104 It needs to be recalled that the choice of the legal basis on which a measure will be adopted prejudges also the number of the Member States that will be bound by the relevant measure.

105 For an excellent categorisation on this point see De Kerchove G., 'Un espace de liberté, de sécurité et de justice aux dimensions incertaines: Quelques réflexions sur le recours aux coopérations renforcées en matière de justice et d'affaires intérieures', *op.cit.*

gen continues to exist as a separate system functioning with its own rules.[106] As it has been cogently argued, a new sub-category of law, the so-called "building upon the Schengen *acquis* law" is further installed within the framework of the EU.[107] A special test, the so-called "Schengen relevance test" has been also created in that respect. By this test, run with regard to each measure that is proposed on the basis of Title IV or Title VI, the Council defines whether a measure is "building upon the Schengen *acquis*" or not and subsequently decides which Member States or third parties need to be involved. The answer to this question affects profoundly the extent and legal character of the association of all the outsiders, meaning the United Kingdom, Ireland, Denmark as well as Norway, Iceland, Switzerland and in the near future also Liechtenstein.[108]

The problems regarding the scope as well as the definition of the Schengen relevance concept are numerous. First of all, it needs to be underlined in this respect that opting-out from Title IV TEC and the specific Danish, British and Irish positions regarding Schengen are two different things. The EU Member States' status regarding Title IV TEC should be clearly distinguished from their position regarding Schengen, since the scope and purpose of the relevant provisions are different. Secondly, the very scope of the Schengen relevance concept proves on certain occasions difficult to define in practice, in particular in view of the overlaps between the Schengen agenda and the more general EU migration agenda. In fact, one should not underestimate the interactions between the recently imported Schengen *acquis* and the Community and Union *acquis* in this area, given that the two regimes are partly overlapping, albeit based on different premises. Thirdly, the scope of the Schengen relevance concept is rather controversial and the relevant decision is often taken on the basis of political rather than legal criteria. On this note, despite the similarities of the legal position of the outsiders inasmuch as Schengen relevant issues is concerned, their political position is not the same.[109]

---

106 In the words of Charles Elsen, "Schengen ne mourra jamais – ancré definitivement dans l'Union par le traité d'Amsterdam et son désormais celèbre Protocole de Schengen". Elsen C., "Incorporation juridique et institutionnelle de Schengen dans l'UE" in Den Boer M. (ed.), *Schengen still going strong: Evaluation and Update*, EIPA, Maastricht, 2000, p.11-20, at p. 11. For a more detailed analysis see Papagianni G., "Schengen: does it still exist? The incorporation and development of the Schengen *acquis* within the framework of the EU" (in Greek), Επετηρίδα Ι.ΔΙ.Σ *2001-2002,* Περράκης Σ. (επιμ.), Εκδόσεις Σάκκουλα, Αθήνα, 2003, σελ. 312-344.

107 Term used by Kuijper. See Kuijper, *op.cit.*

108 See *infra* at 2.2.1.2.

109 For example, the notion of the Schengen *acquis* is not the same for Denmark, which is an EU Member State and a Schengen contracting party, and for Norway and Iceland, whose association serves the narrow objective of establishing an area of free movement of persons. It is interesting to mention the Declaration attached to the Council Decision establishing a list of Schengen relevant issues with regard to the

Unfortunately Member States and the Council have persistently refused until now to define the scope of the Schengen relevance concept.[110] Even the sole example of a sort of list of Schengen relevant issues, which has been adopted within the framework of the association of Norway and Iceland, is so vague that it is not of much help.[111] Despite the fact that the idea of a Council Decision on the definition of the Schengen relevance question had been proposed, it has not been possible to reach consensus on the procedural aspects of such a process.[112] According to the solution that has been adopted, the Schengen relevance issue should be decided by COREPER on the basis of an opinion of the Council Legal Service.[113] In practice, the decision regarding the Schengen relevance matter is adopted informally on an *ad hoc* basis at working group level. The matter does not go up to COREPER unless a delegation objects to the proposed decision. In light of the above, one can deduce that, given the political implications of this concept, the political actors involved preferred to maintain their freedom as to the definition of what is Schengen relevant and what is not on an *ad hoc* basis.

To be sure, the answer to the Schengen relevance test is not always obvious. Whilst, for example, in the case of visas the answer to this question is in the affirmative, this is not always the case for immigration or asylum matters. In principle, legal migration issues did not pose a problem, since these have not been dealt with in the Schengen framework.[114] However, the Schengen States

---

association of Norway and Iceland, where the Council expressly states that the sole purpose of this list is to facilitate the application of the association agreement with the two Nordics and that it does not constitute a list of the entire Schengen *acquis*. See Declaration by the Council, annexed to Council Decision 1999/437/EC, *op.cit.*

110 For example, the adoption of a code of conduct on this issue has been suggested by certain authors. See Kortenberg, "Closer Co-operation in the Treaty of Amsterdam", *op.cit.*

111 See the list of Schengen relevant issues included in Council Decision 1999/437/EC, *op.cit.*

112 Member States could not agree on whether this decision should be taken by simple majority or a unanimous vote.

113 The criteria used by COREPER in order to take this decision are: firstly, whether the measure is necessary for the creation of an area without internal borders, and, secondly, whether the association of Norway and Iceland is indispensable.

114 Nonetheless, the case of the proposal for a Regulation laying down a uniform format for residence permits for third country nationals seems to have been debated, most likely due to the fact that the Schengen States had proceeded to some sort of cooperation in this area. The use of contradictory statements in the relevant Commission proposal reflects an internal debate on the Schengen relevance issue. More specifically, whereas the proposal is not considered as a "building upon the Schengen *acquis*" measure as far as Denmark is concerned, when the situation of Norway and Iceland is examined, it is stated that the adopted measure should be

had developed a consistent *acquis* with regard to illegal migration. Nonetheless, the final objective of Schengen was not identical to that of Title IV TEC. Subsequently, the lack of clear rules in that respect in conjunction with the plethora of political interests at stake not only generates eternal legal confusion but quite often leads to legal solutions that are not only unpredictable but ambiguous as well. The examples are numerous. It is useful to concentrate on two particular examples which are closely linked to the subject matter of this book.[115]

One of the issues that has been the subject of intense debate concerns the question of readmission. Discussions over a Finnish initiative concerning a Council Regulation on the readmission of third-country nationals revealed a lack of consensus over the Schengen relevance question.[116] The question of Schengen relevance was, however, mainly discussed within the framework of readmission agreements. The Council position on the matter is unclear. According to the Council, whereas readmission is *per se* Schengen relevant, readmission agreements are not.[117] However, according to a COREPER decision, the model readmission agreements should be examined for "information, consultation and discussion" in the Mixed Committee with Norway and Iceland.[118] Taking into account the importance of readmission agreements for the Schengen system as well as the consequent need to associate Norway and Iceland and the political difficulty of engaging them with external relations questions,[119] the Council position appears to be another compromise solution. Indeed, the solution that has

implemented by "all Schengen States" as soon as possible "including Norway and Iceland". See Proposal for a Council Regulation laying down a uniform format for residence permits for third-country nationals, COM (2001) 157 final, 23.3.2001. It is likely that the issue was heavily debated internally.

115 There are also a series of interesting examples to be retrieved with regard to asylum, especially with regard to Regulation amending the Dublin Convention. For a detailed discussion on those see Papagianni G. "Free Movement of Persons in the light of the new Title IV TEC: from intergovernmentalism towards a Community policy", *op.cit.*

116 See Initiative of the Republic of Finland with a view to the adoption of a Council Regulation determining obligations as between the Member States for the readmission of third-country nationals, OJ C 353/6, 7.12.1999. See also Council doc. 5599/00 MIGR 9 COMIX 85, 24.1.2000. Negotiations on the initiative have been frozen, mainly due to the limited interest from the part of Member States.

117 House of Lords, *Correspondence with the Ministers*, Select Committee on European Union Sixth Report, Session 2000-2001, London, 27 July 2001, pt. 42-43.

118 See Council document "Recommendations for Council Decisions authorizing the Commission to negotiate re-admission agreements between the European Community and Sri Lanka, Morocco, Pakistan, Russia – 'Schengen relevancy'", 6720/00 MIGR 25, 6.3.2000.

119 Given that there are no provisions regarding external relations in the association agreement between the Community and Norway and Iceland. Moreover, it is obvi-

been adopted consists in the insertion of a standard Joint Declaration attached to the readmission agreement, according to which the contracting parties declare that it is appropriate that the third state concludes a readmission agreement with Norway and Iceland as well as with Denmark in the same terms as the present agreement.[120]

Another issue that was heavily debated concerns the expulsion of third country nationals. Whereas the entry, stay and expulsion within the framework of Title IV TEC concerns third country nationals who have entered both for short and long-term stays, Schengen was only interested and regulated solely the former case, since long-term stays fell under the exclusive competence of the contracting parties. Thus, when this specific issue arose within the framework of a German initiative regarding transit in cases of expulsion by air the Schengen relevant question proved puzzling. According to the initial proposal the issue was treated as purely Schengen relevant but the Council was to take a different position considering the relevant measure partly Schengen relevant and partly non Schengen relevant.[121] More specifically, Denmark, Norway and Iceland were only associated "to the extent that it [the measure] applies to third country nationals who do not fulfil or no longer fulfil the conditions for a short stay applicable within the territory of a Member State by virtue of the provisions of the Schengen *acquis*".[122] The initial proposal was silent on Ireland and the UK, but according to the final text they could participate in the future on the basis of

---

ously not possible for the Commission to negotiate readmission agreements in the name of Norway and Iceland.

120 See Joint Declaration concerning Iceland and Norway and Denmark respectively attached to the first readmission agreement already signed between the Community and Hong Kong. See Agreement between the European Community and the Government of the Hong Kong Special Administrative Region of the People's Republic of China on the readmission of persons residing without authorization, OJ L 17/25, 24.1.2004. Analogous declarations have also been included in the other agreements on which negotiations have been concluded and for which the Commission has presented a draft decision concerning the signing. See *inter alia* Proposal for a Council Decision concerning the signing of the Agreement between the European Community and the Republic of Albania on the readmission of persons residing without authorization and Proposal for a Council Decision concerning the conclusion of the Agreement between the European Community and the Republic of Albania on the readmission of persons residing without authorization, COM (2004) 92 final, 12.2.2004.

121 See recitals 8 and 9 of the Initiative of the Federal Republic of Germany with a view to adopting a Council Directive on assistance in cases of transit for the purposes of removal by air, OJ C 4/4, 9.1.2003, in conjunction with recitals 9, 10 and 11 of Council Directive 2003/110/EC of 25 November 2003 on assistance in cases of transit for the purposes of removal by air, OJ L 321/26, 6.12.2003.

122 See recitals 9 and 10 of Council Directive 2003/110/EC, *op.cit.*

Article 4 of their national Protocol.[123] There was, however, no provision regarding the relations between the UK and Ireland on the one hand, and Norway and Iceland on the other.[124]

The legal and political reasons leading the Council to take such a decision are understandable. That being said, criticism is deserved regarding the lack of legal coherence as well as the problems that arose as to the practical implementation of the decision. Firstly, as relates to the UK/Irish position, in contrast to the principle according to which the UK and Ireland should opt-in in accordance with the Schengen Protocol as far as Schengen relevant issues are concerned, they seem to opt-in on the basis of their national protocol with regard to both long-stay and short-stay related issues. Secondly, given that a distinction is drawn between short and long-term with regard to those States benefiting from a special status, a proper implementation of the measure would require the competent authorities involved – i.e. the national authorities responsible for expulsion- to establish whether the request for transit from the States being partially involved regards a returnee who had entered on the basis of a short or long-stay regime, prior to accepting and enforcing a request for transit. Obviously, given the operational character of these services as well as the lack of any clear provisions in that respect, such control is practically impossible.

As a final point, it is worth highlighting that the Council has not taken a clear position and has not yet proceeded to a serious attempt to confront and align eventual overlaps or contradictions between the former EU and the incorporated Schengen *acquis*. First of all, the case of family members of EU citizens and SIS discussed above could be mentioned. While the Commission has clearly declared that family members of EU citizens can only be listed in the SIS when they represent a threat to the public order in each Schengen State, there are no clear legislative rules regarding this prohibition, which does not seem to be respected in practice.[125] Moreover, it is interesting to note the airport transit

123 See recital 11 of Council Directive 2003/110/EC, *op.cit.*

124 The only case where the issue has been addressed is within the framework of the Decision on joint flights. See recital 12 of Council Decision 2004/573/EC of 29 April 2004 on the organization of joint flights for removals from the territory of two or more Member States, of third country nationals who are subjects of individual removal orders, OJ L 261/28, 6.8.2004.

125 See *supra* at 2.1.1.2. The Commission has in fact already taken legal action against Spain on this matter. See Action brought on 27 November 2003 by the Commission of the European Communities against the Kingdom of Spain (Case C-503/03), OJ C 21/26, 24.1.2004 as well as the Opinion of Advocate General Kokott in this case, *op.cit.* See also *infra* at 6.2.5. Hopefully, this will most likely be rectified following the adoption of the Regulation concerning the establishment of SIS II since according to the relevant Commission proposal family members of EU citizens are excluded from the scope of SIS II. See Articles 3 (e), 15 and 20 (3) of the Proposal for a Regulation of the European Parliament and of the Council on the establish-

visas case, where the list of third countries annexed to the relevant Schengen Executive Committee Decision was more extensive than the list annexed to the relevant EU Joint Action.[126] Taking into consideration the fact that none of the two measures have been formally repealed, the Member States participating within the framework of the Schengen cooperation, as well as Norway and Iceland, will have to apply the Schengen list, whereas the UK and Ireland will most probably continue to be bound by the Community one.[127] Although there have been initiatives proposing the amendment of the Joint Action, no concrete action has been taken.[128] Finally, given that the Schengen *acquis* in particular with regard to visas and external borders has been developed on the basis of a rather piece meal approach, the efforts of consolidation need to be constant and should be stepped up.[129]

---

ment, operation and use of the second generation Schengen information system (SIS II), COM (2005) 236 final, 31.5.2005.

126 Joint Action 96/197/JHA of 4 March 1996, adopted by the Council on the basis of Article K.3 of the Treaty on European Union on airport transit arrangements, OJ L 63/8, 13.3.1996; Annex 3 of the Decision of the Executive Committee of 28 April 1999, on the definitive versions of the Common Manual and the Common Consular Instructions, OJ L 239/317, 22.9.2000.

127 The same situation had also appeared in the case of the Regulation on the visa list, where harmonisation within the framework of Schengen had gone much further than within the Community. Nonetheless, in that case the Council had identified the differences prior to the incorporation of Schengen and had proceeded to the alignment soon after the incorporation of Schengen repealing the relevant parts of the Schengen *acquis*.

128 The Austrian Presidency had tabled a proposal developing the Joint Action by adding two more states and requiring all Member States to grant an exception in favour of persons with residence permits from Member States or Western European States, Japan, US and Canada, but had not been adopted. See Council doc. 12225/98, 16.7.1998, cited in Peers S., *EU Justice and Home Affairs Law*, *op.cit.*, at p. 72. In the post-Amsterdam era an analogous measure under the form of a Regulation has been submitted by Finland. See Draft initiative of the Republic of Finland with the view to the adoption of a Council Regulation on airport transit arrangements, Council doc. 10867/1/99 REV 1 VISA 61 COMIX 224, 8.10.1999. However, no reference was made to the relevant Joint Action or to the Schengen list nor to the position of UK and Ireland. The Council proceeds to amend exclusively the Schengen measure without including any reference in parallel to the relevant Joint Action. See Council Decision 2000/586/EC of 28 July 2003 on amendment of Annex 3, Part I, of the Common Consular Instructions and Annex 5a, Part I of the Common Manual on third country nationals subject to airport visa requirements, OJ 198/15, 6.8.2003.

129 The Council has already proceeded to two exercises of consolidation of the Common Consular Instructions – see OJ C 313/1, 12.12.2003 and OJ C 326/1, 22.12.2005 – whereas it has also, in cooperation with the European Parliament, reached politi-

2.2.1.2 The Association of Norway and Iceland

The association of Norway and Iceland is another source of problems. The very association agreement with Norway and Iceland could be considered an authorised distortion of the EU legal order. As mentioned above, Norway and Iceland already had a cooperation agreement with the Schengen countries since 1996. However, the integration of this agreement into the EU framework was not possible due to the extended rights that were recognised to the two Nordic outsiders, rights that could not possibly have been justified within the EU framework. Therefore, a process of "squaring the circle" was initiated within the Council.[130] The final text granted to these two countries a decision-shaping power, but no decision-making rights.[131] Moreover, according to a *guillotine* clause the Agreement would cease in the case of Norway and/or Iceland not transposing the relevant Schengen or EC/EU legislation.[132] Apart from the innovative type of relations that have been established between the two parties,[133] the Agreement is

---

cal agreement on Commission proposal for the recasting of the Common Manual. See Proposal for a Regulation establishing a Community Code on the rules governing the movement of persons across borders (Schengen Borders code), *op.cit.* An analogous recasting exercise will also be conducted with regard to the visas *acquis*, meaning the recasting of the Common Consular Instructions. See Section 1.7.3 of the Hague Programme and Section 2.9 of the relevant Commission and Council Action Plan, *op.cit.*

130 This expression is coined by Kuijper in order to stress the difficulties of finding the right balance between the prerequisite to preserve the essence of the 1996 Cooperation Agreement and the need to find a solution compatible with EU law. See Kuijper, *op.cit.*

131 See Articles 4 and 5 of the Agreement concluded by the Council of the European Union and the Republic of Iceland and the Kingdom of Norway concerning their association with the implementation, application and development of the Schengen *acquis*, *op.cit.*

132 Article 8 of the Agreement, *op.cit.* As has been rightly argued in a paper examining the relations between Norway and the EU, the EU accepts the association of Norway but under the condition that such an association does not create much "fuss". See Andersen S., "Norway: Insider AND Outsider", Arena Working Paper, No 4, February 2000.

133 One could say that Norway and Iceland have a *quasi* observer status. Whilst according to Article 2 of their Agreement they are associated via a Joint Committee, in practice they have much more extensive rights. According to Article 9 of the Agreement, they will not only be informed about the relevant case law of the Court, but they will further have the right to present written observations with regard to cases pending before the Court. Also in practice all the relevant working groups in the Council meet in an enlarged formula including Norway and Iceland whenever an issue is considered as Schengen relevant. Finally, the relevant operational services are usually open to the two Nordics as well. For example CEPOL will offer its infrastructure to Norwegian and Icelandic senior officials. See Article 6 (3) of Council

notorious in two further respects. On the one hand, the appearance of the Council, and, more specifically, the 'Schengen Council', as a contracting party in an agreement involving both EC and EU elements,[134] and, on the other, the loose definition of the issues to which these two countries are associated.[135]

Furthermore, it is worth highlighting a series of other legal and practical problems linked with the association of the two Nordic outsiders, such as their full association with EC institutional procedures like the comitology process or the sensitive issue of external relations. Inasmuch as the first issue is concerned there has been an exchange of letters in that respect. In practice the issue is usually dealt with in each Committee.[136] The second matter seems to prove much

---

Decision 2000/820/JHA of 22 December 2000 establishing a European Police College (CEPOL), OJ L 336/1, 30.12.2000.

134 According to Kuijper there has been an *ad hoc* delegation of powers from the Member States to the Union. See Kuijper, *op.cit.* Tizzano argues that the participation of the Council as a contracting party can be explained if one accepts that the EU has legal personality. He considers that this Agreement is further proof in this direction. See Tizzano A., "A proposito dell'inserzione dell'*acquis* di Schengen nei Trattati comunitari: l'accordo "del Consiglio" con Islanda e Norvegia", *Il Diritto dell'Unione Europea,* 1999, p. 521-527. This position is also defended by De Witte. See De Witte B., "Chameleonic Member States: Differentiation by means of Partial and Parallel International Agreements", in De Witte B., Hanf D. and Vos E. (eds.), *The Many Faces of Differentiation in EU Law*, Intersentia, Antwerpen, 2001, p. 231.267. For an in-depth analysis regarding the legal personality of the EU, see Tizzano A., "La personnalité internationale de l'Union européenne", *RMUE,* Vol. 4, 1998, p. 11-40. Whilst I am partially receptive to the above comments, I would argue that this Agreement should be rather seen as an act of Schengen closer cooperation.

135 A list of Schengen relevant issues is provided by Council Decision 1999/437/EC on certain arrangements for the application of the agreement concluded by the Council of the European Union and the Republic of Iceland and the Kingdom of Norway, *op.cit.* However, given its general character this list is not very helpful.

136 Initially the only existing Committee concerned the uniform format of visas to which they were associated. See Article 6 of Council Regulation (EC) No 1683/95 laying down uniform format for visas as amended by Article 2 of Regulation (EC) No 334/2002 of 18 February 2002, OJ L 53/7, 23.2.2002. Subsequently the issue has arisen in other occasions as well. It has been usually dealt via the inclusion of a general reference concerning the need to find an arrangement as to comitology within the framework of the preamble. See i.e. recital 11 of Council Decision 2005/267/EC of 16 March 2005 establishing a secure web-based Information and Coordination Network for Member States' Migration Management Services, OJ L 83/48, 1.4.2005 and recital 24 of the Proposal for a Regulation of the European Parliament and of the Council concerning the Visa Information System (VIS) and the exchange of data between Member States on short-stay visas, COM (2004) 835 final, 28.12.2004.

more problematic for a series of reasons. First, there are no clear legal provisions with regard to this matter. Second, whereas it is imperative to associate Norway and Iceland on certain EC agreements with third countries, the Community most probably lacks the competence to negotiate agreements on behalf of two sovereign third States. As mentioned previously the issue was extensively dealt with in the framework of readmission agreements, where the legal solution took the form of a standard Joint Declaration to be attached to the readmission agreements signed by the Community.[137]
One might argue that the main problems regarding the association of the Nordics have been solved since the basic legal framework for their association is in place and functioning. However, every day practice and development of the relevant parts of the *acquis* show clearly that problems continue and will not cease to emerge. Recently the issue of the association of Norway and Iceland to the Agency for the External Borders was posed. Given the difficulties in defining in detail the modalities of their association, the Council has decided to proceed to the conclusion of another specific arrangement with the two Nordic outsiders.[138]

Finally, it is worth underscoring that ironically enough despite the collection of problems stemming from the special status attributed to the two Nordics –leading certain authors to argue for their full membership[139]- the Council has recently decided to associate Switzerland and Liechtenstein in an analogous fashion.[140]

2.2.1.3 The Danish Position

One of the major puzzles in this area is the association of Denmark. The implementation of the Danish Protocol has in fact proved quite problematic. Even in cases where the Danish Protocol expressly provided for the full Danish participation, as in certain aspects of visa policy, things have not been clear or simple. And additionally the opt-in possibilities offered are really scarce.

The first problem that the Council was called to resolve concerned the Danish Association to the visa list Regulation. Given that the scope of the new provision regarding the list of countries (Article 62 (2) (b) (i) TEC) is wider than

137 See *supra* at 2.2.1.1.

138 See recital 23 of the Council Regulation (EC) No 2007/2004 of 26 October 2004 establishing a European Agency for the Management of Operational Cooperation at the External Borders of the Member States of the European Union, OJ L 349/1, 25.11.2004.

139 Bracke N., "Norway and Iceland: an Adventure in the Field of Justice and Home Affairs" in De Kerchove G. and Weyembergh A. (eds.), *Sécurité et justice: enjeu de la politique extérieure de l'Union européenne*, Institut d'Etudes Européennes, Editions de l'Université de Bruxelles, Bruxelles, 2003, p. 225-230.

140 See *supra* at 2.1.1.1.

that of former Article 100C TEC, the Danish participation in the establishment of the 'white list' has been a highly debated issue during the negotiations for the adoption of the new visa Regulation.[141] Eventually the obstacle was bypassed, thanks to a wide interpretation of former Article 100C TEC, according to which the establishment of a white list was also implicitly covered by former Article 100C TEC.[142]

Secondly, given the lack of any transitory law provisions and the silence of the Danish Protocol, Denmark has seen itself excluded from almost all the former third pillar Conventions that have been communitarised. The sole exceptions have been the 1968 Brussels Convention and the Dublin Convention. According to both Regulations replacing the respective Conventions, these remained "in force in relations between Denmark and the Member States that are bound by this Regulation".[143] Obviously, Denmark would be bound on an international law basis. Notwithstanding the positive outcome with regard to the Danish problem and the compatibility of such a solution with public international law, from an EC law point of view the solution can be considered to constitute a distortion of the Danish Protocol.[144] Furthermore, one should also bear in mind

141 The term 'black list' is used to describe the list of counties whose nationals must be in possession of visas, whereas the term 'white list' is used to describe the list of those countries whose nationals are exempted from that requirement. Whereas former Article 100C TEC covered explicitly only the case of a black list, Article 62 (2) (b) (i) TEC states that there will be established a "list of third countries whose nationals must be in possession of visas when crossing the external borders *and those whose nationals are exempt from that requirement*". (emphasis added)

142 See the explanatory memorandum of the first Commission Proposal for a Council Regulation determining the list of third countries whose nationals must be in possession of visas when crossing the external borders and those whose nationals are exempt from that requirement, COM (2000) 27 final, 26.1.2000. Consequently, the final text of the Regulation does not contain any specific provision regarding Denmark. See Council Regulation (EC) No 539/2001 of 15 March 2001 listing the third countries whose nationals must be in possession of visas when crossing the external borders and those whose nationals are exempt from that requirement, OJ L 81/1, 21.4.2001. For a detailed analysis on this point and arguments supporting this position see Papagianni G., "Flexibility in Justice and Home Affairs: an old phenomenon taking new forms", *op.cit.* at p. 123-124.

143 Council Regulation (EC) No 44/2001 of 22 December 2000 on jurisdiction and the recognition and enforcement of judgments in civil and commercial matters, OJ L 12 /1, 15.1.2001 and Council Regulation (EC) No 343/2003 of 18 February 2003 establishing the criteria and mechanisms for determining the Member State responsible for examining an asylum application lodged in one of the Member States by a third-country national, OJ L 50/1, 25.2.2003.

144 According to Articles 3 and 7 of the Danish Protocol, Denmark will not participate in the measures that will be adopted within the framework of Title IV TEC and its sole possibility to 'opt-in' is by waiving its Protocol. The Danish association was

the legal complexity due to the maintenance of the relevant Conventions. In particular, whereas the rest of the Member States would apply among themselves the new Regulation, it would be the old instrument that would continue to apply between them and Denmark.[145]

The Danish position proved rather complicated in cases where it was not clear whether the relevant issues are really Schengen relevant or not, such as for example the cases of Dublin and Eurodac or readmission agreements. The solutions advanced with regard to both issues are testimony to the paranoia of the new regime. As far as the Dublin and Eurodac case is concerned the Council has proposed three different solutions in order to find the right way to associate Denmark.[146] And as relates to the readmission agreements, Denmark is obviously treated as a third state.[147]

Nonetheless, despite the limited possibilities offered by the relevant legal texts, Danish association proves to be, for both practical and political reasons, if not indispensable at least desirable. First, non-association of Denmark to issues

---

made possible due to very specific legal circumstances. In particular, preserving the effects of the 1968 Brussels Convention and the Dublin Convention was possible given the fact that these Conventions had already entered into force and, furthermore, they were not based on former Article K.3 TEU but were pure intergovernmental instruments.

145 It needs to be underlined that in both cases the transformation also brought a number of changes. As far as the Brussels Convention is concerned see Idot L., "Convention Bruxelles – transformation en règlement", *Europe*, Vol. 11, No.3, mars 2001, p. 26.

146 For a detailed discussion on the Schengen or non Schengen relevant character of the Dublin Convention and the association of the Nordics and Denmark see Papagianni G. "Free Movement of Persons in the light of the new Title IV TEC: from intergovernmentalism towards a Community policy", *op.cit.* Initially Denmark was associated to the Dublin II Regulation via the preservation of the effects of the former Dublin Convention. Secondly, Denmark was supposed to be associated via Article 12 of the Dublin parallel agreement associating Norway and Iceland. Finally, the Council has adopted a negotiating mandate in order to adopt a separate agreement with Denmark. See Council Decision authorizing the Commission to negotiate with Denmark the conclusion of an Agreement concerning the criteria and mechanisms for establishing the state responsible for examining a request for asylum lodged in Denmark or any other EU Member State, and to negotiate with Iceland and Norway the conclusion of a Protocol pursuant to Article 12 of the Agreement between the European Community and the Republic of Iceland and the Kingdom of Norway concerning the criteria and mechanisms for establishing the State responsible for examining a request for asylum lodged in a Member State or in Iceland or Norway, Council doc. 8314/03 ASILE 24, 6.5.2003.

147 Denmark benefits from the same status as Norway and Iceland, being associated via a standard Joint declaration attached to readmission agreements. See *supra* at 2.2.1.1. and 2.2.1.2.

closely linked to the Schengen final objective -which, however, are not treated as Schengen relevant by the Council- would inevitably create problems for the proper functioning of the Schengen system or might even lead to the need for reintroduction of border controls with Denmark. Second, it needs to be taken into account that Denmark was bound by all the former third pillar *acquis* and remains willing to be bound by the measures developing this *acquis* or to be associated with other relevant measures.[148]

But neither the current legal framework nor the need to respect the position and interests of all the actors involved facilitate the adoption of a legally coherent solution. Apart from any objections that its partners might have,[149] the special Danish interests do not render things any easier either. First, as it has already been argued, the absence of an opting-in possibility was a Danish preference as well. Therefore, even the extreme scenario of a broad *ad hoc* interpretation of the possibility of Denmark waiving its Protocol does not appear a preferable solution even from a Danish point of view given the Danish constitutional problems.[150] Denmark seems to prefer a solution within the framework of international law both for Schengen relevant and former third pillar issues. Nevertheless, even if this has on certain occasions been possible, it seems that a more stable and concrete framework would be preferable, even within the ambit of an arrangement based on international law. Arrangements such as the one adopted with regard to the Brussels and Dublin Conventions are only casual arrangements offering a temporary solution.[151]

The Danish situation has been and still remains a matter of significant debate both within the Council and the Commission. The option of international law agreements between the Community and Denmark with regard to Title IV TEC issues has led to much debate.[152] The legal problems to be addressed have been

148 Indeed, one should stress the Danish attempts to hang on to pre-existing EU *acquis* whenever this might be possible or acceptable to its partners. See for example the case of the Regulation replacing the 1968 Brussels Convention, or the case of Dublin, *supra*.

149 One could argue that irrespective of all the Danish internal political reasons, it was also Denmark that opted for what was in practice an unworkable Protocol. Now, Denmark will simply have to live with it.

150 Denmark would be obliged to organise a referendum on every measure to which it would 'opt-in'. See Kuijper, *op.cit.*

151 For example Denmark would still be excluded from any developments of the Brussels and Dublin Regulations. Moreover, Denmark is associated to a form of cooperation that has been developed, whereas the interactions with other legal instruments, such as for example the Eurodac Regulation in the case of the Dublin system, are not taken into account.

152 According to Israel there was nothing preventing the Community from entering into negotiations and concluding an agreement with Denmark with regard to Title IV TEC issues. See Israel J., "Conflicts of Law and the EC after Amsterdam: A Change

numerous. One could mention the problem of the legal basis, the scope as well as the extent of both the obligations imposed, and the rights granted to Denmark. Moreover, given that Danish participation in all the instruments based on Title IV TEC would most probably not be acceptable,[153] it has been difficult to decide to which measures the Council would allow Denmark to be associated with as well as the criteria regarding this choice. Any such agreement certainly represents one of the most interesting measures ever adopted by the Community: parallel international agreements between the Community and a Member State concerning the latter's association with major EC instruments.[154] Given the fragile political balances that need to be kept, as well as the legal instruments that need to be respected, the conclusion of such arrangements has been far from an easy task. The right balance between the need to preserve the international law character of the Danish association and the need to assimilate the Danish status to that of a Member State would have to be found, while respecting legal instruments that contravene such a scenario. Finally, the Council has adopted negotiating mandates authoring the Commission to start negotiations for the conclusions

---

for the Worse?", *Maastricht Journal of European and Comparative Law,* 2000, Vol. 7, No 1, p. 81-98. Moreover, an unpublished Council statement expressed interest in a treaty between the EC and Denmark allowing for Danish association with the Eurodac system. See Council doc. 12314/00 ADD 1 COR 1, 21.11.2000, cited in Peers S., "Key Legislative Developments on Migration in the European Union', *EJML*, Vol. 3, 2001, p. 231-255. It is interesting to note that the Belgian Presidency declared that the Council should direct the Commission to engage negotiations with Denmark as soon as possible and that it would take all helpful measures to advance negotiations with Denmark to ensure applicability among the fifteen of the 'Brussels I', 'Brussels II', 'Insolubility' and 'Transmission of deeds' Regulations. See Belgian Presidency, 'Priorities in the field of Justice and Home Affairs', document available at the website of the Belgian Presidency, <http://www.eu.2001.be> Moreover, the Commission also prepared two Working documents on the matter. See Interface entre la mise en oeuvre du Titre IV du TCE et le Protocole sur la position du Danemark: *Est-ce que le Danemark peut participer à la mise en oeuvre des mesures fondées sur le Titre IV du TCE, si oui, sous quelles conditions?*, SEC (2001) 1347, 28.8.2001 and Memorandum for the Commission from Mr Vitorino, in agreement with the President, Mr Prodi, Interface between implementation of Title IV of the EC Treaty and the Protocol on the position of Denmark, SEC (2002) 483 final.

153 Both for political and legal reasons. On the one hand, it is unlikely to be accepted by the other Member States and, on the other, it would constitute a clear circumvention of the Danish Protocol.

154 For an overview and an interesting analysis regarding partial and parallel agreements, see De Witte B., "Chameleonic Member States: Differentiation by means of Partial and Parallel International Agreements", *op.cit.* and De Witte B., "Old-fashioned Flexibility: international Agreements between Member States of the European Union, in de Búrca G. and Scott J. (eds.), *Constitutional Change in the EU – From Uniformity to Flexibility?*, Hart Publishing, Oxford, 2000, p. 31-58.

of three agreements regarding, on the one hand, Dublin II and Eurodac and, on the other, the Brussels I and II Regulations.[155] Up to now, negotiations have been concluded with regard to Brussels I and II Regulations, where the Council has used Articles 61 (c) and 300 (2) as legal bases.[156]

2.2.1.4 The UK and Irish Position

The British and Irish opt-out Protocols are of a much more flexible character but have in any event also proved to be problematic and incoherent. There are several reasons for the inconsistencies encountered in practice.

A close examination of the opting-in clauses used by the Council within the framework of the Title IV acts shows clearly that the relation between the two Protocols – the Schengen Protocol, which concerns Schengen relevant issues, and the respective national Protocols, which concern Title IV issues- is far from clear. Indeed, the drafting used and the opting in procedure enacted each time vary profoundly, even if the cases concerned are analogous. On certain occasions the two Protocols are treated as two equally applicable alternatives and quite often the UK and Ireland opt into Schengen relevant measures on the basis of their

155 Inasmuch as Dublin II and Eurodac is concerned the Commission has been also authorised to open negotiations with Norway and Iceland on the basis of Article 12 of their relevant Association Agreement, See *supra*. For Brussels I and II see Recommendation for a Council Decision authorizing the Commission to open negotiations for the conclusion of two agreements between the European Community and the Kingdom of Denmark, extending to Denmark the provisions of Regulation (EC) No 44/2001 on jurisdiction and the recognition and enforcement of judgments in civil and commercial matters, and the provisions of Regulation (EC) No 1348/2000 concerning the service in the Member States if judicial and extra-judicial documents in civil or commercial matters – Deadline for consultation: Friday, 2 May 2003, Council doc. 8525/03 JUSTCIV 68, 23.4.2003.

156 Council Decision 2005/794/EC of 20 September 2005 on the signing, on behalf of the Community, of the Agreement between the European Community and the Kingdom of Denmark on the service of judicial and extrajudicial documents in civil or commercial matters, OJ L 300/53, 17.11.2005; Agreement between the European Community and the Kingdom of Denmark on the service of judicial and extrajudicial documents in civil or commercial matters, OJ L 300/55, 17.11.2005; Council Decision 2005/790/EC of 20 September 2005 on the signing on behalf of the Community, of the Agreement between the European Community and the Kingdom of Denmark on jurisdiction and the recognition and enforcement of judgements in civil and commercial matters, OJ L 299/61, 16.11.2005; Agreement between the European Community and the Kingdom of Denmark on jurisdiction and the recognition and enforcement of judgements in civil and commercial matters, OJ L 299/62, 16.11.2005. Inasmuch as the Agreement regarding the Dublin and Eurodac Regulations is concerned see "EP/JHA/ASYLUM: EP in favour of extending "Dublin II" and "Eurodac" regulations to Denmark and concluding a Protocol with Iceland and Norway", Bulletin Quotidien Europe No 9093, 20.12.2005.

national Protocol.[157] Yet, in other cases, they are treated as complementary.[158] It is submitted that neither option is legally correct, since the Protocols concern different cases and the relevant procedures differ greatly.[159]

The obvious lack of any clear agreement or code of conduct on the matter has led to all sorts of varying *ad hoc* solutions. So even in cases where the UK and Ireland opt out from Schengen relevant issues the drafting is not consistent. In certain cases there is a reference to the Council Decisions regarding the respective requests for participation to some parts of the Schengen *acquis*, in others there is a reference to their national Protocol.[160] Things are much more complicated where the two States decide to opt-into Schengen relevant meas-

157 The UK has already opted into measures, which were clearly building upon the Schengen *acquis,* on the basis of its national Title IV Protocol on several occasions. See Council Directive 2001/51/EC of 28 June 2001 supplementing the provisions of Article 26 of the Convention implementing the Schengen Agreement of 14 June 1985, OJ L 187/45, 10.7.2001 and Council Directive 2001/40/EC of 28 May 2001 on the mutual recognition of decisions on the expulsion of third country nationals, OJ L 149/34, 2.6.2001. More recently both Ireland and the UK have opted into the draft Directive on joint flights on the basis of Title IV Protocol. See recital 13 of Council Decision 2004/573/EC, *op.cit*. For the relevant requests for participation of the two states see respectively Council doc. 15325/03 MIGR 105 COMIX 728, 27.11.2003 and Council doc. 14595/03 MIGR 95 COMIX 676, 11.11.2003.

158 For instance, in the case of the SIS II Council Regulation there is a reference to both Protocols. See recitals 9 and 11 of the Council Regulation (EC) 2424/2001 of 6 December 2001 on the development of the second generation Schengen Information System (SIS II), L 328/4, 13.12.2001.

159 For example, whereas for Schengen relevant issues there is need for a unanimous decision taken by the Schengen States, opting into Title IV measures is on the basis of a simple majority decision of the Council.

160 An overview of the measures building upon the Schengen visa *acquis* is revealing. See *inter alia* on the one hand, recitals 11 and 12 of Council Decision 2004/512/EC of 8 June 2004 establishing the Visa Information System (VIS), OJ L 213/5, 15.6.2004 and recitals 7 and 8 of Council Regulation (EC) No 415/2003 of 27 February 2003 on the issue of visas at the border, including the issue of such visas to seamen in transit, OJ L 64/1, 7.3.2003 referring to the decisions on the respective requests of UK and Ireland for partial participation to Schengen; and on the other hand recital 4 of Council Regulation 539/2001 listing the third countries whose nationals must be in possession of visas when crossing the external borders and those whose nationals are exempt from that requirement, *op.cit.*, recital 8 of Council Regulation (EC) No 1091/2001 of 28 May 2001 of freedom of movement with a long-stay visa, OJ L 150/4, 6.6.2001 and recital 6 of Council Decision 2002/585/EC of 12 July 2002 on the adaptation of parts III and VIII of the common consular instructions, OJ L 187/44, 16.7.2002 referring to the UK/Irish Protocol. Moreover on certain other occasions a general formula without exact reference has also been used. See recital 7 of Council Regulation (EC) No 453/2003 of 6 March 2003 amending Regulation (EC) No 539/2001 listing third countries whose nationals must be in possession of

ures. First of all, there is an unquestionable preference, mainly on the part of the UK, to opt-in on the basis of the Title IV Protocol, no doubt as result of the much less exacting procedure.[161] The way the Council deals with the matter is rather confusing. Interestingly enough, in some cases the opt-in procedures of both Protocols apply. For instance, in the case of SIS II the UK has notified its intention to opt-in on the basis of the national protocol despite the fact that the measure concerned regards a Schengen relevant issue to which the UK had already opted into on the basis of its request to participate in Schengen.[162] It is interesting to note that on the same occasion the Council remained silent on the Irish position. Ireland opted in at a later stage via an express reference in the Council Decision regarding its request for partial participation in Schengen.[163] On other occasions there is no express reference to a specific provision but a general reference to the provisions of the Treaties.[164] Sometimes there is even a reference to the Irish opt-out in the very text of the measure despite the fact that this is superfluous.[165] And there are also cases in which the two countries have opted in on the basis of different provisions and procedures.[166]

---

visas when crossing the external borders of Member States and those whose nationals are exempt from that requirement, OJ L 69/10, 13.3.2003.

161 See the list of examples cited *supra*. Inasmuch as Council Directive 2001/40/EC on the mutual recognition of decisions on the expulsion of third country nationals is concerned, it is interesting to note that the question regarding the appropriate legal basis for British participation was also raised by the House of Lords. See House of Lords, *Correspondence with the Ministers, op.cit.*, pt. 20.

162 According to the relevant Council Decisions both countries are deemed irrevocably to have notified the Council that they wish to take part in all proposals and initiatives, which build upon the Schengen *acquis*, referred in their respective requests. See Article 8 of Council Decision 2000/365/EC regarding the British request and Article 6 of Council Decision 2002/192/EC concerning the Irish request, *op.cit.* See also recitals 9 and 11 of Regulation (EC) 2424/2001 *op.cit.*

163 Article 5 (1) (d) and (e) of Council Decision 2002/192/EC, *op.cit.*

164 See recital 7 of Council Directive 2002/90/EC of 28 November 2002 defining the facilitation of unauthorized entry, movement and residence, OJ L 328/17, 5.12.2002.

165 See Article 2 of Initiative of the Kingdom of Belgium, the Kingdom of Spain and the French Republic with a view to the adoption by the Council of a Decision amending Article 40 (1) and (7) of the Convention implementing the Schengen Agreement of 14 June 1985 on the gradual abolition of checks at the common borders, OJ C 285/3, 11.10.2001 as well as Article 2 of Council Decision 2003/725/JHA of 2 October 2003 amending the provisions of Article 40 (1) and (7) of the Convention implementing the Schengen Agreement of 14 June 1985 on the gradual abolition of checks at common borders, OJ L 260/37, 11.10.2003.

166 See Directive 2001/40/EC on mutual recognition of expulsion decisions and Directive 2001/51/EC on carrier sanctions, *op.cit.* The UK opted in on the basis of its

It is also curious that different opt-in clauses are used for measures that are complementary and should in principle be treated in the same way. The differences between the Directive on mutual recognition of expulsion decisions and the complementary Council Decision setting out the criteria and practical arrangements for the compensation of the financial imbalances resulting from the application of the relevant Directive are revealing in that regard.[167] Denmark, Norway and Iceland participate in the Decision "to the extent that it applies to third country nationals who do not fulfil or who no longer fulfil the conditions for a short stay applicable within the territory of a Member State by virtue of the provisions of the Schengen *acquis*", and the UK is expressly not affected by the provisions of Article 24 of the Schengen Convention, however there are no clarifications in that respect within the framework of the relevant "parent-Directive".[168] Moreover, Ireland opted into the Directive on the basis of the Decision regarding its request for participation to Schengen and was subsequently not bound by the Decision as a result of its national Title IV Protocol.[169]

Unfortunately, the situation is further complicated due to the fact that certain measures are only partly Schengen relevant or concern horizontal provisions of the Schengen *acquis*. This inevitably leads to the rather confusing statements by the Council. In that regard one could refer to the German initiative on expul-

---

Title IV Protocol whilst Ireland opted in on the basis of its request for participation in some parts of Schengen. See Article 2 (2) of the Council Decision 2002/192/EC on the Irish request for participation to Schengen, *op.cit.*

167 See Directive 2001/40/ on the mutual recognition of expulsion decisions, *op.cit.* and Council Decision 2004/191/EC of 23 February 2004 setting out the criteria and practical arrangements for the compensation of the financial imbalances resulting from the application of Directive 2001/40/EC on the mutual recognition of decisions on the expulsion of third-country nationals, OJ L 60/55, 27.2.2004.

168 See recitals 6, 7 and 8 of Decision 2004/191/EC and recitals 6, 7 and 8 of Directive 2001/40/EC, *op.cit.*

169 See Article 2 (2) of the Decision 2002/192/EC on the Irish request for participation to Schengen, *op.cit.* and recital 9 of the Decision 2004/191/EC regarding the practical arrangements for the compensation of financial imbalances resulting from the application of Directive 2001/40/EC, *op.cit.* It is worth highlighting the practical problems that may arise during the implementation of Directive 2001/40/EC by virtue of the fact that Ireland is not bound by this Decision.

sion by air,[170] the case of ARGO[171] and the Spanish initiative regarding the introduction of some new functions for the SIS.[172]

The inconsistent application regarding the relevant Protocols is also due to a series of political considerations. Firstly, it has already been highlighted that both States have a preference for the national Protocol opting-in procedure. Second, it is interesting to note that the UK systematically – and Ireland to a lesser extent – tends to exercise its opting-in possibility in a quite selective way. In fact both the British and Irish applications to take part in to Schengen have focused on the security aspects of Schengen. Moreover, inasmuch as Title IV measures are concerned, whereas they both systematically opt into measures regarding security characteristics of documents and almost all the illegal migration measures they do not opt into legal migration measures.[173] The selectivity

170 See Council Directive 2003/110/EC on assistance in cases of transit for the purposes of removal by air, *op.cit.* and the discussion *supra* at 2.2.1.1.

171 Despite the hybrid character of ARGO regarding the funding of both Schengen relevant and non-Schengen relevant measures, the UK has opted into ARGO on the basis of its national Protocol without any further clarifications, whereas Ireland is not participating. See recitals 12 and 13 of Council Decision 2002/463/EC of 13 June 2002 adopting an Action programme for administrative cooperation in the fields of external borders, visas, asylum and immigration, (ARGO programme), OJ L 161/11, 19.6.2002.

172 See recitals 10 and 11 of the Initiative of the Kingdom of Spain with a view to adopting the Council Regulation (EC) No .../2002 concerning the introduction of some new functions for the Schengen information system, in particular in the fight against terrorism, OJ C 160/5, 4.7.2002, in conjunction with recitals 9 and 10 of the Initiative of the Kingdom of Spain with a view to adopting the Council Decision 2002/.../JHA concerning the introduction of some new functions for the Schengen information system, in particular in the fight against terrorism, OJ C 160/7, 4.7.2002. Although the UK and Ireland do not participate in the former they do participate and are bound by the latter. Nonetheless, both instruments partly amend to a certain extent the same Schengen provisions – i.e. Articles 103, 108 and 113 of the Schengen Convention – which are of a horizontal character.

173 It is worth underscoring the concerns raised by the House of Lords regarding the position of the UK. First, it questions whether the maintenance of controls is the best way to fight illegal migration. Second, it questions whether an independent policy is feasible, using as an argument the two proposals for Regulation on the third country national workers that are posted in a second Member State. Third, it considers the governement's distinction between illegal migration and positive measures to be artificial. Finally, it considers that the opt-out weakens the negotiating position of the UK and prevents it from contributing to the on going debate on migration. See House of Lords, *A Community Immigration Policy,* Thirteenth Report, 1999-2000 Session, London, 3 April 2001. However, the discussion on the establishment of an identity cards scheme was started in the UK. The Government has already prepared a draft Identity Cards Bill. See House of Commons, House

characterising the exercise of their opting in possibility demonstrates the irony prevailing in the new regime. Britain and Ireland are granted the option, not only to not commit themselves to any obligations arising from Community law in this field, but, furthermore, they are able to participate in all the advantageous aspects, such as the security dimension.[174]

However, despite the fact that one could expect that the two States would opt into the same measures, major differences in approach are evident. For its part, the UK systematically opts into all the illegal migration measures –with the exception of the German initiative on expulsion by air- as well as on visa security issues. The Irish position is not as coherent. In contrast to the UK opting systematically out of all the legal migration Directives, Ireland has opted into the Draft Directive on paid employment as well as into the Directive on the admission of researchers.[175] Nonetheless, whereas the UK has opted into the Regulation regarding the format for residence permits for third country nationals, Ireland has not.[176] And in contrast to the UK, Ireland has not opted in to any of the visa related security measures nor to the ARGO programme for

---

Affairs Committee, *Identity Cards*, Fourth Report of Session 2003-04, available at <http://www.statewatch.org>.

174 Curtin D., 'The Schengen Protocol: Attractive model or poisoned chalice?', in Ehlermann C.D. (ed.), *Multi-Speed Europe-the Legal Framework of Variable Geometry in the European Union,* Bundesazeiger, Bonn, 1999, p. 73-84. Nevertheless, the House of Lords has expressed fears about the weakening of the British negotiating position with regard to Title IV due to the British opt-out. See House of Lords, *A Community Immigration Policy*, *op.cit.*

175 See respectively Council doc. 5084/02 MIGR 1, 8.1.2002 and recital 27 of Directive 2005/71/EC of 12 October 2005 on a specific procedure for admitting third-country nationals for the purposes of scientific research, OJ L 289/15, 3.11.2005.

176 See recitals 14 and 15 of Council Regulation (EC) No 1030/2002 of 13 June 2002 laying down a uniform format for residence permits for third country nationals, OJ L 157/1, 15.6.2002. Furthermore, no reference or clarification of the Irish position is made in the Commission proposal amending the relevant Regulation. See Proposal for a Regulation amending Regulation (EC) 1683/95 laying down a uniform format for visas and proposal for a Council Regulation amending Regulation (EC) 1030/2002 laying down a uniform format for residence permits for third-country nationals, COM (2003) 558 final, 24.9.2003.

administrative cooperation in the fields of external borders.[177] The same applies for most readmission agreements as well.[178]

Surprisingly enough whereas both the UK and Ireland have not opted into any parts of the Schengen *acquis* regarding visa policy and border issues, the UK has opted into both the Regulation regarding the visa format and the Regulation regarding the forms for affixing visas.[179] The UK has also actively participated in operational measures for border management, having also submitted a project for an *ad hoc* Centre of Excellence at Dover.[180] However, despite the patent interest at least on the part of the UK to participate both in the forthcoming Visa

177 See recital 14 of Council Regulation (EC) No 334/2002 of 18 February 2002 amending Regulation (EC) No 1683/95, *op.cit.*; recital 12 of Council Regulation (EC) No 333/2002 of 18 February 2002 on a uniform format for forms for affixing the visa issued by Member States to persons holding travel documents not recognized by the Member State drawing up the form, OJ L 53/4, 23.2.2002; recitals 12 and 13 of Council Decision 2002/463/EC on the ARGO programme, *op.cit.* See also recitals 9 and 10 of the new Commission proposal – Proposal for a Council Decision amending Decision No 2002/463/EC adopting an action programme for administrative cooperation in the fields of external borders, visas, asylum and immigration (ARGO programme), COM (2004) 384 final, 19.5.2004 – where it is clarified that the UK will participate whereas Ireland will not.

178 Ireland, in contrast to the UK, has so far only opted into the EC readmission agreement with Hong Kong. See recital 5 of Council Decision 2004/80/EC of 17 December 2003 concerning the inclusion of the Agreement between the European Community and the Government of the Hong Kong Special Administrative Region of the People's Republic of China on the readmission of persons residing without authorization, OJ L 17/23, 24.1.2004; recitals 5 and 6 of Council Decision 2004/424/EC of 21 April 2004 concerning the conclusion of the Agreement between the European Community and the Macao Special Administrative Region of the People's Republic of China on the readmission of persons residing without authorization, OJ L143/97, 30.4.2004; recitals 5 and 6 of Council Decision 2005/809/EC of 7 November 2005 concerning the conclusion of the Agreement between the European Community and the Republic of Albania on the readmission of persons residing without authorization, OJ L 304/14, 23.11.2005; recitals 4 and 5 of Council Decision 2005/371/EC of 3 March 2005 on the signing of the Agreement between the European Community and the Republic of Albania on the readmission of persons residing without authorisation, OJ L 124/21, 17.5.2005 and recitals 5 and 6 of Council Decision 2005/372/EC of 3 March 2005 concerning the conclusion of the Agreement between the European Community and the Democratic Socialist Republic of Sri Lanka on the readmission of persons residing without authorisation, OJ L 124/41, 17.5.2005.

179 See recital 13 of Council Regulation (EC) No 334/2002, *op.cit.* and recital 11 of Council Regulation (EC) No 333/2002, *op.cit*.

180 See Report on the implementation of programmes, ad hoc centres, pilot project and joint operations, Council doc. 10058/1/03 REV 1 FRONT 70 COMIX 354, 11.6.2003.

Information System and the Agency for the management of the EU's external borders as well as in measures regarding the collection and use of biometric data and eventually also the interest of their partners to take them both on board, finding a legal solution has proved rather problematic.[181] In the end, while the two States have currently been excluded from the VIS and the Regulation on the standards for security features and biometrics in passports and travel documents issued by Member States[182] a strange formula has been inserted in the Regulation concerning the establishment of the Agency for the External Borders. According to this formula "the Agency shall facilitate operational cooperation with Ireland and the United Kingdom in matters covered by its activities and to the extent required for the fulfilment of its tasks", while their representatives "shall be invited to attend the meetings of the Management Board".[183] Nonetheless, despite the existence of the UK Protocol regarding border controls as well as the fact that a solution was also included in the text of the Regulation the UK has informed the Council of its will to be associated.[184] Moreover, the UK has also brought two actions against the Council asking for the annulment of both the Regulation establishing the Agency as well as of the Regulation on the security

---

181 The Commission correctly applying the appropriate Protocols has excluded both countries in its relevant proposals. See recitals 11 and 12 of the Proposal for a Council Decision establishing a Visa Information System (VIS), COM (2004) 99 final, 12.2.2004; recitals 24 and 25 of the Proposal for a Regulation of the European Parliament and of the Council concerning the Visa Information System (VIS), *op.cit.*; recitals 23 and 24 of the Proposal for a Council Regulation establishing a European Agency for the Management of Operational Cooperation at the External Borders, COM (2003) 687 final, 11.11.2003 and recitals 10 and 11 of the Proposal for a Council Regulation on standards for security features and biometrics in EU citizens' passports, COM (2004) 116 final, 18.2.2004.

182 See recitals 11 and 12 of Council Decision 2004/512/EC regarding the Visa Information System (VIS), *op.cit* and recitals 11 and 12 of Council Regulation (EC) No 2252/2004 of 13 December 2004 on standards for security features and biometrics in passports and travel documents issued by Member States, OJ L 385/1, 29.12.2004.

183 See recitals 25 and 27 and Articles 12 and 23 (4) of Council Regulation 2007/2004 establishing a European Agency for the Management of Operational Cooperation at the External Borders, *op.cit.*

184 Communication from the United Kingdom on its intentions to participate in the adoption of the proposal for a Council Regulation establishing a European Agency for the Management of Operational Cooperation at the External Borders, Council doc. 10658/04 FRONT 114 COMIX 413, 17.6.2004. However, the House of Lords rightly stressed that the UK is in an increasingly awkward position in seeking to reconcile its retention of internal frontier controls with more active participation in integrated border management of the EU's external borders. See House of Lords, *Proposals for a European Border Guard,* EU Twenty-ninth Report, 2002-3 Session, London, 10 July 2003, at Chapter 5, and in particular at pts 71 and 76.

standards and biometrics in passports.[185] Even if one shares the substantive legal reasons preventing the UK participation into the above mentioned measures, which is in any case a conscious political choice of the UK, one needs to underscore the practical problems stemming from the exclusion of the two States in particular from VIS. Given that VIS will also contain data regarding Dublin and return related issues, an eventual association of the two outsiders might prove essential.

Last but not least, the UK and Irish selective participation seems to create a series of other practical problems as well. One issue that arises regarding the UK and Irish request for partial participation in Schengen concerns their participation in the Schengen Information System. The SIS contains data regarding both objects and persons. The data on persons are linked both with issues of policing, to which the UK and Ireland have opted in as well as issues of entry and movement of third country nationals to the Schengen territory to which the UK and Ireland are not participating. However, given that the UK and Ireland are not bound by the Schengen provisions on border controls, they should not have access to the data concerning persons inasmuch as this data concerns the entry and movement of persons.[186] There may well be arguments in favour of full UK and Irish participation.[187] But it would not be easy from a political point of view to justify such participation since it would be unfair for the UK and Ireland to have full access without lifting the border controls. It is worth noting that a technical solution consisting in the establishment of a filter between the central SIS server and the UK national server has already been advanced.[188] However, the

185 See Action brought on 17 February 2005 by the United Kingdom of Great Britain and Northern Ireland against Council of the European Union (Case C-77/05), OJ C 82/25, 2.4.2005 and Action brought on 24 March 2005 by United Kingdom of Great Britain and Northern Ireland against Council of the European Union (Case C-137/05), OJ C 132/16, 28.5.2005. For further details on the UK position on these cases see House of Lords, *Correspondence with Ministers June 2004 to February 2005,* EU Committee 4th Report, 2005-6 Session, London, 6 September 2005, at p. 307-310 and 316-317.

186 On the problems arising from UK's partial participation and the discussions in the Council see 'Schengen: UK given rough ride', *Statewatch*, Vol. 9, No 5, September-October 1999, p. 25-26.

187 i.e. "double emploi" of data, since a person might be inserted for two different reasons – i.e. persons under surveillance and expulsion – and need for hierarchic classification, since the UK might already possess the relevant data through another source such as Europol. That said, the technical arguments advanced are not entirely valid, since the double-entry problem is something that already exists within the framework of the SIS.

188 See UK Delegation Note on the Implementation of Schengen in UK, Council doc. 8913/01 SIS 50 COMIX 374, 17.5.2001.

Decision regarding the full application of the SIS provisions by the two States is still to be adopted.[189]

2.2.2 *Problems Arising from the Implementation of the Title IV Institutional Framework*

Apart from the problems arising from the existence of the various protocols establishing special relations with certain Member States, the Title IV decision-making process is further complicated due to the second aspect of this partial communitarisation, namely the partial transfer of the relevant legal bases to the first pillar and the special characteristics of the Title IV TEC.

First of all, the split of the relevant legal bases between the first and the third pillar – some of the legal bases regarding certain security measures remaining in the third pillar- renders the decision-making process even more cumbersome and often leads to skirmishes between institutions. In particular, while migration issues are treated within the framework of Title IV TEC, Member States seem to insist that issues linked with penalties and police cooperation should be treated under the third pillar. Therefore, on certain occasions they opt to split legislative proposals in two.[190] And the Council systematically deletes the provision regarding penalties included in most of the proposals for Directives with regard to legal migration.[191] The position of the Commission is different.

---

189 See recital 2 of Council Decision 2004/926/EC regarding the putting into effect of parts of the Schengen acquis to the UK, *op.cit.*

190 See the French initiatives for a Directive and Framework Decision on unauthorised entry. Initiative of the French Republic with a view to the adoption of a Council Framework Decision on the strengthening of the penal framework to prevent the facilitation of unauthorised entry and residence, OJ C 253/6, 4.9.2000 and Initiative of the French Republic with a view to the adoption of a Council Directive defining the facilitation of unauthorised entry, movement and residence, OJ C 253/1, 4.9.2000. See also Council Directive 2002/90/EC defining the facilitation of unauthorized entry, movement and residence, *op.cit.* and Council Framework Decision 2002/946/EC of 28 November 2002 on the strengthening of the penal framework to prevent the facilitation of unauthorized entry and residence, OJ L 328/1, 5.12.2002.

191 See for example Articles 17 and 28 of the initial Commission proposals for the Directives on family reunification and the status of long-term residents respectively, in conjunction with the final texts of the Directives. See Proposal for a Council Directive on the right to family reunification, COM (1999) 638, 1.12.1999 and Proposal for a Council Directive concerning the status of third-country nationals who are long-term residents, COM (2001) 127 final, 13.3.2001. See also Council Directive 2003/86/EC of 22 September 2003, on the right to family reunification, (2003) OJ L 251/12, 3.10.2003 and Council Directive 2003/109/EC of 25 November 2003, concerning the status of third-country nationals who are long-term residents, OJ L 16/44, 23.1.2004.

More specifically, considering that the Community has a competence on migration, the Commission sustains that it also has the competence to regulate via a Community measure the issue of penalties where necessary. The argument is two-fold. Firstly, the determination of a legal basis must be based on objective criteria relating, in particular, to the aim and content of the measure. And, secondly, if the Community has the competence to regulate behaviour in order to achieve a Community objective, then it also has the competence to decree that the regulated behaviour be sanctioned at national level by criminal sanctions and penalties and this is, particularly, the case where it is considered that only criminal sanctions can assure the respect of Community obligations regarding the regulated behaviour.[192] The Commission's argumentation was recently followed by the European Court of Justice which delivered a judgment concerning the distribution of powers between the first and the third pillar as regards provisions of criminal law. More specifically, the Court has clarified that whereas as a general rule neither criminal law nor the rules of criminal procedure fall within the Community's competence, this does not prevent the Community legislature from taking measures that relate to criminal law which it considers necessary in order to ensure that the rules which it lays down are fully effective.[193] Following the Court's judgement the Commission issued a Communication to which is attached a list of instruments affected by the implications of the judgement and with regard to which the Commission intends to proceed to the necessary steps insofar as these are adopted on the correct legal basis.[194]

Another issue that proves quite problematic is the division of the SIS provisions between the first and the third pillar. Indeed, on all the occasions that the Council has adopted measures developing the SIS a double first and third pillar

192 Commission Staff Working Paper – Position concerning the legal base of the French initiative with a view to the adoption of a Council Directive defining the facilitation of unauthorised entry, movement and residence, and the adoption of a Council Framework Decision on the strengthening of the penal framework to prevent the facilitation of unauthorised entry and residence [SEC (2001) 727, 4.5.2001], Council doc. 8845/01 DROIPEN 45 MIGR 44 COMIX 370, 16.5.2001.

193 See paras 47 and 48 of the Court's judgement of 13 September 2005, Case C-176/03 *Commission v. Council.*

194 See Communication from the Commission to the European Parliament and the Council on the implications of the Court's Judgement of 13 September 2005 (Case C-176/03 Commission v. Council), COM (2005) 583 final, 23.11.2005.

instrument was adopted.[195] In fact, a double instrument is used for the development of SIS II as well.[196]

The existence of legal bases regarding the movement and other rights of third country nationals in other parts of the EC Treaty complicates things even more and leads inevitably to the fragmentation of the legal framework. The application of different decision-making procedures, the diverse role of the EU institutions and, particularly, the different position of the various Member States depending on whether the measure is adopted on the basis of a Title IV TEC legal basis or not, significantly complicates the drafting of the relevant measures. Bearing in mind that certain categories of third country nationals either benefit from a special status or have their position regulated by specific Treaty bases, their exclusion from the scope of the proposed measure was on certain occasions unavoidable.[197]

The final outcome becomes even less transparent if one takes into consideration the lack of any transitory law provisions with regard to the already existing EU *acquis* in conjunction with the actors' unwillingness to clarify the relationship between the former intergovernmental *acquis* and new proposals. First, it needs to be clarified that, unlike the Schengen *acquis*, the instruments of the existing third pillar *acquis* that now fall under Title IV TEC have not automati-

195 See Council Regulation 2424/2001 regarding SIS II, *op.cit.* and Council Decision 2001/886/JHA of 6 December 2001 on the development of the second generation Schengen Information System (SIS II), L 328/1, 13.12.2001 and the Spanish Initiatives concerning the introduction of some new functions for the Schengen information system, in particular in the fight against terrorism, *op.cit.*

196 Proposal for a Regulation of the European Parliament and of the Council on the establishment, operation and use of the second generation Schengen information system (SIS II), *op.cit.* and Proposal for a Council Decision on the establishment, operation and use of the second generation Schengen information system (SIS II), COM (2005) 230 final, 31.5.2005.

197 i.e. family members of EU citizens and workers posted by a service provider for the purposes of cross-border services or as cross-border providers of services. To the extent that this last category is concerned, the UK was to exhibit great resistance to the adoption of the two Directives. See COM (1999) 3 final, 26.2.1999 and for the amended proposal COM (2000) 271 final, 8.5.2000. According to the UK's view "it would be confusing to and inappropriate to adopt any measure which relates to the entry and residence of third country nationals except under Title IV" and the effect of its Title IV Protocol would be "fatally undermined, if questions of immigration policy could be decided under other Titles of the Treaty". See House of Lords, *A Community Immigration Policy, op.cit*. Despite the UK's different view the Commission has included the said categories of persons in its recent proposal on services. See Proposal for a Directive of the European Parliament and the Council on services in the internal market, COM (2004) 2 final, 5.3.2004.

cally become Community *acquis*.[198] According to the Vienna Action Plan, most probably the entirety of this *acquis* should be replaced by Community instruments.[199] However, the Treaty of Amsterdam does not contain any transitory law provisions regulating the actual status of this *acquis* or the obligations of the Member States that have opted out of Title IV TEC, namely Denmark, Britain and Ireland. It seems that the position sustained by the Council is that the Amsterdam Treaty has no retroactive effects.[200] But not only has the Community not adopted any official position on that issue, it also usually avoids to clearly addressing the question whenever it presents proposals developing former third pillar instruments.[201] Despite the marginal legal value of most of the former third pillar instruments,[202] maintaining these instruments when a new Commu-

198 On that point see Hailbronner K., "European immigration and asylum law under the Amsterdam Treaty", *op.cit.* For an overview of the former third pillar *acquis,* see Lo Monaco A., " Actions communes et positions communes dans les domaines de la justice et des affaires intérieures ", in Pauly A., Best E., Guggenbuhl A. and Marinho C. (eds.), *De Schengen à Maastricht : voie royale et course d'obstacles,* EIPA, Maastricht, 1996, p. 45-59.

199 The replacement of the former third pillar *acquis* is stated as one of the priorities included in the Vienna Action Plan. See Action Plan of the Council and the Commission on how best to implement the provisions of the Treaty of Amsterdam on an Area of Freedom, Security and Justice (Vienna Action Plan), OJ C 19/1, 23.1.1999, at pt. 29.

200 For further arguments on that point as well as for an analysis of how the Community has treated the case of the former third pillar conventions that have been communitarised, see Papagianni G., "Flexibility in Justice and Home Affairs: an old phenomenon taking new forms", *op.cit.*

201 The only case where the Commission proposes the repeal of a former Joint Action is within the framework of the proposal for a framework decision on trafficking. See Proposal for a Council Framework Decision on combating trafficking in human beings, COM (2000) 854 final and Council Framework Decision 2002/629/JHA of 19 July 2002 on combating trafficking in human beings, OJ L 203/1, 1.8.2002. However, in the case of proposals regarding first pillar instruments, although the relevant former third pillar instruments are mentioned in the recitals or in the explanatory memorandum of the Commission proposals, the Community fails to take a clear position on their status after the adoption of the Community instruments. See Council Directive 2001/55/EC of 20 July 2001 on minimum standards for giving temporary protection in the event of influx of displaced persons and on measures promoting a balance of efforts between Member States in receiving such persons and bearing the consequences thereof, OJ L 212/12, 7.8.2001; Proposal for a Council Directive on minimum standards for the qualification and status of third country nationals and stateless persons as refugees or as persons who otherwise need international protection, COM (2001) 510 final, 12.9.2001, and Proposal for a Council Directive on the status of long-term residents, *op.cit.*

202 Given that most of these instruments are quite general soft law measures.

nity instrument is adopted that develops the third pillar instrument will inevitably create legal complexity.

This whole issue is not simply of academic interest, it also has important practical consequences. More specifically it is not clear whether the Member States that have opted out of the Title IV relevant measures continue to be bound by the former third pillar *acquis*. Essentially there are two positions that could be taken. One could argue that given that the relevant Member States have clearly expressed, via the relevant Protocols, their political will not to be bound by the Title IV relevant measures they are accordingly no longer bound. Alternatively, one could counter argue that the relevant Member States remain bound given that this *acquis* was negotiated and adopted by them as well. Eventually, they will not be bound by any future measures, if they do not wish so, but they clearly remain bound by what was adopted pre-Amsterdam.

From a practical point of view this is a non-issue in cases where the Council has already adopted measures developing the existing third pillar *acquis*, to which the respective Member States do not opt-in. But it is not really clear how things will turn out in relation to measures that are not yet "developed" or in cases where a relevant measure is adopted but the previous one is not formally repealed. Unfortunately, as already mentioned, the Council avoids taking a clear position by repealing the former third pillar measure. Furthermore, it is interesting to highlight the different positions taken with respect to issues that are closely linked, namely the two visa measures that were both adopted on the basis of former Article 100 C TEC. Whereas the visa list Regulation was replaced by a new Regulation,[203] the proposal for the visa format Regulation was surprisingly enough tabled as an amendment of the previous Regulation.[204] It is likely that the main reasons were of a legal nature, since the legal basis regarding the visa list had been amended by the Amsterdam Treaty and now expressly included a reference to a white list.[205] However, given the Schengen relevant character of the measure and the fact that the UK had not opted into the relevant part of the Schengen *acquis*, the position taken by the Council seems to be rather convenient for British interests.

---

203 Proposal for a Council Regulation determining the list of third countries whose nationals must be in possession of visas when crossing the external borders and those whose nationals are exempt from that requirement, COM (2000) 27 final, 26.1.2000 and Council Regulation (EC) No 539/2001, *op.cit*.

204 Proposal for a Council Regulation amending Regulation (EC) No 1683/95 laying down a uniform format for visas, COM (2001) 577 final, 9.10.2001 and Council Regulation (EC) No 334/2002, *op.cit.*

205 Even if the Commission was arguing that this was implicitly the case also in the former legal basis. See discussion *supra* at 2.2.1.3.

2.2.3 The Competence Debate Still Going Strong

Even though the relevant legal bases have been communitarised, the competence debate between Member States and the Community has not really ended. The issue that received most attention from the Member States was undoubtedly the question regarding external relations competence. More specifically, given the reinforcement of Community competence with regard to the issues that are covered by Title IV TEC, Member States felt the need to preserve their treaty-making power and to safeguard the respect of their foreign policy interests and concerns. Despite the fact that, in principle, the provisions of Title IV TEC do not expressly confer external competence on the Community, it is generally accepted that the Community has implicitly –in accordance with the *ERTA* doctrine- acquired such a competence as a result of it having instantly acquired secondary law in this area.[206] However, most of the Member States were already contracting parties in a series of agreements with third countries,[207] and, most importantly, they were interested in maintaining their treaty-making power in this area, due to national foreign policy concerns.

First of all, according to Article 63 TEC the measures adopted by the Council pursuant to immigration policy shall not prevent Member States from maintaining or introducing in the areas concerned national provisions which are compatible with the Treaty and with international agreements. This provision is rather difficult to interpret and raises questions about the extent of the EC's external competence with regard to migration. Although this provision could not be interpreted as an exemption clause authorising a deviation from Community legislation, nonetheless, it shows clearly that the attribution of the relevant competence to the Community was not supported by all the Member States. However, it is likely to be difficult to distribute powers between the Community and the Member States according to the general principle of subsidiarity due to the political sensitivities of those Member States who were reluctant to give up part of their sovereignty in immigration policy.[208] Moreover, according to

206 Kuijper, *op.cit.*, at p. 364-365. The position regarding the *ERTA* effect on Title IV TEC is also sustained by Peers. See Peers S., *EU Justice and Home Affairs Law*, *op.cit.*, at p. 51. For a general discussion on external competence based on exercised or unexercised internal powers, see O'Keeffe D., "Community and Member State Competence in External Relations Agreements of the EU", *European Foreign Affairs Review*, Vol. 4, 1999, p. 6-36.

207 Furthermore, one should not lose sight of the bilateral agreements concluded within the Schengen framework, as well as the well-known multilateral readmission agreement with Poland. For a general discussion on readmission agreements within the framework of Schengen, see De Noël X., "Les accords de réadmission du Benelux à Schengen et au-delà", *RTDE*, Vol. 29, No 4, oct-déc 1993, p. 635-653.

208 See Hailbronner K., "European Immigration and Asylum Law under the Amsterdam Treaty", *op.cit.*, at p. 1050-1051. See also the discussion *supra* at 2.1.2.2 as well as the Opinion of Advocate General Kokott in case C-540/03, *op.cit.*

a Protocol and a Declaration annexed to the Treaty of Amsterdam, Member States have safeguarded their competence to negotiate and conclude agreements with third countries in domains regarding respectively the crossing of external borders and certain aspects of immigration policy.[209]

Nevertheless, despite this explicit reservation of national competence in external relations, things remained unclear. Indeed, the issue of external relations competence has attracted a great deal of attention from both the Council and the COREPER. In a first phase the discourse focused on the question of readmission agreements and visa policy. The JHA Council, by dissociating readmission agreements from the Community objective of repatriation of illegal residents, arrived at the conclusion that the Community's responsibility with regard to readmission agreements was therefore not exclusive. At the same time it clearly stated that Member States could continue to conclude readmission agreements, in exceptional cases even *after* the conclusion of a Community agreement.[210] However, the Council gave the Commission the necessary mandates in order to negotiate a series of readmission agreements.[211] The Commission traditionally argued for the existence of an exclusive competence on the matter but at the same time can be interpreted as having tacitly accepted the approach of the Member States given that they continued to conclude readmission agreements and the Commission never formally intervened.[212]

---

209 See Protocol on external relations of the Member States with regard to the crossing of external borders and Declaration on Article 63 (3) (a) of the Treaty establishing the European Community. Hailbronner argues that the external relations Protocol indicates clearly the inapplicability of *ERTA* in the field of external border controls. See Hailbronner K., *Immigration and Asylum Law and Policy of the European Union*, *op.cit.*, at p. 65.

210 See Press Release of the meeting of the Council of Justice and Home Affairs, 27/28 May 1999. On this point see De Witte B., "Chameleonic Member States: Differentiation by means of Partial and Parallel International Agreements", *op.cit.* Despite the official Council conclusions on this issue, special national concerns were also expressed during the discussion regarding the readmission agreements with Morocco, Pakistan, Sri Lanka and Russia. See Press Release of the meeting of the Council of Justice and Home Affairs of 29 May 2000.

211 For a detailed discussion see Chapter 4.

212 On this point see Schieffer M., "Community Readmission Agreements with Third-Countries – Objectives, Substance and Current State of Negotiations, *EJML*, Vol. 5, 2003, p. 350-351 and Pastore F., "Visas, Borders, Immigration: Formation, Structure and Current Evolution of the Entry Control System" in Walker N. (ed) *The Area of Freedom, Security and Justice,* Oxford University Press, Oxford, 2004, p. 89-142, at p. 104. The only case on which there is some evidence that the Commission has initiated an infraction procedure concerns an action against Germany which had concluded and signed an ADS agreement, including a readmission clause, with China, despite the fact that the Commission had a mandate to sign an analogous

The question of external relations has also been widely debated in the case of visa policy. Following the full harmonisation of certain aspects of visa policy the Community has arguably acquired exclusive competence with regard to these issues. In contrast to questions regarding the issuing of visas and granting facilitations, where some margin of manoeuvre is left to Member States,[213] the acquisition of an exclusive competence with regard to the list of countries appears to have been resolved.[214] Nonetheless, the question of bilateral visa waiver agreements proved rather problematic. According to Article 20 (2) of the Schengen Convention the Schengen contracting parties had the "right to extend beyond three months an alien's stay in its territory in exceptional circumstances or in accordance with a bilateral agreement concluded before the entry into force of this Convention". In fact several Member States had made use of this provision within the framework of visa waiver agreements. However, the possibility given to Member States by Article 20 (2) leads to a *de facto* contradiction with Article 62 (3) TEC which provides for a maximum three month stay in the Schengen area.[215] In an attempt to solve the issue on an *ad hoc* basis Portugal submitted

agreement. Mariani T., *L'Europe forteresse: mythe ou réalité? Les enjeux de la politique européenne d'immigration*, Assemblée Nationale, Rapport d'Information No 1238, Novembre 2003, at p. 43. However, no case has officially reached the Court yet.

213 For instance according to the visa list Regulation Member States can decide unilaterally to provide visa exemptions to certain categories of persons, such as diplomats or civilian air and sea crew etc. See Article 4 (1) of Council Regulation 539/2001, *op.cit.* Moreover, on the basis of the Schengen Common Consular *acquis* they have some margin of manoeuvre regarding the type of visa that they will issue, i.e. multiple entry, for one to five years etc. Therefore, unless there is a Community action on the matter or a concrete EC negotiating mandate Member States should in principle be able to conclude agreements with third countries, provided that these are compatible with the EC *acquis*. It is worth noting that the Council has already initialled a visa facilitation agreement with Russia – See Summary of discussions of the Ministerial JHA Troika EU/Russia Permanent Partnership Council (PPC) in Luxembourg on 12/13 October 2005, Council doc. 13557/05 JAI 357 RELEX 539 NIS 145, 20.10.2005 – and has also adopted a negotiated mandate for the conclusion of a similar agreement with Ukraine, see Adoption of the Draft Council Decision authorising the Commission to negotiate with Ukraine a Visa Facilitation Agreement between the European Community and Ukraine, Council doc. 13725/05 VISA 268 NIS 147 COEST 180, 27.10.2005.

214 According to the twelfth recital of the visa Regulation, this aspect is fully harmonised. See Council Regulation (EC) No 539/2001, *op.cit.*.

215 Since the third country nationals benefiting from several national bilateral visa waiver agreements could, through the accumulation of the relevant three month periods, stay longer than three months in the EU territory. Therefore, these agreements are not compatible with EC law. And moreover it is worth highlighting that certain of these agreements have been concluded *after* the entry into force of the

an initiative regulating the matter with regard to third countries falling under the 'white visa list', since such agreements were concluded with countries falling under this category.[216] The Commission, on the basis of a combined use of Articles 62 (3) and 63 (3) TEC, instead proposed a global solution setting a general framework for the freedom to travel of third country nationals, which on the one hand, communitarises the relevant Schengen *acquis*, and on the other hand, introduces a specific authorisation to stay for a period up to six months in order to rectify the contradictions between the former Schengen *acquis* and Article 62 (3) TEC.[217] A long and heated debate started within the Council, which was centred around the following central questions:[218] the *ad hoc* approach followed by the Portuguese initiative in contrast to the global approach of the Commission; the illegal character of the existing bilateral agreements; the question of whether the legal bases used by the Commission were correct;[219] and the issue of reciprocity.[220] Given the limited possibilities offered by the existing legal bases for the time being the issue seems to be blocked.[221] However, it is worth noting

Amsterdam Treaty, namely the bilateral visa waiver Agreement between Portugal and the United States.

216 Initiative of the Portuguese Republic with a view to adopting a Council Regulation on the period during which third country nationals exempt from visa requirements are free to travel within the territory of the Member States, OJ C 164/6, 14.6.2000.

217 Proposal for a Council Directive relating to the conditions in which third-country nationals shall have the freedom to travel in the territory of the Member States for periods not exceeding three months, introducing a specific travel authorization and determining the conditions of entry and movement for periods not exceeding six months, COM (2001) 388 final, 10.7.2001.

218 For an overview of the discussions see Outcome of proceedings of the Visa Working Party, Council doc. 11503/02 VISA 120 COMIX 485, 14.8.2002 and Outcome of proceedings of the Visa Working Party, Council doc. 13660/02 VISA 157 COMIX 616, 31.10.2002.

219 In particular, Article 62 (3) did not seem to justify the extension of the freedom of movement beyond three months and its combined use of Article 63 (3) was heavily debated given that Article 62 (3) constituted a *lex specialis*.

220 The issue of reciprocity is in fact closely linked with the visa waiver agreements. More specifically, given that visa reciprocity was on certain occasions established on a bilateral basis, some third States seemed to have problems with the idea of extending reciprocity to all the EU states. However, a reciprocity clause is included in the text of the visa Regulation – See Article 1 (4) of Council Regulation 539/2001, *op.cit.* There are many cases, however, where reciprocity is not a reality. Despite the Community competence on the matter, no concrete action has been taken and Member States seem to have opted to solve the problem nationally, via bilateral visa waiver agreements. For a discussion on reciprocity see infra Chapter 4.

221 Since Article 62 (3) sets a clear maximum limit of three months. However, it needs to be mentioned that the reference to a specific time limit has been abolished within

that the Council and the Commission have already announced their intention to proceed to the conclusion of visa waiver agreements between the EC and third countries on the conditions to move freely within the Union for a period between three and six months.[222]

As the issue of external relations in JHA matters was a new area of Community competence, the need to integrate this new area into the general framework of EC external relations appeared imperative. Thus, during its meeting in June 2000, the General Affairs Council examined a Presidency report that was subsequently submitted and approved by the Feira European Council.[223] This report stressed the need for the Union to integrate JHA matters fully into its external policy so that a comprehensive, integrated, cross-pillar action could be carried out by the Union as a whole. An aspect of this report that was the subject of much debate concerned the question of the institutional framework. The substantial changes between the first and the final version of the report seemed to reinforce the argument regarding the Member States' concerns about the competence question in external relations.[224] The issue arose again during the examination of the new EU strategy for the external dimension of Justice and Home Affairs following the Hague Programme. On this occasion the Council has been even more laconic by simply reaffirming the cross-pillar responsibility of COREPER for ensuring coherence across Council work in this area and inviting the geographical and functional groups and committees which cover JHA and external relations to co-ordinate between themselves and if appropriate to organise joint meetings on an *ad hoc* basis.[225]

---

the framework of the Draft Constitutional Treaty where there is simply a reference to "a short period". See Article III-166 (2) (c) of the Draft Constitutional Treaty.

222 See point 2.9 (h) of the joint Commission and Council Action Plan for the implementation of the Hague Programme, *op.cit.*

223 European Union priorities and policy objectives for external relations in the field of justice and home affairs, Council doc. 7653/00 JAI 35, 6.6.2000. See the Presidency Conclusions of the Santa Maria de Feira European Council, 19 and 20 June 2000; Press Release of the meeting of the Council of General Affairs, 13 June 2000. See also the European Parliament Report on justice and home affairs: EU priorities and policy objectives for external relations, A5-0414/2001, 21.11.2001.

224 For the changes between the two texts, see House of Lords, *Correspondence with the Ministers, op.cit.*, at pt. 44.

225 See point 14 of Note from the Presidency on a Strategy for the External Dimension of JHA: Global Freedom, Security and Justice, Council doc. 15446/05 JAI 488 RELEX 741, 6.12.2005. It is also worth mentioning in that respect the proposal of the Council Secretariat for the establishment of a cross-pillar group. See Note from the Secretariat General of the Council – Contribution to the debate that should lead by the end of 2005 to a Strategy for JHA External Relations, Council doc. 12850/05 JAI 318 RELEX 491, 4.10.2005. See also Communication from the Commission A

Another issue that proved rather sensitive concerned the access of third country nationals to the labour market. In fact, the German Chancellor, in a letter sent to the EU Presidency, clearly informed his partners of the German interpretation of the relevant provision, which is to say the maintenance of exclusive national competence on this specific issue.[226] And, the deletion of the relevant reference to employment, included in the relevant provision of the Maastricht Treaty, could be seen as a sign in this direction.[227] In addition, it is arguable that the existence of Article 137 TEC, which is the only express legal basis on immigration and employment issues, has complicated the debate. It grants a further legal argument to those reluctant to grant Community competence to maintain that there was no such competence under Article 63 (3) (a) TEC.[228] The existence of a Community competence with regard to access to employment has actually been repeatedly questioned by Germany. However, on every occasion the Council Legal Service has confirmed the existence of a Community competence, though on certain occasions on a different legal basis, i.e. Article 137 TEC.[229] In light of the above, it should come as no surprise to find that the pertinent provisions in the relevant migration Directives have been watered down and that the discussions on the proposal for a Directive on paid employment have been completely frozen.[230]

Strategy on the External Dimension of the Area of Freedom, Security and Justice, COM (2005) 491 final, 12.10.2005.

226 See the letter sent by the German Chancellor to the President of the Council after the signature of the Treaty of Amsterdam reproduced in Hailbronner, "European Immigration and Asylum Law under the Amsterdam Treaty", *op.cit.*, at p. 1052 and in Hailbronner K., "The Treaty of Amsterdam and Migration Law", *EJML*, Vol. 1, 1999, p. 9-28, at p. 14.

227 Compare Article K.1 (3) (b) of the Maastricht Treaty with Article 63 (3) (a) of the Amsterdam Treaty.

228 However, it needs to be underscored that Article 137 TEC is found in a rather different context, regulates a different issue – i.e. the employment conditions and not the issue of access to the labour market – and most probably was not meant to be a *lex specialis* as to Article 63 (3) (a) TEC. As Brinkmann rightly points out, Article 137 TEC regulates which kind of conditions apply to third country and is thus the legal basis for 'how' they are employed, while access to employment concerns 'whether' a third country national is admitted. Brinkmann G., "The Immigration and Asylum Agenda", *ELJ*, Vol. 10, Issue 2, March 2004, p. 182-199, at p. 188.

229 The Council Legal Service examined the issue with regard to the temporary protection, reception conditions and paid employment Directives. See Brinkmann G., "The Immigration and Asylum Agenda", *op.cit.*, at p. 188. However, given the existence of the Protocols and the different decision-making procedures applying with regard to the two provisions the relevant legal bases cannot be combined.

230 See *infra* at 4.2.1.

Finally in relation to the competence debate, Member States have continued to exhibit a constant tendency to keep the law-making process under their immediate control. One of the issues that has been fiercely debated concerns the procedures applied for the development of the Schengen *acquis*. Whereas within the Schengen framework a series of implementing measures were adopted by the Schengen Executive Committee, which has been replaced by the Council, within the Community framework implementing powers lie with the Commission on the basis of Article 202 TEC and the relevant Council Decision.[231] This has been disregarded by the Council for it has reserved certain implementing powers, contrary to the opinions of the Commission and the European Parliament, with regard to visa policy and border controls by adopting respectively a Finnish and a Portuguese initiative.[232] Both these cases constitute an *ad hoc* limitation of the scope of Article 202 TEC with regard to Title IV TEC and establish an

231 Council Decision 1999/438/EC of 28 June 1999 laying down the procedures for the exercise of implementing powers conferred on the Commission, OJ L 184/23, 17.7.1999.

232 See Council Regulation (EC) No 789/2001 of 24 April 2001 reserving to the Council implementing powers with regard to certain detailed provisions and practical procedures for examining visa applications, OJ L 116/2, 26.4.2001 and Council Regulation (EC) No 790/2001 of 24 April 2001 reserving to the Council implementing powers with regard to certain detailed provisions and practical procedures for carrying out border checks and surveillance, OJ L 116/2, 26.4.2001. For the relevant initiatives see Initiative of the Republic of Finland with a view to the adoption of a Regulation reserving to the Council implementing powers with regard to certain detailed provisions and practical procedures for examining visa applications, OJ C 164/7, 14.6.2000 and Initiative of the Portuguese Republic with a view to adopting a Council Regulation reserving to the Council implementing powers with regard to certain detailed provisions and practical procedures for carrying out border checks and surveillance, OJ C 73/8, 6.3.2001. Both initiatives have been rejected by the Parliament See also the common Parliament Report A5-0066/2001, 27.2.2001. It is interesting to note that the Council has already exercised its implementing powers. See *inter alia* Council Decision 2001/329/EC of 24 April 2001 updating part VI and Annexes 3, 6 and 13 of the Common Consular Instructions and Annexes 5(a), 6(a) and 8 of the Common Manual, OJ L 116/32, 26.4.2001 and Council Decision 2001/420/EC of 28 May 2001 on the adaptation of Parts V and VI and Annex of the Common Consular Instructions on Visas and Annex 6a to the Common Manual with regard to long-stay visas valid concurrently as short-stay visas, OJ L 150/47, 6.6.2001. See also the Outcome of proceeding of the Visa Group meeting on the Draft Council Regulation on the adaptation of Part VII and Annex 12 of the Common Consular Instructions and Annex 14a of the Common Manual, Council doc. 12796/01 VISA 116 COMIX 673, 16.10.2001. During the discussion the Commission contested the compatibility of the legal basis, considering that the rules in the draft decision should be the subject of a proposal under Title IV TEC and that the consultation of the Parliament would be required.

additional institutional restriction, which has not been provided expressly by the Treaty itself.

According to Article 202 TEC the implementing powers are in principle attributed to the Commission, [233] whereas "the Council may reserve the right, *in specific cases*, to exercise directly implementing powers itself" (Article 202, third indent TEC, emphasis added). Unfortunately, the concept of a "specific case" has never been defined clearly and the case law of the Court is hardly explicit on this point. [234] According to some authors, the vague character of the regime concerning the implementation of Community powers is deeply rooted in the lack of an adequate framework governing executive action, which further reflects the lack of consensus about the constitutional nature of the Community.[235] However, according to the case law of the Court, which has been confirmed by the Comitology Decision, the reservation of implementing powers by the Council is an exceptional situation and the cases where such a reservation takes place must be "specific and substantiated".[236]

The arguments used by the Council were two-fold and mainly linked to the sensitivity of the relevant areas. On the one hand, the fact that under the Schengen regime those powers were attributed to the Schengen Executive Committee, which has been replaced by the Council,[237] and, on the other hand, the "enhanced role" of Member States with regard to the development of visa and border policies.[238] It is interesting that this reservation of implementing powers is limited in time. As is stated in the preamble of the relevant Regulations, the

233 Most commentators accept this position, however, Kortenberg argues that in principle the implementing function is vested in the Member States and that the Commission undertakes only those tasks that the Council as a "collection of Member States confers upon it". See Kortenberg H., "Comitologie: le retour", *RTDE*, 1998, p. 317-327. For a detailed analysis on Comitology, see Lenaerts K. and Verhoeven A., "Towards a legal framework for executive rule-making in the EU? The contribution of the new Comitology decision", *CMLRev,* Vol. 37, 2000, p. 645-686.

234 For an overview of the case law of the Court see Lenaerts K., "Regulating the regulatory process: "delegation of powers" in the European Community", *ELRev*, Vol. 18, 1993, p. 23-49.

235 See Lenaerts and Verhoeven, *op.cit.*, at p. 649.

236 Unfortunately, the Comitology Decision avoids addressing this question directly, by simply consolidating the existing *acquis*. See Council Decision 1999/468/EC, *op.cit.* For an analysis of the Comitology decision see Lenaerts and Verhoeven, *op.cit.*, at p. 666-686. See also the relevant report of the House of Lords. House of Lords, *Delegation of powers to the Commission: reforming Comitology*, Select Committee on the European Union Third Report, Session 1998-99, London, 2 February 1999.

237 See recital 6 of Council Regulation No 789/2001 and recital 3 of Council Regulation No 790/2001, *op.cit.*

238 See recital 8 of Council Regulation No 789/2001 and recital 5 of Council Regulation No 790/2001, *op.cit.*

Council reserves the relevant implementing powers "during the transitional period of five years...pending a review by the Council of the conditions under which such implementing powers would be conferred to the Commission at the end of that transitional period".[239] Clearly it is only supposed to apply during the five-year transitory period. Given the temporarily limited character of the reservation of powers and the lack of any substantial justification, it is arguable that the motivation is based on the Member States tenacious resolve to maintain the intergovernmental character of Title IV TEC as much and for as long as possible. These policy choices aiming at distinguishing Title IV from the classic Community institutional order -at least during this five-year transitory period- by inserting restrictions that are not even expressly provided by the Treaty, cannot be explained satisfactorily except as the products of intergovernmental-nostalgia crises.

Both Regulations were challenged by the Commission before the Court.[240] The Commission argument is two-fold: firstly, the Council's statement of reasons is so generic that it could cover all of Title IV, and, secondly, that the argument regarding the sensitivity of the area is not valid.[241] On the other hand, the Council contends in essence that the reservation of powers is adequately justified and concerns specifically amendments to certain detailed provisions and practical procedures and it also gave concrete examples attesting to the sensitivity of the area.[242] Advocate General Léger in his Opinion, while being rather cautious and not very clear-cut in his reasoning, concluded in favour of the Commission.[243] On the contrary the Court has shown much more sympathy for the Council's position. Considering, on the one hand, that "the Council could reasonably consider itself to be concerned with a specific case and that it duly stated the reasons", whereas on the other hand, that the Commission has not succeeded in

239 See recital 8 of Regulation 789/2001 and recital 5 of Regulation 790/2001, *op.cit.*

240 See Case 257/2001, *Commission v. Council* (hereafter "comitology case"). See Opinion of Advocate General Léger delivered on 27 April 2004.

241 See Opinion of Advocate General Léger, paras. 29-31.

242 *Idem*, paras. 34-37.

243 The Advocate General explains in detail the difficulties that the Court is facing since the reservation of powers "falls within the institution's [Council's] political discretion", see paras. 56-61. Then while he sustains that it is not "the amendments which must be specific but the situation in which the Council reserves implementing powers to itself" and that the Regulation's recitals suggest that there is a "standard form of wording in which the only thing to have changed is the subject matter concerned" he contends that nonetheless "that similarity need not, in my view, preclude the content from being such as to establish that there is a specific situation, justifying the reservation of powers", see paras. 64 and 65. Finally, based on the fact that the Council has established a general procedure for a particular area the Advocate General concludes in favour of the Commission, see paras. 66-68 and 69.

showing the need for a uniform procedure, the Court dismissed the action.[244] As a final note, it is worth mentioning that the Council has already repealed Regulation 790/2001 following the adoption of the Regulation establishing the Code for the crossing of the external borders.[245]

2.3 Perspectives for the Future

2.3.1 The Treaty of Nice: Postponing the Cutting of the 'Umbilical Cord'

The presentation of the process of communitarisation of policies related to the free movement of persons, the examination of the institutional structures of Title IV TEC as well as the brief overview of the first five years following the entry into force of the Amsterdam Treaty had revealed a series of shortcomings due, mainly, to the partial character of this communitarisation. One might well have expected the Treaty of Nice to have been the ideal opportunity to correct and complete the work that was initiated at Amsterdam in order to achieve a full communitarisation of these policies. Unfortunately, this has not been the case. The Heads of State and Government either avoided addressing certain questions, or have managed to reach only extremely complicated compromise solutions for the issues that were finally examined. Once again, they refused to sever completely the intergovernmentalism umbilical cord, winning some more time for themselves and their Ministries to recover from the Amsterdam shock.

As previously discussed, numerous issues could have eventually been dealt with at Nice, but were, unfortunately, not addressed. Some of them even graced the IGC agenda, whereas others remained on the wish lists of the Community institutions and academics. One of the major unresolved questions concerns the role of the Court within the framework of Title IV TEC. Whereas the Heads of State and Government have *de facto* amended certain aspects of Article 67 (2) TEC and have, further, given certain guidance to the Council regarding the unanimous decision for the passage to complete institutional communitarisation regarding certain other aspects,[246] they avoided addressing the question of

244 See in particular paras 59 and 71, 77 and 79 of the Court's judgement of 18 January 2005 in Case C-257/01.

245 See Article 39 of the Community Code on the rules governing the movement of persons across borders, *op.cit.*

246 The term 'de facto' is used given that although the new fifth paragraph that has been added to Article 67 TEC refers expressly to the first paragraph of Article 67 TEC, it amends *de facto* the second paragraph of this Article. Moreover, certain other institutional aspects of Title IV TEC are examined in the Declaration that is attached to the new Article 67 TEC as amended by the Treaty of Nice. See new Article 67 (5) TEC as well as the Declaration (No 5) on Article 67 of the Treaty establishing the European Community.

the role of the Court.[247] Moreover, given that one of the main reasons for the limitation with regard to the preliminary ruling mechanism (Article 68 (2) TEC) was the fear that the Court would not be able to deal with the eventual overload of preliminary requests in this area, the Heads of State and Government did not proceed to any changes of the Statute of the Court in this respect.[248] Finally, there has been no attempt by the IGC to address the many calls for the relaxation of the standing criteria for individuals and private parties under Article 230 TEC.[249]

Another question that has not been dealt with is the problematic relationship between Title IV TEC and the new third pillar (Title VI TEU). As argued above, the separation of the policies related to the free movement of persons between the two pillars inevitably generates a certain degree of confusion and overlap. Further one should take into consideration the traditional inclination

247 Despite the fact that the risks arising from the limitation of the national courts empowered to make references to the Court of Justice were also highlighted by the Court itself in its contribution to the IGC. See "The future of the judicial system of the European Union (Proposals and Reflections)" <http://curia.eu.int/en/txts/intergov/index.htm>.

248 However, the Statute of the Court has been examined and amended in certain respects. Some areas of preliminary rulings are to be transferred to the Court of First Instance, with intellectual property rights being the first candidate. Article 225a TEC provides for the setting up of specialised chambers. According to a Declaration attached to Article 225a TEC, the first chamber will be responsible for staff cases, whereas intellectual property rights seem to be possible candidates as well. See Declaration (No 16) on Article 225a of the Treaty establishing the European Community. For more details regarding the reform of the judicial system Johnston A., "Judicial reform and the treaty of Nice", *CMLRev*, Vol. 38, 2001, p. 499-523 and Barents R., "Some observations on the Treaty of Nice", *Maastricht Journal of European and Comparative Law,* Vol. 8, No 2, 2001, p. 121-132. However, none of these changes seem to affect, at least in the foreseeable future, the Court's jurisdiction under Title IV TEC. Moreover, certain other options that had been proposed, such as the establishment of an "accelerated mechanism" or the setting up of a "filtering" mechanism, do not seem to have been taken into account. See Position Paper, "The Jurisdiction of the European Court of Justice in respect of Asylum and Immigration matters, Human Rights and the EU Intergovernmental Conference 1996-7", *Justice*, May 1997.

249 Despite the central importance of such a change for the judicial protection of individuals, especially with regard to human rights issues, and despite the fact that the Union professes to attach the highest value to the establishment of the 'area of freedom, security and justice'. See Johnston, *op.cit.*; Albors-Llorens, *op.cit.*, and Wouters J., 'Institutional and constitutional challenges for the European Union – some reflections in the light of the Treaty of Nice', *ELRev*, Vol. 26, 2001, p. 342-356.

of the Member States towards the third pillar.[250] Article 42 TEU, the third pillar *passerelle* clause, provides for the transfer of certain aspects of the third pillar to Title IV TEC. Given the express reference to Article 31 TEU by Article 61 TEC, the communitarisation of Article 31 TEU and its transfer to Title IV TEC would be more than welcome. And when the deep political character and special difficulties that the use of Article 42 TEU poses are taken into account – difficulties that could not possibly be surmounted by a simple Council Decision – then it is arguable that the examination of such a possibility within the framework of an IGC would have been a more appropriate approach.[251] In this respect, it is regrettable that the Member States refused to proceed to any further transfer of competences to the EC as this inevitably compromises the process of creating a coherent Community migration policy.

Member States have also persistently refused to re-open the sensitive Schengen file and alter the shaky compromises of Amsterdam. Despite the enormous difficulties that have been encountered in practice, the Schengen relevance concept remains vague. One might, for example, have hoped for an invitation to establish a code of conduct on this issue. Member States, obviously, preferred to leave the hands of the Council free in this respect. Moreover, given the great number of both legal and practical problems that have already been posed with regard to the implementation of the Danish Protocol, one might have expected some sort of review of the Danish position with regard to Title IV TEC. Obviously neither Denmark nor the rest of the Member States, were willing to alter the sensitive balance of the Amsterdam compromise. Furthermore, the Heads of State and Government, clearly too concerned with the big institutional questions, have neglected the importance of certain, admittedly smaller, but, from a practical point of view, equally important questions. It should be recalled that the question of SIS remained open due to a lack of consensus within the Council with regard to the establishment of the appropriate legal bases in the Treaty. However, as mentioned above, sooner or later the Council would have to adopt

250 It is interesting to note that the two French initiatives concerning the question of unauthorised entry, movement and residence had been initially presented as a single proposal in the form of a Council framework decision, but were later divided, following an opinion of the Council Legal Service. However, according to the Commission the French initiative should be based in its entirety on an EC law legal basis. In a working paper submitted to the Council, the Commission states, with regard to the question of sanctions, that "if the Community has – within given competence- the power to regulate behaviour in order to achieve a Community objective, then it has also the competence to decree that the regulated behaviour be sanctioned at national level by *criminal* sanctions and penalties". In support of its arguments, the Commission cites a series of case law of the Court. See Commission Staff Working Paper, SEC (2001) 727 final, *op.cit.*, as well as the discussion *supra* at 2.2.2.

251 See the Danish Declaration regarding Article 42 TEU, *op.cit.*

measures building upon this *acquis* in view of the establishment of SIS II.[252] The creation of an independent Agency responsible for the management of this *acquis* has been proposed as a solution on different occasions, but no legal basis has been adopted in this respect.[253]

The only question that was examined was the application of the co-decision procedure (Article 251 TEC). This formed part of the general debate on the passage of a series of Community policies to the qualified majority voting system. The questions posed could be summarised as follows: on the one hand, whether there was the political will to apply prematurely what was agreed upon in Amsterdam, and, on the other hand, the idea of applying Article 251 TEC was also questioned, given the confidential nature of certain issues. The solutions proposed and the positions taken varied widely. Some proposed an automatic transition to qualified majority, others persistently rejected any transfer to qualified majority, and the solution of a new transitional period or that of a declaration were also examined.[254] The German refusal to renounce unanim-

252 In fact, as already mentioned the Commission has already tabled the relevant proposals for the development of SIS II. See COM (2005) 236 and COM (2005) 230, *op.cit.* Thus, it now falls up to the Council to decide upon the division of SIS between the first and the second pillar.

253 See *supra* at 2.1.1.2.

254 The Benelux countries along with Italy proved to be the most "EC-oriented". See "EU/Institutional reform: Luxembourg Memorandum" (Benelux Memorandum), *Bulletin Quotidien Europe*, No 7832, 31 October 2000. The proposal regarding the introduction of a new transitional period was tabled by France. See "EU/Institutional reform: At IGC, still "too much deadlock", says Barnier, announcing that Commission is prepared to play role in preparing post-Nice", *Bulletin Quotidien Europe*, No 7812, 4 October 2000. Finally, the last Presidency draft proposed a five year transitional period after the entry into force of the Treaty of Nice. See "EU/Institutional reform: Nice Treaty must respect balance between Member States, says Barnier, hoping Commission would have role to play in enhanced cooperation under second pillar also – Commission willing to contribute with Presidency to "post Nice" debate", *Bulletin Quotidien Europe*, No 7858, 7 December 2000. For a general overview see "Special Edition for Nice European Council (7,8 & 9 December 2000)", *Bulletin Quotidien Europe*, No 7860, 12 December 2000.

ity,[255] the constitutional problems invoked by France,[256] as well as the fear of creating risks regarding the ratification process of the new Treaty, resulted in the drafting of a complex compromise.

The compromise between those in favour of the transition to qualified majority and to the 251 TEC procedure and those constantly rejecting it took the form of a new fifth paragraph to be added to Article 67 TEC, according to which:

> By derogation from paragraph 1, the Council shall adopt, in accordance with the procedure provided for in Article 251 … the measures provided for in Article 63 (1) and (2) (a) *provided that the Council has previously adopted, in accordance with paragraph 1 of this Article, Community legislation defining the common rules and basic principles governing these issues* (emphasis added).

Moreover, according to a Declaration attached to Article 67 TEC, Member States established the following agreement with regard to the Decision that the Council would take pursuant to Article 67 (2) TEC: on the one hand, the measures concerning free movement within the EU territory (Article 62 (3) TEC) and illegal

255 The possibility of renouncing unanimity in asylum and immigration issues had been ruled out by Germany on numerous occasions during the IGC. See "EU/IGC/Germany: Schroeder confirms he is open to restricted Commission and keen on unanimity on asylum issues", *Bulletin Quotidien Europe*, No 7847, 23 November 2000; "EU/Institutional reform: informal meeting of Vimont group will examine summary document covering all issues from IGC, except those concerning Commission and weighting of votes in Council", *Bulletin Quotidien Europe*, No 7835, 4 November 2000. Indeed, the German Länder seem to adopt an increasingly unfriendly stance towards the transfer of decision-making capacity to Brussels on immigration and particularly asylum matters. It needs to be recalled that the idea for an automatic transition from unanimity to qualified majority voting after a five year period following the entry into force of the Treaty of Amsterdam – which was foreseen in both the Irish and Dutch drafts – was struck down by Chancellor Kohl during the final days of negotiations, under considerable pressure by the Länder. See Petite, *op.cit.* and Uçarer E., "From the Sidelines to Center Stage: Sidekick No More? The European Commission in Justice and Home Affairs", European Integration Online Papers, Vol. 5 (2001) No. 5, <http://eiop.or.at/eiop/texte/2001-005a.htm>.

256 France claimed that such an amendment would require changes in the French Constitution for which there was no majority. See "EU/Institutional reform: Moscovici gives details in France's position", *Bulletin Quotidien Europe*, No 7829, 26 October 2000. Moreover, the French Minister of Foreign Affairs recalled that the introduction of Title IV TEC at Amsterdam had led to "extremely complex debates" within the French Parliament. See "EU/European Council of Biarritz: Following an initial discussion between Heads of State or Government on institutional reform, Pierre Moscovici hoped that "the Biarritz spirit" was "the will to succeed ambitiously Nice", *Bulletin Quotidien Europe*, No 7820, 14 October 2000.

immigration (Article 63 (3) (b) TEC) would be adopted in accordance with the Article 251 TEC procedure, as from 1 May 2004, and, on the other hand, the Council would decide to act in accordance with the 251 TEC procedure in order to adopt measures regarding the crossing of external frontiers (Article 62 (2) (a) TEC) only *"from the date on which agreement has been reached on the scope of the measures concerning the crossing by persons of the external borders of the Member States"* (emphasis added). Furthermore, a third paragraph of the same Declaration invited the Council to "endeavour to make the procedure referred to in Article 251 applicable from 1 May 2004 or as soon as possible thereafter to the other areas covered by Title IV or to parts of them". Finally, according to a Protocol annexed to the Treaty of Nice, from 1 May 2004, the Council should act by qualified majority in order to adopt the measures referred to in Article 66 TEC.[257]

The legal problems arising from this new fifth paragraph added to Article 67 TEC as well as from the attached Declaration were numerous. Starting with Article 67 (5) TEC, one could observe the following. First, the exact timing of this passage to the co-decision procedure was not clear. According to the new Article 67 (5) TEC, the passage would take place *when* the Council would have defined "the common rules and basic principles". Given that there was no definition regarding the intended scope of this description, it is obvious that interpretations of this could vary.[258] And, even if the issue was brought before the Court, the possibilities for a successful review of legality were much more limited.[259] The Heads of State and Government obviously preferred to leave the Council's hands free with regard to the interpretation of this provision, as well as to provide legitimate grounds of defence should a challenge before the Court arise.

257 Protocol on Article 67 of the Treaty establishing the European Community. Arguably the change regarding Article 66 TEC could not have been included into the Declaration agreed at Nice as to the exercise of the Council's power under 67 (2) TEC, since that power is limited to the substitution of co-decision for the 67 (1) procedure, while the new procedure provided in 66 TEC is the consultation procedure with the Council acting by qualified majority. Thus, drafting a separate Protocol amending Article 66 TEC seemed necessary.

258 First of all, the scope of the term "common" is not clear, especially in view of the fact that the term used in most of the relevant Treaty provisions is "minimum standards". See Article 63 (1) and (2) TEC. Bearing in mind that there can be "common" measures at a very low level as well, one could argue that the two terms are not necessarily contradictory. Moreover, given that the measures mentioned in the new fifth paragraph of 67 TEC regard asylum, the question of whether the condition regards the first or the second stage of the asylum process could be raised as well.

259 However, given the new interpretative role of the Court in Title IV TEC, a request for a ruling on the interpretation of this provision could be submitted. See Article 68 (3) TEC.

Moreover, the way that this passage to co-decision would take effect was not clear. From the way Article 67 (5) TEC was drafted it did not seem that there would be a Council Decision on this issue. One could reasonably argue that this would most likely take place on a case-by-case basis.[260] Furthermore, the relationship between the new fifth paragraph and the second paragraph of 67 TEC or the Declaration was not addressed. Thus, taking the scenario in which the "common rules and basic principles" had not been adopted in relation to one of the areas covered by the fifth paragraph by the time the five year period lapses, it was not clear what institutional framework would apply to the measures included in 67 (5) TEC.[261]

Unfortunately the Declaration did not provide any clarification on the points that have been raised. On the contrary, one could say that it further complicated Article 67 TEC. First of all, even if the part of the Declaration concerning Articles 62 (3) and 63 (3) (b) TEC was quite clear, the part that referred to the borders issue was rather obscure.[262] One might have arguably sustained that

260 According to Van Nuffel it was up to the Commission to affirm this and in the future to present proposals within the framework of the co-decision procedure. It would then be up to the Council when it examined the proposal to determine whether the condition was fulfilled. See Van Nuffel P., 'Le traité de Nice: Un commentaire', *Revue du Droit de l'Union Européenne,* Vol. 2, 2001, p. 329-387. However, it was not clear whether these issues should be treated as a package or whether a basic measure would have to be put in place for *every* separate issue. For example given that in the case of temporary protection logically the "common rules" regarding temporary protection are already in place, – see Council Directive 2001/55/EC on temporary protection, *op.cit.* – should the Council pass to co-decision even if many of the other asylum proposals have not been adopted? Given that the question of temporary protection is easily distinguishable from the other measures, it seemed likely that the Council would have to move to the co-decision procedure. However, this was a matter to be judged on an *ad hoc* basis, while keeping in mind the interactions among the different measures that needed to be adopted.

261 Even if this scenario might be highly unlikely, given that all the proposals with regard to these provisions have already been tabled, one should keep in mind that decision-making in JHA can be a very long process. It took six years in total for the adoption of the temporary protection Directive and almost two years for the adoption of the Eurodac Regulation, a proposal that had already been extensively discussed in the form of a Convention. The European Parliament was consulted four times on that issue. Thus, in case this scenario might arise it was not clear whether it was Article 67 (2) TEC that would apply, or the Declaration, or even whether the obligation for the prior adoption of "common rules" would be still valid. Given that the scope of 67 (5) was to accelerate the passage to co-decision this last hypothesis would not seem probable, even if from a legal point of view it is debatable.

262 According to certain academics the change in procedure was contingent on the resolution of a long-running dispute as to the application of the measures in question with respect to Gibraltar. See Dashwood A., "The constitution of the European

it was not certain that Article 62 (2) (a) TEC would pass to the co-decision procedure after the lapse of the five-year period. The vague phrase that was used is striking given that this part of the Declaration clearly referred to the Decision that the Council was obliged to take by the end of the five-year period. Finally, the lack of reference to Articles 62 (1), 63 (2) (b), 63 (3) (a) and 63 (4) TEC, in conjunction with the last paragraph of the Declaration, created a certain ambiguity with regard to the application of the co-decision procedure to these provisions after the lapse of the five-year period. One could make two observations in that respect. First, this last paragraph of the Declaration did not come under the same heading as the previous three, which referred expressly to the Article 67 (2) TEC Decision. Second, Article 67 (2) TEC referred to *all* the provisions of Title IV TEC. However, one should also examine such legally binding character as the Declaration possesses as well as its political weight.

One might persuasively argue that the provisions of the Treaty of Nice have complicated rather than clarified the already complex Amsterdam *status quo*.[263] However, they also brought to light important policy considerations with regard to this area. First, it becomes clear that the Member States were determined not to renounce their veto right or to allow any major interference by the Community institutions until they shaped a common ground with regard to these areas. This consideration is further reinforced if one recalls the remainder of the temporary restrictions with regard to Title IV TEC and, in particular, the crucial impact of the five-year time limit. Given, on the one hand, the limited expertise of the Community institutions in these areas as well as the considerable differences among their national policies, Member States wanted to make sure that the task of forging the bases of this new Community policy would principally lie on their side, with each one of them on an equal footing. This transitional period should accordingly not be seen as simple restrictions but as a trust-building period as well, not only between the Community institutions and Member States but also among the Member States. Moreover, one cannot fail to observe the sensitivity of the external borders question. External borders seemed to be one of the last points within the new Title IV on which Member States trust their partners or would like Community institutions to meddle. This consideration is further reinforced by the new Article 18 (3) TEC, as amended by the Treaty of Nice, as well as by Article 6 of the new visa Regulation.[264]

Union after Nice: law-making procedures", *ELRev,* Vol. 25, No 3, 2001, p. 215-238.

263 Following the Treaty of Nice there were nine decision-making procedures within the framework of Title IV TEC. For a detailed enumeration of these procedures see Van Nuffel, *op.cit.*

264 Council Regulation 539/2001, *op.cit.* One should keep in mind all the safety nets and restrictions with regard to the borders' question. See *supra* at 2.1.2.2.

The outcome of the Nice Summit has certainly not been clear. It does, however, seem that the addition of these legally ambiguous provisions might have been at this stage the only way to overcome differences and political objections. And in the long run it might be capable of having a positive effect if one takes into account that it would grant the Heads of State and Government as well as their Ministries the necessary time to learn to work together and overcome their fears.[265]

Following the lapse of the five-year time limit two questions became rather pressing. Firstly, what would be the fate of Member States initiatives still under negotiation in view of the acquisition of exclusive right of initiative by the Commission.[266] Secondly, would there be any passage to co-decision for any of the areas not passing automatically. Inasmuch as the former is concerned, the Council seems to have taken a rather restrictive approach. In particular, on the occasion of the Italian initiative on joint flights and the Spanish initiative on the communication of passenger data –draft Decisions on which the Council had reached a common approach but on which the European Parliament had not given its opinion and could subsequently not be officially adopted- the Council took a clear position stating that due to the fact that as of 1 May 2004 the Council could no longer act on an initiative of the Member States the said Decisions would be adopted without the opinion of the Parliament.[267] Inasmuch as the second issue is concerned, it seems that the focus during the Irish Presidency was transferred to the negotiations under the IGC. However, the Dutch Presidency has brought the issue to the forefront by including it in the more general framework of the preparations of the political guidelines for the new multi-annual

265 Position expressed by Romano Prodi. See Special Nice Edition, *Bulletin Quotidien Europe*, *op.cit.*

266 Strictly speaking on the basis of Article 67 (2) TEC Member States could not submit and the Council should not anymore negotiate on, or act upon, Member State initiatives after the 1 May 2004. Nonetheless, one needs to take into consideration the political implications of the matter in question, since there were measures based on Member States initiatives on which negotiations in the Council were already advanced or on which there was already even political agreement but the measure had not yet been officially adopted. Therefore it was not clear whether 67 (2) also prevented the Council from finalising pending negotiations.

267 See recitals 5, 6 and 7 of Council Decision 2004/573/EC on the organization of joint flights, *op.cit.*, as well as the relevant Note to Coreper included in Council doc. 8773/04 MIGR 33 COMIX 280 OC 447, 26.4.2004. See also recitals 4, 5 and 6 of Council Directive 2004/83/EC of 29 April 2004 on the obligation of carriers to communicate passenger data, OJ L 261/24, 6.8.2004 as well as the relevant Note to Coreper -Draft Council Directive on the obligation of carriers to communicate passenger data – Common Guidelines, Council doc. 8842/04 FRONT 77 COMIX 288 OC 450, 26.4.2004.

programme for the area of freedom, security and justice.[268] Bearing in mind the extreme complications in the decision-making process, the position of the Commission as well as the considerable pressure from the European Parliament, the European Council invited the Council the examine the issue at the latest until 1 April 2005.[269] Indeed, the Council has already adopted the relevant Decision regarding the passage to the co-decision procedure for the entire Title IV, with the exception of measures regarding legal migration, as from 1 January 2005.[270]

2.3.2 The Draft Treaty Establishing a Constitution for Europe

In contrast to the Treaty of Nice, the Constitutional Treaty as it has been proposed by the Convention and agreed upon by the Heads of State during the European Council of 17 and 18 June 2004 is much more ambitious. The legal bases regarding policies on border checks, visa policy and immigration have been clarified and extended.[271] There are now specific legal bases for issues already currently examined by the Council such as readmission policy, integration policy, integrated management of external borders, solidarity and fair sharing of responsibility.[272]

Moreover, the relevant policies have been completely integrated into the classic Community framework and submitted under the usual decision-making and judicial process. Qualified majority voting and co-decision have become the rule for the entire Title IV and the jurisdiction of the Court is no longer subject

268 See the Agenda of the Justice and Home Affairs Council of 19 July 2004 as well as the Presidency Note on the Preparation for the political orientations for the multi-annual programme building the area of freedom, security and justice, Council doc. 11122/04 JAI 258, 9.7.2004.

269 See point 15 of the Presidency Conclusions of the European Council of Brussels, 4-5 November 2004 as well as point 1.2 of the Hague Programme, *op.cit.*

270 See Council Decision 2004/927/EC, *op.cit.*

271 See Articles III-257 to III-268 of the Treaty establishing a Constitution for Europe, OJ C 310, 16.12.2004. See also Draft Treaty establishing a Constitution for Europe adopted by consensus by the European Convention on 13 June and 10 July 2003, OJ C 169, 18.7.2003 as well as the Final Report of Working Group X "Freedom, Security and Justice", CONV 426/02. It needs to be highlighted that the text of the relevant provisions proposed by the Convention have been adopted as such by the Intergovernmental Conference and the Heads of States. For interesting discussion, see Walker N., "Freedom, Security and Justice", *in* De Witte B. (ed.) *Ten Reflections for the Constitutional Treaty in Europe,* European University Institute, San Domenico di Fiesole, 2003, p. 163-185 and Walker N., "In Search of The Area of Freedom, Security and Justice: A Constitutional Odyssey", in Walker N. (ed.) *The Area of Freedom, Security and Justice,* , Oxford University Press, Oxford, 2004, p. 3-38.

272 Articles III-265, III-267 and III-268.

to any limitations.[273] Furthermore, whereas the Commission's right of initiative is *de jure* exclusive, the newly established right of the European Council to define the strategic guidelines for legislative and operational planning was seen as a broader if less direct qualification of the Commission's right.[274]

However, certain traces of Member State reluctance to attributing the relevant competence to the Community are evident. The area of freedom, security and justice is clearly now considered an area of shared competence,[275] the usual clause on national competence for safeguarding internal security remains[276] and, following a German request, another safeguard clause regarding admission for employment has been added.[277] A new mechanism that establishes the possibility for national parliaments to check the correct application of the subsidiarity principle was set up.[278] In the case of integration policy it is clearly stated that harmonisation of national laws is excluded.[279] Member States have also reaffirmed their wish to maintain their treaty-making power with regard to certain aspects of external relations.[280] They have also tried to safeguard the respect of

273 The application of qualified majority voting and the co-decision process flow from the establishment of the unity principle. To the extent that the jurisdiction of the Court is concerned, it is worth highlighting that the exception with regard to state responsibilities in the maintenance of law and order and the safeguarding of internal security are retained for the former third pillar issues. See Article III-283. For a brief presentation of the institutional changes see Walker N., "In Search of The Area of Freedom, Security and Justice: A Constitutional Odyssey", *op.cit.*

274 Article III-258. See also Walker N., "In Search of The Area of Freedom, Security and Justice: A Constitutional Odyssey", *op.cit.*

275 See Article I-14 (j). However, according to Article I-13 (2) the Union shall have exclusive competence for the conclusion of an international agreement when its conclusion is provided for in a legislative act of the Union or is necessary to enable the Union to exercise its internal competence, or insofar as its conclusion may affect common rules or alter their scope.

276 Articles III-262.

277 Article III-267 (5). Dehousse F. and Garcia Martinez J., "The Area of Freedom, Security and Justice in the European Convention", in Dehousse F. and Coussens W. (eds.), *The Convention's Draft Constitutional Treaty: Old Wine in New Bottle?,* Studia Diplomatica, Vol. LVI: 2003, No 1-2, p. 135-151, at p. 144.

278 Article III-259. It is worth stressing that that the role of the nationals Parliaments has generally been reinforced. See Protocol No 1 on the role of Member States' national parliaments in the European Union, OJ C 310/204, 16.12.2004.

279 Article III-267 (4).

280 Protocol No 21 on external relations on the Member States with regard to the crossing of external borders, OJ C 310/204, 16.12.2004. Nonetheless, within the framework of the Declaration regarding Article III-325 concerning the negotiation and conclusion of international agreements by Member States relating to the area of freedom, security and justice there is no reference to Section 2 regarding external

the fundamental – mainly financial – aspects of their security systems within the framework of the establishment of a European immigration policy.[281] And, finally, a new rather unclear distinction between legislative and operational measures, which has been severely criticised, was created.[282]

Despite the series of problems that have emerged due to the Schengen and the other Protocols it has, unfortunately, not been possible either within the framework of the Convention or within that of the IGC to take any major action to simplify the *status quo* and alleviate the impact of the problems stemming from the opt-out Protocols. The text of the British-Irish Protocols have more or less been kept intact,[283] and that of the Schengen Protocol received merely minor changes to take into account recent developments.[284] The most important changes concern the status of Denmark, which might radically change should Denmark decide so in line with its constitutional rules, most likely a referendum. An opting in mechanism based largely, and almost copying, the pick and choose opting in system applied in the case of the UK and Ireland has been annexed to the text of the Protocol, which as far as the rest is concerned remains mainly the same. In a new Article 9 it is stated that at any time Denmark may notify its

---

borders, and immigration issues. See Declarations concerning provisions of the Constitution, OJ C 310/420, 16.12.2004.

281 Declaration re Article III-136 and Article III-267. According to the Declaration "the Conference considers that in the event that a draft European law or framework law based on Article III-267 (2) would affect fundamental aspects of the social security system of a Member State, including its scope, cost or financial structure, or would affect the financial balance of that system as set out in Article III-136 (2), the interests of that Member States will be duly taken into account."

282 See "The birth of the EU's Interior Ministry?", *Statewatch,* Issue 1, 2003, p. 21.

283 The title of both Protocols has been amended. See Protocol No 18 on the application of certain aspects of Article III-14 of the Constitution to the United Kingdom and Ireland and Protocol No 19 on the position of the United Kingdom and Ireland on policies in respect of border controls asylum and immigration, judicial cooperation in civil matters and on police cooperation. Inasmuch as the text is concerned the amendments are limited. A new Article 4 and a reference to Article III-265 has been added to the former, whereas there is just one amendment regarding Article 5 on financial consequences inasmuch as the latter is concerned.

284 i.e. the fact that the *acquis* has been already integrated and the accession of the new Member States. See Protocol No 17 on the Schengen *acquis* integrated into the framework of the European Union. There is now reference to the new Member States in Article 1, the legal bases with regard to integration of Schengen have been deleted as well as the reference to the obligations of Denmark, which has been transferred to the new Danish Protocol. One needs also to highlight the new British-Spanish Declaration on Gibraltar. See Declaration No 45 by the Kingdom of Spain and the United Kingdom of Great Britain and Northern Ireland, according to which the Treaty applies to Gibraltar as a European territory for those external relations a Member State is responsible.

partners that the opting in process with regard to JHA issues will be replaced by the one that is provided in the annex of the Protocol. Additionally, in such a case, six months after the date on which such notification takes effect the entire former Schengen *acquis* as well as the measures building upon this *acquis* that had been adopted in the meantime and which until then had been binding on Denmark as obligations under international law, shall be binding upon Denmark as Union law.[285]

The important institutional improvements accomplished by the new Treaty are to be welcomed. It is regrettable, however, that the Amsterdam Protocols were not dispensed with. The result has been to preserve a complicated and fragmented legal framework.[286] In any case it remains to be seen whether the new Treaty will eventually pass the ratification test, which is expected to prove difficult for certain countries.

Concluding Remarks

This brief presentation of the institutional framework post-Amsterdam as established by Title IV TEC enables one to generate some preliminary conclusions of relevance to the core issue of this book.

First of all, the analysis of the relevant Protocols clearly indicates that we cannot, at least for the moment and the foreseeable future, talk about *common* policies in this area, at least in the traditional sense of this term. The reason is two-fold. On the one hand, not all the Member States are participating, And, on the other, even if the abstaining Member States decide to participate in the future, this will probably be on a 'pick and choose' basis, as shown by the British and Irish requests and is likely to also happen in the future with respect to Denmark. Secondly, it is in any case debatable whether we can talk about a pure *Community* policy given that at least one Member State – Denmark – is bound exclusively on an international law basis and that three outsiders – Norway, Iceland and Switzerland – are deeply involved. Indeed, as has been argued in detail previously, the present arrangements do not constitute closer cooperation but are rather a tailor-made codification of national preferences, making the use of the term communitarisation *à la carte* much more representative of the flexibility-related *status quo* regarding Title IV TEC.

A second important point, is that the integration of Schengen introduced not only a valuable set of substantial rules into the EU framework, allowing the establishment of an 'area without internal frontiers' immediately after the entry into force of the Treaty of Amsterdam, but a considerable number of legal

285 Protocol No 20 on the position of Denmark.

286 For a comparative study of the necessary improvements and the outcome of the Convention see Dehousse F. and Garcia Martinez J., "The Area of Freedom, Security and Justice in the European Convention", *op.cit.*

problems as well. In fact, the price to be paid in terms of clarity, legal certainty and effectiveness proves rather high.

Finally, having briefly analysed these institutional deviations from the classic Community legal order one could undoubtedly conclude that these restrictions constitute clear signs of a certain mistrust being exhibited towards the Community institutions, due to the Member States fear of losing control over areas that are politically extremely sensitive. Member States are determined to preserve their freedom to decide the degree of interference in their legitimate right of sovereignty, even if in certain cases this would only be for a limited period of time.[287] This conclusion is further reinforced by the introduction of a series of additional safety nets within the framework of Title IV TEC. It is clearly the case that the passage to the co-decision procedure has already been a big step and the eventual entry into force of the new draft Constitutional Treaty in the long-term will constitute another major step towards a complete communitarisation in this area. However, one should not neglect the fact that both the effect of the opt-out Protocols is maintained and the new Treaty is accompanied by a series of safeguard clauses. Therefore, it might be a long time before we can talk about a definitive cutting of the umbilical cord from intergovernmentalism and the birth of a Community policy on migration. However, one should not lose sight of the fact that there is no doubt that the Amsterdam Treaty constitutes the turning point, the beginning of the end, a sort of Rubicon line for intergovernmentalism in JHA and the birth of a Community migration policy. It is to be hoped that future developments will contribute and build positively upon this major step.

287 Since a part of the restrictions would either be automatically, or on the basis of a Council decision, waived after the lapse of the five-year transitory period.

PART II: Substantive Law – The Emergence of a European Migration Policy

Chapter 3: The Intergovernmental and EU *Acquis* before 1999

Introduction

Aside from all the criticism regarding the decision-making process before Amsterdam, the lack of clarity regarding the exact legal value of these acts as well as the limited added value of the vast majority of them, the intergovernmental and EU *acquis* before Amsterdam is substantial. The most vital part of this *acquis* was undoubtedly adopted within the framework of the Schengen cooperation. Indeed, the Schengen mark on European affairs in this area is unquestionable. Apart from the fact that the Schengen *acquis* has been literally 'renamed' EU law in the post-Amsterdam era, Schengen had deeply influenced EU policy even before. In this chapter, it will be argued that the Maastricht era *acquis* had been deeply influenced by the Schengen approach, and to a large extent even literally 'copied' Schengen measures.

An overview of the intergovernmental and EU *acquis* is also important from a policy-making point of view. The first policy documents adopted since the 1970s and up to Maastricht show clearly that there were definitely segments of migration policy since the very early days of the Community. Whilst the later documents adopted under the Maastricht Treaty provide a clear idea of how migration policy was perceived and contribute in evaluating the developments in policy-making in the last decade.

The chapter is divided into four sections covering, respectively, the early days up to 1985, the Single European Act era, developments within the framework of Schengen and, finally, developments under the Maastricht Treaty.

3.1 Segments of a European Migration Policy

Bearing in mind the limited number of relevant legal bases as well as the lack of any clear objectives in this respect, it is not surprising that migration is examined almost exclusively in relation to the free movement of EU nationals and within the framework of international agreements between the Community and third countries. Residence rights are granted to third country nationals who are family members of EU nationals moving within the Community by a series of acts adopted on the basis of the relevant EEC Treaty provisions.[1] And, on the basis of Article 238 EEC, the Community had signed a series of association agreements with third countries, providing for a series of rights for third country nationals.[2]

It is clear that there were segments of migration policy since the 1970s notwithstanding a lack of any concrete legislative steps. An overview of a series of non legally binding or policy-making instruments, such as European Council Conclusions, Council Resolutions and Commission legislative proposals or Communications, as well as the existence of intergovernmental cooperation on related issues, support this conclusion.

First of all, a series of initiatives touching upon aspects of migration policy have been taken by the Heads of State themselves. During their Conference in Paris in 1972 they expressed the importance that they were attaching to vigorous action in the social field, inviting the Community institutions to adopt an action programme. In 1974 the European Council proceeded to set up a working party on passport union and the introduction of a common passport, a decision that was seen as envisaging the stage-by-stage harmonisation of the law affecting aliens.[3] In 1975, at the Rome European Council, Heads of State decided for the first time to proceed to cooperation as far as the security aspects of JHA are concerned.[4] Moreover, among the measures envisaged by the *ad hoc* Committee on "people's Europe", set up by the 1984 Fontainebleau European Council, was the abolition of all customs and police controls at the crossing of intra-Community borders.[5]

Secondly, the Commission had been quite active as well. Already in 1974 and in 1976 it had issued two proposals for Directives concerning certain specific aspects of migration policy. The first concerned the inclusion of the children of non-Community nationals in a Directive on the education of children of migrant workers.[6] Interestingly enough the Council, while deleting the relevant provision of the Commission proposal, reaffirmed the political will of the Member States to extend the implementing measures to the children of non-Community

1 All the relevant EEC Regulations provided expressly the possibility of movement for family members irrespective of their nationality. See *supra* at 1.1.1.

2 For a detailed discussion see Guild E., *Immigration Law in the European Community, op.cit.,* Chapters 3 to 6.

3 See Handoll, *op.cit.*, at p. 354. Handoll also provides a useful overview of all the major steps for the period 1970-1985, see p. 353-355.

4 De Lobkowicz W., *L'Europe et la sécurité intérieure Une élaboration par étapes, op.cit.*, at p. 11-14.

5 Fontainebleau European Council, 25 and 26 June 1984, Bull. EC 6-1984.

6 See Article 1 of the Commission Proposal for a Council Directive on the education of the children of migrant workers, OJ C 213/2, 17.9.1975.

nationals in a Declaration attached to the Council minutes.[7] The second Commission proposal concerned the harmonisation of Member State law to combat illegal migration and illegal employment.[8]

The Commission also proved extremely dynamic with regard to issues concerning consultation among the Member States on immigration policy. In 1979 it presented a Communication on consultation on immigration policies *vis-à-vis* third counties.[9] And, in 1985 it adopted the famous Decision on the organization of relevant consultations, which was partially annulled by the Court of Justice, and it also presented guidelines on migration policy.[10]

Finally, the Commission also began exploring the idea of abolishing border controls. In 1984, it presented the first proposal for a Directive regarding the easing of border controls.[11] The proposal itself was limited for 'psychological' reasons to EU citizens. However, in the relevant explanatory memorandum and in the recitals the Commission clarified that the present proposal was just a first step. It further initiated an analysis of the relation between the abolition of internal border controls and the need for legislation on foreigners and visa policy. Interestingly enough the Commission added that its approach was inspired by the 1984 Franco-German Saarbrücken Agreement.

As for the Council, though it refused to adopt any concrete legislative measures, it adopted a series of relevant Resolutions either on its own initiative or at the request of the European Council. In 1974, at the request of the Paris European Council of 1972, it adopted a Resolution concerning a social action

7 Council Directive 77/486/EEC of 25 July 1977 on the education of children of migrant workers, OJ L 199/32, 6.8.1977.

8 Proposal for a Council Directive on the harmonisation of laws in the Member States to combat illegal migration and illegal employment, OJ C 277/2, 23.11.1976. The Commission further submitted an amended proposal in 1978. For this second proposal see Amended proposal for a Council Directive concerning the approximation of the legislation of the Member States, in order to combat illegal migration and illegal employment, OJ 1978 C 97/9, 22.4.1978. Nonetheless, the Council never adopted the relevant act.

9 Communication of the Commission on Guidelines for a Community labour market policy, COM (79) 115 final, 23.3.1979.

10 Commission Decision 85/381/EEC, *op.cit.*; Commission Guidelines for a Community policy on migration, COM (85) 48 final, 1.3.1985. See also the discussion *supra* at 1.1.2.

11 Proposal for a Council Directive on the easing of controls and formalities applicable to nationals of the Member States when crossing intra-Community borders, COM (84) 749 final, 24.1.1985. For the amended proposal see Amendment to proposal for a Council Directive on the easing of controls and formalities applicable to nationals of the Member States when crossing intra-Community borders, COM (85) 224 final, 7.5.1985.

programme.[12] Among the measures to be adopted in accordance with this Resolution figured the promotion of consultation on migration policies *vis-à-vis* third countries and the achievement of equality of treatment for Community and non-Community workers and members of their families in respect of living and working conditions. Given that one of the priorities set was the establishment of an action programme, the Commission prepared a Communication on the matter. Subsequently, the Council came back to this issue with another Resolution in 1976.[13] Within the framework of this second Resolution the Council reaffirmed the principle of equality between workers who are nationals of third countries and those who are nationals of the Member States and stressed the need to promote consultation on migration policies *vis-à-vis* third countries. It also underlined therein, and for the first time, the importance of strengthening cooperation between Member States in the campaign against illegal immigration of workers who are nationals of third countries. In that respect it underscored the need to ensure that appropriate sanctions are laid down to repress trafficking and abuses linked with illegal migration and that the obligations of employers are fulfilled.

Then, in 1980, following the Commission Communication on guidelines for a Community labour market policy, the Council adopted a new Resolution on this issue where it stressed the need to take into account the "priority to be afforded to workers who are nationals of Member States and to contain access to the Community labour market by labour from third countries and by appropriate consultation on migration policies *vis-à-vis* third countries".[14] It also reaffirmed the importance of seeking effective means to combat illegal immigration and illegal employment. The importance of the migration component was further stressed within the framework of its 1984 Conclusions for the medium-term action program.[15] In fact within the framework of its 1980 Resolution the Council had already strongly 'invited' the Commission to take the necessary initiatives. And, in 1985, while taking note of the Commission's intention of drawing up an appropriate procedure to this end, it declared its desire to promote

12 Council Resolution of 21 January 1974 concerning a social action programme, OJ C 13/1, 12.2.1974.

13 Council Resolution of 9 February 1976 on an action programme for migrant workers and members of their families, OJ C 34/2, 14.2.1976. For a discussion on the Commission action see Handoll, *op.cit.*, at p. 353.

14 Council Resolution of 27 June 1980 on guidelines for a Community labour market policy, OJ C 168/1, 8.7.1980.

15 Conclusions of the Council of 22 June 1984 concerning a Community medium-term social action programme, OJ C 175/1, 4.7.1984.

cooperation and consultation between the Member States and the Commission as regards migration policy, including *vis-à-vis* third countries.[16]

In parallel to this intense dialogue among EEC institutions there was also rigorous cooperation taking place at the intergovernmental level. Justice and interior officials had been working on an *ad hoc* basis mainly with regard to security issues since 1975. As examples of the first attempts to cooperate in this area, one could mention the Trevi group, which was established at the request of the Rome European Council (1 December 1975).[17]

3.2 The Single European Act: A Promise Not Kept

Migration policy received a new impetus via the process of completing the internal market following the adoption of the Single European Act and the presentation of the Commission's White Paper.[18] Unfortunately, no concrete legislative acts were adopted. Nonetheless, the issue received major attention from the part of all the policy actors involved, leading to an intense proliferation of documents.

First of all, the importance of convergence among Member States' migration policies was highlighted by the Commission in its White Paper for the Internal Market. Coordination of national policies regarding the entry and residence of third country nationals, along with transferring the current border controls to the Community's external borders and harmonisation of visa policy, were among the major prerequisites for reaching the objective of abolition of internal border controls for persons. The Commission announced its intention to table a series of proposals for Directives regarding all these issues. As it turns out, none were presented. Despite the lack of any substantive progress with regard to the free movement of persons having been systematically highlighted in all

16 Council Resolution of 16 July 1985 on guidelines for a Community policy on migration, OJ C 186/3, 26.7.1985.

17 The Trevi Group – whose name is chosen as an indirect reference to its first President Mr. Fonteijn – was initially working mainly on terrorism. Subsequently, during a meeting in Athens in December 1988 it was decided to extend its mandate in order to examine the security aspects of the free movement of persons. In that respect a special Working group "Trevi 1992" was created. For a brief presentation of the Trevi Group see De Lobkowicz W., *L'Europe et la sécurité intérieure Une élaboration par étapes, op.cit.*, at p. 17-21 and 34-35. For other *fora* see Elsen C., "Les mécanismes institutionnels: Trevi, Schengen, Dublin, Maastricht", in Pauly A. (ed.), *Schengen en panne,* EIPA, Maastricht, 1994, p. 43-53 and Papademetriou, *op.cit.*, at p. 32-33.

18 White Paper from the Commission to the European Council "Completing the Internal Market", COM (85) 310 final, 14.6.1985.

the Commission progress reports on the completion of the internal market, no concrete measures were taken within the Community framework.[19]

Migration policy issues were, however, extensively discussed and heavily debated in the newly institutionalised *fora*, specifically the Ad Hoc Group for Immigration, created in 1986 under the UK Presidency, and the Group of Coordinators established in 1988 by the Rhodes European Council. For its part, the Coordinators Group elaborated a working programme, the famous "Palma document", which was submitted to the European Council of Madrid (26 and 27 June 1989).[20] The Palma document drew up a catalogue of measures to be adopted, making a distinction between "necessary" and "desirable" measures. It also defined the authority that should be responsible for adopting each measure and suggested target dates for their adoption.[21]

The basic legal document discussed in these *fora* was a draft Convention for the crossing of external borders, based on an initiative of the French Presidency during the second semester of 1989. Despite the fact that the Council had almost reached agreement in June 1991 largely thanks to the efforts of the Luxembourg Presidency, the whole issue was finally blocked at the very last minute due to a disagreement between Spain and the UK over Gibraltar.[22] The draft Convention was centred on four main principles: firstly, the definition of external borders; secondly, the definition of the controls exercised at these frontiers; thirdly, the establishment of a basic mechanism for a common approach on visa policy; and, fourthly, establishing the principle of mutual recognition of visas. Nonetheless, the Convention remained silent on the question of internal borders in order to get British agreement.[23]

---

19 See Progress Report required by Article 8b of the Treaty "Completing the Internal Market: an area without internal frontiers", COM (90) final, 23.11.1990; Sixth Report of the Commission to the Council and the European Parliament concerning the implementation of the White Paper on the Completion of the Internal Market, COM (91) 237 final, 19.6.1991.

20 It was named after the place where it was adopted, at Palma de Majorca. It was not officially published. The document is reproduced in Guild and Niessen, *op.cit.*, at p. 443-448.

21 For more details see De Lobkowicz W., *L'Europe et la sécurité intérieure Une élaboration par étapes, op.cit.*, at p. 34-35.

22 De Lobkowicz W., "Intergovernmental cooperation in the field of Migration – From the Single European Act to Maastricht", *op.cit.* The Gibraltar quarrel dates back to the Treaty of Utrecht in 1713, which put an end to the Spanish war of succession and which ever since set Spain and the UK against one another on this issue. It proved impossible to find a compromise on whether or not Gibraltar should be included in the geographical scope of the Convention.

23 On this point see De Lobkowicz W., *L'Europe et la sécurité intérieure Une élaboration par étapes, op.cit.*, at p. 32.

In parallel, migration policy was also examined under a much broader context, this time within the framework of the Community and mainly at the request of the European Council. In 1989, at the request of the Hanover European Council, the Commission presented a Report on the integration of third country nationals.[24] The Report did not really take up the question of admission. Rather it focused on presenting a substantive account of the situation of third country nationals living in the Member States but failed to include any recommendations for improving their situation. Subsequently, at the request of the Strasbourg European Council –which had asked for an inventory of the national positions on migration- the Commission presented a second Communication on the issue of social integration of migrants.[25] In contrast to the former, the second Communication did offer several recommendations, proposing, *inter alia,* the drawing up of a list of basic principles on integration. However, the Council merely took note of the reports, without proceeding to any further concrete initiatives on the matter.[26]

Finally, in view of the Maastricht Treaty negotiations, the Commission presented a general Communication on migration in order to stimulate discussions for the upcoming IGC.[27] After summarising the major problems that Member States were confronted with –i.e. abuse of asylum procedure, the need to manage the effects of steady migration pressure, the control of migration pressure and the integration of legal migrants- as well as the work taking place at the intergovernmental level, it further recommended the reinforcement of association and cooperation with countries of emigration in order to counter migration pressure.[28]

3.3 Schengen: The Successful *Laboratoire d'essai*

Legislative developments within the framework of the Schengen closer cooperation constitute beyond any doubt the most important set of legislative rules in the pre-Amsterdam era. First of all, Schengen has managed to accomplish what the EU had failed to do in 1993, namely the abolition of internal border controls. Indeed, the 26 March 1995, the date of full entry into force of the Convention Implementing the Schengen Agreement, should be seen as the date

24 Commission Report on the social integration of third country migrants residing on a permanent and lawful basis in the Member States, SEC (89) 924 final, 22.6.1989. See also Hanover European Council, 27 and 28 June, Bull. EC 6-1988.

25 Policies on Migration and the Social Integration of Migrants in the European Community, SEC (90) 1813 final, 28.9.1990. Strasbourg European Council, 8 and 9 December 1989, *op.cit.*

26 Guild and Niessen, *op.cit.*, at p. 14.

27 Commission Communication to the Council and the European Parliament on Migration, SEC (91) 1855 final, 23.10.1991.

28 For a commentary see Guild and Niessen, *op.cit.*, at p. 16.

of the accomplishment of an area without internal borders, albeit only for some Member States.[29] For certain others this has been fully accomplished at some later dates, the last ones being the Nordics, on the 26 March 2001.[30] However, and despite the incorporation of Schengen within the EU framework, for two Member States, namely the UK and Ireland, this remains a deliberately unaccomplished goal.[31] Nonetheless, Schengen has certainly been a successful *laboratoire d'essai* for European integration in this area.

As already stated, the ultimate goal of Schengen being the abolition of internal border controls the Schengen Contracting Parties have limited themselves to the very essential measures that would ensure the abolition of controls at internal borders, and would offer the essential security counterbalance. Schengen has been limited to regulating issues linked with short-term stays, i.e. crossing of external borders, short-stay visas and combating illegal migration. Whilst those matters concerning the entry of third country nationals for long-term stays as well as issues of residence remained under the exclusive competence of the Contracting Parties.

Given that the Schengen *acquis* constitutes, following its incorporation within the EU framework in Amsterdam, the basic EU *acquis* regarding the abolition of internal border controls as well as issues linked with visa policy, management of external borders and illegal migration issues, it is worth discussing briefly the key legislative steps taken in the Schengen framework. For systematic reasons the relevant legislative measures are presented under two major headings, representing to a certain extent the philosophy behind Schengen. Accordingly, the basic provisions creating the basis for an area without internal borders will be presented followed by a brief overview of the flanking measures whose introduction was considered indispensable for the abolition of internal border controls. Finally, given the importance attached to maintaining the integrity as well as the high standards of the Schengen system, some final provisions of the

29 The Convention was initially fully applied only by seven of the nine signatory parties (the five founding countries plus Spain and Portugal). Italy and Greece had been unable to meet certain requirements with regard to external border controls. Austria only signed the Agreements in April 1995 and Denmark was still in the process of applying. For further discussion see De Ceuster, *op.cit.*

30 Council Decision 2000/777/EC of 1 December 2000, on the application of the Schengen *acquis* in Denmark, Finland and Sweden and in Iceland and Norway, OJ L 309/24, 9.12.2000.

31 Indeed, as it has already been mentioned neither the UK nor Ireland have in their respective applications for opting into parts of the Schengen *acquis* opted into the parts regarding border controls. See *supra* at 2.1.1.1 and 2.2.1.4.
On the UK and Ireland's non-accession to Schengen see O' Keeffe D., "Non-Accession to the Schengen Convention: The cases of the United Kingdom and Ireland", in Pauly A. (ed.), *Schengen en panne,* European Institute of Public Administration, Maastricht, 1994, p. 43-53.

Schengen Convention aiming at safeguarding the aforementioned principles will be discussed.[32]

3.3.1 An Area without Internal Borders

Article 2 (1) of the Schengen Convention sets out the basic principle according to which: "internal borders may be crossed at any point without any checks on persons being carried out". Articles 19 to 24 clarify that the freedom of movement within the Schengen area includes third country nationals. More specifically, three basic categories of third country nationals can move freely within the Schengen area for a period of up to three months: third country nationals who hold uniform Schengen visas;[33] third country nationals who are nationals of third countries not subject to a visa requirement;[34] and, third country nationals holding valid residence permits, or even provisional residence permits, issued by one of the Contracting Parties.[35] Finally, the right of transit for a maximum five days is granted to the holders of national long-stay visas.[36] However, each Contracting Party had the possibility to reinstate temporarily controls at the internal borders, albeit this was an exceptional measure.[37]

Even though Schengen did not regulate any issues regarding substantive conditions for admission of third country nationals for long-term stays, the inclusion of certain provisions regulating some aspects of legal migration was deemed indispensable. Firstly, given that the right of free movement is granted to holders of national residence permits, the Contracting Parties were requested to communicate to the Executive Committee a list of the documents that they were issuing as valid travel documents, residence permits or provisional residents permits "within the meaning of this Article".[38] In fact it needs to be clarified that the right of freedom of movement is not granted to all third country nationals legally residing in a Contracting Party, but just to those who hold a residence permit that has been communicated by the Contracting Party concerned to its Schengen partners. Furthermore, the Schengen States had decided to implement

32 The present analysis is based on the Schengen *acquis* as published in the Official Journal of the European Communities, OJ L 239, 22.9.2000.

33 Article 19 (1) CISA.

34 Article 20 (1) CISA.

35 Article 21 (1) and (2) CISA.

36 Article 18 CISA.

37 Article 2 (2) CISA. See also Decision of 20 December 1995 (SCH/Com-ex (95) 20 rev.2), OJ L 239/133, 22.9.2000. For an overview of the cases in which Article 2 (2) has been used see Groenendijk K., "Reinstatement of Controls at the Internal Borders of Europe: Why and Against Whom", *ELJ*, Vol. 10, Issue 2, March 2004, p. 150-170.

38 Article 21 CISA. For the relevant list see Annex 4 of the Common Consular Instructions, OJ L 239/356, 22.9.2000.

the EU Joint Action establishing a uniform format for residence permits.[39] Last but not least, the Schengen Contracting Parties had also established some general rules in order to deal with cases where a Contracting Party had already issued, or was considering issuing, a residence permit to a third country national for whom an alert had been issued for the purposes of refusing entry by another Contracting Party.[40]

3.3.2 Flanking Measures

3.3.2.1 Visa Policy for Short-stays

Visa policy clearly constitutes one of the cornerstones of Schengen cooperation. It is one of the issues on which the Schengen Contracting Parties have focused their efforts and embodies one of the biggest parts of the Schengen *acquis*. One could convincingly argue that short-stay visa policy has been almost completely harmonised within the Schengen framework.

The general rules regarding the issuing of short-stay uniform visas are established by Articles 9 to 17 of the Schengen Convention. The detailed provisions regarding both the different types of visas and the conditions and procedures for their issuing are established in detail in a specific decision of the Schengen Executive Committee, the so-called "Common Consular Instructions" (CCI),[41] as well as in a series of Decisions of the Executive Committee and the Schengen Central Group.

According to the Common Consular Instructions there are five basic types of visas: uniform visas (Visa Type C), transit visas (Visa Type B), Airport Transit Visas (Visa Type A), visas with limited territorial validity (usually called VTL)[42] and national long-stay visas (Visa Type D). Most of these types of visa have several variations depending on the number of entries, and the length of the stay, to which the holder is entitled. The Schengen Contracting Parties had managed to harmonise almost completely the list of countries whose nationals were either under a short-stay visa obligation or exempted from such an obliga-

---

39 See Decision of the Executive Committee of 15 December 1997 on the implementation of the Joint Action concerning a uniform format for residence permits (SCH/Com-ex (97) 34 rev.), OJ L 239/187, 22.9.2000. For the relevant Joint Action see Joint Action 97/11/JHA of December 1996 adopted by the Council on the basis of Article K.3 of the Treaty on European Union concerning a uniform format for residence permits, OJ L 7/1, 10.1.1997.

40 Article 25 CISA.

41 The latest consolidated version is published in OJ C 326/1, 22.12.2005.

42 This being the visa that is granted to a third country national, who does not fulfil all the entry conditions. The validity of this visa is limited to the territory of the Contracting Party that issued it. This type of visa is granted on exceptional circumstances and the issuing Contracting Party is requested to inform its partners accordingly.

tion.[43] Moreover, the Common Consular Instructions lay down the procedures and conditions for issuing short-stay visas. In particular, they define the authorities that are competent for issuing the relevant visas, which are in principle the consular services of the Member States of the main destination. They establish the detailed rules on the examination of the relevant applications -i.e. necessary supporting documents, decision-making process, relevant reply times- as well as the practical guidelines regarding the filling of the visa stickers which includes examples of stickers. Insofar as the uniform format of the visa sticker is concerned, it is noteworthy that the Schengen Contracting Parties have been using the same technical specifications and security features as those of the EU since 1996.[44] And they have also compiled a detailed manual on documents to which a visa may be affixed.[45]

It is worth noting that the Schengen Contracting Parties have also established between themselves a system of representation whereby another State can issue a visa on behalf of a partner that does not have its own consular authority in the relevant third country.[46] Moreover, according to Article 17 of the Schengen Convention in certain cases issuing a visa is subject to consultation with the central authorities of other Contracting Parties.[47] The Schengen Contracting

43 The only country appearing in the Schengen grey list was Colombia. See Annex 1 of the Common Consular Instructions, OJ L 239/344 22.9.2000. The harmonisation of this aspect of visa policy has been achieved progressively. See Decision of the Executive Committee of 15 December 1997 on the harmonisation of visa policy (SCH/Com-ex (97) 32), OJ 239/186, 22.9.2000, and Decision of the Executive Committee of 16 December 1998 on the abolition of the grey list of States whose nationals are subject to the visa requirement by certain Schengen States (SCH/Com-ex (98) 53 rev. 2), OJ L 239/206, 22.9.2000.

44 See Annex 8 of the Common Consular Instructions, OJ L 239/371 22.9.2000. For the relevant EU measure see Council Regulation (EC) No 1683/95 of 29 May 1995 laying down a uniform format for visas, OJ L 164/1, 14.7.1995.

45 This manual constitutes a complete inventory of all the travel documents issued by third countries and recognised by each Contracting Party. See Decision of the Executive Committee of 18 December 1998 concerning the compilation of a manual of documents to which a visa may be affixed (SCH/Com-ex (98) 56), OJ L 239/297, 22.9.2000 as well as Decision of the Executive Committee of 28 April 1999 on the compilation of a manual of documents to which a visa may be affixed (SCH/Com-ex (99) 14), OJ L 239/298, 22.9.2000.

46 As for the general rules on representation see point II.1.2 of the Common Consular Instructions, OJ L 239/324, 22.9.2000.

47 A computerised system for consulting the central authorities has been established in that respect, the so-called VISION system. See Decision of the Executive Committee of 21 November 1994 introducing a computerised procedure for consulting the central authorities referred to in Article 17 (2) of the Convention (SCH/Com-ex (94) 15 rev.), OJ L 239/165, 22.9.2000.

Parties have also laid down some basic general rules regarding consular cooperation at the local level.[48] Finally, special attention has been given to the exchange of visa statistics.[49]

3.3.2.2 The Management of External Borders

The second basic precondition for the abolition of internal controls was the application of uniform principles regarding the checks that were carried out at the crossing of external borders. The general rules regarding the crossing of external borders are set out in Articles 3 to 8 of the Convention itself. In particular, the basic conditions that the third country national must fulfil in order to be able to enter the Schengen area are enumerated in Article 5 (1) of the Convention. However, the detailed rules regarding border controls on persons and surveillance of external borders are established by a specific decision of the Schengen Executive Committee, namely the Common Manual.[50]

External borders may in principle only be crossed at border crossing points and during fixed opening hours.[51] The basic conditions that third country nationals need to fulfil in order to be able to enter are: a) possession of a valid travel document; b) possession of a valid visa, if required; c) possession, if necessary, of documents justifying the purpose and conditions of the intended stay and of sufficient means of subsistence, both for the period of the intended stay and for their return; d) lack of any alert for the purposes of refusing entry in their regard; and e) that they are not considered to be a threat to public policy, national security or the international relations of the Contracting Parties.[52] A separate Convention provision underlines that checks on persons include not only the verification of travel documents and other conditions governing entry, residence, work and exit but also checks to detect and prevent threats to the national security and public policy of the Contracting Parties.[53]

Furthermore, the Schengen Implementing Convention provided the necessary legal basis for the cooperation among Contracting Parties with a view to the effective implementation of checks and surveillance.[54] In that respect the Contracting Parties were requested to harmonise as far as possible the instruc-

48 See Part VIII of the Common Consular Instructions, OJ L 239/342, 22.9.2000.

49 Decision of the Executive Committee of 22 December 1994 on the exchange of statistical information on the issuing of uniform visas (SCH/Com-ex (94) 25), OJ L 239/173, 22.9.2000 and Decision of the Executive Committee of 21 April 1998 on the exchange of statistics on issued visas (SCH/Com-ex (98) 12), OJ L 239/196, 22.9.2000.

50 Recently published in the Official Journal, OJ C 313/97, 16.12.2002.

51 Article 3 CISA.

52 Article 5 (1) (a) to (e) CISA.

53 Article 6 CISA.

54 Article 7 CISA.

tions given to their border guards, to promote standard basic and further training of officers manning checkpoint and the eventual exchange of liaison officers was also recommended. Finally, special attention was attributed to the exchange of statistics.[55]

In addition to the basic rules set out by the Convention itself, the Common Manual establishes all the detailed rules regarding checks at the borders while also providing a practical guide for border guards. The Common Manual is divided into two main parts: a first part setting the conditions for entering and residing in the territory of the Contracting Parties, and, a second part, establishing the principles, objectives and practical procedures regarding border checks on persons. Around twenty annexes are also included containing lists, technical specifications and other useful information for border guards. Despite the fact that the vast majority of provisions on borders are included in the Common Manual, certain specific aspects that are not covered, at least not in detail, are regulated by special Decisions of the Executive Committee.[56]

3.3.2.3 The Fight against Illegal Migration

Whereas Schengen has not dealt with legal migration issues, it has examined extensively aspects of illegal migration policy, which were considered to be accompanying measures.

Article 23 of the Schengen Convention establishes the principle of removal of third country nationals not fulfilling, or no longer fulfilling, the short-stay conditions applicable within the Schengen territory and the readmission obligations between Contracting Parties. Article 24 provides the legal basis in order to set the appropriate criteria and practical arrangements for compensation among the Contracting Parties of any financial imbalances which may result from the obligation to expel as provided for in the previous Article. Articles 26 and 27 establish rules regarding carriers' liability as well as the principle that appropriate penalties should be imposed on any person who for financial gain assists or tries to assist a third country national to enter or reside within the territory of one of the Contracting Parties in breach of its laws on the entry and residence of third country nationals.

55 Article 7 CISA as well as Decision of the Executive Committee of 20 December 1995 on the swift exchange between the Schengen States of statistical and specific data on possible malfunctions at the external borders (SCH/Com-ex (95) 21), OJ L 239/176, 22.9.2000.

56 i.e. the stamping of travel documents both at the entry and exit of third country nationals and the introduction and application of the Schengen arrangements in airports and aerodromes. See respectively Decision of the Executive Committee of 21 November 1994 on the acquisition of common entry and exit stamps (SCH/Com-ex (94) 16 rev.), OJ L 239/166, 22.9.2000 and Decision SCH/Com-ex (94) 17 rev. 4, OJ L 239/168, 22.9.2000.

Furthermore, the Schengen States had also elaborated practical rules, and an Action Plan, for the fight against illegal migration,[57] guiding principles for means of proof within the framework of readmission agreements among themselves,[58] and measures to be taken against third States posing problems with regard to the issuing of travel documents required for expulsion.[59] They also established cooperation mechanisms among themselves for the purposes of return by air.[60] Finally, in 1991 the Schengen Group also signed a multilateral readmission agreement with Poland.[61]

3.3.2.4 The Schengen Information System

The most important and most notorious Schengen flanking measure is undoubtedly its special database of undesirable persons, the so-called "Schengen Information System" (SIS).[62] The system is composed of a central database based in Strasbourg, France (C.SIS), to which all the national databases (N.SIS) are connected. Each national database has a separate complementary database – the so-called SIRENE- that contains all the detailed information regarding the alerts within the SIS.

The SIS contains data both on persons and on objects. It has a dual objective. It aims to both curb illegal migration and also to provide a major tool for police cooperation. According to Article 96, which is the central provision

57 Decision of the Executive Committee of 27 October 1998 on the adoption of measures to fight against illegal immigration (SCH/Com-ex (98) 37 def. 2), OJ L 239/203, 22.9.2000 and Decision of the Central Group of 27 October 1998 on the adoption of measures to fight against illegal immigration (SCH/C (98) 117), OJ L 239/205, 22.9.2000.

58 Decision of the Executive Committee of 15 December 1997 on the guiding principles for means of proof and indicative evidence within the framework of readmission agreements between Schengen States (SCH/Com-ex (97) 39 rev.) OJ L 239/188, 22.9.2000.

59 Decision of the Executive Committee of 23 June 1998 on measures to be taken in respect of countries posing problems with regard to the issue of documents for expulsion form the Schengen territory, (SCH/Com-ex (98) 18 rev.) OJ L 239/197, 22.9.2000.

60 Decision of the Executive Committee of 21 April 1998 on cooperation between the Contracting Parties in returning foreign nationals by air (SCH/Com-ex (98) 10) OJ L 239/193, 22.9.2000.

61 See Guild and Niessen, *op.cit.*, at p. 29-30, and Schieffer M., "The Readmission of Third Country Nationals within Bilateral and Multilateral Frameworks", in Den Boer M. (ed.), *The Implementation of Schengen: First the Widening, Now the Deepening,* EIPA, Maastricht, 1997, p. 97-108. It is worth highlighting that the text of the agreement was not published and does not appear in the list of the Schengen *acquis* that has been integrated within the EU framework.

62 Articles 92 to 112 CISA.

concerning the alerts on persons, decisions for issuing an alert may be based on a threat to public policy or public security or to national security, which the presence of a third country national may pose. This situation may arise in particular in the case of a conviction carrying a penalty involving deprivation of liberty of at least one year, or where there are serious grounds for believing that the person concerned has committed serious criminal offences or there is clear evidence of an intention to commit such offences. It is important to note that one of the basic conditions for entry and movement within the Schengen territory is the absence of an alert to the SIS.[63]

3.3.3 Safeguarding the Integrity and High Security Standards of the Schengen System

The Schengen States attached major importance to the security level within the Schengen area without internal borders. The best proof of this consists in the Schengen double-check adhesion mechanism. According to a Joint Declaration on Article 139 of the Schengen Implementing Convention, "the Convention shall not be brought into force until the preconditions for its implementation have been fulfilled in the Signatory States and checks at external borders are effective".[64] Three of the deadlines for the entry into force of the Schengen Convention were actually missed as a result of inadequate security standards, mainly due to the fact that the SIS was not fully operational. Indeed, the main reason for not taking Greece and Italy on board from the beginning, notwithstanding that by 1995 they had both already signed the Schengen Convention, was their inability to prove that they were able to 'seal' their external borders.[65] It is in general considered that the screening before the full implementation of the Convention and the abolition of internal controls is a rather long process and proves quite rigorous for the candidate State. For instance, Greece had signed the Convention in 1992 but it was not until March 2000 that internal border controls were lifted.[66]

63 See Article 5 (1) (d) CISA.

64 Final Act, Joint Declaration on Article 139, OJ L 239/55, 22.9.2000.

65 The three deadlines for the entry into force of the Schengen Convention that had been missed were 1st July 1993, 1st December 1993 and 1st February 1994. See De Ceuster, *op.cit.*

66 See the Agreement on the Accession of the Hellenic Republic, signed at Madrid on 6 November 1992, OJ L 239/83, 22.9.2000, as well as Council Decision 1999/848/EC of 13 December 1999 on the full application of the Schengen *acquis* in Greece, OJ L 327/58, 21.12.1999, setting the 25 of March 2000 as the date of lifting of internal border controls with Greece.

In 1998 the Schengen States had also established the Schengen Standing Committee.[67] The role of the Committee is of a dual nature. Firstly, to establish on the basis of visits by experts whether all the preconditions for bringing the Convention into force in a candidate State have been fulfilled. Secondly, to ensure that the Schengen *acquis* is properly applied by the States already implementing the Convention. In other words there is a constant screening process, as the controls apply both to the newcomers and the States that have already passed the 'screening test'.

A final point to note is Article 136 of the Convention which sets certain limitations to the Contracting Parties' external relations competence in order to safeguard the integrity of the system. Thus, "no Contracting Party shall conclude with one or more Member States agreements simplifying or abolishing border checks without prior agreement of the other Contracting Parties", the only agreements being excluded from this quite strict rule being those on local border traffic.[68]

3.4 Maastricht: Copying Schengen or Creating Something New?

The Maastricht Treaty clearly gave migration policy a strong impetus. As it has been argued, migration was for the first time seen independently having previously been linked exclusively with the free movement of persons objective.[69]

Preparations for the implementation of the new Treaty's third pillar commenced well before the Treaty was even signed. In addition to the Interior Ministers' Palma document and the Commission's Communication of 1991,[70] the Council, at the request of the Luxembourg European Council (28 and 29 June 1991),[71] further prepared a report containing a work programme, which was submitted to the European Council of Maastricht itself.[72]

67 Decision of the Executive Committee of 16 September 1998 setting up a Standing Committee on the evaluation and implementation of Schengen (SCH/Com-ex (98) 26 def.), OJ L 239/138, 22.9.2000.

68 Article 136 (3) CISA.

69 For more details see De Lobkowicz W., *L'Europe et la sécurité intérieure Une élaboration par étapes, op.cit.*, at p. 37-40.

70 See *supra* at 3.2.

71 The German proposal apart from communitarising the relevant policy further proposed to ask the immigration Ministers to put forward a work programme on these questions without waiting for the future Treaty to come into force. For more details see De Lobkowicz W., "Intergovernmental cooperation in the field of Migration – From the Single European Act to Maastricht", *op.cit.*

72 Report from the Ministers responsible for immigration to the European Council meeting in Maastricht on immigration and asylum policy, SN 4038/91 WGI 930, reproduced in Guild and Niessen, *op.cit.*, at p 449-491.

Both the Council and the Commission in their respective documents submitted to the European Council seem to proceed for the first time to a more general analysis of the phenomenon of migration, albeit in a cautious way. Migration is seen within a more general spectrum and is linked with external relations issues and the need for a comprehensive approach is stressed. The Commission proposed three main considerations on which proposals for action should be based: first, action on migration pressure -by making migration an integral part of external relations- second, controlling migration flows -including mainly measures to combat illegal migration- and third, strengthening the integration policies for the benefit of legal immigrants. These three main axes were further developed in a second, considerably more comprehensive, and a great deal more ambitious, Commission Communication in 1994.[73] However, an overview of the measures adopted under the Maastricht era shows clearly that while the Schengen system had a strong influence, the results in the area of legal migration were rather mediocre.

In the light of the above, this section seeks to highlight both these aspects. The section first attempts to demonstrate that the implementation of Maastricht was to a certain extent a copy of Schengen, and an incomplete one at that. Subsequently, it purports to highlight the innovative aspects of Maastricht or at least their added value with regard to the way migration had been perceived under the lenses of the EEC Treaty and the Schengen system.

3.4.1 Copying the Schengen System

3.4.1.1 Visa Policy

Both the structure and the content of the emerging EU visa policy under the Maastricht Treaty were evidently based on the Schengen *acquis*. Visa policy concerned exclusively short-stay visas, whereas long-stay visas remained national. Moreover, the basic criteria for issuing a visa, the types of visas and the various safeguard clauses and derogations were similar to those established within the Schengen framework.

Given the partial and mainly disputed communitarisation of visa policy the visa *acquis* is formed by both first and third pillar measures. Whilst the objectives of setting up of a list of countries whose nationals are subject to a visa requirement and the establishment of a uniform format for visas are achieved via two Regulations adopted on the basis of Article 100C TEC,[74] it is within the

---

73 Communication from the Commission to the Council and the European Parliament on Immigration and Asylum policies, COM (94) 23 final, 23.2.1994.

74 Council Regulation 2317/95, *op.cit*. This Regulation has been challenged by the European Parliament due to lack of re-consultation, and was subsequently annulled by the Court of Justice. It has been re-adopted in 1999. See Council Regulation 574/1999, *op.cit*. For discussion see *supra* at 1.4.2. See also Council Regulation 1683/95 on the uniform format of visas, *op.cit*. It has been rightly argued that the

framework of the proposal for a Convention for the crossing of the external borders that all the details regarding the issuing of the visas were to be regulated.[75] Unfortunately this Convention was never adopted.

All the above measures were manifestly copying Schengen. But they did not manage to reach either the level of harmonisation achieved within the Schengen framework nor the detailed character of the provisions therein. First of all, insofar as the visa list is concerned, the Schengen countries had already managed to form not only a "positive/white" list but also a "negative/black" list and a "grey" list and they continued their efforts until they reached almost complete harmonisation. Secondly, the idea of setting a uniform format for visas already existed within the framework of Schengen. As mentioned previously, the Schengen States had also immediately after the adoption of the EC Regulation decided to align themselves to the EU *acquis*. Thirdly, the relevant provisions of the Convention on the External borders are similar to those of the Schengen Convention, albeit not so detailed.[76]

The Member States have also, and in this respect they again follow the example of the Schengen States, adopted a Joint Action setting up a list of countries whose nationals are under the obligation to have an airport transit visa, albeit the EU list of countries was shorter than the Schengen one.[77] Furthermore, the Council adopted a series of soft-law measures regarding certain other aspects of visa policy, such as local consular cooperation and honorary consuls, issues that were also regulated within the framework of Schengen.[78] Finally, an Ital-

validity of this document was initially purely symbolic, since it was used for the granting of "national" visas, i.e. visas whose territorial validity was limited to the territory of the Member State that issued them. See De Ceuster, *op.cit.* For a critical analysis of the limited scope of the communitarised aspects of visa policy see Cruz A., "Visa Policy under the First Pillar : A meaningless Compromise", in Den Boer M. (ed.), *Schengen, Judicial Cooperation and Policy Coordination,* EIPA, Maastricht, 1997, p. 213-239.

75 For the relevant Commission proposal see COM (93) 684 final, *op.cit.* See also the discussion *supra* at 1.4.2. For a discussion see Hailbronner K., "Visa Regulations and third-country nationals in EC law", *CMLRev,* Vol. 31, 1994, p. 969-995.

76 See Articles 17 to 25 of the proposed Convention in conjunction with Articles 9 to 18 of the Schengen Implementing Convention as well as the Schengen Common Consular Instructions.

77 Joint Action 96/197/JHA, *op.cit.* See also Annex III of the Common Consular Instructions containing the Schengen list, OJ L 239/351, 22.9.2000. The Schengen list contains all the States mentioned in the EU list plus two more as well.

78 Council recommendation of 4 March 1996 relating to local consular cooperation regarding visas, OJ C 80/1, 18.3.1996; Honorary consuls already empowered to issue visas who, as a transitional measure, will be allowed to issue uniform visas (Text adopted by the Council on 20 June 1994), OJ C 274/58, 19.9.1996. See also respectively, Part VIII of the Common Consular Instructions (on local consular

ian proposal for an EC common consular visa handbook is likely to have been premature.[79]

3.4.1.2 Border Issues

As far as border issues are concerned, legislative developments within the EU framework during the Maastricht era are almost non-existent. It should though be acknowledged that the Schengen stain is rather evident and strong on most of the proposed measures in this area as well.

The focal external borders instrument was undoubtedly the proposal for the relevant Convention. Negotiations were now based on a Commission proposal, which simply revised the text on which the Council had already been negotiating since 1989 and on which agreement had almost been reached in 1991.[80] The proposed Convention was not only inspired by the Schengen Convention but literally copied central Schengen provisions, such as, for example, the criteria for allowing entry or the criteria for listing someone on the list of undesirable persons.[81] This proposal was, however, never adopted as the Council did not manage to find a formula satisfying both the UK and Spain over the highly disputed issue regarding the application of the Convention to Gibraltar.[82] It was therefore limited to adopting a few soft law instruments regarding minor aspects of external frontier policy.[83]

---

cooperation), OJ L 239/342, 22.9.2000, and Annex 6 of the Common Consular Instruction on honorary consuls, OJ L 239/367, 22.9.2000.

79 Peers S., *EU Justice and Home Affairs Law*, *op.cit.*, at p. 73.

80 See COM (93) 684 final, *op.cit.* As clearly mentioned in the preamble of the proposal the Commission proceeded exclusively to those changes that were necessary due to a number of developments which had taken place since the negotiations on the earlier draft broke off (i.e. entry into force of the Maastricht Treaty, Community competence on internal borders and visa policy, signature of the EEA Agreement, competence of the Court of Justice). Furthermore, it was also stressed that despite the lack of formal conclusion of the agreement beforehand all the provisions of the draft Convention apart from those concerning the territorial scope would be deemed to have been accepted by the Member States. For more details see the Explanatory Memorandum of the Commission's proposal. See also O'Keeffe D., "The Convention on the Crossing of the External Frontiers of the Member States" in Pauly A., Best E., Guggenbuhl A., Marinho C. (eds.), *De Schengen à Maastricht : voie royale et course d'obstacles,* EIPA, Maastricht, 1996, p. 33-44.

81 See Articles 7 and 10 of the proposed Convention in conjunction with Articles 5 and 96 CISA.

82 However, the Council had even prepared Draft Conclusions on the implementation of controls on persons under the Convention on the crossing of external borders, reproduced in Guild and Niessen, *op.cit.*, at p. 493-506.

83 i.e. Council Recommendation of 28 May 1998 on the provision of forgery detection equipment at ports of entry to the European Union, OJ C 189/19, 17.6.1998.

As far as internal border controls are concerned, there have not been any considerable comprehensive legislative developments. Mainly this has been due to the strongly contested character of both the competence as well as the objective in question. First of all, the Commission correctly considering the matter to fall under Community competence in its revised proposal for the Convention on external borders not only did not include a relevant provision but has further replaced the definition of internal borders that existed in the previous draft with a reference to "instruments enacted under the Treaty establishing the European Community".[84] The Commission has subsequently presented a package of three proposals for Directives on the matter, the well-known "paquet Monti", named after the Commissioner responsible for internal market issues. This package consisted of three proposals for Directives: one requiring the abolition of border controls, another granting to all third country nationals the right to move for a maximum period of three months, and a third amending EC free movement legislation to take account of the first two proposals.[85] While the first two were based on Article 100 TEC the third was based on the provisions regarding the free movement of EU nationals. Inasmuch as the substance is concerned they were closely linked to the relevant provisions of the Schengen *acquis* and the abovementioned draft Convention for the external borders. Nonetheless, the Commission has been rather cautious in its approach,[86] stating, *inter alia,* that the proposal on the elimination of internal border controls "would take effect only when the flanking measures were themselves in force".[87] In any case, the proposals immediately faced political difficulties stemming mainly from the British side. In an attempt to overcome political problems the Irish Presidency proposed a third pillar joint action with a more limited scope, albeit this time

84 See the explanatory memorandum of the relevant Commission proposal – at p. 9 – as well as Article 1 (h) of the proposal.

85 Proposal for a Council Directive on the right of third country nationals to travel in the Community, COM (1995) 346 final, 12.7.1995; Proposal for a Council Directive on the elimination of controls on persons crossing internal borders, COM (95) 347 final, 12.7.1995, and Proposal for a European Parliament and Council Directive amending Directive 68/360/EEC on the abolition of restrictions on movement and residence within the Community for workers of Member States and their families and Directive 73/148/EEC on the abolition of restrictions on movement and residence within the Community for nationals of Member States with regard to establishment and the provision of services, COM (95) 348 final, 12.7.1995.

86 For a detailed discussion on this point see Guild E., *Immigration Law in the European Community, op.cit*, at p. 225-228.

87 See the explanatory memorandum of the proposal on the elimination of controls of persons crossing internal frontiers, *op.cit.*, at p. 2.

facing a categorical reservation by the Commission and by Belgium which had been sympathetic to the Commission's view for a first pillar legal basis.[88]

In the end, the only aspect that was actually regulated was that of school pupils travelling within the framework of a school excursion.[89] It is worth mentioning that the German Presidency's initial proposal envisaged a measure of a much wider scope providing for the abolition of the visa obligation with regard to travelling within the Community for certain categories of third country nationals while awaiting agreement on the external frontier Convention, but the Council limited itself to regulating solely the case of school pupils.[90]

3.4.1.3 Illegal Migration

The EU approach to illegal migration, while being to a large extent influenced by Schengen had also moved further on certain points.[91]

First of all, provisions regarding illegal migration were included in the draft Convention on the crossing of the external borders. They concerned issues such as illegal residence and obligation to expel, readmission agreements and carriers' liability and mainly reproduced the relevant provisions of the Schengen Convention.[92] The Council has also adopted a series of recommendations on matters that were also dealt with in the framework of Schengen and the draft Convention for external borders. Mention could be made of the Recommendation on cooperation in cases of transit for the purposes of expulsion by air,[93] as well as the Conclusions on the issuing of residence permits to persons appearing on the list of undesirable persons and the readmission obligation in cases of illegal resi-

88 Peers S., *EU Justice and Home Affairs Law*, *op.cit.*, at p. 75.

89 Council Decision 94/795/JHA of 30 November 1994 on a joint action adopted by the Council on the basis of Article K.3.2.b of the Treaty on European Union concerning travel facilities for school pupils from third countries resident in a Member State, OJ L 327/1, 19.12.1994.

90 For a more detailed discussion on the initial German initiative see Peers S., *EU Justice and Home Affairs Law*, *op.cit.*, at p. 74.

91 The relevant measures will not be discussed in detail. For an overview and analysis see Peers S., *EU Justice and Home Affairs Law*, *op.cit.*, at p. 94-99 and Guild and Niessen, *op.cit.*

92 See Articles 14 to 16 of the draft Convention on the crossing of external borders in conjunction with Articles 23, 24 and 26 CISA.

93 See the Recommendation regarding transit for the purposes of expulsion, Council doc. 19579/92 IMMIG 2 Annex F to Annex II, reproduced at Guild and Niessen, *op.cit.*, at p. 239-249, as well as the Council Recommendation of 22 December 1995 on concerted action and cooperation in carrying out expulsion measures, OJ C 5/3, 10.1.1996 and the Recommendation concerning transit for the purposes of expulsion, OJ C 5/5, 10.1.1996. See also the Decision of the Executive Committee of 21 April 1998 on cooperation between the Contracting Parties in returning foreign nationals by air, *op.cit.*

dents holding a residence permit of another Member State.[94] Moreover, given the serious problems that the majority of Member States were facing with regard to the lack of travel documents of the apprehended illegal immigrants, the issue was examined under both frameworks though with different perspectives. Whereas the Schengen States focused on measures to be taken against those third States,[95] the EU Member States created a standard travel document for expulsion.[96]

In some respects the EU has also moved beyond the Schengen framework. The Council adopted a Recommendation on concerted cooperation in carrying out expulsion operations[97] and further examined the possibility of placing the arrangements for expulsion by charter flights on a more formal footing.[98] In the readmission domain, a special specimen for readmission agreements was adopted[99] and the Council also adopted guiding principles to be followed in drawing up protocols for the implementation of readmission agreements.[100] It is undoubtedly the case that most of the attention was focused on forced return measures, however, Member States have expressed some interest in voluntary return issues as well. Nonetheless, the relevant Decision merely establishes a framework for exchanging information on the matter.[101]

---

94 Conclusions on conditions for the readmission of persons who are illegally resident in a Member State but who hold a residence permit of another Member State, General Affairs Council, 31.10.1994, reproduced in Guild and Niessen, *op.cit.*, at p. 507-510. See also Articles 25 and 23 SIC and Articles 8, 11 and 15 of the draft External Frontiers Convention as well as the Decision of the Executive Committee of 15 December 1997 on the guiding principles for means of proof and indicative evidence within the framework of readmission agreements between Schengen States, *op.cit*.

95 Decision of the Executive Committee of 23 June 1998 on measures to be taken in respect of countries posing problems with regard to the issue of documents for expulsion form the Schengen territory, *op.cit*.

96 Council Recommendation of 30 November 1994 concerning the adoption of a standard travel document for the expulsion of third-country nationals, OJ C 274/18, 19.9.1996.

97 Council Recommendation of 22 December 1995 on concerted action and cooperation in carrying out expulsion measures, *op.cit*.

98 Peers S., *EU Justice and Home Affairs Law*, *op.cit.*, at p. 98-99.

99 Council Recommendation of 30 November 1994 concerning a specimen bilateral readmission agreement between a Member State and a third country, OJ C 274/20, 19.9.1996.

100 Council Recommendation of 24 July 1995 on the guiding principles to be followed in drawing up protocols on the implementation of readmission agreements, OJ C 274/25, 19.9.1996.

101 Council Decision 97/340/JHA of 26 May 1997 on the exchange of information concerning assistance for the voluntary repatriation of third-country nationals, OJ L 147/3, 5.6.1997.

Furthermore, via a series of Recommendations Member States have set a series of general principles regarding illegal residence adding special emphasis to specific problems linked with admission policy,[102] such as the illegal employment of third country nationals[103] and the problem of marriages of convenience.[104] And, finally, the first legal steps concerning the major problem of human trafficking were also taken in the form of a Joint Action.[105]

3.4.2 Legal Migration

It is beyond any doubt that measures regarding legal migration have an authentic EU stamp on them since this issue was not really examined in the Schengen framework. The sole 'common' measure between the two systems was the EU Joint Action establishing a uniform format for residence permits of third country nationals that the Schengen States had decided to implement as well.[106]

However, legislative developments on legal migration did not really offer much by way of added value with regard to the policies already applied at national level. They were rather limited, with a strongly restrictive character and since they principally took the form of Resolutions were mainly non-binding.

The first legal act adopted was a Resolution on family reunification.[107] Despite the use of the term harmonization, the provisions included were rather

102 Recommendation of Immigration Ministers on 30 November/1 December 1992 regarding practices followed by Member States on expulsion, Council doc. SN 4678/92 WGI 1266, 16.11.1992, not published in the Official Journal. Reproduced in Guild and Niessen, *op.cit.,* at p. 219-238.

103 This is based on a three-step process. See Recommendation concerning checks on and expulsion of third country nationals residing or working without authorisation, Brussels, 25 May 1993, SN 3017/93 WGI 1516, reproduced in Guild and Niessen, *op.cit.,* p. 275-293; Council Recommendation of 22 December 1995 on harmonising means of combating illegal immigration and illegal employment and improving the relevant means of control, OJ C 5/1, 10.1.1996 and Council Recommendation of 27 September 1996 on combating the illegal employment of third-country nationals, OJ C 304/1, 14.10.1996.

104 Council Resolution of 4 December 1997 on measures to be adopted on the combating of marriages of convenience, OJ C 382/1, 16.12.1997.

105 Joint Action 97/154/JHA of 24 February 1997 adopted by the Council on the basis of Article K.3 of the Treaty on European Union concerning action to combat trafficking in human beings and sexual exploitation of children, OJ L 63/2, 4.3.1997.

106 Joint Action 97/11/JHA, *op.cit.*, and Council Decision 98/701/JHA of 3 December 1998 on common standards relating to filling in the uniform format for residence permits, OJ L 333/8, 9.12.1998. See also Decision of the Executive Committee of 15 December 1997 on the implementation of the Joint Action concerning a uniform format for residence permits (SCH/Com-ex (97) 34 rev.), OJ L 239/187, 22.9.2000.

107 Resolution on the harmonisation of national policies on family reunification, Ad Hoc Group Immigration, Copenhagen, 1 June 1993, SN 2828/1/93 REV 1 WG I

loose. In particular, they were not legally binding and the principles were not supposed to afford a ground of action for individuals. Moreover, they were rather restrictive. The definition of family was quite restrictive, the requirements for entry rather extensive and it was further made clear that the principles set out in the Resolution would not affect national legislation or practice in respect of the rights of reunited families in areas which had no direct bearing on the right of entry and stay. The Resolution has been in general criticised for its failure to contain a clear positive statement, the lack of coherent harmonisation measures and its questionable compatibility with international law instruments.[108]

The second set of acts regarding admission policy, adopted a year later, set a series of limitations regarding the admission of third country nationals for employed or self-employed activities.[109] Both measures emphasized the need for restrictive policies on the matter, granting extremely limited leeway for admission. Some months later the Council adopted another Resolution regarding the admission of another category of third country nationals, namely students.[110] Moreover, the Council has also adopted a Resolution regarding the status of long-term residents.[111] Nonetheless, the present act was much more of a Declaration, since it did not really contain any legally binding provisions.

It is also worth recalling that the Agreement on Social Policy attached to a Protocol to the EC Treaty further allowed the Council to adopt measures on equal working conditions for non-EC nationals.[112] A Franco-German initiative

1497, text reproduced in Guild and Niessen, *op.cit*, p. 251-273. For a brief discussion of the family reunification Resolution as well as of the rest of the Maastricht era legal migration Resolutions see Hailbronner K., "Migration Law and Policy within the Third Pillar of the Union Treaty", *op.cit.*, and Peers S., "Building Fortress Europe: The development of EU Migration law", *CMLRev*, Vol. 33, 1998, p. 1235-1272.

108 See Handoll, *op.cit.*, at p. 367-370.

109 Council Resolution of 20 June 1994 on limitation on admission of third country nationals to the territory of the Member States for employment, OJ C 274/3, 19.9.1996 and Council Resolution of 30 November 1994 relating to the limitations on the admission of third country nationals to the territory of the Member States for the purpose of pursuing activities of self-employed persons, OJ C 274/7, 19.9.1996.

110 Council Resolution of 30 November 1994 on the admission of third-country nationals to the territory of the Member States for study purposes, OJ C 274/10, 19.9.1996.

111 Council Resolution of March 4 1996 on the status of third-country nationals residing on a long-term basis in the territory of the Member States, OJ C 80/2, 18.3.1996. For a discussion see Peers S., "Justice and Home Affairs- Undercutting Integration: Developments in Union Policy on Third-Country Nationals, *ELRev*, Vol. 22, 1997, p. 76-84.

112 Peers S., *EU Justice and Home Affairs Law*, *op.cit.*, at p. 69.

for the creation of a Union-level Consultative Commission on combating racism and xenophobia was submitted at the June 1994 Corfu Council and subsequently led to the creation of a European Observatory on Racism and Xenophobia.[113]

In July 1997, shortly after political agreement on the Amsterdam Treaty was reached, the Commission tabled a proposal for a Convention on Admission.[114] The Convention was clearly based upon the five Resolutions on admission that had previously been adopted by the Council. Given the transitory character of this proposal –the Commission having already announced, in the framework of the explanatory memorandum, that it would redraft the proposal as a Directive after the entry into force of the Amsterdam Treaty- it will not be discussed in detail.[115] Still it is worth underlining that that Member States reacted rather negatively.[116]

3.4.3 Related Issues

The Treaty of Maastricht also provided the necessary legal bases in order to establish a series of horizontal functions that would contribute to the forging of a common approach on immigration policy and to confronting common problems more effectively.

Firstly, one of the most innovative points of the Maastricht Treaty consisted in bringing JHA issues under the EU umbrella and subsequently granting to the Member States the possibility to make use of the Union's financial resources. Attention was mainly focused on the financing and burden sharing of costs regarding displaced persons and refugees, obviously due to the extreme increase of these categories of persons following the war in Iraq and the crisis in the Balkans.[117] Nonetheless, the Council also adopted a series of Joint Actions

---

113 Papademetriou, *op.cit.*, at p. 88-89.

114 Proposal for a Council Act establishing the Convention on the rules for the admission of third-country nationals to the Member States, COM (1997) 387 final, 30.7.1997.

115 For a discussion see Hedemann-Robinson M., "From Object to Subject?: Non-EC Nationals and the Draft Proposal of the Commission for a Council Act Establishing the Rules for the Admission of Third Country Nationals to the Member States", *YEL*, Vol. 1998, p. 289-335 and Peers S., *EU Justice and Home Affairs Law*, *op.cit.*, at p. 90-91.

116 De Lobkowicz W., *L'Europe et la sécurité intérieure Une élaboration par étapes, op.cit.*, at p. 79-80.

117 See the Council Resolution of 25 September 1995 (OJ C 262/1, 7.10.1995) and Council Decision 96/198/JHA (OJ L 63/10, 13.3.1996) on burden-sharing with regard to the admission and residence of displaced persons on a temporary basis, as well as Joints Actions 98/304/EC (OJ L 138/6, 9.5.1998), 98/305/EC (OJ L 138/8, 9.5.1998), 97/477/JHA (OJ L 205/3, 31.7.1997), and 97/478/JHA (OJ L 205/5, 31.7.1997) concerning the financing of specific projects in favour of displaced persons who have found temporary protection in the Member States, asylum seekers and refugees.

establishing programs of training, exchanges and cooperation in the field of migration and other related policy issues.[118]

Another issue that is worth discussing briefly is the implementation of Article K.5 regarding cooperation in external relations. Despite the possibility to do so, the adoption of Common Positions proved to be a rare event. However, the Council agreed on a system of holding meetings at ministerial level with certain third countries on important topics, while leaving the responsibility of further contacts to the Presidency. The Presidency was assisted by the Council Secretariat and was usually working in close association with the Commission. The meetings with the representatives of third States were principally held at working party or senior level. The tradition of each Presidency drawing up an external relations work programme setting out a list of the planned meetings was also established.[119]

Additionally, the importance of exchanging information was recognised by the Member States and they took the first tentative legislative steps in this direction. Following the creation of the relevant Asylum Clearing House (CIREA),[120] they established a Centre for Information, Discussion and Exchange on the cross-

---

See also the Decision regarding burden sharing in an area not linked with refugees. Council Decision 98/243/JHA of 19 March 1998 on the sharing of the costs of preparing film masters for the uniform format for residence permits, OJ L 99/1, 31.3.1998.

118 Joint Action 96/637/JHA of 28 October 1996 adopted by the Council on the basis of Article K.3 of the Treaty on European Union introducing a programme of training, exchanges and cooperation in the field of identity documents ('Sherlock'), OJ L 287/7, 8.11.1996; Joint Action 98/244/JHA of 19 March 1998 adopted by the Council on the basis of Article K.3 of the Treaty on European Union, introducing a programme of training, exchanges and cooperation in the field of asylum, immigration and crossing of external borders (Odysseus-programme), OJ L 99/2, 31.3.1998; Joint Action 96/700/JHA of 29 November 1996 adopted by the Council on the basis of Article K.3 of the Treaty on European Union, establishing an incentive and exchange programme for persons responsible for combating trade in human beings and the sexual exploitation of children, OJ L 322/7, 10.1.1996; Joint Action 97/12/JHA of 20 December 1996 adpted by the Council on the basis of Article K.3 of the Treaty on European Union providing a common programme for the exchange and training of, and cooperation between , law enorcement authorities ('Oisin'), OJ L 7/5, 10.1.1997.

119 It needs to be noted that several third countries had established contacts with the EU on JHA matters even before Maastricht. For more details regarding cooperation on external relations and references to Council documents see Peers S., *EU Justice and Home Affairs Law*, *op.cit.*, at p. 33-34.

120 Interior Ministers had set up CIREA at their meeting on 11-12 June 1992. See Second activity report on the Centre for Information, Discussion and Exchange on Asylum (Cirea) (Text adopted by the Council on 20 June 1994), OJ C 274/55, 19.9.1996.

ing of Frontiers and Immigration, the so-called "CIREFI group".[121] Later, they have also set up a database for false documents, known as FADO.[122] Moreover, the first steps towards cooperation among national authorities were also taken. In particular, the Council laid down some preliminary general rules regarding cooperation between liaison officers.[123]

Furthermore, realising that one of the major shortcomings of the third lay in the fact that the measures adopted were not in practice implemented, emphasis was placed on monitoring the implementation process. In an effort to monitor the fulfilment of the obligations stemming from the first five admission Resolutions as well the from the implementation of all the illegal migration, expulsion and readmission measures the Council adopted a Decision providing for an annual review of implementation.[124]

Finally, and rather interestingly considering the institutionalisation offered by the Treaty of Maastricht, migration issues kept being dealt with in the framework of a series of parallel "Clubs" or "Groups" situated outside the EU. One could mention the Vienna, Berlin and Budapest initiatives.[125]

---

121 The establishment of CIREFI is based on a first decision in 1992 -Decision setting up a Center for Information, Discussion and Exchange on the Crossing of Borders and Immigration (CIREFI), 30.11.92, text reproduced in Guild and Niessen, *op.cit.*, p. 205-217 – which was further developed and published in the Official Journal in 1996. See Council Conclusions of 30 November 1994 on the organization and development of the Centre for Information, Discussion and Exchange on the Crossing of Frontiers and Immigration (Cirefi), OJ C 274/50, 19.9.1996. In early 1998 the Council agreed a reform of CIREFI, due to problems linked with the analysis and dissemination of information. Thus, it was decided that migration statistics would be compiled by the Commission's Eurostat service, while non statistical information would be compiled by the Council Secretariat with each supposed to draw up reports analysing the information. See Peers S., *EU Justice and Home Affairs Law*, *op.cit.,* at p. 98-99.

122 Joint Action 98/700/JHA of 3 December 1998 adopted by the Council on the basis of Article K.3 of the Treaty on European Union concerning the setting up of a European Image Archiving System (FADO), OJ L 333/4, 9.12.1998.

123 Joint Action 96/602/JHA of 14 October 1996 adopted by the Council on the basis of Article K.3 of the Treaty on European Union providing for a common framework for the initiatives of the Member States concerning liaison officers, OJ L 268/2, 19.10.1996.

124 See Council Decision of 22 December 1995 on monitoring the implementation of instruments already adopted concerning admission of third-country nationals, OJ C 11/1, 16.1.1996, and Council Decision 1996/749/JHA of 16 December 1996 on monitoring the implementation of instruments adopted by the Council concerning illegal immigration, readmission, the unlawful employment of third country nationals and cooperation in the implementation of expulsion orders, OJ L 342/5, 31.12.1996.

125 For an overview see Papademetriou, *op.cit.*, at p. 35-37.

Concluding Remarks

This brief overview of the legislative developments and the documents of more general interest that were adopted from the 1970s until the adoption of the Amsterdam Treaty enable us to reach some conclusions.

Firstly, it is worth reiterating that discussion over migration related issues was initiated quite early. Obviously the migration debate lacked coordination and coherence and though it was not structured until the late 1980s there were still quite a few steps that had already been taken. And, surprisingly enough, more general issues such as integration policy, management of migration flows and partnership with third countries were already examined in the late 1980s and the beginning of the 1990s.

Secondly, in terms of legislative developments, the vast majority of legal acts that were adopted were centred on the predominant Schengen logic and structure. However, whereas the Schengen experiment has, despite its purely intergovernmental character, proved successful and extremely efficient, the EU *acquis* did not offer much added value in terms of law-making.

Nonetheless, as the following Chapter seeks to demonstrate both policy-discussion and legislative developments under the Maastricht era have undoubtedly set the policy agenda for the Amsterdam era as well.

Chapter 4: The Treaty of Amsterdam: Forging a European Migration Law

Introduction

As already analysed in detail within the framework of the second chapter, the Amsterdam Treaty endeavoured to provide a coherent and comprehensive solution within the EC framework. Detailed legal bases for the adoption of the necessary flanking measures with regard to the abolition of internal border controls and measures that aspire to the formation of a comprehensive approach towards the entry, residence and movement of third country nationals were established.[1] The whole migration agenda was placed in the more general policy framework of an "area of freedom, security and justice".

More specifically, inasmuch as migration policy is concerned, the Treaty of Amsterdam established special legal bases for the adoption of measures regarding the abolition of internal border controls, the crossing of external borders – including rules on short-stay visas – and the fight against illegal migration. It also aimed to regulate not simply the mere movement of third country nationals, but also to establish rules on their entry and residence as well as the rights and conditions concerning their stay in another Member State. Additionally, the relevant Schengen *acquis,* having also been incorporated within the EU framework, offered a well-established and tested "area without internal borders" and a solid basis for the further development and accomplishment of certain aspects –primarily linked with security – of the emerging European migration law.

Preparations for the implementation of the new Treaty legal bases commenced shortly after its adoption. In the first three years after the signature of the Treaty efforts were mainly focused on preparations for the incorporation of Schengen and on the drafting and presentation of more general documents setting the broader lines of Europe's new area of freedom, security and justice.

First of all, JHA Ministers, in cooperation with the Commission, had prepared a timetable for the adoption of the measures mentioned in the Treaty. This was adopted by the Council during its meeting in Vienna in December 1998,

1 Articles 61-69 TEC.

the so-called "Vienna Action Plan".[2] Secondly, the Commission presented two Communications. The first focused on more general, and mainly procedural, issues -such as practicalities concerning the transition from the former Treaty to the Treaty of Amsterdam, especially with respect to the proposals that were already on the negotiating table- and provided a definition of the concepts of freedom, security and justice.[3] And, the second, focused exclusively on migration policy.[4]

The central migration policy document, however, was signed by the Heads of State and Government during the special meeting of the European Council in Tampere, on 15 and 16 October 1999, and is known as the "Tampere milestones".[5] The basic elements that immigration policy should include are presented under three major headings. Firstly, "management of migration flows": under this heading the Heads of State and Government included measures regarding border controls and the fight against illegal migration. Secondly, "fair treatment of third country nationals": here the European Council presents its views on the admission of third country nationals and places special emphasis on their integration and the granting of rights comparable to those of EU citizens. Finally, in a third part, entitled "partnership with countries of origin" Heads of State emphasised their intention to form a comprehensive approach addressing more general political and development issues. The need for a stronger link and coherence between internal and external EU action is also further discussed in a separate section of the Tampere Conclusions.

The European Council has recently reaffirmed its commitment to establish an area of freedom, security and justice and to enhance EU action in these areas during its November 2004 Summit, when it adopted the new EU multi-annual programme on freedom, security and justice, the so-called Hague Programme.[6] On the basis of this Programme the Commission presented a Communication

2 OJ C 19/1, 23.1.1999.

3 Communication from the Commission Towards an Area of Freedom, Security and Justice, COM (1998) 459 final, 14.7.1998.

4 Communication from the Commission to the Council and the European Parliament on a Community Immigration policy, COM (2000) 757 final, 22.11.2000. An analysis of the relevant Commission Communication is not provided in this book because both the approach of the Commission and the EU post-Amsterdam action are based on the political guidelines established within the framework of the Tampere European Council Conclusions.

5 This title was chosen by the European Council itself. See Tampere European Council, 15 and 16 October 1999, Presidency Conclusions.

6 See OJ C 53/1, 3.3.2005 *op.cit.*

with its main priorities and has jointly with the Council adopted an Action Plan to be the frame of reference for their work in this area for the next five years.[7]

The measures that have been adopted within the framework of the implementation of the Tampere milestones during the subsequent five years as well as more recently within the framework of the implementation of the Hague Programme have been numerous.[8] The basic aim of this chapter is to highlight those measures that are closely linked with, and most comprehensively illustrate, the content of the emerging European migration policy. The structure of the chapter follows that of the relevant Tampere European Council Conclusions. The first two sections briefly present the key legislative developments inasmuch as the management of migration flows and the fair treatment of third country nationals are concerned. And a third section provides a general presentation of other related issues and seeks to place migration in its broader contextual setting. More recent developments stemming from the implementation of the Hague Programme will be briefly presented at the end of each section.

4.1 The Management of Migration Flows

4.1.1 Visa Policy and the Management of External Borders

Most of the measures regarding visa policy and the crossing of the EU's external borders have already been almost completely harmonized within the framework of the Schengen cooperation. Thus, the vast majority of the acts adopted

7 Communication from the Commission to the Council and the European Parliament The Hague Programme: Ten priorities for the next five years The Partnership for European renewal in the field of Freedom, Security and Justice, COM (2005) 184 final, 10.5.2005. For the joint Council and Commission Action Plan implementing the Hague Programme see OJ C 198/1, 12.8.2005, *op.cit.*

8 For a complete overview of all the proposals examined by the Council and the measures that have been adopted, see the eight versions of the Scoreboard and a final assessment on the progress of the implementation of the Tampere program prepared by the Commission. See respectively COM (2000) 167 final/2, 13.4.2000, COM (2000) 782 final, 30.11.2000, COM (2001) 278 final, 23.5.2001, COM (2001) 628 final, 30.10.2001, COM (2002) 261 final, 30.5.2002, COM (2002) 738 final, 16.12.2002, COM (2003) 291 final, 22.5.2003, COM (2003) 812 final, 30.12.2003 and COM (2004) 402 final, 2.6.2004 and SEC (2004) 680, 2.6.2004. For a brief presentation and analysis of the relevant measures see the six-month surveys regularly updated by Steve Peers and published in the *EJML*. See Peers S., "Key Legislative Developments on Migration in the European Union, *EJML* Vol. 3 2001, p. 231-255; *EJML* Vol. 4, 2002, p. 85-126; *EJML* Vol. 4, 2002, p. 339-367; *EJML* Vol. 5, 2003, p. 107-141, and *EJML*, Vol. 5, 2003, p. 387-410. Lastly, for a review of the most recent developments see Balzacq T. and Carrera S., *Migration, Borders and Asylum Trends and Vulnerabilities in EU Policy,* Centre for European Policy Studies, Brussels, 2005.

following the entry into force of the new Treaty were aimed at developing the Schengen *acquis*.

As regards visa policy, the Council, in an obvious attempt to bring in to line the existing Schengen and EC *acquis*, has, on the basis of the new Treaty provisions providing for complete harmonisation, adopted a Regulation determining the list of countries whose nationals must be in possession of visas when crossing the external borders and those whose nationals are exempt from that requirement.[9] The list is regularly amended and updated.[10] Moreover, via an amendment of Article 18 of the Schengen Convention the possibility of movement within the Schengen area has been extended to the holders of national long-stay visas for the first three months of validity of their visa.[11] Furthermore, via the adoption of a series of Regulations and mainly Decisions, the Council updated and developed the provisions of the Common Consular Instructions (CCI) regarding certain aspects linked with the issuing of visas. More specifically, a Council Regulation developed the procedure for issuing visas at the border and to seamen in transit,[12] and another Regulation updated the relevant CCI procedure on forms for affixing visas on travel documents that are not recognised.[13] The Council also developed other parts of the CCI concerning the requirements, or the procedural aspects, for the issuing of visas by *inter alia* inserting an obligation for medical insurance,[14] providing for the possibility to ask for additional documents in "risk cases",[15] clarifying and developing the representation procedure,[16] harmonising the visa fees[17] and the visa application

9 Council Regulation 539/2001, *op.cit.*

10 For the subsequent amendments of that list see Council Regulation (EC) No 2414/2001 of 7 December 2001, OJ L 327/1, 12.12.2001 and Council Regulation (EC) No 453/2003 of 6 March 2003, OJ L 69/10, 13.3.2003.

11 Council Regulation 1091/2001 and Council Decision 2001/420/EC, *op.cit.*

12 Council Regulation 415/2003, *op.cit.*

13 Council Regulation 333/2002, *op.cit.*

14 Council Decision 2004/17/EC of 22 December 2003 amending Part V, point 1.4, of the Common Consular Instructions and Part I, point 4.1.2 of the Common Manual as regards inclusion of the requirements to be in possession of travel medical insurance as one of the supporting documents for the grant of a uniform entry visa, OJ L 5/79, 9.1.2004.

15 Council Decision 2004/14/EC of 22 December 2003 amending the third subparagraph (Basic criteria for examining applications) of Part V of the Common Consular Instructions, OJ L 5/74, 9.1.2004.

16 Council Decision 2004/15/EC of 22 December 2003 amending point 1.2 of Part II of the Common Consular Instructions and drawing up a new Annex thereto, OJ L 5/76, 9.1.2004.

17 Council Decision 2002/44/EC of 20 December 2001 amending Part VII and Annex 12 to the Common Consular Instructions and Annex 14a to the Common Manual,

form,[18] and by developing the provisions regarding group visas issued by tour operators.[19] The necessary updates of the CCI Annexes, either at the request of the interested Member States[20] or those deemed necessary for other reasons were also examined by the Council.[21] Finally, certain parts of the CCI were downgraded or declassified.[22]

In addition, the Council was called to address two mainly political problems, which also had considerable practical ramifications. In both cases a solution was found via a broad interpretation and flexible use of certain provisions of the Schengen *acquis*. Thus, a Regulation was adopted establishing certain limited amendments to the classic visa issuing procedure regulating the entry of the members of the Olympic family for the 2004 Athens Olympic Games while maintaining the right balance between the requirements set by the International Olympic Committee and the provisions of the Schengen *acquis*.[23] Two

---

OJ L 20/5 23.1.2002 and Council Decision 2003/454/EC of 13 June 2003 amending Annex 12 of the Common Consular Instructions and Annex 14a of the Common Manual on visa fees, OJ L 152/82, 20.6.2003. It is worth noting that the French Delegation has recently submitted a proposal regarding the increase of visa fees in view of the establishment of the Visa Information System. See Note from the French Delegation – Proposal to increase the fees to be charged corresponding to the administrative costs of processing visa applications, Council doc. 13111/05 VISA 242 COMIX 648, 10.10.2005.

18 Council Decision 2002/354/EC of 25 April 2002 on the adaptation of Part III of, and the creation of an Annex 16 to, the Common Consular Instructions, OJ L 123/50, 9.5.2002.

19 Council Decision 2002/585/EC, *op.cit.*

20 i.e. Council Decision 2003/585/EC of 28 July 2003 amending Annex 2, Schedule A, of the Common Consular Instructions and Annex, Schedule A, of the Common Manual on the visa requirements for holders of Pakistani diplomatic passports, OJ L 198/13, 6.8.2003 and Council Decision 2000/586/EC of 12 July 2002 on the amendment of part VI of the common consular instructions, OJ L 187/48, 16.7.2002.

21 i.e. following the full accession of the Nordics to Schengen. Council Decision 2001/329/EC of 24 April 2001 updating part VI and Annexes 3, 6 and 13 of the Common Consular Instructions and Annexes 5(a), 6(a) and 8 of the Common Manual, OJ L 116/32, 26.4.2001.

22 Council Decision 2004/16/EC of 22 December 2003 on downgrading Annex 5 to the Common Consular Instructions and the corresponding Annex 14b to the Common Manual and on declassifying Annexes 9 and 10 to the Common Consular Instructions and the corresponding Annexes 6b and 6c to the Common Manual, OJ L 5/78, 9.1.2004.

23 According to the Olympic International Charter the Members of the Olympic family were supposed to be exempted from the visa obligation. Nonetheless, such an exemption as for those persons that were nationals of third states appearing in the "black" list of the visa Regulation would clearly violate the EU *acquis* on the matter. In an effort to keep the right balance between the wishes of the Olympic Commit-

other Regulations provided some flexible and acceptable solutions to the thorny Kaliningrad issue.[24]

Special attention was also devoted to the relevant security aspects and, in particular, to the security characteristics of visas. The Council first adopted a

---

tee and the need to respect the EU *acquis*, the Council adopted a rather innovative solution. The visa obligation remained. However, whereas the check on persons, necessary for security purposes, was in substance maintained, this would be carried out in a discrete way. More specifically, visa applications would be examined within the framework of the accreditation process and the visa serial number would be put behind the accreditation card, which would have the same security characteristics as Schengen visas. See Council Regulation (EC) No 1295/2003 of 15 July 2003 relating to measures envisaged to facilitate the procedures for applying for and issuing visas for members of the Olympic family taking part in the 2004 Olympic and Paralympic Games in Athens, OJ L 183/1, 22.7.2003. The same solution was subsequently applied with regard to the 2006 Turin Winter Olympics. See Regulation (EC) No 2046/2005 of the European Parliament and of the Council of 14 December 2005 relating to measures envisaged to facilitate the procedures for applying for and issuing visas for members of the Olympic family taking part in the 2006 Olympic and/or Paralympic Winter Games in Turin, OJ L 334/1, 20.12.2005. For the Commission proposal see Proposal for a Regulation of the European Parliament and of the Council relating to measures envisaged to facilitate the procedures for applying for and issuing visas for members of the Olympic family taking part in the 2006 Olympic and /or Paralympic Winter Games in Turin, COM (2005) 412 final, 7.9.2005.

24 The situation of the residents of the Kaliningrad area, which following EU enlargement would need to cross the territory of the EU in order to reach the rest of the territory of the Russian Federation, has proved to be rather problematic. The EU had initially refused the granting of a visa free regime to Russian citizens (Russia is on the black list of the visa Regulation). Certainly the full application of the relevant *acquis* with regard to visas would render very difficult the movement of the persons concerned. After long and arduous negotiations with Russia, the Council adopted two Regulations maintaining the visa obligation but providing for a facilitated procedure for the granting of the relevant visas. Council Regulation (EC) No 693/2003 of 14 April 2003, establishing a specific Facilitated Transit Document (FTD), a Facilitated Rail Transit Document (FRTD) and amending the Common Consular Instructions and the Common Manual, OJ L 99/8, 17.4.2003 and Council Regulation (EC) No 694/2003 of 14 April 2003, on uniform formats for facilitated Transit Documents (FTD) and Facilitated Rail Transit Documents (FRTD) provided for in Regulation (EC) No 693/2003, OJ L 99/15, 17.4.2003. For a detailed presentation of the Kaliningrad problem and the positions of the countries involved see Communication from the Commission to the Council "Kaliningrad: Transit", COM (2002) 510 final, 18.9.2002 and Communication from the Commission to the Council: the EU and Kaliningrad, COM (2001) 26 final, 17.1.2001. See also Potemkina O., "Some Ramification of Enlargement on the EU-Russia Relations and the Schengen Regime", *EJML,* Vol. 5, 2003, p. 229-247.

Regulation inserting a photograph in visas.[25] Then, in the aftermath of September 11 and under pressure both from the US and certain EU countries the Council also decided to insert biometric data in visas and residence permits, as well as in passports and travel documents issued by Member States.[26] The idea of establishing a new system for the exchange of visa data between Member States – the so-called Visa Information System (VIS)- was also intensively promoted. The Commission, following a feasibility study on the matter, has tabled initially a proposal for a Council Decision aiming at allowing the development of the VIS to take place by means of Community financing as of 2004, and subsequently, a fully fledged proposal for a Council Regulation concerning the establishment of VIS.[27] Indeed, the Council has already adopted the Decision for the establishment of VIS,[28] whereas negotiations on the relevant Council Regulation have not been concluded yet.

The EC has also dealt with certain external aspects of visa policy. Firstly, it has signed a Memorandum of Understanding with China on visa and related

25 Council Regulation 334/2002, *op.cit.* See also Council Decision 2002/586/EC, *op.cit.*

26 Following a request by the Council, the Commission presented the relevant proposal in September 2003. The Commission proposal covered both visas and residence permits of third country nationals. See Proposal for a Regulation amending Regulation (EC) 1683/95 laying down a uniform format for visas and proposal for a Council Regulation amending Regulation (EC) 1030/2002 laying down a uniform format for residence permits for third-country nationals, *op.cit.* However, technical problems as to the storage of biometric identifiers in visas have delayed the adoption of the relevant Regulation. See Integration of biometric identifiers into the uniform format for visa stickers and residence permits for third-country nationals, Council doc. 5748/05 VISA 24 COMIX 62, 1.2.2005. Inasmuch as passports and travel documents issued by Member States are concerned, the Council has already adopted the relevant Regulation. See Council Regulation (EC) No 2252/2004, *op.cit.*

27 Apart form the feasibility study the Commission has also prepared a report on possible synergies with SIS II. See Communication from the Commission to the Council and the European Parliament on the Development of the Schengen Information System II and possible synergies with a future Visa Information System, *op.cit.* See also Proposal for a Council Decision establishing a Visa Information System (VIS), *op.cit.* as well as Proposal for a Regulation of the European Parliament and of the Council concerning the Visa Information System (VIS), *op.cit.* See also Draft Council Conclusions on access to the VIS by Member States authorities responsible for internal security, Council doc. 6899/05 VISA 56 CODEC 121 COMIX 150, 1.3.2005 and Proposal for a Council Decision concerning access for consultation of the Visa Information System (VIS) by the authorities of Member States responsible for internal security and by Europol for the purposes of the prevention, detection and investigation of terrorist offences and of other serious criminal offences, COM (2005) 600 final, 24.11.2005.

28 Council Decision 2004/512/EC, *op.cit.*

issues concerning tourist groups from China, the so-called "ADS Agreement".[29] Secondly, in response to continuous requests by Russia and in order to accelerate negotiations on the relevant readmission agreement, the Council has approved a negotiating mandate for the conclusion of a visa facilitation agreement with Russia.[30] In fact negotiations on the visa facilitation and the readmission agreements were holding in parallel ("back to back negotiations") and were successfully concluded at the course of the EU-Russia Summit in October 2005.[31] An analogous mandate has been given to the Commission regarding Ukraine,[32] whereas the issue of visa facilitation is further examined by the Council.[33]

Moreover, the Commission, under pressure from several Member States, whose nationals are under visa obligation in third countries being on the EU "white list", decided to address the visa reciprocity issue and has presented a proposal for the amendment of the reciprocity mechanism.[34] Following the

29 Council Decision of 8 March 2004 concerning the conclusion of the Memorandum of Understanding between the European Community and the National Tourism Administration of the People's Republic of China on visa and related issues concerning tourist groups form the People's Republic of China (ADS), OJ L 83/12, 20.3.2004 and Memorandum of Understanding between the European Community and the National Tourism Administration of the People's Republic of China on visa and related issues concerning tourist groups form the People's Republic of China (ADS), OJ L 83/14, 20.3.2004.

30 See Draft negotiating directives for an agreement between the EC and the Russian Federation on the facilitation of the issuance of short-stay visas to Union and Russian citizens, Council doc. 11071/04 NIS 100 VISA 130, approved by Coreper, Part 2, 30.6.2004 and EU Council Press Release, Joint Statement on EU Enlargement and EU Russia Relations, Luxembourg, 27 April 2004, Council doc. 8664/04 (Press 122), 27.4.2004. However, it seems that Russia had already entered into negotiations with at least three Member States, namely Germany, France and Italy. See 'Russia presses for first moves towards visa free travel', <www.euobserver.com>, 18.5.2004.

31 See Summary of discussions of the Ministerial JHA Troika EU/Russia Permanent Partnership Council (PPC) in Luxembourg on 12/13 October 2005, *op.cit.*

32 See Council doc. 13725/05, *op.cit.*

33 See Common approach on visa facilitation, Council doc. 16030/05 VISA 328 RELEX 776, 21.12.2005.

34 According to Article 1 (4) of Regulation 539/2001 in case a third state reinstates the visa obligation for a Member State the Member State in question *may* notify the Council and Member States are obliged to subject the nationals of the third country concerned to the visa obligation within a provisional period of 30 days following the notification unless the Council acting by qualified majority had decided otherwise. In fact, there are numerous cases where third States whose citizens are exempted from visa obligation for entry into the Community request a visa for the citizens of certain Member States. The most representative case concerns the US request for visas for Greek citizens and for the citizens of all the new Member States. Given

adoption of the relevant Regulation Member States have transmitted to the Commission the list of third countries appearing in the EU "white list" in which their nationals are under visa obligation.[35] Subsequently, the Commission, in close cooperation with Member States, delivered verbal notes to the third countries concerned and held bilateral meetings with their authorities.[36]

Finally, it is worth noting that the Hague Programme and the subsequent joint Commission and Council relevant Action Plan are much more ambitious inasmuch as visa policy measures are concerned. More specifically, these include proposals for establishing common application centres already in 2005 and common visa offices in 2007 as well as suggestions for negotiations of EC visa waiver agreements.[37]

In contrast to the massive legislative developments that pertain to visa policy, external border management developments have initially been mainly of a more organisational and operational nature. The first Decisions regarding the Common Manual focused on the need to declassify certain of its parts.[38] Actu-

---

that the mechanism provided in Article 1 (4) was not flexible and never used for that reason, the Commission has presented a proposal amending this system. Proposal for a Council Regulation amending Regulation (EC) No 539/2001 as regards the reciprocity mechanism, COM (2004) 437 final/2, 19.7.2004.

35 Council Regulation (EC) No 851/2005 of 2 June 2005 amending Regulation (EC) No 539/2001 listing the third countries whose nationals must be in possession of visas when crossing the external borders and those whose nationals are exempt from that requirement as regards the reciprocity mechanism, OJ L 141/3, 4.6.2005. See also Statement on Council Regulation (EC) No 851/2005 of 2 June 2005 amending Regulation (EC) No 539/2001 as regards the visa reciprocity, OJ C 172/1, 12.7.2005. The notifications of the Member States are also published in the Official Journal. See i.e. editions C 163, C 251, C 277, and C 310 of the 2005 Official Journal.

36 For an overview as to the implementation of Regulation 851/2005 so far see Report from the Commission to the Council on visa waiver reciprocity with certain third countries in accordance with Article 2 of Council Regulation (EC) 851/2005 of 2 June 2005 amending Regulation (EC) No 539/2001 listing the third countries whose nationals must be in possession of visas when crossing the external borders and those whose nationals are exempt from that requirement as regards the reciprocity mechanism, COM (2006) 3 final, 10.1.2006.

37 See Section 1.7.3 of the Hague Programme, *op.cit.* and Section 2.9 of the Council and Commission Action Plan implementing the Hague Programme, *op.cit.*

38 Council Decision 2002/353/EC of 25 April 2002 on declassifying Part of the Common Manual adopted by the Executive Committee established by the Convention implementing the Schengen Agreement of 14 June 1985, OJ L 123/49, 9.5.2002 and Council Decision 2000/751/EC of 30 November 2000 on declassifying certain parts of the Common Manual adopted by the Executive Committee established by the Convention implementing the Schengen Agreement of 14 June 1985, OJ L 303/29, 2.12.2000.

ally the Common Manual was not published until late 2002.[39] Subsequently, the Council has focused on a process of bringing the Common Manual in to line with the EU *acquis* and repealing certain redundant or outdated provisions.[40] The wider need to recast the Common Manual proved to be a much more complex and time consuming issue than expected, mainly due to the Manual's hybrid character and its contested legal value. The recasting of the Common Manual was discussed several times in the Council, the first discussions dating back to early 1999 when the Finnish Presidency had circulated a questionnaire on the matter. In early 2003 the Commission tabled a Working Document proposing a three step approach: first, reviewing in detail the *acquis* on external borders, then identifying the gaps that exist and the problems arising from the current structure of the Common Manual and, finally, proceeding to the drafting of concrete proposals for recasting the *acquis* on external borders.[41] On the basis of this analysis the Commission prepared a questionnaire containing certain basic questions,[42] which was sent to the Member States at the end of July 2003. On the basis of the replies – the vast majority of which came out in favour of the Commission's proposals on separating clearly the legal instrument and the practical handbook and on the need to go beyond a mere clean-up – the Commission tabled a legislative proposal for a Regulation establishing a Community Code on the rules governing the movement of persons across borders, both internal and external on which the Council and the European Parliament have already reached political agreement.[43]

The urgency of certain matters has, however, led the Commission to table beforehand concrete legislative proposals regarding certain parts of the Common Manual. More specifically the Council has already adopted a Regulation regard-

39 OJ C 313/97, 16.12.2002. With the exception of those parts that were confidential.

40 Council Decision 2002/587/EC of 12 July 2002 on the revision of the Common Manual, OJ L 187/50, 16.7.2002 and Council Decision 2002/352/EC of 25 April 2002 on the revision of the Common Manual, OJ L 123/47, 9.5.2002.

41 Commission Staff Working Document on the Recasting of the Common Manual, *op.cit.*

42 i.e. whether there should be a clear distinction between the legislative instrument and the practical handbook for border guards, whether to restrict the operation to a simple clean-up of the current Manual or to expand certain parts and whether it might be worth extending the scope of the Manual to cover internal borders.

43 For the Commission proposal see Proposal for a Council Regulation establishing a Community Code on the rules governing the movement of persons across borders, *op.cit.* For the final text as this was approved by the Council and the Parliament see Council doc. 3643/05, *op.cit.* It is worth noting that the Commission intends to table a supplementary proposal for a practical handbook for border guards.

ing the systematic stamping of travel documents upon entry and exit[44] and two Decisions regarding respectively the establishment of a standard form for refusal of entry and indications on signs at external frontiers crossing points in order to take into account the EEA Agreement and the EU-Swiss Agreement on the free movement of persons.[45] The content of these measures has been included in the more wide-ranging proposal for a Regulation establishing a general Code, and once this proposal enters into force it will replace them as well as Articles 2-8 of the Schengen Convention and the entire Common Manual.[46]

Moreover, the Commission has also attempted to resolve certain issues that have proved rather problematic in the post enlargement era, meaning on the one hand the local border traffic issue, and on the other hand, the problems regarding circulation of third country nationals in the new Member States. More specifically, the Commission has presented a discussion document and legislative proposals regarding the issue of local border traffic, a matter that for the time being is regulated by diverging bilateral agreements at national level.[47] Furthermore, it

44 See Council Regulation (EC) No 2133/2004 of 13 December 2004 on the requirement for the competent authorities of the Member States to stamp systematically the travel documents of third country nationals when they cross the external borders of the Member States and amending the provisions of the Convention implementing the Schengen agreement and the common manual to this end, OJ L 369/5, 16.12.2004. For the Commission proposal see Proposal for a Council Regulation laying down the requirement for the competent authorities of the Member States to stamp systematically the travel documents of third country nationals when they cross the external borders of the Member States and amending the convention implementing the Schengen agreement and the common manual to this end, COM (2003) 664 final, 6.11.2003.

45 See respectively Council Decision 2004/574/EC of 29 April 2004 amending the Common Manual, OJ L 261/36, 6.8.2004 and Council Decision 2004/581/EC of 29 April 2004 determining the minimum indication to be used on signs at external border crossing points, OJ L 261/119, 6.8.2004.

46 See Article 39 of the new Community Code on the rules governing the movement of persons across borders, *op.cit.*

47 See Commission Working Document Developing the *acquis* on local border traffic, SEC (2002) 947 final. Subsequently the Commission in order to facilitate the entry and movement of third country nationals living in border areas both at the new external EU borders as well as at the temporary EU external borders submitted the following legislative proposals: Proposal for a Council Regulation on the establishment of a regime of local border traffic at the external land borders of the Member States and Proposal for a Council Regulation on the establishment of a regime of local border traffic at the temporary external land borders between Member States, COM (2003) 502 final, 14.8.2003. However, there have been certain problems during the negotiations leading the Irish Presidency to ask for a reaffirmation of the Council's mandate to the Commission to draw up proposals for local border traffic. See Presidency Note on the Proposal for a Council Regulation on the establishment of

has also presented a proposal regarding the unilateral and optional recognition by the new Member States of travel documents granted to third country nationals living in Member States applying fully the Schengen Convention.[48]

In parallel the more general issue of the management of external borders has been also extensively discussed at the EU level. The issue was first put on the EU agenda during the Laeken Summit, when Heads of State underlined the importance of the effective management of the EU's external borders.[49] The Commission also prepared a Communication on the matter and the issue was extensively discussed in certain informal *ad hoc fora* where certain interesting documents have been presented, such as the report prepared by Austria, Sweden and Finland within the framework of the OISIN programme or the Feasibility

---

a regime of local border traffic at the external borders of the Member States and the Proposal for a Council Regulation on the establishment of a regime of local border traffic at the temporary external land borders between Member States, Council doc. 8083/04 VISA 62 COMIX 240, 1.4.2004. Moreover, it needs to be recalled that following the lapse of the five year transitory period the entire Article 62 (2) (b) TEC concerning visa policy automatically passed to the co-decision procedure. Nonetheless, unanimity and consultation of the European Parliament remained the rule for Article 62 (2) (a) regarding the crossing of external borders. As the legal basis for the relevant legislative measure was Article 62 (2) there were certain implications and the submission of a new proposal proved necessary. See Proposal for a Regulation of the European Parliament and of the Council laying down rules on local border traffic at the external land borders of the Member States and amending the Schengen Convention and the Common Consular Instructions, COM (2005) 56 final, 23.2.2005. For the final amendments agreed by the Council see Proposal for a Regulation of the European Parliament and of the Council laying down rules on local border traffic at the external land borders of the Member States and amending the Schengen Convention – Approval of the final amendments of compromise, Council doc. 15760/05 FRONT 212 VISA 323 CODEC 1184 COMIX 852, 16.12.2005.

48 This has been rendered necessary in order to alleviate the burden on the consular offices of the new Member States to the old Member States. An analogous proposal has been tabled with regard to Switzerland. See Proposal for a Decision of the European Parliament and of the Council introducing a simplified regime for the control of persons at the external borders based on the unilateral recognition by Czech Republic, Estonia, Cyprus, Latvia, Lithuania, Hungary, Malta, Poland, Slovenia, Slovakia of certain documents as equivalent to their national visas for the purposes of transit through their territories & Proposal for a Decision of the European Parliament and the Council establishing a simplified regime for the control of persons at the external borders based on the unilateral recognition by the Member States of certain residence permits issued by Switzerland and Liechtenstein for the purpose of transit through their territory, COM (2005) 381 final, 22.8.2005.

49 European Council meeting in Laeken, 14 and 15 December 2001, Presidency Conclusions, pt. 42.

Study for a European Border Police prepared by Italy.[50] On the basis of these three documents the Spanish Presidency prepared an Action Plan, which was adopted by the Council in June 2002.[51] The basic aim of the Plan was to improve the coordination of operational activities of those in charge of the control and surveillance of the external borders, within the framework of an integrated strategy.

The issue was then examined in detail at the Seville Summit. The Heads of State proposed the establishment of an institutional framework to examine the management of the external borders and set specific goals for June 2003, when the Greek Presidency was expected to prepare a progress report for the Thessaloniki Summit.[52] Heads of State requested, among other things, the implementation of joint operations at the external borders and the immediate initiation of pilot projects open to all interested Member States before the end of 2002. They also asked for the preparation of a Common Risk Analysis Model in order to achieve a common and comprehensive risk evaluation as well as for the establishment of a Common Core Curriculum for border guard training before June 2003.

Within the framework of the implementation of the Seville Conclusions, the Council established a Practitioner's Unit which was composed of external border practitioners and was meeting within the framework of SCIFA, the so-called SCIFA+. And the Danish Presidency initiated the Roadmap process in order to keep the relevant process under constant review.[53] On the basis of the Plan for the management of external borders, which constituted a practical guide containing a list of measures to be implemented in the short as well as in the long-term, Member States have submitted a series of initiatives, which were subsequently approved by SCIFA+. Within this framework two *Ad Hoc* Centres have been set up – i.e. a centre for land borders in Berlin and a Centre of Excellence for developing new technologies to facilitate border controls at Dover; some first reports on a Common Risk Analysis Model and a Common Core Curriculum have been prepared by Finland and Austria/Sweden respec-

50 See Communication from the Commission to the Council and the European Parliament "Towards integrated management of the external borders of the Member States of the European Union", COM (2002) 233 final, 7.5.2002.

51 Plan for the management of the external borders of the Member States of the European Union, Council doc. 10019/02 FRONT 58 COMIX 398, 14.6.2002.

52 Seville European Council, 21 and 22 June 2003, Presidency Conclusions, pts 31, 32 and 39.

53 The first Roadmap was already presented in July 2002, at the very beginning of the Danish Presidency. See Council doc. 10525/2/02 REV 2 JAI 152, 31.7.2002. The Roadmap has been regularly updated both under the Danish and the Greek Presidencies.

tively; and several Member States have also organised a series of pilot projects on various issues as well as common operations at sea, land and air borders.[54]

The border management issue was further examined at the Thessaloniki Summit. Heads of State and Government, on the basis of the Presidency report and a second Commission Communication[55] called for the setting up of a special institutional framework.[56] Subsequently, in early November 2003 the Commission tabled a proposal for the establishment of an Agency for the management of external borders.[57] In parallel the Council, following a concrete request by the European Council,[58] decided, in addition to the Berlin Centre for land borders, on the establishment of *Ad Hoc* Centres for sea and air borders as well. The centre for air borders was located in Italy[59] and the two sea border centres were based in Greece and Spain respectively.[60] Additionally, in relation to sea borders

54 For an overview of all the programmes, ad hoc centres, pilot projects and joint operations initiated within the framework of the implementation of the Seville Conclusions see the relevant Report prepared by the Greek Presidency in view of the Thessaloniki European Council, *op.cit.*.

55 Communication from the Commission to the European Parliament and the Council in view of the European Council of Thessaloniki on the development of a common policy on illegal immigration, smuggling and trafficking of human beings, external borders and the return of illegal residents, COM (2003) 323 final, 3.6.2003.

56 Thessaloniki European Council, 19 and 20 June 2003, Presidency Conclusions, pts 12 to 14. See also Council Conclusions on more effective management of external borders of EU States, Council doc. 10059/1/03 REV 1 FRONT 71 COMIX 355, 4.6.2003 as well as the Presidency Conclusions of the European Council of Brussels, 16 and 17 October 2003, pt 28.

57 Proposal for a Council Regulation establishing a European Agency for the Management of Operational Cooperation at the External Borders, *op.cit.*

58 European Council of Brussels, 16 and 17 October 2003, Presidency Conclusions, pt 27.

59 See Note form the Italian Delegation on International Airports Plan – Air Borders Centre project (Italy), Council doc. 13524/1/03 REV 1 FRONT 141 COMIX 612, 1.12.2003. It needs to be recalled that within the framework of the implementation of the Plan for the Management of the external borders Italy had been the leading country for a project on air borders.

60 It needs to be recalled that within the framework of the implementation of the Plan for the Management of the external borders Greece and Spain had been the leader countries for operations regarding maritime borders. Inasmuch as the sea borders centres are concerned Spain and Greece had initially submitted two separate proposals and were competing but in the end submitted a joint document proposing the establishment of two centres. See Note of the Spanish Delegation on a Proposal to set up a Cooperation Centre of EU external maritime borders, Council doc. 6445/03 FRONT 14 COMIX 105, 17.2.2003; Note of the Greek Delegation on a Proposal to establish a Joint Sea Borders Coordination Centre (JSBCC), Council doc. 7491/03 FRONT 27 COMIX 178, 14.3.2003 and Note of the Spanish and Greek delegations

and following earlier discussions at European Council level,[61] Council Conclusions[62] and a recent Commission study on maritime borders, the Council, following an express request of the European Council of October 2003,[63] adopted an Action Plan in November 2003.[64] In late March 2004 the Council also reached political Agreement on the Commission's proposal for the establishment of an Agency for the management of external borders.[65] The Agency finally took up its responsibilities as from 1 May 2005[66] and is based in Warsaw (Poland).[67] The first evaluation report on the Agency is set for 2007, whereas it is worth noting that the Council has not abandoned the idea of a system of European border guards.[68] Moreover, following an invitation by the European Council to enhance

---

on Sea Borders Centres, Council doc. 13779/1/03 REV 1 FRONT 145 COMIX 628, 29.10.2003.

61 The issue has been discussed at the Nice European Council following a letter from the Spanish and Italian Prime Ministers. More specifically, Heads of State recalled the need to promote operational cooperation between the competent authorities of the Member States in controlling the Union's sea borders, with a view in particular to curbing illegal migration. Nice European Council 7, 8 and 9 December 2000, Presidency Conclusions, pt. 51.

62 Council Conclusions on measures to be applied to prevent and combat illegal immigration and smuggling and trafficking in human beings by sea and in particular on measures against third countries which refuse to cooperate with the European Union in preventing and combating these phenomena, Council document 10017/02 JAI 142 RELEX 122 MIGR 57, 14.6.2002.

63 European Council of Brussels, 16 and 17 October 2003, Presidency Conclusions, pts 27 and 29.

64 Programme of measures to combat illegal immigration across the maritime borders of the Member States of the European Union, Council doc. 15445/03 FRONT 172 COMIX 731, 28.11.2003.

65 Council Regulation (EC) No 2007/2004 of 26 October 2004 establishing a European Agency for the Management of Operational Cooperation at the External Borders of the Member States of the European Union, OJ L 349/1, 25.11.2004. See also Press Release of the Justice and Home Affairs Council meeting of 30 March 2004.

66 According to a European Council request the Agency should in principle have become operational by 1 January 2005. See European Council of Brussels, 12 December 2003, Presidency Conclusions, pt 17.

67 Council Decision 2005/358/EC of 26 April 2005 designating the seat of the European Agency for the Management of Operational Cooperation at the External Borders of the Member States of the European Union, OJ L 114/13, 4.5.2005. The Management Board has also already named its director, Colonel Ilkka Laitinen, former director of the Finnish Border Police. See Balzacq and Carrera S, *op.cit*.

68 See section 2.8 of the joint Council and Commission Action Plan implementing the Hague Programme, *op.cit*. There, it is announced that there will be a proposal on the setting up of teams of national experts to provide technical and operational assistance to Member States in the control and surveillance of external borders as well

cooperation regarding the management of sea borders[69] as well as the events in Ceuta and Melilla and the situation in Malta, Lampedusa as well as in some Greek islands the Commission has recently proposed the establishment of a Mediterranean Coastal Patrol Network.[70]

Another issue on which both the Commission and the Council have been working intensively concerns the preparation of the SIS II system, a technically upgraded version of SIS.[71] As already mentioned in the course of the integration of the Schengen *acquis*, the Council had not managed to reach an agreement on the legal bases with regard to SIS and so the SIS *acquis* was integrated provisionally *en bloc* in the third pillar. The upgrading of the system was an issue of vital importance following enlargement – since the existing system could only operate with a maximum of eighteen Member States. As a result, the Council has already adopted the necessary legislative measures regarding the financial aspects of the development of SIS II.[72] And the Commission has prepared a feasibility study on the matter, referring occasionally to the Council in order to get the political agreement on the various choices to be made, and has also launched the relevant call for tenders.[73] In parallel, the Council has introduced some new

as a feasibility of a system of European border guards. See also Annex Section III, p. 21-22 of the Communication from the Commission to the European Parliament, the Council, the European Economic and Social Committee and the Committee of the Regions Unlocking Europe's full potential Commission Legislative and Work Programme 2006, COM (2005) 531 final, 25.10.2005.

69 See sections 1.6.1 and 1.7.1 of the Hague Programme, *op.cit.*

70 See Communication from the Commission to the Council and the European Parliament Priority actions for responding to the challenges of migration: First follow-up to Hampton Court, COM (2005) 621 final, 30.11.2005. This proposal has been subsequently supported by the Council and the European Council as well. See Council Conclusions – Global approach to migration: Priority actions focusing on Africa and the Mediterranean, Council doc. 15744/05 ASIM 66 RELEX 761, 13.12.2005 and Annex 1 of the Presidency Conclusions of the European Council of Brussels, 15 and 16 December 2005.

71 For a brief overview of the functioning of SIS and the discussions regarding the preparation of SIS II see Vandamme L., "Le nouveau cadre du Système d'Information Schengen", in Marinho C. (ed), *Asylum, Immigration and Schengen Post-Amsterdam – A First Assessment,* EIPA, Maastricht, 2001, p. 119-130.

72 Council Regulation 2424/2001, *op.cit.* and Council Decision 2001/886/JHA, *op.cit.*

73 See SIS II functions, Council doc. 10125/04 SIRIS 69 COMIX 378, 3.6.2004. The issue of synergies between the different databases has been also extensively discussed. See the Commission Communication on the Development of the Schengen Information System II and possible synergies with a future Visa Information System, *op.cit.*, as well as the Communication from the Commission to the Council and the European Parliament on improved effectiveness, enhanced interoperability

functions in SIS in particular in the fight against terrorism.[74] Moreover, it has also adopted the relevant framework legislative measures as for the amendments of SIRENE.[75] Finally, the Commission has already presented the legislative proposals for the development of SIS II.[76]

Lastly, despite the fact that the freedom of movement of third country nationals within at least the Schengen area is regulated *grosso modo* by Schengen, it is rather unfortunate that the Council has not managed to adopt a comprehensive legislative framework on the matter. As already mentioned, Portugal and France in their initiatives on freedom to travel regarding respectively nationals of countries exempted from the visa obligation and long-stay visas have attempted to provide *ad hoc* solutions and the relevant comprehensive proposal of the Commission has been frozen.[77] However, it is worth recalling that the Council and the Commission have recently announced their intention to proceed to the conclusion of agreements with third countries on the conditions to move freely within the Union for a period between three and six months.[78]

---

and synergies among European databases in the area of Justice and Home Affairs, COM (2005) 597 final, 24.11.2005.

74 Council Regulation (EC) No 871/2004 of 29 April 2004 concerning the introduction of some new functions for the Schengen Information System, including in the fight against terrorism, OJ L 162/29, 30.4.2004 and Council Decision 2005/211/JHA of 24 February concerning the introduction of some new functions for Schengen Information System, including in the fight against terrorism, OJ L 68/44, 15.3.2005. These measures have been adopted following a double Spanish initiative. See Initiatives of the Kingdom of Spain with a view to adopting a Council Regulation and a Council Decision concerning the introduction of some new functions for the Schengen information system, in particular in the fight against terrorism, *op.cit.*

75 Council Regulation (EC) No 378/2004 of 19 February 2004 on procedures amending the Sirene Manual, OJ L 64/5, 2.3.2004 and Council Decision 2004/201/JHA of 19 February 2004 on procedures amending the Sirene Manual, OJ L 64/45, 2.3.2004. For the basic text of the Sirene Manual see Sirene Manual, OJ C 38/1, 17.2.2003.

76 See Proposal for a Regulation of the European Parliament and of the Council on the establishment, operation and use of the second generation Schengen information system (SIS II) and Proposal for a Council Decision on the establishment, operation and use of the second generation Schengen information system (SIS II), *op.cit.*

77 See discussion *supra* at 2.2.3. The Commission proposal took on board both these initiatives. See the explanatory memorandum and Article 20 of the relevant Commission Proposal for a Council Directive relating to the conditions in which third-country nationals shall have the freedom to travel in the territory of the Member States for periods not exceeding three months, introducing a specific travel authorization and determining the conditions of entry and movement for periods not exceeding six months, *op.cit.*

78 See point 2.9 (h) of the joint Commission and Council Action Plan for the implementation of the Hague Programme, *op.cit.*

4.1.2 Return Policy

One of the areas where most of the attention was focused in the post-Amsterdam era was the fight against illegal migration and the formation of a European return policy. The acts adopted took two main forms. On the one hand, there were concrete legislative measures, and on the other, documents of more general interest or of a programmatic value such as Action Plans or Communications.

The vast majority of the legislative measures adopted were either replacing or developing parts of the relevant Schengen *acquis*. Firstly, the Council through the adoption of a Directive and a Framework Decision on the unauthorised entry and residence of third country nationals,[79] and a Directive supplementing the relevant Schengen rules with regard to carriers' liability,[80] has developed the relevant provisions of the Schengen *acquis*.[81] Moving beyond the Schengen provisions, it has also adopted a Directive obliging carriers to communicate, in advance, passenger data to the competent authorities,[82] and has signed an agreement with the US regarding the transfer of passenger data to US authorities.[83] Furthermore, in an attempt to facilitate expulsion of third country nationals it adopted a Directive, albeit of rather limited scope, for the mutual recognition of expulsion decisions.[84] On the basis of Article 7 of this Directive the Council adopted a Decision which both set the criteria and practical arrangements for compensation between Member States and also constituted the basis for establishing the criteria and practical arrangements for the implementation of Article 24 of the Schengen Convention.[85] It is worth highlighting that the Commission considering the scope of the mutual recognition Directive to be rather limited and not establishing a binding framework has presented a global proposal for a

---

79 Council Directive 2002/90/EC, *op.cit.*, and Council Framework Decision 2002/946/EC, *op.cit.*

80 Council Directive 2001/51/EC, *op.cit.*.

81 Articles 27 and 26 CISA respectively.

82 Council Directive 2004/83/EC, *op.cit.*

83 Council Decision 2004/496/EC of 17 May 2004 on the conclusion of an Agreement between the European Community and the United States of America on the processing and transfer of PNR data by Air Carriers to the United States Department of Homeland Security, Bureau of Customs and Border Protection, OJ L 183/83, 20.5.2004 and Commission Decision 2004/535/EC of 14 May 2004 on the adequate protection of personal data contained in the Passenger Name Record of air passengers transferred to the United States' Bureau of Customs and Border Protection, OJ L 235/11, 6.7.2004.

84 Council Directive 2001/40/EC, *op.cit.*

85 Council Decision 2004/191/EC, *op.cit.*

Directive on minimum standards for return procedures and mutual recognition of return decisions.[86]

On the basis of a German initiative, the Council also adopted a Directive on assistance in cases of transit for the purposes of removal by air.[87] And following an initiative of the Italian Presidency the Council has adopted a Decision on the organisation of joint flights for removals.[88] Both issues had been examined in the past either within the EU or within the Schengen framework or in both. In addition, the Commission has also prepared, in close cooperation with the Member States, draft guidelines on security provisions for removals by air which have been included as an annex to the final text of the Italian initiative on joint flights.[89] The Council has also examined in depth the organisation of pilot projects, the exchange of experience among Member States and the involvement of the Agency for the External Borders.[90] In an attempt to cover the cases of transit by land and sea borders, the Italian Presidency also presented an initiative for another Directive complementing the German initiative on air transit which was later transformed into Council Conclusions.[91] Furthermore, the Council has

86 Proposal for a European Parliament and Council Directive on common standards on procedures in Member States for returning illegally staying third country nationals, COM (2005) 391 final, 1.9.2005.

87 Council Directive 2003/110/EC, *op.cit*. See also the relevant Initiative of the Federal Republic of Germany, *op.cit*. Germany had also previously proposed this initiative in the form of a Joint Action. However, certain Member States were not particularly interested since they had direct flights (i.e. the UK, France and the Netherlands usually have direct flights). Thus, regulating the question of transit was considered superfluous.

88 Council Decision 2004/573/EC, *op.cit*. See also Initiative of the Italian Republic with a view to adopting a Council decision on the organisation of joint flights for removals of third country nationals illegally present in the territory of two or more Member States, OJ C 223/3, 19.9.2003.

89 See Annex of Council Decision 2004/573/EC, *op.cit.*

90 All these issues have been discussed by the Informal Justice and Home Affairs Council in Dublin on 22-23 January 2004. See Presidency Note – Implementing Decision on the shared organisation of joint flights for removals, from the territory of two or more Member States, of third country nationals who are subject of individual removal orders, Council doc. 6144/04 MIGR 5 COMIX 90, 10.2.2004. For the final text see Draft Council Conclusions on ways of giving practical effect to the draft Council Decision on shared organisation on joint flights for removals, from the territory of two or more Member States, of third country nationals who are subject of individual removal orders, Council doc. 8540/04 MIGR 30 COMIX 275, approved by Coreper, Part 2, 30.6.2004.

91 See Draft Council Conclusions on assistance in cases of short-term transit by land or sea through the territory of another Member State in the course of effecting a removal order adopted by a Member State against a third-country national in

paid special attention to the issue of the EU travel document.[92] A letter was sent to third countries,[93] subsequent Presidencies have prepared questionnaires on the matter,[94] and, on the basis of a Greek initiative, the Council adopted a handbook of best practices for return.[95] The Council has also asked the Commission to re-examine its legal basis and format and to present proposals for legislative measures on the EU travel document.[96]

Finally, following a series of tragic events special attention has been devoted to trafficking in human beings.[97] A Framework Decision on combating trafficking was adopted in 2002.[98] Subsequently the Council has adopted another Commission proposal with regard to the granting of short-term residence permits to victims of trafficking.[99] The Council has also endorsed the recommenda-

---

the framework of the operational cooperation among Member States, Council doc. 15998/1/03 REV 1 MIGR 111 COMIX 757, 12.12.2003. For the initial Italian initiative for a draft Directive see Council doc. 10909/03, MIGR 61 COMIX 412, 3.7.2003.

92 The relevant document had been established by a Council Recommendation in 1994, *op.cit.*

93 Letter to third countries concerning the use of standard travel documents for the expulsion of third country nationals, Council doc. 7665/99 MIGR 27, 26.4.1999.

94 See Council doc. 6071/02 MIGR 8, 7.2.2002 [questionnaire prepared by the Belgian Presidency]; Council doc. 6445/04 MIGR 9 COMIX 110, 18.2.2004 [questionnaire prepared by the Irish Presidency] and Council doc. 11223/04 MIGR 61 COMIX 463, 7.7.2004 [questionnaire prepared by the Dutch Presidency].

95 Draft Manual of Best Practices on the acquisition of travel documents and the removal of third-country nationals from Member States' territory, Council doc. 8499/3/03 REV 3 MIGR 27 COMIX 246, 26.5.2003. See also the Recommendations drafted within the framework of Schengen. Council of the European Union, EU Schengen Catalogue – External border control, Removal and Readmission: Recommendations and Best Practices, February 2002.

96 Draft Council Conclusions on the re-examination of the legal basis, format and use of the EU Travel Document, Council doc. 9581/04 MIGR 40, 17.5.2004.

97 For a detailed presentation of the European actions with regard to trafficking and the more general global legal regime and practical aspects of this phenomenon see Twomey P., "Europe's Other Market – Trafficking in People", *EJML*, Vol. 2, 2000, p.1-36.

98 Council Framework Decision 2002/629, *op.cit.* For the Commission proposal see COM (2000) 854 final, *op.cit.*

99 Council Directive 2004/81/EC of 29 April 2004 on the residence permit issued to third country nationals who are victims of trafficking in human beings or who have been the subject of an action to facilitate illegal immigration, who cooperate with the competent authorities, OJ L 261/19, 6.8.2004. Despite the fact that this proposal regulates the issuing of a residence permit to victims of trafficking and has been examined by the "Migration-Admission" working party, it consists in a legislative

tions included in the so-called Brussels Declaration, which is the outcome of the European Conference on Preventing and Combating Trafficking in Human Beings in September 2002, and the Commission has set up a consultative group on the matter.[100] More recently, the Council has authorised the Commission to negotiate a draft European Convention on the fight against trafficking in human beings,[101] whereas it has also adopted an Action Plan on Trafficking.[102]

Without underestimating the value of the legislative acts that have been adopted, the most interesting part of return policy in the post-Amsterdam era definitely lies in the series of documents of a more general character issued either by the Commission or by the Council. The first Commission Communication was presented in November 2001.[103] The Communication was divided into two parts, a general part setting guidelines and targets, and, a second part, which was a sort of Action Plan proposing concrete measures. The Commission identified six areas for possible action: visa policy, infrastructure for information exchange, cooperation and coordination, border management, police cooperation, aliens and criminal law and return and readmission policy. Shortly after, in February 2002, and on the basis of the Commission Communication, the Spanish Presidency prepared a Council Action Plan, which was largely inspired by the second part of the Communication.[104] Subsequently, and in an effort to initiate discussion on the matter, the Commission launched a Green Paper on

---

measure aiming primarily at the fight against illegal migration. See also Proposal for a Council Directive on the short-term residence permit issued to victims of action to facilitate illegal immigration or trafficking in human beings who cooperate with the competent authorities, COM (2002) 71 final, 11.2.2002.

100 Council Conclusions of 8 May 2003 – Brussels Declaration on Preventing and Combating Trafficking in Human Beings, OJ C 137/1, 12.6.2003. See also the Commission Decision 2003/209/EC of 25 March 2003 setting up a consultative group, to be known as the 'Experts Group on Trafficking in Human Beings', OJ L 79/25, 26.3.2003.

101 See Proposal for a Council Decision authorising the Commission to negotiate a draft European Convention on the fight against trafficking in human beings, SEC (2004) 519 final, 30.4.2004. See also Proposal for a Common Position of the Council, on the basis of Article 34 of the Treaty on European Union, on negotiations relating to the draft European Convention on Action against Trafficking in Human Beings being undertaken in the Council of Europe, Council doc. 12314/04 CRIMORG 78 JUSTCIV 122 MIGR 71, 13.10.2004. The final text is not published since it is confidential.

102 EU plan on best practices, standards and procedures for combating and preventing trafficking in human beings, OJ C 311/1, 9.12.2005.

103 Communication from the Commission to the Council and the European Parliament on a Common Policy on Illegal Immigration, COM (2001) 672 final, 15.11.2001.

104 Proposal for a Comprehensive Plan to combat illegal migration and trafficking of human beings in the European Union, OJ C 142/23, 14.6.2002.

return policy.[105] A questionnaire was distributed to Member States and a Public Hearing was organised in late July 2002.[106]

On the basis of the discussions held within the Council, and within the framework of the Public Hearing, the Commission prepared a new Communication on return policy.[107] Following this second Communication and at the request of the Seville Summit asking for the adoption of a European return program the Danish Presidency prepared a draft of such a return programme, which was adopted in December 2002.[108] This general return program included a list of measures to be adopted in the short, medium and long-term, which was annexed to the text. In fact most of the actions taken and the measures adopted subsequently follow this timetable. On this basis the Council has adopted a special return program for Afghanistan which was intended to serve as a test case,[109] Subsequently, the Council has also adopted conclusions on best practices of return as well as on voluntary return.[110]

However, one needs to underscore the fact that illegal migration and return are seen as part of the more general EU policy on the management of external borders, including visa policy.[111] In fact, the various Action Plans regarding borders and return issues are partly overlapping.[112] Important measures regarding the fight against illegal migration are also included in the Action Plan for the management of the external borders and a series of the projects initiated within

105 Green paper on a Community return policy on illegal residents, COM (2002) 175 final, 10.4.2002.

106 Hearing on a Community Return Policy on Illegal Residents, Brussels, 16 July 2002.

107 Communication from the Commission to the Council and the European Parliament on a Community Return Policy on illegal residents, COM (2002) 564 final, 14.10.2002.

108 Proposal for a Return Action Programme, Council doc. 14673/02 MIGR 125 FRONT 135 VISA 172, 25.11.2002.

109 Afghanistan return plan, Council doc. 14654/02 MIGR 124 RELEX 248, 25.11.2002. See also Commission Staff Working Paper Review of the Afghanistan Return Plan, SEC (2005) 340, 4.3.2005.

110 See Adoption of draft Council conclusions on best practice on return with regard to specific countries of third-country nationals illegally staying on the territory of Member States, Council doc. 15122/04 MIGR 107 COMIX 713, 23.11.2004 and Draft Council Conclusions on voluntary return, Council doc. 12806/05 MIGR 46 COMIX 626, 3.10.2005.

111 The link between visa facilitation and readmission policy proves largely this point.

112 See Plan for the management of the external borders of the Member States of the European Union, *op.cit.* and Proposal for a Return Action Programme, *op.cit.*

this framework concerned illegal migration issues.[113] As mentioned previously, one of the issues extensively discussed at the EU level concerned the fight against illegal migration by sea, an issue closely linked with the effective management of sea borders.[114]

Therefore, illegal migration and return of illegal residents were also examined as part of the more general migration and border management package at the European Council level during the Thessaloniki Summit on the basis of the Commission Communication.[115] Heads of State have had the possibility to overview progress in this area and give further guidelines to the Council. One of the most important decisions taken at Thessaloniki and further elaborated at the Heads of State level during the Italian Presidency was the establishment of a special financial instrument aimed at supporting a common approach in the area of return. The Commission was invited to present the relevant proposal at the beginning of 2004.[116] The Council has, in fact, adopted Conclusions on elements for establishing preparatory actions for a financial instrument for return management and has called upon the budgetary authority to provide appropriate funding.[117]

Finally, one of the issues extensively debated within the Council and to which the Community has focused a lot of its efforts is readmission policy and more

---

113 See Plan for the management of the external borders of the Member States of the European Union, *op.cit*. For instance, within the framework of the implementation of the Plan, France tabled an initiative for a pilot project on the standardisation of security measures concerning the repatriation of aliens by ship, airplane and other means.

114 See Council Conclusions on measures to be applied to prevent and combat illegal immigration and smuggling and trafficking in human beings by sea, *op.cit*. and Draft Council conclusions evaluating the progress made with regard to the implementation of the programme of measures to combat illegal immigration across the maritime borders of the Member States of the European Union, Council doc. 15087/04 FRONT 201 COMIX 709, 22.11.2004. See also the discussion on the Plan for the maritime borders, *supra* at 4.1.1.

115 Communication of the Commission in view of the European Council of Thessaloniki, *op.cit*.

116 See Thessaloniki European Council, Presidency Conclusions, pt. 14; Brussels European Council, 16 and 17 October 2003, Presidency Conclusions, pt. 31; and Brussels European Council, 12 December 2003, Presidency Conclusions, pt. 21.

117 Council Conclusions on elements for establishing preparatory actions for a financial instrument for return management in the area of migration, Council doc. 10375/04 MIGR 51, 9.6.2004. Indeed the Call for proposals has already been published. See Preparatory Actions for return management in the area of migration – Call for proposals 2005, OJ C 224/11, 13.9.2005.

specifically readmission agreements.[118] Despite the fact that the issue of readmission between Member States has also been discussed at some point within the framework of the Council, albeit without reaching any concrete conclusions,[119] the Union's efforts have clearly focused on concluding readmission agreements with third countries. The Commission was given the mandate to negotiate a series of readmission agreements with third countries.[120] So far negotiations have been concluded with Hong Kong, Macao, Sri Lanka and Albania.[121] In

118 For an excellent overview of Community readmission policy see Schieffer M., "Community Readmission Agreements with Third-Countries – Objectives, Substance and Current State of Negotiations", *op.cit.* As far as the model of readmission agreement that it is followed see Reermann O., "Cooperation with Countries of Origin and Transit : Readmission Agreements", in Faria C. (ed.), *Managing Migration Flows and Preventing Illegal Immigration – Schengen-Justice and Home Affairs Colloquium,* EIPA, Maastricht, 2002, p. 13-24.

119 Finland had tabled a proposal which was discussed quite a few times but there has not been any decision most likely due to the sensitive character of the issue.

120 The Council so far authorised the Commission to negotiate readmission agreements with 11 third countries/entities: Morocco, Sri Lanka, Russia, Pakistan (September 2000), Hong Kong, Macao (May 2001), Ukraine (June 2002) and Albania, Algeria, China, Turkey (November 2002). Negotiations have so far been concluded with Hong Kong (agreement signed in November 2002), Macao (October 2002), Sri Lanka (May 2002), and Albania (November 2003).

121 Council Decision 2004/80/EC concerning the inclusion of the Agreement between the European Community and the Government of the Hong Kong, *op.cit.*; Council Decision 2004/424/EC concerning the conclusion of the Agreement between the European Community and the Macao Special Administrative Region of the People's Republic of China on the readmission of persons residing without authorization, *op.cit.*; Council Decision 2005/372/EC concerning the conclusion of the Agreement between the European Community and the Democratic Socialist Republic of Sri Lanka on the readmission of persons residing without authorisation, *op.cit.*; Council Decision 2005/371/EC on the signing of the Agreement between the European Community and the Republic of Albania on the readmission of persons residing without authorisation, *op.cit.* and Council Decision 2005/809/EC concerning the conclusion of the Agreement between the European Community and the Republic of Albania on the readmission of persons residing without authorization, *op.cit.* See also Information on the entry into force of the Agreement between the European Community and the Government of the Hong Kong Special Administrative Region of the People's Republic of China on the readmission of persons residing without authorization, OJ L 64/38, 2.3.2004; Information concerning the entry into force of the Agreement between the European Community and the Macao Special Administrative Region of the People's Republic of China on the readmission of persons residing without authorization, OJ L 285/17, 6.8.2004 and Information relating to the entry into force of the Agreement between the European Community and the Democratic Socialist Republic of Sri Lanka on the readmission of persons residing without authorisation, OJ L 138/17, 1.6.2005.

2004, following an invitation by the European Council the Commission has produced a report identifying in particular the priorities of a common readmission policy and the measures taken to ensure the successful development of such a policy.[122] On the basis of this Communication the Council has adopted Conclusions defining the line to take in this area.[123] As a final point, it is worth noting that readmission policy remains high on the agenda of the Hague Programme as well. In this framework, besides the usual invitation for conclusion of the Community readmission agreements, Heads of State invited the Commission to appoint a Special Representative for a common readmission policy.[124]

4.2 Fair Treatment of Third Country Nationals

4.2.1 Admission Policy

In contrast to the spectacular developments as far as measures on the management of migration flows are concerned, progress with regard to legal migration is relatively modest. In fact, negotiations proved extremely difficult and slow and the content of the final outcome is far from innovative.

Discussions were initially centred on four Commission proposals. All originate from the 1997 global Convention on rules for admission, which was essentially divided into four pieces and re-proposed as four proposals for Directives.[125] Most of the relevant proposals are based on exhaustive comparative studies prepared either by the Commission itself or by research institutions on behalf of the Commission.[126] The first proposal concerned the right to family reunification

122 Communication from the Commission to the Council and to the European Parliament – Report on the priorities for the successful development of a common readmission policy, SEC (2004) 946 final, 19.7.2004. See also Brussels European Council, 16 and 17 October 2003, Presidency Conclusions, pt. 31.

123 Draft Conclusions on the priorities for the successful development of a common readmission policy, Council doc. 13758/04 JAI 389 MIGR 92 RELEX 459, 27.10.2004.

124 See Section 1.6.4 of the Hague Programme, *op.cit.* as well as Section 2.6 of the Hague Action Plan, *op.cit.*

125 The Commission had already indicated that it would redraft its proposed Convention on Admission as soon as the new Treaty communitarising the relevant issues entered into force. See the relevant Convention proposal, *op.cit.*

126 See Groenendijk K., Guild E. and Barzilay R., *The Legal Status of Third Country Nationals who are Long-Term Residents in a Member States of the European Union*, Center for Migration and Law, University of Nijmegen, Netherlands, 2000 [For a summary of the relevant research and some preliminary comments in view of the negotiation of the relevant Directive within the framework of the Council see Groenendijk K. and Guild E., " Converging Criteria: Creating an Area of Security of Residence for Europe's Third Country Nationals, *EJML*, Vol. 3, Issue 1, 2001, p. 37-59]; Ecotec-Research and Consulting, *Admission of Third Country Nationals for Paid Employment or Self-Employed Activity, Study carried out on behalf of the Euro-*

and was presented in late 1999.[127] The second was presented almost a year and a half later and concerned the status and rights of long-term residents.[128] Some months later the Commission presented another proposal regarding admission for paid employment and self-employed activities.[129] The last proposal, completing this first set of legislative proposals, was presented in late 2002 and concerns admission for purposes of studies, vocational training or voluntary service.[130] In March 2004, the Commission has also presented a new Communication and proposals for related legislative instruments for the admission and mobility of researchers, which are seen as complementary to the students' Directive.[131]

The aforementioned proposals close the first circle of Commission proposals for admission of third country nationals. The Commission had announced its intention to present a proposal governing the admission of third country nationals for other purposes not provided for in the other proposals for Directives. It was finally decided however that such a proposal would not be presented at this stage due to the fact that the number of persons falling under this category was relatively low and could be dealt with adequately by the Member States' domestic law at the current stage of approximation of migration legislation.[132]

---

pean Commission, DG JHA, Ecotec, Brussels, 2000; ICMPD & European Commission, DG JHA, *Admission of third country nationals to an EU Member State for the purposes of study or vocational training, and admission of persons not gainfully employed,* DG JHA-ICMPD, August 2000.

127 Proposal for a Council Directive on the right to family reunification, *op.cit.*

128 Proposal for a Council Directive concerning the status of third-country nationals who are long-term residents, *op.cit.*

129 Proposal for a Council Directive on the conditions of entry and residence of third-country nationals for the purpose of paid employment and self-employment economic activities, COM (2001) 386 final, 11.7.2001.

130 Proposal for a Council Directive on the conditions of entry and residence of third-country nationals for purposes of studies, vocational training or voluntary service, COM (2002) 548 final, 7.10.2002.

131 Communication from the Commission to the Council and the European Parliament on the presentation of a proposal for a Directive and two proposals for Recommendations on the admission of third-country nationals to carry out scientific research in the European Community; Proposal for a Council Directive on a specific procedure for admitting third-country nationals to carry out scientific research in the European Community; Proposal for a Council Recommendation to facilitate the admission of third-country nationals to carry out scientific research in the European Community and Proposal for a Council Recommendation to facilitate the issue by the Member States of uniform short-stay visas for researchers from third countries travelling within the European Community for the purpose of carrying out scientific research, COM (2004) 178 final, 16.3.2004.

132 See the explanatory memorandum of the Proposal for a Council Directive on the conditions of entry and residence of third-country nationals for purposes of studies, *op.cit.*

Negotiations on the first two proposals were eventually concluded after three and a half years of difficult negotiations and substantive pressure by the European Council.[133] The Council managed to reach political agreement on the Directive on family reunification in late February 2003[134] and on the Directive on the status of long-term residents in early June 2003.[135] It needs, however, to be stressed that the content of both these proposals has been substantially weakened to reach the lowest common denominator. Subsequently in 2004 and 2005 respectively the Council also reached political agreement on the students Directive[136] and on the legislative measures regarding the admission of researchers.[137]

For systematic reasons and given the tendency of the Council to use as a precedent provisions on which it has reached agreement, the relevant legislative measures will each be presented in turn and following the sequence of discussions in the Council.

4.2.1.1 The Family Reunification Directive

The first Commission proposal on family reunification was submitted in late 1999.[138] The Directive was negotiated for more than three years and the Com-

---

133 The European Council of Seville had set the end of June 2003 as the deadline for the adoption of the family reunification and the long-term residents Directives. See European Council of Seville Conclusions, pt. 37.

134 Council Directive 2003/86/EC, *op.cit*. See also Press release of the Justice and Home Affairs Council meeting of 27 and 28 February 2003.

135 Council Directive 2003/109/EC, *op.cit*. See also Press release of the Justice and Home Affairs Council meeting of 5 and 6 June 2003.

136 Council Directive 2004/114/EC of 13 December 2004 on the conditions of admission third-country nationals for the purposes of studies, pupil exchange, unremunerated training or voluntary service, OJ L 375/12, 23.12.2005.

137 Council Directive 2005/71/EC of 12 October 2005 on a specific procedure for admitting of third-country nationals for the purposes of scientific research, OJ L 289/15, 3.11.2005; Council Recommendation 2005/762/EC of 12 October 2005 to facilitate the admission of third country nationals to carry out scientific research in the European Community, OJ L 289/26, 3.11.2005 and European Parliament and Council Recommendation 2005/761/EC of 28 September 2005 to facilitate the issue by the Member States of uniform short-stay visas for researchers from third countries travelling within the Community for the purpose of carrying out scientific research, OJ L 289/23, 3.11.2005.

138 For a presentation of the proposal see Brinkmann G., "Family Reunion, Third Country Nationals and the Community's New Powers", in Guild E. and Harlow C. (eds.), *Implementing Amsterdam: immigration and asylum rights in EC law*, Hart Publishing, Oxford, 2001, p. 241-266 and Boeles P., "Directive on Family Reunification: Are the Dilemmas Resolved?" *EJML*, Vol. 3, Issue 1, 2001, p. 61-71.

mission had to submit two modified proposals in 2000 and 2002 respectively.[139] In contrast to the first modified proposal, which did not embark on major changes, the second modified proposal submitted at the request of the Laeken European Council, attempted to resolve the most important problems that had arisen during the negotiations. In fact, this second modified proposal was definitely much closer to the Council position and also satisfied specific concerns of certain Member States. The final text may well change slightly– since the European Parliament has already brought an action for the annulment of certain provisions.[140] Still it is worth examining briefly the content of the final text as it stands particularly in comparison with the first, and occasionally also the second, Commission proposal.[141]

The main objective of the Directive, as announced in its very first Article, is to determine the conditions for the exercise of the right to family reunification by third country nationals residing lawfully in the territory of the Member States. Whereas the objective of the first Commission proposal was to harmonise Member States' legislation, a "new approach" recognizing the need of various stages for harmonization was put forward in the Commission's second modified proposal. In this second modified proposal, the Commission proposed the inclusion of a general "stand still clause" in order to "freeze" the harmonization accomplished during this first stage as to the central provisions of the Directive.[142] Nonetheless, this general clause was finally deleted, most probably due to the hostility that Member States expressed and the fact that the exact conse-

139 See respectively COM (2000) 624 final 10.10.2000 and COM (2002) 225 final, 2.5.2002.

140 Action brought on 22 December 2003 by the European Parliament against the Council of the European Union, Case C-540/03, OJ C 47/21, 21.2.2004. The European Parliament seeks the annulment of Articles 4 (1) third sub-paragraph, 4 (6) and 8 of the Directive.

141 For a general discussion on the negotiation process within the Council and on the content of the Directive see Ferraiolo S., "Immigrazione, asilo, accoglienza: gli effeti pratici del "vento di Tampere" Direttive, regolamenti e applicazione nei diritti nazionali", *Diritto & Giustizia*, No 20, 2004, p. 54-80.; Mariani T., *"L'Europe forteresse": mythe ou réalité? Les enjeux de la politique européenne d'immigration*, Assemblée Nationale, Rapport d'Information No 1238, Novembre 2003 and Peers S., "Key Legislative Developments on Migration in the European Union, *EJML*, Vol. 5, 2003, p. 387-410.

142 Article 3 (6) of the second modified Commission proposal. Stand still clauses concerning national migration law in force at the date of the adoption of the Community measure are to be found, *inter alia*, in Article 4 (3) of Directive 64/221 and Article 13 of Decision 1/80 of the Association Council EC/Turkey. See Brinkmann G., "Family Reunion, Third Country Nationals and the Community's New Powers", *op.cit.*, at p. 266.

quences of the implementation of this clause were not entirely clear.[143] However, special *ad hoc* "stand still clauses" were introduced with respect to certain derogation clauses inserted in the Directive.[144] Further, a new provision regarding the possibility to adopt or apply more favourable provisions has been added, mainly due to the various stages of harmonization.[145]

The personal scope of the Directive is limited to third country nationals holding a residence permit, which is valid for one year or more. The sponsor has to have reasonable prospects of obtaining permanent residence though the Directive does not clarify how this is to be assessed. Asylum applicants and persons residing under temporary or subsidiary protection schemes are excluded. Family members of EU citizens are also excluded, albeit for different reasons.[146]

The definition of "family" is quite restrictive. Family reunification is obligatory only for the spouse and the unmarried minor children and the admission of vast categories of persons falls under the optional clauses of the second and third paragraph of Article 4. A series of express derogations limit the scope of the sole binding paragraph as well. Some of them have been introduced by the Commission itself and others have been inserted by the Council.[147]

143 It was, *inter alia*, not clear what would be the consequences for Member States that did not have at the time of the adoption of the Directive legislation regarding certain provisions covered by the stand still clause, such as for example family reunification of unmarried partners or children falling under the optional clauses. It was also not clear whether and which standards those Member States that would introduce relevant legislation at a later stage would have to follow.

144 Apart from the specific stand still clauses that the Commission has inserted with regard to the derogatory clauses of Articles 4 (1) third sub-paragraph and Article 8 second sub-paragraph, the Council has inserted a stand still clause also in the derogation clause of Article 4 (6) of the Directive.

145 Article 3 (5) of the Directive. Both the solution of the more favourable clause as well as that of the stand still clause had been proposed by Boeles who had expressed fears about the watering down of the proposal. See Boeles P., "Directive on Family Reunification: Are the Dilemmas Resolved?", *op.cit.*, at p. 71.

146 Given that their status is still diverse and generally more positive.

147 The first concerns children over 12 years old who need to meet a condition for integration (Article 4 (1)). The second concerns the possibility of requiring the sponsor and his/her spouse to be of a minimum age and a maximum age of 21 before the spouse is able to join him/her (Article 4 (5)). Finally, the third one concerns the possibility to request that the application regarding minor children be submitted before the age of 15 (Article 4 (6)). The first two have been introduced by the Commission – though the Council has further reinforced the second one – whilst the third was introduced by the Council itself, most probably after difficult negotiations, since its meaning is somewhat contradictory. So according to the first sentence the application has to be submitted before the age of fifteen, yet according to the second sentence even if the application is submitted after the age of fifteen Member States who

As far as the requirements for the exercise of the right and the documentary evidence that need to be submitted are concerned, the persons concerned are required to prove that the sponsor has accommodation, sickness insurance and stable and regular resources.[148] The possibility of a waiting period of two years – which according to the Commission's second modified proposal can be extended to three years – is also provided.[149] Furthermore, the usual provisions regarding public security have been considerably reinforced and the Council has also included a reference to terrorism within the preamble.[150] Interestingly the Council adopted a statement according to which the above public security provisions do not constitute a precedent for other relevant negotiations which is certainly indicative of concerns with regard to the standards of protection laid down therein.[151] Finally, a new requirement regarding the compliance with integration measures has been added.[152]

There is also considerable departure from the initial Commission proposal as far as certain procedural aspects linked with the exercise of the right are concerned. The application for family reunification may be submitted either by the sponsor or by the family member. In principle, it should be submitted when the family member is outside the territory of the Member States though exceptionally it could also be accepted if submitted when the family member is already in the territory of the country.[153] As relates to the time limit imposed on the authorities to reply, the Commission proposal provided for a maximum six-month deadline, however, this was extended to nine months by the Council. The Council also added a new clause according to which, in exceptional cases, the time limit may be extended without any concrete deadline for reply.[154] In any case, Member States shall ensure that the persons concerned have the right

apply this derogation "shall authorize the entry and residence of such children on grounds other than family reunification".

148 Article 7 (1) of the Directive.

149 Article 8 of the Directive.

150 Article 6 of the Directive and recital 14 in the preamble.

151 See Statement to be added to the Council minutes Ad Article 6, reproduced in Council doc. 10755/03 MIGR 58, 9.7.2003. According to this statement "The Council considers that the content and the scope of Article 6 of this Directive is without prejudice to the content and scope of similar clauses on the public policy and public security contained in other Community Directives in the area of legal immigration which are currently being considered or which will be considered by the Council bodies."

152 Article 7 (2) of the Directive.

153 Article 5 (1) and (3) of the Directive.

154 See Article 5 (4) of the Directive.

to mount a legal challenge, even if the initial Commission proposal was much clearer and recognised an express access to justice.[155]

The duration of the residence permit of the family member is for at least one year and it cannot be longer than that of the sponsor.[156] At least two points are worth highlighting in relation to the renewal of residence permits. Firstly, in contrast to the Commission proposal providing for a re-checking of the conditions of entry only on the occasion of the first renewal, it now seems that Member States can perform such a check at every stage.[157] Secondly, the list of reasons to reject an application or refuse to renew a family member's residence permit has been considerably lengthened.[158] There is now a reinforced clause on marriages of convenience which almost establishes a sort of presumption that the marriage contracted after the sponsor had been issued his residence permit is one of convenience.[159] And there is also a clause referring to the rather controversial issue of rupture of family relationship.[160] The existence of a reinforced clause against expulsion is to be welcomed. According to this clause Member States will have to take into account the length of stay of the person concerned as well as a series of other important reasons which function as a safety net for the persons concerned.[161]

Two other provisions have also been subject to serious limitations. First, according to a new derogation clause the access of family members to the labour market may be limited for twelve months.[162] The second regards the autonomous

155 See Article 18 of the Directive and Article 16 of the initial Commission proposal according to which "the applicant and the members of his family have the right to apply to courts of the Member State concerned".

156 Article 13 (2) and (3) of the Directive.

157 Article 16 (1) (a) introduces a general provision according to which an application may be rejected or withdrawn or renewal may be refused where the conditions laid down by the Directive are no longer satisfied. In practical terms this appears to mean that the requirements introduced by Articles 6 and 7 are checked at every stage.

158 See Article 16 of the Directive in conjunction with Article 14 of the initial Commission proposal.

159 See the new clause inserted in Article 16 (2) (b) of the Directive. See also the cross-reference in the introductory phrase of Article 4.

160 Article 16 (1) (b) of the Directive. See in that respect the *Sen* Judgment of the European Court of Human Rights. *Sen v. the Netherlands*, Judgment of the European Court of Human Rights of 21 December 2001. For a discussion see *infra* at 6.4.

161 Article 17 of the Directive.

162 Article 14 (2) of the Directive. It provides that Member States may decide according to national law the conditions under which family members shall exercise an employed or self employed activity. These conditions shall set a time limit, which shall in no case exceed 12 months, during which Member States may examine the

residence permit. In principle, this is granted no later than after five years of residence. However, according to an express optional derogation Member States may limit the granting of an autonomous residence permit only to the spouse in cases of breakdown of the family relationship.[163] The procedural details regarding the granting of this permit as well as the conditions concerning its granting and its duration are established by national law.[164] A considerable margin of manoeuvre thus seems to be left to the Member States.

Finally, one of the new clauses introduced by the Commission in the second modified proposal is the "*rendez-vous* clause" of Article 19. According to this clause two years after the implementation of the Directive the Commission shall report to the Council and shall propose amendments that may appear necessary, by way of priority in relation to the central provisions of the Directive.[165]

4.2.1.2 The Long-Term Residents Directive

The Directive on the status and rights of long-term residents is the second proposal for a Directive submitted by the Commission and examined by the Council. The Directive, establishes a new status at EC level, the EC long-term resident status. The first two Chapters of the Directive determine the terms for conferring and withdrawing this status as well as the rights pertaining thereto. In the third Chapter, and undoubtedly the most innovative part of the Directive, the conditions under which EC long-term residents may reside in a Member State other than that where they have acquired the status are laid down. In fact, it is the first time that the conditions for the mobility and residence of third country nationals in a second Member State have been established. It is useful to clarify in that respect that, while the Directive does not replace the relevant national regimes, third country nationals that have acquired the status on the basis of national law do not benefit from the advantages of the Directive.[166] The Directive itself differs in many ways from the initial Commission proposal and it is

---

situation of their labour market before authorizing family members to exercise an employed or self-employed activity.

163 See Article 15 (1) of the Directive. See also the two positive optional clauses of paragraphs 2 and 3 according to which the autonomous residence permit may be granted to other categories of persons, such as adult children or relatives in the ascending line, or under special circumstances, such as death of the sponsor, divorce or separation. This option becomes obligatory for the Member States in the event of particularly difficult circumstances.

164 Article 15 (4) of the Directive.

165 Articles 3 (scope of the Directive), 4 (definition of family members), 7 (conditions for entry), 8 (waiting period) and 13 (right to entry and residence).

166 See Article 13 of the Directive, where it is clearly stated that the persons having acquired the "national" long-term resident status do not benefit of the right of mobility within the EU as described in Chapter III of the Directive.

helpful while presenting briefly the Directive to highlight the main differences between the two texts.

The main requirement for acquiring the status of long-term resident is the duration of residence, which is set at five years of continuous and legal residence, immediately prior to the application for the acquisition of the status.[167] Illegal residents and persons residing on a temporary basis are excluded from the scope of the Directive.[168] In contrast to the Commission proposal students of every level, and refugees, are excluded from the scope of the Directive.[169] However, periods of study *may* be taken into account though only half the period of study will count,[170] and the Council has welcomed the Commission's commitment to present within one year a proposal for extending the Directive to refugees and persons enjoying subsidiary protection.[171]

Inasmuch as the calculation of the period of residence is concerned, there are specific provisions regulating the issue of absences so that account can be taken of circumstances in which a person might have to leave the territory on a temporary basis. In contrast to the detailed provisions for the calculation of the five-year period and the calculation of the periods of absence proposed by the Commission, the Council has opted for a much more general and open-ended drafting which leaves a large margin of manoeuvre to the Member States.[172]

In addition to the temporal requirement, the persons concerned will have to prove compliance with several further substantive conditions in order to acquire the status of long-term resident. They have to prove that they have stable and regular resources as well as sickness insurance.[173] There is also an optional clause regarding compliance with integration conditions.[174] Furthermore, a series of

167 Article 4 (1) of the Directive.

168 Article 3 (1) and (2) of the Directive. It is useful to underline also that the provisions of the Directive are applied without prejudice to more favourable provisions of bilateral agreements.

169 According to the Commission proposal doctoral students were included in the scope of the Directive – see Article 3 (2) (b) of the Commission proposal – and there were also specific provisions for refugees, see Article 3 (5) and 6 (2) (a) of the Commission proposal.

170 Article 4 (2) second sub-paragraph of the Directive. In the Commission proposal this was an obligation. See Article 5 (2) (b) of the Commission proposal.

171 See the Council Statement on Article 3 in the Minutes of the 2546th meeting of the Council.

172 Article 4 (3) of the Directive in conjunction with Article 5 (3) of the Commission proposal.

173 Article 5 (1) of the Directive.

174 Article 5 (2) of the Directive.

"clarifications" that are included either in the preamble[175] or in the framework of Article 7 referring to the documentary evidence supporting the application[176] seem to lead to the establishment of additional conditions for the acquisition of the status. Finally, Member States may refuse to grant the status on grounds of public policy or public security.[177]

The national competent authorities are bound to give a written notification of the decision as soon as possible and, save in exceptional circumstances, no later than six months from the date on which the application is lodged.[178] Although the status is permanent, the EC long-term residence permit is granted for an initial duration of at least five years instead of the ten years that had been proposed by the Commission.[179]

The status is lost or withdrawn in cases of fraudulent acquisition, adoption of an expulsion measure or where the person concerned constitutes a threat to public policy though the threat itself is not a reason for expulsion.[180] The status is also in principle lost or withdrawn in cases of absences exceeding twelve consecutive months, unless otherwise decided by the Member State concerned. Whereas the Commission proposal provided for a two-year absence with a list of concretely specified exceptions including a more generally drafted, and rather confusing, exception-clause, the Council opted for a shorter time-limit and more open-ended drafting.[181]

---

175 i.e. contributions to the pension system and fulfilment of tax obligations. See recital 7.

176 Where there is an express reference to appropriate accommodation. See Article 7 (1) second sub-paragraph of the Directive.

177 Article 6 of the Directive. However, the Council has further reinforced the relevant provision. According to recital 8 the notion of public policy and public security may cover a conviction for committing a serious crime and a Declaration on terrorism was also included in the Council minutes at the time of the adoption of the Directive. Moreover, the express reference to the "personal conduct" of the person concerned has been deleted. See Article 7 (1) of the Commission proposal. The Member States are, however, bound to proceed to a balancing test between the severity or type of offence or the danger that emanates from the person and the personal situation and interests of the person concerned.

178 Article 7 (2) of the Directive.

179 See Article 8 (1) as well as Article 8 (2) of the Directive in conjunction with Article 9 (1) of the Commission proposal.

180 Article 9 (1) and (3) of the Directive. In cases where the loss of status does not lead to removal Member States shall authorise the person concerned to remain in its territory if the person fulfils the relevant conditions of national law and does not constitute a threat to public policy. See Article 9 (7).

181 Article 9 (1) (c) and 9 (2) of the Directive. See also Article 10 (1) (a) and 10 (3) of the Commission proposal.

Inasmuch as the provisions regarding the residence in a second Member State are concerned while the Council maintained the basic principle that the status is lost or withdrawn once acquired in a second Member State it has nonetheless substantially amended the system regarding certain aspects linked to the mobility of long-term residents. According to the Commission proposal, absences related to the exercise of the right of movement to another Member State did not entail withdrawal of the status and the status in the first Member State was maintained unless acquired in the second Member State. The Council, however, opted for the establishment of a time-limit of six years after which the status is in any case withdrawn or lost. In parallel, it has also established, clearly as a compensatory measure, a fast-track re-acquisition procedure in cases of withdrawal or loss due to absence.[182] The reasons leading to these changes seem to be two-fold. Firstly, the ambiguity of the Commission proposal with regard to certain cases, i.e. where the long-term resident did not apply for the status in the second Member State or where the status in the second Member State was refused. Secondly, the practical need to put a time-limit on the responsibility of the first Member State granting the status,[183] while not penalising severely those long-term residents who make use of their right to move.

Inasmuch as the rights granted to persons having acquired the status are concerned, both the Commission and the Council adopted the approach of listing certain rights instead of accepting the general principle of equality and listing the exceptions.[184] Taking into account the various derogations and restrictions attached to the general list of rights, it becomes clear that the rights finally granted to long-term residents are considerably restricted in comparison with the Commission proposal. The rights that have been subject to the most severe restrictions are those regarding access to employment,[185] education and study

182 See Articles 10 (2), 23 and 27 of the Commission proposal, in conjunction with Article 9 (4) and (5) of the Directive.

183 In principle the Member State that has granted the status remains in some way "responsible" for the long-term resident as long as the status is maintained, since there is an obligation to readmit the third country national concerned in case he/she is expelled from the second Member State. See Article 22 (2) of the Directive. Moreover, the persons concerned also maintain in principle their rights in the first Member State, until their status is lost or withdrawn.

184 See Article 12 of the Commission proposal, which became Article 11 in the final text of the Directive.

185 See Article 11 (1) (a) in conjunction with Article 11 (3) (a), establishing an optional derogation for posts reserved to nationals, EU and EEA citizens.

grants,[186] social assistance and social protection[187] as well as the access to goods and services.[188]

The provisions on residence and pertaining rights in other Member States are established by Chapter III of the Directive, which has been considerably redrafted by the Council. EC long-term residents may reside in a second Member State on the following grounds: exercise of an economic activity, pursuit of studies or for other purposes.[189] Following an intensive debate on whether certain additional restrictions should be established the Council decided to allow, firstly, the maintenance of existing national quota systems;[190] and, secondly, the possibility to proceed to a prior examination of the labour market before permitting the entry for employment purposes and also the requirement of a work permit.[191]

Long-term residents as well as their family members will have to comply with a series of conditions described in detail in Articles 15 and 16. The structure of the initial Commission proposal has been completely changed, however, there are no major amendments as far as the substance is concerned,[192] except with regard to four specific points: firstly, persons entering for employment will also have to prove that they have financial resources;[193] secondly, there is a new condi-

186 See Article 11 (1) (b) in conjunction with Article 11 (2), establishing a possibility to limit the right to cases where the usual place of residence remains to the first Member State, and Article 11 (3) (b) establishing the possibility to require proof of appropriate language proficiency as well as fulfilment of education prerequisites with regard to access to university. Inasmuch as study grants are concerned it is interesting to note the reference to national law and the further eventual limitations mentioned in the fifteenth recital of the preamble regarding grants financed under social assistance schemes as well as the reference to the reciprocity rule. See also recital 14 safeguarding at least the access of minors to education.

187 See Article 11 (1) (d) in conjunction with Article 11 (2) – establishing an eventual limitation linked with the usual place of residence – and Article 11 (4) granting to Member States the possibility to limit treatment in that respect to "core benefits". For an indicative list of "core benefits" see recital 13. The reference to social benefits initially included in the Commission proposal – see Article 12 (1) (f) of the Commission proposal – has been deleted.

188 See Article 11 (1) (f) in conjunction with Article 11 (2) regarding the usual place of residence limitation. It is interesting also to note that the final text refers to access to "procedures for obtaining housing" and no longer to "housing" thus giving the impression that the right has been watered down.

189 Article 14 (2) of the Directive.

190 Article 14 (4) of the Directive.

191 Article 14 (3) of the Directive.

192 See Articles 16 and 17 of the Commission proposal.

193 Since the said clause has now become horizontal. See Article 15 (2) of the Directive.

tion regarding proof of appropriate accommodation for all categories; [194] thirdly, there is a new optional integration requirement;[195] and, fourthly, the provisions on family members have been aligned with the outcome of the negotiations on the family reunification Directive.[196] Moreover, the Council has also included in the very beginning of Chapter III a reference to Community legislation on social security, meaning the recently adopted Regulation extending the relevant Community Regulations on social security to third country nationals.[197]

The public policy clause and its procedural aspects are almost identical to those of the first part of the Directive, albeit there is a new specific clause for public health and the time limits are considerably limited.[198] As far as the rights of long-term residents in the second Member State are concerned, they are in principle identical to those granted in the first Member State.[199] There has, however, been a considerable limitation of the right of access to employment.[200]

Furthermore, the long-term resident may acquire the status in the second Member State under the same conditions as applied in the first Member State.[201] The Directive sets detailed rules regarding the withdrawal of the residence in the second Member State and the obligation for readmission of the first Member State.[202] A network of contact points in order to facilitate the cooperation among Member States is also established.[203]

Finally, it is worth underlining the existence of a "*rendez-vous* clause" obviously deemed necessary due to the character of the Directive as a 'test measure' whose practical implications could not be foreseen.[204]

---

194 See Article 15 (3) of the Directive.

195 See Article 15 (4) second sub-paragraph of the Directive.

196 See Article 16 of the Directive in conjunction with Article 18 of the Commission proposal.

197 Council Regulation (EC) No 859/2003 of May 14, 2003, extending the provisions of Regulation (EEC) No 1408/71 and Regulation (EEC) No 574/72 to nationals of third countries who are not already covered by those provisions solely on the ground of their nationality, (2003) OJ L 124/1, 20.5.2003.

198 See Articles 17 to 20 of the Directive. Here the time limit for examination of the application is four months with a possible extension for three further months.

199 Article 21 of the Directive.

200 See Article 21 (2) of the Directive.

201 Article 23 of the Directive.

202 Article 22 of the Directive.

203 Article 25 of the Directive.

204 Article 24 of the Directive. According to which the Commission shall present a report proposing the necessary amendments no later than five years after the full implementation of the Directive. The proposals for amendments shall be made by way of priority in relation to Articles 4, 5, 9, 11 and to Chapter III.

4.2.1.3 The Draft Directive on Admission for Paid Employment and Self-Employed Activities

This Draft Directive should undoubtedly be considered as the cornerstone of migration policy, since the development of a comprehensive Community migration policy is impossible without addressing this issue. Nonetheless, the establishment of a common policy at European level on this issue has proved, and still remains, extremely difficult. The very competence of the Community on the matter has been strongly contested [205] and a series of practical and political reasons have rendered the formation of a common agenda a rather difficult task.[206] In fact discussions on this Draft Directive were frozen as soon as the Council concluded the first reading of the text. However, it is useful to review briefly the content of this first Commission legislative proposal on this issue.

The main objective of the Draft Directive consisted in defining common conditions, standards and procedures for entry and residence of third country nationals for the purposes of employment. When drafting this proposal the Commission based itself on a series of principles that were divided into two main categories. Firstly, the need to establish a mechanism that is transparent, rational, based on clear and simple procedures that address the need of the market to recruit successfully and quickly. And, secondly, the need to respect the domestic labour market situation of the Member States.

The Commission introduced a new "one stop shop procedure", meaning a single national application procedure leading to a combined title. The application would be submitted either by the employer or by the third country national concerned. It could be lodged either via the representation of the competent Member State or directly in the territory of the State concerned, if the applicant was already resident or legally present there.[207] Article 5 (3) provided a long list of conditions that third country nationals would have to comply with in order to be admitted.

An economic need test was also established. According to this test it should be demonstrated that the post could not be filled in the short-term by a series of persons –nationals or third country nationals legally established- who had a preference. The said requirement was deemed to be fulfilled if the specific vacancy had been made public via national employment services and the EURES system for at least four weeks.[208] Nonetheless, the proposal provided for a series of exceptions to which Member States could have recourse in order to be able to exclude certain categories of persons from the aforementioned requirement. These concerned either a specific number of jobs in specific sectors for

205 See discussion *supra* at 2.2.3.

206 See discussion *infra* at 6.1.1.4.

207 See Articles 4 and 5 of the proposal.

208 Article 6 (1) and (2) of the proposal.

a limited time period or in specific regions or certain thresholds of income or guarantees.[209] Moreover, Member States had the right to maintain or introduce more favourable provisions regarding certain categories of employees.[210] Finally, the Commission acknowledged the right of Member States to limit admission, if they considered that it was necessary to apply horizontal measures to that effect, i.e. ceilings or quotas.[211]

The duration of the first residence permit was limited up to three years.[212] During the initial three-year period there were strictly enumerated restrictions as to the exercise of specific professional activities or fields of activities.[213] The main reason for withdrawal of the permit was that of fraudulent acquisition.[214] It was also clearly stated that unemployment in itself should not constitute a sufficient reason for revoking the permit unless it exceeded a certain duration.

The proposal also established a list of rights linked mainly with movement, equal treatment in working conditions and social security, access to goods and services and freedom of association. Third country national workers' right to request and obtain payment of their contributions in case they left the Member State was also recognized.[215]

Finally, the proposal provided special rules for certain categories of employees such as seasonal workers, trans-frontier workers, intra-corporate transferees, trainees and persons entering in the context of youth exchange or youth mobility schemes.[216]

The procedure for admission of employees applied *mutatis mutandis* in the case of self-employed persons.[217] In this case the economic need test was replaced by a beneficial effect test.[218]

Given the considerable resistance from certain Member States to attribute such competences to the Community, discussions were frozen. Moreover, the mechanism proposed by the Commission was severely criticised as cumbersome and unable to fulfil the need for a flexible and rapid mechanism that enables

209 Article 6 (3) to (5) of the proposal. Thus, different systems such as quotas or specific calls for certain types of employees – i.e. hi-tech – may be maintained.

210 i.e. researchers, academic specialists, sport professionals. Article 3 (4) of the proposal.

211 Article 26 of the proposal.

212 Article 7 of the proposal.

213 Article 8 of the proposal.

214 Article 10 of the proposal.

215 For the full list of rights see Article 11 of the proposal.

216 Articles 12 to 16 of the proposal.

217 Articles 17 to 24 of the proposal.

218 Article 19 of the proposal.

businesses to recruit the necessary migrant labour.[219] The Commission has subsequently decided to adopt a much more prudent approach and launched an extensive consultation process. First, it tabled a Green Paper on legal migration and labour and organised a Public Hearing.[220] Then, and following an express request from the European Council the Commission prepared a Policy Plan on Legal Migration, which was presented in December 2005.[221] This document does not contain any legislative or operational proposal. It rather defines a roadmap for the remaining period of the Hague Programme (2006-2009) and lists actions and legislative initiatives that the Commission intends to take, so as to pursue the coherent development of EU legal migration policy. Inasmuch as the legislative proposals are concerned these will consist of a general framework Directive defining the basic rights of all immigrant workers admitted in the EU and of four specific Directives addressing the conditions of entry and residence of certain categories of immigrants, i.e. highly skilled and seasonal workers, intra-corporate transferees and remunerated trainees. Emphasis is also placed on cooperation regarding the exchange of information, integration policy and circular migration aspects. As a final point, it needs to be highlighted that it also aims to meet the objectives of the Lisbon Strategy.

4.2.1.4 The Directive on Admission for the Purposes of Studies, Pupil Exchange, Unremunerated Training or Voluntary Service

This proposal was submitted to the Council in October 2002, but its examination only started in mid 2003, after the Council had reached agreement on the family reunification and long-term residents Directives. The Council reached a common approach during the Justice and Home Affairs Council meeting of 30 March 2004.[222] Despite the fact that it is frequently called the "students' Directive", the proposal covers four different categories of third country nationals: students, school pupils, unremunerated trainees and volunteers. However, in contrast to the initial proposal providing for binding provisions with regard to

219 House of Lords, *A Community Immigration Policy, op.cit.*, pts 90-93.

220 Green Paper on an EU approach to managing economic migration (COM (2004) 811 final, 11.1.2005. A public hearing took place on 14 June 2005 closing the official phase of the public consultation.

221 Communication from the Commission Policy Plan on Legal Migration, COM (2005) 669 final, 21.12.2005. See also European Commission Press Release, "Policy Plan on Legal Migration", MEMO/05/494, 21.12.2005; "EU/JHA/LEGAL IMMIGRATION: Commission unveils "Policy Plan on Legal Migration" with aim of attracting highly qualified workers – Importance of integrating immigrants", Bulletin Quotidien Europe No 9095, 22.12.2005, and "Commission pushes ahead with EU green card scheme", <www.euobserver.com>, 22.12.2005.

222 See Press release of the relevant Council meeting. The text was published in the Official Journal only a few months later. See Directive 2004/114/EC, *op.cit.*

all four categories, the final draft has rendered the regulation of the last three categories optional.[223]

A series of general conditions for admission apply to all four categories of persons that are covered by the Directive [224] with specific conditions for admission of each of the categories being laid down separately. Thus, apart from proof that they have a valid travel document, a parental authorisation in case of minors, health insurance cover for all risks and that they have paid the fee for handling the application, the persons concerned must also submit documentary evidence that they fulfil a series of specific conditions varying depending on the specific category concerned.[225] Moreover, a new horizontal provision regarding the need to submit all the necessary documentary evidence showing that the said conditions are fulfilled has been inserted.[226] Member States are also left sufficient room for manoeuvre to refuse admission or withdraw a residence permit for public security reasons.[227]

The Commission's initial proposal included detailed provisions with regard to the application procedure, the issuing of visas and residence permits and set specific deadlines for the process of the application.[228] The final text is, however, drafted in much more general and laconic terms. The provisions regarding the issuing of the visas and the submission of the application have been deleted.[229] And there are no longer any concrete deadlines for a reply from the administration.[230] While the final text includes a series of provisions regarding the issuing, withdrawal and length of the residence permits,[231] it states in parallel in a newly inserted provision in rather obscure language that "by way of derogation" from these provisions "Member States are not obliged to issue permits in accordance with this Directive in the form of a residence permit for a period of up to two

223 See Article 3 of the Directive.

224 Article 6 of the Directive.

225 See Articles 7 and 9 to 11 of the Directive respectively.

226 Article 5 of the Directive.

227 Article 6 (1) (d) and Article 16 of the Directive. See also the text of the new recitals re Articles 6 (1) (d) and 7 that have been inserted in the preamble, i.e. recitals 14 and 15. While the former copies the text regarding the public policy text that was also in the Directives on family reunification and long-term residents the latter establishes a catch-all clause in case the Member State concerned has doubts with regard to an application.

228 Articles 17, 19 and 20 of the proposal.

229 Articles 17 and 19 of the proposal.

230 According to the Directive a decision shall be taken and the applicant shall be notified of it within a period that does not hamper the pursuit of the relevant studies, whilst leaving the competent authorities sufficient time to process the application. See Article 20 of the Directive.

231 Articles 12 to 16 of the Directive.

years, after the period determined by Article 29 [i.e. the implementation deadline of two years] expires".[232] As is customary, third country nationals have the right to mount a legal challenge.[233] Finally, Member States may apply a fast-track admission procedure on the basis of agreements to be concluded between Member States immigration authorities and educational establishments or exchange organizations.[234]

Students may have limited access to the labour market up to a maximum number of weekly hours to be set by each Member State between 10 to 20 hours and Member States are allowed to request that those concerned report in advance or otherwise to a designated authority.[235] The final text, however, has been accompanied by a series of safeguard clauses concerning the possibility to take into account the situation in the labour market, the need for a prior authorisation and the possibility to restrict the right for the first year of residence.[236]

One aspect of this Directive which clearly has added value is the provision on the mobility of third country nationals studying in another Member State.[237] However, it is worth noting that the Council has inserted a provision clarifying once more that for the purposes of granting the long-term resident status the Member States are not obliged to take into consideration the time during which the persons concerned have resided in their territory.[238]

4.2.1.5 The Researchers Package

The so-called researchers package is composed of four different documents: a Communication and three related legislative proposals. As far as the legislative instruments are concerned the Commission followed a three-fold step by step approach. It submitted to the Council a proposal for a Directive on a specific procedure for admitting third country nationals for the purposes of research and two proposals for Recommendations that deal respectively with certain specific aspects of the admission procedure, such as family reunification, operational cooperation and the procedure for issuing uniform short stay visas in cases where researchers from third countries travel within the EU for the purposes of carrying out research. The main aim of the two Recommendations is to create some degree of approximation of national legislation in advance of the Directive.

232 New Article 23 of the Directive.

233 Article 18 (4) of the Directive.

234 Article 19 of the Directive.

235 Article 17 of the Directive.

236 Article 17 (1), (3) and (4) of the Directive.

237 Article 8 of the Directive.

238 Article 24 of the Directive. See also Article 4 (2) of the long-term residents Directive.

The whole issue of promoting and facilitating the admission of researchers from third countries is seen in close connection with the EU initiative for the creation of a European Research Area and the Sixth Framework Programme for Research as well as in the context of the Lisbon process, which aims at making the EU the most dynamic and competitive economy in the world. Starting with the assumption that 700 000 researchers are needed by 2010,[239] the proposals seek to achieve the objective of attracting researchers from third countries by providing favourable conditions for being admitted in the Member States and facilitating their mobility within the EU.

The Directive revolves around three key elements.[240] Firstly, it grants to authorised research organisations a central role in the admission procedure. The said organisations will be responsible for the task of checking if the research project is credible, they will subsequently sign a hosting agreement with the third country national concerned, and will be responsible for, and guarantee, the researcher's living expenses, health costs and return travel costs.[241] Consequently, following the division of roles between research organisations and Member States, the admission procedure is rather fast, simplified and streamlined and there is no work permit obligation.[242] Secondly, the interpretation of the concept of the researcher is broad and adapted to the needs of the EU and the concept of research institutions includes also the private sector.[243] Thirdly, steps are taken to promote the mobility of researchers in the EU. The Directive allows researchers in possession of a residence permit and a passport or travel document to pursue activities related to their research project in a second Member State.[244] And, further, the proposal lists a series of other rights to which the said persons have access.[245]

In order to achieve a certain degree of harmonisation as soon as possible, and facilitate the implementation of the Directive, the Commission calls on the Member States via the first Recommendation to adopt a number of practical

239 With regard to this specific point see also the Commission Communication on Investing in research: a action plan for Europe, COM (2003) 226 final, 30.4.2003.

240 See Directive 2005/71/EC, *op.cit.*

241 Articles 1, 5 and 6 of the Directive.

242 According to Article 7 of the Directive Member States will ask for the documents issued by the research organisation, whereas they will only check the identity of the person concerned and ascertain that he/she does not constitute a threat for public policy and public health. Member States can always check whether the hosting agreement has been signed in compliance with the relevant terms. See Articles 6 and 7 (2) of the Directive. As far as the lack of the work permit obligation is concerned see Recital 11 of the Directive.

243 See Article 2 of the Directive.

244 Article 13 of the Directive.

245 Article 12 of the Directive.

measures without delay in advance of transposition of the Directive.[246] The relevant points concern the abolition of the work permit obligation and any eventual quota restrictions or time limits, measures concerning procedural aspects, the right to family reunification as well as operational cooperation.

Finally, the second Recommendation aims at providing ways for facilitating certain aspects of the procedure for issuing short-term visas, by applying to researchers certain flexible provisions regarding *bona fide* persons, reducing the evidence required for the acquisition of a visa as well as the relevant fees.[247]

4.2.2 Integration Policy

One of the main policy issues included in the Tampere European Council Conclusions was the need for a more rigorous integration policy aimed at granting third country nationals rights and obligations comparable to those of EU citizens. Therefore, and notwithstanding the lack of any Treaty provision on integration policy,[248] both the Commission and the Council have dealt extensively with the issue in the post-Tampere era.

First of all, it is worth highlighting the fact that one of the central aspects of establishing an integration policy consists in consolidating the relevant legislative framework. The Council has already adopted two Directives implementing the principle of equal treatment: one of a more general character,[249] and, a second, concerning specifically equal treatment in employment and occupation.[250] Furthermore the Council established an action programme to combat discrimination.[251] However, discrimination on the basis of nationality and issues regarding the entry and residence of third country nationals is excluded from the

246 See Council Recommendation 2005/762/EC, *op.cit.*

247 See Council Recommendation 2005/761/EC, *op.cit.*

248 It is only in the Draft Constitutional Treaty that a relevant provision has been included. See *supra* at 2.3.2.

249 Council Directive 2000/43/EC of 29 June 2000 implementing the principle of equal treatment between persons irrespective of racial or ethnic origin, OJ L 180/22, 19.7.2000. For a discussion of the negotiation process see Tyson A., "The negotiation of the European Community Directive on Racial Discrimination", *EJML,* Vol. 3, 2001, p. 199-229 and Ellis E., "The Principle of Non-Discrimination in the Post-Nice Era", in Arnull A. and Wincott D. (eds.), *Accountability and Legitimacy in the European Union*, Oxford University Press, 2002, p. 291-305.

250 Council Directive 2000/78/EC establishing a general framework for equal treatment in employment and occupation, OJ L 303/16, 2.12.2000.

251 Council Decision 2000/750/EC of 27 November 2000 establishing a Community action programme to combat discrimination (2001 to 2006), OJ L 303/23, 2.12.2000.

scope of the relevant Directive[252] even though they are of obvious importance for the integration of immigrants in the life of the host society.

Moreover, the Council has also included provisions regarding integration on the two Directives that have already been adopted on legal migration, namely the family reunification[253] and the long-term residents Directives.[254] Nonetheless, the meaning of these provisions is rather general and open-ended, and might prove quite problematic in practice.[255]

More recently, integration policy was also examined independently and under a much broader framework. The issue as such was first discussed at the informal JHA Council meeting in Copenhagen in September 2002, following a conference organized by the Danish Presidency in July 2002.[256] At the first formal Council meeting during the Danish Presidency, on 14 and 15 October 2002, Justice and Interior Ministers adopted some preliminary Conclusions on integration.[257] After a short overview of existing Community initiatives such as measures against racism and xenophobia and the European Social Agenda endorsed by the Nice European Council,[258] Ministers have reaffirmed that integration policy is an important element in the establishment of a European migration policy. Furthermore, they defined some elements of the emerging

252 See Article 3 (2) of Directive 2000/43/EC, *op.cit.*

253 Article 7 (2) of the family reunification Directive.

254 Article 5 (2) and 15 (3) of the long-tem residents Directive.

255 More specifically, in the case of the long-term residents Directive it is rather clear that integration is seen as a condition for acquiring the status but in the case of family reunification it is not clear whether it concerns a condition that needs to be fulfilled *a priori* or whether it concerns the post entry phase, i.e. courses that the persons concerned need to follow, or who pays for such courses. The second subparagraph of the relevant provision excluding refugees from any integration conditions prior to entry points towards the conclusion that integration measures might take the form both of conditions for entry as well as measures applicable after the entry into the country. The clarification regarding refugees reinforces this reading. Besides the very position of the relevant provision – within the framework of the Article regarding requirements – further reinforces this interpretation.

256 European Conference on Successful Integration on the Labour Market, Copenhagen 4-5 July 2002.

257 Integration of third country nationals – Draft Council conclusions, Council doc. 12492/02 MIGR 85, 1.10.2002.

258 Nice European Council, 7, 8 and 9 December 2000, Presidency Conclusions, Annex I – European Social Agenda. There, it is stated *inter alia* that a policy to fight poverty and social exclusion must be accompanied also by action to ensure equal treatment for all third country nationals residing lawfully on Union territory.

Community position on integration policy.[259] On the basis of a Council request, a list of national contact points was set up in December 2002.

The issue was high on the Greek Presidency's agenda as well. Ministers had the opportunity to proceed to a further exchange of views during the informal JHA meeting in Veria, on 28-29 March 2003, and the Greek Presidency also organized a conference on migration where the issue was further discussed.[260]

Subsequently, the Commission issued a Communication on the interlinked issues of immigration, integration and employment in early June 2003.[261] In its Communication the Commission reviewed current practice and experience on integration –providing a synthesis report on national integration policies at the request of the Veria Council – and further outlined policy orientations and priorities, including actions at EU level to promote integration. It is worth noting that the issue was examined under a rather wide spectrum and there were also useful links with a series of different EU initiatives and policies, i.e. the Lisbon strategy, the European Employment Strategy, the European Social Agenda. Major questions such as the economic role of immigration and its impact on employment, the impact of the demographic change on employment and economic growth and the extent to which immigration could contribute in tackling Europe's demographic problems, are also addressed. Furthermore, the Commission advocated a "holistic" approach that takes into account various aspects, such as integration in the labour market, education, social and urban issues, culture and political issues, closer dialogue with third countries, while further encouraging the involvement of all actors. Finally, the Commission also promoted the idea of "civic citizenship"[262] and political rights for third county nationals.

259 i.e. approximation of rights and obligations of third country nationals to those of EU citizens, continued effort against discrimination and xenophobia, active participation of migrants in community life and labour market, promotion of exchange of information among Member States which could lead to gradual drafting of best practices.

260 Greek Presidency's Conference on "Managing Migration for the Benefit of Europe", Athens 15 and 16 May 2003.

261 Communication from the Commission to the Council, the European Parliament, the European Economic and Social Committee and the Committee of the Regions on immigration, integration and employment, COM (2003) 336 final, 3.6.2003.

262 The "civic citizenship" concept was actively supported by the Commission and consists in granting to third country nationals that have resided lawfully in principle for a long period of time a core set of rights and obligations. It is a status somewhere between the level of lawful migrant and naturalisation.

Following the Commission Communication the Council adopted Conclusions on the development of integration policy in June 2003.[263] The issue was brought to the attention of Heads of State during the Thessaloniki Summit.[264] Whereas both Ministers and Heads of State supported the Commission's approach and proposals, they conspicuously failed to take up the suggestions of developing the concept of civic citizenship or giving third country nationals rights of political participation even at the local level.

Progress on integration policy has certainly been constant. National contact points meet on a regular basis. The Commission is already financing a series of pilot projects. And on the basis of a Commission request and funding the Erasmus University of Rotterdam has prepared an interesting report on benchmarking in immigrant integration, providing an overview of integration models in Europe and drawing up a list of indicators on the matter.[265] In 2004, the Commission has also prepared its first annual report on migration and integration.[266] Furthermore, in autumn 2004 the results of the exchanges of information among the contact points have also been presented in the form of a handbook on integration for policy makers and practitioners.[267] Integration policy was also high at the agenda of the Dutch Presidency, which organised a Ministerial Conference at Kroningen in November 2004.[268] On the basis of this Conference the Council has adopted Conclusions on the matter in November 2004.[269]

---

263 Council Conclusions on the development of a policy at European Union level on the integration of third country nationals residing in the territory of the European Union, Council doc. 10622/03 MIGR 52, 17.6.2003.

264 European Council of Thessaloniki, 19 and 20 June 2003, Presidency Conclusions, pts 28 to 35.

265 Entzinger H. and Biezeveld R., *Benchmarking in Immigrant Integration*, European Research Centre on Migration and Ethnic Relations (ERCOMER), Erasmus University, Rotterdam, August 2003.

266 Communication from the Commission to the Council, the European Parliament, the European Economic and Social Committee and the Committee of the Regions – First Annual Report on Migration and Integration, COM (2004) 508 final, 16.7.2004.

267 European Commission, DG Justice, Freedom and Security, *Handbook on integration for policy makers and practitioners,* November 2004, written by the Migration Policy Group, Brussels, available at <http://europa.eu.int/comm/justice_home/doc_centre/immigration/integration/doc/handbook_en.pdf>.
For an overview of the Commission activities in 2004 see Vitorino Antonio, "What EU strategy for integrating migrants", SPEECH/04/340, Brussels, June 30 2004.

268 Presidency Conclusions on the Integration Policy Conference, 9-11 November 2004, Groningen, The Netherlands.

269 Draft Conclusions of the Council and the Representatives of the Governments of the Member States on the establishment of Common Basic Principles for immigrant integration policy in the European Union 14776/04 MIGR 105, 18.11.2004.

Integration policy remains a top priority within the framework of the Hague Programme as well. In 2005 the Commission has presented a new Communication on the matter.[270] On the basis of this second Communication the Council has adopted Conclusions in November 2005.[271] Moreover, the Commission has tabled a Proposal for the creation of an Integration Fund.[272] Finally, following a request from the European Council the Commission is planning to present a second Handbook on integration as well as to establish a website on integration.[273]

4.3 Migration in a Broader Context

4.3.1 Relations with Third Countries and Co-development

Stronger external action and the inclusion of JHA in the more general EU external action as well as the need to intensify relations with third countries were among the fundamental objectives laid down at Tampere.[274] The Tampere Conclusions identify four main categories of external partners: acceding countries, neighbouring countries, countries with which the EU has structured relations and international organisations.[275] During its subsequent meeting at Feira, the European Council identified the guiding principles for establishing priorities for the JHA dimension of the Union's external policy and drew up a list of priorities and partners.[276] This list is regularly updated and each Presidency presents an updated version of the multi-annual JHA external programme.[277]

270 Communication from the Commission to the Council, the European Parliament, the European Economic and Social Committee and the Committee of the Regions A Common Agenda for Integration Framework for the Integration of Third-Country Nationals in the European Union, COM (2005) 389 final, 1.9.2005.

271 Draft Conclusions of the Council and the Representatives of the Governments of the Member States on a common agenda for integration, Council doc. 14613/05 MIGR 69, 18.11.2005.

272 See Proposal for a Council Decision establishing the European Fund for the Integration of third-country nationals for the period 2007-2013 as part of the General programme 'Solidarity and Management of Migration Flows', COM (2005) 123 final, 2.5.2005.

273 See Section 1.5 of the Hague Programme and Section 2.5 of the joint Council and Commission Action Plan implementing the Hague Programme, *op.cit.*

274 For a general discussion on the need to include migration on the EU foreign policy agenda and a brief overview of EU action see Niessen J., "International Migration on the EU Foreign Policy Agenda", *EJML*, Vol. 1, 1999, p. 483-496.

275 De Lobkowicz W., *L'Europe et la sécurité intérieure Une élaboration par étapes, op.cit.*, at p. 172.

276 See Council doc. 7653/00, *op.cit.*

277 See Note from the Secretariat on EU commitments vis-à-vis third countries, Council doc. 9166/04 RELEX 169 PESC 337 JAI 140, 4.5.2004 and Note of the Netherlands Presidency on JHA External Relations Multi-Presidency Programme, Council

Most external relations issues are dealt with in the framework of the High Level Working Group for Migration and Asylum (hereafter High Level Working Group), created in 1999. The initial terms of reference for this specialised external relations group were limited to the elaboration of five country-oriented Action Plans,[278] but have since been amplified.[279] Thus, the High Level Working Group has been responsible for the examination of a series of much more wide-ranging matters of cross-pillar character, such as development policy and foreign policy issues. However, its role has been heavily criticised.[280]

Initially relations with third countries were seen mainly through the lenses of forced return policy, and more specifically readmission policy. Thus, one of the first issues to be dealt with in the post-Amsterdam agenda concerned the elaboration of a model readmission clause to be included in Community agreements.[281] Then the Council adopted criteria for the identification of third countries with which readmission agreements should be negotiated. Five criteria were identified: migratory pressure, geographical position in relation to the EU, eventual added value for Member States with respect to bilateral relations, exclusion of candidate countries but inclusion of countries with which the EU has already signed cooperation agreements and the need to keep a geographical balance between the various regions of origin and transit.[282] It is on the basis of these criteria that the Council has asked the Commission to submit the last series of relevant negotiating mandates for Albania, Algeria, Turkey and China, which were presented in autumn 2002.

---

doc. 11044/04 JAI 255 RELEX 317, 30.6.2004. For the latest JHA External Relations Multi-Presidency Work Programmes of the UK and Austrian Presidencies see respectively Council doc. 10728/05 JAI 244 RELEX 355, 1.7.2005 and 5003/06 JAI 1 RELEX 1, 3.1.2006.

278 Terms of reference of the High Level Working Group on Asylum and Migration, Preparation of Action Plans for the most important countries of origin and transit of asylum seekers and migrants, Council doc. 5264/2/99 REV 2 JAI 1 AG 1, 22.1.1999.

279 Modification of the terms of reference of the High Level Working Group on Asylum and Migration (HLWG), Council doc. 9433/02 JAI 109AG 20 ASIM 18, 30.5.2002.

280 The cross pillar strategy of the High Level Working Group was considered as a tool to press third States to readmit persons. Peers S., *EU Justice and Home Affairs Law*, *op.cit.*, at p. 102-103.

281 Council decision on the inclusion of model readmission clauses in Community agreements and in agreements between the European Community, its Member States and third countries, Council doc. 13409/99 MIGR 69, 25.11.1999.

282 Draft Council Conclusions – Criteria for the identification of third countries with which new readmission agreements need to be negotiated, Council doc. 7990/02 COR 1 MIGR 32, 16.4.2002.

Subsequently, emphasis was placed on the need to cooperate more closely with third countries. In the light of the seriousness of the situation created by the increase of illegal immigration by sea in the EU, in its April and June 2002 Conclusions the Council underlined the absolute necessity of effective cooperation with the countries of boarding, departure and transit of illegal migration flows.[283] The Council stressed the need for an integrated approach, while also identifying some of the operational measures to be taken by the EU and the preventive measures to be adopted by the countries of boarding, departure or transit respectively.

The European Council of Seville highlighted the importance of ensuring the cooperation of countries of origin and transit in the joint management of migration as well as in border control and readmission issues.[284] On the same occasion, the European Council asked for a systematic assessment of relations with third countries that do not cooperate in combating illegal migration. This assessment should be taken into account in relations between the EU and its Member States and the country concerned, in all relevant areas. Insufficient cooperation by a country could hamper the establishment of closer relations with the Union. Certain Member States had been in favour of a harsher drafting and were actively promoting the idea of imposing sanctions on third countries, in the end a much more neutral drafting was chosen.[285]

In its Conclusions of November 2002 the Council reaffirmed these concepts and provided further elaboration. The following set of criteria have been used to identify countries of origin or transit with whom the Council considered that intensified cooperation should be established: nature and size of migratory flows towards the EU; geographical position in relation to the EU; need for capacity building concerning migration management; existing framework for cooperation and attitude towards cooperation on migration issues. Based on these criteria the Council identified the following nine countries with which relations should be intensified: Albania, China, Federal Republic of Yugoslavia, Morocco, Russia, Tunisia, Ukraine, Libya and Turkey.[286] The only country

283 Council Conclusions on measures to be applied to prevent and combat illegal immigration and smuggling and trafficking in human beings by sea and in particular on measures against third countries which refuse to cooperate with the European Union in preventing and combating these phenomena, *op.cit*.

284 European Council of Seville, 19 and 20 June 2002, Presidency conclusions, pts 34 to 36.

285 It seems that while the idea of sanctions was promoted by the UK and Spain, it was blocked by France and Sweden. See 'Les Quinze ne sanctionneront pas les pays d'émigration illégale', Le Monde.fr, 22.6.2002.

286 General Affairs Council Conclusions of November 2002 on intensified cooperation on the management of migrations flows with third countries, 13894/02 ASIM 47 RELEX 227, 14.11.2002.

with which there was not already a more general framework for cooperation was Libya. It is worth noting that the Commission has subsequently prepared a first report on the relations with the nine countries identified in the November 2002 Council Conclusions.[287]

The matter was addressed again at the European Council level at Thessaloniki. Heads of State recognised the importance of developing an evaluation mechanism to monitor relations with third countries which do not cooperate with the EU in combating illegal migration and also drew up a list of elements to be taken into consideration. The Commission was invited to report annually on the results of the above monitoring.[288] Following the Seville and Thessaloniki European Council Conclusions concerning the necessity to carry out a systematic assessment of relations with third countries which do not cooperate in combating illegal immigration and the importance of developing an evaluation mechanism to that end, the Council adopted Conclusions on the matter in November 2003.[289] In accordance with the Council Conclusions the aim of the mechanism should be to monitor the migratory situation in the third countries concerned. The Commission was invited again to report annually on the results of the monitoring and assessment activity and to make proposals and recommendations, as it deemed appropriate. While underlining the need of a case-by-case based examination, a list of indicators was established.[290] The monitoring activity should be carried out, where possible, in partnership with the third country concerned within the framework of existing agreements. In principle the mechanism should cover all relevant countries. However, in order to test its functioning a pilot phase was considered recommendable. Therefore, for the first year, the mechanism would cover a limited number of third countries on the basis of the

287 Commission Staff Working Paper Intensified Cooperation on the management of Migration flows with third countries – Report by the Commission's Services on the implementation of the Council Conclusions on intensified cooperation on the management of migration flows with third countries of 18 November 20002, SEC (2003) 815 final, 9.7.2003.

288 Thessaloniki European Council, Presidency Conclusions, pts 19 to 21.

289 Draft Council Conclusions on the establishment of a monitoring and evaluation mechanism of the third countries in the field of the fight against illegal migration, Council doc. 15292/03 ASIM 72 RELEX 447, 25.11.2003.

290 Such as existing national legislation aimed at preventing and combating illegal migration as well as participation in international instruments; efforts in migration management, border control and interception of illegal immigrants; cooperation in readmission and return issues; and cooperation on visa policy and possible adaptation of their visa systems.

priorities identified by the Council in its November 2002 Conclusions. Indeed, in July 2005, the Commission has presented its first annual report.[291]

More recently, cooperation with third countries has been also viewed with a broader lens. The Commission issued a Communication regarding external relations and in particular development issues.[292] The Communication endeavoured to put migration policy back in its broader context taking into account the driving forces of international migration and discussing issues such as push and pull factors and brain drain. After providing a useful overview of migration policy issues that are already integrated in Community external cooperation programmes and policies, the Commission attempted to identify possible policy developments, such as including the migration component in the mid-term review of country strategy papers, putting systematically the migration-development nexus on the agenda of the Union's political dialogue or seeing readmission agreements as part of a broader cooperation agenda which takes due account of the problems encountered by partner countries in seeking to effectively address migration issues. While the Commission's Communication is to be welcomed, one could marshal a series of criticisms both as to the assumptions on which it is based as well as the quality and successful character of the proposed recommendations.[293]

291 Communication from the Commission to the Council on the monitoring and evaluation mechanism of the third countries in the field of the fight against illegal immigration, COM (2005) 352 final, 28.7.2005.

292 Communication from the Commission to the Council and the European Parliament "Integrating migration Issues in the European Union's relations with third countries: I. Migration and Development, II. Report on the effectiveness of financial resources available at Community level for repatriation of immigrants and rejected asylum seekers, for management of external borders and for asylum and migration projects in third countries", COM (2002) 703 final, 3.12.2002.

293 First in contrast to the Commission considering development as a factor diminishing emigration there are plausible grounds for arguing that economic development tends to promote rather than reduce migration pressure. See House of Lords, *A Community Immigration Policy, op.cit.*, at pt 43. For instance whilst many countries in Sub-Saharan Africa are among the most important recipients of development funds, they are not found among the highest migrant generating countries. See "Migration and Development: Preliminary observations by NGOs active in the migration, refugee protection and the development field on the European Commission's Communication on "Integrating Migration Issues in the European Union's Relations with Third Countries", COM (2002) 703 final of 3 December 2002 [paper provided by Caritas Europa, Brussels]. Moreover, while the Commission seems to neglect the impact of eventual pull factors, it has been argued that economic, social, political and demographic disparities alone do not cause migration. See Schulte B., "Implications of Labour Migration for Social Security Systems in European Countries – Activities of the Council of Europe", *EJML*, Vol. 4, Issue 4, 2002, p. 477-489. See also the discussion in Chapter 6 on the balance between legal and illegal migration.

The Council, after examining thoroughly the Communication within the framework of joint meetings of the High Level and the Development groups, has adopted Conclusions on migration and development.[294] The Council Conclusions try to strike a fair balance between migration and development interests and contain a series of short and mid-term policy measures for the Commission to follow, with a view to paving the way for an increasing synergy between migration and development cooperation. According to the Council, migration related assistance to third countries should be focused on strengthening capacity to manage migration. Moreover, it asked the Commission to further elaborate proposals on its suggestions on ways to regulate demand and supply and organise access of labour as well as to step up its efforts on readmission agreements. Finally, it also asked the Commission to present, following consultations with Member States, a comprehensive report to the Council that includes migration statistics and data as well as policy recommendations on further action in the field of migration and development by the second half of 2004. Indeed, the Commission has presented a second Communication on migration and development in September 2005.[295] This second Communication focuses on a number of specific topics that are associated primarily with South-North migration, such as remittances, circular migration and brain drain.

Meanwhile, the idea of establishing at the European level quotas for the entry of third country nationals has also been examined. The issue was debated during the informal JHA Council meeting of Rome in September 2003 under the Italian Presidency and proved to be rather controversial. After a heated debate within the Council, the European Council of Brussels recognised that each Member State is responsible for the number of legal immigrants admitted to its territory. It also took note of the Commission's initiation of a study not on the quota system specifically but on the more general issue of the relationship between legal and illegal immigration and invited Member States to cooperate fully with the Commission to this end.[296] The Commission presented a Communication on the matter in June 2004 which is limited to a fact-finding exercise conducted in cooperation with the Member States' experts.[297] The Communication is divided into three parts. The first two parts provide respectively an

294 Draft Council Conclusions on migration and development, Council doc. 8927/03 DEVGEN 59 RELEX 160 JAI 123 ASIM 25, 5.5.2003.

295 Communication from the Commission to the Council, the European Parliament, the European Economic and Social Committee and the Committee of the Regions Migration and Development: Some concrete orientations, COM (2005) 390 final, 1.9.2005.

296 Brussels European Council, 16 and 17 October 2003, Presidency Conclusions, pt 32.

297 Communication from the Commission to the Council, the European Parliament, the European Economic and Social Committee and the Committee of Regions

interesting overview of the existing national ways of managing migration and a rather limited examination of the impact of bilateral labour agreements, visa policy and cooperation with third countries on illegal migration flows. In the third part, the Commission provides a series of policy recommendations which are in essence limited to an overview of current policy developments and repetition of existing policy proposals for future action.

The external dimension of migration policy and cooperation with third countries remains high on the EU policy agenda within the framework of the Hague Programme as well.[298] Following an express request by the European Council the Council and the Commission have elaborated the EU Strategy for the external dimension of JHA, one of the key thematic objectives of which remains migration.[299] In parallel, special attention was paid to the need for a comprehensive approach to tackle migration issues, in particular in close cooperation with third countries. The matter was examined during the informal meeting of Heads of State and Government at Hampton Court on 27 October 2005. Subsequently the Commission has presented a Communication developing a list of priority actions for improving global migration, with a special focus on Africa and the Mediterranean region.[300] On the basis of this Communication the Council has adopted Council Conclusions, which also focused on Africa and the Mediterranean region.[301] Bearing in mind the increased migration pressure from North Africa, the enhanced efforts of the EU to develop cooperation with the Mediterranean and African countries and the focus on this region in related EU documents and initiatives is not a surprise.[302]

– Study on the links between legal and illegal migration, COM (2004) 412 final, 4.6.2004.

298 See Section 1.6 of the Hague Programme and Section 2.7 of the Hague Action Plan, *op.cit.*

299 See section 4 of the Hague Programme, *op.cit.;* Note from the Presidency on a Strategy for the External Dimension of JHA: Global Freedom, Security and Justice, *op.cit.* and Communication from the Commission A Strategy on the External Dimension of the Area of Freedom, Security and Justice, *op.cit.*

300 Communication from the Commission to the Council and the European Parliament Priority actions for responding to the challenges of migration: First follow-up to Hampton Court, *op.cit.*

301 Council Conclusions – Global approach to migration: Priority actions focusing on Africa and the Mediterranean, Council doc. 15744/05 ASIM 66 RELEX 761, 13.12.2005.

302 See Conclusions of the Brussels European Council on 16 and 17 June 2005; Communication from the Commission to the Council, the European Parliament and the European Economic and Social Committee EU Strategy for Africa: Towards a Euro-African pact to accelerate Africa's development, COM (2005) 489 final, 12.10.2005; Council Conclusions on Migration and External Relations, Council doc. 14769/05 ASIM 58 DEVGEN 228 RELEX 674, 21.11.2005 and the EU Strategy on Africa

4.3.2 Exchange of Data and Cooperation among Member States

Special emphasis was also placed on certain more practical issues of real importance for the successful implementation of a European migration policy, such as the exchange of information and operational cooperation among Member States.

First of all, the issue of exchange of statistics had been extensively discussed in the discussions for the EU return policy, since some preliminary discussions on the definitions of the Commission Green Book have shown clearly that the terms used were not always compatible. Moreover, all the actors involved recognised the need to collect and exchange liable statistics. In 2003 the Commission presented an Action Plan for the collection and analysis of Community statistics in the field of migration.[303] And in 2005 it has also presented a proposal for a Regulation on Community statistics on immigration and asylum.[304] Furthermore, following a Commission proposal the Council has decided to set up a new secure database containing statistics, the so-called Iconet.[305] Finally, following an express request from the Council the Commission has tabled a proposal on the establishment of a mutual information procedure.[306] More specifically, bearing in mind the indirect impact that asylum and migration measures taken by one Member State are likely to have on other Member States, this procedure would

---

adopted by the European Council at its meeting on 15 and 16 December 2005, The EU and Africa: Towards a Strategic Partnership, Council doc. 15961/05, 19.12.2005. Moreover, a strong migration strand has been included in the new Euromed five year work programme that was adopted in Barcelona during the Euromed Conference on 27 and 28 November 2005. See "EU/EUROMED: Barcelona Summit adopts code of conduct for fight against terrorism, five year working plan and "declaration of President", Bulletin Quotidien Europe No 9077, 29.11.2005, p. 3-4. Finally, special attention was put in enhancing cooperation with Libya. See Council Conclusions on initiating dialogue and cooperation with Libya on migration issues, Council doc. 9796/05 ASIM 24 RELEX 291 LIBYE 5, 6.6.2005.

303 Communication from the Commission to the Council and the European Parliament to present an Action Plan for the collection and analysis of Community Statistics in the field of migration, COM (2003) 179 final, 15.4.2003.

304 Proposal for a Regulation of the European Parliament and of the Council on Community statistics on migration and international protection, COM (2005) 375 final, 14.9.2005.

305 Council Decision 2005/267/EC of 16 March 2005 establishing a secure web-based Information and Coordination Network for Member States' Migration Management Services, OJ L 83/48, 1.4.2005. See also Proposal for a Council Decision Establishing a secure web-based Information and Coordination Network for Member States' Migration Management Services, COM (2003) 727 final, 25.11.2003.

306 Proposal for a Council Decision on the establishment of a mutual information procedure concerning Member States' measures in the areas of asylum and immigration, COM (2005) 480 final, 10.10.2005.

request Member States to communicate to the other Member States and to the Commission –through a web-based network run by the Commission- measures which they intent to take in the areas of migration and asylum and which are susceptible to have an impact on other Member States or on the Community as a whole.

At the same time, the idea of establishing a European Migration Observatory, which had already been launched in the past by the Commission, was extensively discussed. Following the invitation of the Laeken European Council to establish a "system for exchanging information on asylum, migration and countries of origin" the Commission launched, at the end of 2002, a preparatory action for the creation of a European Migration Network (EMN). The EMN provided for the establishment of a network of national focal points for exchanging and following up information relating to political, economic, demographic and social dimension of migratory phenomena and identifying their root causes. In the initial three-year pilot phase, which comes to an end in 2005, a network of focal points, which now includes nearly all Member States, has been set up. The Thessaloniki European Council endorsed the creation of the network and stated that it would "examine the possibility of creating a permanent structure in the future". The Commission initially announced its intention to put forward a legal basis for the Network's longer-term future.[307] However, at the end it chose to proceed in a much more prudent way by presenting a Green Paper on the future of the Network.[308]

Another issue that received major attention was the establishment of a network of Immigration Liaison Officers (ILO Network). On the basis of some preliminary Council Conclusions of May 2001 an ILO Network was initially established in the Western Balkans.[309] This operation was led by Belgium.[310] Subsequently, in June 2002 the Seville European Council asked for the establishment of a general ILO Network by the end of 2002.[311] In early June 2002, the Danish Presidency had already tabled a Presidency Note on the establishment of such

307 Vitorino Antonio, "What EU strategy for integrating migrants", *op.cit*.

308 Green Paper on the future of the European Migration Network, COM (2005) 606 final, 28.11.2005.

309 See Guidelines for the establishment of an EU Immigration Liaison Officers Network for the Western Balkans, annexed to the Press release of the Justice and Home Affairs Council meeting of 28 and 29 May 2001. For the text of the Conclusions see I/A Note – Adoption of Council conclusions concerning the creation of national immigration liaison officers to help control illegal migration flows through the Western Balkan region, Council doc. 8684/01 CIREFI 31 COMIX 344, 10.5.2001.

310 It was also included among the operations that were initiated within the framework of the Plan for the management of external borders.

311 Seville European Council, 19 and 20 June 2002, Presidency Conclusions, pt. 32.

a network, while identifying the third countries concerned.[312] On the basis of a questionnaire sent to the Member States, the Commission also prepared a report on the current level of cooperation between liaison officers in third countries. The Council then adopted Conclusions on the improvement of the ILO Network in November 2002,[313] as well as a Decision on the common use of liaison officers posted abroad.[314] The Greek Presidency has further promoted the issue by organising a special seminar, drafting a series of notes and emphasising the need for acceleration of works on the adoption of an appropriate legal instrument.[315] Finally, on the basis of a Greek initiative, the Council has adopted a Regulation establishing a network of liaison officers.[316]

4.3.3 Financing

Special attention has also been placed on the financial aspects of the relevant policies. Recognising the growing financial needs and the fact that they should match the increasing political ambitions of the Union in the area of JHA, the issue of financing was brought vigorously to the forefront of the EU agenda.

---

312 Presidency Note on the initiation of the creation of network of liaison officers envisaged by the Plan for the management of the external borders of the Member States of the European Union, Council doc. 10917/02 FRONT 69 CIREFI 42 COMIX 452, 11.7.2002. The following countries were identified: Russia, Turkey, Thailand, Pakistan, Albania, Hungary, Poland, Romania, Morocco, Nigeria, Colombia and China.

313 Council Conclusions on the improvement of the Immigration Liaison Officers Network, Council doc. 14464/02 CIREFI 69 FRONT 134 COMIX 659, 20.11.2002.

314 Council Decision 2003/170/JHA of 27 February 2003 on the common use of liaison officers posted abroad by the law enforcement agencies of the Member States, OJ L 67/27, 12.3.2003. The UK has recently tabled a proposal for the amendment of Council Decision 2003/170 in order to take account of current practice relating to the use by Member States of Europol liaison officers posted abroad. See Council Decision 2005/.../JHA of amending Decision 2003/170/JHA on the common use of liaison officers posted abroad by the law enforcement agencies of the Member States, OJ C 188/19, 2.8.2005.

315 Presidency Note on the establishment of ILO network in third countries, 7462/03 CIREFI 10 MIGR 20 COMIX 170, 14.3.2003.

316 Council Regulation (EC) No 377/2004 of 19 February 2004 on the creation of an immigration liaison officers network, OJ L 64/1, 2.3.2004. See also Initiative of the Hellenic Republic with a view to adopting a Council Regulation on the creation of an immigration liaison officers network, OJ C 140/12, 14.6.2003. Recently, the Commission adopted a Decision on the format of the report on the activities of liaison officers. See Commission Decision 2005/687/EC of 29 September 2005 on the format for the report on the activities of immigration liaison officers network and on the situation in the host country in matters relating to illegal migration, OJ L 264/8, 8.10.2005.

First of all, the Council adopted a new general financial instrument, the so-called "ARGO program".[317] However, given the limited possibilities for financing and the increasing needs, the issue was brought to the attention of the European Council itself. Thus, at the request of the Seville European Council the Commission prepared a Report on the financial aspects of JHA.[318] Having been extensively discussed at Council level,[319] the issue was further examined within the framework of a second Communication of the Commission and was taken up again at the European Council level at Thessaloniki.[320] There, it was decided to release a sum of 140 million euros for the period of 2004-2006, with the matter to be discussed further within the framework of the Community financial perspectives after 2006.[321]

Apart from the general debate regarding the financing perspectives of JHA matters, financing was examined within the framework of external relations as well. An annex to the Commission Communication on external relations provided a useful list of the amounts spent for JHA related issues within external relations policy. And, a new budgetary line was created in 2001 mainly in order to finance the projects handled by the High Level Working Group within the framework of the implementation of the relevant Action Plans, budget line B7-667. In 2004 a new programme for financial and technical assistance to third counties has been established, the so-called AENEAS.[322]

---

317 Council Decision 2002/463/EC, *op.cit.* This programme is for five years with a financial reference of 25 million euros. Recently, the Council has amended the initial ARGO Decision in order to make the programme more accessible to national administrations. See Council Decision 2004/867/EC of 13 December amending Decision 2002/463/EC adopting an action programme for administrative cooperation in the fields of external borders, visas, asylum and immigration (ARGO programme), OJ L 371/48, 18.12.2004.

318 Communication from the Commission to the Council and the European Parliament "Integrating migration Issues in the European Union's relations with third countries: I. Migration and Development, II. Report on the effectiveness of financial resources available at Community level for repatriation of immigrants and rejected asylum seekers, for management of external borders and for asylum and migration projects in third countries", COM (2002) 703 final, 3.12.2002.

319 On the basis of a Presidency Note prepared by the Greek Presidency. See Council doc. 6731/03 JAI 55 RELEX 75 ASIM 14 FIN 87, 24.2.2003.

320 See the relevant Commission Communication in view of Thessaloniki, *op.cit.*

321 Thessaloliki European Council, 20 and 21 June 2003, Presidency Conclusions, pts 22 and 23.

322 Regulation (EC) No 491/2004 of the European Parliament and of the Council of 10 March 2004 establishing a programme for financial and technical assistance to third countries in the areas of migration and asylum (AENEAS), OJ L 80/1, 18.3.2004. The first call for proposals (2004) was closed on 30 March 2005 and allowed the

Special funding was reserved with regard to integration policy as well. The first pilot projects on integration that the Commission is financing are funded by a new special budget line, line B5-815. And the Commission has announced its intention to provide a sum of 12 million euros over 3 years.[323]

In view of the extreme and disproportionate pressure under which certain Member States find themselves, mainly due to their geographical position, and following considerable pressure from the Member States concerned, the Council has also started examining the question of burden-sharing under a much more general spectrum.[324] The Commission in its May 2002 Communication on the management of external borders has supported the idea of financial and operational burden-sharing in the relevant area.[325] Subsequently, at the request of the Seville European Council the Commission prepared, on the basis of a questionnaire sent to the Member States, a study with regard to burden-sharing between the Member States and the Union concerning the management of external borders.[326] Following extensive discussions within the Council, the Commission identified four criteria to be taken into account in evaluating the burden of each Member State and gave an overview of the financial perspectives in the short and long-term.

Moreover, as mentioned earlier, the Council has adopted, at the request of the European Councils of Thessaloniki and Brussels, Conclusions on preparatory actions for a financial instrument for return management, while the Commission has set up a 30 million euros Framework Preparatory Action for Returns to run during 2005/2006.[327]

---

submission of 83 projects. See Annex 1 of the 2005 Commission Communication on Migration and Development, *op.cit.*

323 See Communication of the Commission on immigration, integration and employment, *op.cit.*, at p. 34-35. A funding programme for preparatory actions promoting integration, the so-called INTI, was established in that regard. It amounted to 6 million euros for 2004. See 'INTI – Integration of third country nationals', <http://europa.eu.int/comm/justice_home/funding/inti/funding_inti_en.htm>.

324 This issue was previously examined almost exclusively with regard to displaced persons and refugees.

325 See Report on the effectiveness of financial resources available at Community level for repatriation of immigrants and rejected asylum seekers, for management of external borders and for asylum and migration projects in third countries", COM (2002) 703 final, *op.cit.* and Communication of the Commission on the integrated management of the external borders of the EU, *op.cit.*, at pts 45-46.

326 Communication of the Commission in view of the European Council of Thessaloniki, *op.cit.*, at p. 14-16.

327 See Council Conclusions on elements for establishing preparatory actions for a financial instrument for return management in the area of migration, *op.cit.*. See also Presidency Note – Implementing Decision on the shared organisation of joint flights for removals, from the territory of two or more Member States, of third

Additionally, one should not ignore that a major part of financing in JHA has been directed at the acceding countries. It is estimated that between 1997 and 2001 356 million euros were given to acceding countries within the framework of the pre-accession strategy under the National Phare Programmes.[328] Moreover, 970 million euros will be also granted to the acceding States for the period 2004-2006, under the so-called "Schengen facility" initiative, in order to help them put in place the necessary prerequisites for fully participating in Schengen.[329]

As a final note, one needs to underline the radical increase of the EU budget in this area within the framework of the EU's 2007-2013 financial perspectives. Matters related to the area of freedom security and justice are now gathered under a separate heading -Heading 3- of the new financial perspectives. Migration policy related matters constitute one of the main thematic areas for external relations thematic programmes.[330] And, last but not least, the Commission has presented legal instruments for the establishment of four Funds concerning respectively refugees, borders, integration and return policy.[331]

---

country nationals who are subject of individual removal orders, *op.cit.*, and "EU agrees fund for return of illegal immigrants", <www.euobserver.com> 23.1.2004.

328 See Commission Report of the effectiveness of financial resources available at Community level, *op. cit*, at p. 39. According to Pastore the amount allocated within the PHARE programme for activities in the JHA sector is 541 million euros. See Pastore F., "Visas, Borders, Immigration: Formation, Structure and Current Evolution of the Entry Control System", *op.cit.*, at p. 135. For a detailed list of funding allocated per country within the framework of the PHARE programme in the period 1997-1999 see De Lobkowicz W., "La perspective de l'élargissement dans le domaine de la Justice et des Affaires intérieures", in Marinho C. (ed), *Asylum, Immigration and Schengen Post-Amsterdam – A First Assessment,* EIPA, Maastricht, 2001, p. 107-118.

329 See the general Commission Communication on the development of a common policy on illegal migration, external borders and return submitted to the European Council of Thessaloniki, *op. cit.*, at p. 18.

330 Communication from the Commission to the Council and the European Parliament – External Actions through Thematic Programmes under the Future Financial Perspectives 2007-2013, COM (2005) 324 final, 3.8.2005.

331 Communication from the Commission to the Council and the European Parliament establishing a framework programme on Solidarity and the Management of Migration Flows for the period 2007-2013

- Proposal for a Decision of the European Parliament and the Council establishing the European Refugee Fund for the period 2008-2013 as part of the General programme 'Solidarity and Management of Migration Flows'
- Proposal for a Council Decision establishing the European Fund for the Integration of third-country nationals for the period 2007-2013 as part of the General programme 'Solidarity and Management of Migration Flows'
- Proposal for a Decision of the European Parliament and Council establishing the European Return Fund for the period 2007-2013 as part of the General

Concluding Remarks

Having briefly presented the major legislative developments and policy themes on which discussions were focused in the post-Amsterdam era, it becomes crystal-clear that the position of migration among the major EU policies and objectives has now been cemented. That said, one cannot fail to recognise the evident similarities between the pre and post-Amsterdam era with regard to the general policy themes and the vast majority of the specific legislative developments and also the fact that post-Amsterdam developments seem to fall short of the indisputably ambitious Tampere milestones. The legislative texts seem to limit themselves to a crystallisation of the Schegnen and Maastricht *acquis*, the policy is evidently unbalanced towards flanking measures and developments on legal migration do not manage to live up to the public's expectations post-Tampere. But putting the criticism of this first stage of policy-making to one side, it needs to be recognised that both the Amsterdam Treaty and the subsequent Tampere conclusions signal a new era with respect to migration policy. Migration policy has undoubtedly been brought into the European policy sphere, though it is still facing many of its infancy diseases.

---

programme 'Solidarity and Management of Migration Flows', COM (2005) 123 final/2, 2.5.2005.

PART III: Policy-making in Migration

Chapter 5: Policy-Making in Migration (Part I): The Role of Different Actors

Introduction

Developments regarding Europe's nascent migration law cannot be fully understood unless the role of different policy actors is examined. Accordingly this chapter provides an analysis of the day-to-day institutional practice in the area of migration and draws upon elements of "political sociology".[1]

A general analysis of the role of different EU policy actors is beyond the scope of this book. There have already been various excellent pieces of work in that respect.[2] The aim of the present work is rather to provide a comprehensive examination of the impact of the position of the various actors with respect to policy-making in migration. The analysis herein will adopt a two-prong approach. Firstly, on the basis of the general institutional features of the relevant actors it will evaluate and analyse their interaction with regard to migration issues. Secondly, it will endeavour to highlight any eventual specific interests, goals and weaknesses as well as their negotiating weight in the said area. The approach taken is pragmatic and practice oriented. The analysis is based on Treaty provisions and official documents, emphasis is however placed on the everyday practice as well as on certain factors and practices that are rather informal and in principle intentionally un-codified.[3]

---

1 The term "political sociology" is used by Guiraudon. See Guiraudon V., "The constitution of a European immigration policy domain: a political sociology approach", *Journal of European Public Policy*, Vol. 10:2, April 2003, p. 263-282.

2 See Nugent N., *The European Commission,* Palgrave, Hampshire, 2001; Hayes-Renshaw F. and Wallace H., *The Council of Ministers,* MacMillan Press, London, 1997; Cini M., *European Union Politics,* Oxford University Press, Oxford, 2003; Wallace H. and Wallace W. (eds.), *Policy-Making in the European Union*, Oxford University Press, Oxford, 2000, and, Hix S., *The political system of the European Union*, MacMillan Press, London, 1999.

3 It has been correctly highlighted with regard to the role and functions of the Council that there is an intentional effort to not formalise key aspects of the Council's

The chapter divides into four main sections. These examine respectively the role of the four institutions that are currently implicated in the policy-making process with regard to migration, namely the Council, the Commission, the Parliament and the Court. Given the varying impact of the relevant institutions on policy-making, the four parts are not equally balanced in terms of length. The biggest part of the analysis will be devoted to the Council and the Commission, since these are the main policy actors, at least as things stand.

The first section will examine the role of the Council, which one could say has for several decades been, and to a certain extent still remains, the predominant actor. Firstly, it will highlight the role of the various sub-actors that are involved in policy-making within the Council itself. Whilst to the external observer the Council is frequently perceived as a unified actor, it is in reality sub-divided in to different sub-actors, which often have diverse characteristics and functions. Considering that the major sub-actors are the Member States, the Presidency, the Council Secretariat and the European Council, successive subsections will be devoted to each of them. The objective is to provide the reader with a pragmatic analysis of the decision-making process within the Council. The presentation will focus on two main issues: first, on certain practical aspects of the negotiation process, and second, on the impact of a series of other general background factors, i.e. factors not expressly stated and of a primarily political character.

The second section will examine the role of the Commission. First of all, an overview of the Commission's position within the framework of policy-making in migration is sketched. Emphasis is placed on the Commission's strategic choices in this field during the last two decades. Moreover, considering that a comprehensive examination and full understanding of the Commission's role requires more than a black letter analysis of Treaty provisions and official texts, the analysis seeks to bring into light some additional aspects that highlight some of the Commission's hidden strong points or weaknesses.

The last two sections will examine briefly the roles of the European Parliament and the Court of Justice. Given the institutionally, but also *de facto*, limited role of these two actors until now, the analysis will unavoidably be rather limited. Inasmuch as the Parliament is concerned, a brief overview of its activi-

rules and that some of the most significant powers of the Council have an informal footing. Lewis J., "Informal integration and the supranational construction of the Council", *Journal of European Public Policy*, Vol. 10:6, December 2003, p. 996-1019.

While sharing the above comments, I would add that up to a certain degree the entire negotiation process is much more informal, pragmatic and political than it might seem to the external observer. Thus, much of the information included is based on interviews as well as on my personal experience with the everyday functioning of the Council and the interaction among the various EU actors in this area.

ties and negotiating position will be presented with the emphasis on its limited role, at least until the passage to the co-decision procedure. The analysis of the Court's role will be even more limited and to a certain degree speculative, since it is based exclusively on an overview of the few judgments already delivered and speculation as to the role the Court might play.

5.1 The Council: The Key Actor

5.1.1 The Council's Many Faces

5.1.1.1 Member States: Identifying the Main Policy Concerns and Actors

Given the Council's deeply national character – since the Council has been created and organised in such a way as to ensure a specifically national, as opposed to supranational, input to EU affairs – to most observers it is the Member States.[4] Indeed, notwithstanding the reference to an ever closer union among the 'peoples of Europe' and not between Member States, the EC policy-making system is constructed in a way that makes it crystal clear that the Member States are at the heart of the Community.

Additionally, to the extent that migration related issues are concerned Member States have always managed to secure their central role as well as to reserve a predominant position in that area. Initially they were cooperating exclusively at intergovernmental level and under the Maastricht Treaty's third pillar their role was almost exclusive. Even under the Amsterdam Treaty's communitarised framework the role of the Member States remained for several years predominant.[5] Both the shared right of initiative and the unanimity rule facilitated the securing of their vital interests, be they individual or collective. Therefore, one could argue that this reinforced institutional role of Member States also renders them to a large extent co-responsible, if not primarily responsible, since they cannot hide themselves behind the choices or the inactivity of the Commission inasmuch as the formation of Europe's migration law and policy are concerned.[6]

While up to a certain extent Member States share similar interests and concerns, their positions and negotiating weight are at the same time deeply varying. The analysis herein will be centred around these two main themes: on the

4 The Council's national character is rightly highlighted by Hayes-Renshaw and Wallace. See Hayes-Renshaw and Wallace, *op.cit.*, at p. 211.

5 Meaning until, on the one hand, the reacquisition of the right of initiative by the Commission after the lapse of the five-year transitory period, and on the other hand, the recent passage to the co-decision procedure and the qualified majority voting rule for the vast majority of matters falling under Title IV TEC. This is still the case inasmuch as measures in the field of legal migration are concerned. See discussion on the passage to the co-decision procedure *supra* at 2.3.1.

6 De Lobkowicz W., *L'Europe et la sécurité intérieure Une élaboration par étapes, op.cit.*, at p. 52.

one hand, the main policy concerns of the Member States, and on the other, the identification of the most influential States and their eventually diverging interests and positions.

5.1.1.1.1 Main Policy Concerns and Trends

It is true that in general Member States have a strong interest in cooperating, however, one should not forget that the entry and residence of foreigners in each Member State's national territory is primarily perceived as a sovereign right, the exercise of which is based on principally national economic, social and political considerations.[7] This could in fact be considered as the common denominator, which explains, to a certain degree, Member States' actions and reactions to the process of forging a common policy at the EU level. Under these premises, despite the sometimes diverging interests and clashes among them, one could undoubtedly distinguish a series of common policy concerns guiding Member States' policy actions and options at the EU level.

First of all, there is an indisputable preference for intergovernmentalism and 'flexible solutions'. At every stage of policy-making with regard to migration policy, Member States have clearly shown their dislike for rigid legal frameworks and their preference for flexible solutions that would allow them to 'keep their hands free'. This was initially facilitated by the lack of any legal bases with regard to migration in the Treaty of Rome. Nonetheless, it soon became clear that the continuous 'lack' of Community legal bases and competence was a conscious policy option of Member States. The legal action against the Commission in the 1980s, the reluctance to attribute competence to the Community via the subsequent Treaty amendments and the unwillingness to adopt any binding legal instruments on migration policy are to a certain extent revealing of a Member State preference for intergovernmental cooperation.[8]

One might have expected this stage to have been overcome as a result of the Amsterdam Treaty establishing a Community competence on migration. Member States, however, continued to act *à l' intergovernmentale*. It is indicative that even during the time of euro-euphoria of 1998 and 1999 – when the JHA Council had issued the Vienna Action Plan extending the five-year deadline to issues regarding legal migration and the Heads of State delivered the Tampere

7 It needs to be underscored that whereas the principle of admission of own nationals is well established within the framework of international law, States are free to decide whom to admit inasmuch as third country nationals are concerned, within of course the limits set by international law regarding specific cases of a mainly humanitarian character such as refugees and family members. See Guild E., *Immigration Law in the European Community, op.cit.*, at p. 1-2, and De Ceuster, *op.cit.*

8 Obviously this is only one of the factors since the lack of any Community action was initially also due to certain Member States – notably the UK and Denmark – refusing to cooperate under a Community framework.

milestones- Member States had already safeguarded their turf via the various legal safety nets inserted into the Treaty of Amsterdam and some of them had also officially taken a restrictive position.[9]

Subsequently, even within the framework of the implementation of the Tampere agenda Member States constantly exhibited a clear preference, on the one hand, for soft-law documents, such as Conclusions and operational plans, and on the other, for rather open-ended and vague drafting inasmuch as legislative measures are concerned. Additionally, one could identify a more general reluctance in bringing issues under Community competence. Despite the communitarisation of the main aspects of migration policy the competence debate does not seem to have ended. Subsidiarity is generally considered one of the central guiding principles of the Council's action with regard to JHA matters.[10] There is still an obvious, though not always expressly stated, position that certain issues – such as the number of immigrants admitted mainly for work purposes- should remain exclusively within the national sphere. The abolition of the reference to the case of admission for employment purposes in the respective Treaty provision during the Amsterdam IGC,[11] the freezing of the relevant Commission proposal after the completion of the first reading and the inclusion of a specific provision clarifying that the number of migrants admitted for employment purposes fall under the competence of the Member States in the Draft Constitutional Treaty[12] are some examples that show clearly the Council's position on the matter. It is worth highlighting that the question of access to employment proved so sensitive for certain delegations, primarily the German, that they were willing to block the adoption of an entire Directive and to reopen a text on which a political agreement was reached.[13] And the Council was further

9 See the legal analysis of the relevant provisions in Chapter 2 and in particular the position taken by Germany.

10 According to the Vienna Action Plan EU action should be based on the following principles: subsidiarity, solidarity, operational efficiency, responsibility for safeguarding of internal security resting with the Member States and realistic approach. See Part II.A of the Vienna Action Plan, *op.cit.*

11 See Article K.1 (3) of the Maastricht Treaty as compared with Article 63 (3) (a) of the Amsterdam Treaty.

12 Article III-257 (5) of the Draft Constitutional Treaty.

13 More specifically Germany has reopened negotiations on the text of the reception conditions Directive on which the Council had reached political agreement on April 2002. It took almost one year of further negotiations and the considerable watering down of the relevant provision for the Council to reach political agreement on the Directive. For more details see Peers S., "Key Legislative Developments on Migration in the European Union, *EJML*, Vol. 5, 2003, p. 387-410, at p. 388-389. See also Article 11 of Council Directive 2003/9/EC of 27 January 2003 laying down minimum standards for the reception of asylum seekers, OJ L 31/18, 6.2.2003.

compelled to examine the said issue with extreme cautiousness.[14] The limitations that were inserted took the following forms: they either blocked the access to the labour market for a certain period of time and/or made it conditional to an examination of the labour market and/or they created a principle of preference for EU citizens.[15]

The second main characteristic of Member States action is also linked with the alleged sensitivity and sovereignty implications of migration related issues. It consists of a certain rigidity, a secrecy obsession and mistrust by the Member States towards both the general public and the other national and EU actors. Confidentiality, sovereignty and sensitivity of the relevant issues are arguments that are quite often advanced by the Council. They were among the central arguments of the Council both within the framework of the migration policy case in the 1980s as well as within the comitology case in the post-Amsterdam era.[16] Moreover, it is worth highlighting the fact that instead of following the Scoreboards that the Commission prepared, as expressly requested by the Heads of State at Tampere, the Council usually adopts and follows its own Action Plans and Road-maps. Furthermore, inasmuch as the involvement of the European Parliament and the general public are concerned, given the sensitivity of migration related issues as well as the strong security tradition developed within and inherited by the Schengen era, Member States tend to adopt a rather secretive approach during negotiations. Documents are only partly accessible and usually only after the Council has reached political agreement. A lack of mutual trust among the Member States also seems to exist.[17]

---

14 As illustrated in the analysis of the relevant provisions in Chapter 4 a series of safeguard clauses regarding the issue of access to employment have been inserted in all the legal migration Directives and the paid employment Directive was frozen. See *supra* at 4.2.1.

15 See Article 11 (1), (2) and (4) of the reception conditions Directive, *op.cit.*; Article 12 of the temporary protection Directive, *op.cit.*; Article 14 (2) of the family reunification Directive, *op.cit.*; Articles 11 (3) and 14 (3) of the long-term residents Directive, *op.cit.*; Article 17 (1), (3) and (4) of the student's Directive, *op.cit.* and Article 6 (1) of the Commission proposal for a Directive on paid employment. On this point see Brinkmann G., "The Immigration and Asylum Agenda", *op.cit.*, at p. 188.

16 Joined cases C-281, 283 to 285 and 287/85, *Germany and Others v Commission of the European Communities, op.cit.* and case C-257/01, *Commission v Council*, pending. See Opinion of the Advocate General Léger delivered on 27 April 2004. For discussion see respectively Chapter 1 at 1.1.2 and Chapter 2 at 2.2.3.

17 See for instance the difficulties faced as to abolition of border controls within the framework of Schengen, *supra* at 3.3, and the disapproval of some Member States of certain decisions of their partners at national level, i.e. regularisation processes, *infra* at 6.1.1.4. Nonetheless, on certain occasions this lack of trust might be explained by the lack of Community legislation on issues that are interlinked, i.e. definition of public order clause, admission conditions.

Thirdly, Member States usually adopt a rather pragmatic and security oriented approach. Solidarity, operational efficiency and realism have been placed expressly among the guiding principles of EU action in the post Amsterdam era.[18] Moreover, the impact of the Schengen system is strong. In this respect one could highlight the relevant Declarations attached to the Amsterdam Treaty, the maintenance of the Schengen evaluation system as well as the safeguard clauses included within the accession Treaties.[19] There is also an undeniable preference to deal with illegal migration and to adopt measures of a primarily operational character. An overview of Member State initiatives in the post-Amsterdam era reveals a clear preference for compensatory measures. In fact, Member States have traditionally opted for maximised cooperation in illegal migration, but for national competence with regard to legal migration.

Finally, inasmuch as legal migration measures are concerned, Member States, at least a considerable part of them, usually tend to adopt a cautious and rather restrictive approach. In the Maastricht era there was an obvious trend for limitations of admission both at national and European level. However, avoiding the creation of "pull factors" remains a major concern even in the post-Amsterdam era. An overview of the amendments brought by the Council to the relevant Commission legislative proposals provides clear evidence of this. The Council systematically renders the requirements for admission and residence a great deal stricter.[20] It has also been remarkably reluctant to recognise equal treatment inasmuch as social rights and benefits are concerned to immigrants[21] and has further erected a wall between the entry and residence of third country nationals and the possibility of recourse to the non-discrimination principle.[22] Somewhat revealing in this respect is the fact that migratory pressures have led to the redefinition of the criteria for entitlement for social rights at national

18 See the list of principles enumerated in the Vienna Action Plan, *op.cit.*

19 For the Declarations attached to the Amsterdam Treaty see *supra* at 2.1.2.2 and 2.2.2; whereas for the safeguard clauses in the accession Treaties see De Lobkowicz W., "La sécurité intérieure de l'Union européenne élargie" in De Kerchove G. and Weyembergh A. (eds.) *Sécurité et justice: enjeu de la politique extérieure de l'Union européenne*, Institut d'Etudes Européennes, Editions de l'Université de Bruxelles, Bruxelles, 2003, p. 31-65, at p. 47.

20 See the analysis on the post-Amsterdam legal admission Directives *supra* at 4.2.1.

21 The considerable watering down of the relevant provision of the long-term residents Directive (Article 11) is revealing.

22 More specifically, issues regarding the entry, admission and movement of third country nationals are excluded from the scope of the Directive on racial discrimination. See Article 3 (2) of Directive 2000/43/EC, *op.cit.* See also Cahn C., "Racial Preference, Racial Exclusion : Administrative Efforts to Enforce the Separation of Roma and Non-Roma in Europe through Migration Controls", *EJML*, Vol. 5, 2004, p. 479-490, at p. 488-489.

level,[23] and that yet few Member States have signed and ratified the Code of Social Security and the relevant Protocols and Conventions of the Council of Europe.[24] Therefore, the existence of a Declaration seeking to protect the fundamental aspects of social security systems in the Draft Constitutional Treaty does not come as a surprise.[25]

One could argue that most of the conclusions drawn above represent merely the position of only a part of the Member States. This is in fact correct, in particular with regard to legal migration issues. Nonetheless, these conclusions are drawn on the basis of the outcome of negotiations at Council level, even if this outcome is simply the lowest common denominator due to the unanimity rule imposing the need to reach consensus.

5.1.1.1.2 The Role of Specific Member States

Despite the undeniable existence of common policy concerns and interests, which function as strong links bonding the Member States, one could also identify a series of different approaches, sub-groups or individual Members States that either marshal special interests or undoubtedly play a leading role.

In the course of the first decades of EU policy-making in migration and up to Amsterdam, the United Kingdom undoubtedly played a leading role. The occasions on which progress with regard to migration related issues had been blocked due to British opposition have been numerous. The quite diverse approach of British policy -consisting mainly in the lack of identity cards and the island mentality- as well as its strong attachment to sovereignty and to a certain degree a mistrust of its partners, led the UK to block a series of proposals and Treaty amendments in that regard. For example, when the Monti package was presented the UK immediately announced its intention to block it,[26] and even its initiative to establish an Ad Hoc Group for Immigration under its Presi-

23 In Germany for example increased migration has prompted a rethink of the status of '*Aussiedler*' (ethnic German). See Geddes A., *Immigration and European Integration – Towards fortress Europe?,* Manchester University Press, Manchester, 2000, at p. 154.

24 For an overview see Schulte B., "Implications of Labour Migration for Social Security Systems in European Countries – Activities of the Council of Europe", *op.cit.* Schulte also presents the reactions of the Member States to the Council of Europe Conventions. While in some cases these influence legislation and policy despite the lack of ratification, in others the interpretation has been rather restrictive. Moreover, as Guild highlights none of the Member States have ratified the 1990 United Nations Convention on the protection of the rights of all migrant workers and only ten Member States have ratified the 1977 Council of Europe Convention on the Legal Status of Migrant Workers. Guild E., *Immigration Law in the European Community, op.cit.*, at p. 10.

25 Declaration regarding Article III-136 and Article III-267. See *supra* at 2.3.2.

26 See Guild E., *Immigration Law in the European Community, op.cit.*, at p. 228.

dency in 1986 was considered a UK attempt to safeguard the intergovernmental character of the cooperation. The same dislike towards cooperation at the Community level was also somewhat characteristic of Denmark's position as well, even if the Danish concerns are in a way different from the British concerns.[27] The opt-out Protocols of the Amsterdam Treaty manage to put an end to the Union being held hostage by the British and Danish positions, albeit at the price of creating a rather complex decision-making mechanism. Interestingly enough, in contrast to their exclusionary position in the past, nowadays the UK, Ireland and Denmark are keen to be associated.[28]

Secondly, the more general political negotiating weight of specific Member States as well as the number of immigrants present in the national territory are also important factors with regard to the position that Member States take and their negotiating power as to European integration in migration policy. Therefore, as one would have expected, France and Germany are amongst the leading players in the migration field.[29] However, in contrast to other areas of EU law, the Franco-German axis does not really seem to function in the sphere of migration policy. At least, when it comes to aspects of legal migration the position of the two States seem to be rather diverse. Whereas Germany takes a considerably restrictive approach, France in principle aligns itself with those Member States that are taking a much more liberal approach.[30] In contrast to France, which seems to have a much more balanced and coherent position, the German position was to a certain extent rather contradictory. For example, whereas in 1985 Germany was one of the leading countries within the framework of the Schengen initiative, at the same time it headed the 'coalition' of the five Member States that attacked the Commission for taking relevant initiatives within the EEC framework.[31] And though it was the leading country advocating the communi-

---

27 For an analysis of the Protocols and the national positions of the Member States concerned see *supra* at 2.1.1.1.

28 See for example the willingness of the UK to be associated in the Border Agency, VIS and other biometric data related projects and the attempts to associate Denmark to readmission policy and the Dublin system. See the discussion *supra* at 2.2.1.

29 See the relevant table regarding statistics on migration for 1985, 1990, 1995 and 1998 in De Lobkowicz W., *L'Europe et la sécurité intérieure Une élaboration par étapes, op.cit.*, at p. 126. Moreover, one should not lose sight of the fact that German concern and anxieties have been a key factor for the development of a common policy with regard to migration. See Den Boer M. and Wallace W., "Justice and Home Affairs – Integration through Incrementalism?" in Wallace H. and Wallace W. (eds.), *Policy-Making in the European Union*, Oxford University Press, 2000, p. 493-519, at p. 496.

30 See Mariani, *op.cit.*, at p. 20-21.

31 See the migration policy case, discussed *supra* at 1.1.2.

tarisation of the relevant areas during the Maastricht IGC, by the Amsterdam and Nice IGCs it was one of the countries objecting strongly to the attribution of the relevant competence to the Community and effectively blocked the introduction of a qualified majority voting rule in the area of migration.[32]

In contrast to the more eurosceptic attitudes of certain Member States there is also a core of States taking a more European stand, among which the Benelux club is rather predominant. It is worth recalling that during the Amsterdam IGC, the Benelux countries issued a joint memorandum in which they adopted the strongest pro-integration stance and called for the supranationalisation of migration, the incorporation of Schengen and the inclusion of provisions on the protection of civil, social and political rights regardless of racial origins.[33]

Certain Member States also have special links, and share common problems and concerns mainly due to geographical reasons. Apart from those which already have long-standing cooperation, such as the Benelux countries, the Nordics and the UK and Ireland,[34] there has recently emerged what could effectively be seen as a coalition among the countries that are mainly in the southern outer frontiers of Europe: namely Spain, Italy and Greece. The three countries holding their presidencies almost consecutively strongly promoted issues such as the management of the external frontiers, the fight against illegal migration as well as the principle of solidarity, mainly in financial terms, with regard to the relevant issues.[35] Subsequently, and following the increasing migration pressure from Northern Africa as well as the tragic incidents in Ceuta and Melilla and the situation in Lampedusa, Malta and certain Greek islands, an extended informal Euro-Mediterranean circle of Member States has systematically promoted and actively supported initiatives regarding the fight against illegal migration, in par-

32 See Monar J., "Decision-making in the Area of Freedom, Security and Justice", in Arnull A. and Wincott D. (eds.), *Accountability and Legitimacy in the European Union*, Oxford University Press, Oxford, 2002, p. 63-80, at p. 66. During the Amsterdam IGC Germany's change of stance is considered the most decisive event during the negotiations. This opposition stemmed from the migratory pressures faced by Germany, the involvement of Länder competences for immigration, the 1998 federal elections and the desire of the centre-right coalition to take a tough line on immigration and asylum policy. See Geddes A., *Immigration and European Integration – Towards fortress Europe?, op.cit.*, at p. 117.

33 Geddes A., *Immigration and European Integration – Towards fortress Europe?, op.cit.*, at p. 117.

34 For a presentation of these three closer cooperation frameworks, i.e. Benelux, the Nordic Passport Union and the Common Travel Area see Handoll, *op.cit.*, at p. 53-56.

35 See the discussion in Chapter 4.

ticular in the Mediterranean region, and the enhancement of the cooperation with regard to the management of the sea borders.[36]

Last but not least, one should not lose sight of the emergence of certain new 'clubs' outside the framework of the Council whose establishment is prompted mainly by the concerns raised by terrorism and the difficulties in reaching consensus and progressing fast at the EU level. The predominant group among them seems to be the so-called 'G5' or 'Big Five' group.[37] It is an informal group established by the Interior Ministers of the UK, France, Spain, Italy and Germany. They have already met several times.[38] Their agenda follows closely the EU agenda and they seem to consider themselves a pioneer group.[39] They have launched rather ambitious initiatives such as the establishment of a *chef de fils* responsible for negotiating readmission agreements on behalf of the five.[40] More

---

36 See the discussion *supra* at 4.1.1, 4.1.2 and 4.3.1. More specifically, the initiatives taken with regard to maritime borders and the fight against illegal migration as well as those taken following the informal European Council at Hampton Court as to the Mediterranean region need to be mentioned. See also "Amnesty criticises Spain over Mellila", <www.euobserver.com>, 7.10.2005; "Migrant clashes expose EU shortcomings", <www.euobserver.com>, 4.10.2005; "Malta calls for EU help on illegal migration", <www.euobserver.com>, 11.7.2005; "EU leaders back Franco-Spanish migrant plan", <www.euobserver.com>, 28.10.2005 and "EU/INFORMAL SUMMIT/IMMIGRATION: Member States unanimously support Franco-Spanish project at Hampton Court – Franco Frattini continuous tour of Euro-Mediterranean capitals", Bulletin Quotidien Europe No 9059, 29.10.2005.

37 'L'elite europea si chiama g5', at invetati.org, 27.10.2003, <http://www.invetati.org/mailman/publi/borderzerolist/2003-October/000471.html>.

38 In Jerrez (Spain) in May 2003, in La Baule (France) in October 2003, in Garmisch-Partenkirchen (Germany) in February 2004, in Sheffield (UK) in July 2004, in Florence (Italy) in October 2004, in Paris (France) in May 2005 and in Evian (France) in July 2005. See 'EU: New 'G-5' group of Interior Ministers meet for second time in France', <http://statewatch.org/news/2003/oct/23g5.htm>,'Big five meet to discuss security issues' <www.euobserver.com>, 6.7.2004, and "G-5 meeting marked by immigration split", <www.euobserver.com>, 12.5.2005.

39 'Bilan des actions de coopération internationale', Audition du Ministre devant la Commission des Affaires étrangères de l'Assemblée Nationale sur les actions de cooperation internationale en matière de lutte contre le terrorism et l'immigration illégale, 11.2.2004, available at the website of the French Interior Ministry, <http://www.interieur.gouv.fr>; 'EU's "G5" discuss fight against terrorism, immigration', Euractive.com, 19.10.2003, <http://eubusiness.com/afp/031019103213.px2r95i4> and "Charter flights to deport illegal immigrants", <www.euobserver.com>, 6.7.2005.

40 'Les G5 prend des measures contre le terrorism et l'immigration clandestine', Le Monde.fr, 20.10.2003, <http//www.lemonde.fr> and 'Les propositions du G5 à la Baule: pour une meilleure sécurité en Europe', Press Release of the French Ministry of Interior, 22.10.2003, <http://www.interieur.gouv.fr>.

recently another club composed of the Benelux countries plus Austria and Germany focusing more on the anti-terror fight has emerged.[41] Could we talk about Schengen II or simply about the need of certain Ministers for '*affichage politique*'? Arguably it is rather early to be able to assess the depth of the political will of the pioneers to move further, the viability of these new 'clubs' as well as their eventual future list of members and agendas, especially in the post-enlargement era.[42]

5.1.1.2 The Presidency: A Source of Dynamism or Incoherence?

Given the loose character of the institutional framework with regard to, and the limited involvement of European institutions in, JHA, the role of the Presidency has been traditionally pivotal in this area. This was the case not only within the intergovernmental framework, but remains so within the EU framework as well. Beyond its customary role of agenda-shaping[43] and its *porte-parole* function *vis-à-vis* the rest of the EU institutions, third countries and other international organisations, the Presidency's role is much stronger in this area given that it has been the main drafter of the vast majority of Member States' initiatives.

The communitarisation of the relevant policies in Amsterdam has increased the weight of the EU institutions –initially mainly that of the Commission and subsequently, following the passage to the co-decision procedure, that of the Parliament as well- but it has not really diminished the power of the Presidency. The role of the Presidency remains vital given the extent and character of the competences and tasks attributed to it combined with the still predominant in certain respects role of the Council in general. Nonetheless, whilst recognising the focal character of the tasks of the Presidency one should not lose sight of the fact that the impact of its rotating character is both positive and negative and that there are real difficulties in keeping a balance between neutrality and national interests.[44]

41 'Five EU states move ahead on anti-terror fight', www.euobserver.com, 8.6.2004.

42 During a recent G5 meeting the French Minister, Mr Sarkozy, suggested extending the group and adding Poland to form a G6. See "Charter flights to deport illegal immigrants", <www.euobserver.com>, 6.7.2005.

43 For an analysis on the agenda-shaping role of the Presidency see Tallberg J., "The agenda-shaping powers of the EU Presidency", *Journal of European Public Policy*, Vol. 10:1, February 2003, p. 1-19.

44 The Presidency is supposed to be an actor distinct from the national delegation, which maintains its own place at the negotiation table and is supposed to defend the national position. However, the dividing line between the two is usually blurred. For an analysis of the balance between neutrality and its role as a policy actor promoting national interests, see Schout A., "The Presidency as Juggler – Managing Conflicting Expectations", Eipascope, No 1998/2, p. 2-10.

5.1.1.2.1 The Presidency's Positive Impact

Taking into account the importance that holding the EU Presidency for six months represents for each Member State, it is evident that the rotating character of the EU Presidency proves to be central to the Council's dynamism. In contrast to officials of the Commission and the Council for whom having a leading role in EU affairs becomes at some point a mere "job", national politicians, diplomats and bureaucrats are usually extremely fascinated and enthusiastic to find that the Union's decision-making process centres around them for six months. Moreover, they tend to invest their best efforts in order to achieve what is usually perceived as a national goal or challenge. Furthermore, it is worth highlighting that the right of initiative of the Member States was in principle exercised by the Presidency. In fact very few Member States, apart from those holding the Presidency, actually exercised their right of initiative.[45]

The rotating character of the EU Presidency can also prove beneficial for EU affairs in another respect: that is, in terms of achieving quicker progress. More specifically, it could be argued that Member States holding, or about to take over, the Presidency are more willing to lift their reservations under the pressure of getting results at the Council level or in order to avoid finding themselves in a rather embarrassing situation. The balance between a reservation on a concrete legislative proposal and the more general national interest of achieving a result on a major dossier obviously leans towards the latter, unless the relevant reservation is pivotal. It is interesting in that regard to highlight the lifting of a series of Greek reservations on the family reunification and long-term residents Directives under the Greek Presidency or the waiving of the Greek and Italian concerns with regard to the Dublin II Regulation at the very end of the Danish Presidency in late 2002.[46]

Finally, in the post-Amsterdam era the various Presidencies have launched general debates and a tradition of organising major Conferences has been established. One could mention, *inter alia,* the general debate on immigration launched following the presentation of the UN report and the several Conferences organised by the French Presidency,[47] the Ministerial Conference organ-

45 De Lobkowicz W., *L'Europe et la sécurité intérieure Une élaboration par étapes, op.cit.*, at p. 100.

46 For a list of the points of incompatibility between the Greek legislation and the Directives on family reunification and long-term residents and an analysis of the Greek position towards the Dublin Regulation see Naskou-Perraki P. and Papagianni G., "Migration and Asylum Law and Policy: National Report for Greece", in Higgins I. (ed.) and Hailbronner K. (General Rapporteur), *Migration and Asylum law and Policy in the European Union – FIDE 2004 National Reports*, Cambridge University Press, Cambridge, 2004, p. 135-160.

47 Apap J., "Shaping Europe's Migration Policy – New regimes for Employment of Third-Country Nationals: A Comparison of Strategies in Germany, Sweden, the

ised by the Belgian Presidency in October 2001 in view of the mid-term review of the Tampere programme,[48] the Danish Presidency conference on integration,[49] the Greek Presidency's general conference aiming primarily at restating the balance of the migration agenda[50] and the Ministerial Conference on integration organised by the Dutch Presidency in November 2004.[51] One needs further to underscore the contribution of the Presidency with regard to the establishment and evolution of the more general migration agenda through its shaping of the European Council agenda. One could mention in that respect apart from the eminent Tampere Summit, the Laeken, Seville, Thessaloniki and Brussels European Councils which have all extensively examined migration related issues as well as the November 2004 Brussels European Council which adopted the second multi-annual EU work programme in the area of freedom, security and justice, the well-known Hague Programme.[52]

5.1.1.2.2 The Presidency's Negative Impact

The impact of the Presidency can also be rather harmful, both in terms of coherence, comprehensiveness and effectiveness as well as from an inter-institutional balance perspective.

First of all, when one takes into account that for most Member States the Presidency is the best opportunity to promote their own national interests, its rotating character constitutes one of the reasons for a lack of consistency and coherence in EU policy-making. Moreover, in principle, the approach taken with regard to the initiatives tabled by the Presidency has been piecemeal. The reason for not tabling comprehensive and ambitious initiatives is two-fold. The Presidency lacks the necessary resources to draft wide-ranging legislative proposals and, in any case, is overly-concerned with achieving concrete results by the end of the six-month period in office. The Portuguese initiative on the free movement of third country nationals and the French initiatives on long-term visas and mutual recognition of expulsion decisions are representative of this sort of action.[53] In fact it is rather indicative that all of them have been rejected

---

Netherlands and the UK", *EJML*, Vol. 4, Issue 3, 2002, p. 309-328 at p. 314.

48 Held in Brussels on the 16 and 17 October 2001.

49 European Conference on Successful Integration on the Labour Market, Copenhagen 4-5 July 2002.

50 Greek Presidency's Conference on "Managing Migration for the Benefit of Europe", Athens 15 and 16 May 2003.

51 Held in Kroningen on the 9-11 November 2004.

52 For further information on the European Council Summits' role see *infra* at 5.1.1.4.

53 Initiative of the Portuguese Republic with a view to adopting a Council Regulation on the period during which third country nationals exempt from visa requirements are free to travel within the territory of the Member States, *op.cit.*; Initiative of

by the European Parliament and that the Commission has already presented proposals taking them on board.[54]

Furthermore, the dynamism of the Presidency, though generally beneficial, can not only be counter-productive, but can also disturb the decision-making process and the inter-institutional balance. Indeed, the lack of experience and in depth knowledge of the system on the part of the Presidency constitutes a major weakness. And, due to the eagerness of the Presidency to achieve agreement before the end of its term -since the relevant measure frequently serves national interests and there is the fear that the next Presidency will not promote the issue- there is often a palpable risk either of bringing matters to a higher level when these are not yet mature or of not consulting the European Parliament.[55] The case of the Italian initiative on joint flights is revealing.[56]

Last but not least, the impact of national internal coordination, which becomes paramount during the Presidency since its absence affects the functioning of the entire EU, should be taken into account.[57] Bearing in mind the wide-ranging character of migration related issues and the fact that the definition of a national position usually requires the prior consultation of a series of Ministries, it sometimes proves difficult for the Presidency to act in a swift and effective way, given that decisions often need to be taken almost on the spot. A lack of a clear predetermined position and internal coordination quite often delays considerably the decision-making process and creates confusion.

The abovementioned problems are relatively well known and the EU has already tried to find solutions. Thus, in order to overcome the problem of inconsistency among Presidencies, the rule of the multi-presidency programme has

---

the French Republic with a view to adopting a Council Regulation on freedom of movement with long-stay visa, *op.cit.* and Initiative of the French Republic with a view to adopting a Council Directive on mutual recognition of decisions on the expulsion of third country nationals, *op.cit.*

54 See the discussion *supra* at 2.2.3 and 4.1.

55 De Ceuster, *op.cit.*

56 Initiative of the Italian Republic with a view to adopting a Council decision on the organisation of joint flights for removals of third country nationals, *op.cit.* The Council has reached a general approach in record time without waiting for the opinion of the European Parliament. See Press Release of JHA Council meeting on the 6 November 2003. Finally, the decision was adopted without the opinion of the Parliament. See the discussion *supra* at 2.3.1.

57 Moreover, internal coordination during the Presidency has to take a different form, since there needs to be centralised coordination. And in many countries rivalries between Ministries increase during the course of the Presidency, since most Ministries do not like to be controlled by diplomats of Foreign Affairs, which usually takes the central coordinating role. On the need for a different type of coordination see Schout A., "The Presidency as Juggler – Managing Conflicting Expectations", *op.cit.*

been established and subsequent Presidencies are also requested to present a common annual operational programme.[58] Moreover, the EU institutions, mainly the Council Secretariat and the Commission, are to a certain degree compensating for the weaknesses of the Presidency.[59] It is worth highlighting that the problems linked with the working methods in JHA have also been examined at the initiative of the Presidency itself. In January 2001 the Swedish Presidency commenced a critical analysis on the Council's function in the JHA area, the so-called "Haga process", named after the Swedish castle where it began.[60]

5.1.1.2.3 The Council Secretariat: The Driving Force behind the Scenes

In contrast to the general perception that its work is mainly administrative – an impression that is often reinforced by the lack of codification of its real role-the Council Secretariat is one of the vital policy-making actors in JHA. While the vast majority of Council Secretariat staff are geared towards organising, facilitating and documenting Council meetings, there is a smaller inner circle of A-grade officials who are closely tied to EU policy-making and whose role is almost entirely informal and largely invisible to the outside world.[61] The special JHA Directorate General (DG H) was established after Maastricht and its role has been *de facto* strengthened given the growth of work under the third pillar and the limited role of the Commission. As a result the Council Secretariat is in general now considered much more of an actor in the policy process than hitherto.[62] The role of the Secretariat is rather strong at every stage and each level of the decision-making process as well as under every aspect of the more general policy-making process.

According to the relevant provision of the Council Rules of Procedure, the Secretariat is "closely and continually involved in organising, coordinating and ensuring the coherence of the Council's work and implementation of its annual programme" and "under the responsibility and the guidance of the Presidency,

58 Article 2 (4) and (5) of Council Decision 2004/338/EC of 22 March 2004 adopting the Council's Rules of Procedure, OJ L 106/22, 15.4.2004. See the operational programme of the Council submitted by the Greek and Italian Presidencies, Council doc. 15881/02 POLGEN 83, 20.12.2002. See also the Multi-Presidency programme on JHA external relations, Council doc. 11091/03, JAI 202 RELEX 269, 2.7.2003.

59 See *infra* 5.1.1.2.3 and 5.2.

60 See Council doc. 10336/01, JAI 66, 26.6.2001. Amongst the various issues examined within the framework of the "Haga process" it is worth mentioning the suggestions on the improvement with regard to the Member States initiatives, i.e. the need to follow the Council Legal Service guidelines, to consult other Member States and inform the Parliament in time. See Monar J., "Decision-making in the Area of Freedom, Security and Justice", *op.cit.*, at p. 72-74.

61 Lewis, *op.cit.*, at p. 1003-1005.

62 Wallace and Wallace, *op.cit.*, at p. 18.

it shall assist the latter in seeking solutions".[63] However, its role is much more vital than the modest drafting of this Article would seem to suggest. It is in practice deeply involved in the drafting of the vast majority of the documents that are circulated in the Council, a fact that does not always appear in the title of the document. The main types of documents prepared *ex officio* by the Secretariat are the outcome of proceedings of each meeting and the briefings for the chair at Coreper and Council level. However, the reality is that it is also quite often the co-author of a considerable number of the Presidency's notes, such as action programmes, draft Council Conclusions etc. Moreover, in practice most of the compromises presented officially by the Presidency originate from the Secretariat. To a certain extent the Secretariat has taken away from the Commission its honest-broker role and is considered a competitor of the Commission. Some Council officials estimate that upwards of ninety percent of all compromises originate from the pen of the Council Secretariat rather than the Presidency or the Commission.[64]

Additionally, the Council Legal Service, which is part of the Secretariat, plays a central role. Traditionally, its role is to review the legality of the measures that are examined by the Council and to defend it before the Court. But of late, and given the shared right of initiative and the obligation to publish Member States' initiatives, it has become more and more involved in the drafting process. First, it has issued a series of guidelines for the drafting of the relevant Member State's initiatives.[65] It has also vested the role of conducting a pre-screening of Member States initiatives, before these are officially submitted to the Council, a practice that has considerably improved their quality.[66] When account is taken of the Member States' natural mistrust towards the Commission's Legal Service –leading Member States to follow in principle the opinion of the Council Legal Service- and the comparatively limited legal knowledge of the Presidency and national delegates, the importance of the role of the Council Legal Service becomes evident.

In parallel, the Secretariat is involved in relations with other EU actors and its role is also strong with regard to external relations aspects. It briefs the Ministers chairing the Council before their appearances in front of the Parliament. The Secretary General may also represent, with the agreement of the Presidency, the Council before the Parliament or its committees.[67] The Secretariat is also

63 Article 23 (3) of Council Decision 2004/338/EC, *op.cit.*

64 Lewis, *op.cit.*, at p. 1004.

65 Guidelines of the Council Legal Service for Member States' initiatives within the framework of Title IV and Part II of the TEC and Title VI of the TEU, SN 3606/2/00, 26.10.2000.

66 See Article 22 as well as the statement concerning this Article, of Council Decision 2004/338/EC, *op.cit.*

67 Article 26 of Council Decision 2004/338/EC, *op.cit.*

deeply involved in the drafting of the Council's replies to European Parliament questions. Moreover, it keeps informal strong contacts with the Commission. Finally, it holds an official role in meetings with third countries and it also assists the Presidency with the organisation of coordinating meetings among Member States in order to formulate a common position prior to a meeting within the framework of international organisations, such as the Council of Europe.

In the light of the above it becomes clear that the Secretariat manages to a certain degree to counterbalance the disadvantages stemming from the rotation of the Presidencies. It manages to balance the lack of coherence among different Presidencies, by acting as a sort of historic memory of the Council and it counterbalances the inevitable lack of experience and know-how of the Presidency. It is thus usually considered 'the Presidency's best friend'.

Finally, the Secretariat has a more general policy-making role. Apart from the useful advice to the Presidency during the whole course of the latter's term in office, it is often also involved in the process of preparing the European Council Summit and the drafting of the relevant Conclusions.[68] It has been rightly highlighted that a very symbolic moment in the independent, supranational influence of the Secretary-General's office is the now famous "Trumpf-Piris Report", produced by a high-level working party of thirteen officials of the Secretariat and chaired by the then Secretary-General Jürgen Trumpf.[69]

68 Even if the European Council Conclusions are entitled 'Presidency Conclusions' the other EU actors – i.e. the Commission, the Council Secretariat, the Council of Ministers and its preparatory bodies- are, in principle, also actively involved in the drafting. Officially a draft of the 'Presidency Conclusions' is circulated to delegations only in the course of the European Council and is in principle adopted by consensus. However, while the Presidency has the sole responsibility for the final text and the issue is in principle dealt with at a very high political level – i.e. cabinet of Prime Minister- some parts have either been discussed in the Council preparatory bodies as part of Council Conclusions and others come directly from the pen of the Commission or the Secretariat. For the preparation of the European Councils of Tampere and Thessaloniki see respectively Elsen C., "L'esprit et les ambitions de Tampere: une ère nouvelle pour la coopération dans le domaine de la Justice et des Affaires Intérieures?", *RMC,* Issue 433, 1999, p. 659-663 and Elsen C., "Le Conseil européen de Thessalonique – Un nouveau pas vers une politique commune en matière d'asile d'immigration et de contrôle aux frontiers", *RMC,* Issue 471, 2004, p. 516-518.

69 Lewis, *op.cit.*, at p. 1005. The report makes over a hundred specific recommendations for Council reform in anticipation of Eastern enlargement and became the virtual blueprint for the relevant Declaration that was adopted at the 1999 Helsinki European Council. See Annex III of the Presidency Conclusions to the 1999 Helsinki Summit "An effective Council for an enlarged Union – Guidelines for reform and Operational Recommendations – which captures the letter and the spirit of the "Trumpf-Piris Report". For the text of the Report see Council doc. SN 2139/99.

5.1.1.2.4 The European Council: Political Impetus or Empty Promises?

In contrast to the Secretariat's rather veiled status, the European Council is a body with which the general observer is much more familiar. The Summits are usually the subject of major attention by the media. Nonetheless, the exact role, competences and functions of the European Council and particularly its position in the EU institutional structure are not fully comprehended.[70] It is not entirely clear whether it is the highest level in the Council hierarchy or a rather independent policy actor.

Given the principally intergovernmental characteristics of policy-making with regard to JHA matters, the role of the European Council has been vital. In fact, a vast part of developments in relation to migration policy have been initiated by the Heads of State themselves. The impact of the European Council on migration related issues can be examined from three angles: first, its impact on the formation of the more general policy agenda and goals; second, its impact on the institutional and legal framework; and, third, its direct involvement in the legislative process of the Council.

Firstly, defining the general political guidelines is the role traditionally attributed to the European Council.[71] Due to the lack of any concrete legal bases up to Maastricht, the Union's agenda on these issues was formed mainly at the European Council level and then implemented within a purely intergovernmental framework. Issues such as terrorism, external borders, integration of migrants and the fight against racism were dealt with following an express request of the European Council.[72] Subsequently, the European Council has through the practice of requesting reports and action plans not only kept close control but also geared the policy-making process within the Council.[73] While bearing in

70 For an interesting overview of the creation, role, strong points and weaknesses of the European Council see De Schoutheete P., "Forces et faiblesses du Conseil européen", in Vandersanden G. and de Walsch A. (eds.), *Mélanges en hommage à Jean-Victor Louis(Vol. I)*, Editions de l'Université de Bruxelles, Bruxelles, 2003, p. 109-118.

71 Article 4 TEC.

72 Cooperation against terrorism was the first issue that Heads of State decided to promote, during their 1975 meeting in Rome; the issue of integration of third country nationals was examined in the late 1990s when the European Councils of Hanover and Strasbourg asked for the preparation of reports; the Vienna Centre for Racism and Xenophobia was set up following a Franco-German initiative presented at the Corfu European Council in 1994; finally, the issue of external borders and burden sharing in return were promoted by the European Council itself within the scope of the work of the Coordinators Group and the implementation of the Palma document. For more details and references see Chapter 3.

73 One could mention, *inter alia*, the practice of annual reports on JHA in the Maastricht era that was established by the 1993 Brussels European Council – see Brussels European Council, 10-11 December 1993, Bull. EC 12-1993 –; the Vienna Action

mind that both the agenda and the documents examined and adopted by the European Council are prepared in principle by other policy actors,[74] it is worth highlighting that recently the instructions of the European Council towards not only the Council, but also towards the Commission have been so detailed that one could even argue that it is exercising agenda-setting functions. One could mention in that regard the specific call of the Feira European Council to the Commission and the incoming French Presidency to take forward the issues of smuggling,[75] and also the detailed lists of measures to be promoted and adopted that are included in the Conclusions of the European Councils of Seville, Thessaloniki and Brussels.[76]

The fact that the Heads of State have decided to draw the guidelines for the implementation of the Amsterdam Treaty themselves, in the framework of a special Summit convened for this purpose during the Finnish Presidency, the famous Tampere Summit, and have subsequently kept a close overview of its implementation reveals the political importance they were attributing to this operation. The Tampere Summit was the second thematic Summit in EU history.[77] The Council seems to have devoted a great deal of effort to the prepara-

---

Plan which was drafted at the request of the Cardiff European Council – Cardiff European Council, 15 and 16 June 1998, Presidency Conclusions; the Spanish Presidency Action Plan on illegal migration and return, which was drafted at the request of the Laeken European Council – see point 40 of the Laeken Conclusions; the report on the effectiveness of the financial resources that was drafted at the request of the Seville European Council; the European return program which was drafted at the request of the Seville European Council; the annual reports that the Thessaloniki European Council requested respectively on the monitoring of the evaluation mechanism and on integration policy – see points 21 and 33 of the Thessaloniki Presidency Conclusions; the report on readmission agreements that the Commission was asked to prepare by the Brussels European Council, see point 31 of the Conclusions of the Brussels European Council of 16 and 17 October 2003.

74 i.e. the JHA and the General Affairs Council, the Council Secretariat, the Commission, the Presidency as well as individual or groups of Member States. In fact, as will be argued later, the infrequent character of the European Council's meetings and its obvious dependence on the other actors present agenda-setting opportunities in particular for the Commission. See Nugent, *op.cit.*, at p. 118. See also *infra* at 5.2.2.1.

75 Santa Maria da Feira European Council, 19 and 20 June 2000, Presidency Conclusions.

76 See points 26-39 of the Seville European Council; points 8-35 of the Thessaloniki European Council; points 25-32 of the October 2003 Brussels European Council; points 17-23 of the December 2003 Brussels European Council; points 24-30 of the December 2004 European Council and points 7-10 as well as Annex 1 of the December 2005 European Council.

77 The first being the Summit on Employment in Luxembourg in 1997.

tion of the Tampere Conclusions. The Finnish Prime Minister Paavo Lipponen had already sent a letter to his colleagues in April 1999, followed by a tour of capitals in May and intensive discussions with other EU actors and NGOs.[78] The Scoreboard method – used in the case of the internal market – was employed.[79] The European Council has also kept constant control of the implementation process.[80] Moreover, it is certain that the role of the European Council will remain central in the coming years. In 2004 it adopted the new multi-annual programme, the well known Hague Programme, and it monitors closely its implementation,[81] while its institutional role in this area is further reinforced by the Draft Constitutional Treaty.[82]

Secondly, the European Council has also contributed to the development of a proper institutional structure in JHA. Initially, this contribution was structured on a rather *ad hoc* basis either via the setting up of a series of groups, which were given a concrete mandate or via the establishment of loose frameworks examining related issues. It was often the case that *ad hoc* groups would be developed to form part of a more coherent process. The Trevi group set up by the 1975 Rome Summit;[83] the *ad hoc* Committee for "people's Europe" established by the 1984 Fontainebleau Council;[84] the Ad Hoc Group for Immigration initi-

78 For a concise presentation of the preparation of the Tampere European Council see Eslen C., 'L'esprit et les ambitions de Tampere: une ère nouvelle pour la coopération dans le domaine de la Justice et des Affaires Intérieures?', *op.cit*. For a rather different overview of the preparations of Tampere see 'History of Tampere An Undemocratic process excluding civil society', *Statewatch*, Vol. 9, No 5, September-October 1999, p. 1-3.

79 See Elsen C., 'L'esprit et les ambitions de Tampere: une ère nouvelle pour la coopération dans le domaine de la Justice et des Affaires Intérieures?', *op.cit*. at p. 660. The Commission has presented in total eight versions of the Scoreboard and a final assessment of the Tampere programme. See respectively COM (2000) 167 final/2, 13.4.2000, COM (2000) 782 final, 30.11.2000, COM (2001) 278 final, 23.5.2001, COM (2001) 628 final, 30.10.2001, COM (2002) 261 final, 30.5.2002, COM (2002) 738 final, 16.12.2002, COM (2003) 291 final, 22.5.2003, COM (2003) 812 final, 30.12.2003 and COM (2004) 402 final, 2.6.2004 and SEC (2004) 680, 2.6.2004.

80 A mid-review Presidency report was submitted at the Laeken Council. The European Councils of Seville, Thessaloniki and the two Brussels European Summits during the Italian Presidency have proceeded to a detailed screening of the implementation of the timetable giving further detailed instructions to the Council.

81 See Conclusions of the November 2004 Brussels European Council as well as the Hague Programme, *op.cit.*

82 Article III-258 of the Draft Constitutional Treaty. See also the discussion *supra* at 2.3.2.

83 De Lobkowicz W., *L'Europe et la sécurité intérieure Une élaboration par étapes, op.cit.*, at p. 17-21 and 34-35.

84 Fontainebleau European Council, 25 and 26 June 1984, Bull. EC 6-1984.

ated under the British Presidency by the 1986 London Summit[85] and the Group of Coordinators set up by the 1988 Rhodes European Council[86] are examples of this institutional-forging aspect of the European Council. In addition to this, the European Council is the central body responsible for the negotiation of Treaty amendments. In the successive Treaty revisions of Maastricht, Amsterdam, and the last IGC, it was the Heads of State that finally decided upon the extent of competence attributed to the Community and/or Union as well as the form of the institutional structure and the role of the various European institutions in the decision-making process. In fact, it was also the Heads of State that, on the one hand, finally decided the passage to the co-decision procedure in November 2004,[87] and on the other hand, invited the Commission to submit a proposal on means to enable the Court to handle requests for preliminary rulings n the area of freedom, security and justice.[88]

Thirdly, the European Council frequently involves itself directly in the legislative process in the Council by providing the necessary political impetus. In fact, when major initiatives were blocked the Heads of States often proceeded to strong appeals to the relevant actors. Setting a deadline for the adoption of a concrete measure became one of the classic techniques used by the European Council to put pressure on the Council. The consecutive deadlines set for the adoption of the external borders draft Convention in the early 1990s[89] and more recently the Seville, Thessaloniki and Brussels European Council's deadlines for the adoption of the first two legal migration Directives or the deadlines for the measures regarding the management of the external borders could all be cited as examples.[90]

85 London European Council, 5 and 6 December 1986, Bull. EC 12-1986.

86 Rhodes European Council, 2 and 3 December 1988, Bull. EC 12-1988.

87 Despite the reluctance of Interior Ministers to proceed to the co-decision procedure at this stage. In fact the matter had been discussed during the October 2005 JHA Council, but the Ministers failed to agree on this. See point 15 of the Presidency Conclusions of the European Council of Brussels, 4-5 November 2004; point 1.2 of the Hague Programme, *op.cit.* as well as "EU asylum policy passed on to Summit", <www.euobserver.com>, 26.10.2005.

88 See point 3.1 of the Hague Programme, *op.cit.*

89 See Presidency Conclusions of the Strasbourg European Council, 8 and 9 December 1989, Bull. EC 12-1989; the Luxembourg European Council, 28 and 29 June 1991, Bull. EC 6-1991; the Essen European Council, 9 and 10 December 1994; the Cannes European Council, 26 and 27 June 1995; and the Madrid European Council, 15 and 16 December 1995.

90 See points 26-39 of the Seville European Council; points 8-35 of the Thessaloniki European Council; points 25-32 of the October 2003 Brussels European Council; and points 17-23 of the December 2003 Brussels European Council.

Nonetheless, the role of the European Council may not be in reality as 'positive' as it might seem. A comparative reading of the European Council Conclusions with a close examination of their follow-up leads to the conclusion that the Heads of State on certain occasions seem to limit themselves to merely a citizen-friendly general discourse while being rather cautious when they are supposed to deliver a proper follow-up.[91] In fact, there are two types of inconsistency that are not easy to explain. On the one hand, the inconsistencies between the positions taken in the European Council Conclusions and the position of Heads of State during the IGCs. And, on the other, the discrepancies between the Heads of State level and the working party and/or JHA Council level.

First of all, the very relationship between the European Council and the JHA Council is rather puzzling. The Council of General Affairs and the Foreign Ministers are obviously rather close to the Heads of State, however, this is not always the case for Interior Ministers and the officials of their Ministries. Treaty amendments are negotiated mainly by Foreign Ministers and Heads of State, whereas Interior Ministers are almost exclusively *a posteriori* called upon to implement.[92] In addition, quite often the Heads of State opt to be directly involved in the handling of certain files due to their cross-pillar character, such as external relations. One could mention the Declaration on the principles governing external aspects of migration policy attached to the Edinburgh European Council Conclusions,[93] the reports of the High Level Working Group submitted directly to the Nice European Council[94] and the establishment of the post-Amsterdam external relations agenda from the European Council itself at its

91 For instance Tampere has been accused of being inconsistent with EU practice which traditionally favoured security measures. According to Statewatch the main objective was to spin policies in such a way that passive citizens 'accept' and support what is being done in their name. See 'History of Tampere An Undemocratic process excluding civil society', *Statewatch*, *op.cit.* and 'Tampere: A victory for 'spin' over content?', *Statewatch*, Vol. 9, No 5, September-October 1999, p. 27-29.

92 According to Guiraudon the introduction of the Schengen Protocol, which constituted a source of major problems, was also due to the fact that the Amsterdam Treaty was negotiated by Ministries of Foreign Affairs who were not acutely concerned with the consequences of the Protocol, a task that their colleagues at Interior Ministries would have to undertake. See Guiraudon V., "European Integration and Migration Policy: Vertical Policy-making as a Venue Shopping", *Journal of Common Market Studies*, Vol. 38, No 2, 2000, p. 251-271, at p. 265.

93 See Annex 5 of Part of Edinburgh European Council, 11 and 12 December 1992, Bull. EC 12-1992. See also Handoll, *op.cit.*, at p. 360-361.

94 See the Presidency Conclusions of the Nice European Council, 7, 8 and 9 December 2000. For the text of the report see Council doc. 13993/00 + ADD 1 JAI 152 AG 76, 29.11.2000.

meetings, first, at Feira in June 2000, and more recently at Hampton Court and Brussels in autumn 2005.[95]

Furthermore, apart from the institutional disjunction between the two bodies there seems to be a rather puzzling difference of approach inasmuch as their substantive positions are concerned. The European Council in principle shows a rather positive attitude – though it has become harsher mainly in the aftermath of September 11[96] – and occasionally puts pressure on the JHA Council with regard to progress on legal migration issues. For its part, however, the JHA Council has traditionally shown a restrictive approach and a preference for security measures.

Eventually this difference in approach might be partly explained by the character of the texts examined and adopted by the two bodies. While the European Council Conclusions are political documents and are in principle drafted in a rather open-ended way –the classic example being the "as far as possible" formula of the Tampere Conslusions with regard to the equal treatment of migrants- the texts adopted by the JHA Council are primarily legally binding. Subsequently, it is in principle much easier to agree on aims and on broad worded 'milestones' or guidelines. However, it is a very different exercise to define the details – since abstract conclusions are always open to interpretation – and to examine and reach consensus on legal texts. Therefore, despite the very positive character of the discourse at European Council level, the difficulties in adopting decisions during every-day negotiations in the JHA Council bodies is often insurmountable. Nonetheless, this deep divergence of views and apparent lack of coherence is rather bizarre, especially if one considers the fact that the national delegates at working party level and the Ministers at Council level represent the government position and that the Heads of State have certainly some sort of control or authority over them. In the light of the above one could question the extent of the sincerity of the citizen-friendly discourse employed by the Heads of State.

95 See the Presidency Conclusions of the Santa Maria da Feira European Council, 19 and 20 June 2000, which approved the external relations program included in Council doc. 7653/00, *op.cit.* as well as the follow-up of the Hampton Court informal meeting of the European Council on 27 and 18 November 2005 and the Global Approach to Migration that was adopted by the December 2005 Brussels European Council. See discussion *supra* at 4.3.1.

96 In fact the Hague Programme has been criticised as giving excessive attention to security and sidelining freedom and justice. See House of Lords, *Evidence by Commissioner Franco Frattini, Commissioner for Justice, Freedom and Security on Justice and Home Affairs Matters, op.cit.* and Balzacq and Carrera, *op.cit.*

5.1.2 The Decision-making Process within the Council: From Theory to Practice

5.1.2.1 The Council Structure and Negotiation Stages

Negotiation within the Council is based on concrete written proposals – mainly of a legislative nature, but also of a more political or operational character- which are in principle submitted either by the Commission or by the Member States.[97] Whereas, in the case of the latter, reaching consensus does not really present a problem, due to their soft law and more operational and mainly political character, the former require thorough preparation and their negotiation often takes months or even years. Both types of documents are in principle mainly examined at the lower Council levels, the Ministers themselves eventually being involved at the later stages of the negotiations and focusing on the few pending reservations.[98] The agenda of each meeting at every level is set by the Presidency. Despite the *de jure* freedom of the Presidency as pertains to the setting of the agenda, it usually respects a more generally agreed work timetable, while obviously promoting its own initiatives and interests.

In principle, the first level to which new initiatives and legislative proposals are presented to, and first negotiated at, is the working party level. Nonetheless, it is worth highlighting that quite often certain issues and/or documents are mainly dealt with, or at least first presented to, higher levels of the Council hierarchy. The main reasons leading the initiators, usually the Presidency or the Commission or a group of Member States, to opt for this choice are two-fold. Firstly, the attempt to reach some sort of political consensus or 'test the waters' before coming up with a concrete legislative proposal that would eventually fail. Secondly, the legal and practical difficulties in transforming these new ideas, at least in the short-term, into legislative proposals due to the eventual lack of the necessary legal bases or to deep divergences of views among Council members. Thus, *fora* of a more political nature, such as the European Council or informal Council meetings or meetings of highly ranked Committees are usually the appropriate place for the launching of such ideas or initiatives. One could mention as examples of this top-down approach the new Borders Agency, the estab-

97 Quite often there are also other types of documents on the agenda, such as reports of special organs or international organisations or reports regarding developments at, or outcomes of, meetings usually held by the Presidency or the Commission with third countries. But these in principle are treated as points of information. Moreover, the Council might have, usually on the basis of a Note, a general discussion and mere oral exchange of views on a specific issue, albeit without adopting any conclusions on the matter. This is usually the practice followed during informal Council meetings.

98 According to research, 70% of Council texts are agreed in working groups, another 10-15% in Coreper or other senior committees, leaving 10-15% to the Ministers themselves. See Wallace and Wallace, *op.cit.*, at p. 18.

lishment of a financial instrument for return purposes and the Italian initiative for the establishment of quotas at EU level.[99]

The working parties dealing with migration related issues are numerous.[100] They could be divided into three main types of groups on the basis of the character of the issues that they examine. Firstly, the central working party responsible for migration policy issues is the "Migration Admission and Expulsion" working party. It is actually divided into two sub-groups: the "Migration-Admission" sub-group, dealing with legal migration and the "Migration-Expulsion" sub-group, dealing with illegal migration and return policy matters and recently also being vested with the role of assisting the Commission in the readmission Agreements.[101] Despite the common origin of the two sub-groups they are in practice distinct, since both the matters that they examine and their members are diverse. The former is composed of officials of the Ministries of Interior whilst the latter is composed either of Interior Ministry officials, albeit attached to a different unit, or mainly police officers. More recently, a new sub-section has been established within the framework of the "Migration-Expulsion" working party, the so-called "Migration-Expulsion+", which is composed of practitioners and is responsible for examining practical return issues.[102] Secondly, there is the CIREFI working party, which is composed of officials of the Ministries of Interior or police officers and examines several migration related issues, such as exchange of statistics, reports on the situation in third countries and cooperation among immigration liaison officers. Relatedly, there is the High Level Working Group on Asylum and Migration, a cross-pillar group composed by senior officials, who is nonetheless referring not to the JHA but to the General Affairs Council.[103] Thirdly, there are a series of working parties examining migration related issues of mainly Schengen relevant character, such as the "Visa Working

99 The first two were first examined at European Council level before the Commission presented a concrete legislative proposal. The third was launched at the informal JHA Council of Rome and then, following the deep divergences of view among Member States, led subsequently to the preparation of a Commission Communication on the relationship between legal and illegal migration. See Study on the links between legal and illegal migration, *op.cit*.

100 For a list of the Council preparatory bodies in the area of JHA see Council doc. 14132/01 POLGEN 32, 16.11.2001 and Council doc. 6582/1/02 JAI 29 REV 1, 1.3.2002.

101 Appointment of the Migration and Expulsion Working Party as the responsible body for assistance and consultations to the Commission in relation to the negotiation of readmission agreements, Council doc. 15649/02 MIGR 134, 13.12.2002.

102 Presidency Note on Meetings between Member States' return practitioners, Council doc. 13541/02 MIGR 106, 29.10.2002.

103 For the terms of reference and a presentation of the issues examined by this group see *supra* at 4.3.1.

Party", which is in principle composed of diplomats and examines visa policy issues; the "Frontiers Working Party", which gathers employees of the border management national authorities; as well as a series of purely Schengen related groups dealing with institutional or technical aspects of the Schengen *acquis* (i.e. Schengen *acquis*, SIS, SIS-Tech, SIRENE and Schengen Evaluation Working Parties).

The second layer of decision-making in the post-Amsterdam era consists of the Strategic Committee for Immigration, Frontiers and Asylum (SCIFA). It is comprised of senior officials –in principle of Interior Ministries- and was initially set up for a transitory period of five years.[104] SCIFA essentially functions as a clearing house for all Title IV working parties. Its function is twofold: to discuss outstanding issues in order either to resolve them or to make a substantive contribution towards discussion at Coreper level and to conduct policy discussions and formulate a strategic approach with regard to the relevant policy areas. Following the increasing importance of borders issues SCIFA, at the request of the Seville Council, has been split in to two branches: its usual formation and SCIFA+, which is composed of the Heads of external border control services. Although one could have expected that SCIFA had all the credentials in order to, on the one hand, act as a sort of Coreper III specialised on the communitarised part of JHA, and on the other, to give political guidance and impetus where necessary, its function has not been considered satisfactory. It is often criticised for a lack of political vision and guidance and for acting simply as a working party, albeit of a higher level.

Issues are forwarded to Coreper level, more specifically Coreper II. As this is also the case for other areas of EU law, the main role of Coreper consists in preparing the relevant points for the Ministers. In general, Coreper is considered to be the 'place to make the deal'.[105] However, the largely technical characteristics of JHA matters – far from appealing to ambassadors who in principle show a strong preference for much more political issues- and the lack of familiarity of Coreper II with technical issues,[106] results in JHA matters often being treated as "*le parent pauvre*" in comparison to other areas.

In this context, it is worth examining briefly the role of JHA Counsellors. They are a group of national officials, employees of either the Ministry of Foreign Affairs or other Ministries, though in the case of migration they are in

104 SCIFA is the body dealing with the communitarised branch of the policies that were previously examined by the former K.4 Committee, which has been now renamed the Article 36 Committee and examines the current third pillar issues. See Council doc. 6166/2/99 CK4 12 REV 2. The mandate of SCIFA has been extended.

105 For the role of Coreper in general see Article 207 TEC; Lewis, *op.cit.*, at p. 1001, and Hayes-Renshaw and Wallace, *op.cit,*, at p. 72-84.

106 In contrast to Coreper I which habitually examines technical aspects of European law, this is more the exception for Coreper II.

principle employees of the Ministry of Interior, who are attached to the national Permanent Representations in Brussels. Their main function is to brief and keep informed the Permanent Representative, mainly prior to Coreper and Council meetings. As they are based in Brussels they are also the link between their government and the EU institutions. It is not easy to determine the exact position of this group in the decision-making hierarchy, since JHA Counsellors usually intervene at various stages but always on an *ad hoc* basis. The group is in principle convened in order to examine specific outstanding points with regard to documents that are already forwarded to Coreper or the Council when there is no time to convene a working party or SCIFA meeting. Given the fact that it is composed of people who are familiar both with the national and the EU system and who are living permanently in Brussels and usually keep close contacts with their colleagues from other Permanent Representations, the Council Secretariat and the Commission, the role of the group is fundamental.

Finally, the entire bulk of files is forwarded to the Ministers, who are those competent to take the final decisions and adopt the relevant measures. In most cases the role of the Ministers is purely formal, since political agreement has already been reached and the relevant files are put as 'A-points'. However it is frequently the case that they have to discuss pending issues, in particular with regard to important files. Ministers are accompanied by the Permanent Representative, and eventually also the SCIFA representative. The legal expert or the JHA Counsellor responsible for the file also follows the discussions either in the back seats or in a separate '*salle d'écoute*'. Even if the Minister has been in principle briefed before the meeting by the team of experts, their presence proves vital in case new compromise proposals are circulated, since Ministers are usually not familiar with the legislative evolution of the file and the technicalities. Discussions at Council level have a primarily political character with the legal implications often being ignored by the Ministers. Also it is quite often the case, and particularly during informal JHA Council meetings, that the discussion takes the form of a general exchange of views on specific issues.

5.1.2.2 The Negotiation Process

The negotiation method and process varies profoundly depending both on the stage of the negotiation as well as on the character of the file. Soft law documents or documents of more general political value or interest, such as Action Plans and Council Conclusions, are usually rather quickly adopted. But the negotiation of legislative documents, such as Directives, Regulations and Decisions, proves rather lengthy and demanding both in terms of time as well as in terms of the efforts required. Moreover, in the course of the first reading positions are rather general, however, at later stages they become much more succinct. In principle, during the course of the first reading almost every delegation takes the floor and this usually is the best place to explain in detail the national position, whilst at later stages discussions are mainly focused around those provisions that are the most controversial and among those delegations that have the major objections. Furthermore, whereas it is generally the case that discussions are much more legal and technical at the working party level, in Coreper and at the Council they have a rather political character.

However, there are certain common characteristics almost at every stage of the decision-making process, albeit their intensity may vary at each level for a series of reasons. First of all, in contrast to what one could expect, voting is somewhat rare. Even if at first sight efforts to reach consensus are to be expected, since unanimity was until recently the rule in this area, in practice even in cases where the qualified majority voting procedure applies the Council proceeds to voting only where attempts to reach a consensus were unfruitful.[107] It is much more the threat of the possibility to proceed to voting on the basis of the qualified majority rule –which inevitably leads to the loss of a major negotiating weapon, though rarely used- that renders the actors more flexible than the actual recourse to voting. This could be easily explained if one takes into account the existence of a certain type of solidarity within the Council. Each member is aware that they could in turn find themselves isolated on a different point or issue the next day.[108] Moreover, it is not certain that a qualified majority voting system would be more efficient than unanimity, even if one would *a priori* expect this to be the case. It has been convincingly argued that qualified majority voting presupposes the existence of alliance systems that are difficult to forge with regard to long legal texts. Therefore the existence of contradictory alliances might also be a blocking factor equally as strong as unanimity.[109] That said, it is in any case certain that the dynamics within the framework of the co-decision and qualified majority voting process are considerably diverse.

Secondly, discussions within the Council bodies are not so much geared by the will to forge a common policy at European level but rather focus on defending the national legislation, which Member States are not willing to amend.[110] Ministers and officials meeting in the Council are servants of their governments, affiliated to national political parties, and accountable to national electorates. Thus, their first priority is generally to pursue whatever seems to be the pre-

107 For some useful information on the recourse to the qualified majority voting procedure in general see Dony M., "La majorité qualifiée au Conseil du traité de Rome à la Convention sur l'avenir de l'Union", in Vandersanden G. and de Walsch A. (eds.), *Mélanges en hommage à Jean-Victor Louis(Vol. I)*, Editions de l'Université de Bruxelles, Bruxelles, 2003, p. 139-164.

108 On this point see Lewis, *op.cit.*, at p. 1008.

109 El Kaim G., "Quelques remarques du point de vue du négotiateur", paper presented at the 3rd Congress of the Academic Network of Legal Studies on immigration and asylum in Europe "European immigration and Asylum polic"', Paris, 10 and 11 June 2004.

110 Ferraiolo, *op.cit.*

ferred objective of national policy.[111] The main objective of the negotiations is drafting a provision that does not hinder any, or at least the vast majority of, national legislation –a sort of compromise among national policies- rather than searching for what would be the best solution at the EU level. The negotiation of mainly the Directives on family reunification and long-term residents has shown that usually reservations are not lifted until the delegation concerned is offered a compromise solution that makes sure that the national legislation will not have to be amended.[112] The fact that negotiations within the Council are often blocked due to the fact that a Member State is in the process of revising its national legislation is rather indicative of the mentality and attitude prevailing within the Council.

Thirdly, it is worth highlighting the fact that in contrast to what the general public may believe the decision-making process is relatively informal. First of all, consensus on the vast majority of outstanding points is often not achieved inside the Council's meeting rooms and during the course of official meeting hours, but rather in the corridors, over coffee breaks, lunches and dinners. The limited time available to each delegate to express his point, interpretation problems and the formal character of meetings are rather cumbersome and prevent a substantive and sincere exchange of views.

Moreover, one of the central factors that facilitate the achievement of consensus lies in documents, *prima facie* neutral, such as the outcomes of proceedings that are prepared by the Secretariat or the Notes prepared by the Presidency in collaboration with the Secretariat, to be forwarded to the next level of decision-making. Even if these documents are in principle neutral, since by all accounts they summarise the outcome of discussions, it is worth highlighting that the way that discussions are summarised and a national position is presented can be decisive. They can have a positive or negative effect on the negotiating position of the Member State concerned. They can either put pressure on a certain delegation or promote a specific position. For example, providing detailed explanations of a national position might prove extremely helpful for clarifying certain points that the national delegate has not been able to explain orally. On the other hand, stating that the vast majority of delegations are contrary to a particular national position, mentioning the efforts and any eventual previous compromise proposals submitted by the Presidency in order to reach consensus on that point, quite often puts the delegation concerned in a rather awkward and isolated position. Interestingly enough, Council documents might even be beneficial in terms of internal coordination at national level in case there is not good communication between the low ranked officials and the Minister or the Permanent Representation and the capital or among different Ministries. On certain occasions the drafting of these documents or draft compromise pro-

111 Wallace and Wallace, *op.cit.*, at p. 19.

112 Ferraiolo, *op.cit.*

posals that are submitted by the Presidency have been agreed *a priori* or even literally drafted by the officials of the Member State having the reservation and might form part of a package deal. The reasons for which these are presented by the Presidency are numerous. For example, helping the Member State concerned to overcome internal problems and rendering the solution more palatable at the national level, or facilitating the consensus of both the other Member States and the Member State concerned, since the former are in principle more friendly to Presidency proposals and the latter avoids in that way the risk of losing face.

Furthermore, efficient and fruitful negotiation requires a long-standing experience with regard to, and deep knowledge of, both the EU negotiating system and the different substantive positions and negotiating traditions of Member States. Every reservation has its own merit and importance. There are reservations of a primarily political nature that can only be lifted at Ministerial level. There are also points where reaching a compromise is a question of legal drafting. There are reservations that are substantive and others that are mainly kept for tactical purposes. There are also informal "clubs", in the sense that a delegation inserts a reservation not because it is contrary to the actual drafting but in order to support another Member State. There are delegations that prefer not to be isolated at Ministerial level, whilst others are much more ready to block even at this level if they are not satisfied with the outcome. An in-depth knowledge of the system renders the decision-making process much more effective –since there is a reasonable division of time spent on each point and files are moved to the next decision-making level only when they are mature enough- and facilitates fruitful unofficial horse trading and achieving the necessary package deals.

Last but not least, one of the central catalysts for reaching compromise is the nature of personal relations among the negotiators involved. Regularity of contact and a pattern of socialisation mean that the Council and especially its preparatory bodies develop a kind of insider amity.[113] The creation of *esprit de corps* and special links, and the friendships which sometimes grow out of them, can be instrumental in solving problems which might otherwise hold up the entire decision-making process.[114] This is especially the case among people working on a more stable basis together, such as Commission and Council Secretariat officials and JHA Counsellors.

5.1.2.3 Techniques in Order to Reach Compromise

In addition to what has already been said, reaching a compromise usually involves a series of either formalised or more informal techniques. There are two main types of techniques: negotiation techniques and drafting techniques.

113 Wallace and Wallace, *op.cit.*, at p. 19.

114 Hayes-Renshaw. and Wallace, *op.cit.*, p. 236.

First of all, it is worth mentioning briefly the practice of bilateral meetings that are held mainly at the initiative of the Presidency. These usually take place between, on the one hand, the Presidency, the Council Secretariat –and eventually, though not always, the Commission – and on the other, either one delegation, which has a series of reservations in order to examine eventually a package deal, or with two or more delegations that have contradictory positions with regard to one or two central points. In principle the outcome of these meetings is subsequently submitted formally to the relevant Council body as Presidency compromise proposals. It is interesting to mention the fact that these kinds of bilateral meetings can eventually take place also in the margins of a Council meeting. This is the well-known technique of the 'confessional' that has been applied for example by the Luxembourg Presidency in order to reach agreement on the external frontiers Convention in 1991.[115]

Another formula that is used of late is the "Friends of the Presidency Group" pattern.[116] These meetings usually take the form of drafting sessions. The participants either coincide with those of the working parties or are the JHA Counsellors. Their informal character and the fact that participants have to express themselves in a common language, given the absence of interpreters, generate a sincerer exchange of views and often lead to successful compromises. Their outcome is subsequently submitted officially to the working party. They are in general considered constructive, since, even if their outcome is not supported by all the delegations, they contribute to working in the right direction. Moreover, from a political point of view they further legitimise and reinforce considerably the proposal submitted by the Presidency, since this is usually shared and supported by the vast majority of the participants.

More recently, two other methods that have not been formalised have also been applied. The first such technique is a type of 'tacit approval method'.[117] In this case the Presidency submitted, at Council level, a final package deal which delegations were invited to examine within a specific time-limit of one week. Were there no objection within the set deadline it would be considered that there was political agreement. Under this procedure it is difficult for individual Member

115 That is, parallel meetings between the Presidency and delegations in the course of a Council meeting. For more details see De Lobkowicz W., *L'Europe et la sécurité intérieure Une élaboration par étapes, op.cit.,* at p. 32. The same technique was used more recently by the 2002 Danish Presidency in order to reach a common approach on the Dublin II Regulation.

116 This group was improvised during the Agenda 2000 negotiations. See Lewis, *op.cit.*, at p. 1002.

117 This method – which Peers coins the 'silent procedure' – has been applied successfully by the Danish Presidency during the negotiation of Dublin II Regulation. See Peers S., "Key Legislative Developments on Migration in the European Union", *EJML*, Vol. 5, 2003, p. 387-410, at p. 390.

States to predict whether someone else will object. And under the political pressure of being the "*bouc émissaire*" they usually give in, unless the matter is of extreme national importance. The second of these informal techniques consists in freezing negotiations during a Council meeting, conducting a parallel drafting experts meeting the outcome of which is subsequently presented to Ministers at a later stage the same day.[118]

It is also worth noting that quite often the most difficult files, on which the Council has reached political agreement but official adoption was not possible, are placed as "A-points" in another Council's agenda and not in that of the JHA Council.[119] Given the difficulties of reaching a compromise as well as the fragile character of the package deal obtained, avoiding any eventual risk of re-opening discussion could well be among the reasons for this reshuffling among various Council formations.

The second series of techniques is linked with the drafting process. One could identify several types of techniques in that regard.[120] First of all, the lack of agreement on a point leads to opting either for a rather vague and open-ended drafting[121] or for an optional clause, the so-called "may provisions".[122] Furthermore, the technique of drafting an optional derogation clause proved to be rather successful. In this case, while the principle is clearly stated, it is accompanied by a series of express optional derogation clauses. The notorious German clause for the integration criteria imposed on twelve year old children,[123] the Austrian clauses for the submission of the application before the age

118 This technique has been applied successfully by the Greek Presidency during the February 2003 JHA Council meeting with regard to the family reunification Directive.

119 i.e. both the family reunification and long-term residents Directives have been officially adopted by other Council formations.

120 For a detailed presentation of the relevant Directives and a discussion of the relevant examples retrieved from the Directives see the analysis in Chapter 4. For some useful comments see also El Kaim, *op.cit.*

121 i.e. Article 5 (4) of the family reunification Directive and Articles 7 (2) and 20 of the long-term residents Directive on the procedural aspects; Articles 4 (3) and 9 (2) of the long-term residents Directive on the issue of absences, their reasons and their calculation; Article 18 of the family reunification Directive and Articles 10 (1) and 20 of the long-term residents Directive on the redress procedures.

122 i.e. Article 4 (2) and (3) of the family reunification Directive on the categories of persons that are covered; Article 7 (2) of the family reunification Directive and Articles 5 (2) and 15 (2) of the long-term residents Directive on the integration condition. It is worth highlighting the fact that in the case of the draft Directive on studies, the application of the Directive has been rendered optional to the rest of the categories with the exception of students, see Article 3 (1) of the Directive.

123 Article 4 (1) of the family reunification Directive.

of fifteen and the extension of the waiting period up to three years[124] and the derogation clauses to the right of access to the labour market[125] are representative examples of this technique via which the said States succeeded in maintaining their national political position on the aforementioned matters.[126] On certain occasions these derogations may even go so far as to water down the very substance of the rights enumerated. For instance one could mention the long list of derogation clauses included within the framework of Article 11 enumerating the rights of long-term residents; the exclusion clauses regarding the movement of long-term residents; and the limitation of the right to an autonomous residence permit in the case of the family reunification Directive.[127]

Moreover, the deletion of a 'problematic' provision has also been used as another way of circumventing an existing problem. For example, the Council has deleted the reference regarding the granting of the residence permit free of charge. If one takes into consideration the very high level of the fees imposed by certain Member States, it becomes clear that this provision has most probably been the subject of intense debates within the Council.[128]

Another technique consists in transferring or inserting into the preamble certain provisions on which there is no consensus. This approach represents a rather useful compromise when it is not possible to apply the aforementioned approaches or in case a specific delegation is insisting on having a reference somewhere in the text to which others are objecting.[129] If the inclusion into the

124 Article 4 (6) and 8 of the family reunification Directive.

125 Article 14 (2) of the family reunification Directive and Articles 14 (3) and 21 (2) of the long-term residents Directive.

126 On these points see Ferraiolo, *op.cit.*, and Mariani, *op.cit.*, at p. 20-21.

127 Read Article 11 (1) in conjunction with 11 (2) (3) and (4) and recitals 13 and 15 of the long term residents Directive; Article 14 (1) in conjunction with Article 14 (2) and (3) of the long term residents Directive, and Article 15 (1) first sub-paragraph in conjunction with Article 15 (1) second sub-paragraph and 15 (4) of the family reunification Directive.

128 The fees in the Netherlands and in Greece are nearly 900 euros. See Written question E-0652/03 by Erik Meijer to the Commission on Conflict between the large increase in the price of residence permits in the Netherlands and promotion of freedom of establishment in the EU, OJ C 11E/103, 15.1.2004, and Article 71 of the basic Greek Immigration Act, Law 2910/2001, Government Gazette A No 91, 21.5.2001.

129 i.e. recital 10 of the family reunification Directive regarding the case of movement of family members falling under the optional categories; recital 14 of the family reunification Directive, recital 8 of the long-term residents Directive and recital 14 of the Directive on studies with regard to public order; recitals 7 and 15 of the long-term residents Directive establishing respectively additional requirements with regard to the condition of stable and regular resources and the exercise of the right regarding the access to study grants and recital 15 of the Directive on studies with regard to the fight against abuse of the procedure.

preamble is not possible, quite often due to the fact that the objections of those disagreeing are strong, then as a solution of last resort there is the option of declarations. These can be either Council or unilateral Declarations. The Declarations attached to the family reunification and long-term residents Directives are examples of the latter in operation.[130]

In addition, the literal copying of compromises reached within similar frameworks has proved to be relatively successful. The Council has copied a series of provisions from the family reunification Directive in to the long-term residents Directive and subsequently in to the Directive on studies. Of particular note are the provisions on the conditions for acquiring the relevant rights, the public policy clause, the provision regarding the procedural aspects and the legal redress clause.[131] Moreover, the employment exclusion clauses, which were used for the first time in the reception conditions and temporary protection Directives, were subsequently transposed in to the family reunification and long-term residents Directives as well as in to the Directive on studies.[132]

Finally, two new techniques that the Commission introduced in the framework of its second modified proposal for family reunification can be highlighted: the "stand still clause" and the "*rendez-vous* clause".[133] The former has generally proved unsuccessful – at least in the form of a general clause, though in specific cases it contributed positively in preventing the extensive application of derogation clauses. The latter was widely accepted by all Member States and was subsequently incorporated in the long-term residents Directive as well.[134] To be sure, the reasoning behind the positive reaction of certain delegations was probably different from that of the Commission or certain other Member States. From a negotiation point of view, however, this clause proved beneficial for both sides. Those opting for restrictive clauses used it as an argument in order to make the

130 See Declaration regarding Article 6 of the family reunification Directive, Council doc. 10755/03; and Declarations regarding Articles 3 and 6 of the long-term residents Directive, Council doc. 14679/03. See also the Unilateral Dutch Declaration with regard to the family reunification Directive, Addendum to I/A Item Note – Council Directive on the right to family reunification, Council doc. 10755/03 ADD 1 MIGR 58 OC 439, 14.7.2003.

131 Read respectively Articles 7 (1), 6 (1) and (2), 5 (4) and 18 of the family reunification Directive in conjunction with Articles 5 (1), 6 (1), 7 (2), 10 (1) and 20 of the long-term residents Directive, and Article 6 and 18 (4) of the Directive on studies.

132 See Article 11 of the reception conditions Directive and Article 12 of the temporary protection Directive in conjunction with Article 14 (2) of the family reunification Directive, Articles 11 (3) and 14 (3) of the long-term residents Directive and Article 17 of the Directive on studies.

133 Articles 3 (6) and 19 of the Commission's second modified proposal on family reunification. For an in-depth discussion of these clauses see *supra* 4.2.1.

134 Article 24 of the long-term residents Directive.

derogations they were asking for more acceptable to the rest of their colleagues in the short-term. And those of a more liberal persuasion –the Commission included- were likely to have in mind the possibilities that would be opened up in the long-term following the passage to qualified majority voting since it is likely that the renegotiation might well take place with the qualified majority voting rule applying.

This overview of the practical drafting techniques used by the Council in order to reach consensus raises certain additional considerations. Recourse to all the aforementioned techniques has proved rather beneficial for the purposes of reaching consensus but these techniques might have somewhat of a boomerang effect since they defer the conflict to a later stage such as the renegotiation of the measure, the implementation at the national level or interpretation by the courts. The first scenario might seem some way off, however, the other two are quite visible. Thus, the degree of harmonisation depends on the extent to which Member States have recourse to the derogation clauses. And, as it has been convincingly argued, while these techniques may be a tempting way to reach a political compromise, it is very doubtful whether it is wise to leave essentially political issues to the European Court.[135]

5.1.2.4 The Impact of General Background Factors

The decision-making process within the Council, and in particular the pace with which there is progress and subsequently agreement on a specific file, is also affected by a series of other factors that are not always apparent to the external observer. These are usually linked with the internal organisation and the political situation within each single Member State as well as with the institutional and/or political challenges that the EU as such needs to address.

First of all, effective intra and inter-ministerial coordination at national level is pivotal to the well-functioning of the EU, since the success of a meeting depends to a large extent on the clarity of the national position and on the margin of manoeuvre allowed to the participating national delegate.[136] Whereas the lack of the former eventually leads to inconsistencies diminishing the national positions and slowing down the EU decision-making process, the lack of the latter not only increases the number of points having to be examined by the Ministers themselves, but might even block the whole decision-taking process.

---

135 Hailbronner K., "European Immigration and Asylum Law – FIDE Conference – Introductory remarks", paper distributed at the XXI FIDE Congress, Dublin, 2-5 June 2004. The risk of interference of the Court to the competences of the Community legislator was also highlighted by Advocate General Kokkot in her Opinion concerning the annulment of certain provisions of the family reunification Directive. See Opinion of Advocate General Kokkot in case C-540/03, *op.cit.*

136 Hayes-Renshaw and Wallace, *op.cit.*, at p. 214-218.

To start with, the formulation of a single point national position does not come about naturally or necessarily easily but is normally the result of debate and frequently of compromise between several Ministerial departments,[137] or internal political actors. Moreover, there are obviously different traditions. Certain countries such as, for example, the UK, France and Germany are usually well prepared and the participating officials regularly have written instructions. Smaller countries are in principle much more flexible. Indeed, the idiosyncrasies of particular countries, such as the German Länder system, or the Danish and Dutch scrutiny systems increasingly slow down the EU decision-making process. It has been rightly questioned whether the Council could cope with more than one or two monitoring systems of such severity.[138]

The more general internal political situation, such as the existence of a coalition government, as well as political developments at national level, such as elections or referenda or intra-government reshuffling of portfolios or majority-opposition clashes, inevitably affect the representation of the Member States in the Council since they considerably slow down the coordination process at national level. Further, the dependence of Ministers on the media and public concerns in conjunction with heated internal debates often provoked by interlinked issues – such as a large influx of illegal immigrants, the existence of a strong presence of extreme right parties, or other parallel policy developments, such as economic problems, changes of the pension or social security systems- inevitably affect the national position and render Ministers much less flexible.[139] In countries where immigration is a salient issue, national politicians may try to secure votes by being 'tough' on immigration.[140] Another factor is the independent changes of national legislation – a significant phenomenon in the post-Amsterdam era- which often transformed EU policy-making in to a "hostage" of national developments,[141] particularly where this proved to be not only a long but also a painful process, such as in the case of Germany.[142]

---

137 Hayes-Renshaw and Wallace, *op.cit.*, at p. 216.

138 On the national traditions see Hayes-Renshaw and Wallace, *op.cit.*, at p. 230-233.

139 Ministers being politicians having to reply to their constituencies' concerns in order to be re-elected are deeply affected by media and political coverage both at the European but mainly at the national level.

140 In contrast to Commissioners and Commission officials that do not have to bother about re-election. Geddes A., *Immigration and European Integration – Towards fortress Europe?, op.cit.*, at p. 139.

141 El Kaim, *op.cit.*

142 For the process of amendment of the German national legislation see Schmidt D. "Die aktuellen Debatten uber das neue deutsche Zuwanderungsgesetz", paper distributed at the ERA Conference "EC Asylum and Immigration Law: Reaching the Tampere Milestones?" held at Trier on the 11 and 12 March 2004. After several years of negotiations the German Immigration Act was passed in early July 2004.

In addition, it is worth underscoring the fact that the pace of negotiations is also affected by the sensitivity of the file in question. Member States have been much more cautious with regard to issues concerning the admission of third country nationals for labour purposes than with regard to other categories of persons. The exclusion clauses entered in relation to the labour market access provisions of the Directives as well as the "freezing" of the paid employment Directive can be contrasted with the relatively quick negotiation of the Directive on students – a case in principle seen not through the lens of immigration but as a temporary phenomenon – and show clearly this difference in approach.

There are also a series of developments at European level that have an impact on decision-making progress. Firstly, the upcoming enlargement and the consequent fear of having to reach consensus among twenty-five has certainly functioned as an accelerating factor for reaching consensus on a series of pending legislative proposals. Secondly, the existence of consensus on the need for a European response to a certain political development functions as a catalyst. The spur provided by the Austrian crisis for the adoption of the equal treatment Directive is revealing.[143] Finally, pressure from external actors such as third countries also constitutes a vital factor. The change of US policy on visa issues has clearly accelerated developments with regard to biometrics and visa policy at the EU level.[144]

5.2 The Commission: Hovering between Vision and *Realpolitik*

The second major actor in this area is definitely the Commission. Its role has not always been strong from an institutional point of view but thanks to its global and pro-European approach it has been the locomotive for a series of developments at the EU level. Nonetheless, one should not forget that the Commission is a political actor pursuing on certain occasions its own interests and is both affected by internal situations and reacting to external factors. In fact, one could enumerate a series of occasions on which the Commission has adopted a rather pragmatic approach or has even failed to take actions that one would have expected it to take. In the light of the above, while focusing on the contrast between the visionary and *realpolitik* approach of the Commission, this section will present the Commission's position and strategic choices as well as certain of its strong and weak points which are not always evident. In contrast with the preceding section on the Council, this section takes mainly a chronological approach.

See 'German immigration law favours highly skilled foreigners', <www.euobserver.com>, 15.7.2004.

143 Guiraudon V., "The constitution of a European immigration policy domain: a political sociology approach", *op.cit.*, at p. 275.

144 "Biometric ID documents herald a global identification system", *Statewatch*, Vol. 13, No 3/4, May-July 2003, p. 1.

5.2.1 The Commission's Position and Strategic Choices

The first part of this book has already discussed the rather limited role of the Commission up to the mid 1980s. Not only was there not any obvious Community competence on migration but the Commission was also excluded from any cooperation at the intergovernmental level, such as Trevi.[145] That being said, the Commission did purport to bring the migration issue under Community competence. The proposal for a Directive on illegal migration, the proposal for inclusion of third country nationals' children under the scope of the education Directive as well as the adoption of the famous Decision on the organisation of consultations on migration policy can be held up as examples of such efforts, even if they proved unsuccessful.

The Commission's approach appeared to become a great deal more constructive following the inclusion of certain aspects of migration policy within the framework of the Single Market objective and the famous Commission White Paper. It has been argued that "in Delors's thinking the move to abolish frontiers between EC countries would in turn convince Member States of the need to cooperate on admission and other border control measures, thus creating a context for subsequent efforts to bring immigration policy into the institutional framework of the EC. Although the EC did not include mention of common immigration policies, Article 8a of the SEA set policy goals that, realistically, could not be fully realized without EC-wide policies on migration."[146] One should however highlight that the Commission's approach at the time was rather contradictory. It repeatedly stressed the lack of any progress in its general reports on the progress towards the completion of the internal market[147] and on numerous occasions took a clear position on the fact that the abolition of internal border controls should necessarily apply to third country nationals[148] and even threatened to taking legal action against those Member States that contin-

145 De Lobkowicz W., *L'Europe et la sécurité intérieure Une élaboration par étapes, op.cit.*, at p. 19.

146 Papademetriou, *op.cit.*, at p. 22.

147 Progress Report required by Article 8b, *op.cit.*; Sixth Report of the Commission to the Council and the European Parliament concerning the implementation of the White Paper on the Completion of the Internal Market, *op.cit.*

148 Communication of the Commission on the abolition of controls of persons at intra-Community borders, COM (88) 640 final, 16.1.1989; Communication from the Commission to the Council and the Parliament "Abolition of frontier controls", COM (91) 549 final, 18.12.1991; Commission Communication on Abolition of Border Controls, *op.cit.*

ued to carry out internal frontier checks on persons.[149] Yet the Commission did not table any initiatives until 1993.[150]

Moreover, on a series of occasions the Commission has softened its tone and adopted a rather pragmatic approach. For instance, in its 1988 Communication it took a much more modest approach by adopting the Palma document's distinction between necessary and desirable measures,[151] and thus itself restricting its ambitious internal market programme. Furthermore, it seems to have agreed with the Member States' decision on approaching the matter in an intergovernmental framework, placing greater importance on the outcome rather than the method, and arguably renounced its right of initiative.[152] The need for dialogue and close cooperation between the Member States and the EC institutions was also emphasised by the Commission.[153]

The Commission's pragmatism was most probably based on a series of realistic considerations. First of all, Community competence was strongly contested by Member States, and it is very likely that they would have considered any eventual Commission proposals as a breach of their sovereignty.[154] For its part the Commission probably hesitated to make any proposals being fearful of the British reaction and waiting for the Schengen Convention to come into effect

149 See the Commission Statement to the European Council in Copenhagen on the implementation of Article 8a of the Treaty of Rome with regard to the movement of persons, *op.cit*. For further discussion see *supra* at 1.2.2.

150 The Commission could have submitted a proposal on the basis of Article 100 EEC, which is in fact the Article that it used when it presented the Monti package. On the possible use of Article 100 as a legal basis see Timmermans C.W.A., "Free Movement of Persons and the Division of Powers between the Community and its Member States – Why do it the intergovernmental way?", in Schermers et al. (eds.), *Free Movement of Persons in Europe, Legal Problems and Experiences*, T.M.C. Asser Institute, The Hague, 1993, p. 352-368, at p. 359 and De Zwaan J. W., "Institutional problems and Free Movement of Persons – The legal and political framework for cooperation", in Schermers et al. (eds.), *Free Movement of Persons in Europe, Legal Problems and Experiences*, T.M.C. Asser Institute, The Hague, 1993, p. 335-351, at p. 347.

151 De Ceuster, *op.cit.*

152 More specifically, in its 1989 report on the abolition of border controls it proposed that Community legislation in this field should be applied only to those cases where the legal security and uniformity provided by Community law constituted the best instrument for achieving the desired goal. See Van Den Brink and Vierhout R., "Democratic control without frontiers? The European parliament and free movement of persons", in Schermers et al. (eds.), *Free Movement of Persons in Europe, Legal Problems and Experiences*, T.M.C. Asser Institute, The Hague, 1993, p. 379-390, at p. 384-385.

153 See Guild and Niessen, *op.cit.*, at p. 41.

154 De Ceuster, *op.cit.*

first.[155] In fact, given the uncertainty as to whether the experiment of a frontier-free area would work in practice the Commission traditionally saw Schengen as a necessary, albeit temporary, step pending the adoption of Community measures to achieve the objective of Article 7a of the EC Treaty.[156]

In the light of the above, while the lack of any concrete proposals was criticised and the Commission's 1991 Communication received criticism for its restrictive and exclusionary tone, in retrospect, it needs to be stressed that it is rather unlikely that Member States would have been receptive to Commission appeals for additional policy harmonisation in the migration field and that any Commission initiative might have only served to isolate the Commission further.[157] However, ironically enough, it was the Commission that was subject to the backlash resulting from the inactivity and lack of political will of the Member States. The European Parliament, apparently not best pleased with the Commission's pragmatic approach, brought an action for failure to act against the Commission before the Court of Justice.[158] It has been convincingly argued that the fact that the Commission chose the line of least resistance consequently rendered the Parliament inoperative.[159]

Unfortunately the post-Maastricht era remained a "*période probatoire*" for the Commission, which was still seen as a "*partenaire toleré*".[160] Yet the Commission exhibited political realism as well. First of all, the Commission was rather cautious within the framework of the preparation for the IGC.[161] And later it proved rather pragmatic and cautious in the process of implementing the Treaty provisions. Even at the internal level, in contrast to the transformation of the Directorate General within the Secretariat into a full Directorate General (DG IA) following the expansion of the competence for second pillar issues, the Commission did not proceed to a comparable exercise with regard to the third pillar.[162] The tabling of legislative proposals has also not seen the Commission at its most active, indeed quite to the contrary. Apart from the external borders Convention and the visa Regulation, both of which had their origins in the intergovernmental era, it has only presented the Monti package, which to a certain extent was seen as a self-defence action. Indeed, the Commission's decision to

155 Peers S., *EU Justice and Home Affairs Law*, *op.cit.*, at p. 74.

156 Handoll, *op.cit.*, at p. 52-53. See also COM (88) 640 final.

157 Papademetriou, *op.cit.*, at p. 53-55.

158 See case C-445/93, *op.cit.*

159 Van Den Brink and Vierhout, *op.cit.*, at p. 386 and 389.

160 De Lobkowicz W., *L'Europe et la sécurité intérieure Une élaboration par étapes, op.cit.*, at p. 49-50.

161 Guild and Niessen, *op.cit.*, at p. 42. See also Contribution of the Commission to the IGC, Bulletin EC, Supplement 2/91.

162 Den Boer and Wallace, *op.cit.*, at p. 500.

push ahead despite the hostile climate was seen as an effort to pre-empt a ruling by the European Court of Justice on the case brought against it two years earlier by the European Parliament for failing to implement the Single European Act.[163] It was also cautious inasmuch as the substance of these limited proposals was concerned.[164] Furthermore, the Commission has for several years clearly avoided addressing the issue of internal border controls. The issue was not dealt with until 1995 under the pressure of the pending action of the European Parliament.[165] Finally, it is worth underlining that the main legislative proposal regarding legal migration was only presented in 1997 on the eve of the official signature of the Amsterdam Treaty and was mainly seen as a preparatory action for the implementation of the new Treaty.[166]

But the picture is not all one-sided for there have also been limited exceptions to this pragmatic and rather restrictive approach. The Commission's 1994 Communication is most certainly among them. It has been rightly considered to be the most comprehensive blueprint of Commission thinking.[167] Indeed, it could even be argued that this document is even more comprehensive and ambitious than the first Commission Communications in the post-Amsterdam era.[168] However, an immediate follow-up was completely absent. This leads one to suspect that this excellent document was definitely badly timed and that it is unlikely that its presentation was sufficiently contemplated or strategically planned by the Commission itself beforehand.

Following the communitarisation of migration related policies and the increasing responsibilities that were assigned to the Commission by the Amsterdam Treaty, its action became considerably more constructive. A special Directorate General for JHA, the so-called "Freedom, Security and Justice Directorate General" (JLS) -bringing together the relevant Unit of the former DG XV and the Maastricht era Task Force that was located in the Secretariat General-was created, an initiative that was rightly seen as a result of the Commission's increasing role in this area.[169] Keeping in mind that the new DG employs around

163 Papademetriou, *op.cit.*, at p. 99. The lack of genuine interest of the Commission in this project is also confirmed by the fact that it was soon superseded by the 1997 proposal for a draft admission Convention.

164 See the discussion *supra* at 1.4. and 3.4.

165 Within the framework of the Monti package. For a presentation and references see *supra* at 3.4.1.2. It is interesting that the legal basis used by the Commission was Article 100 TEC, a provision that existed since the very early days of the Community and which the Commission could have used before.

166 Proposal for a Council Act establishing the Convention on the rules for the admission of third-country nationals, *op.cit.*

167 Papademetriou, *op.cit.*, at p. 83.

168 COM (2000) 757 final, *op.cit.*

169 Nugent, *op.cit.*, at p. 135.

300 persons in contrast to the Task Force that did not employ in excess of 50[170] – while it had started with five[171] – this decision is also indicative of the importance that the Commission was willing to attach to the matters concerned.

Unfortunately, the entry into force of the Amsterdam Treaty came at one of the most troubling periods in the history of the Commission. With the Santer Commission resigning *en bloc* following strong accusations of malfunctioning on the basis of a report of an independent group, it was difficult to take any decisions. No substantial decisions were taken before September 1999 when the new Commission was nominated.[172] The two documents adopted between the signature and the entry into force of the new Treaty –namely the July 1998 Communication and the December 1998 Vienna Action Plan- were of a primarily organisational character. The former mainly examined aspects of transitory law and, the latter, to which the Commission was only a co-author, does not seem to have been adequately thought-through beforehand. The actions announced therein were rather confusing. Further, they were far from ambitious and hardly went beyond the pre-Amsterdam agenda.[173] The Action Plan has in practice been abandoned by the Commission and the Council.[174]

The first substantial Commission document was a general Communication, which was presented in autumn 2000.[175] The Commission presented in detail its views on the more general framework of the emerging migration policy and initiated the new approach it proposed to follow. In substance the Commission was following closely the ideas launched at Tampere with the Communication

170 Barbe E., *Justice et affaires intérieures dans l'Union européenne – Un espace de liberté, de sécurité et de justice,* La Documentation française, Paris, 2002, at p. 27.

171 Geddes A., *Immigration and European Integration – Towards fortress Europe?, op.cit.*, at p. 104.

172 De Lobkowicz W., *L'Europe et la sécurité intérieure Une élaboration par étapes, op.cit.*, at p. 153. Almost immediately after its resignation, the Santer College announced it would stay in office in a caretaker capacity until a replacement College was appointed. During this period it would not launch any significant new initiatives or take any major policy decisions. To emphasise the transitional nature of the operation Commissioners were at the time referred to as Acting Commissioners. On the Santer Commission see Nugent N., *The European Commission, op.cit.,* at p. 49-55.

173 This point is raised by Monar J., "Decision-making in the Area of Freedom, Security and Justice", *op.cit.*,at p. 68.

174 Since it was soon superseded by the Tampere Conclusions and the Commission Scoreboard and was never followed in practice.

175 Communication from the Commission on a Community immigration policy, *op.cit.*

focusing exclusively on aspects of legal migration. The first Communication on illegal migration came only a year later.[176]

Inasmuch as its legislative proposals are concerned, the Commission initially chose to focus on those aspects of migration regarding admission policy. The first document on illegal migration, of November 2001, took the form of a Communication. Whilst the first major legislative proposal in this field was only presented in September 2005.[177] There are several justifications for this choice. An obvious lack of resources is one important contributory factor and arguably rendered the need to make a choice inevitable. It is also likely that the Commission may have speculated that Member States would be mainly active with regard to illegal migration, due to their stronger interest and long-standing expertise in this field.

The Commission's second major choice in the post-Amsterdam era lies in the sequence of issues it decided to examine inasmuch as legal migration is concerned. Firstly, the choice of initially tabling proposals for Directives concerning corollary rights –i.e the right to family reunification- and to regulate first the subsequent stage of acquisition of the long-term resident status and residence in a second Member State, before confronting the very heart of migration policy, could arguably be justified by the fact that it was considered at the time that Member States were not yet ready to confront this conundrum.[178] Although this

176 COM (2001) 672 final, *op.cit*.

177 Meaning the draft Directive concerning common standards on procedures for return. Beforehand the Commission had only presented a proposal for a Decision regarding the arrangement of the financial imbalances within the framework of the implementation of the Directive on the mutual recognition of expulsion decisions as well as a Decision for the establishment of a database for the exchange of statistics. For references see *supra* at 4.1.2.

178 Inasmuch as the family reunification proposal is concerned which was the very first Commission proposal an additional reason lies in the fact that this was the largest group of migrants entering the EU and it was considered that it would be the easiest area to regulate. Moreover, it is likely that the humanitarian aspects of this category as well as the existence of a series of international law documents on the matter suggested a greater convergence among Member States' national law and that reaching an agreement would be rather quick and easy.

choice inevitably created a series of practical problems during the negotiation of the relevant proposals,[179] in the long run it proved to be rather wise.[180]

Furthermore, the Commission's position shifted over time. Initially it appeared rather dynamic and ambitious in its approach but its tone was progressively moderated and it became rather pragmatic. The unexpected difficulties in reaching agreement on the family reunification Directive, revealing an undeniable reluctance on the part of the Member States to proceed to any substantial harmonisation of legal migration, is likely to have played an important role. It was soon realised that it needed to be sympathetic to the sensitivities both of the Council as a whole and sometimes of its individual members as well. As a consequence of this need to be sensitive to the position of national governments, the Commission frequently moderated, or retreated from positions it would like to take, and sometimes ought to take, were it to be acting in a wholly mechanical way.[181]

First of all, as negotiations were getting harder and harder, instead of taking drastic measures – i.e. withdrawing the proposal – it would accept a watering down of its own proposals. The example of the family reunification Directive is revealing. The objective of the first Commission proposal was to harmonise Member States' legislation in order to restrict the choice of the Member State in which third country nationals decided to reside by providing broadly the same conditions for family reunification irrespective of the Member State. However, the Commission's second modified proposal was endowed with

179 Given the strong divergence among national policies as related to the conditions for the first entry and for the first renewals as well as the lack of any approximation at the EU level of these policies, it proved rather difficult to negotiate the establishment of common conditions for the acquisition of the long-term resident status. More specifically, certain Member States choose to effectuate strict scrutiny before the issuing of the first residence permit, others apply measures such as massive regularisations. Also certain Member States choose to control the situation of the third country national exclusively before the issuing of the first residence permit and do not run any strict controls as far as renewals are concerned – and subsequently do not consider it logical for instance to ask for accommodation condition after five years of residence. Certain others run strict checks also during the course of renewals and perceive the check for the acquisition of the long-term resident status as the final check that has to be passed before this new advantageous status is acquired.

180 It is likely that the paid employment Directive would have failed anyway. Whilst the adoption of the rest of the legal migration Directives at least achieves a certain, albeit limited, approximation of national legislation that will be useful before proceeding to the next step of legislative integration.

181 This argument is pointed out by Nugent within a more general framework. Nonetheless, I consider it to also be applicable with regard to migration policy. See Nugent, *op.cit.*, at p. 197.

a "new approach" recognizing the need for various stages of harmonization.[182] Likewise, it seems to have given in to a series of Member State requests to lower down the standards of protection of the Directive.[183] In addition, it has also accepted the watering down of a series of provisions inasmuch as all its proposals are concerned.[184]

Secondly, right from the beginning it took a cautious approach in relation to those proposals that were expected to provoke major resistance, such as the paid employment Directive, and tried not to encroach on the sensitivities and competence of the Member States. Despite the efforts of the Commission to keep the balance between the will to regulate the matter at Community level and the need to respect Member States' discretion on the matter, the reaction of the Member States has been negative. Subsequently, when it became obvious that there was no political will, the Commission has almost silently accepted the Council's decision to freeze the proposal and decided to try again later. Indeed, even at the second attempt to regulate the matter the Commission opted for an extremely prudent approach based on a prior long consultation process and using both legislative and non-legislative tools, while stressing repeatedly that the number of migrants to be admitted fall under national competence.[185]

Thirdly, there has been an evident shift in the Commission's priorities with illegal migration progressively acquiring increasing importance. The September 11 effect inevitably provoked a strong shift in the Commission's agenda as well. However, when the intensive dialogue between the European Council and the Commission is taken into account, it could convincingly be argued that this shift in the Commission's agenda represents, to some extent, the need to reply to specific Council and Member State requests and to adapt itself to the political ambience in the Council. In the year and a half following autumn 2001, the Commission has issued five major communications dealing with issues of illegal migration, return and border management; a report on the available financial resources as well as two proposals regarding the security features of visas and

182 In parallel the Commission had proposed the inclusion of a general "stand still clause" in order to "freeze" the harmonization accomplished within this first stage as for the central provisions of the Directive. See the discussion *supra* at 4.2.1.

183 See Article 4 (1) regarding the clause on the 12 year children and Article 8 (2) regarding the extension of the waiting period. Both clauses have been challenged by the European Parliament as violating the European Convention on Human Rights (ECHR) standards. See discussion *supra* – at 4.2.1 – and *infra*, at 6.4.

184 See the discussion of all the Directives *supra* at 4.2.1.

185 See the discussion on the Legal Migration Policy Plan *supra* at 4.2.1.4. See also the replies of Commissioner Frattini during his appearance at the House of Lords, where he underlined his respect for subsidiarity and clarified that he prefers to talk about "common principles" rather than about "European law on immigration". See House of Lords, *Evidence by Commissioner Franco Frattini, op.cit.*

residence permits and various feasibility studies on security measures.[186] It has also been receptive to Member States requests both for the proposal of new security measures as well as for the diminution of the protection of individuals in its legislative proposals.[187]

Fourthly, it is worth highlighting the fact that there have been numerous occasions where the Commission chose to remain silent instead of entering into a strong conflict with the Member States. Noteworthy in this respect is readmission policy where notwithstanding that the Commission considers this an exclusive Community policy it has tacitly accepted the opinion of Member States by not intervening in cases where they have continued negotiating parallel agreements.[188] On certain occasions one could go as far as suggesting that the Commission fails to fulfil its role as guardian of the Treaties. For example, the visa waiver agreements clearly violate Article 62 (3) of the Treaty according to which third country nationals are expected to move up to a maximum of three months within the EU territory. The vast majority of Member States have such agreements, in particular, with the US. The Commission representative in the visa working party has been systematically reminding Member States of the fact that their agreements were illegal. And yet the Commission has not formally intervened even in cases where these agreements have been signed after the Treaty of Amsterdam came into force.[189] Moreover, for several years the Commission avoided taking a strong position with regard to certain deeply political situations such as, for example, the lack of reciprocity notably with the US inasmuch as the abolition of the visa obligation is concerned, despite the fact that reciprocity is among the principles mentioned in the relevant Community Regulation.[190]

---

186 For references and discussion see *supra* at 4.1.

187 Guild E., "Immigration, Asylum, Borders and Terrorism: The Unexpected Victims of 11 September 2001", in Gökay B. and Walker R.B.J.(eds.), *11 September 2001 War, Terror and Judgement,* Frank Cass, London, 2003, p. 175-194.

188 Schieffer M., "Community Readmission Agreements with Third-Countries – Objectives, Substance and Current State of Negotiations", *op.cit.*, at p. 351.

189 The Commission has tabled a proposal on the matter, which has raised considerable legal and political concerns, but the issue remains unresolved. See Proposal for a Council Directive relating to the conditions in which third-country nationals shall have the freedom to travel in the territory of the Member States for periods not exceeding three months, introducing a specific travel authorization and determining the conditions of entry and movement for periods not exceeding six months, *op.cit.* For a discussion and references see *supra* at 2.2.3.

190 Notwithstanding the reciprocity clause included in the Council visa Regulation and despite the US appearing in the "white list" of the EU visa Regulation, there was at least one EU country that was under a visa obligation *vis-à-vis* the US, namely Greece. The thorny question of a lack of reciprocity, especially with the US, was in fact accentuated not only following the new regulations regarding entry into the US -requiring that most foreign visitors travelling to the US on a visa have their two

That the Commission has finally decided to act is likely to be attributable to the pressure of enlargement as it was no longer only one of the Member States that appears on the US black list but nearly half of the Member States. [191]

Finally, the Commission's position at some points became rather puzzling. On the one hand, it followed a discourse of harmonisation and rather high standards, and yet at the very same time it proposed, despite the lack of any legal basis in that respect, the introduction of an Open Method of Coordination (OMC) in migration, a method that is primarily used in areas where the Community does not have legislative powers and which is difficult to reconcile with the strive for harmonisation in law-making terms.[192] According to the Commission the two methods need to be seen as complementary and their combination provides the necessary policy mix for the migration area.[193] Even if this is so, the Commission's Communication does not exhibit a coherent and carefully thought-through approach to the matter. The six main guidelines proposed by the Commission primarily copy the broad strategic aims of the Tampere Conclusions and the explanatory objectives that are enumerated are rather unclear and generic. Moreover, it is surprising to find in the list issues that clearly demand legislative approximation[194] as well as areas that relate to mere exchange of information or operational cooperation or to work that is already done by Council

index fingers scanned and a digital photo taken- but also due to the fact that none of the new Member States has signed a visa waiver agreement with the US and they accordingly all remain under the visa obligation. For more information on the new US-VISIT Program and on the US Visa Waiver Program see respectively <http://www.dhs.gov/us-visit> and <http://travel.state.gov/vwp.html>.

191 See Proposal for a Council Regulation amending Regulation (EC) No 539/2001 as regards the reciprocity mechanism, *op.cit*. On the visa reciprocity issue see also *supra* at 4.1.1.

192 Communication from the Commission to the Council and the European Parliament on an open method of coordination for the Community immigration policy, COM (2001) 387 final, 11.7.2001. For a commentary on the OMC method in immigration see Fletcher M., "EU Governance techniques in the Creation of a Common European Policy on Immigration and Asylum", *European Public Law,* Vol. 9, Issue 4, 2003, p. 533-562.

193 See the relevant Communication on the OMC, *op.cit.*, at p. 5 as well as Vitorino A., 'Interview with Antònio Vitorino, European Commissioner for Justice and Home Affairs', in European Economic and Social Committee, *Immigration, Asylum and Social Integration*, Office for Official Publications of the European Communities, Luxembourg, 2002, p. 7-15.

194 i.e. adopting adequate level of sanctions for criminal activities associated with illegal migration flows, reviewing legislation which restricts the possibility for migrants to move freely between their country of residence and their country of origin, or notification of national measures implementing Community legislation.

working parties.[195] Indeed, both the European Parliament and various commentators have expressed concerns about using the OMC in this area.[196] Given the strong competence debate in this field, the Commission may well have seen in the OMC process a nice compromise between the wish for EU action and the desire of Member States to maintain some degree of control. The Commission also seems to use the informational asymmetries as an opportunity for supranational activity, positioning itself in a central coordinating role.[197] However, the Commission proposal has not been taken up by the European Council of Laeken and the Council seems to prefer the traditional Community method.[198] Interestingly enough even the Commission itself seems to have abandoned this initiative.

To some extent, the Commission's decisions and choices can be explained by the lack of complete communitarisation. The sharing of the right of initiative has definitely deprived the Commission of a major negotiating weapon, i.e. the threat of withdrawing its proposals. With Member States making extensive use of their right of initiative the Commission had to struggle to live up to its traditional role of policy initiator.[199] Nonetheless, the role of the Commission is expected to be reinforced, not only in the sense that it has already reacquired its exclusive right of initiative, but also because the Community will shortly enter in to the implementation phase where its role is likely to prove pivotal since there is an obvious need to keep a close track of implementation.[200]

195 i.e. the collection and analysis of statistics, cooperation between consular authorities and pre-frontier cooperation.

196 See European Parliament report, A5-224/2003. See also de Búrca G., "The Constitutional Challenge of New Governance in the EU", *ELRev*, Vol. 28, No 6, December 2003, p. 814-839, and Geddes A., *The Politics of Migration and Immigration in Europe,* SAGE Publications, London, 2003, at p. 141.

197 See Geddes A., *The Politics of Migration and Immigration in Europe, op.cit.*, at p. 141.

198 See Reply of the Council to Oral question No II-572/02 by Robert Evans during the questions time of the European Parliament Session of September 2002.

199 Monar J., "Decision-making in the Area of Freedom, Security and Justice", *op.cit.*, at p. 75 and 76 respectively.

200 Indeed the Commission has already brought actions against Member States for non implementation of Community legislation. See Cases C-449/04 *Commission v. Luxembourg*, OJ C 314/7, 18.12.2004; C-516/04 *Commission v. Belgium*, OJ C 31/17, 5.2.2005; C-460/04 *Commission v. Netherlands*, OJ C 314/8, 18.12.2004; C-450/04 *Commission v. France*, OJ C 314/7, 18.12.2004; C-448/04 *Commission v. Luxembourg*, OJ C 314/6, 18.12.2004; C-462/04 *Commission v. Italy*, OJ C 6/30, 8.1.2005; and C-474/04 *Commission v. Greece*, OJ C 314/10, 18.12.2004. Moreover, the excessive importance placed to implementation and monitoring within the framework of the Hague Programme reinforces this thesis.

5.2.2 *The Commission's Well-hidden Arsenal and Weak Points*

Having briefly examined the Commission's position and strategic choices, it is worth highlighting certain additional aspects –which are often not sufficiently highlighted or taken into consideration- in order to be able to fully comprehend some of the Commission's choices and to have a fuller picture of the Commission's policy-making role and position.

5.2.2.1 Strong Points

First of all, the major advantage of the Commission is its deep knowledge and familiarity with the EU system along with the fact that it follows a dossier through every stage of the decision-making process. It has been convincingly argued that the Commission is well placed as a mediator and broker: first, due to its neutrality –which renders it an honest broker- and second, because of its knowledge and experience, since in most cases it is very well-placed to judge how a problem may be resolved and what approach is likely to command support amongst decision makers.[201]

Secondly, apart from being a facilitator, a role that it in principle shares with the Council Secretariat, the Commission is definitely the Union's 'think tank'. To some extent the Council is dependent on the Commission for ideas, initiatives, specific proposals and guidance, in particular with regard to legal migration issues.[202] This is somewhat understandable, since the Commission is usually willing and able to invest both the resources and the time in conducting surveys. Moreover, it has at its disposal a good network of academics willing to conduct surveys on its behalf. It is indicative that the Commission has conducted major comparative studies, itself or by commission, with regard to each of the legislative proposals that it has presented and it has also commissioned a series of studies on various other matters.[203]

---

201 For a discussion on this point in general see Nugent, *op.cit.*, at p. 13. Inasmuch as migration policy is concerned one needs to take into consideration two factors: first, all the legislative proposals on legal migration are based on comparative analysis of national legislation, a fact that gives the Commission an overview of the national positions and margins of manoeuvre of the Member States; and, second, despite its limited institutional role the Commission has been participating in the discussions and has a long-standing experience on Member States' positions and negotiation methods and techniques.

202 Where illegal migration is concerned the expertise lies with the Member States. For a more general discussion of the Council's dependence on the Commission for ideas see Nugent, *op.cit.*, at p. 118.

203 i.e. the studies conducted for the purposes of preparing its legislative proposals – for references see *supra* at 4.2.1 – as well as the major feasibility studies on several issues, such as integration policy, or more technical issues, such as maritime borders and the Visa Information System.

Thirdly, the Commission is usually the actor with the more general overview and Community approach. The internal inter-service consultation preceding the presentation of important documents is beneficial even if it inevitably slows down the process. The Commission's legislative proposals and other documents manage to bring together various aspects of Community law, coherence in EU law policy-making in general and contribute to maximising the means for attaining the Community objectives. Some examples of the Commission's global European view are the links between the researchers package and the European Research Area project,[204] the references to the Bologna Declaration of the Education Ministers in the Directive on studies,[205] the cross references between the legal migration Directives and other Community instruments on third country nationals – i.e. the format of residence permits, social security issues, bilateral agreements – the respective cross references between the European Employment Strategy and the Communications on migration and finally the inclusion of certain migration aspects in the EC guidelines for the employment policies of Member States.[206]

However, the Commission is also a policy actor and to some extent is intent on pursuing its own political goals and reinforcing its own institutional position. Therefore, on certain occasions it prepares and presents reports and creates a series of parallel structures, in an attempt to increase its competence. For instance, during the post-Maastricht era the Commission, despite the absence of formal agenda-setting powers, sought to develop credible policy ideas in the expectation that this would tempt the EU governments to delegate this function to the Commission in the next round of institutional reform. And, in fact, between 1994 and 1996 it was extremely active.[207] More recently, the establishment of the Committee on Immigration and Asylum, the so-called CIA –an informal forum of exchange of information and experiences- as well as the creation of the European Migration Network, and the passage of the external borders management competence in to the Commission's remit via the creation of an Agency in this field could arguably be seen as attempts by the Commission to increase the impact of its position. Moreover, some of these *fora*, in particular the CIA, could be interpreted as an effort by the Commission to render Member States co-responsible for the drafting of further EU proposals.

204 See the explanatory memorandum of the Commission's researchers package, *supra* at 4.2.1.

205 See the explanatory memorandum of the Commission's proposal on studies, *supra* at 4.2.1.

206 i.e. reduction of the unemployment gaps between non-EU and EU nationals (guideline No 7). See Council Decision 2003/578/EC of 22 July 2003 on guidelines for the employment policies of the Member States, OJ 197/13, 5.8.2003.

207 Hix S., *The political system of the European Union*, *op.cit.*, at p. 327-328.

Furthermore, the Commission succeeds in taking advantage of the weaknesses of other players, such as the Presidency and the European Council. Inasmuch as the former is concerned, it is worth highlighting the fact that the preparation of the compromise proposals is usually the outcome of extensive discussion with the Commission and the Council Secretariat. The Commission also manages to have its own position prevail by taking advantage of the extreme pressure under which the Presidency is often found combined with its lack of familiarity with specific dossiers.[208] As for the European Council, its institutional weaknesses – it meets infrequently and when it does meet is hampered by internal divisions – make it difficult for the European Council to act in a dynamic, innovative and independent manner. It is, accordingly, necessarily heavily dependent on ideas and proposals being presented to it. This provides agenda-setting opportunities for the Commission, which, alongside various parts of the Council of Ministers machinery, is actively involved in helping to prepare European Council meetings. Over half of the documents that are presented to normal EU Council sessions usually originate from the Commission, some of which are presented at the request of earlier Summits whilst others are launched at the Commission's own initiative.[209]

One further factor that is often not given sufficient weight and can either cash out positively or negatively is the impact of the personality of a particular Commissioner and also that of the Commission President. Whereas the President can of course determine the general tempo of the Commission which impacts upon developments in JHA matters[210] the personality of the JHA Commissioner is of immense importance.[211]

---

208 Two of the main reasons for which the Commission uses this technique are that the internal Commission inter-service procedure is rather heavy and that sometimes a proposal is better received if it comes from the Presidency rather than from the Commission.

209 For the impact of the Commission on the European Council see Nugent, *op.cit.*, at p. 186-187.

210 Even under the Delors Presidency, developments on JHA issues were not spectacular. Despite his evident dynamism, Delors would not pursue a course of action without having reason to believe that there was likely to be a considerable measure of support for at least the principle of such action at senior governmental levels. See Nugent, *op.cit.*, at p. 75. However, Santer's lack of interest in expanding the competences of the Commission – his motto being "less action but better action" – most probably contributed to the Commission's lack of dynamism in the implementation of the Maastricht Treaty. On the Santer Commission see Nugent, *op.cit.*, at p. 49-55.

211 Since he/she in principle decides on the Commission's agenda in the field and defines the approach to be taken. For instance, the lack of a sufficiently dynamic leadership was seen as one of the reasons affecting the Commission's position in the Maastricht era. See Uçarer, *op.cit.*

5.2.2.2 Weak Points

The Commission's weaknesses are of two main kinds. Those of an organisational nature and those linked with internal conflicts.

First of all, the Commission is an institution with significant organisational problems.[212] It is revealing that each document – be it a simple letter or a major Communication or legislative proposal – is only sent out or presented after having been circulated within the same DG and sent to the Legal service and/or other DGs that might have partial competence on the matter. Such a process is beneficial in terms of coherence and comprehensiveness but it obviously requires time and resources and diminishes considerably the dynamism of the Commission. On certain occasions it might even risk becoming counter productive.

Inasmuch as the second source of weaknesses is concerned, there are three general types of inter-service conflict: territorial, ideological and conflict over resources.[213] Frictions often arise in the college, especially in cross-sectoral policy areas, over who is responsible for particular aspects. This has, for example, long been a problem in the sphere of external relations policy where Commissioners' portfolios are not wholly self-contained but rather overlap at the edges. The progressive development of the external aspects of JHA and the logical request of the Freedom, Security and Justice DG to have a say on the matter, combined with the consequent limitation of the competence, authority and budget allocation of the external relations DG renders the debate between the two clearer. Another common problem is differences between DGs over policy priorities and policy methods. The difference in approach between the Employment and Social Affairs DG, which is considerably more open and migrant friendly, and the Freedom Security and Justice DG, which is a great deal more security oriented, are representative. Finally, several commentators relate such policy content and policy style differences to cultural differences within the Commission, with the behaviour and actions of officials being seen to be partly influenced by identities officials have either assumed or brought with them.[214]

5.3 The European Parliament: *Le Partenaire Ignoré*

5.3.1 An Overview of the European Parliament's Activities

Notwithstanding its limited institutional role, the European Parliament has been rather active with regard to the movement of persons and migration related issues. It has traditionally not only followed closely the relevant developments but has also taken strong positions which were noticeably pro-European and of a liberal orientation.

212 Nugent, *op.cit.*, at p. 4.

213 This categorisation is provided by Nugent. See Nugent, *op.cit.*, at p. 159-160. Although he uses it at the more general level it appears to be particularly applicable to the field of migration.

214 Nugent, *op.cit.,* at p. 9.

Even if its political stance had initially emerged from, and is primarily linked to, its long standing concern for human rights and for the free movement of workers, from 1985 and the Single European Act it started to develop a more comprehensive position on migration issues.[215] In the 1980s and early 1990s, the European Parliament issued a series of own initiative reports,[216] and has taken a position with regard to all the major developments in this area. Its position was plainly pro-European and traditionally argued in favour of Community competence though this position is said to have stemmed from, *inter alia*, its irritation due to the fact that it had not had any opportunity to have a say.[217] For instance, it has been argued that in its intervention to the migration policy case "the Parliament was more clear-sighted about the fundamental issue at stake and argued that if the Decision was annulled for lack of competence this in fact would alter the division of powers between the Community and the Member States in the field to the detriment of the Community".[218] It also took a strong position on the universal application of Article 8a EEC and called for its implementation by the Council and the Commission.[219] Moreover, in a number of Resolutions it criticised strongly the failure to take action on migration policy under the EEC Treaty.[220]

---

215 Monar J., "The European Parliament and Immigration Policy: Its Positions and Possibilities of Control", in Korella G.D. and Twomey P.M. (eds.), *Towards a European Immigration Policy*, European Interuniversity Press, Bruges, 1993, p. 123-137, at p. 124. Monar also provides an interesting overview of the Parliament's position up to 1993 and its relations with the Commission.

216 For an overview of the European Parliament's Reports and activities see Van Den Brink and Vierhout, *op.cit.*, at p. 385-388.

217 Van Den Brink and Vierhout, *op.cit.*, at p. 386 and 389.

218 See Guild E., *Immigration Law in the European Community, op.cit.*, at p. 236 and Handoll, *op.cit.*, at p. 34. See also Parliament's Resolution on the matter, Resolution on free movement of persons pursuant to Article 8a of the EEC Treaty, OJ C 176/35, 28.6.1993.

219 Report of the Committee on Civil Liberties and Internal Affairs on the abolition of controls at internal borders and free movement of persons within the European Community, K. Tsimas, 2 October 1992, A-3 0284/92. See Guild E., *Immigration Law in the European Community, op.cit.*, at p. 225.

220 Resolution on the harmonisation of policies on entry to the territories of the EC Member States with a view to the free movement of persons (Article 8a of the EEC Treaty) and the drawing up of an intergovernmental Convention among 12 Member States of the EC (OJ C 72/213, 18.3.1991), Resolution on the free movement of persons and security in the European Community (OJ C 267/197, 14.10.1991), Resolution on the European Labour Market after 1992 (OJ C 241/51, 21.9.1992), Resolution on the abolition of controls at internal frontiers and free movement of persons within the European Community (OJ C 337/211, 21.12.1992), Resolution on the free movement of persons (OJ C 72/136, 15.3.1993), Resolution on migrant

The Parliament was also active in the post-Maastricht era, albeit exhibiting less interest for the third pillar than for Common Foreign and Security Policy (CFSP) issues.[221] Its position has been of a liberal nature. So during the Maastricht IGC it criticised the Commission's Communication for being compliant with the restrictive drift.[222] Taking traditionally a pro-European position and considering that the only positive point in Maastricht was Article K.9, it had asked the Commission to pronounce on this.[223] Further, it is worth highlighting that already as early as 1993 the European Parliament had proposed the drawing up of a Charter of rights and obligations of nationals of non-member countries in the EU, calling for the need for equal rights to be enjoyed by Community and non-Community citizens.[224] Finally, the European Parliament was also interested and active both with regard to Schengen cooperation and the integration of the Schengen *acquis* within the framework of the EU.[225]

The post-Amsterdam era also saw the Parliament playing a lively role. It participated actively and adopted a liberal position during the course of the Amsterdam IGC.[226] It contributed to the more general inter-institutional discussion on the implementation of the new Treaty by issuing an own initiative report on migration policy.[227] Inasmuch as its role during the implementation of the Treaty is concerned, the activities of the Parliament took various forms. Firstly, through its official institutional role in the decision-making process it followed policy developments closely both within the Commission and the Council and

---

workers from third countries (OJ C 175/180, 16.7.1990), Resolution on European Immigration policy (OJ C 337/94, 21.12.1992), Resolution on the European Council meeting in Luxembourg on 28 and 29 June 1991 (OJ C 240/132, 16.9.1991) and Resolution on the results of the Intergovernmental conferences (OJ C 125/81, 18.5.1992). See also Handoll, *op.cit.*, at p. 358.

221 Den Boer and Wallace, *op.cit.,* at p. 499.

222 On the Maastricht IGC see Geddes A., *Immigration and European Integration – Towards fortress Europe?, op.cit.*, at p. 89-91. See also the European Parliament Resolutions on the European Council meeting in Luxembourg on 28 and 29 June 1991, OJ C 240/132, 16.9.1991, and on the Maastricht IGC, OJ C 125/81, 18.5.1992.

223 Resolution A3-0402/93 of 19 January 1994, p. 28 to 33. Of course, Article K.9 was the so-called *passerelle* clause included in Maastricht's third pillar, according to which the Council could decide unanimously the transfer of a certain policy area from the third to the first pillar. For more details see Chapter 1.

224 European Parliament Report on the status of nationals of non-member countries in the European Union, A3-0332/93, 5.11.1993. For a brief discussion see Melis B., *Negotiating Europe's Immigration Frontiers,* Kluwer, The Hague, 2001, at p. 30.

225 See the Report of Anne Van Lancker on Schengen, OJ C 104/144, 14.4.1999.

226 Geddes A., *Immigration and European Integration – Towards fortress Europe?, op.cit.*, at p. 120.

227 See the report of Viviane Reding on migration, OJ C 219/106, 30.7.1999.

issued reports and resolutions on the matters, whether legislative measures or documents of more general interest, discussed. In spite of its limited negotiating weight, the Parliament tries to be an equal partner in the inter-institutional debate, producing a considerable number of reports and Resolutions. Secondly, it systematically asks the Commission and the Council oral and written questions. Thirdly, the Parliament does not limit itself to taking a position whenever this is required institutionally or on documents presented by the other institutional actors. Rather it is active in relation to more general or future developments. The own initiative reports and Resolutions are an example of this and usually reflect awareness and interest by MEPs in bringing an issue not only to the attention of the Commission and the Council but also the broader public.[228] For instance, the Parliament holds an annual debate on the Area of Freedom Security and Justice,[229] as well as public hearings on several issues,[230] and its research unit frequently prepares relevant working papers.[231]

Inasmuch as the substance of its position is concerned, the Parliament has consistently argued for a comprehensive and migrant-friendly approach.[232] Firstly, the Parliament is sensitive to issues such as human rights. Good examples are provided by its legal challenge to the family reunification Directive and its position with regard to the data protection issues linked with the transfer of

228 Maurer A., "The Evolution of the Legislative Powers of the European Parliament : an Impact Assessement", in Vandersanden G. and de Walsch A. (eds.), *Mélanges en hommage à Jean-Victor Louis (Vol. I)*, Editions de l'Université de Bruxelles, Bruxelles, Bruxelles, 2003, p. 309-336, at p. 317.

229 See, for instance, the European Parliament Resolution on progress in 2002 in implementing an area of Freedom, Security and Justice – 2002 Annual debate on an area of freedom, security and justice, OJ C 62E/176, 11.3.2004. These meetings also have a 'think tank' function. In its 2003 annual debate, for example, it examined in depth the case of Tampere II and proposed a series of policy guidelines that EU action should follow.

230 For example, the 2000 European Parliament Hearing: "The European Union and Data Protection", available at <http://www.europarl.ep.ec/dg2/hearings/20000222/libe/subject/en/default.htm> as well as the 2001 European Parliament Hearing: "The situation of fundamental rights in the European Union and the establishment of the European area of freedom, security and justice", 21.3.2001.

231 It is the so-called LIBE series. See, *inter alia*, European Parliament Working paper "Free Movement of persons in the European Union – An Overview" LIBE 100 EN and European Parliament Working paper "Freedom, Security, Justice: An Agenda for Europe" Civil Liberties Series, LIBE 106, 1999.

232 For a brief presentation of the position of the Parliament see Watson G., "EU Asylum and Immigration Policies: The Point of View of the European Parliament", in Marinho C. (ed.), *Asylum, Immigration and Schengen Post-Amsterdam – A First Assessement,* EIPA, Maastricht, 2001, p. 47-53.

passenger data agreement with the US.[233] And even with respect to the Commission legislative proposals its position was much more liberal.[234] For example, by touching upon issues that are considered "taboo" by the Member States, such as voting rights for migrants.[235] It has also not hesitated in rejecting a series of Member States' initiatives, due mainly to their piecemeal or overlapping character.[236] It has been cogently argued that this liberal approach can be explained by the lack of any immediate electoral pressure.[237] However, it is difficult to assess the position of MEPs since their attitude differs profoundly depending on their relationship with their respective Member State, their party affiliation, their personal convictions and how seriously they perceive their work.[238]

5.3.2 The European Parliament's Negotiating Position

Legally speaking, that is if one refers to the relevant Treaty provisions, the institutional role of the European Parliament has until recently been rather limited. Everyday practice, however, reveals a different reality. On the one hand, sometimes its existing formal powers are not as strong as they may seem, but, on the other hand, it exercises powers that are not always evident.

233 See Case C-540/03, *European Parliament v Council*, pending. See also "Parliament set to challenge EU-US data deal in court", <www.euobserver.com>, 16.6.2004.

234 See, for example, the European Parliament Reports on the proposal for a Directive on the right to family reunification, A5-0201/2000 and A5-0086/2003 or the Report on short-term residence permits issued to victims, OJ C 27E/140, 30.1.2004.

235 See European Parliament Report on the proposal for a Council Directive concerning the status of third-country nationals who are long-term residents, A5-0436/2001, 30.11.2001.

236 For a list of all the Member States initiatives that have been rejected by the Parliament see the two editions of the Scoreboard for 2001. For an analysis on the reasons of their rejection see Papagianni G., "Free Movement of Persons in the light of the new Title IV TEC: from intergovernmentalism towards a Community policy", *op.cit*.

237 Guiraudon V., "The constitution of a European immigration policy domain : a political sociology approach", *op.cit.*, at p. 273.

238 According to one interesting paper, the behaviour of MEPs is influenced by three main factors: re-election, policy seeking and office-seeking. See Hix S., Raunio T. and Scully R., *An Institutional Theory of Behaviour in the European Parliament*, EPRG Working Paper, No 1, Manheim, <http://personal.lse.ac.uk/HIX/Working-Papers.HTM>. One commentator focusing on migration policy has sustained that the right-left construct has an organising power among parties in the European Parliament regarding migration policy preferences. See Lahav G., "Ideological and Party Constraints on Immigration Attitudes in Europe", *Journal of Common Market Studies,* Vol. 35, No 3, September 1997, p. 377-406.

5.3.2.1 *Partenaire Ignoré*

Traditionally the role of the Parliament has been rather limited, a mere consultation obligation being the extent of its role in most cases. Inasmuch as the Maastricht Treaty is concerned, a consultation obligation was not expressly established. The Commission systematically consulted the European Parliament but this was not the case for Member State initiatives, for which the European Parliament was usually informed only *a posteriori*. A tradition was, however, established for the Presidency to present in front of the competent European Parliament Committee once or twice each semester.[239]

The Amsterdam Treaty has clarified the obligation of consultation and the progressive passage to the co-decision procedure has further reinforced the powers of the Parliament. However, in the post-Amsterdam era and until the passage to the co-decision procedure, despite the official obligation to consult the Parliament, its *de facto* role was extremely limited. A comparison of the amendments proposed by the Parliament with the final texts adopted by the Council show clearly that the Council almost never took into consideration the opinion of the Parliament. Moreover, there has been a growing tendency to reach political agreement within the Council without even waiting for the opinion of the Parliament. The consultation thus being transformed into a mere formality.[240] And the Council continues to adopt strategy documents on which the Parliament is not consulted.[241]

In the light of the above, it is fair to say that up to the passage to the co-decision procedure the Parliament was a *partenaire ignoré*. To be sure, the passage to the co-decision procedure has significantly enhanced its role in the relevant fields.[242] It has also been convincingly argued that the application of the co-decision process has a considerably positive impact on the "functional professionalisation" and policy linked "specialisation" of MEPs, since they are "condemned

239 De Lobkowicz W., *L'Europe et la sécurité intérieure Une élaboration par étapes, op.cit.*, at p. 51; Van Den Brink and Vierhout, *op.cit.*, at p. 388.

240 For instance, this was the case with the family reunification Directive, the Directive on the short-term residence permit for victims of trafficking and the Directive on transit in cases of expulsion by air. It is worth highlighting that with regard to the Italian initiative on joint flights and the Spanish Initiative on the obligation of communication of passenger data, the Council adopted the relevant measures without the opinion of the Parliament. See recitals 5, 6 and 7 of Council Decision 2004/573/EC on the organization of joint flights, *op.cit.*, as well as the relevant Note to Coreper included in Council doc. 8773/04, *op.cit*. See also recitals 4, 5 and 6 of Council Directive 2004/83/EC on the obligation of carriers to communicate passenger data, *op.cit.*

241 Monar J., "Decision-making in the Area of Freedom, Security and Justice, *op.cit.*, at p. 77-78.

242 Inasmuch as the passage to the co-decision process is concerned see the discussion *supra* at 2.3.

to become experts in technical and complex issues".[243] However, given the limited time frame that the co-decision procedure applies in this area it is for the moment rather premature to judge its impact.[244]

5.3.2.2 Indirect Powers

Despite the long standing restricted character of its institutional powers, through an innovative use of its limited powers and thanks to a series of more general factors, the Parliament has nevertheless on several occasions managed to increase its institutional weight and influence.

Firstly, there is the main institutional weapon of the Parliament, namely the budget, and the possibilities for interfering that this grants to the Parliament. Indeed, in the early post-Maastricht days, the Council was somewhat distrustful of the Parliament on this point.[245] Secondly, Article 192 TEC grants to the Parliament the possibility to ask the Commission to submit a proposal.[246]

Thirdly, the Parliament can make use of some more general political weapons to put pressure on the Commission and the Council. In the case of the Commission this can be much more direct –since the college needs to be approved by the Parliament and it can even call for the collective resignation of the college.[247] The most recent example regarding the resignation of the candidate Italian Commissioner for JHA, Mr Buttiglione, following the extreme pressure and

---

243 Maurer, *op.cit.*, at p. 319. He also provides an interesting overview of the development of the legislative powers of the European Parliament as well as of the recent amendments of the co-decision procedure. See specifically p. 312-313.

244 However, the experience of the first major legislative instrument that has been adopted under the co-decision procedure – i.e. the Community Code for the crossing of borders – has been rather positive bearing in mind that they the two institutions managed to reach political agreement during the first reading.

245 The operational JHA expenses were non-obligatory, which means that the Parliament had the last word. The inclusion of such expenses in the budget was therefore a way to implicate itself in the third pillar. Nonetheless, Member States have been extremely distrustful fearing that via the funding there would be a risk of communitarisation. In fact, while in 1995 the Parliament had included to the budget expenses regarding Europol, Member States have opted to leave the relevant financial credits and opted for national funding. See De Lobkowicz W., *L'Europe et la sécurité intérieure Une élaboration par étapes, op.cit.*, at p. 82-83.

246 However, to my knowledge this provision has not been used by the Parliament in the migration field.

247 The Commisioners' cabinets and each DG has officials responsible for relations with the EP and there is also a special directorate in the Commission's Secretariat General which has a general responsibility for ensuring that the Commission's relations with the European Parliament are handled in an efficient and expeditious manner. See Nugent, *op.cit.,* at p. 193.

strong criticisms from the European Parliament, is revealing.[248] The Parliament also uses to good effect its limited legislative powers to exercise pressure over the Council. Ministers holding the Presidency need to appear in front of the Parliament, a process that can be rather tough. Moreover, the Parliament often delays the legislative process when the Commission and the Council are deemed to be insufficiently sympathetic to its amendments.[249] And quite often the Parliament brings pressure to bear through written and oral questions as well as through the interviewing of MEP's by the media.

Fourthly, the Parliament has used its judicial *locus standi* possibilities in order to oblige the Council and the Commission to listen to its voice. In 1993 it did not hesitate to act against the Commission. The main argument of the Parliament in its 1993 action was that "the Commission was wrong to acquiesce in the Member States' wish to act outside the EC Treaty framework by means of intergovernmental agreements". Adding that, "since under the EC Treaty, only the Commission has the right to initiate legislation, it was bound to introduce the requisite proposals".[250] More recently, it 'showed its teeth' when the Council ignored completely its position with regard to the family reunification Directive – the Council adopted a common approach before the Parliament's consultation and waited for its opinion for merely formal reasons. Using its newly acquired active *locus standi*, the Parliament asked for the annulment of the Directive. This was considered an innovative and courageous step. On the one hand, it was the first time that the Parliament brought an action as a privileged actor under Article 230 (2) TEC, and on the other it was the first time that it brought an action regarding human rights.

Fifthly, the Parliament has managed to overcome its limited institutional role via an innovative use of media coverage and access to the Court by certain of its members. As an example, one could mention the "Croisades cyclistes" where an MEP refused to present identification documents at the crossing of the border (Dieter Rogalla).[251] An analogous action was also taken some years

---

248 See "Parlement européen: les convictions morales de Buttiglione", *Figaro*, 6.10.2004.; "Rocco Buttiglione devant le Parlement européen", *La Croix*, 6.10.2004, and "Italian Commissioner struggles to beat off criticism" <www.euobserver.com>, 5.10.2004.

249 In general on this point see Nugent, *op.cit.*, at p. 189. It needs to be recalled that the Council had twice, due to the urgency of the particular issue, adopted measures without waiting for the opinion of the Parliament, i.e. the Italian initiative on joint flights and the Spanish initiative on the transfer of passenger data.

250 Handoll, *op.cit.*, at p. 34-35.

251 De Lobkowicz W., *L'Europe et la sécurité intérieure Une élaboration par étapes, op.cit.*, at p. 24.

later by another MEP, Mr Wijsenbeek, leading to the well-known case law of the Court.[252]

5.4 The European Court of Justice: The Unknown Factor

In contrast to the general perception, albeit well-based from an institutional point of view, according to which the Court does not officially participate in the decision-making process, it needs to be underscored that the Court influences strongly the outcome of the decision-making process not only *ex post* but also *ex ante*. The *ex post* influence of the Court is obviously more evident. Through its case law the Court can establish a narrower or broader interpretation of the legal texts than the Council has adopted. On some occasions it might even repeal certain provisions or, through creative interpretation, establish rights that are not expressly mentioned.

However, the Court also has an important *ex ante* impact over the decision-making process. In fact, the fear of judicial activism frequently influences the position of the Member States, since it regularly renders them much more cautious and restrictive in their approach.[253] Three examples are worth citing. First, and in line with academic commentary, the content and in general the text of the Declarations attached to the Single European Act were eventually affected by the then pending migration policy case.[254] Secondly, the case of the public order provisions of the recently adopted legal migration Directives. In contrast to the Commission proposals recommending a drafting close to that of Directive 64/221, Member States deleted the reference to "personal conduct" and accompanied this with a series of clarifications in the preamble and declarations which have limited even further the scope of the relevant provisions.[255] It is likely that the impact of cases such as *Rutili* still loomed large in the minds of the negotiators.[256] Thirdly, the impact of the *Chen* case in Ireland has been swift.[257] Following the relevant request for a preliminary reference, the govern-

252 Case C-378/97, *Wijsenbeek*, *op.cit.*

253 It is likely that one of the reasons for the limitation of the role of the Court most likely was that certain Member States were against establishing the possibility of preliminary references for lower courts in this sensitive policy area given the Court's past record in social policy. Beach, *op.cit.*, at p. 105. For an overview of the current limitations of the role of the Court see our discussion in Chapter 2.

254 See Guild E., *Immigration Law in the European Community, op.cit.*, at p. 240.

255 See Article 6 in conjunction with recital 14 of the family reunification Directive and Article 6 in conjunction with the relevant Declaration and recital 8 of the long-term residents Directive, as well as the relevant clauses of the initial Commission proposals.

256 Case C-36/75, *Rutili* [1975] ECR 1219.

257 Case C-200/02 *Man Lavette Chen*. See the Judgement of the Court of 9 October 2004 as well as the Opinion of Advocate General Tizzano, delivered on 18 May

ment called for a referendum on the basis of which Irish nationality law has been amended and the *ius soli* nationality is limited now to cases where at least one of the parents is Irish.[258]

As was already demonstrated in previous chapters – mainly chapters one and two – there is a patent and continuous attempt by the Member States to limit to the greatest degree possible the role and the competence of the Court. Moreover, the occasions on which the Court has had a chance to examine migration policy issues have been somewhat limited, since its case law on third country nationals is mainly concerned with persons that are family members of EU citizens or are nationals of countries with which the Community had signed an association agreement.[259] The cases directly linked with migration policy as such were limited and concerned almost exclusively institutional issues like the competence question and the inter-institutional skirmishes.[260]

Following the integration of the Schengen *acquis* and with a view to the full implementation of Community legal instruments on migration the role of the Court is sure to be of the utmost importance. The lack of judicial control and protection was one of the main criticisms with regard to the lack of a uniform application of the Schengen *acquis*. However, Schengen relevant provisions such

---

2004. The case concerns a preliminary reference from a British court where a Chinese mother, who, having arranged to give birth to her child in the North of Ireland, was claiming a right to stay permanently in the UK on the basis of the Irish (and by definition also European) citizenship of the baby. Indeed, the Court has recognised the right of the mother to reside with the child in the host Member State on the basis that a refusal to allow the parent to reside with the child would deprive the child's right of residence of any useful effect.

258 Point raised by Richard Plender in his paper "Forced Migrations – Grounds and Limits to States' Action", distributed at the IX Convengo SIDI "Le migrazioni: una sfida per il diritto internazionale, comunitario e interno" held in Rome, 17 and 18 June 2004. It is worth underlining that Ireland proceeded to the amendment of its legislation even before the judgement of the Court.

259 For a brief discussion on this case law see Guild E., *Immigration Law in the European Community, op.cit.*; Van Raepenbusch S., " La jurisprudence de la Cour de justice des Communautés européennes vis-à-vis des ressortissants de pays tiers", in Den Boer M. (ed.), *The implementation of Schengen: First the Widening, Now the Deepening,* EIPA, Maastricht, 1997, p. 41-69 and Hedemann-Robinson M., "An overview of recent legal developments at Community level in relation to third country nationals resident within the European Union, with particular reference to the case law of the European Court of Justice", *CMLRev*, Vol. 38, 2001, p. 525-586. For a more general brief overview of the case law and the competence of the Court with regard to migration see Guild and Peers, *op.cit*.

260 Joined cases C-281, 283 to 285 and 287/85, *Germany and Others v Commission of the European Communities* (migration policy case); Case C-170/96, *Commission v Council* (the airport transit visas case) and Case 257/2001, *Commission v. Council,* (the comitology case).

as SIS blacklisting or refusal of entry are extremely sensitive for individuals. And as discussed earlier, the vague drafting of a series of legal provisions in the post-Amsterdam Directives and the deferral of consensus for later stages increase the importance of the Court, which is expected to provide an authoritative interpretation of the relevant provisions. The role of the Court to ensure a uniform implementation of EU law thus becomes more important than ever.

The issues that the Court will eventually have to address are both numerous and complex. First of all, given that one of the favourite Council techniques in order to reach compromise lies in the insertion of references to national legislation or to the preamble, the Court would inevitably have to set the borders of what the obscure phrase "according to national law" really means and where are the limits of national competence as well as the value of additional restrictions included in the preamble. For example, could national legislation refuse to grant the specific right to third country nationals? What if the conditions that are imposed as far as the exercise of the right is concerned are so difficult to respect that to all intents and purposes they partly annul the substance of the right? All these and many more issues would probably have to be the subject of a case-by-case examination. Moreover, the Court would have to provide a common interpretation for a series of provisions that have been consciously drafted in an open-ended way, as well as to find common definitions for concepts such as "core benefits", social assistance or "legal residence", whose meaning differs profoundly from one Member State to another. Last but not least, given the human rights implications with regard to the issues in question the Court will also be performing the role of guardian for the respect of human rights.[261]

Nonetheless, it is rather difficult for the moment to predict the position that the Court will take in the future. Currently there are few cases already judged or pending and these are of a primarily institutional or more general character.[262]

261 For some interesting comments on the development of human rights issues in the case law of the Court of Justice as well as the relationship between the courts of Strasbourg and Luxembourg see Frangakis N., "Human Rights and European Integration – From the European Convention on Human Rights to the Charter of Fundamental Rights of the European Union", in Vandersanden G. and de Walsch A. (eds.), *Mélanges en hommage à Jean-Victor Louis (Vol. I)*, Editions de l'Université de Bruxelles, Bruxelles, 2003, p. 189-201.

262 i.e. Case C-257/01 on comitology; Case C-540/03 on the family reunification Directive; the two actions of the UK against the Council for rejection of opt-in requests – Cases C-77/05 and C-137/05 – as well as Commission actions against Member States for non implementation of Directives, *op.cit.* The only cases that concern substantive law Schengen relevant issues are, on the one hand, Case C-503/03 *Commission v. Spain* on the SIS listing of family member of EU citizens, *op.cit.*, and on the other hand, a preliminary ruling concerning the concept of first entry within the Schengen framework, Case C-241/05, *Bot v. Préfecture du Val-de-Marne,* OJ C 193/19, 6.8.2005, both of them pending.

It is expected that in the period following the implementation of the Directives the number of cases brought to the Court of Justice will considerably increase.[263] In a rather preliminary attempt to examine the position of the Court one could take into consideration a series of factors. Firstly, experience has shown that the limits with regard to the competence of the Court are permeable. The airport transit visas case is evidence in this regard.[264] Concepts of a primarily national character, such as that of public order are not unknown to the Court.[265] Secondly, the Court traditionally takes a rather Community favourable approach. The judgment on the migration policy case, its recent judgement on the border line between first and third pillar regarding criminal law penalties and the traditionally positive stance taken with regard to the more European-centred institutions such as the Parliament and the Commission are good examples.[266] Third, there is a growing case law with references to human rights issues and ECHR provisions[267] and it is expected that the role of the Court will grow especially in light of the incorporation of the Charter of Human Rights in the Draft Constitutional Treaty.

On the other hand, it is not yet clear whether the Court will be as activist as it has been in the past. First, the case of citizens is most probably rather different from the case of third country nationals. Even in the case of citizens the Court had for a long time hesitated taking a clear position on their rights. It was not

263 However, it has already been noted that the Court does not have the competence to examine preliminary references from lower courts. In fact, the Court has already declared expressly its lack of competence. See Cases C-45/03 and C-555/03, *op. cit.*, which concerned preliminary references from lower courts and which have been removed from the register.

264 Case C-170/96, *op.cit.* For discussion see *supra* at 1.4.2.

265 For a discussion on the public policy proviso see Arnull A. and Jacobs F.G., "Applying the common rules on the free movement of persons – The role of the national judiciary in the light of the jurisprudence of the European Court of Justice", in Schermers et al. (eds.), *Free Movement of Persons in Europe, Legal Problems and Experiences*, T.M.C. Asser Institute, The Hague, 1993, p. 272-285, at p. 278-281. The authors highlight the fact that responsibility for the application of the concept of public policy in specific cases rests ultimately with the national courts however they also emphasise the need for national courts to give proper weight to the Community interest.

266 For a discussion on the migration policy case see *supra* at 1.1.2. For a discussion on Case C-176/03 on penalties see *supra* at 2.2.2. Moreover, one should not lose sight of the fact that the European Parliament has established its consultation rights to some extent thanks to the case law of the Court.

267 Case C-413/99 *Baumbast and R v Secretary of State for the Home Department* [2002] ECR I-7091; Case C-60/00 *Carpenter v Secretary of State for the Home Department* [2002] ECR I-6279; Case C-109/01 *Secretary of State for the Home Department v Hacene Akrich*, judgment of 23 September 2003.

until 1997 and the famous *Martinez Sala* case that it decided to deal with this issue.[268] Second, the limits between national competence and that of the Court as far as the supervision of human rights are concerned is highly contested.[269] Hitherto and with regard to third country nationals having a special link with EU citizens, the approach of the Court has been expansive. It is interesting that in the *Akrich* case, while acknowledging that there was no Community competence on the matter in question, the Court still chose to give some 'human rights lessons' to the Member States.[270] Nonetheless, even if the Court has been traditionally rather progressive with regard to EU citizens or their family members[271] it remains to be seen whether it will be as progressive where it is exclu-

268 For a discussion on the 'missed opportunities' of the Court as far as the establishment of substantive rights deriving from the EU citizenship as well as on the *Martinez Sala* case see "La circulation des citoyens de l'Union: de Maastricht à Amsterdam et au délà", *Actualités de droit*, Vol. 4, 1999, p. 625-665.

269 For a detailed discussion on this point as well as a brief summary of the position taken by the ECJ itself see Tridimas T., *The General Principles of EC Law*, Oxford University Press, Oxford, 1999, p. 202-243 and Craig P. and de Búrca G., *EC Law Text, Cases & Materials,* Third edition Oxford University Press, Oxford, 2003, at p. 337-349. See also Weiler J.H.H., "Thou Shalt not oppress a stranger (Ex. 23:9): on the judicial protection of the human rights of non-EC nationals", in Schermers et al. (eds), *Free Movement of Persons in Europe, Legal Problems and Experiences*, T.M.C. Asser Institute, The Hague, 1993, p. 248-271, at p. 262. According to Weiler, even in the absence of positive Community law defining with precision many of the conditions for its application, and in a situation which leaves much liberty to the individual Member States in setting these conditions, the Court retains jurisdiction (and a duty) to ensure that the fundamental human rights of migrants in relation to their right of residence should not be violated either by the Community or by its Member States. In contrast to Weiler's liberal view, Hailbronner and Plender seem considerably more restrictive in their approach. They consider that the Council cannot be held responsible for any violation of the ECHR as a result of the Member States' decision to make use of eventual options or reservations that are included in Community measures. Furthermore, they are both rather critical of the *Ackrich* case law in that regard. See Hailbronner K., "European Immigration and Asylum Law – FIDE Conference – Introductory remarks", paper distributed at the XXI FIDE Congress, 2-5 June 2004. Plender R., "Quo vadis? Nouvelle orieantation des regles su la libre circulation des personnes suivant a l'affaire Akrich", paper distributed at the IX Convegno SIDI "Le migrazioni: una sfida per il diritto nazionale, communitario e interno", held in Rome, 17 and 18 June 2004.

270 Case C-109/01 *Akrich, op.cit.*, at para. 61, fourth intent.

271 For an overview of the Court's case law see Wouters J., "European citizenship and the case-law of the Court of Justice of the European Communities on the free movement of persons", in Marias E. A. (ed.), *European citizenship,* EIPA, Maastricht, 1994, p. 25-61 and Mattera A., "La libre circulation des travailleurs à l' intérieur de la Communauté européenne", *RMUE*, No 3, 1993, p. 47-108.

sively third country nationals that are involved. It is certainly possible that the Court might take into consideration political considerations that will render it more cautious.[272] Taking into account the impact of the public policy case law on negotiations in the Council and the recent amendment of the Irish citizenship law following the relevant preliminary reference request, it appears that the factors that the Court will have to take into consideration are numerous, since ultimately excessive judicial activism, might impact negatively on the rights of individuals.

Concluding Remarks

The main conclusion that could be drawn on the basis of the examination of the position and role of, and interactions among, the different policy actors is that these are much more complex than they might seem at first sight. Each of the actors has a series of sensitivities or policy objectives as well as a series of strong and weak points that, while not always evident, affect deeply the decision-making process.

Secondly, the decision-making process within the Council is much more informal than it might seem and one could identify the establishment of a series of patterns or techniques. While some of them are rather useful in terms of efficiency, certain others, and in particular the technique of deferring compromises to a later stage, could eventually prove rather dangerous. Moreover, the entire negotiation process is heavily influenced by a series of political considerations that may not always be evident to the external observer.

Thirdly, the decision-making process as well as the position of the two main policy actors in this area, namely the Council and the Commission, is primarily pragmatic. To be sure, pragmatism is not without its positive effects but it can have negative impacts on comprehensiveness, legal clarity and certainty which should also be recognised.

Bearing in mind the complex character of policy-making in the field of migration and the fact that as of May 2004 the Council has to take decisions with twenty-five Member States at the table, one really wonders whether it could possibly function effectively in the future.

272 For example it has been sustained that on the occasion of the *Demirel* case the Court was very much aware of the presence of 1,500,000 Turkish immigrants in Germany and the problems this posed. See Alexander W., "Free movement of non-EC nationals – A review of the case-law of the Court of Justice", in Schermers et al. (eds.), *Free Movement of Persons in Europe, Legal Problems and Experiences*, T.M.C. Asser Institute, The Hague, 1993, p. 485-496, at p. 496.

Chapter 6: Policy-making in Migration (Part II): An Overall Critical Analysis of Europe's Nascent Migration Law and Policy

Introduction

Having presented the main legislative developments regarding migration law as well as the role of, and interaction among, the key policy actors, this last chapter will endeavour to draw an overall critical analysis of Europe's nascent migration law and policy. The analysis will be centred around two main axes: first, an overview of the general features and framework of policy-making with regard to migration; and, second a critical analysis of the content and quality of Europe's migration policy, in particular in the post-Amsterdam era.

Considering that the existence of a clear, and most importantly a commonly accepted, framework and ultimate goal is a *sine qua non* condition for the development of a coherent and effective migration policy, this chapter will first examine this specific issue. A first sub-section will draw attention, in particular, to the fact that policy-making in migration traditionally did not have a consistent or clear-cut objective, but was rather, and still is, heavily influenced by a series of internal and mainly external factors. This is followed by an attempt to define the scope of migration policy at EU level and to highlight the existence of a two track approach concerning, on the one hand, aspects regarding the entry for short-term purposes and mere circulation of third country nationals – which is defined herein as migration *stricto sensu* – and on the other hand, more general issues regarding entry and residence for long-term purposes, which is defined as migration in the classic sense. Further, this first sub-section strives to identify the causes impeding the formation of a coherent and effective migration policy at European level.

Taking into account that the Treaty of Amsterdam constitutes a major turning point for European migration policy, a second sub-section examines in depth the extent and the meaning of the changes resulting from Amsterdam. The major question that will be posed and analysed concerns the extent to which the Treaty of Amsterdam provisions and the way these have been implemented really mark the beginning of a new era, or whether these are not quite so innovative and what is being witnessed is merely a crystallisation of the pre-existing *acquis*.

The second main section of this chapter examines the content and quality of the emerging Community migration policy. More specifically, it purports to assess the extent to which migration law lives up to the Tampere milestones which call for a common, comprehensive and balanced policy. The main policy issues and questions that will be examined in that respect concern: first, the breadth in terms of comprehensiveness of EU's migration policy; second, the desired or necessary depth of the EU integration -which will be seen under the oft-posed dilemma of harmonisation or coordination; and, finally, the quite controversial issue of balance. This section will also endeavour to scrutinise the quality of the emerging European migration policy. To this end, the analysis will focus on two main issues: firstly, transparency and accountability; and secondly, human rights. Inasmuch as transparency is concerned the analysis will focus, on the one hand, on policy-making and democratic accountability issues, and on the other, on issues of legal certainty and clarity of substantive law. The human rights analysis seeks to examine the extent to which human rights considerations are important in the process of policy-making at the European level as well as the extent to which the texts that are adopted live up to international human rights standards.

6.1 An Overview of the General Features and Framework of the Emerging Migration Law and Policy

6.1.1 The Challenge of Setting a Common Framework and Goal

It has been convincingly argued that in contrast to the classic European integration process, integration in JHA is not based on a predetermined objective transformed in to law but rather on a "*pyramide inversée*".[1] Cooperation in this area started under the pressure of events, and not on the basis of a pre-existing political will, it was then institutionalised but a coherent and well-articulated political concept only emerged much later.[2] While the same reasoning applies with regard to migration policy, certain additional facets need to be highlighted: first, the strong spill over effect that is characterising policy-making with regard to migration in conjunction with the fact that the ultimate rationale seems to change constantly, or at least there are several overlapping aims;[3] second, the subsequent uncertainty with regard to the material and personal scope of the relevant policy and the development of two policy tracks; and, third, the existence of factors that are impeding the setting of a clear-cut objective and the formation of a coherent and effective EU policy.

1 De Lobkowicz W., *L'Europe et la sécurité intérieure Une élaboration par étapes, op.cit.*, at p. 11-14.

2 *Idem*.

3 Den Boer and Wallace, *op.cit.*, at p. 497.

6.1.1.1 The Overarching Rationale: The Spill Over Effect and the 'Moving Target'

The EU's approach and action with regard to migration related issues up to Maastricht most certainly failed to reveal a single *a priori* commonly agreed objective and any comprehensive approach. One could distinguish a series of different eras, under each of which the final objective seems to be different, rendering the ultimate aim somewhat of a 'moving target'. During the first stages of policy-making, migration policy was guided by a strong spill over effect.[4] More specifically, migration policy was seen not as a policy *per se*, but as an issue that had to be regulated in order to accomplish a different Community objective or to address specific related common problems. Consequently, EU action was piecemeal and its approach lacked coherence. Absent the existence of various sporadic instruments and attempts to examine migration related issues and the relentless competence debate, one could have concluded that migration was not included among the EEC's objectives. During the early stages of EU integration, migration related issues were examined under several rather diverse perspectives. First, the security aspects of migration policy, which were linked with, and motivated by, citizen's security concerns, were examined by the Trevi group. Second, Member States, most probably motivated by the concrete need to face a social problem, were also interested in examining certain aspects of integration policy. Third, certain admission policy issues were also regulated, albeit exclusively those that were linked with family members of EU citizens due to the need to facilitate the free movement of citizens. Finally, issues linked with equal treatment were examined within the framework of agreements with third countries.

Progressively the approach of the EU became a great deal more structured and the spill over effect became more evident. The completion of the internal market, including as one of its main components the free movement of persons, has functioned as a catalyst.[5] This is because an area without internal frontiers for EU citizens was not feasible unless internal frontier controls were abolished for *all* persons and following such abolition governments would be affected by

4 For the spill over effect of the internal market over the entire JHA field see Monar J., "The Area of Freedom, Security and Justice: Institutional and Substantial Dynamics in the perspective of the European Union", Collegium No 22, December 2001, Special Edition-Proceedings of the Conference "Integrated security in Europe, a democratic perspective", Bruges, 14-17 November 2001, p. 11-24.

5 As O'Keeffe rightly highlighted on the eve of the Maastrict IGC the then existing legislation in the area of the free movement of persons was no longer sufficient given the strains of the objective of the single market and external pressures. A common immigration policy concerning entry into the Community should be achieved, otherwise the Schengen Agreement would remain the only viable alternative. O'Keeffe D., "The free movement of persons and the Single Market", *op.cit.*

each other's decisions about border controls and immigration.[6] It should be emphasised, however, that the Member States have pursued a minimalist agenda by choosing in the main to deal with what was necessary and not what was desirable.[7]

At Maastricht the agenda was amplified. A series of legal bases regarding migration related issues were inserted into the Treaty, albeit in a separate pillar, and it seems that migration policy was seen in its own right. The Commission's 1994 Communication on migration policy reinforces this reading. However, a close examination of the Maastricht Treaty's provisions and the main legislative developments thereafter reveal that the links with the objective of establishing an area without internal frontiers for EU citizens were still rather strong.[8] The more general political context as well as the content and character of the legislative measures that have been adopted support the argument that migration policy was seen manifestly as a security issue. Its aim was limited to restricting migration movements towards Europe and consequently lacked a comprehensive approach. To a certain extent this was to be expected and can be explained by a general political context favouring a restrictive approach and the fact that this was a very new competence for the Community and the Union.

6 Geddes A., *Immigration and European Integration – Towards fortress Europe?, op.cit.*, at p. 3; Hix S., *The political system of the European Union*, *op.cit.*, at p. 322. See also the discussion in Chapters 1 and 3 with regard to the developments and the position of the Member States during this period.

7 See the analysis of the Palma document drawing a clear distinction between necessary and desirable measures, an approach followed both by the Member States and by the Commission, *supra* at 3.2. A contrasting approach is taken by certain commentators according to whom the so-called 1992 operation really marked the beginning of the recognition that there were no longer national answers to the phenomenon of international migration. This thesis is based on the argument that the removal of internal border controls for persons meant that Member States would share external borders and, as a consequence, would need to develop at least common admission policies. Guild E. and Niessen J., *The Developing Immigration and Asylum Policies of the European Union Adopted Convention, Resolutions, Recommendations, Decisions and Conclusions*, *op.cit.*, at p. 21. This proposition is compelling in relation to border control issues, but when it comes to admission policy a more cogent argument would be that the Palma document approach remained valid and was in practice applied. See *infra* the discussion on the dual connotation of the free movement of persons and the dual track of EU migration policy.

8 As Guild rightly argues, the Maastricht Treaty's third pillar is linked with Articles 3 and 14 regarding the completion of the internal market. See Guild E., *Immigration Law in the European Community, op.cit.*, at p. 258. Indeed, according to Article K.1 the main purpose of Member States' cooperation is the achievement of the objectives of the Union and "in particular the free movement of persons". Moreover, as argued in Chapter 3, developments in the post-Maastricht era largely copied Schengen's much more limited rationale.

6.1.1.2 The Impact of Internal and External Factors

It has been convincingly argued that JHA EU policy has been a reactive policy.[9] EU policy-making was not only deeply affected but often also guided, or prompted, by more general political developments. In fact, to a certain degree, the very origins, development and content of migration policy have been shaped and determined by a series of internal and external factors.

First of all, initial action at the European level was a response to pressing national problems.[10] The first decision regarding cooperation in JHA matters was taken under the pressure of terrorist attacks in Italy and Germany in the 1970s.[11] And the early interest of Member States in integration policy lay with the social problems with which they were faced due to what were initially expected to be temporary migrants remaining indefinitely.

Secondly, the introduction of the migration relevant provisions in the Treaty of Maastricht was rightly viewed as a reaction to the perceived threat and resulting fear of a massive asylum and migration influx from Eastern Europe, the Soviet Union and the States of the Mediterranean basin.[12] In fact, it was not until the fall of the Berlin Wall and the collapse of the Soviet bloc exposing the region's vulnerability to potentially uncontrollable immigration flows from Eastern Europe and the former Soviet Union that Member States really began to consider the value of harmonising their migration policies and the possibility of bringing these policies into the EU institutional framework.[13] It is indeed within this framework that the German proposal at the European Council of Luxembourg in 1991 needs to be analysed.[14]

---

9 See Lobkowicz W., *L'Europe et la sécurité intérieure Une élaboration par étapes, op.cit.*, at p. 11-14 and Walker N., "Freedom, Security and Justice", *op.cit.* For the exogenous pressure as a factor explaining EU freedom and security policies see Hix S., *The political system of the European Union, op.cit.*, at p. 318-321.

10 For a detailed discussion of the question of europeanisation of national problems and its impact as a driving factor for the genesis and the development of a JHA policy at the EU level see Monar J., "The Area of Freedom, Security and Justice: Institutional and Substantial Dynamics in the perspective of the European Union", *op.cit.*

11 At the European Council of Rome in 1975. See Lobkowicz W., *L'Europe et la sécurité intérieure Une élaboration par étapes, op.cit.*, at p. 11-14.

12 This pressure was even perceived as the result of a conscious attempt of the said countries to put pressure on the EU for financial help or indeed as part of their development policy. See De Lobkowicz W., "Intergovernmental cooperation in the field of Migration – From the Single European Act to Maastricht", *op.cit.*

13 Papademetriou, *op.cit.*, at p. 12-13 and Guild E., *Immigration Law in the European Community, op.cit.*, at p. 218-219.

14 Since it was mainly under the asylum pressure caused by the considerable increase of asylum seekers that solidarity among EU Member States became a priority for

Thirdly, EU policy-making has traditionally been deeply affected by more internal political developments within the Member States, whether these are relevant to Europe or not. For instance, the ratification problems that certain Member States had faced in the post-Maastricht era, the electoral triumph of centre-right parties in France on a wave of anti-foreigner public opinion[15] and the increasing public concern due to the sense of lack of security, inevitably affected the implementation of the Maastricht Treaty and obviously affected also the EU political stance on migration issues.[16]

Finally, even the Amsterdam amendments should be seen within the framework of this policy mix of internal and external factors. Indeed, voter concerns and demands for EU action with regard to free movement and internal security were among the reasons for placing this policy area so high up the Amsterdam IGC agenda.[17] Moreover, given that the globalisation of migration increased the number of countries that were affected –more specifically former countries of emigration such as Greece, Italy, Portugal and Spain became countries of immigration- there has been a much stronger plea for EU action with regard to migration. Furthermore, the likely forthcoming membership of eastern European countries raised the salience of migration policy at EU level in particular with regard to the challenge of managing its new external borders.[18] As a final note, it is worth underlining that pressing national problems and concerns of individual Member States traditionally play a crucial role as to the shaping of the EU policy agenda.[19]

6.1.1.3 The Scope and Two Track Approach to Migration Policy at EU Level

In contrast to how migration policy is traditionally perceived at the national level – which is to say, entry and residence of foreigners both for shorter and longer stays and for various purposes – migration policy at the European level has a rather different scope and is organised in quite a different way. The reason

---

Germany. See Guild E., *Immigration Law in the European Community, op.cit.*, at p. 260.

15 Papademetriou, *op.cit.*, at p. 61-63.

16 De Lobkowicz W., "Intergovernmental cooperation in the field of Migration – From the Single European Act to Maastricht", *op.cit.*

17 See Hix S., *The political system of the European Union*, *op.cit.*, at p. 323.

18 Geddes A., *Immigration and European Integration – Towards fortress Europe?, op.cit.*, at p. 17 and Batt J., "Managing the EU's New External Border", Arnull A. and Wincott D. (eds.), *Accountability and Legitimacy in the European Union*, Oxford University Press, Oxford, 2002, p. 453-467.

19 The recent example of the impact of the events in Ceuta and Melilla and the situation in Malta, Lampedusa as well as in some Greek islands on EU policy with regard to the management of sea borders as well as to the external relations focusing on the Mediterranean region is revealing. See *supra* at 4.1.1 and 5.1.1.1.

for this lies mainly in the fact that the EU represents a different layer of policy-making. As a consequence, it has to regulate issues that do not appear to be a problem at national level – i.e. the abolition of internal border controls and freedom of circulation within the EU territory. It is also not so easy for it to regulate certain other issues such as admission policy, since this requires *a priori* the approximation of all the relevant national legislation which proves difficult both in terms of the political will of the Member States and in terms of efficiency.

The initial lack, and subsequently strongly contested character, of Community competence in this field has strongly affected both the material and personal scope of migration policy as it is included in the area of freedom, security and justice. First, the various categories of migrants having been dealt with at different stages, it is accordingly not easy to define the personal scope of Title IV which gathers the vast majority of the provisions regarding migration policy. Adopting a rather simplistic approach one could consider that European migration policy in the light of Title IV covers those categories of third country nationals that are not covered by another more specific legal framework at the EU level, i.e. legislative measures concerning EU citizens and their family members, association agreements and Article 49 TEC concerning workers posted to another Member State as employees of an EU company.[20] Nonetheless one needs to underscore that the vast majority of the Title IV provisions encompass all the third country nationals – and in some cases EU citizens as well – albeit with certain variations.[21] Moreover, the linkage with the case of refugees is rather ambiguous. Although asylum policy is rightly considered as an interlinked but separate policy, there are references to refugees in some of the Directives whilst in others there are no such references.[22]

Additionally, the existence of a strong competence debate inevitably creates uncertainty with regard to the material scope of the EU migration policy. It has been convincingly argued that the Amsterdam Treaty legal bases do not provide for a general Community competence over every aspect of migration policy, but they rather attribute competence on a series of limited and *a priori* enumerated areas. The lack of the classic non-exhaustive clause "in particular" was considered as confirming this point of view.[23] Moreover, it is not easy to assess the limits of the existing legal bases due to the fact that they are drafted

20 Article 49, second sub-paragraph TEC.

21 i.e. the rules regarding the crossing of borders are different in the case of citizens and their family members as well as the rules regarding public policy and SIS listing.

22 i.e. the family reunification Directive includes a Chapter on refugees, whereas in the case of the long-term residents Directive the relevant provisions initially included in the Commission proposal were deleted.

23 De Lobkowicz W., *L'Europe et la sécurité intérieure Une élaboration par étapes, op.cit.*, at p. 125-127.

in a rather general and open-ended way, which appears to have been a conscious choice by the Member States as they were most probably willing to maintain some sort of flexibility as to the margins of the provisions and the legal obligations stemming from them. The example of Article 63 (3) (b) TEC regarding illegal migration is revealing. Although at the beginning of the Amsterdam IGC process it was much more detailed, by the end of the process a more general drafting prevailed.[24]

And most importantly, it needs to be highlighted that following the step-by-step development of an EU migration competence and policy, the EU responses to the migration challenge have been progressively shaped in two different policy sets, which are closely linked with the dual connotation that the free movement of persons has at EU level. One facet concerns entry for short-term purposes and mere circulation following the abolition of internal border controls. This could be called 'migration *stricto sensu*'. The other facet concerns the right of third country nationals to enter for long-term purposes as well as their right to reside in another Member State and takes the more classic migration approach. The former is mainly linked with border and visa policy issues as well as with certain aspects of return policy, and fits comfortably into the Schengen formula.[25] The latter is seen under a much more general and inclusive spectrum, and takes a similar form to how migration policy is usually perceived at national level, a sort of 'migration in the classic sense'. It concerns issues of admission policy, employment, social rights, more general aspects of return policy and a series of other related policies, such as external relations, development policy etc.

In the light of the above, and bearing in mind the existence of the opt-out Protocols, it is not very easy to give a definition or to determine the exact scope of EC's migration policy. It varies profoundly depending on the personal and material scope of the Treaty provisions and the use that Member States make out of them as well as whether and by which legislative measures Member States are bound.

24 See Guild E., *Immigration Law in the European Community, op.cit.*, at p. 322-323. Guild further considers that grey zones remain, i.e. the status of persons that can not be expelled either in law or in practice and readmission agreements. In fact, the actual legal bases are rather broadly formulated and most likely cover the aforementioned areas as shown by the EU action in the post-Amsterdam era. The clarifications of the Draft Constitutional Treaty are, however, useful.

25 On the more limited character of the Schengen rationale see Monar J., "The impact of Schengen on Justice and Home Affairs in the European Union: An Assessment on the Threshold to its Incorporation", in Den Boer M. (ed.), *"Schengen still going strong: Evaluation and Update"*, EIPA, Maastricht, 2000, p. 21-35, at p. 26-30.

6.1.1.4 The Factors Impeding the Setting of a Clear-cut Objective and the Formation of a Coherent and Effective EU Migration Policy

Developments as well as discussions in the Council have clearly shown that the establishment of a coherent and effective migration policy at European level has certainly not been, nor is it expected to become, an easy process. The setting of a clear-cut objective and the formation of a coherent strategy proves to be an extremely difficult task due to a series of varying reasons and factors.

The sensitivity of the area in question, the need to preserve national sovereignty and the lack of mutual trust are usually cited among the main difficulties in forging a common migration policy. Such factors should not be underestimated, however, it can be argued that they are not of a decisive character inasmuch as the lack of progress is concerned. European history shows that when strong political will existed, legal and practical problems could be overcome. The example of the internal market and the European Monetary Union are testimony to this. Numerous also are the examples in the JHA field itself. The adoption of the European arrest warrant within the record time of three months as well as the adoption of a series of other security measures in remarkably short time spans, and most importantly, the success of Schengen illustrate what can be achieved when political will exists.[26] Of course within the Schengen framework integration was no easy process. Greece and Italy faced major difficulties in adapting themselves to Schengen standards, but never questioned the need to do so. France more than once was to express doubts about Italy's capacity to seal its borders, and repeatedly criticised the Dutch drug policy. And after initially demanding the extension of the intermediate period to the end of 1995, France finally decided to maintain controls at its external borders. During the years of the continual postponement of the Convention's implementation, it became clear that Member States did not have enough mutual trust in each other's policies.[27] At the end of the day, the experiment did however succeed.

It is therefore tempting to argue that the decisive factor in the establishment of a common, coherent and effective Community migration policy lay less with the sovereignty concerns of the area and more with the lack of a clear political will due to the deep divergence of views over a series of vital issues. Issues, such as, the existence of a need to promote European integration, the depth and final objective of such integration, the form that this should take and the means via which it would be achieved. Bearing in mind the deeply diverging socio-economic situation, labour market needs, internal organisation and differences in approach to immigration among Member States' national policies, it is evident

26 For the European arrest warrant see Council Framework Decision 2002/584/JHA of 13 June 2002 on the European arrest warrant and the surrender procedures between Member States, OJ L 190/1, 18.7.2002; for security measures post-Amsterdam see Chapter 4; for a discussion on Schengen see Chapter 3.

27 Guild and Niessen, *op.cit.*, at p. 30.

that finding common ground and promoting common goals consistently and efficiently is no easy task.

Member States have traditionally been deeply divided on central policy aspects of migration, such as the attribution of competence to the Community and the treatment of third country nationals. So, for example, right from the beginning the nationality limitation was applied by the Member States in the case of the free movement of workers in contrast to the approach adopted to the free movement of goods.[28] The need for the completion of the internal market and the Single European Act was also to constitute a conundrum for the Member States. A balance needed to be found between the desire, for economic reasons, to abolish intra-Member State border controls and the lack of consensus on the treatment of third country nationals.[29] Progressively two clear trends emerged. Those Member States that wanted to move further and those that were not willing to attribute any competence to the Community. Subsequently, this led to a need to compromise the two trends in order to keep a balance and reach consensus. In fact the Maastricht Treaty confirms the existence of a '*double verrou*': on the one hand additional competences are attributed, but only to the extent necessary for the completion of the single market, and on the other the competences were mainly kept within the unanimity safety net, as well as at a safe distance from the EU institutions.[30] The formula used at Amsterdam is much more revolutionary since it leaves outside all those not willing to follow. However, the institutional chaos created by both Maastricht and Amsterdam inevitably rendered the implementation of these treaties a long and testing road.[31]

A clear consensus as to the very existence of a need to address migration issues, at least those linked with labour migration, at EU level is arguably absent. As far as illegal migration is concerned there appears to be a consensus over the existence of a concrete need to cooperate at European level in order to confront more effectively common problems. Such a consensus is lacking in legal migration issues. The reasons are numerous. First of all, it is generally much easier to define what is not wanted than what is wanted. Thus, it is considerably easier to

28 The nationality limitation has been viewed as a false step that caused confusion as regards the creation of the internal market in labour. Elspeth Guild arrives at this conclusion on the basis of a comparison with the free movement of goods and capital. See Guild E., *Immigration Law in the European Community, op.cit.*, at p. 343.

29 See Guild E., *Immigration Law in the European Community, op.cit.*, at p. 253.

30 De Lobkowicz W., *L'Europe et la sécurité intérieure Une élaboration par étapes, op.cit.*, at p. 44.

31 For a detailed discussion see Chapter 2. Additionally, it is worth highlighting the fact that the extent of exceptions that one finds with regard to the free movement of persons could have never been accepted in the area of free movement of goods. O'Keeffe, FIDE XXI Congress, Dublin, 2-5 June 2004.

define common objectives in the areas of illegal migration and security than it is with regard to legal migration.

Secondly, admission for labour has been a taboo for most of the Member States since the 1970s when they started applying the "zero immigration policy".[32] One could argue that following the impact of globalisation, the current debate about the eventual beneficial impact of immigration to the EU's demographic problem and the feeling that the EU is likely to suffer from labour shortages, political leaders now appear ready to reopen the immigration discourse.[33] Both the Commission and several academics have marshalled a series of arguments about the need to reopen legal channels for migration. These include: the need to cooperate since Member States will be competing in order to attract immigrants;[34] arguments of certain academics that "policy-making in the area of immigration is driven less by a zero immigration policy and increasingly by a policy of market necessity";[35] that it should be linked with social and economic policies and take into account the positions of the relevant stakeholders;[36] and that the EU approach needs to be consistent in its response to the globalisation of the market.[37] Nonetheless, every day negotiations at EU level did not

---

32 Even if immigration in the EU has continued at a relatively high level despite the official 'zero immigration policy'. House of Lords, *A Community Immigration Policy, op.cit.*

33 As for the demographic issue it is worth recalling the relevant UN Report which examined the idea of 'replacement migration', i.e. the idea that by importing younger immigrant workers Western societies could preserve the balance between young and old within their populations. However, both the European Commission and academics have argued that 'replacement migration' cannot by itself solve the demographic problems facing the EU Member States. See House of Lords, *A Community Immigration Policy, op.cit.*, pts 25-27 and 64-69. See also "Commission says immigration cannot correct the effects of Europe's ageing population", IP/02/774, 29.5.2002. On the possible contribution of migration to the solution of demographic problems see also Communication from the Commission Green Book on demographic changes solidarity between generations, COM (2005) 94 final, 16.3.2005.

34 Commission Study on the links between legal and illegal migration, *op.cit.*, at p. 4.

35 Dell'Olio F., "Immigration after Nice : From 'Zero Immigration' to Market Necessity", in Arnull A. and Wincott D. (eds.), *Accountability and Legitimacy in the European Union*, Oxford University Press, Oxford, 2002, p. 469-483.

36 i.e. employers, trade unions, NGOs as well as the EU objectives regarding the employment and social agenda and the obligations stemming from GATS. See Niessen J., "Overlapping Interests and Conflicting Agendas: The Knocking into Shape of EU Immigration Policies", *EJML*, Vol. 3, Issue 3/4, 2001, p. 419-434.

37 Guild provides an overview of the impact of the globalisation of markets on the movement of persons. According to Guild there is a strange paradox: whereas the EU on the one hand tries to enhance mobility among Member States, there is a discourse against primary migration from outside the EU. See Guild E., "Pri-

seem to support the need to reopen legal channels for migration.[38] Even today, the admission of migrants for employment purposes is the main category for admission of third country nationals in only two Member States.[39] Furthermore, it needs to be stressed that it is particularly difficult to quantify the economic effects of migration and even more difficult to relate these to the formulation of a new policy at the EU level.[40]

Thirdly, the approach taken by each Member State varies dramatically, since it reflects its own experience, socio-economic development and foreign labour needs and often is also based on a series of other issues linked with foreign policy. For example, former colonial powers, such as Portugal, Spain, France, the United Kingdom and the Netherlands, had, or still have, special obligations to citizens of their former colonies in terms of admission, residence and acquisition of nationality. Further, countries such as Finland, Germany and Greece grant, under certain conditions, residence rights to so-called ethnic Finns, Germans and Greeks respectively. All these differences add to the difficulties in designing and implementing common policies on entry and residence.[41]

The approach taken by the Member States in particular with regard to labour migration is also diverse. The form taken varies considerably according to historical circumstances. Whilst ex-colonial powers could make use of labour from their colonies or former colonies, other Member States instead had to set up labour recruitment systems in order to bring in temporary foreign workers.[42] And even within the latter camp there is a great variety of methods employed. Some apply the method of prior examination of the labour market, or a point system, and others apply quota systems or often organise massive regularisa-

---

mary migration: the Great Myths", in Guild E. and Harlow C. (eds.), *Implementing Amsterdam: immigration and asylum rights in EC law*, Hart Publishing, Oxford, 2001, p. 65-94.

38 In fact Apap has rightly highlighted the fact that the Commission's liberal approach post-Amsterdam represented a clear rupture with former immigration policies at EU level. Apap J., "Shaping Europe's Migration Policy – New regimes for Employment of Third-Country Nationals: A Comparison of Strategies in Germany, Sweden, the Netherlands and the UK", *op.cit.*, at p. 315.

39 Commission Study on the links between legal and illegal migration, *op.cit.*, at p. 5.

40 House of Lords, *A Community Immigration Policy, op.cit.*, at pt 49. In light of these difficulties as well as due to a series of other reasons that will be examined subsequently, the choice of the Commission for a much more flexible long-term solution combining both legislative and non legislative tools comes as no surprise. See also the discussion on the Legal Migration Policy Plan *supra* at 4.2.1.4.

41 Guild and Niessen, *op.cit.*, at p. 12.

42 Schulte B., "Implications of Labour Migration for Social Security Systems in European Countries – Activities of the Council of Europe", *EJML*, Vol. 4, Issue 4, 2002, p. 477-489, at p. 479.

tions, methods that are heavily contested by their partners.[43] Additionally, the position of Member States is rather divisive on issues of equal treatment and the integration of third country nationals.[44] Whereas certain Member States, in particular Germany and Austria, are rather restrictive and adopt exclusionary models, others are much more liberal and consider measures such as equal treatment or access to the labour market as ways of facilitating integration.[45] Indeed, this difference in approach in conjunction with the lack of mutual trust among Member States and the consequent need to preserve control over who is entering the country has been more than evident during the negotiations of the provisions regarding the movement of long-term residents.[46]

Fourthly, the needs of the Member States are also rather diverse. Some are very selective and focus exclusively on categories such as highly qualified migrants, others are much more interested in low-skilled seasonal migration that would cover their needs in sectors such as agriculture. Some observers posited that the failure to provide an adequate legal framework for immigration is due primarily to business interests in preserving a black market for migrant labor,

43 For an overview see Commission Study on the links between legal and illegal migration, *op.cit.* and Apap, *op.cit.* See also Mariani, *op.cit.* at p. 30-33. For an overview of the regularisations processes organised recently see De Bruycker (ed.), *Regularisations of illegal immigrants in the European Union,* Bruylant, Bruxelles, 2000 and Apap J., De Bruycker P. and Schmitter C., "Regularisation of Illegal Aliens in the European Union. Summary Report of a Comparative Study", *EJML*, Vol. 2, 2000, p. 263-308.

44 There are Member States that have been recipients of immigrants for decades –and have subsequently already developed an integration policy, which is now much more oriented to immigrants of the second or third generation. Certain others have only been affected by the immigration challenge recently, integration policy is thus not surprisingly at a rather primitive stage. According to recent research conducted by the Erasmus University of Rotterdam, on the basis of a Commission request and funding, there are three different integration models in Europe: differential exclusion (Germany and the southern countries), assimilationist (the UK, France and the Netherlands), pluralist (only outside Europe in the classical immigration countries that deliberately use migration in their process of nation-building). According to others the categorisation is slightly different: guest-worker model in Germany, assimilation in France, ethnic minorities in the UK. See Entzinger and Biezeveld, *op.cit.*

45 For the positions regarding the discussions on the equal treatment issue within the framework of the long-term residents Directive and that over the link between access to the labour market and integration see Mariani, *op.cit.*, at p. 25 and 39.

46 More specifically, certain Member States, mainly Germany and Austria, strongly opposed the idea of free mobility. Indeed, according to the final version of the text long-term residents seeking residence in a second Member State could be treated as new-comers. See Articles 14 and 15 of the long-term residents Directive as well as Mariani, *op.cit*, at p. 26.

particularly in such industries as agriculture.[47] In fact, it had been argued that regulating migration policy contradicted the position of southern European countries which considered the black market a means of economic growth and viewed cooperation at EU level as a sign of Europeanisation.[48]

Returning to the impediments to the formation of a common policy on both legal and illegal migration aspects, a further constraint consists in the differences of terminology and administrative organisation among the Member States. Discussions over the list of social rights attributed to long-term residents have clearly shown that the same terms do not have the same meaning in all Member States.[49] This makes it difficult to gather statistics at the European level and thus to provide a common assessment. For example, even the term "lawfully within the territory" is far from having a common meaning in the Member States. There are cases or systems where people have not been officially admitted, but are nonetheless tolerated in the country.[50] The example of the German '*Duldung'* is revealing.[51] This lack of uniform definitions complicates any attempt at benchmarking in integration policy as well.[52] Finally, there are major discrepancies as far as administrative law is concerned. Indeed, the amendments of the procedural law provisions of the Commission proposals for Directives in legal migration are revealing of a reluctance by the Member States to amend their administrative law and to adopt fully harmonised legally binding Community provisions.[53]

---

47 Cahn, *op.cit.*, at p. 481. Also according to the Commission the shadow economy within the EU is estimated to be between 7-16% of the EU GDP. See Commission Study on the links between legal and illegal migration, *op.cit.*, at p. 11.

48 The black or underground economy was considered a major structural feature of all southern countries. In the case of Italy and Greece even the official GDP figures were boosted by 15-30 per cent. See Baldwin-Edwards M., "The Emerging European Immigration Regime: Some Reflections on Implications for Southern Europe", *Journal of Common Market Studies,* Vol. 35, No 4, December 1997, p. 497-519, at p. 508 and 519.

49 Ferraiolo, *op.cit.*

50 For an interesting discussion on this point see Schermers H., "Human Rights and Free Movement of Persons : the Role of the European Commission and Court of Human Rights", in Schermers et al. (eds.), *Free Movement of Persons in Europe, Legal Problems and Experiences*, T.M.C. Asser Institute, The Hague, 1993, p. 235-247, at p. 238.

51 A *Duldung* ("toleration") is not a residence permit, it is a sort of temporary protection mechanism. See Cahn, *op.cit.*, at p. 480.

52 According to the relevant Erasmus University research, benchmarking is only possible if there is a basic consensus on definitions. See Entzinger and Biezeveld, *op.cit.*

53 See Article 5 (4) of the family reunification Directive and Article 7 (2) of the long-term residents Directive.

A further constraint to the formation of a common migration policy is the possible fear of the unknown. For the moment it is not easy to predict whether new and more liberal legislation at the EU level will constitute a pull factor, as in the case of family reunification, or how many people will wish to make use of the relevant provisions, as in the case of the long-term residents Directive, or, more importantly, what costs would be imposed for the national budget.

Moreover, the negotiation of certain legislative measures is rendered much more difficult due to the fact that even though they are covering partly overlapping issues, they are negotiated simultaneously. One could mention in that regard the linkages between the Directive on long-term residents and the Directives regarding the first entry of third country nationals. In like vein, there were linkages between the migration Directives and the Directives on the reception and acquisition of the status of refugee. Worthy of mention are the cross references between the family reunification and the long-term residents Directives;[54] trainees being included in both the students and paid employment Directives; and the Commission Declaration regarding the extension of the long-term residents Directive to refugees once the issue of transfer of responsibility is solved.[55]

Finally, harmonisation of migration legislation might require in principle a much deeper integration in other areas of EC law, such as social policy and foreign policy, or the establishment of a certain type of solidarity among Member States in sharing the responsibilities that such a process entails. The case of readmission policy is revealing. Bearing in mind the need to offer some incentives to third countries and the limited possibilities of doing so, it becomes clear that establishing an effective policy at EU level is no easy task. Experience has shown that the leverage that could eventually be brought to bear by the Community is rather limited.[56] A visa-free regime and imposing pressure through exter-

54 See recital 10 of the family reunification Directive and Article 16 of the long-term residents Directive.

55 See Declaration ad Article 3, Council doc. 14679/03 MIGR 96 OC 705, 14.11.2003. According to this Declaration "the Council welcomes the commitment of the Commission to table within one year and possibly by the end of 2003 a proposal for the extension of long-term resident status to refugees and persons under subsidiary protection, taking into account the study on transfer protection status".

56 It needs to be clarified that although the obligation to readmit own nationals is well established under international law, in the absence of a readmission agreement this obligation is usually subordinated to the issuing of a *laissez-passer* by the consular authorities. However, certain countries often refuse to deliver such a document when the person is undocumented and the identity cannot be proved. Within the framework of readmission agreements States agree on the procedure and set commonly accepted deadlines. Furthermore, the second main added value of readmission agreements lies in the establishment of an obligation to readmit also third country nationals that are legal residents or have transited through the particular third country. In fact these prove to be some of the most difficult points

nal relations or offering the possibility to cooperate in order to combat common problems may well work with respect to certain countries but it seems that this is not enough for the vast majority of third countries.[57] Recently, the offer of a parallel visa facilitation agreement was successfully used as part of a political package deal with regard to Russia.[58] However, visa facilitation is certainly not, and should not be used as, panacea. The lack of a common foreign policy at the EU level and the incoherence in approach – the target countries are designated by the Council without taking into consideration the priorities defined by the European Commission in terms of humanitarian assistance and development- are also important factors impeding the establishment of an effective readmission policy and need to be examined in an approapriate fashion.[59] It is to be hoped that the adoption of the new multi-annual cooperation programme allocating 250 million euros will not only give some much-needed leveraging power to the Commission, but will further contribute to the establishment of a more integrated approach to readmission policy.[60]

---

in the negotiation of a readmission agreement. Bearing in mind that the EU states choose to negotiate agreements with countries constituting a major source of, or are a transit country for, illegal immigration towards the EU, the advantages stemming from the signature of a readmission agreement are much greater for the European country than for the third state. Therefore, readmission agreements usually are seen as part of a more general political package deal, where third countries are offered some kinds of advantages. For example Germany while negotiating its readmission agreements with Poland and the Czech Republic in 1993 decided to allocate then respectively a lump sum of 120 and 60 million DM. On these points see Bouteillet-Paquet D., "Passing the Buck: A Critical Analysis of the Readmission Policy Implemented by the European Union and Its Member States", *EJML*, Vol. 5 2003, p. 359-377.

57 The signature of a readmission agreement was seen as part of a political package deal lifting visa obligations for citizens of Macao and Hong Kong; the status of candidate and the on-going negotiation for a Stabilisation and Association Agreement proved also enough for Turkey and Albania respectively, and the promise for closer law enforcement cooperation, including measures against the financing of terrorist activities, satisfied the relevant request of Sri Lanka. However, with regard to Morocco, Pakistan Russia Ukraine, China and Algeria, it is not easy to identify sufficiently attractive compensation. See Schieffer M., "Community Readmission Agreements with Third-Countries – Objectives, Substance and Current State of Negotiations", *op.cit*.

58 See *supra* at 4.1.1.

59 Bouteillet-Paquet, *op.cit.*, at p. 370-371.

60 The nexus between the new programme and the issue of leverage is highlighted by Schieffer M., "Community Readmission Agreements with Third-Countries – Objectives, Substance and Current State of Negotiations", *op. cit.,* at p. 356-357.

6.1.2 The Treaty of Amsterdam: The Beginning of a New Era or Simply Going Round in Circles?

The Treaty of Amsterdam undoubtedly represents a major turning point in migration policy at the European level. In the first place, it clearly resolves many of the institutional problems that were impeding progress in the past. And in contrast to the patent absence of a clear objective in the past, the Treaty of Amsterdam purported to offer an overall perspective in migration policy within the more general framework of an area of freedom, security and justice which is seen as one of the new main objectives of the Union, as the internal market had been in the 1980s. The added value of the Amsterdam changes and the new impetus with regard to the achievement of these goals are of real importance, but one could strongly question their innovative character. The doubts are twofold and concern, firstly, the novelty of the content of the new Treaty bases; and, secondly, the substance and innovative character of the new discourse and developments in the post-Amsterdam era.

6.1.2.1 The Treaty of Amsterdam: New Terms v Old Interpretation

In the Maastricht Treaty migration policy formed part of the cooperation on "Justice and Home Affairs" matters but as a result of the Amsterdam Treaty it became part of the new "Area of Freedom, Security and Justice". Notwithstanding the change in terminology, the new communitarised legal bases, while bringing migration policy within the Community sphere, are far from being innovative.

First of all, a comparative reading of the two series of relevant Treaty provisions enables one to seriously question the added value of the new provisions. Apart from the provision regarding the freedom of movement and residence of third country nationals in a second Member State (Article 63 (4) TEC), certain useful clarifications with regard to visa policy, the freedom of movement of third country nationals and an express reference to repatriation policy[61] the rest already existed.[62] Indeed it could be argued that in relation to certain provisions the Treaty of Amsterdam has been somewhat of a retrograde step. For instance, the deletion of the reference to "the access to employment" seems to reveal a strong political message as to the limits of the scope of the provisions regarding the establishment of a common admission policy.[63] This reading is further reinforced in light of the new Article III-267 (5) of the Draft Constitutional

61 See Articles 62 (2) and 63 (3) TEC.

62 De Lobkowicz W., *L'Europe et la sécurité intérieure Une élaboration par étapes, op.cit.*, at p. 125.

63 See Article 63 (3) TEC in conjunction with former Article K.1 (3) TEU.

Treaty.[64] Also direct effect does not seem to have been the intention for any of the provisions of Title IV.[65]

Moreover, the objective of the famous area of freedom, security and justice is not mentioned anywhere and no definition is provided.[66] Although the creation of the area goes further than the objective of the free movement of persons,[67] it is doubtful whether migration policy is seen as an objective *per se*. A careful reading of Article 61 TEC, the introductory provision of Title IV, reveals that the traditional links with the internal market objective and the classic distinction between migration related measures being necessary and desirable remain. More specifically, while the first point of Article 61 TEC includes those measures that are indispensable to achieving the objective of Article 14 TEC, which is to say measures regarding border controls, visa policy and freedom of circulation within the area without internal borders, the points regarding a more general approach on immigration are included in a separate point.[68] And the five-year deadline only covers the first category of measures. The existence of close links with the internal market objective is also reinforced by the fact that Article 3, which sets out the activities for the achievement of the internal market, was extended to include a reference to the free movement of persons under Title IV.[69]

The fact that Title IV TEC in part applies to Community nationals and third country nationals and in part to third country nationals only reveals that the main concern, at least initially, was the achievement of the free movement of EU citizens. Such an interpretation can be bolstered by a careful reading of the Tampere Conclusions. To be sure, there is a reference to a "common immigration policy" therein, but one could raise serious doubts as to whether the establishment of such a policy was initially seen as an objective itself. Rather, it appears that the main objective of the new area centered around the EU citizen.

64 According to this provision "This Article shall not affect the right of Member States to determine volumes of admission of third-country nationals coming from third countries to their territory in order to seek work, whether employed or self-employed".

65 See Guild E., *Immigration Law in the European Community, op.cit.*, at p. 296-297.

66 *Idem*. For some comments on the concepts of 'area', 'freedom' and 'security' see Boeles P., "Introduction: Freedom, Security and Justice for All", in Guild E. and Harlow C. (eds.), *Implementing Amsterdam: immigration and asylum rights in EC law*, Hart Publishing, Oxford, 2001, p. 1-12.

67 The division between the establishment of the area and its deepening is clearly shown by De Lobkowicz. See De Lobkowicz W., *L'Europe et la sécurité intérieure Une élaboration par étapes, op.cit.*, p. 120-128.

68 See Article 61 (1) points (a) and (b) TEC.

69 Articles 2 and 3 TEC. See Guild E., *Immigration Law in the European Community, op.cit.,* at p. 296-297.

In fact, one of the main driving forces, and the main objectives, for the Tampere Summit was to send a strong political message to EU citizens that the objective of European integration is not to create a bureaucratic Europe but a Europe for the citizens that takes into account their concerns for freedom, security and justice.[70]

In light of the above, it could be argued that although the Amsterdam Treaty employs new terms, their interpretation and real content is not necessarily markedly different from that of the Maastricht Treaty provisions particularly since the new legal bases have been viewed to a certain extent with lenses similar to those of the pre-Amsterdam era.

6.1.2.2 The Implementation of the New Treaty: A New Beginning or a Mere Crystallisation of the Pre-Amsterdam *Acquis*?

A comparative reading of the strategic documents that were presented and the legislative measures that have been adopted under the Maastricht and Amsterdam eras reveals certain close similarities in terms of policy-making and thinking. For example if one takes, on the one hand, the Commission Communication of 1994, and on the other hand, the Tampere Conclusions and the Commission Communication of 2000, the similarities are striking.[71] They follow the same structure and are essentially based on the same principles and ideas. In this respect it can convincingly be argued that the broad lines for the formation of a European migration policy have not really changed.

As it turns out, most of the measures adopted in the post-Amsterdam era are also to a large extent redrafted proposals based on legislative acts that have either already been adopted under the Maastricht era or build upon the Schengen *acquis* and do not go much further than the initial acts.[72] Moreover, the Union's approach to migration policy remains to a certain extent rather piecemeal. At least for the moment, and despite the general political discourse, a comprehensive legislative framework for the entry, movement and return of third country nationals is still missing.

One could counter argue that in the post-Amsterdam era there has been an immense proliferation of documents of more general interest and operational or programmatic value, which are establishing the bases for the formation of a new policy and evince a certain dynamism. The reality, however, is that the vast majority of these documents merely reproduce earlier versions and on certain occasions almost copy parts of documents that have already been presented in a

70 Elsen C., "L'esprit et les ambitions de Tampere: une ère nouvelle pour la coopération dans le domaine de la Justice et des Affaires Intérieures? ", *op.cit.*, at p. 660.

71 For the Commission Communications see respectively COM (94) 23 and COM (2000) 757, *op.cit.* For a discussion of the relevant Communications see respectively *supra* at 3.4, 4 and 5.2.1.

72 See *supra* Chapter 4.

slightly different framework.[73] One might view this as confirmation of a certain level of coherence, less generously one could question the benefits of all this "recycling" of documents.

This does not mean that the conclusion should simply be reached that developments under the Treaty of Amsterdam are largely a mere crystallisation of the *acquis* and the ideas that already existed in the pre-Amsterdam era. A more balanced picture would need to acknowledge that the framework is now considerably different.[74] Firstly, migration policy has been communitarised. Although it is true that the new legislative measures do not go much further than their predecessors and seem to follow a long-standing piecemeal approach, they are at least legally binding. Secondly, there is definitely now a new political impetus. The Council has really devoted a lot of effort to the preparation of the Tampere Conclusions, and the relevant issues have since remained high on both the Council and the European Council agendas.[75] Even if the character of the documents that are circulated is partly repetitive, the scale of activity within the field of JHA is steadily increasing.[76]

Additionally, certain ideas that already existed in the past now take progressively a more concrete form whilst there are also certain new issues that are examined within this much broader debate on migration policy. It is interesting that certain issues, initially examined without the existence of any concrete legal provisions within the Treaty, such as the management of external borders, solidarity and integration policy, were mature enough to be the objective of concrete legal actions and subsequently have gained their own place in the new

73 See, for example, the similarities among on the one hand, the Commission Communications on illegal migration, return, and integration policies as well as the Commission Scoreboards, and on the other, the Council Action Plan on illegal migration, the Return Action Programme, the Conclusions on integration of third country nationals and the Council Roadmaps. One can further notice a series of overlaps between the various Council Actions Plans and Roadmaps. See for example the Plan for the External Borders, the Plan for illegal migration, the Return Action Programme and the various Roadmaps. See also the 2003 best practices for return and the Schengen 2002 best practices on the same matter or the recent proliferation of questionnaires on return policy issues.

74 Nonetheless, as O'Keeffe rightly argued in 1999 it is only the implementation that would show how substantive the changes really are. O'Keeffe D., "Can the Leopard Change its Spots? Visas, Immigration and Asylum – Following Amsterdam", in O'Keeffe D. and Twomey P. (eds.), *Legal Issues of the Amsterdam Treaty,* Hart Publishing, Oxford, 1999, p. 271-288.

75 For a short discussion on the preparation of Tampere and its follow-up see *supra* at 5.1.1.4.

76 It was estimated that in 1997 one-third of the meetings and 40 per cent of the documents circulated in the Council concerned third pillar issues. See Den Boer and Wallace, at p. 503.

Draft Constitutional Treaty. Moreover, an extensive debate on issues such as external relations, or on whether Europe needs migrants or not, or the need to attract researchers, or the establishment of links with other policy areas such as the employment strategy has been launched. Even if Europe has not yet reached the point of concrete action in a number of areas, the debate is taking place and it appears to be merely a matter of time before action is taken.[77]

In any case, it is crucial that crystallisation should not necessarily be seen as a retrograde step or as stalling, but rather as a necessary step in a process of evolution. Therefore, despite the fact that communitarisation has come at a price, the Treaty of Amsterdam has considerably improved the legal framework and provided the necessary political impetus for action in the sphere of migration. It is essential however to keep in mind that Title IV is a work in progress.

6.2 A Critical Analysis of the Content and Quality of EU Migration Law and Policy: The Challenge of Living up to Europe's Goals and Values

6.2.1 The Challenge of a Comprehensive Approach

Forging a comprehensive approach to migration policy was one of the objectives set by the Tampere Conclusions and subsequently reaffirmed in a series of other documents of political character. The exact meaning of the notion of comprehensiveness remains elusive. In the Tampere Conclusions, the term seems to be mainly linked with the external aspects of migration. The concept of comprehensiveness is primarily seen in terms of linkages with other policies that the formation of a migration policy needs to take into consideration and *vice versa*, such as political, human rights and development issues.[78] It is submitted, however, that it should be further examined under the perspective of the width and the scope of the European migration policy *per se*. And it is on this second approach that the present analysis will focus. Taking into account the many phases and aspects of migration policy at EU level, and in particular the existence of a dual policy track upon which migration policy is developed at EU level, the analysis herein will examine its comprehensiveness under both the *stricto sensu* and classical perspectives.

6.2.1.1 Comprehensiveness and Migration S*tricto* S*ensu*

On the basis of the overview of legislative measures in chapter four one could conclude that the EU approach to migration *stricto sensu* is in principle comprehensive. The competence for dealing with the relevant issues is unambiguously attributed to the Community. The legal bases are rather clear and, most

77 The extensive references to the Lisbon and Employment Strategies in the new Policy Plan for Legal Migration as well as in the Hague Programme reinforce this argument.

78 It is found under the heading of "Partnership with countries of origin". See point 11 of the Tampere Conclusions.

importantly, almost all the elements regarding the policy of entry for short-term periods and movement within the Schengen area are already in place. Therefore, one could convincingly argue that this first policy track had already *grosso modo* been completed primarily via the Schengen cooperation. The EU has definitely entered the phase of fine-tuning and monitoring.

Nonetheless, one needs to underscore the fragmented character of the existing legislative framework and the piecemeal approach taken to the development of existing legislative measures. At times this could be explained by the following factors: the diversity of the legal bases, which are not easy to combine;[79] the varying EU approach with regard to specific categories of persons;[80] the existence of specific obligations that the EU needs to respect.[81] On certain other occasions the explanation for a piecemeal approach probably lies with factors that are mainly of a practical or psychological nature such as the 'habit' of adopting a pragmatic approach stemming from the strong legacy of the Schengen tradition, or the limited resources of the Presidency and individual Member States, which usually prevents them from tabling far-reaching legislative proposals.[82] However, the Commission has already consolidated the *acquis* with regard to borders issues,[83] has submitted a comprehensive proposal for return policy and has further announced its intention to present a legal instrument for the consolidation of the visa *acquis*.[84]

6.2.1.2 Comprehensiveness and Migration in the Classic Sense

The entry, short-term stay and the mere circulation of third country nationals within the EU territory has been *grosso modo* accomplished within the Schengen framework. In contrast, the accomplishment of migration policy in the "classic sense" forms part of a more general policy with regard to migration, a policy that the EU is currently trying to build.

79 i.e. Article 49 TEC and Title IV, Article 62 (3) TEC regarding the movement of third country nationals and Article 62 (2) regarding visa policy or Article 63 (3) regarding long-term visas and admission. More specifically, the existence of the Protocols and the fact that the procedures applied were different and have been further diversified given that some of these provisions will pass to the co-decision procedure.

80 i.e. the difference in approach between those that have a link with EC law and other third country nationals.

81 i.e. third country nationals falling within the scope of international agreements.

82 See the discussion on the piecemeal approach of the Member States and on the negative impact of the Presidency in Chapter 5.

83 See Community Code on the rules governing the movement of persons across borders, *op.cit.*

84 Meaning the recasting of the CCI. The Commission has also presented a comprehensive proposal for the movement of third country nationals. See COM (2001) 388, *op.cit.* For further discussion and references see *supra* at 4.1.1 and 4.1.2.

The analysis of the existing Treaty bases and the more general policy-making framework is testimony to the difficulty of this task.[85] Both the Commission and the Council in their respective documents of more general interest adopt a holistic approach, however, the competences that *de jure* exist are not only limited, but are also strongly contested and the approach regarding legislative documents is far from ambitious. Moreover, the EU has not reached the necessary level of integration in a series of areas that are interlinked, such as foreign policy, development policy and employment policy, though it is currently in the process of examining the interactions among all these areas at the EU level.

A root question that needs to be asked is whether the formation of a migration policy in the classic sense is feasible or even effective at the EU level. When account is taken of the deep divergences among not only the approach of the Member States, but also among their real needs, it is doubtful whether the adoption of such a policy is realistic.[86] The difficulties in addressing successfully the migration challenge at national level, where in principle coordination among the different actors is much easier and the *status quo* considerably more homogenous, generates doubts as to the successful management of a migration policy in the classic sense at the EU level.[87]

6.2.2 Harmonisation or Coordination?

6.2.2.1 The Myths and Realities about Harmonisation and Coordination

The terms harmonisation and coordination represent, in principle, the depth of European integration in a certain area. But not only is the use of this terminology confusing but it can often be misleading. While it is generally established that the former is in principle much deeper than the latter, and remains often the long-term objective, it is not at all clear whether these integration methods could be complementary, or could be seen as steps in a single process or whether one needs to choose among them.[88]

---

85 For further discussion see *surpa* 6.1.1.4.

86 According to the House of Lords the shared assessment of the economic and demographic developments within the EU that Tampere called for will be rather difficult given the wide variations among Member States. The same report concludes that it may not be possible to device an effective EU-wide policy in this area. See House of Lords, *A Community Immigration Policy, op.cit.*, at pt 68.

87 Since the key levers for migration policy – i.e. employment policy, social policy and external relations- come within the remit of different Directorates General at the Commission, different committees in the European Parliament and different Ministries at national level – with the usual barriers thus created to developing a coordinated strategy.

88 The lack of clarity as to the limits to, and ultimate objective of, Community activity in this area means that this will be a matter of policy judgment to be made in accordance with the principles of subsidiarity and proportionality. See House of Lords, *A Community Immigration Policy, op.cit.*

Inasmuch as migration policy is concerned it is not clear which integration method is, or should be, used and there does not seem to exist any agreement on the matter among the policy actors involved. In the early stages of EU integration in this area, consultation and a loose form of cooperation was the maximum that actors expected or wished for. Subsequently, within the framework of the Single European Act, it became clear that some form of legislative harmonisation was necessary. However, the lack of consensus both over the legal form and the content impeded the adoption of any concrete measures. The Maastricht Treaty rendered things a little bit clearer, by providing in general for the legislative harmonisation of certain aspects of migration policy – i.e. visas – and for "cooperation" with regard to the rest of migration policy covered by the Treaty.[89]

Despite the communitarisation of the relevant legal bases by the Amsterdam Treaty, the final objective of European integration in migration policy has not been entirely clarified. Whereas in the first Presidency Note during the Amsterdam IGC in 1996 there was reference to harmonisation, the term subsequently disappeared.[90] The Treaty legal bases do not provide for any clear indications or guidelines and the position taken at Tampere is ambiguous. The title of the relevant section talks about a "common" EU migration policy.[91] It is worth noting though that the term "common" was preferred by the Council of Ministers over the Commission's proposal for a "single immigration and asylum system".[92] As far as the rights attributed to third country nationals are concerned, the famous "as far as possible" formula is used, rendering the final objective rather obscure and leaving enough space for those objecting to invoke "impossibilities".

In its 2000 Communication on immigration policy, the Commission suggested a "two-tier" approach.[93] It announced its intention to define a common legal framework on the admission of migrants and to launch an open coordination mechanism on Community immigration policy. Almost a year later it returned to the same theme and proposed the establishment of the Open Method of Coordination in immigration policy.[94] However, before examining the merits of this new method and examining whether and how it could be used in an effective way it is necessary to highlight a series of other factors.

89 As far as visa policy was concerned, harmonisation under the first pillar was not completed and the dividing line between the first and the third pillar was also blurred.

90 See Guild E., *Immigration Law in the European Community, op.cit.*, at p. 322. For an overview of the drafting history see in particular p. 297-305.

91 See Title of Part A of the Tampere Conclusions.

92 Dell'Olio, *op.cit.*, at p. 474.

93 COM (2000) 757 final, *op.cit.*

94 COM (2001) 387 final, *op.cit.*

First of all, the choice between harmonisation and coordination is a misleading one, since in principle this is not an all or nothing issue. Two main sets of factors that prove decisive on the policy method to be employed concern, on the one hand, the character of the EU policy concerned, in particular with regard to the way that it could be more efficiently managed, and on the other hand, the depth of divergences among national policies. There are areas in which it is practically impossible to achieve effective and efficient integration without proceeding to, even complete, harmonisation. There are other areas in which a more flexible form of mere coordination proves not only easier to achieve but also more efficient. For example, within the framework of Schengen cooperation it became clear that this system could not function properly unless issues relating to visa policy and the legal aspects of checks at external borders were fully harmonised. This is also the case with regard to issues such as, for example, the attribution of the long-term resident status or the acquisition of the right to family reunification, since the lack of harmonisation could eventually lead to status-shopping and secondary movements within the EU. On the contrary, certain other issues, such as admission for employment purposes are more difficult to harmonise given the different needs of Member States and the necessity to maintain a certain degree of flexibility. In the long run harmonisation could even prove detrimental in that it would impose a rigid system that does not correspond to the needs of the labour market. This is likewise applicable in integration policy where the deep discrepancies among Member States' factual situations and approaches makes it difficult to find one-size-fits-all solutions applicable to all possible states of affairs existing in the different Member States.

Another factor to take into consideration is the nature of the specific policy issue concerned as many aspects of JHA policy have a manifestly operational nature. In many respects integration with regard to JHA does not depend as much on drawing up legislative texts as does the 'traditional' economic and social integration pursued by the European Community. Rather it is weighted far more towards the exchange of information and the joint or coordinated cooperation of national administrations.[95] That said, it is frequently the case that operational cooperation is either combined with legislative action – i.e. visa policy, external borders – or is a first step before proceeding to legislative harmonisation, such as in the case of return policy.

In the light of the above it becomes clear that the 'magical formula' for integration with regard to migration policy must be based on an appropriate policy mix of aspects of both the harmonisation and coordination method.[96] It is most likely under these premises that the Commission had proposed the

95 Peers S., *EU Justice and Home Affairs Law*, *op.cit.*, at p. 2.

96 As Commissioner Vitorino clarified the open coordination approach should be complementary to the classic common approach. See Vitorino A., "Interview with

method of open coordination as a complement to the classic Community common approach. However, the discussion in chapter five has shown that the relevant method has not been sufficiently thought through. The open coordination method is premised on a rational approach based on the identification of needs, the availability of information and the fact that the actors are able to fulfil the objectives that they set. Nonetheless, migration policy in particular with regard to labour immigration is better understood as being rather unstable, information is not always available and state actors are not always able to meet their objectives.[97] Given the need for a rapid and flexible mechanism, the proposed method consisting in the preparation of regular national reports which will then be summarised into further reports is too cumbersome to keep pace with the speed of developments in the labour market.[98] *Ab initio* this model has an appealing feel to it as in principle the open method of coordination is the equivalent of "seminar diplomacy", comparing national experiences and developing sets of best practices in a range of new socio-economic policy areas where formal policy-making competencies remain in the hands of national and subnational authorities.[99] Yet, if it is not well designed, it risks creating a cumbersome bureaucratic mechanism that offers little in terms of efficiency.

A wiser approach might well be to move in the direction of more informal forms of coordination and exchange of best practices, which should in any case be combined with legislative action.[100] First of all, there needs to be a step-by-step approximation of national legislation based on shared assessment of economic, social and demographic developments within the EU and further taking into account the reception capacity of each Member State and the historical and cultural links with countries of origin. In that respect it is worth recalling that the Commission is also expected in the next five years after the implementation of each Directive to prepare a report and propose the necessary amendments on the basis of the practical experience gained in the meantime. Subsequently, it might be necessary to have studies conducted as to the actual situation and needs of the Member States in order to find some common denominators for common policy action, and to proceed to exchange of best practices and operational cooperation. In fact, most of these actions are already operating within the framework of several *fora* both within the Council and the Commission, i.e.

Antònio Vitorino, European Commissioner for Justice and Home Affairs", *op.cit.*, at p. 8.

97 Geddes A., *The Politics of Migration and Immigration in Europe, op.cit.*, at p. 141.

98 House of Lords, *A Community Immigration Policy, op.cit.*, at pts 90-91.

99 Lewis, *op.cit.*, at p. 1012.

100 Indeed, this seems to be the approach taken by the Commission within the framework of its recently published Policy Plan on Legal Migration. See *supra* at 4.2.1.4. However, it is for the moment quite early to foresee the final form and content that the proposed by the Commission procedure will take.

EMN, CIA, High Level Group, Agency for external borders, CIREFI. Now what may well be imperative is a rationalisation and better coordination of all the above-mentioned *fora*.

6.2.2.2 The Risks Stemming from the Lack of Harmonisation

The overview of the legislative measures in the post-Amsterdam era has clearly shown that Member States have chosen to adopt a rather restrictive approach, by limiting harmonisation to the lowest common denominator and opting for flexible and open-ended drafting as well as for a series of optional derogation clauses. Consequently, as previously mentioned, the level of harmonisation is heavily dependent on the recourse of Member States to the numerous options set out in the various Directives.

While understanding at this stage of policy-making both the difficulties in reaching complete harmonisation and the reluctance of the Member States to pursue such an agenda, the eventual risks stemming from the lack of harmonisation should also be highlighted. These could be divided in two main categories. Firstly there is a risk of rights shopping which has mainly practical implications. Secondly, there is the risk of the much-touted race to the bottom which raises primarily political considerations and fundamental rights issues.

6.2.2.2.1 Rights Shopping

The lack of a harmonised system of entry and residence in the EU combined with the abolition of internal border controls could lead to considerable distortions of the "area without internal borders" system.

The existence of major differences in the process of visa issuing is of importance. Where the embassies and consulates of some Member States are more lenient in their screening process this can create pull factors. And once in the EU territory, third country nationals can easily move from one Member State to another. The same applies also in the case of border controls. Those Member States that are applying more relaxed controls are creating pull factors for illegal entry which constitute gaps in the efficient functioning of the system.

In fact, all of these risks were sufficiently highlighted, and up a certain degree dealt with, within the Schengen system. So the list of countries whose nationals are subject to, or exempted from, the visa obligation has been progressively fully harmonised, the procedure and the conditions for issuing a visa and the controls at the external borders have been standardised, and a system of monitoring their correct implementation has been established. Following the integration of the Schengen *acquis,* these efforts have continued and have been intensified at the EU level. An Agency for the management of the external borders has been set up and a database for the visas that have been issued and for those that have been refused (VIS) is shortly to be established.

The need for a harmonised approach to the admission policy for long-term entry and residence is based partly on inter-related considerations. Thus, the objective of the first Commission proposal on family reunification was to harmonise Member States' legislation in order to restrict the choice of the Member State in which third country nationals decide to reside by providing broadly the same conditions for family reunification irrespective of the Member State concerned. Moreover, in the proposal for the long-term residents Directive the Commission endeavoured to harmonise as far as possible the conditions regarding the acquisition of the status, the conditions of residence and the extent of equal treatment granted to third country nationals in the various Member States in order to prevent any eventual rights shopping.[101]

However, the open-ended drafting and the plethora of derogation clauses in the final versions of both these Directives render these risks rather palpable.[102] The need for a common approach was compromised by a series of factors, such as the existence of optional provisions, the possibility of Member States to apply additional conditions, requirements and limitations and the numerous references to national legislation, which allow for greater diversity and flexibility. All the relevant Directives also contain a more favourable provisions clause. Unfortunately, it is not possible at this stage to estimate the extent to which these will contribute to secondary movements within the EU. Nonetheless, it could be argued that from a practical point of view rights shopping might not be as widespread as might be feared, since the main reasons for choosing a county to migrate to are principally linked with labour opportunities or special family or cultural links with the country. It is most likely that the market itself will take the final decisions and make sure that there is migrant-sharing on the basis of the labour needs of each Member State. All the aforementioned arguments aside, some level of harmonisation is still necessary to deter migrants from country shopping.[103]

6.2.2.2.2 Race to the Bottom

Member State reluctance to proceed to a widespread harmonisation at the EU level creates a risk that Member States will enter into a progressive lowering of their standards of protection in order to avoid creating pull factors, the so-called "race to the bottom" phenomenon.

First of all, it has been convincingly argued that the fact that the positive legal integration thus far achieved mainly focused on strengthening controls on

101 Inasmuch as the content of the rights is concerned this inevitably varies since the criterion that has been used for equal treatment is the rights of citizens of the Member State concerned.

102 Ferraiolo, *op.cit.*

103 Hailbronner K. and Higgins I., "General Report", in Higgins I. (ed.) and Hailbronner K. (General Rapporteur), *Migration and Asylum law and Policy in the European Union – FIDE 2004 National Reports*, Cambridge University Press, Cambridge, 2004, p. 455-476, at p. 467.

illegal migration does not prevent a "race to the bottom" towards more unfavourable treatment of third country nationals, but in principle encourages or compels Member States to engage in such a race.[104] Moreover, the main criticism with regard to the non-binding character and the optional provisions of the Resolutions adopted under the Maastricht era consisted in the fact that Member States could use Europe as their excuse to impose more restrictive policies whenever this proved necessary.[105]

Inasmuch as the post-Amsterdam era is concerned, the fact that the implementation process has not been completed for any of the Directives means that it is too early to predict the validity and extent of these fears. For the moment evidence and political signs are contradictory. On the one hand, in certain cases Member States have already proceeded to a pre-mature transposition of Directives by lowering down their standards even before a Directive was adopted[106] and there are serious concerns that the Directives may lead to such a lowering of the standards even in other countries.[107] While on the other hand, it appears that the majority of Member States that apply higher standards do not currently envisage that the Directives will result in a lowering of these standards.[108] However, the deadline for implementation still remains some way off and the situation in most countries is not clear. The existence of a wide range of optional derogatory clauses render these fears palpable, even if it would be unfortunate if European legislation was the catalyst for a race to the bottom. Hopefully, the drafting of these clauses is often accompanied by a series of stand-still clauses preventing a race to the bottom or managing to "freeze", at least to some extent, the harmonization accomplished within this first stage.

Finally, it should be stressed that despite the low standards of the newly adopted Directives, in particular with regard to family reunification, these can have a positive impact on certain national legislation where standards are even lower.[109] In any case, the long-term residents Directive certainly has an added value, since it grants to third country nationals a right that had hitherto been negated, i.e. to reside on the basis of a facilitated procedure in a second Member State. It needs also to be acknowledged that following the accession of the new

104 Peers S., *EU Justice and Home Affairs Law*, *op.cit.*, at p. 6.

105 In fact, it has been highlighted that the perverse effects of this were two-fold: not only did they not harmonise but they could be used as a political justification. De Lobkowicz W., *L'Europe et la sécurité intérieure Une élaboration par étapes, op.cit.*, at p. 79-80.

106 France has lengthened the period for acquiring the long-term resident status from 3 to 5 years even before the adoption of the relevant EC Directive. See Mariani, *op.cit.,* at p. 9 and 23 and El Kaim, *op.cit.*.

107 Hailbronner and Higgins, *op.cit.*, at p. 466.

108 *Idem.*

109 For a list with examples see Hailbronner and Higgins, *op.cit.*, at p. 465.

States, the Directives are likely to contribute positively in reaching some level of approximation between the legislation not only of the fifteen but of the twenty-five Member States.

6.2.3 The Challenge of a Balanced Approach: Towards a Fortress Europe?

The term "balanced approach" is usually understood in terms of a contrast between the progress achieved in legal and illegal migration. There is no doubt that this is the main theme. There is though another aspect which is less obvious but worth examining, namely, the lack of balance in terms of restrictions imposed and rights granted to third country nationals within the framework of the legal migration instruments themselves. Considering that this second aspect is equally important to a final assessment, the concept of balance will be analysed under both these heads.

6.2.3.1 Legal v Illegal Migration

A simple balance sheet of developments since Amsterdam is enough to prove that the policy is heavily unbalanced in favour of security measures. This disequilibrium is rather obvious both in internal as well as in external action. Counting on the one hand the number of proposals and adopted legislative measures that aim at the fight of illegal migration or the reinforcement of security aspects, and on the other hand, examining the quality in terms of substance of the first few measures on legal migration confirms the disequilibrium between legal and illegal migration. There is also a curious disparity in terms of time-frames for political agreement. In the case of the majority of the legislative measures on security matters such agreement took between three months to one year. In contrast, it took three and a half years for the Council to reach agreement on its first legal migration Directive.

It is also the case that the EU's approach towards third countries has traditionally been seen primarily through a security lens. It has been sustained that the new partnership policy has proved to be a euphemism for a policy orientation that is rooted in the well-known phenomenon of "burden shifting".[110] The EU approach to the development sector was criticised as well. According to several NGOs, there is a clear risk of making development funding conditional on migration prevention measures. While the EU is correct to point to the potential of development policy in migration, it fails to adequately acknowledge this in

110 Bouteillet-Paquet, *op.cit.*, at p. 372-373. For a proposal for an alternative approach see Hakura F., " The External EU Immigration Policy : The need to Move beyond the Orthodoxy ", *European Foreign Affairs Review*, Vol. 3, 1998, p. 115-134. Indeed, the absence of eight Heads of State from the south of the Mediterranean at the November 2005 Barcelona Euromed Summit is symbolic. See "EU/EUROMED: Barcelona Summit adopts code of conduct for fight against terrorism, five year working plan and "declaration of President", *op.cit.*

its proposed actions.[111] Furthermore, there is undue reference to the aid that needs to be granted to the third countries without taking into consideration the European side of the coin, which is to say the eventual pull factors that *de facto* exist.[112] Finally, strong concerns have been voiced as to the successful character of such an undue emphasis on combating and preventing illegal migration.[113]

The preceding discussion concerning the overwhelming focus on security is well-known, of more interest are the reasons for which the disequilibrium exists. First of all, European integration in migration related issues has traditionally been seen under a security perspective,[114] since migration policy was for a long time, and to a degree remains, one of the flanking measures needed for the abolition of internal border controls. In fact the creation of the link between internal and external border controls and between border crime security and third country nationals, led to the construction of migration as a security issue.[115] The main factors contributing to the promotion of European integration in this area, such as the fall of the Berlin Wall and the collapse of the Soviet Union, have also contributed to the increase of security concerns.[116] And the fear of massive arrivals of immigrants and the political pressure that was created by right-wing dema-

111 See "Migration and Development: Preliminary observations by NGOs active in the migration, refugee protection and the development field on the European Commission's Communication on "Integrating Migration Issues in the European Union's Relations with Third Countries", *op.cit.* However, it is worth underlining that issues such as remittances and circular migration are extensively discussed within the framework of the 2005 Commission Communication on Migration and Development. See *supra* at 4.3.1.

112 See the criticism of the Commission Communication on development policy, *supra* at 4.3.1. As Schulte argues, migration is the result of the interdependence between sending and receiving countries within the political economy of the world market and in Europe within the process of European integration. See Schulte, *op.cit.*, at p. 480. That said it needs to be highlighted that the issue of informal economy and employment with regard to migration are included both in the Hague Programme and in the relevant Action Plan. See Section 1.4 of the Hague Programme, *op.cit.* and section 2.6 of the joint Council and Commission Action Plan implementing the Hague Programme, *op.cit.*

113 Cholewinski R., "The EU acquis on Irregular Migration : Reinforcing Security at the expense of Rights", *EJML*, Vol. 2, 2000, p. 361-405.

114 For an overview of the reasons leading to the development of a restrictive migration policy and the social construction of migration into a security issue see Huysmans J., "The European Union and the Securization of Migration", *Journal of Common Market Studies,* Vol. 38, No. 5, p. 751-777.

115 See Guild E., *Immigration Law in the European Community, op.cit.*, at p. 244.

116 De Lobkowicz W., "Intergovernmental cooperation in the field of Migration – From the Single European Act to Maastricht", *op.cit.*

gogues who politically exploited national passions have helped to further push the Union elites towards a security-oriented approach.[117]

This initial tendency for illegal migration measures to be placed at the forefront was to be reinforced in the post-Amsterdam era by a series of additional factors. Firstly, the Schengen stain remained strong on EU migration policy-making thanks to the existence of a strong and disciplined legal framework which does not grant Member States a wide margin of manoeuvre. Second, as argued earlier, there is much more convergence among Member States' interests in the area of illegal migration, since policy-making is seen as a means of confronting common problems. Additionally, the mainly operational nature of illegal migration measures inevitably renders their adoption much easier and quicker.

Another factor is that the political will of the Member States to go further in this area is much stronger due to the fact that it coincides with a political desire to respond to the security concerns of citizens.[118] It is worth highlighting that in the post-Amsterdam era there have been three Presidencies that were deeply interested in illegal migration and border matters. There was also a change in the political scenery of Europe with more right wing parties in government resulting in a move away from *une Europe rose* in 1999 at Tampere to *une Europe bleue* in 2003. It has been correctly noted that parties offering coded or explicit anti-migrant platforms have entered government in Austria, France, Denmark, Italy and the Netherlands and frequently centrist governments have adopted restrictive anti-migrant rules in an effort to dissuade voters from voting for the extreme right.[119] Moreover, phenomena like the massive arrival of illegal migrants harden national positions. The reaction of the Italian Presidency to the Lampedusa drama as well as the impact of the events in Ceuta and Melilla and the situation in Malta as well as in some Greek islands on EU policy are symbolic.[120] Other parallel developments such as economic problems, changes of pension or social security systems inevitably affect the position of the Member States as well.

Finally, international developments continued to have a strong impact on the EU migration agenda. A seismic event being the attacks of the 11th September-

117 Papademetriou, *op.cit.*, at p. 107-109.

118 According to Bigo, migration control is not a policy response to an existing social problem, but rather a social construction of a threat established and fed by political, media and bureaucratic elites who compete among themselves to have their objectives included in politicians' platforms since their importance and budget is dependent on the degree to which the threat is accepted as real. See Bigo D., "Migration and Security", in Guiraudon V. and Joppke C. (eds.), *Controlling a New Migration World,* Routledge, London, 2001, p. 121-149.

119 Cahn, *op.cit.*, at p. 481.

120 Mariani, *op.cit.*, at p. 37. See also *supra* at 4.1.1 and 5.1.1.1.

ber, which seems to have overturned not only the Belgian Presidency's agenda,[121] but to a certain extent the entire EU approach on the matter. Its impact has been strong on every aspect of policy-making and on every institution. An undeniable turn towards security measures resulted and it is a turn which was reinforced by the subsequent attacks in Madrid and in London which revived and intensified a trend that already existed.[122] Indeed, even if the tragic events of September 11 did not lead immediately to major concrete proposals with regard to movement of persons, they marked a shift in the agenda and have constantly been used as the justification for a consolidation of the existing preference for security measures.[123] Certainly the root of some measures predates the events of September 11, however its impact was not only to accelerate progress in illegal migration but also to slow down progress with regard to legal migration and led to a diminution of the protection of individuals.[124]

121 Speech given by Guy Verhofstadt, President in office of the European Council to the European Parliament, Brussels, 17 December 2001. While stating that the Belgian Presidency had great expectations with regard to asylum and migration, Guy Verhofstadt admits that this issue lost salience in the wake of the events of 11 September.

122 Two new extraordinary declarations on Terrorism have been adopted following the Madrid and London attacks – see Declaration of 25 March 2004 as well as the new Declaration on the EU response to the London bombings adopted by the Extraordinary JHA Council on 13 July 2005 – whereas the old Roadmap has been revived and constantly updated. See *inter alia* EU Plan of Action on Combating Terrorism, Council doc. 10010/2/04 REV 2 JAI 185, 8.6.2004 and Report to the Council on the implementation of the Declaration on combating terrorism, Council doc. 10009/2/04 REV 2 JAI 184, 8.6.2004. See also "Terror at the top of the UK presidency agenda", <www.euobserver.com>, 15.7.2005.

123 See Brouwer E., "Immigration, Asylum and Terrorism: A Changing Dynamic – Legal and Practical Developments in the EU in Response to the Terrorists Attacks of 11.09", *EJML*, Vol. 4, 2003, p. 399-424.

124 For an overview and an analysis of the impact of September 11 on immigration, visas and external borders policies see Bribosia E. et Weyembergh A., "L'impact de la lutte contre le terrorism sur les politiques d'asile et d'immigration de l' Union européenne", in Vandersanden G. and de Walsch A. (eds.), *Mélanges en hommage à Jean-Victor Louis (Vol. I)*, Editions de l'Université de Bruxelles, Bruxelles, 2003, p. 63-82 and Guild E., "Immigration, Asylum, Borders and Terrorism: The Unexpected Victims of 11 September 2001", *op.cit.* The 11 September effect has led to the adoption of several concrete measures: i.e. the strengthening of the public order clauses, the process of establishing VIS and the agreement within the Article 36 Committee on a definition of a terrorist threat of exceptional gravity, which would justify the re-establishment of internal border controls. See European Commission Working Document, The Relationship between Safeguarding Internal Security and Complying with International Protection Obligations and Instruments, COM (2001) 743 final, 5.12.2001, p. 21-23 and Council doc. 14181/1/01 ENFOPOL 134,

6.2.3.2 The Interests of States v the Interests of Individuals

The lack of balance and the existence of a strong preference towards restrictive measures is evident within the framework of legal migration instruments as well. As for the establishment of a model of rights for migrants, various approaches have been proposed and could have been applied.[125] The EU has opted for the approximation of their rights either with those of EU citizens or with those of citizens of the Member State concerned. The reality is that such approximation remains some way off. The provisions regarding control over migrants have been reinforced and the drafting of the provisions that attribute rights to third country nationals is rather loose. It is as if there are two competing issues at stake. On the one hand, there is the interest of the State in safeguarding internal security, having a strict control over the admission process and eventually also over its budget, and on the other hand, the interests of the individual for fair and equal treatment.

Firstly, the public policy provisions included in the legal migration Directives have been considerably reinforced. It is not only the drafting of the relevant provisions that has been reinforced but further references have also been included in the preamble or in the Council minutes. In particular, the reference to "personal conduct" has been deleted from the text and the drafting is broad enough to leave the Member States the room for manoeuvre they need in order to refuse

30.11.2001. See also Monar J., "The European Union's Role in the Fight against International Terrorism: An Evaluation in the Light of the Response to 11 September 2001", in Vandersanden G. and de Walsch A. (eds.), *Mélanges en hommage à Jean-Victor Louis (Vol. I)*, Editions de l'Université de Bruxelles, Bruxelles, 2003, p. 337-354, at p. 348.

125 i.e. the use of national immigration legislation as the starting point, using existing international standards or the extension of rules regarding specific categories of third country nationals and using the rights of EU citizens as a reference point. For a list and analysis see Groenendijk K., "Security and Residence and Access to Free Movement of Settled Third Country Nationals under Community Law", in Guild E. and Harlow C. (eds.), *Implementing Amsterdam: immigration and asylum rights in EC law*, Hart Publishing, Oxford, 2001, p. 225-240. Groenendijk comes to the conclusion that in both the cases of movement within the EU and the legal status in the Member State of residence the model that the EU has chosen is that of EU citizens rights. This may well be so as far as the case of movement is concerned, however to the extent that the status in the Member State of residence is concerned it needs to be clarified that although the status of third country nationals is compared to that of EU citizens – see Tampere Conclusions – in the long-term resident Directive the criterion is the status of nationals of the Member State concerned. Moreover, there is no general equality as such, rather it is focused on specific areas. For an analogous categorisation see Peers S., "Aliens, Workers, Citizens or Humans: Models for Community Immigration Law", in Guild E. and Harlow C. (eds.), *Implementing Amsterdam: immigration and asylum rights in EC law*, Hart Publishing, Oxford, 2001, p. 291-308.

admission for public security. And according to the preamble, the notion of public order may cover the conviction of a serious crime and also cases in which a third country national belongs to an association which supports terrorism, supports such an association or has extremist aspirations.[126]

Secondly, the process of issuing and withdrawal of the relevant residence permits grants the Member States a considerable margin of manoeuvre should they wish to apply strict scrutiny. The initial issuing of the residence permits is subject to the fulfilment of a series of rather strict conditions, their duration is rather short, Member States maintain the right to control the fulfilment of these conditions in the course of renewals and there is also a series of rather broadly defined reasons justifying the withdrawal of the residence permits.

Thirdly, the rights that are granted to migrants have been considerably limited or subject to optional derogatory clauses. This is most evident in the case of the rights of long-term residents.[127] The reaction of the Member States is comprehensible when one considers the breakdown of social assistance systems and the extra burden that results for national budgets. This conclusion is further reinforced by the text of the relevant Declaration of the Draft Constitutional Treaty.[128] However, it needs to be highlighted that the problem of equal treatment is primarily focused on first-generation migrants, since citizenship is usually attributed to second-generation migrants and is seen as an integration measure.[129] Member States have also proved reluctant to grant other types of rights as well. They display a lack of support for inititatives such as the establishment of civic citizenship or the granting of political rights to third country nationals.[130]

---

126 See recital 14 and Article 6 of the family reunification Directive and recital 14 and Article 8 of the long-term residents Directive.

127 See the discussion of this Directive and in particular its Article 11 *supra* at 4.2.1.

128 Declaration regarding Article III-136 and Article III-267, *op.cit.*

129 Large scale post-war immigration and the need to integrate a large and often growing resident population of third country nationals created pressure for reform of nationality law. It has additionally been argued that for migrants in Europe 1992 was the end of European citizenship, not the beginning, and that for the foreseeable future inclusion will be negotiated at national level, and the attribution of citizenship will be an integral part of this process. Hansen R. and Weil P., "Introduction: Citizenship, Immigration and Nationality : Towards a Convergence in Europe ?", in Hansen R. and Weil P. (eds.), *Towards a European Nationality – Citizenship, Immigration and Nationality Law in the EU*, Palgrave Publishers, New York, 2001, p. 1-23.

130 See the discussion *supra* at 4.2.2.

6.2.4 *The Challenges of Transparency and Accountability*

Transparency, accountability and the democratic deficit are issues that have traditionally raised concerns with regard to the development of a JHA policy.[131] These terms, however, raise a series of varying issues. For example, whereas the issue of democratic deficit seems to be perceived by the European Parliament as primarily the lack of parliamentary intervention, the Council and the Commission put more the emphasis on the need to increase the legitimacy of *all* the institutions.[132]

The issues of transparency and accountability in EU migration policy-making can be seen from two perspectives. Firstly, in the sense of the democratic accountability of the institutional actors and the possibility of participation, and access to information, of all interested actors and especially citizens. Secondly, in terms of the clarity and legal certainty of the substantive legislative measures adopted. The importance of the former is frequently emphasised and this is rightly so, however, the significance of the latter should not be neglected. It is equally important both for the EU citizens and for the third country nationals concerned to have a clear idea of the EU position and legislation on migration, and accordingly of their rights and obligations.

6.2.4.1 Policy-making in Migration: Forging a Policy for the Citizens without the Citizens?

The lack of democratic accountability at the EU level is often strongly criticised. Those concerns become accentuated with regard to JHA issues. Both Schengen and the third pillar have been the subject of substantial criticism.[133] It has even been argued that avoiding judicial control and transparency and the wish to find venues that were more favourable to restrictive control policies were among the

131 For a discussion on the free movement of persons and democracy in Europe at the beginning of the 1990s see Groenendijk C.A., "Three questions about free movement of persons and democracy in Europe", in Schermers et al. (eds.), *Free Movement of Persons in Europe, Legal Problems and Experiences*, T.M.C. Asser Institute, The Hague, 1993, p. 391-402.

132 On these points see Franck C., "Le déficit démocratique: une notion en débat", in Vandersanden G. and de Walsch A. (eds.), *Mélanges en hommage à Jean-Victor Louis (Vol. I)*, Editions de l'Université de Bruxelles, Bruxelles, 2003, p. 175-188.

133 Given the fact that there was no scrutiny of the Schengen *acquis*, its transformation to EU *acquis* was considered a striking example of a democratic deficit. Plender R., "The Treaty of Amsterdam and the Free Movement of Persons", *European Business Law Review*, Vol. 9, No 11 & 12, 1998, p. 400-406. On the criticism regarding the third pillar see among many others Tizzano A., "Brevi note sul "terzo pilastro" del Trattato di Maastricht", *Il Diritto dell'Unione Europea*, Issue 2, 1996, p. 391-403 and Den Boer M., "Steamy Windows: Transparency and Openness in Justice and Home Affairs", in Deckmyn V. and Thomson I. (eds.), *Openness and Transparency in the European Union*, EIPA, Maastricht, 1998, p. 91-105.

reasons prompting Member States to cooperate at the European level.[134] Taking into account the strengthened role of the Member States in migration issues and in contrast to the general conception of the Commission's lack of accountability,[135] it will be argued herein that the main source of concern lies within the decision-making process in the Council. The examination will focus on two main issues: first, the limited participation of non-governmental actors; and, second, the issue of access to documents.

6.2.4.1.1 Democratic Accountability in the Decision-making Process

The involvement of mainly non-state actors, and also state actors that are not closely linked to the central administration – which in principle holds a dominant position during the Council negotiations – are, if not excluded from the decision-making process, at least dependent on national legislation or the will of each national government. The same argument could be made in relation to those EU actors that do not officially participate in negotiations in the Council, namely the European Parliament, the Economic and Social Committee and the Committee of the Regions.[136] To the extent that national actors are considered this position is expected due to the institutional autonomy of Member States, however, it is necessary to have a similar degree of representation of the interests of all the European citizens. Given the implications that JHA related issues have on the life of citizens, it is rather unfortunate, to say the least, that decisions are taken almost behind closed doors without any input from civil society.

First of all, it is worth examining briefly the role of each of these marginalised actors. Inasmuch as the role of the directly elected assemblies is concerned, as argued earlier, in the vast majority of cases the participation of the European Parliament was limited to mere consultation without any real decision-making power. As for the role of national parliaments, this depends on the legal system of each Member State, since the relations between national parliaments and the

134 Giraudon V., "European Integration and Migration Policy: Vertical Policy-making as a Venue Shopping", *op.cit*. The so-called 'escape to Europe' hypothesis is also supported by Geddes and others. See Geddes A., *The Politics of Migration and Immigration in Europe, op.cit.*, at p. 127-128.

135 It has been convincingly argued that claims of an over-zealous out-of-touch Commission are indeed unfounded. See Crombez C. and Hix S., Unaccountable Brussels Bureaucrats? Implications of the EU Constitutional Reforms for the Accountability of the Commission, 12 June 2003, <http://personal.lse.ac.uk/HIX/WorkingPapers.HTM >.

136 Inasmuch as the period prior to the passage to the co-decision procedure and the areas to which the co-decision procedure does yet not apply are concerned. From a legal point of view the consultation of the Parliament is an obligation for the Council but it has been clearly shown that its opinion is rarely taken into account.

Council are indirect.[137] It is only the individual governments of each Member State that are accountable to their respective parliamentary bodies. However, whereas all national parliaments have some type of monitoring system, which usually takes the form of specialised committees, the degree of monitoring and scrutiny that they exercise varies substantially. Some national parliaments have managed to secure greater scrutiny as a *quid pro quo* for their agreement to ratify the Treaty of Maastricht.[138] Others, such as the Dutch parliament, have employed considerable pressure to make sure that their governments are prevented from taking any decisions with regard to JHA related issues without prior referral to the national parliament.[139] More recently, the Treaty of Amsterdam, following French proposals for the strengthening of the role of national parliaments, provides for a legally binding protocol on the powers offered to these actors,[140] a role which has been significantly bolstered by the Draft Constitutional Treaty.[141]

Secondly, the role of other national interlocutors, such as national interest groups and sub-national governmental authorities, varies even more and is heavily dependent on the system of each Member State.[142] Insofar as the role of the regions is concerned, in contrast to the case of countries that have a centralised system of governance – where their role is almost non-existent – in countries that have a federal system it is a remarkably strong role that they play. The case of the German Länder is the best example of the strong role of regional actors. Their role appears to be considerably influential during internal negotiations that form the national position – both with regard to legislative measures as well as in the IGC processes. Further, a representative of the Länder is always present during the Council preparatory bodies and Council level meetings.

Thirdly, the role of NGO's in migration policy-making is quite limited notwithstanding the civil liberties and human rights implications of the measures concerned. Their involvement usually takes the form of bilateral meetings with, or letters sent to, the Presidency, individual Ministries or European institutions. As far as the practice of the Council is concerned, this is limited to distribut-

137 Hayes-Renshaw and Wallace, *op.cit.*, at p. 225-228.

138 It needs to be mentioned in that regard that a Declaration in that regard was also attached to the Treaty of Maastricht as well. See Declaration No 13 on the role of the national parliaments in the European Union.

139 Hayes-Renshaw and Wallace, *op.cit.*, at p. 226.

140 See Protocol on the role of the national parliaments in the European Union. Maurer, *op.cit.*, at p. 312. Moreover, according to the same Protocol as well as the Council's rules of procedure, Title VI measures cannot be put on a Council's agenda before the lapse of a six-week period. See Point I.3 of the Protocol and Article 3 (3) of Council Decision 2004/338/EC, *op.cit.*

141 Nascimbene B., "Il progetto di Constituzione europea e l'immigrazione", *Diritto Immigrazione e Cittadinanza,* anno VI, No 1, 2004, p. 13-23.

142 Hayes-Renshaw and Wallace, *op.cit.*, at p. 228-230.

ing the letter or document without in principle holding a debate on the matter. Their impact is, however, much stronger at bilateral level with Member State representatives or mainly with EU officials. The Commission is usually the main target of interest groups. Their relations prove to be mutually beneficial. In fact the Commission sponsors and co-opts interest groups into consultation processes[143] as a way of enhancing the legitimacy of supranational processes and facilitating the consolidation of its role as a policy actor.[144] Moreover, interest groups seem to have a strong impact on the European Parliament and individual MEPs. The pressure exercised over MEPs for the legal challenge to the family reunification Directive attests to this.[145]

The, in principle, limited impact of NGOs on the decision-making process, lies not only in the limited interest or even contradictions between their position and that of governments or EU institutions, mainly the Council, but also on a series of more general factors of a mainly structural nature. Migration policy is usually seen from the humanitarian angle of asylum, and NGOs are mainly interested in cases where the persons concerned are facing an expulsion order.[146] In fact their presence during the public hearing with regard to the Green Book for Return was remarkably strong. However, migration does not have solely humanitarian aspects but also raises economic considerations as well, which are not sufficiently considered. Another explanatory factor for the absence of a significant NGO impact is that there are no remarkably strong NGOs focusing exclusively in the area of migration. This can be contrasted with for example the fields of asylum and fundamental rights where they have a much stronger presence. Moreover, the vast majority of existing NGOs seem to have sectoral interests, i.e. rights of children and women and human rights issues, a fact that diminishes their influence. Additionally, there is also a more general problem of formulating a 'migrants interests' agenda that exhibits some coherence, given the sheer diversity of migrant and migrant-origin communities living in EU Member States and the fear that through participation they will legitimise policy developments.[147] It is also apparent that pro-immigrant lobby groups operating

143 The Commission systematically emphasises the contribution of NGOs to the strengthening of participatory democracy. See Niessen J., "Consultations on Immigration Policies in the European Union", *EJML*, Vol. 4, Issue 1, 2002, p. 79-83.

144 Geddes A., *Immigration and European Integration – Towards fortress Europe?, op.cit.*, at p. 135 and 144.

145 It seems that the NGOs launched a campaign directed at MEPs with the objective of pursuing a legal challenge. Ferraiolo, *op.cit.* and Mariani, *op.cit.*, at p. 22.

146 For an overview of the NGOs present in the migration area see Niessen J., "Consultations on Immigration Policies in the European Union", *EJML*, Vol. 4, Issue 1, 2002, p. 79-83.

147 On the role, positions and fears of migrant interest groups see Geddes A., *Immigration and European Integration – Towards fortress Europe?, op.cit.*, at p. 134-137 and

at the EU level do not command the resources of powerful and well-entrenched interest groups such as business, trade unions and agriculture, their lobbying arenas usually being at the sub-national and national level.[148]

Finally, it is worth highlighting a series of factors that increase this lack of democratic accountability in the decision-making process. Firstly, there is an inherent tension between democracy and efficiency.[149] The two concepts are usually perceived as contradictory and the EU does not seem to manage to find the right balance between them. Secondly, another major problem aggravating this obvious lack of democratic accountability lies in the fact that the vast majority of the decisions are taken at working party level where officials are accountable only via their Minister.[150] Certain authors have also questioned the accountability of the European Council.[151] Thirdly, a major part of legislative proposals, namely Member States' initiatives, were exempted from the scope of the Protocol attached to the Treaty of Amsterdam concerning the role of the national parliaments.[152] Fortunately this has ended since 1 May 2004 when Member States have lost their right of initiative. Fourth, the lack of transparency is also linked with the operational nature of JHA.[153] This issue is likely to be accentuated in view of the establishment of a series of operational structures, such as the centres and the overriding Agency for the control of the external borders.

6.2.4.1.2 Access to Documents and Information v Confidentiality

Up to the early 1990s, access to documents was almost wholly excluded. First of all, it was excluded with regard to intergovernmental cooperation and within

142-148.

148 Geddes A., *Immigration and European Integration – Towards fortress Europe?, op.cit.*, at p. 143.

149 Hayes-Renshaw and Wallace, *op.cit.*, at p. 227. See also the comments of Maurer with regard to the co-decision procedure, which was initially heavily criticised as cumbersome and seen as symptomatic of a "general trade-off" between the efficiency of EU decision-making on the one hand and parliamentary involvement on the other. Maurer, *op.cit.*, at p. 310.

150 Curtin D., "Democracy, Transparency and Political Participation: Some Progress Post-Amsterdam" in Deckmyn V. and Thomson I. (eds.), *Openness and Transparency in the European Union*, EIPA, Maastricht, 1998, p. 107-120 at p. 109, and Hayes-Renshaw and Wallace, *op.cit.*, at p. 227.

151 Monar J., "Decision-making in the Area of Freedom, Security and Justice", *op.cit.*, at p. 69-70.

152 For a discussion on this point see Peers S., *EU Justice and Home Affairs Law*, *op.cit.*, at p. 42.

153 Peers S., *EU Justice and Home Affairs Law*, *op.cit.*, at p. 3. In particular, strong concerns have been raised with regard to the operational aspects of the management of external borders. See House of Lords, *Proposals for a European Border Guard, op.cit.*, at pt. 58.

the Schengen framework. It was not until the Maastricht Treaty adopted a Declaration on the right of access to information, and mainly once the Danish and French referenda with regard to the ratification of the Maastricht Treaty made it urgent to act upon the relevant Declaration, that the transparency issue came to the forefront of the EU agenda.[154] The lack of transparency nonetheless remained one of the main criticisms even with regard to the former third pillar.[155] The issue was initially developed through the case law of the Court of Justice.[156] The European Ombudsman has also played a role although its competence has been forcefully contested by the Council.[157]

Transparency in terms of access to documents in the post-Amsterdam era has definitely increased.[158] The Amsterdam Treaty includes a specific provision on access to documents, namely Article 255 TEC. A special Regulation was

154 See Declaration 17 of the Maastricht Treaty on the basis of which the Council and the Commission adopted in 1993 a common Code of Conduct on public access to documents which each of them implemented through a decision. For an overview on the development of the right to access to documents see Dyrberg P., "Accountability and Legitimacy: What is the Contribution of Transparency?", in Arnull A. and Wincott D. (eds.), *Accountability and Legitimacy in the European Union*, Oxford University Press, Oxford, 2002, p. 81-96; Peers S., "From Maastricht to Laeken: The Political Agenda of Openness and Transparency in the European Union", in Deckmyn V. (ed.), *Increasing Transparency in the European Union?,* EIPA, Maastricht, 2002, p. 7-32 and Peers S., "Access to Information on EU External Relations and Justice and Home Affairs", in Deckmyn V. (ed.), *Increasing Transparency in the European Union?,* EIPA, Maastricht, 2002, p. 209-232.

155 Peers S., *EU Justice and Home Affairs Law*, *op.cit.*, at p. 36-37.

156 For an overview of the relevant case law see Naômé C., "The Case-Law of the Court of Justice and of the Court of First Instance of the European Communities on Transparency: From Carvel to Hautala II (1995-2001)", in Deckmyn V. (ed.), *Increasing Transparency in the European Union?,* EIPA, Maastricht, 2002, p. 147-198.

157 At the occasion of a complaint submitted by Tony Bunyan, editor of *Statewatch*, the Council took the view (by a vote of 9-6) that the Ombudsman had no competence to hear complaints over the Council's administration of the Decision where third pillar documents were involved. But the Ombudsman maintained the view that it had such competence, and in June 1997 the Council decided that it would answer the complaint insofar as it related to the application of the Decision but not the substance of the documents. Peers S., *EU Justice and Home Affairs Law*, *op.cit.*, at p. 32-33. See also Söderman J., "The Role and the Impact of the European Ombudsman in Access to Documentation and the Transparency of Decision-Making", in Deckmyn V. and Thomson I. (eds.), *Openness and Transparency in the European Union,* EIPA, Maastricht, 1998, p. 75-83.

158 For an overview on the process of establishing a right of access to information and some useful comments see Curtin D., "The Developing Right of Citizen Access to Information on Asylum and Immigration Decision-Making", in Guild E. and

adopted on the matter,[159] and relevant provisions have also been included in the Council's Rules of Procedure.[160] Moreover, the right of access to documents is enshrined in the Charter of Fundamental Rights.[161] For its part, the Council has taken considerable efforts to make public the Schengen *acquis* by declassifying the biggest part of it and in principle Member States' initiatives now have an explanatory memorandum and are published. And since 1999 a large part of Council documents are now available in the Council's public register.[162]

The situation, however, is far from being perfect. The traditional dilemma between transparency and confidentiality remains strong. The legislative process remains rather secretive with many documents not available or only partly available to the public at critical times. The need to preserve the integrity of the Council's decision-making process and confidentiality with regard to individual Member States' positions should be recognised but this should not outweigh the public's interest in transparency, especially in such a sensitive area.

6.2.4.2 Transparency in Terms of Legal Certainty and Clarity of Substantive Law

The legal certainty and clarity of the legislative measures adopted is another important aspect of the emerging area of freedom, security and justice. It is undoubtedly the case that the EU migration *acquis* is far from clear. The two main sources of this lack of clarity are: first, the existence of a series of different statuses combined with the lack of a consolidated legal framework and the impact of the Title IV opt-out Protocols; and, second, the contested legal value of a major part of this *acquis*.

The lack of a clear Community competence on migration for several decades, the fragmented EU approach and the unwillingness of the Member States to extend the same rights that had already been recognised to certain categories of third country nationals to all third country nationals have led to the estab-

Harlow C. (eds.), *Implementing Amsterdam: immigration and asylum rights in EC law*, Hart Publishing, Oxford, 2001, p. 35-63.

159 Regulation 1049/2001 of 30 May 2001 regarding public access to European Parliament, Council and Commission documents, OJ L 145/43, 31.5.2001. For a presentation see Maes M, "The "New" Regulation on Access to Documents", in Deckmyn V. (ed.), *Increasing Transparency in the European Union?,* EIPA, Maastricht, 2002, p. 199-208.

160 See Annex II to Council Decision 2004/338/EC, *op.cit*.

161 Article 42 of the Charter of Fundamental Rights of the European Union, OJ C 264/1, 18.12.2000.

162 Council Decision 2000/23/EC of 6 December 1999 on the improvement of information on the Council's legislative activities and the public register of Council documents, OJ L 9/22, 13.1.2000. See also <http://ue.eu.int/docCenter.asp?lang=en&cmsid=245>.

lishment of a complex system of multiple statuses inasmuch as admission of migrants is concerned. These could be divided in to three main categories: family members of EU citizens, third country nationals who are citizens of a country with which the EU has signed a bilateral agreement and the rest of the third country nationals. In addition, the evolution of the Schengen and subsequently the EU *acquis* with regard to the crossing of borders and the movement of third country nationals has led to the formation of a rather complex framework which calls for the adoption of consolidated texts.

The first series of EU legislative acts on migration in the post-Amsterdam era not only reveal an unwillingness to remedy the extant fragmentation, but they further appear to create new partitions. In all the relevant Directives the two main categories of immigrants already covered by EU law – i.e. family members and persons moving within the framework of a Community firm – are excluded from their scope.[163] There are also two new types of more favourable clause provisions: first, a clause on more favourable provisions laid down by bilateral international agreements signed either by the Community or by the Member States; and, second, a more general type of catch-all clause stating that the Directive applies without prejudice to any more favourable national provisions.[164] Consequently, apart from the already existing partitions at EU level, a series of "national" statuses is further maintained. However, in principle, the migrants who are admitted on the basis of this second more favourable clause are excluded from any possible additional advantages provided by the Directive.[165]

In like vein, account needs to be taken of the deeply partitioning effect of the opt-out Protocols as well as of the participation of Norway, Iceland and Switzerland, and shortly also of Liechtenstein, in certain central aspects of migration policy.[166] It is not easy for the persons concerned to know which States are bound by a legislative measure and to what extent, given that the application

163 i.e Article 3 (3) of the family reunification Directive, Article 3 (2) of the students' Directive and Article 15 (5) of the long-term residents Directive.

164 i.e Articles 3 (4) and 3 (5) of the family reunification Directive, Articles 3 (3) and 13 of the long-term residents Directive and Article 4 of the students' Directive.

165 For instance in the case of the long-term residents Directive they cannot move and reside in another Member State – see Article 13 of the long-term residents Directive- whereas in the case of the family reunification Directive where such a reunification is based on optional more favourable clauses, the rest of the Member States are not obliged to recognise these persons as family members, see recital 10 of the family reunification Directive.

166 Additionally, one needs to underscore the existence of a series of closer cooperation or special legal frameworks such as the Benelux Cooperation, the Nordic passport Union and the Common Travel area. See Cullen D., "Variable Geometry and Overlapping Circles: in Search of a Suitable Model for Justice and Home Affairs", in Bieber R. and Monar J. (eds.), *Justice and Home Affairs in the European Union*

of the Protocols is not always consistent and the opting in and out policy of the UK and Ireland with regard to Title IV measures is not coherent. It is ironic that third country nationals living in the three, shortly to become four, outsiders have greater rights than those living in the UK and/or Ireland, whose entry into the Schengen area could possibly also be subject to a visa obligation.

While understanding the legal and political obstacles preventing the adoption of a comprehensive and consolidated legal framework as well as the need for differentiating between different categories of migrants – since even at the national level one witnesses the existence of different statuses – it is imperative that the EU invests greater efforts in providing a clear and comprehensive framework. Issues that call out for action are the need for a consolidation of the former Schengen *acquis* on visas;[167] the establishment of a comprehensive system for the movement of third country nationals within the EU territory;[168] and eventually further harmonisation in the area of admission for long-term purposes.

The second major source of confusion concerns the contested character of the value of a considerable part of the EU *acquis*. The first source of confusion lies in the value of the various soft law measures that the EU has inherited from the Maastricht era. Of course, the non-exhaustive character of Article 249 TEC does not preclude the Council from adopting non-legally binding measures such as Resolutions or Conclusions. However, this use of soft law is deserving of criticism not only because of its limited impact, but also because it often was relatively detailed and definitive.[169] In fact, the value of the relevant *acquis* adopted in the Maastricht era was highly debated.[170] The second major source of per-

---

The Development of the Third Pillar, European Interuniversity Press, Brussels, 1995, p. 65-91.

167 Meaning the recasting of the CCI. It needs to be recalled that the relevant Schengen *acquis* on borders issues has already been consolidated. See Council Regulation establishing a Community Code on the rules governing the movement of persons across borders, *op.cit*.

168 However, one needs to take into consideration the legal obstacles in the Treaty of Amsterdam. See discussion *supra* at 2.2.3.

169 Peers S., *EU Justice and Home Affairs Law*, *op.cit.*, at p. 29-30.

170 Publication in the L series of the Official Journal and the wording used were considered as determing factors in that regard. See Fernhout, *op.cit.*, at p. 385 and 390. Moreover, there has been strong controversy over the legal effect of Joint Actions: thirteen Member States supported by the Council Legal Service considered all Joint Actions to be "obligatory in law and that the extent of the obligation on the Member States depends on the content and the terms of each Joint Action", whereas the UK and Portugal argued that they "were not automatically ... legally binding ... the whole question of whether [a Joint Action] was legally binding depended on its actual text". The Council Legal Service even invited the Court to settle this point in the airport transit visas case, but the ECJ considered this question irrelevant. See

plexity lies in the nature of considerable parts of the Schengen *acquis*, which are somewhere between operational measures, best practices and legally binding provisions.[171] Fortunately, following the recasting of the Common Manual the Commission is planning to present a proposal for a Regulation concerning the recasting of the CCI on visas.[172]

Finally, it is rather unfortunate that the need to find imaginative drafting methods in order to reach consensus during the negotiation process renders a considerable part of the post-Amsterdam *acquis* rather obscure. First of all, it is difficult to interpret the plethora of references to national legislation, especially if one takes into consideration the fact that Directives need to be implemented via national legislation. Moreover, it is rather difficult to assess the value of the vague drafting as well as that of the series of new conditions that are included as a type of clarification in the preamble. In fact, the final outcome on certain occasions takes the form of a strange legal text trying to reconcile deeply varying legal traditions and resulting in an '*objet juridique non identifié*'.[173] Consequently, as an immediate result of this deferral technique a part of the legislative power is *de facto* transferred to the Court. One could well argue that in terms of legal certainty the ideal solution is not for rights to be established or negated via jurisprudence but rather for the legislator to provide either a concrete legislative framework or at least clear and coherent guidelines. The dilemmas of policy-making also remain at the implementation stage.[174]

---

minutes of K.4 Committee of 7 April 1995, Council doc. 6684/95, 4.5.1995. See also case C-170/96 *op.cit*. On these points see Peers S., *EU Justice and Home Affairs Law*, *op.cit.*, at p. 28-29.

171 Following the adoption of the Regulation on a Community Code on Borders the Schengen Common Manual – the hybrid character of which has been a source of major legal uncertainty – has been finally communitarised. On the hybrid character of the Common Manual see the discussion *supra* at 2.1.1.2 and 4.1.1. However, it is worth noting that the Schengen States have been systematically drafting recommendations and best practices regarding the application of the *acquis*. See the three volume series prepared and published after the integration of Schengen within the EU. Council of the European Union, EU Schengen Catalogue – External border control, Removal and Readmission: Recommendations and Best Practices, February 2002; Council of the European Union, EU Schengen Catalogue – Schengen Information System SIRENE: Recommendations and Best Practices, December 2002; and Council of the European Union, EU Schengen Catalogue – Issuing of Visa: Recommendations and Best Practices, March 2003.

172 See *supra* at 4.1.1.

173 Term used by Gilbert El Kaim. See El Kaim, *op.cit*.

174 See the interesting general report of the IAPASIS research project of the European University Institute published in a special issue of the Journal of Ethnic and Migration Studies. See Jordan B., Stråth B. and Triandafyllidou A., "Contextualis-

6.2.5 *Fundamental Rights Issues*

One of the major challenges that the Community is facing in view of the process of the establishment of an area of freedom, security and justice is that of living up to international human rights standards. Bearing in mind the width of the eventual linkages between, and implications of, immigration law and human rights, proceeding to an exhaustive analysis of the issues in question is beyond the scope of this book. Rather, the focus will be on two sets of issues. First, the human rights implications that migration policy presents and the Member States and the Union's general approach with regard to human rights issues. Secondly, certain human rights issues that might eventually arise in relation to a number of recently adopted substantive migration law measures.

It is axiomatic that migration law opens up many fundamental rights questions. However, notwithstanding the visible implications, the long-standing international *acquis* and the importance of compliance with human rights standards with regard to asylum, the human rights factor has been given insufficient attention in the field of migration. Admission of migrants is in principle considered a sovereign right of each State. In contrast to the special links between the State and its own citizens, States do not consider these kind of links to exist in relation to third country nationals. Therefore, immigrants are not to be attributed the same rights as citizens. This position also appears to have been confirmed at the EU level, since the recently adopted EU Charter itself seems to be "balancing between a human rights declaration and an incipient constitution incorporating human rights".[175]

Member States have traditionally been reluctant to expressly recognise the applicability of fundamental rights to third country nationals. In addition to the sovereignty dogma explored earlier in this chapter, this reticence can be explained by a series of other factors. In the first place, fundamental rights are seen as contradicting the need to safeguard internal security and as a threat to the national budget. Moreover, immigration has traditionally been considered a temporary phenomenon and consequently immigrants have often seen themselves excluded from a series of rights linked with long-term situations. The official 'zero migration model' in conjunction with migration pressure and more recently the fear of terrorism risks has further led to a focus on the security dimension of migration both at the national and European level. And the rise of xenophobia in many countries has most likely further reinforced Member States' exclusionary policy towards migrants. Thus, the Member States frequently, and subsequently also

---

ing immigration policy implementation in Europe", *Journal of Ethnic and Migration Studies,* Vol. 29, No 2, March 2003, p. 195-224, at p. 211.

175 Guild E., "Citizens, Immigrants, Terrorists and Others", in Peers S. and Ward A. (eds.), *The European Union Charter of Fundamental Rights*, Hart Publishing, Oxford, 2004, p. 231-246, at p. 233. For the text of the Charter see Charter of Fundamental Rights of the European Union, OJ C 264/1, 18.12.2000.

the EU, face a certain type of dilemma between security implications and the need to respect international human rights standards with the latter being seen much more as a problem than an obligation.

In the light of the above it is not surprising that the EU position has been rather restrictive. The difference in the EU's internal and external approach is noteworthy. The EU is keen on imposing exacting human rights standards on third countries with which it has relations whilst at the same time following a much more moderate discourse internally. The juxtaposition between, on the one hand, the conditionality doctrine that has been developed with regard to external relations and the enlargement process, where a patent lack of trust towards the new-comers leads the EU to impose on third countries criteria that might not be respected by the fifteen, and on the other, the serious concerns raised over compliance with human rights standards by the fifteen, is rather revealing.[176] Serious concerns have been raised with regard to the lack of adequate scrutiny of human rights issues.[177] The annual reports of human rights implementation by Member States show that problems with regard to the respect of human rights within the EU are a reality.[178]

The general EU approach with regard to migration relevant issues seems to favour security-oriented aspects over human rights considerations. Even if the Austrian Presidency's draft strategy paper on asylum and immigration in September 1998, which was eventually adopted in a much lighter version following the vigorous attacks to which it was subjected,[179] constitutes an extreme example, the initiatives taken with regard to the promotion of rights of migrants are considerably more limited as compared with those regarding security aspects.

---

176 For a definition of conditionality and an overview of its application with regard to third countries, its inconsistencies and contested value see Smith K., "The Use of Political Conditionality in the EU's Relations with Third Countries: How Effective?", *European Foreign Affairs Review,* Vol. 3, 1998, p. 253-274. For a discussion on human rights and EU membership see De Witte B. and Toggenburg G., "Human Rights and Membership of the European Union", in Peers S. and Ward A. (eds.), *The European Union Charter of Fundamental Rights*, Hart Publishing, Oxford, 2004, p. 59-82. For a discussion on human rights and enlargement see De Schutter O., "La réunification de l'Europe et les droits de l'homme" in De Kerchove G. and Weyembergh A. (eds.), *Sécurité et justice: enjeu de la politique extérieure de l'Union européenne*, Institut d'Etudes Européennes, Editions de l'Université de Bruxelles, Bruxelles, 2003, p. 31-65.

177 'Amnesty criticizes EU states for violating human rights', Euobserver.com, 25.7.2004, < http://euobserver.com/?aid=16306&sid=9>.

178 A network of independent experts has been established in that respect in 2000. See 'A Network of independent experts to assess the safeguarding of fundamental rights by the European Union Member States', <http://europa.eu.int/comm/justice_home/cfr_cdf/index_en.htm>.

179 Den Boer and Wallace, *op.cit.*, at p. 504.

Furthermore, there are also practical reasons for the lack of a proactive EU approach to human rights issues in the migration field. Most of the migration legislative developments have for a long time been taking place at the intergovernmental level. It is therefore not surprising that what is essentially a precedence for Member State competence was recognised and the issue was not dealt with at EU level. Some argue that even in the Maastricht era the human rights debate lay essentially at the national rather than the EU level given the recognition of wide and potentially restrictive reserved powers to the Member States.[180]

There has however been somewhat of a transformation of late as the EU has become a great deal more active in the human rights sphere. A series of factors have contributed to this development. Firstly, the EU has been attributed its own competence to adopt legally binding legislation with regard to migration. Moreover, the Schengen *acquis* has been integrated into the EU. Human rights implications consequently became extremely relevant given the very discretionary nature of procedures such as that for visa allocation and the decision to allow entry to a person into the territory of a State[181] as well as the tendency of States to interpret strictly the rights attributed to third country nationals. Secondly, enlargement is rightly considered as a leitmotiv for human rights in the EU.[182] Thirdly, the Union has drafted and adopted its own Charter of fundamental rights, a process that has brought human rights issues to the forefront of the EU agenda and generated heated discussions, mainly due to the expectations that it had raised and its legal form being that of a solemn declaration.[183]

The issues that the adoption of the Charter raised are numerous. Its scope and added value, its relationship both to the European Convention on Human Rights (ECHR) and the case law of the Strasbourg Court and with national constitutions are some such complex issues.[184] A detailed analysis of the Charter

180 Handoll, *op.cit.*, at p. 370. In the Maastricht era, the sole positive Community action on migration related to fundamental rights was included in the social protocol and concerned the conditions of employment for third country nationals legally residing in the Member States. Guild and Niessen, *op.cit.*, at p. 49.

181 Cahn, *op.cit.*, at p. 487.

182 De Schutter, *op.cit.*

183 For an overview of the migration relevant rights included in the Charter and some preliminary comments regarding its scope see Vitorino A., "La Charte des droits fondamentaux de l'Union européenne", *Revue du Droit de l'Union Europénne*, No 1, 2001, p. 27-64; Peers S., "Immigration, Asylum and the European Union Charter of Fundamental Rights", *EJML,* Vol. 3, 2001, p. 141-149 and Groenendijk K., "Long-term Immigrants and the Council of Europe", in Guild E. and Minderhout P. (eds.), *Security of Residence and Expulsion – Protection of Aliens in Europe,* Kluwer, The Hague, 2001, p. 7-22, at p. 18-20.

184 For useful legal analyses of these issues see Peers S., "Taking Rights Away? Limitations and Derogations", in Peers S. and Ward A. (eds.), *The European Union Charter of Fundamental Rights*, Hart Publishing, Oxford, 2004, p. 141-179; Lemmens

is beyond the scope of this book, the objective is merely to highlight some issues that are of central importance to migration policy. The general consensus within the literature is that the Charter does not create any new competence for the EU with regard to human rights issues, since it was not the intention of the drafters to change the legal, political and constitutional *status quo*. The Charter rather proceeds to a codification of existing rights within the limits provided by EU law.[185] Consequently, the rights recognised to third country nationals are limited by existing or future secondary Community law on the matter. In any case, certain types of rights – i.e. social rights – require positive legislative action.[186] Indeed, there are valid arguments claiming that the Charter has restricted EU competence on human rights issues that had been established by the case law of the Court.[187] Notwithstanding much of the criticism as to the lack of added value provided by the Charter and its legally non-binding character, the Charter does have an impact on EU policy-making.[188] The Commission has already announced its intention to scrutinise any proposal for legislation and any draft instrument for compatibility with the Charter and adopted a standard formula as a formal statement of compatibility.[189] Finally, it needs to be underscored that regardless of the status of the Charter the respect of human rights was already an obligation for the EU and remains so.[190]

P., "The Relation between the Charter of Fundamental Rights of the European Union and the European Convention on Human Rights – Substantive aspects", *Maastricht Journal of European and Comparative Law,* Vol. 8, No 1, 2001, p. 49-67; Carozza P., "The Member States", in Peers S. and Ward A. (eds.), *The European Union Charter of Fundamental Rights*, Hart Publishing, Oxford, 2004, p. 35-58, at p. 39-40 and De Witte B., "The Status of the Charter: Vital Question or Non-Issue?", *Maastricht Journal of European and Comparative Law,* Vol 8, No 1, 2001, p. 49-67.

185 Vitorino A., "La Charte des droits fondamentaux de l'Union européenne", *op.cit.*

186 De Witte B., "The Status of the Charter: Vital Question or Non-Issue?", *op.cit.*

187 Carozza rightly highlights the fact that whereas the Charter is addressed to the Member States "only when they are implementing Union law" the Court in its *ERT* judgement sustained that EU human rights law applies to Member States not merely when they are implementing EU law, but whenever they are "acting within the scope of Community law". See Carozza, *op.cit.*, at pp. 39-40 and 43. See also De Witte B., "The Status of the Charter: Vital Question or Non-Issue?", *op.cit.*

188 De Witte B., "The Status of the Charter: Vital Question or Non-Issue?", *op.cit.*

189 European Commission, Memorandum from the President and Mr Vitorino – Application of the Charter of Fundamental Rights of the European Union, SEC (2001) 380/3, 13.3.2001.

190 Article 6 TEC. Moreover, fundamental rights are among the general principles of Community law and the Court had already developed a long-standing case law on the matter. See Tridimas T., *The General Principles of EC Law*, *op.cit.*, at p. 202-243 and Craig P. and De Bùrca G., *EC Law Text, Cases & Materials,* Third edition, *op.cit.*, at p. 337-349.

However, despite the expectations that the Charter has raised and the political statements of the various actors, EU policy-making and substantive law has been severely criticised for falling short of human rights standards on several occasions. The examples are numerous. There has been a rather heated debate with regard to the recently adopted EU-US Agreement on the transfer of passenger data to the US,[191] as well as on the controversial proposal on data retention.[192] Concerns regarding the compliance with human rights also affect areas that are unlikely to make the front pages of newspapers but which are nonetheless very important. Noteworthy in this respect are concerns expressed with regard to the Action Plans and the general approach of the High Level Working Group,[193] readmission agreements[194] and the Italian initiative on the organisation of joint flights which was considered a method of massive expulsions.[195] Schengen relevant and return policy issues are also a source of constant concerns.[196] The very arbitrary nature of the procedures of visa issuing and border controls,[197] and the listing in SIS are some of the main sources of concern in this

191 "Parliament supports legal action over EU-US data deal", <www.euobserver.com>, 20.6.2004; "Brussels seek to sooth nerves on data exchange", <www.euobserver.com>, 5.10.2005 and "No EU air data to US, says top judge", <www.euobserver.com>, 22.11.2005.

192 See "MEP up in arms about data privacy law", euobserver.com, 4.5.2005 and "EU moves slowly ahead with data retention law", <www.euobserver.com>, 9.9.2005.

193 'Globalising immigration controls', *Statewatch*, Vol. 9, No 5, September-October 1999, p. 29-31.

194 In particular as far as asylum issues are concerned such as the respect of the principle of non-refoulement. In that regard it is worth highlighting the calls of the European Parliament for a human rights impact assessment and its proposal for the adoption of an appropriate monitoring mechanism. See the report of Graham Watson MEP on the Hong Kong-EC readmission agreement, A5-0381/2002. On this point see Bouteillet-Paquet, *op.cit.*, at p. 371. See also "EU: buffer states & 'processing' centres", *Statewatch,* Vol. 13, No 2, March-April 2003, p. 1-2 and Balzacq and Carrera, *op.cit.*

195 In fact the measure was finally adopted without the approval of the European Parliament. On the issue of deportation by charter flights see "EU: Mass deportations by Charter flight – enforcement and resistance", *Statewatch,* Vol. 13, No 2, March-April 2003, p. 19-21.

196 Cholewinski R., "The EU acquis on Irregular Migration: Reinforcing Security at the expense of Rights", *op.cit.*

197 Cahn, *op.cit.*, at p. 487 and Cholewinski R., *Borders and Discrimination in the European Union,* ILPA, London, 2001. See also the proposal for a Draft Directive on minimum guarantees for individual freedom, security and justice in relation to decisions regarding movement of persons prepared by Boeles et al. See Boeles P. et al, *Border control and movement of persons – Towards effective legal remedies for indi-*

area.[198] In fact, the rejection of an asylum application and rejection of subsequent visa applications due to SIS listing has already been examined by French Courts,[199] whilst an action on the same matter has been brought by the Commission against Spain.[200]

There are also serious difficulties in applying the non-discrimination principle to establish a violation of third country nationals' rights particularly with regard to assessing whether there is an arbitrary application of legal provisions with regard to migrants. It has been correctly highlighted that the relevant Treaty clause, being framed as a classical legal base, does not appear to create a free-standing principle or to be capable of direct effect.[201] Furthermore, issues regarding the entry and residence of third country nationals are excluded from the scope of the relevant Directive.[202] Moreover, the relevant provision of the Commission proposals in the area of legal migration has been transferred to the preamble.[203]

---

viduals in Europe, Standing Committee of Experts in International Immigration, Refugee and Criminal Law, Utrecht, 2003.

198 In particular, with regard to supervision and data protection issues. See Colvin M., "The Schengen Information System: A Human Rights Audit", *E.H.R.L.R.*, Issue 3, 2001, p. 271-279 and *The Schengen Information System – A human rights audit,* Justice report, Justice, London, 2000.

199 The well-known *Forabosco* case decided by the French Council of State on 9 June 1999. Ms Forabosco's request for a visa to a French Consulate was rejected as she had been listed in the SIS by Germany because she had asked and been refused asylum in Germany. The Council of State ruled that it was competent to examine the case and that the German authorities had made an error in law. See Gortazar C., "Abolishing Border Controls : Individual Rights and Common Control of EU External Borders", in Guild E. and Harlow C. (eds.), *Implementing Amsterdam: immigration and asylum rights in EC law*, Hart Publishing, Oxford, 2001, p. 121-140.

200 Case C-503/03, *op.cit.* See *supra* at 2.1.1.b.

201 Langrish S., "The Treaty of Amsterdam : Selected Highlights", *ELRev*, 1998, Vol. 2, p. 3-19, at p. 15 and Melis, *op.cit.*, at p. 38.

202 It needs to be recalled that according to Article 3 (2) of Council Directive 2000/43/EC implementing the principle of equal treatment between persons irrespective of racial or ethnic origin, *op.cit.*, the Directive does not cover difference of treatment based on nationality and is without prejudice to provisions and conditions relating to the entry, residence and treatment of third country nationals. Despite the relevant reassurances of the Commission arguing that admission policies were not included in the material scope of the Directive, Member States had insisted on the inclusion of an express clause on the matter since they feared that other differences of rights, i.e. access to social benefits and to employment, might be covered. For a discussion of the negotiation process see Tyson, *op.cit.*

203 According to Brinkmann the reason is two-fold: initially the inclusion of a non-discrimination clause was opposed by the Member States since it would confer special

In addition to the legal problems that the limitation of the non-discrimination principle might cause there have been serious concerns over a series of substantive provisions in particular in the family reunification Directive. The provision establishing a possibility for the State to withdraw or refuse to renew a family member's residence permit where the sponsor and the family member do not or no longer live in a real family relationship, the possibility to withdraw a residence permit or refuse its renewal on the basis of failure to fulfil conditions such as integration, the lack of an upper procedural limit for the reply of the administration and the weak reference to the possibility to "mount a legal challenge" have been severely criticised.[204] The Dutch Unilateral Declaration stating its intention to interpret the Directive's provisions with full respect to family life reveals that the issue of compliance of some of the provisions of the Directive is likely to have been heavily debated in the course of negotiations within the framework of the Council itself.[205]

The European Parliament has already submitted an action for annulment challenging the compatibility of certain provisions of the Directive with human rights. The provisions challenged by the Parliament are: Article 4 (1) concerning minors above twelve who might not be able to join their family if they cannot fulfil the integration criterion; Article 8 establishing a waiting period of up to three years; and Article 4 (6) concerning the need for minors to submit the application before the age of fifteen.[206] The case is of central importance and is expected to prove rather controversial. Despite the fact that of late the Court

non-discrimination rights only on those persons covered by the relevant proposal, whereas later when it became clear that the Charter of Fundamental Rights would be included in the Constitutional Treaty a special non-discrimination clause was considered superfluous. See Brinkmann G., "The Immigration and Asylum Agenda", *ELJ,* Vol. 10, Issue 2, March 2004, p. 182-199, at p. 184-185. Nonetheless, another reason for the deletion of the relevant clause from the texts of the Directives might lie in the fact that the relevant clause is a legal basis and could therefore not be used as a free-standing provision in the text of a Directive.

204 Peers S., "Family Reunion and Community Law", in Walker N. (ed.), *The Area of Freedom, Security and Justice,* Oxford University Press, Oxford, 2004, p. 143-197.

205 See Council doc. 10755/03 ADD 1 MIGR 58 OC 439, 14.7.2003. According to the text of the Declaration "The Netherlands underlines that the provisions of the Directive on the right to family reunification should be interpreted with full respect to family life. This Directive should be applied in conformity with Article 8 of the European Convention for the protection of human rights and fundamental freedoms".

206 See the action brought by the Parliament against the Council, Case C-540/03, *op.cit.* See also the Opinion of Advocate General Kokott delivered on 8 September 2005. It needs to be underlined that in contrast to the case of the first two provisions, meaning Articles 4 (1) and 8, where the State has the right to refuse family reunification, in the third one, meaning Article 4 (6), the State cannot refuse the family

has extensively dealt with and referred to human rights provisions,[207] it is the first time that a migration relevant legislative measure is challenged for a lack of compliance with human rights standards. The difficulties that the Court will face are two-fold, even if these are closely interlinked. First, it might prove difficult to pronounce in the abstract on whether the relevant provisions are violating human rights or not. And second, given that all three challenged provisions are optional derogations and much depends on whether and how these will be implemented via national law by the Member States, one could argue that it might be difficult to establish that the Directive itself, meaning the EU law as opposed to the national law, falls short of relevant human rights standards. According to the Parliament the aforementioned provisions of the Directive violate international human rights, namely the right to family life and the right not to be discriminated.[208] One could additionally mention, inasmuch as Articles 4 (1) and 4 (6) are concerned, the rights of children. The EU Charter of fundamental rights, the preamble of the Directive and the general principles on which the EU is based include references to all these rights.[209]

While international human rights instruments invoke the principle of family reunification they do not go so far as to recognise it as a right.[210] The ECHR does not create any right to enter a country of which one is not a national and the extent to which a State is obliged to permit family members to join their sponsor remains unclear in the Strasbourg case law.[211] The violation of the family reunifi-

reunification. The last provision was added by the Council whilst the other two were proposed by the Commission in its second modified proposal.

207 For an overview of the recent case law of the court see Peers S., "Family Reunion and Community Law", *op.cit.*

208 See Case C-540/03, *op.cit.*

209 See Articles 7, 21 and 24 of the EU Charter; recitals 2, 5 and 11 of the Directive; Articles 8 and 14 of ECHR and the 1989 New York Convention of the Rights of the Child ratified by all the Member States. For an overview of the relevant international law provisions see the Opinion of Advocate General Kokott in the family reunification case, *op.cit.,* in particular paras 24 to 30.

210 Niessen J., "Overlapping Interests and Conflicting Agendas: The Knocking into Shape of EU Immigration Policies", *EJML,* Vol. 3, Issue 3/4, 2001, p. 419-434, at p. 275.

211 Brinkmann G., "Family Reunion, Third Country Nationals and the Community's New Powers", *op.cit.*, at p. 247. For an overview of case law see Van Dijk P., "Protection of 'Integrated' Aliens against Expulsion under the European Convention on Human Rights", in Guild E. and Minderhout P. (eds.), *Security of Residence and Expulsion – Protection of Aliens in Europe,* Kluwer, The Hague, 2001, p. 23-39; Harvey C., "Promoting Insecurity: Public Order, Expulsion and the European Convention on Human Rights", in Guild E. and Minderhout P. (eds.) *Security of Residence and Expulsion – Protection of Aliens in Europe,* Kluwer, The Hague, 2001, p. 41-58 and Peers S., "Family Reunion and Community Law", *op.cit.*

cation provision is not a 'black-white issue', since it is usually based on a balance test between the interests of the State in terms of public policy and the interests of the individual on the basis of the principle of proportionality.[212]

It is worth discussing briefly in that regard some of the cases that have been brought in front of the court of Strasbourg with regard to the right to family life.[213] More specifically, according to the Strasbourg Court:

(a) The extent of a State's obligation to admit to its territory relatives of settled immigrants will vary according to the particular circumstances of the persons involved and the general interest.
(b) As a matter of well-established international law and subject to its treaty obligations, a State has the right to control the entry of non-nationals into its territory.
(c) Where immigration is concerned, Article 8 cannot be considered to impose on a State a general obligation to respect immigrants' choice of the country of their matrimonial residence and to authorise family reunion in its territory.[214]

On the basis of these principles the Court has already reached the conclusion that there was no violation of Article 8 in cases of refusal of the right of family reunification due *inter alia* to the lack of a real family relationship and the possibility to conduct a common family life in the country of origin. Moreover, in a recent case, *Sen v. The Netherlands*, which concerned the right of a minor child, who was living with her aunt in Turkey, to join her family in the Netherlands, the main reason for which the Court judged that the refusal to grant a residence permit to the child violated Article 8 ECHR was that the family had two other children in the Netherlands and it would not be easy for the family to move back to Turkey.[215] Had the Sen family not have had the two other children, or had these children not been following a Dutch school, it is likely that on the basis of the *Gül* and *Ahmut* judgements the Court would not have recognised a violation of Article 8.

In the light of the above it becomes clear that is not easy to assess in the abstract whether a provision constitutes a violation of a human rights clause.

212 In accordance with the second paragraph of Article 8 ECHR a limitation of the exercise of the right might be justified under certain circumstances.

213 For an overview of the case law of both the Strasbourg and Luxembourg Courts see the Opinion of Advocate General Kokott, in paricular paras 59 to 78.

214 See Case of *Ahmut v. the Netherlands*, Judgement delivered by the European Court of Human Rights on 26 October 1996. See point 67 of the Judgement. The *Ahmut* case follows the precedent set by Case *Gül v. Switzerland*, Judgement of 19 February 1996.

215 See Case *Sen v. the Netherlands*, Judgement of the Court of 21 December 2001. See more specifically, point 40.

Most likely, the decisive factor for the Court will be whether the relevant derogation clauses of the Directive fall under the derogation clauses provided by the ECHR itself, concerning in particular public security and issues of economic well-being.[216] The following factors could prove useful for the assessment of the Court. First, in relation to Article 4 (6), there is in any case an obligation of the State concerned to admit the minor, even if the application of family reunification is rejected. However, in such a case it is not clear what will be the content of the rights granted to the minor. Second, inasmuch as Article 8 and, to a certain extent, Article 4 (6) of the Directive are concerned, it is likely that a balancing test between the public security and economic well-being interests of the State and the interest of individuals will need to be performed, since this provision is linked with the application of quota systems. Third, the provision of Article 4 (1) will be difficult to assess. The justification invoked by the Council in the preamble, i.e. better integration at a younger age,[217] does not figure among the exceptions mentioned in the ECHR. However, in view of the *Ahmut* and *Sen* case law the issue seems to be rather controversial even within the framework of the Strasbourg Court. Moreover, it is not at all clear what form the integration test will take and whether there will be any exceptions to the rule. The rights of the child might also prove a useful factor for the Court in this respect. Finally, the Court might find it difficult to use the non-discrimination principle since the entry and residence of third country nationals is clearly excluded from the scope of the non-discrimination Directive.

Furthermore, the relevant clauses are optional derogations and are vaguely drafted, so much will also depend on *whether* Member States will apply them and most importantly *how* they will apply them.[218] All the relevant clauses concern the specific request of a Member State and are accompanied by a stand-still clause. Therefore, it is likely that they will not have a wide-ranging impact but will just allow the States concerned to continue to apply their national legislation. In contrast to the case of Article 8, which is rather clear, much will depend on the concrete legal framework concerning the application of the other two contested provisions of the Directive. The issue stemming from the optional character is

216 According to the second paragraph of Article 8 ECHR: "There will be no interference by a public authority with the exercise of this right except such as is in accordance with the law and is necessary in a democratic society in the interests of national security, public safety or the economic well-being of the country, for the prevention of disorder and crime, for the protection of health or morals, or for the protection of the rights and freedoms of others".

217 Recital 12 of the preamble of the family reunification Directive.

218 The point regarding the importance of the interpretation of derogatory clauses in order to assess whether they violate human rights or not was raised by Richard Plender during the IX Convengo SIDI "Le migrazioni: una sfida per il diritto internazionale, comunitario e interno" held in Rome, 17 and 18 June 2004.

two-fold. First, can the Court annul a discretionary provision? The answer to this should be in the affirmative since the EU can not permit lower standards even as a matter of discretion.[219] Bearing in mind Article 6 TEC as well as the political but also legal obligations stemming from the very principles on which the EU is based and the existence of the EU Charter of fundamental rights, the EU should not shirk its responsibility. However, are the relevant provisions such clear-cut violations of Article 8? This second question brings us back to the issue regarding the difficulties of an assessment in the abstract.[220]

In September 2005 Advocate General Kokott has delivered her opinion on this case. While proposing the dismissal of the case as non-admissible due to the partial character of the action for annulment, Advocate General Kokott raises a series of important points. First, as to the argument of Germany regarding the possibility of adopting unilateral national measures which would supersede Community law, she rightly underscores that the provision of Article 63 second sub paragraph cannot limit the binding character of the measures taken under Articles 63 (3) and (4).[221] Second, with regard to whether the action for annulment concerns national or Community measures, she correctly observes that the provisions of Community law that allow the adoption of measures that are not compatible with fundamental rights are themselves incompatible with those rights.[222] Thirdly, she rightly underlines the fact that the partial annulment of the Directive would amend the essence of the Directive and would lead the Court in intervening to the competence of the Community legislator.[223] Finally, using as a guiding principle the possibility of taking into account exceptional circumstances or not, she concludes -in a rather subjective way and without any concrete references to the ECHR provisions or case law one might say- that Articles 4 (1) and 4 (6) are compatible with fundamental rights whereas Article 8 is not. In the light of the above and bearing in mind the importance of the case one looks forward to the judgement of the Court.

The communitarisation of migration policy and the adoption of legislative measures inevitably entails a concrete legal responsibility for the EU. On the

219 This view is also supported by Peers S., "Family Reunion and Community Law", *op.cit.*

220 In a recent case the Court does not seem to exclude the possibility of examining the compatibility of Directives with human rights. However, it states, at least in the case under examination where there was a need for a balance to be found between different rights that "... it is rather at the stage of the application at national level of the legislation implementing Directive 95/46 in individual cases that a balance must be found between the rights and interests involved". See Case C-101/01 *Lindqvist,* Judgement of 6 November 2003, paras 72 to 90 and in particular paras 84 and 85.

221 Opinion of Advocate General Kokott, paras 34 to 42.

222 *Idem.* Paras 43 to 45.

223 *Idem.* Paras 46 to 49.

one hand, a responsibility for the drafting of measures, which need not only to be compliant with human rights, but to further avoid creating loop-holes for violations, and on the other hand, as to the protection of individuals in terms of control over the implementation process and the establishment of substantive legal remedies. The EU also has a much more general political obligation to live up to the expectations both of its citizens and the international Community. In that respect the decision of the Heads of States to include the Charter of fundamental rights in the Draft Constitutional Treaty,[224] to create the necessary legal bases for the accession of the Union to the European Convention on Human Rights,[225] and last but not least, their decision to agree to build upon the existing European Monitoring Centre on Racism and Xenophobia and to extend its mandate to become a Human Rights Agency in that effect are worthy of praise.[226]

Concluding remarks

Within the last two decades and in particular in the post-Amsterdam era, the EU has raised a series of expectations with regard to the establishment of an area of freedom and security for both its citizens and for third country nationals. However, forging a migration policy matching the expectations of the European but also of the international community, in particular in light of the growing character of these expectations in the post-Amsterdam era, is not an easy task. Policy-making with regard to migration at the EU level is facing a series of institutional and structural shortcomings, since there does not seem to exist neither a commonly accepted clear-cut objective to be reached, nor a general and comprehensive EU competence. There are also a series of more political and practical factors impeding the setting of such an objective and the formation of a coherent and effective policy at EU level.

---

224 See Part II of the Draft Constitutional Treaty, OJ C 310, 16.12.2004.

225 See Article I-9 of the Draft Constitutional Treaty as well as Protocol No 32 relating to Article I-9 (2) of the Constitution on the Accession of the Union to the European Convention on the Protection of Human Rights and Fundamental Freedoms, OJ C 310, 16.12.2004.

226 See Communication of the Commission on the assessment of the Tampere programme, *op.cit.*, at p. 8. Indeed, the Commission has already presented the relevant proposal. See Proposal for a Council Regulation establishing a European Union Agency for Fundamental Rights and Proposal for a Council Decision empowering the European Union Agency for Fundamental Rights to pursue its activities in areas referred to in Title VI of the Treaty on European Union, COM (2005) 280 final, 30.6.2005. However, in parallel one needs to recall the criticism with regard to the Hague Programme, in particular that excessive attention has been given to security as opposed to fundamental rights. See House of Lords, *Evidence by Commissioner Franco Frattini, Commissioner for Justice, Freedom and Security on Justice and Home Affairs Matters, op.cit.*

As it has been argued in detail, migration policy at the EU level still cannot be seen, at least under the current policy and political framework, as a policy *per se*, at least in the classic meaning of this term. The Amsterdam Treaty, on the one hand, codifies the pre-existing dual connotation of migration policy at EU level, and on the other hand, the completion of the internal market and citizens' concerns seem to preserve their predominant position within the policy-making process. The operational character of some aspects of migration policy as well as the difficulties in establishing a common policy with regard to other aspects render any efforts towards harmonisation for the moment not only contestable but also unproductive. And most importantly, Member States do not seem to be convinced of the need and the added value of transferring certain aspects of migration policy to the EU level. To a certain extent these are also some of the reasons for which there is a strong disequilibrium between the approach to illegal and legal migration. We have seen that although a consensus as to the former does seem to exist, a consensus in relation to the latter does not.

However, post-Amsterdam developments, while mainly codifying the pre-Amsterdam *acquis*, constitute nonetheless, first, a qualitative step – since the legislative measures are legally binding – and second, set the bases for an in-depth discussion on, and eventually the formation of, a common policy.

An overview of the policy-making process and of the legislative measures that have been adopted, lead to series of serious concerns, in particular with regard to transparency, accountability and human rights. The reasons that have led to and reinforced these shortcomings are to a certain degree understandable but it is to be hoped that the EU will manage to find the right balance between the interests of States and the interests of individuals.

General Conclusions: EU Migration Law and Policy in a Nutshell

This book has attempted to coherently and comprehensively present the historical evolution, the institutional characteristics and major legislative steps that have been taken with regard to the formation of migration law and policy at EU level. Some insights as to the EU decision-making process and the role of, and interactions among, the different actors have been teased out as a means to provide a sounder evaluation of both the policy-making choices and the content of the new policy. The concluding chapter has presented and analysed the challenges faced and difficulties encountered during this process while also raising a series of concerns with regard to the content and quality of the emerging EU migration law. With this in mind, and in addition to the conclusions already drawn at the end of each chapter as well as those discussed in detail in the concluding chapter, these general conclusions will seek to capture in a concise manner certain focal points of this on-going process towards the formation of a migration law and policy at EU level.

1. Forging an EU Migration Policy: A Long and Evolving Process

The overview of the intergovernmental and EU *acquis* up to Amsterdam showed clearly that despite the fact that the migration debate obviously lacked coherence and structure there were definitely segments of migration policy since the very early days of European integration. On various occasions both Member States and the Community institutions have underscored the need and have taken a series of actions at the European level with regard to certain migration issues. In fact, the evident similarities between the *ante* and *post* Amsterdam era inasmuch as the general policy themes are concerned and between the vast majority of the specific legislative developments that have taken place under the respective policy eras prove to a large extent that the Union had already started exploring the main themes of the migration policy agenda well before Amsterdam and Tampere brought the issues to the forefront of the EU agenda. It has been argued that the legislative developments in the post-Amsterdam era to a certain degree constituted a mere crystallisation of the Schengen and Maastricht *acquis*.

Nonetheless, forging an EU agenda on migration related issues has encountered, and to some extent is still facing, certain vital structural obstacles that render EU integration in this field a difficult process. Firstly, it is a policy that touches upon sensitive chords of national sovereignty and is deeply politicised. In principle Member States are reluctant to transfer competence and/or act at the European level unless there is a clear need to do so and added value can be provided. This is indeed the case with regard to certain facets of migration, in particular the security dimension. However, not all Member States appear convinced that the communitarisation of certain other issues, in particular those regarding admission for labour purposes, is either needed or desired. Secondly, for several decades the vast majority of Member States have been applying a 'zero immigration policy'. The rest of the Member States were not affected, and in the case of the new Member States might still not be affected, by the immigration challenge. Moreover, there have been, and still are, major divergences among Member States inasmuch as their actual situation, needs and policy options are concerned. Therefore, the forming of a common agenda at the EU level is neither a self-evident proposition nor an easy process. Thirdly, migration policy has a strong horizontal character in the sense that it is being affected and affects a series of other policy areas. This strong spill over effect has a both positive and negative impact. On the positive side, the EU has decided to examine a series of migration related issues in order to accomplish other policy objectives –i.e. the free movement of EU citizens, the internal market- or to face common challenges, i.e. public concerns linked in particular with security. Whilst on the negative side, the development of a comprehensive migration policy is obstructed by the fact that there is no Community competence or concerted action in interlinked areas, such as external relations, employment and social policy. The impact of all the above factors have inevitably affected, and to a certain degree explain, the way that the EU has dealt with the migration challenge as well as the way that the institutional and legislative framework have been shaped until now.

Inasmuch as the institutional framework is concerned, EU migration policy has been characterised by an intense competence debate due primarily to the existence of a strong preference by the Member States for migration issues to be addressed via intergovernmental co-operation. The institutional choices have traditionally hovered between intergovernmentalism and the Community method. The *sui generis* institutional models chosen in both the Maastricht and Amsterdam Treaty are examples of these policy options. And consequently the decision-making process was burdened by a series of legal problems with the fragmented legal framework precluding the adoption and enforcement of a comprehensive approach.

The Amsterdam Treaty clearly constituted a major turning point, indeed a Rubicon line of sorts. While preserving a certain amount of safety nets and respecting Member States' claim for a pragmatic approach, it marks a major step towards full communitarisation and further attempts to shape the bases for the formation of a comprehensive migration policy at the European level. However, one should not lose sight of two realities. First, this is just a communitarisation *à la carte*, inevitably creating a series of problems, and second, the competence debate is far from over and the limits of EU policy-making remain to some extent hazy.

As far as the legislative framework is concerned, EU policy and action has for several decades been based on an *ad hoc* approach that lacks an overall comprehensive and balanced framework. The reasons are numerous. First of all, while Member States have been flirting with certain issues, such as addressing together illegal migration or establishing burden-sharing mechanisms, they were reluctant to lose control over the entire process and assume possible risks or an extra financial burden. Further, not all Member States were interested, and most importantly did not share, a common view on what the Union's approach should be. To some extent there was a certain degree of convergence over security related issues. However, there were pronounced divergences in relation to legal migration policy. It is as such no surprise that progress in security aspects of migration was to proceed much faster than in legal migration, nor that the approach adopted in the domain of legal migration was to be rather limited. Finally, the absence of integration in interlinked areas, such as external relations, employment and social policy, has added further hurdles to the formation of a comprehensive migration agenda.

2. A Two Track Approach

On the basis of the analysis of the historical evolution of migration policy, it has been demonstrated that migration policy at the EU level was largely a response to concrete national needs and that this policy centred around EU citizens and the internal market objective. The abolition of the internal border controls for EU citizens as well as the need to respond to major public concerns for security have been, and arguably still remain, the driving force for an EU migration policy. Migration policy, it has been argued herein, was a policy traditionally viewed through the lenses of other EU policy objectives and not as a policy in its own right.

Subsequently, two different sets of policy responses have been progressively shaped with regard to migration related issues, which this work has defined as 'migration *stricto sensu*' and 'migration in the classic sense'. The difference in the EU's approach to these two tracks is considerable. The framework and final objective of migration *stricto sensu* is clearly defined and *a priori* commonly accepted, its added value also being well established. However, and unfortunately, this is not yet the case for migration in the classic sense. Indeed, the development of the two tracks is heavily unbalanced. The objectives of the former are *grosso modo* achieved and the legislative framework almost completely harmonised but EU policy-making with regard to the latter remains at a rather primitive stage. The difficulties in forging a common agenda with regard to central aspects of migration policy render any efforts and progress towards harmonisation for the time being not only slow but also very contested.

3. The Policy *Status Quo* and a Debate for the Future

The much contested character of EU competence on migration policy and the profound divergences among Member States have perhaps not surprisingly led to the formation of a deeply fragmented policy and institutional framework. Both the existence of the opt-out Protocols and the special institutional characteristics of Title IV as well as the lack of a clear-cut policy objective agreed by all Member States and a respective convergence of views on central issues have hitherto prevented the formation of a comprehensive, balanced and efficient policy.

Firstly, throughout the analysis it has been made clear that for the time being it is not accurate to talk about *common* policies in this area, at least as the term is traditionally understood. The reason is two-fold. On the one hand, not all the Member States are participating, whereas on the other, even when the abstaining Member States decide to participate, this is on a 'pick and choose' basis. This has already been proved by the British and Irish opting-in patterns and will eventually also happen with Denmark given the eventual application of an analogous opting-in system. Furthermore, it is in any case debatable whether one can talk about a pure *Community* policy, given that one Member State, namely Denmark, is, at least for the moment, bound exclusively on an international law basis and three outsiders, namely Norway, Iceland and Switzerland, are intensely involved.

Secondly, the actual *acquis* is often far from clear and its legal value far from certain. As a result of the complex legal framework created by the opt-out Protocols it is not clear which Member States or third States are bound by which measure. Moreover, the EU is still in the process of absorbing the legal problems in terms of legal clarity, certainty and transparency that were caused following the incorporation of the Schengen *acquis* into the EU framework. Despite the key steps already taken, the major task of fully communitarising Schengen is still to be fully accomplished. Additionally, the overview of the first legislative measures adopted in the post-Amsterdam era has revealed a series of ambiguities that might lead to interpretative problems and eventually to litigation. The piecemeal approach with regard to policy-making, the series of optional derogations included into the legislative measures and the cross-references among different texts complicate matters further and make it very difficult for the individuals concerned to have a clear picture of the actual EU regulatory framework.

Thirdly, there are certain problems that to an extent can be seen as consequences of the long-standing, albeit considerably differentiated, patterns of the intergovernmental era and the infancy diseases of the communitarisation process. For instance, an analysis of the institutional framework and the negotiation process makes it clear that the right balance between Member States freedom of action and Community competence still need to be found. A well-functioning *modus vivendi* among the various policy actors is also absent. In addition, an overview of the policy-making process and the legislative measures that have been adopted trigger a host of concerns particularly with regard to the balanced and comprehensive character of the new policy as well as in terms of transparency, accountability and the protection of human rights.

The Amsterdam Treaty and the subsequent Tampere Conclusions have undoubtedly signalled a new era of migration policy. And crucially the EU has raised a series of expectations with regard to the establishment of an area of freedom and security for both its citizens and for third country nationals. Therefore, in parallel to the difficult process of solving what are primarily legal problems stemming from the past, the EU has launched an intensive debate of a more political character concerning the formation of a comprehensive common migration policy. The Commission has prepared a series of Communications and Feasibility Studies and the Council has prepared a significant number of Action Plans for future action. Member States have intensified, at least at the operational level, their co-operation and their experts have been meeting frequently to exchange information and best practices. Issues such as external relations, return, integration policy and the links between migration and other inter-related policies, i.e. social, employment and development policies, have indeed already been examined.

Following the lapse of the transitory period provided in the Amsterdam Treaty, a large consultation process with a view to establishing the new political multi-annual programme has been launched by the Dutch Presidency and the Commission, leading to the adoption of the so-called Hague Programme. Even if the Hague Programme could be considered to a large extent as a rather formal exercise – since in most areas the EU is entering in to the consolidation phase and such an operation should further take into consideration the amendments brought about by the Draft Constitutional Treaty – one could not but welcome the launching of a wide-ranging debate on migration policy. In like vein, one cannot but welcome the passage to the co-decision procedure for most areas of Title IV, the launching of a wide consultation process regarding economic migration on the basis of the Commission's recent Policy Plan on Legal Migration as well as the substantive increase of the financial resources in the JHA field within the framework of the 2007-2013 financial perspectives of the EU.

4. The Challenges and Perspectives for the Future

Three major challenges for the EU with regard to migration policy can be identified.

– *Monitoring of the Implementation Process and Consolidation of the EC Acquis*

Having proceeded to a preliminary approximation of national legislation the EU is now entering the phase of monitoring and consolidating the *acquis*. The difficulties that are likely to be encountered and the challenges to be faced are two-fold. Firstly, the loose character of most of the legislative measures adopted and the great number of derogations allowed mean that it is necessary for the EU to follow closely the implementation process at national level in order to ensure a uniform application of the *acquis*. The role of both the Commission and the Court is expected to prove vital. Secondly, it becomes imperative to proceed to an assessment of this first stage of policy-making with a view to preparing and proposing the necessary improvements for the next stage of integration. Two simultaneous operations need to take place. One being the patent need for a recasting of part of the *acquis* as the piecemeal approach hitherto employed has given the *acquis* a fragmented character – a process already initiated with regard to border issues and return policy. The other being the need for a process of peer review with a view to achieving further harmonisation.

– *Enlargement*

The second major challenge is linked with the recently accomplished enlargement. This could be seen under three perspectives. Firstly, there is the pressing need for the new Member States to associate themselves fully to the migration *stricto sensu* track. Despite the fact that they have all accepted in full the Schengen *acquis*, the abolition of the border controls at internal borders and their full association is expected to be a long and trying process. Secondly, the new States will have to implement the recently adopted legislative measures with regard to migration. While for the fifteen Member States the new Directives might not prove all that innovative, since most of the old Member States have managed to safeguard the respect of their national legislation, this is not the case for the new Member States who have not participated in the negotiations and might also not have a fully-fledged immigration legislation, since most of them are emigration countries. Third, the future policy agenda of, and the measures taken by, the EU will have to be based and accommodate also the needs and views of all the twenty-five Member States, a task that is, to say the least, expected to prove difficult.

– ***Forging a Comprehensive, Balanced and Transparent EU Migration Policy***

In the course of the last decade a considerable set of legislative measures have been adopted, political issues have been debated and operational experience has been gained. The EU has had the possibility to define and start implementing some broad policy guidelines and most importantly to identify the problems linked with the formation of a common policy at the EU level. Furthermore, while being unable to solve major political Gordian knots, such as the issue of the Protocols, the new Draft Constitutional Treaty provides for a new institutional and legal framework alleviating the policy-making process from a number of the problems that have dogged it in the past. Moreover, the debate for the future has already been launched and some preliminary research has been conducted. Additionally, the Hague Programme has reaffirmed the political impetus of the EU concerning the formation of a common migration policy.

Therefore, the EU is clearly now on the verge of entering into a phase of peer review and future planning. On the one hand, the EU needs to reflect upon the well-known existing problems both of an institutional and policy-related nature and to find the appropriate responses at the EU level. Additionally, a well functioning *modus vivendi* among the various policy actors has to be found, in particular following the passage to the co-decision procedure for most of the areas of Title IV. And, on the other hand, it needs to proceed to a sincere exchange of views as to both the content of the policy that should and could be effectively implemented at EU level and the form that this should take. It is to be hoped that the next integration stage of migration law and policy at European level will be more balanced, comprehensive and transparent, that the EU will manage to find the appropriate and most effective integration method for each area, and crucially that it will live up to the expectations that it has already created for its citizens and the international Community.

General Bibliography

A. Academic and Policy Literature

Adam R., "La cooperazione in materiae di justizia e affairi interni tra communitarizzazione e metodo intergovernativo", *Il Dirittto dell'Unione Europea,* Vol. 2-3, 1998, p. 481-509.

Albors-Llorens A., "Changes in the jurisdiction of the European Court of Justice under the Treaty of Amsterdam", *CMLRev,* Vol. 35, 1998, p. 1273-1294.

Alexander W., "Free movement of non-EC nationals – A review of the case-law of the Court of Justice", in Schermers et al. (eds.), *Free Movement of Persons in Europe, Legal Problems and Experiences*, T.M.C. Asser Institute, The Hague, 1993, p. 485-496.

Andersen S., "Norway: Insider AND Outsider", Arena Working Paper, No 4, February 2000.

Anderson M., "Border Regimes and Security in an Enlarged European Community: Implications of the entry into force of the Amsterdam Treaty", EUI Working Papers, RSC No 2000/8.

Apap J., De Bruycker P. and Schmitter C., "Regularisation of Illegal Aliens in the European Union. Summary Report of a Comparative Study", *EJML*, Vol. 2, 2000, p. 263-308.

Apap J., "Shaping Europe's Migration Policy – New regimes for Employment of Third-Country Nationals: A Comparison of Strategies in Germany, Sweden, the Netherlands and the UK", *EJML*, Vol. 4, Issue 3, 2002, p. 309-328.

Arnull A. and Jacobs F.G., "Applying the common rules on the free movement of persons – The role of the national judiciary in the light of the jurisprudence of the European Court of Justice", in Schermers et al. (eds.), *Free Movement of Persons in Europe, Legal Problems and Experiences*, T.M.C. Asser Institute, The Hague, 1993, p. 272-285.

Aubin E., "Le juge administratif français face à l'application de la Convention de Schengen dans ses positions sur le droit d'asile. Bilan juridictionnel de l'application en France des Accords de Schengen", *Revue du Droit Public et de la Science Politique en France et à l'étranger*, No 3, 2000, p. 829-862.

Ayral M., "La suppression des contrôles aux frontières intra-communautaires", *RMUE*, Issue 1, 1993, p. 59-90.

Baldwin-Edwards M., "The Emerging European Immigration Regime : Some Reflections on Implications for Southern Europe", *Journal of Common Market Studies,* Vol. 35, No 4, December 1997, p. 497-519.

Balzacq T. and Carrera S., *Migration, Borders and Asylum Trends and Vulnerabilities in EU Policy,* Centre for European Policy Studies, Brussels, 2005.

Barbe E., *Justice et affaires intérieures dans l'Union européenne – Un espace de liberté, de sécurité et de justice,* La Documentation française, Paris, 2002.

Barents R., "Some observations on the Treaty of Nice", *Maastricht Journal of European and Comparative Law,* Vol. 8, No 2, 2001, p. 121-132.

Batt J., "Managing the EU's New External Border", in Arnull A. and Wincott D. (eds.), *Accountability and Legitimacy in the European Union*, Oxford University Press, Oxford, 2002, p. 453-467.

Beach D., *Between Law and Politics – The relationship between the European Court of Justice and EU Member States,* DJØF Publishing, Copenhagen, 2001.

Bieber R., Lyon A.-C., Monar J. (eds.), *Justice et Affaires Intérieures – L'Union européenne et la Suisse,* Staempfli Editions SA, Berne, 1997.

Bigo D., "Migration and Security", in Guiraudon V. and Joppke C. (eds.), *Controlling a New Migration World,* Routledge, London, 2001, p. 121-149.

Boeles P., "Directive on Family Reunification: Are the Dilemmas Resolved?", *EJML*, Vol. 3, Issue 1, 2001, p. 61-71.

Boeles P., "Introduction: Freedom, Security and Justice for All", in Guild E. and Harlow C. (eds.), *Implementing Amsterdam: immigration and asylum rights in EC law*, Hart Publishing, Oxford, 2001, p. 1-12.

Boeles P. et al, *Border control and movement of persons – Towards effective legal remedies for individuals in Europe,* Standing Committee of Experts in International Immigration, Refugee and Criminal Law, Utrecht, 2003.

Bouteillet-Paquet D., "Passing the Buck : A Critical Analysis of the Readmission Policy Implemented by the European Union and Its Member States", *EJML*, Vol. 5 2003, p. 359-377.

Bracke N., "Norway and Iceland: an Adventure in the Field of Justice and Home Affairs" in De Kerchove G. and Weyembergh A. (eds.), *Sécurité et justice: enjeu de la politique extérieure de l'Union européenne*, Institut d'Etudes Européennes, Editions de l'Université de Bruxelles, Bruxelles, 2003, p. 225-230.

Bribosia E. et Weyembergh A., "L'impact de la lutte contre le terrorisme sur les politiques d'asile et d'immigration de l' Union européenne", in Vandersanden G. and de

Walsch A. (eds.), *Mélanges en hommage à Jean-Victor Louis (Vol. I)*, Editions de l'Université de Bruxelles, Bruxelles, 2003, p. 63-82.

Brinkmann G., "The Immigration and Asylum Agenda", *ELJ*, Vol. 10, Issue 2, March 2004, p. 182-199.

Brinkmann G., "Family Reunion, Third Country Nationals and the Community's New Powers", in Guild E. and Harlow C. (eds.), *Implementing Amsterdam: immigration and asylum rights in EC law*, Hart Publishing, Oxford, 2001, p. 241-266.

Brouwer E., "Immigration, Asylum and Terrorism: A Changing Dynamic – Legal and Practical Developments in the EU in Response to the Terrorists Attacks of 11.09", *EJML*, Vol. 4, Issue 4, 2002, p. 399-424.

Cahn C., "Racial Preference, Racial Exclusion : Administrative Efforts to Enforce the Separation of Roma and Non-Roma in Europe through Migration Controls", *EJML*, Vol. 5, 2004, p. 479-490.

Carozza P., "The Member States", in Peers S. and Ward A. (eds.), *The European Union Charter of Fundamental Rights*, Hart Publishing, Oxford, 2004, p. 35-58.

Castillo de la Torre F., "La libre circulation des services et les ressortissants des pays tiers: quelques réflexions au sujet de l'arrêt Vander Elst", *RMUE*, Vol. 2, 1995, p. 405-433.

Cholewinski R., *Borders and Discrimination in the European Union,* ILPA, London, 2001.

Cholewinski R., "The EU acquis on Irregular Migration : Reinforcing Security at the expense of Rights", *EJML*, Vol. 2, 2000, p. 361-405.

Cini M., *European Union Politics,* Oxford University Press, Oxford, 2003.

Colvin M., "The Schengen Information System: A Human Rights Audit", *E.H.R.L.R.*, Issue 3, 2001, p. 271-279.

Craig P. and De Búrca G., *EU Law Text, Cases & Materials,* Third edition, Oxford University Press, Oxford, 2003.

Crombez C. and Hix S., *Unaccountable Brussels Bureaucrats? Implications of the EU Constitutional Reforms for the Accountability of the Commission,* 12 June 2003 http://personal.lse.ac.uk/HIX/WorkingPapers.HTM.

Cruz A., " Visa Policy under the First Pillar : A meaningless Compromise ", in Den Boer M. (ed.), *Schengen, Judicial Cooperation and Policy Coordination,* EIPA, Maastricht, 1997, p. 213-239.

Cullen D., "Variable Geometry and Overlapping Circles: in Search of a Suitable Model for Justice and Home Affairs", in Bieber R. and Monar J. (eds.), *Justice and Home Affairs in the European Union The Development of the Third Pillar*, European Interuniversity Press, Brussels, 1995, p. 65-91.

Curtin D., "The Developing Right of Citizen Access to Information on Asylum and Immigration Decision-Making", in Guild E. and Harlow C. (eds.), *Implementing*

Amsterdam: immigration and asylum rights in EC law, Hart Publishing, Oxford, 2001, p. 35-63.

Curtin D., "The Schengen Protocol: Attractive model or poisoned chalice?", in C.D. Ehlermann C.D. (ed.), *Multi-Speed Europe-the Legal Framework of Variable Geometry in the European Union,* Bundesazeiger, Bonn, 1999, p. 73-84.

Curtin D., "Democracy, Transparency and Political Participation: Some Progress Post-Amsterdam", in Deckmyn V. and Thomson I. (eds.), *Openness and Transparency in the European Union*, EIPA, Maastricht, 1998, p. 107-120.

Curtin D. and Meijers H., "The principle of open government in Schengen and the European Union: democratic retrogression?, *CMLRev,* Vol. 32, 1995, p. 391-442.

Dashwood A., "The constitution of the European Union after Nice : law-making procedures", *ELRev,* Vol. 25, No 3, 2001, p.215-238.

D'Oliveira J., " Expanding External and Shrinking Internal Borders : Europe's Defence Mechanisms in the Areas of Free Movement, Immigration and Asylum ", in Twomey P. M. (ed.), *Legal issues of the Maastricht Treaty* , Wiley, Chichester, 1994, p. 261-278.

De Bruycker (ed.), *Regularisations of illegal immigrants in the European Union,* Bruylant, Bruxelles, 2000.

De Búrca G., "The Constitutional Challenge of New Governance in the EU", *ELRev*, Vol. 28, No 6, December 2003, p. 814-839

De Ceuster J., "De Europese Unie En De Verblyfsreglemententering", in De Feyter K. (ed.), *Migratie- En Migrantenrecht: Recente Ontwikkelingen,* Die Keure, Brugge, 1995, p. 147-237.

De Kerchove G., "Un espace de liberté, de sécurité et de justice aux dimensions incertaines: Quelques réflexions sur le recours aux coopérations renforcées en matière de justice et d'affaires intérieures", in Den Boer M., Guggenbuhl A. and Van Hoonacker S. (eds.), *Coping with Flexibility and Legitimacy after Amsterdam,* EIPA, Maastricht, 1998, p. 197-204.

De Lobkowicz W., "La sécurité intérieure de l'Union européenne élargie" in De Kerchove G. and Weyembergh A. (eds.) *Sécurité et justice: enjeu de la politique extérieure de l'Union européenne*, Institut d'Etudes Européennes, Editions de l'Université de Bruxelles, Bruxelles, 2003, p. 31-65.

De Lobkowicz W., *L'Europe et la sécurité intérieure Une élaboration par étapes,* La documentation Française, Paris, 2002.

De Lobkowicz W., "La perspective de l'élargissement dans le domaine de la Justice et des Affaires intérieures", in Marinho C. (ed.), *Asylum, Immigration and Schengen Post-Amsterdam – A First Assessment,* EIPA, Maastricht, 2001, p. 107-118.

De Lobkowicz W., "Intergovernmental cooperation in the field of migration – From the Single European Act to Maastricht", in Monar J. and Morgan R. (eds.), *The Third*

Pillar of the European Union – Co-operation in the fields of Justice and Home Affairs, European Interuniversity Press, Brussels, 1994, p. 99-122.

De Noël X., "Les accords de réadmission du Benelux à Schengen et au-delà", *RTDE*, Vol. 29, No 4, oct-déc 1993, p. 635-653.

De Schutter O., "La réunification de l'Europe et les droits de l'homme" in De Kerchove G. and Weyembergh A. (eds.), *Sécurité et justice: enjeu de la politique extérieure de l'Union européenne*, Institut d'Etudes Européennes, Editions de l'Université de Bruxelles, Bruxelles, 2003, p. 31-65.

De Schoutheete P., "Forces et faiblesses du Conseil européen" in Vandersanden G. and de Walsch A. (eds.), *Mélanges en hommage à Jean-Victor Louis (Vol. I)*, Editions de l'Université de Bruxelles, 2003, p. 109-118.

De Witte B. and Toggenburg G., "Human Rights and Membership of the European Union", in Peers S. and Ward A. (eds.), *The European Union Charter of Fundamental Rights*, Hart Publishing, Oxford, 2004, p. 59-82.

De Witte B., "Chameleonic Member States: Differentiation by means of Partial and Parallel International Agreements", in De Witte B., Hanf D. and Vos E. (eds.), *The Many Faces of Differentiation in EU Law*, Intersentia, Antwerpen, 2001, p. 231-267.

De Witte B., "The Status of the Charter: Vital Question or Non-Issue?", *Maastricht Journal of European and Comparative Law,* Vol. 8, No 1, 2001, p. 49-67.

De Witte B., "Old-fashioned Flexibility: International Agreements between Member States of the European Union", in De Búrca G. and Scott J. (eds.), *Constitutional Change in the EU: from Uniformity too flexibility?*, Hart Publishing, Oxford, 2000, p. 31-58.

De Zwaan J.W., "Opting in and opting out of rules concerning the free movement of persons: problems and practical arrangements", *Cambridge Yearbook of European Legal Studies*, Vol. 1, 1998, p. 107-124.

De Zwaan J.W., "Schengen and its Incorporation into the New Treaty: The Negotiating Process", in Den Boer M. (ed.), *Schengen's Final Days? The Incorporation of Schengen into the New TEU, External Borders and Information Systems*, EIPA, Maastricht, 1998, p. 13-24.

De Zwaan J. W., "Institutional problems and Free Movement of Persons – The legal and political framework for cooperation", in Schermers et al. (eds.), *Free Movement of Persons in Europe, Legal Problems and Experiences*, T.M.C. Asser Institute, The Hague, 1993, p. 335-351.

Dehousse F. and Garcia Martinez J., "The Area of Freedom, Security and Justice in the European Convention", in Dehousse F. and Coussens W. (eds.), *The Convention's Draft Constitutional Treaty: Old Wine in New Bottle?,* Studia Diplomatica, Vol. LVI: 2003, No 1-2, p. 135-151.

Dehousse F. et Van Den Hende L., "Plaidoyer pour la réforme du troisième pillier", *RMC*, No 103, décembre 1996, p. 714-718.

Dell'Olio F., "Immigration after Nice : From 'Zero Immigration' to Market Necessity", in Arnull A. and Wincott D. (eds.), *Accountability and Legitimacy in the European Union*, Oxford University Press, Oxford, 2002, p. 469-483.

Den Boer M., " Steamy Windows : Transparency and Openness in Justice and Home Affairs ", in Deckmyn V. and Thomson I. (eds.), *Openness and Transparency in the European Union*, EIPA, Maastricht, 1998, p. 91-105.

Den Boer M., *Taming the Third Pillar : Improving the Management of Justice and Home Affairs Cooperation in the EU*, EIPA, Maastricht, 1998.

Den Boer M. and Corrado L., "For the Record or Off the Record: Comments About the Incorporation of Schengen into the EU", *EJML*, 2000, p. 397-418

Den Boer M. and Wallace W., "Justice and Home Affairs – Integration through Incrementalism?", in Wallace H. and Wallace W. (eds.), *Policy-Making in the European Union*, Oxford University Press, Oxford, 2000, p. 493-519.

D'Oliveira J., " Expanding External and Shrinking Internal Borders : Europe's Defence Mechanisms in the Areas of Free Movement, Immigration and Asylum ", in Twomey P. M. (ed.), *Legal issues of the Maastricht Treaty*, Wiley, Chichester, 1994, p. 261-278.

Dony M., "La majorité qualifiée au Conseil du traité de Rome à la Convention sur l'avenir de l'Union", in Vandersanden G. and de Walsch A. (eds.), *Mélanges en hommage à Jean-Victor Louis (Vol. I)*, Editions de l'Université de Bruxelles, Bruxelles, 2003, p. 139-164.

Dyrberg P., "Accountability and Legitimacy: What is the Contribution of Transparency?", in Arnull A. and Wincott D. (eds.), *Accountability and Legitimacy in the European Union*, Oxford University Press, Oxford, 2002, p. 81-96.

Ecotec-Research and Consulting, Admission of Third Country Nationals for Paid Employment or Self-Employed Activity, Study carried out on behalf of the European Commission, DG JHA, Ecotec, Brussels, 2000.

Ehlermann C.D., "Différentiation, flexibilité, coopération renforcée: les nouvelles dispositions du traité d'Amsterdam", *RMUE*, Issue 3, 1997, p. 53-90.

Ehlermann C.D., "Différentiation accrue ou uniformité renforcée", *RMUE*, Issue 3, 1995, p. 191-208.

El Kaim G., "Quelques remarques du point de vue du négotiateur", paper presented at the 3rd Congress of the Academic Network of Legal Studies on Immigration and Asylum in Europe "European immigration and Asylum policy", held in Paris, 10 and 11 June 2004.

Ellis E., "The Principle of Non-Discrimination in the Post-Nice Era", in Arnull A. and Wincott D. (eds.), *Accountability and Legitimacy in the European Union*, Oxford University Press, Oxford, 2002, p. 291-305.

Elsen C., "Le Conseil européen de Thessalonique – Un nouveau pas vers une politique commune en matière d'asile d'immigration et de contrôle aux frontières", *RMC*, Issue 471, 2004, p. 516-518.

Elsen C., "Incorporation juridique et institutionnelle de Schengen dans l'UE" in Den Boer M. (ed.), *Schengen still going strong: Evaluation and Update*, EIPA, Maastricht, 2000, p. 11-20.

Elsen C., "L'esprit et les ambitions de Tampere : une ère nouvelle pour la coopération dans le domaine de la Justice et des Affaires Intérieures ?", *RMC*, Issue 433, 1999, p. 659-663.

Elsen C., " Schengen et la coopération dans les domaines de la justice et des affaires intérieures. Besoins actuels et options futures ", in Den Boer M. (ed.), *The implementation of Schengen : First the Widening, Now the Deepening*, EIPA, Maastricht, 1997, p. 3-9.

Elsen C., "Les mécanismes institutionnels: Trevi, Schengen, Dublin, Maastricht", in Pauly A. (ed.), *Schengen en panne*, EIPA, Maastricht, 1994, p. 43-53.

Entzinger H. and Biezeveld R., *Benchmarking in Immigrant Integration*, European Research Centre on Migration and Ethnic Relations (ERCOMER), Erasmus University, Rotterdam, August 2003.

Fennelly N., "The Area of "Freedom, Security and Justice" and the European Court of Justice-A Personal View", *International and Comparative Law Quarterly*, Vol. 49, 2000, p. 1-14.

Fennelly N., "Preserving the Legal Coherence within the New Treaty", in Den Boer M., Guggenbuhl A. and Van Hoonacker S. (eds.), *Coping with Flexibility and Legitimacy after Amsterdam*, EIPA, Maastricht, 1998, p. 69-84.

Fennelly N., "Where power now lies – Institutional reform", *Irish Journal of European Law*, 1998, Issue 7, No 1, p. 10-20.

Fernhout R., "Justice and Home Affairs: Immigration and Asylum Policy: From JHA co-operation to communautarisation", in Winter J., Curtin D., Kellerman A. and de Witte B. (eds.), *Reforming the Treaty on European Union – The Legal Debate*, T.M.C. Asser Instituut, Kluwer Law International, The Hague, 1996, p. 377-399.

Ferraiolo S., "Immigrazione, asilo, accoglienza: gli effeti pratici del "vento di Tampere" Direttive, regolamenti e applicazione nei diritti nazionali", *Diritto & Giustizia*, No 20, 2004, p. 54-80.

Filliez F., "Le rapprochement de la Suisse à l'Espace pénal européen à l'exemple des négociations en cours avec l'Union européenne", in De Kerchove G. and Weyembergh A. (eds.), *Sécurité et justice: enjeu de la politique extérieure de l'Union européenne*, Institut d'Etudes Européennes, Editions de l'Université de Bruxelles, Bruxelles, 2003, p. 231-246.

Fletcher M., "EU Governance techniques in the Creation of a Common European Policy on Immigration and Asylum", *European Public Law*, Vol. 9, Issue 4, 2003, p. 533-562.

Franck C., "Le déficit démocratique: une notion en débat", in Vandersanden G. and de Walsch A. (eds.), *Mélanges en hommage à Jean-Victor Louis (Vol. I)*, Editions de l'Université de Bruxelles, Bruxelles, 2003, p. 175-188.

Frangakis N., "Human Rights and European Integration – From the European Convention on Human Rights to the Charter of Fundamental Rights of the European Union", in Vandersanden G. and de Walsch A. (eds.), *Mélanges en hommage à Jean-Victor Louis (Vol. I)*, Editions de l'Université de Bruxelles, Bruxelles, 2003, p. 189-201.

Gaja G., "How flexible is flexibility under the Amsterdam Treaty?", *CMLRev,* Vol. 35, 1998, p. 855-870.

Geddes A., *The Politics of Migration and Immigration in Europe*, SAGE Publications, London, 2003.

Geddes A., *Immigration and European Integration – Towards fortress Europe?,* Manchester University Press, Manchester, 2000.

Gialdino C., "Schengen et le troisième pilier: Le contrôle juridictionnel organise par le traité d'Amsterdam", *RMUE,* Vol. 2, 1998, p. 89-124.

Girend P., "L'article 68 CE: un renvoi préjudiciel d'interpétation et d'application incertaines", *RTDE*, Vol. 4-6, 1999, p. 239-260.

Gortazar C., "Abolishing Border Controls : Individual Rights and Common Control of EU External Borders", in Guild E. and Harlow C. (eds.), *Implementing Amsterdam: immigration and asylum rights in EC law*, Hart Publishing, Oxford, 2001, p. 121-140.

Groenendijk C.A., "Three questions about free movement of persons and democracy in Europe", in Schermers et al. (eds.), *Free Movement of Persons in Europe, Legal Problems and Experiences*, T.M.C. Asser Institute, The Hague, 1993, p. 391-402.

Groenendijk K., "Reinstatement of Controls at the Internal Borders of Europe : Why and Against Whom", *ELJ*, Vol. 10, Issue 2, March 2004, p. 150-170.

Groenendijk K., "Long Term Immigrants and the Council of Europe", in Guild E. and Minderhout P. (eds.), *Security of Residence and Expulsion – Protection of Aliens in Europe,* Kluwer, The Hague, 2001, p. 7-22.

Groenendijk K., "Security and residence and Access to Free Movement of Settled Third Country Nationals under Community Law", in Guild E. and Harlow C. (eds.), *Implementing Amsterdam: immigration and asylum rights in EC law*, Hart Publishing, Oxford, 2001, p. 225-240.

Groenendijk K. and Guild E., " Converging Criteria: Creating an Area of Security of Residence for Europe's Third Country Nationals, *EJML*, Vol. 3, Issue 1, 2001, p. 37-59.

Groenendijk K., Guild E. and Barzilay R., "The Legal Status of Third Country Nationals who are Long-Term Residents in a Member States of the European Union", Center for Migration and Law, University of Nijmegen, Netherlands, 2000.

Guild E., "Citizens, Immigrants, Terrorists and Others", in Peers S. and Ward A. (eds.), *The European Union Charter of Fundamental Rights*, Hart Publishing, Oxford, 2004, p. 231-246.

Guild E., "Immigration, Asylum, Borders and Terrorism: The Unexpected Victims of 11 September 2001", in Gökay B. and Walker R.B.J. (eds.), *11 September 2001 War, Terror and Judgement,* Frank Cass, London, 2003, p. 175-194.

Guild E., *Immigration Law in the European Community,* Kluwer, The Hague, 2001.

Guild E., "Primary migration : the Great Myths", in Guild E. and Harlow C. (eds.), *Implementing Amsterdam: immigration and asylum rights in EC law*, Hart Publishing, Oxford, 2001, p. 65-94.

Guild E., "Adjudicating Schengen: National Judicial control in France", *EJML*, Vol. 2, 2000, p. 419-439.

Guild E. and Niessen J., *The Developing Immigration and Asylum Policies of the European Union Adopted Convention, Resolutions, Recommendations, Decisions and Conclusions,* Kluwer, The Hague, 1996.

Guild E. and Peers S., "Deference or Defiance ? The Courts of Justice's Jurisdiction over Immigration and Asylum", in Guild E. and Harlow C. (eds.), *Implementing Amsterdam: immigration and asylum rights in EC law*, Hart Publishing, Oxford, 2001, p. 267-289.

Guiraudon V., "The constitution of a European immigration policy domain : a political sociology approach", *Journal of European Public Policy*, Vol. 10 :2, April 2003, p. 263-282.

Guiraudon V., "European Integration and Migration Policy: Vertical Policy-making as a Venue Shopping", *Journal of Common Market Studies*, Vol. 38, No 2, 2000, p. 251-271.

Hailbronner K., "European Immigration and Asylum Law – FIDE Conference – Introductory remarks", paper distributed at the XXI FIDE Congress, Dublin, 2-5 June 2004.

Hailbronner K., *Immigration and Asylum Law and Policy of the European Union*, Kluwer, The Hague, 2000.

Hailbronner K., "The Treaty of Amsterdam and Migration Law", *EJML,* Vol. 1, 1999, p. 9-28.

Hailbronner K., "European Immigration and Asylum Law under the Amsterdam Treaty", *CMLRev*, Vol. 35, 1998, p. 1047-1067.

Hailbronner K., " The New Title on Free Movement of Persons, Asylum and Immigration in the TEC ", in Den Boer M. (ed.), *Schengen, Judicial Cooperation and Policy Coordination*, EIPA, Maastricht, 1997, p. 201-212.

Hailbronner K., "Migration Law and Policy within the Third Pillar of the Union Treaty", in Bieber R. and Monar J. (eds.), *Justice and Home Affairs in the European Union*

The Development of the Third Pillar, European Interuniversity Press, Brussels, 1995, p. 95-126.

Hailbronner K., "Visa Regulations and third-country nationals in EC law", *CMLRev,* Vol. 31, 1994, p. 969-995.

Hailbronner K. and Higgins I., "General Report" in Higgins I. (ed.) and Hailbronner K. (General Rapporteur), *Migration and Asylum law and Policy in the European Union – FIDE 2004 National Reports*, Cambridge University Press, Cambridge, 2004, p. 455-476.

Hakura F., " The External EU Immigration Policy : The need to Move beyond the Orthodoxy ", *European Foreign Affairs Review*, Vol. 3, 1998, p. 115-134.

Handoll J., *Free Movement of Persons in the EU,* John Wiley & sons, Chichester, 1995.

Hansen R. and Weil P., "Introduction : Citizenship, Immigration and Nationality : Towards a Convergence in Europe ?", in Hansen R. and Weil P. (eds.), *Towards a European Nationality – Citizenship, Immigration and Nationality Law in the EU*, Palgrave Publishers, New York, 2001, p. 1-23.

Harvey C., "Promoting Insecurity: Public Order, Expulsion and the European Convention on Human Rights", in Guild E. and Minderhout P. (eds.), *Security of Residence and Expulsion – Protection of Aliens in Europe,* Kluwer, The Hague, 2001, p. 41-58.

Hayes-Renshaw F. and Wallace H., *The Council of Ministers,* MacMillan Press, London, 1997.

Hedemann-Robinson M., "An overview of recent legal developments at Community level in relation to third country nationals resident within the European Union, with particular reference to the case law of the European Court of Justice", *CMLRev*, Vol. 38, 2001, p. 525-586.

Hedemann-Robinson M., "From Object to Subject?: Non-EC Nationals and the Draft Proposal of the Commission for a Council Act Establishing the Rules for the Admission of Third Country Nationals to the Member States", *YEL*, Vol. 1998, p. 289-335.

Hix S., Raunio T. and Scully R., *An Institutional Theory of Behaviour in the European Parliament,* EPRG Working Paper, No 1, presented at the Joint Sessions of the European Consortium for Political Research, 26-31 March 1999, Manheim, <http://personal.lse.ac.uk/HIX/WorkingPapers.HTM>.

Hix S., *The political system of the European Union*, MacMillan Press, London, 1999.

Hreblay V., *Les accords de Schengen: origine, fonctionnement, avenir*, Bruyland, Bruxelles, 1999.

Hurwitz A., "The 'Schengen' practice and case-law in Belgium", *EJML*, Vol. 2, 2000, p. 37-48.

Huysmans J., "The European Union and the Securization of Migration", *Journal of Common Market Studies,* Vol. 38, No. 5, p. 751-777.

ICMPD & European Commission, DG JHA, *Admission of third country nationals to an EU Member State for the purposes of study or vocational training, and admission of persons not gainfully employed,* DG JHA-ICMPD, August 2000.

Idot L., "Convention Bruxelles – transformation en règlement", *Europe*, Vol. 11, No.3, mars 2001, p. 26.

Israel J., "Conflicts of Law and the EC after Amsterdam : A Change for the Worse ?", *Maastricht Journal of European and Comparative Law,* 2000, Vol. 7, No 1, p. 81-98.

Jacqué J.-P., "Affaires intérieures et justice Quelques reflections" in Mattera A. (sous la direction de), *La Conférence Intergouvernementale sur l'UE – Répondre aux défis du XXI siècle,* Clément Juglar, Paris, 1996, p. 337-343.

Johnston A., "Judicial reform and the treaty of Nice", *CMLRev*, Vol. 38, 2001, p.499-523.

Jordan B., Stråth B. and Triandafyllidou A., "Contextualising immigration policy implementation in Europe", *Journal of Ethnic and Migration Studies,* Vol. 29, No 2, March 2003, p. 195-224.

Kolliker A. and Milner F., *How to make use of Closer Co-operation? The Amsterdam clauses and the dynamics of European Integration,* European Commission, Forward Studies Unit, 1999. A definitive version of this paper is available at <http://www.europa.eu.int/comm/cdp/working-paper/index_en.htm>.

Kortenberg H., "Closer Co-operation in the Treaty of Amsterdam", *CMLRev*, Vol. 35, 1998, p. 833-854.

Kortenberg H., "Comitologie: le retour", *RTDE*, 1998, p. 317-327.

Kuijper P. J., "Some legal problems associated with the communitarization of policy on visas, asylum and immigration under the Amsterdam Treaty and incorporation of the Schengen *acquis*", *CMLRev,* Vol. 37, 2000, p. 345-366.

Labayle H., "La coopération européenne en matière de justice et d'affaires intérieures et la Conférence intergouvernementale", *RTDE,* Vol. 33, Issue 1, janv.-mars 1997, p. 1-35.

Labayle H., "Un espace de liberté, de sécurité et de justice", *RTDE*, Vol. 33, No 4, oct.-déc. 1997, p. 813-881.

Lahav G., "Ideological and Party Constraints on Immigration Attitudes in Europe", *Journal of Common Market Studies,* Vol. 35, No 3, September 1997, p. 377-406.

Langrish S., "The Treaty of Amsterdam : Selected Highlights", *ELRev*, 1998, Vol. 2, p. 3-19.

Lemmens P., "The Relation between the Charter of Fundamental Rights of the European Union and the European Convention on Human Rights – Substantive aspects", *Maastricht Journal of European and Comparative Law,* Vol. 8, No 1, 2001, p. 49-67.

Lenaerts K. and Verhoeven A., "Towards a legal framework for executive rule-making in the EU? The contribution of the new Comitology decision", *CMLRev,* Vol. 37, 2000, p. 645-686.

Lenaerts K., "Regulating the regulatory process : "delegation of powers" in the European Community", *ELRev*, Vol. 18, 1993, p. 23-49.

Lepoivre M., "Le domaine de la Justice et des Affaires Intérieures dans la perspective de la Conférence Intergouvernementale de 1996", *CDE*, Issues 3-4, 1995, p. 323-349.

Lewis J., "Informal integration and the supranational construction of the Council", *Journal of European Public Policy*, Vol. 10:6, December 2003, p. 996-1019.

Lo Monaco A., " Actions communes et positions communes dans les domaines de la justice et des affaires intérieures ", in Pauly A., Best E., Guggenbuhl A. and Marinho C. (eds.), *De Schengen à Maastricht : voie royale et course d'obstacles,* EIPA, Maastricht, 1996, p. 45-59.

Louette J.-S., *Les Etats Benelux et la France face aux accords de Schengen*, Courrier Hebdomadaire, No 1586-1587, CRISP, 1998.

Maes M, "The "New" Regulation on Access to Documents", in Deckmyn V. (ed.), *Increasing Transparency in the European Union?,* EIPA, Maastricht, 2002, p. 199-208.

Maresceau M.. "Editorial : L'Union européenne et l'immigration au début du nouveau millénaire", *Revue des Affaires Européennes,* Vol. 1-2, April 2000, p. 3-6.

Mariani T., *L'Europe forteresse: mythe ou réalité ? Les enjeux de la politique européenne d'immigration*, Assemblée Nationale, Rapport d'Information No 1238, Novembre 2003.

Martin D., "Comments on *Florus Ariël Wijsenbeek* (Case C-378/97 of 21 September 1999) and *Arblade* (Joined Cases C-369/96 and C-376/96 of 23 November 1999), *EJML*, Vol. 2, 2000, p. 101-107.

Mattera A., "La libre circulation des travailleurs à l' intérieur de la Communauté européenne", *RMUE*, No 3, 1993, p. 47-108.

Mattera A., "Un espace sans frontières intérieures: le défi de l'Europe 1993", Issue 1, 1993, *RMUE*, p. 5-10.

Maurer A., "The Evolution of the Legislative Powers of the European Parliament : an Impact Assessment", in Vandersanden G. and de Walsch A. (eds.), *Mélanges en hommage à Jean-Victor Louis (Vol. I)*, Editions de l'Université de Bruxelles, Bruxelles, 2003, p. 309-336.

Mazzi-Zissis S., 'Les Accords de Schengen et la libre circulation des personnes dans l'Union européenne: exemple à suivre ou dangereux précédent?', in Ehlermann C.D. (ed.), *Multi-Speed Europe – the Legal Framework of Variable Geometry in the European Union,* Bundesanzeiger, Bonn, 1999, p. 47-66.

Mc Mahon R., "Maastricht's Third Pillar: Load bearing or purely decorative?", *Legal Issues of European Integration,* Vol. 1, 1995, p. 51-64.

Meijers et al., *Schengen Internationalisation of central chapters of the law on aliens, refugees, privacy, security and the police*, Stichting NJCM-Boekerij, The Netherlands, 1992.

Melis B., *Negotiating Europe's Immigration Frontiers,* Kluwer, The Hague, 2001.

Metcalfe L., "Flexible integration in and after the Amsterdam Treaty", in Den Boer M. (ed.), *Coping with flexibility after Amsterdam,* EIPA, Maastricht, 1998, p. 11-30.

Monar J., "The European Union's Role in the Fight against International Terrorism: An Evaluation in the Light of the Response to 11 September 2001", in Vandersanden G. and de Walsch A. (eds.), *Mélanges en hommage à Jean-Victor Louis (Vol. I)*, Editions de l'Université de Bruxelles, Bruxelles, 2003, p. 337-354.

Monar J., "Decision-making in the Area of Freedom, Security and Justice", in Arnull A. and Wincott D. (eds.), *Accountability and Legitimacy in the European Union*, Oxford University Press, Oxford, 2002, p. 63-80.

Monar J., "The Area of Freedom, Security and Justice: Institutional and Substantial Dynamics in the perspective of the European Union", Collegium No 22, December 2001, Special Edition-Proceedings of the Conference "Integrated security in Europe, a democratic perspective", Bruges, 14-17 November 2001, p. 11-24.

Monar J., "The impact of Schengen on Justice and Home Affairs in the European Union: An Assessment on the Threshold to its Incorporation", in Den Boer M. (ed.), *"Schengen still going strong: Evaluation and Update"*, EIPA, Maastricht, 2000, p. 21-35.

Monar J., "Justice and Home Affairs in the Treaty of Amsterdam: Reform at the Price of Fragmentation", *ELRev*, Vol. 23, 1998, p. 320-335.

Monar J., 'European Union – Justice and Home Affairs: a balance sheet and an agenda for reform', in Edwards G. and Pijpers A. (eds.), *The Politics of European Treaty Reform – The 1996 Intergovernmental Conference and beyond*, Printer, London, 1997, p. 326-339.

Monar J., 'Schengen and Flexibility in the Treaty of Amsterdam: Opportunities and Risks of Differentiated Integration in the EU Justice and Home Affairs' in M. Den Boer (ed.), *Schengen, Judicial Co-operation and Policy Coordination,* EIPA, Maastricht, 1997, p. 9-28.

Monar J., "The European Parliament and Immigration Policy: Its Positions and Possibilities of Control", in Korella G.D. and Twomey P.M. (eds.), *Towards a European Immigration Policy*, European Interuniversity Press, Bruges, 1993, p. 123-137.

Montaut I., "La Communautarisation du Second et du Troisième Piliers du Traité de l'Union européenne, dans la perspective de la Réforme Institutionnelle de la CIG de 1996", *RMC,* No 408, mai 1997, p. 335-348.

Müller-Graff P.-C., "The legal bases of the Third Pillar and its position in the framework of the Union Treaty", *CMLRev*, Vol. 31, 1994. p. 493-510.

Nanz K. P., "The Schengen Agreement: preparing the free movement of persons in the European Union", in Bieber R.and Monar J. (eds.), *Justice and Home Affairs in the European Union The Development of the Third Pillar*, European Interuniversity Press, Brussels, 1995, p. 29-48.

Naômé C., "The Case-Law of the Court of Justice and of the Court of First Instance of the European Communities on Transparency: From Carvel to Hautala II (1995-2001)", in Deckmyn V. (ed.), *Increasing Transparency in the European Union?,* EIPA, Maastricht, 2002, p. 147-198.

Nascimbene B., "Il progetto di Constituzione europea e l'immigrazione", *Diritto Immigrazione e Cittadinanza,* anno VI, No 1, 2004, p. 13-23.

Naskou-Perraki P. and Papagianni G., "Migration and Asylum Law and Policy: National Report for Greece", in Higgins I. (ed.) and Hailbronner K. (General Rapporteur), *Migration and Asylum law and Policy in the European Union – FIDE 2004 National Reports,* Cambridge University Press, Cambridge, 2004, p. 135-160.

Niessen J., "Consultations on Immigration Policies in the European Union", *EJML*, Vol. 4, Issue 1, 2002, p. 79-83.

Niessen J., "Overlapping Interests and Conflicting Agendas: The Knocking into Shape of EU Immigration Policies", *EJML*, Vol. 3, Issue 3/4, 2001, p. 419-434.

Niessen J., "International Migration on the EU Foreign Policy Agenda", *EJML*, Vol. 1, 1999, p. 483-496.

Nugent N., *The European Commission,* Palgrave, Hampshire, 2001.

O'Keeffe D., "Can the Leopard Change its Spots? Visas, Immigration and Asylum – Following Amsterdam", in O'Keeffe D. and Twomey P. (eds.), *Legal Issues of the Amsterdam Treaty,* Hart Publishing, Oxford, 1999, p. 271-288.

O'Keeffe D., "Community and Member State Competence in External Relations Agreements of the EU", *European Foreign Affairs Review*, Vol. 4, 1999, p. 6-36.

O'Keeffe D., "A Critical View of the Third Pillar", in Pauly A., Best E., Guggenbuhl A. and Marinho C. (eds.), *De Schengen à Maastricht : voie royale et course d'obstacles,* EIPA, Maastricht, 1996, p. 1-16.

O'Keeffe D., "The Convention on the Crossing of the External Frontiers of the Member States" in Pauly A., Best E., Guggenbuhl A. and Marinho C. (eds.), *De Schengen à Maastricht : voie royale et course d'obstacles,* EIPA, Maastricht, 1996, p. 33-44.

O'Keeffe D., "Recasting the Third Pillar", *CMLRev*, Vol. 32, 1995, p. 893-920.

O'Keeffe D., "Reforming the Third Pillar: Transparency and structural reform n the long term perspective", in Bieber R. and Monar J. (eds.), *Justice and Home Affairs in the European Union The Development of the Third Pillar,* European Interuniversity Press, Brussels, 1995, p. 397-421.

O'Keeffe D., "The emergence of a European Immigration Policy", *ELRev*, Vol. 20, 1995, 20-36.

O'Keeffe D., " Non-Accession to the Schengen Convention : The cases of the United Kingdom and Ireland ", in Pauly A. (ed.), *Schengen en panne,* EIPA, Maastricht, 1994, p. 43-53.

O'Keeffe D., "The free movement of persons and the Single Market", *ELRev,* Vol. 2, 1992, p. 3-19.

O'Keeffe D., "The Schengen Convention : A Suitable Model for European Integration?", *YEL*, Vol. 11, 1991, p. 185-219.

Pallett L., "The United Kingdom Position: Implementing the Schengen Protocol", in Marinho C. (ed), *Asylum, Immigration and Schengen Post-Amsterdam – A First Assessment,* EIPA, p. 91-105.

Papademetriou D., *Coming together or pulling apart? The European Union's struggle with immigration and asylum,* Carnegie Endowment for International Peace, Washington, 1996.

Papagianni G., "Schengen: does it still exist? The incorporation and development of the Schengen *acquis* within the framework of the EU" (in Greek), *Επετηρίδα Ι.ΔΙ.Σ 2001-2002,* Περράκης Σ. (επιμ.), Εκδόσεις Σάκκουλα, Αθήνα, 2003, σελ. 312-344.

Papagianni G. "Free Movement of Persons in the light of the new Title IV TEC: from intergovernmentalism towards a Community policy", *YEL*, 2002, p. 107-162.

Papagianni G., "Flexibility in Justice and Home Affairs: an old phenomenon taking new forms", in De Witte B., Hanf D. and Vos E. (eds.), *The Many Faces of Differentiation in EU Law*, Intersentia, Antwerpen, 2001, p. 101-128.

Papagianni G., "La circulation des citoyens de l'Union: de Maastricht à Amsterdam et au delà", *Actualités de droit*, Vol. 4, 1999, p. 625-665.

Pastore F., "Visas, Borders, Immigration: Formation, Structure and Current Evolution of the Entry Control System" in Walker N. (ed.), *The Area of Freedom, Security and Justice,* Oxford University Press, Oxford, 2004, p. 89-142.

Peers S., "Family Reunion and Community Law", in Walker N. (ed.), *The Area of Freedom, Security and Justice,* Oxford University Press, Oxford, 2004, p. 143-197.

Peers S., "Taking Rights Away? Limitations and Derogations", in Peers S. and Ward A. (eds.), *The European Union Charter of Fundamental Rights*, Hart Publishing, Oxford, 2004, p. 141-179.

Peers S., "Key Legislative Developments on Migration in the European Union, *EJML*, Vol. 5, 2003, p. 107-141.

Peers S., "Key Legislative Developments on Migration in the European Union, *EJML*, Vol. 5, 2003, p. 387-410.

Peers S., "Access to Information on EU External Relations and Justice and Home Affairs", in Deckmyn V. (ed.), *Increasing Transparency in the European Union?,* EIPA, Maastricht, 2002, p. 209-232.

Peers S., "From Maastricht to Laeken: The Political Agenda of Openness and Transparency in the European Union", in Deckmyn V. (ed.), *Increasing Transparency in the European Union?,* EIPA, Maastricht, 2002, p. 7-32.

Peers S., "Key Legislative Developments on Migration in the European Union, *EJML*, Vol. 4, 2002, p. 85-126.

Peers S., "Key Legislative Developments on Migration in the European Union, *EJML*, Vol. 4, 2002, p. 339-367.

Peers S., "Aliens, Workers, Citizens or Humans: Models for Community Immigration Law", in Guild E. and Harlow C. (eds.), *Implementing Amsterdam: immigration and asylum rights in EC law*, Hart Publishing, Oxford, 2001, p. 291-308.

Peers S., "Immigration, Asylum and the European Union Charter of Fundamental Rights", *EJML,* Vol. 3, 2001, p. 141-149.

Peers S., "Key Legislative Developments on Migration in the European Union, *EJML*, Vol. 3, 2001, p. 231-255.

Peers S., *EU Justice and Home Affairs Law*, Longman, London, 2000.

Peers S., "Justice and Home Affairs: decision-making after Amsterdam", *CMLRev*, Vol. 25, 2000, p. 183-191.

Peers S., "The EC-Switzerland Agreement on Free Movement of Persons : Overview and Analysis", *EJML,* Vol. 2, 2000, p. 127-142.

Peers S., "Caveat emptor? Integrating the Schengen *acquis* into the European Union legal order", *Cambridge Yearbook of European Legal Studies*, Vol. 2, 1999, p. 87-123.

Peers S., "Building Fortress Europe: The development of EU Migration law", *CMLRev*, Vol. 33, 1998, p. 1235-1272.

Peers S., "Who's Judging the Watchmen? The Judicial System of the 'Area of Freedom Security and Justice", *YEL*, Vol. 18, 1998, p. 337-413.

Peers S., "Justice and Home Affairs- Undercutting Integration: Developments in Union Policy on Third-Country Nationals, *ELRev*, Vol. 22, 1997, p. 76-84.

Petite M., "The Treaty of Amsterdam", *Harvard Working Papers,* 5 October 1997, available at http://www.jeanmonnetprogram.org/papers/98/98-2-.html.

Piçarra N., "La mise en oeuvre du protocole intégrant l'*acquis* de Schengen dans le cadre de l'Union europeéenne: règles et procedures", in Den Boer M. (ed.), *Schengen's Final Days? The Incorporation of Schengen into the New TEU, External Borders and Information Systems*, EIPA, Maastricht, 1998, p. 25-58.

Plender R., "Forced Migrations – Grounds and Limits to States' Action", paper distributed at the IX Convengo SIDI "Le migrazioni: una sfida per il diritto internazionale, comunitario e interno" held in Rome, 17 and 18 June 2004.

Plender R., "The Treaty of Amsterdam and the Free Movement of Persons", *European Business Law Review*, Vol. 9, No 11 & 12, 1998, p. 400-406.

Pollet K., "The Amsterdam Treaty and Asylum and Immigration Policies: A Legal Analysis", *Revue des Affaires Européennes,* Vol. 1-2, April 2000, p. 57-80.

Potemkina O., "Some Ramification of Enlargement on the EU-Russia Relations and the Schengen Regime", *EJML,* Vol. 5, 2003, p. 229-247.

Reermann O., "Cooperation with Countries of Origin and Transit : Readmission Agreements", in Faria C. (ed.), *Managing Migration Flows and Preventing Illegal Immigration – Schengen-Justice and Home Affairs Colloquium,* EIPA, Maastricht, 2002, p. 13-24.

Schermers H.G., "Human Rights and Free Movement of Persons : the Role of the European Commission and Court of Human Rights", in Schermers et al. (eds.), *Free Movement of Persons in Europe, Legal Problems and Experiences*, T.M.C. Asser Institute, The Hague, 1993, p. 235-247.

Schermers H.G., "The effect of the date 31 December 1992", *CMLRev,* Vol. 28, 1991, p. 275-289.

Schieffer M., "Community Readmission Agreements with Third-Countries – Objectives, Substance and Current State of Negotiations", *EJML*, Vol. 5, 2003, p. 343-357.

Schieffer M., " The Readmission of Third Country Nationals within Bilateral and Multilateral Frameworks ", in Den Boer M. (ed.), *The Implementation of Schengen : First the Widening, Now the Deepening,* EIPA, Maastricht, 1997, p. 97-108.

Schmidt D., "Die aktuellen Debatten über das neue Zuwanderungsgesetz", paper presented at Conference entitled "EC Asylum and Immigration Law: reaching the Tampere Milestones?" organised by the Academy of European Law (ERA), Trier, 11 and 12 March 2004.

Schout A., "The Presidency as Juggler – Managing Conflicting Expectations", Eipascope, No 2, 1998, p. 2-10.

Schulte B., "Implications of Labour Migration for Social Security Systems in European Countries – Activities of the Council of Europe", *EJML*, Vol. 4, Issue 4, 2002, p. 477-489.

Schutte J., "The Incorporation of the Schengen *Acquis* in the European Union", in Cullen P. and Gilmore W. (eds.), *Crime Sans Frontières: International and European Legal Approaches*, Edinburgh University Press, Edinburgh, 1998, p. 124-132.

Schutte J., "Schengen : Its meaning for the free movement of persons in Europe", *CMLRev*, 1991, Vol. 28, p. 549-570.

Simon D., *Le système juridique communautaire*, puf, Paris, 1997.

Smith K., "The Use of Political Conditionality in the EU's Relations with Third Countries: How Effective?", *European Foreign Affairs Review,* Vol. 3, 1998, p. 253-274.

Söderman J., "The Role and the Impact of the European Ombudsman in Access to Documentation and the Transparency of Decision-Making" in Deckmyn V. and Thomson I. (eds.), *Openness and Transparency in the European Union,* EIPA, Maastricht, 1998, p. 75-83.

Staples H., "Adjudicating the Schengen Agreements in the Netherlands", *EJML*, Vol. 2, 2000, p. 49-83.

Tallberg J., "The agenda-shaping powers of the EU Presidency", *Journal of European Public Policy,* Vol. 10:1, February 2003, p. 1-19.

Timmermans C.W.A., "Free Movement of Persons and the Division of Powers between the Community and its Member States – Why do it the intergovernmental way ?", in Schermers et al. (eds.), *Free Movement of Persons in Europe, Legal Problems and Experiences*, T.M.C. Asser Institute, The Hague, 1993, p. 352-368.

Tizzano A., 'A proposito dell'inserzione dell'*acquis* di Schengen nei Trattati comunitari: l'accordo "del Consiglio" con Islanda e Norvegia', *Il Diritto dell'Unione Europea*, 1999, p. 521-527.

Tizzano A., "La personnalité internationale de l'Union européenne", *RMUE,* Vol. 4, 1998, p. 11-40.

Tizzano A., "Brevi note sul "terzo pilastro" del Trattato di Maastricht", *Il Diritto dell'Unione Europea*, Issue 2, 1996, p. 391-403.

Toth A. G., "The legal status of the declarations annexed to the Single European Act", *CMLRev*, Vol. 23, 1986, p. 803-812.

Tridimas T., *The General Principles of EC Law*, Oxford University Press, Oxford, 1999.

Trotta R., " La dimension extérieure de la circulation des personnes après Amsterdam ", in Dony M. (ed.), *L'Union européenne et le monde après Amsterdam,* Université de Bruxelles, Bruxelles, 1999, p. 107-141.

Twomey P., "Europe's Other Market – Trafficking in People", *EJML*, Vol. 2, 2000, p. 1-36.

Tyson A., "The negotiation of the European Community Directive on Racial Discrimination", *EJML,* Vol. 3, 2001, p. 199-229.

Uçarer E., "From the Sidelines to Center Stage: Sidekick No More? The European Commission in Justice and Home Affairs", European Integration Online Papers, Vol. 5, No 5, 2001, <http://eiop.or.at/eiop/texte/2001-005a.htm>

Van de Rijt W., "Le fonctionnement des institutions Schengen. "Pragmatisme toujours"", in Den Boer M. (ed.), *Schengen's Final Days? The Incorporation of Schengen into the New TEU, External Borders and Information Systems*, EIPA, Maastricht, 1998, p. 59-66.

Van Den Brink and Vierhout R., "Democratic control without frontiers? The European parliament and free movement of persons", in Schermers et al. (eds.), *Free Movement of Persons in Europe, Legal Problems and Experiences*, T.M.C. Asser Institute, The Hague, 1993, p. 379-390.

Van Dijk P., "Protection of 'Integrated' Aliens against Expulsion under the European Convention on Human Rights", in Guild E. and Minderhout P. (eds.), *Security of Residence and Expulsion – Protection of Aliens in Europe,* Kluwer, The Hague, 2001, p. 23-39.

Van Nuffel P., 'Le traité de Nice: Un commentaire', *Revue du Droit de l'Union Européenne,* Vol. 2, 2001, p. 329-387.

Van Raepenbusch S., " La jurisprudence de la Cour de justice des Communautés européennes vis-à-vis des ressortissants de pays tiers ", in Den Boer M. (ed.), *The implementation of Schengen : First the Widening, Now the Deepening,* EIPA, Maastricht, 1997, p. 41-69.

Vandamme L., "Le nouveau cadre du Système d'Information Schengen", in Marinho C. (ed.), *Asylum, Immigration and Schengen Post-Amsterdam – A First Assessment,* EIPA, Maastricht, 2001, p. 119-130.

Vignes D., "Plaidoyer pour le IIIème Pilier", *RMC*, No 397, avril 1996, p. 273-281.

Vitorino A., "What EU strategy for integrating migrants", SPEECH/04/340, Brussels, June 30.2004.

Vitorino A., 'Interview with Antònio Vitorino, European Commissioner for Justice and Home Affairs', in European Economic and Social Committee, *Immigration, Asylum and Social Integration*, Office for Official Publications of the European Communities, Luxembourg, 2002, p. 7-15.

Vitorino A., "La Charte des droits fondamentaux de l'Union européenne", *Revue du Droit de l'Union Européenne*, No 1, 2001, p. 27-64.

Wagner E., "The integration of Schengen into the framework of the European Union", *Legal Issues of European Integration*, Vol. 2, 1998, p. 1-60.

Walker N., "In Search of The Area of Freedom, Security and Justice: A Constitutional Odyssey", in Walker N. (ed.), *The Area of Freedom, Security and Justice,* Oxford University Press, Oxford, 2004, p. 3-38.

Walker N., "Freedom, Security and Justice", in De Witte B. (ed.), *Ten Reflections for the Constitutional Treaty in Europe,* European University Institute, San Domenico di Fiesole, 2003, p. 163-185.

Wallace H. and Wallace W. (eds.), *Policy-Making in the European Union*, Oxford University Press, 2000.

Watson G., "EU Asylum and Immigration Policies: The Point of View of the European Parliament", in Marinho C. (ed.), *Asylum, Immigration and Schengen Post-Amsterdam – A First Assessment,* EIPA, Maastricht, 2001, p. 47-53.

Weiler J.H.H., "Thou Shalt not oppress a stranger (Ex. 23:9): on the judicial protection of the human rights of non-EC nationals", in Schermers et al. (eds.), *Free Movement of Persons in Europe, Legal Problems and Experiences*, T.M.C. Asser Institute, The Hague, 1993, p. 248-271.

Wiener A., "Forging Flexibility – the British 'No' to Schengen", Arena Working Paper, No 1, January 2000.

Wouters J., 'Institutional and constitutional challenges for the European Union – some reflections in the light of the Treaty of Nice', *ELRev*, Vol. 26, 2001, p. 342-356.

Wouters J., "European citizenship and the case-law of the Court of Justice of the European Communities on the free movement of persons", in Marias E. A. (ed.), *European citizenship,* EIPA, Maastricht, 1994, p. 25-61.

B. EC/EU Legislation

Common Consular Instructions on visas for the Diplomatic Missions and Consular Posts, C 326/1, 22.12.2005.

Regulation (EC) No 2046/2005 of the European Parliament and of the Council of 14 December 2005 relating to measures envisaged to facilitate the procedures for applying for and issuing visas for members of the Olympic family taking part in the 2006 Olympic and/or Paralympic Winter Games in Turin, OJ L 334/1, 20.12.2005.

Council Decision 2005/809/EC of 7 November 2005 concerning the conclusion of the Agreement between the European Community and the Republic of Albania on the readmission of persons residing without authorization, OJ L 304/14, 23.11.2005.

Council Decision 2005/794/EC of 20 September 2005 on the signing, on behalf of the Community, of the Agreement between the European Community and the Kingdom of Denmark on the service of judicial and extrajudicial documents in civil or commercial matters, OJ L 300/53, 17.11.2005.

Agreement between the European Community and the Kingdom of Denmark on the service of judicial and extrajudicial documents in civil or commercial matters, OJ L 300/55, 17.11.2005.

Council Decision 2005/790/EC of 20 September 2005 on the signing on behalf of the Community, of the Agreement between the European Community and the Kingdom of Denmark on jurisdiction and the recognition and enforcement of judgements in civil and commercial matters, OJ L 299/61, 16.11.2005.

Agreement between the European Community and the Kingdom of Denmark on jurisdiction and the recognition and enforcement of judgements in civil and commercial matters, OJ L 299/62, 16.11.2005.

Council Directive 2005/71/EC of 12 October 2005 on a specific procedure for admitting third-country nationals for the purposes of scientific research, OJ L 289/15, 3.11.2005.

Council Recommendation 2005/762/EC of 12 October 2005 to facilitate the admission of third country nationals to carry out scientific research in the European Community, OJ L 289/26, 3.11.2005.

European Parliament and Council Recommendation 2005/761/EC of 28 September 2005 to facilitate the issue by the Member States of uniform short-stay visas for researchers from third countries travelling within the Community for the purpose of carrying out scientific research, OJ L 289/23, 3.11.2005.

Commission Decision 2005/687/EC of 29 September 2005 on the format for the report on the activities of immigration liaison officers network and on the situation in the host country in matters relating to illegal migration, OJ L 264/8, 8.10.2005.

Statement on Council Regulation (EC) No 851/2005 of 2 June 2005 amending Regulation (EC) No 539/2001 as regards the visa reciprocity, OJ C 172/1, 12.7.2005.

Council Regulation (EC) No 851/2005 of 2 June 2005 amending Regulation (EC) No 539/2001 listing the third countries whose nationals must be in possession of visas when crossing the external borders and those whose nationals are exempt from that requirement as regards the reciprocity mechanism, OJ L 141/3, 4.6.2005.

Information relating to the entry into force of the Agreement between the European Community and the Democratic Socialist Republic of Sri Lanka on the readmission of persons residing without authorisation, OJ L 138/17, 1.6.2005.

Council Decision 2005/371/EC of 3 March 2005 on the signing of the Agreement between the European Community and the Republic of Albania on the readmission of persons residing without authorisation, OJ L 124/21, 17.5.2005.

Agreement between the European Community and the Republic of Albania on the readmission of persons residing without authorisation, OJ L 124/22, 17.5.2005.

Council Decision 2005/372/EC of 3 March 2005 concerning the conclusion of the Agreement between the European Community and the Democratic Socialist Republic of Sri Lanka on the readmission of persons residing without authorisation, OJ L 124/41, 17.5.2005.

Agreement between the European Community and the Democratic Socialist Republic of Sri Lanka on the readmission of persons residing without authorisation, OJ L 124/43, 17.5.2005.

Council Decision 2005/358/EC of 26 April 2005 designating the seat of the European Agency for the Management of Operational Cooperation at the External Borders of the Member States of the European Union, OJ L 114/13, 4.5.2005.

Council Decision 2005/267/EC of 16 March 2005 establishing a secure web-based Information and Coordination Network for Member States' Migration Management Services, OJ L 83/48, 1.4.2005.

Council Decision 2005/211/JHA of 24 February concerning the introduction of some new functions for Schengen Information System, including in the fight against terrorism, OJ L 68/44, 15.3.2005.

Council Decision 2004/927/EC of 22 December 2004 providing for certain areas covered by Title IV of Part Three of the Treaty establishing the European Community to be governed by the procedure laid down in Article 251 of that Treaty, OJ L 396/45, 31.12.2004.

Council Decision 2004/926/EC of 22 December 2004 on the putting into effect of parts of the Schengen *acquis* by the United Kingdom of Great Britain and the Northern Ireland, OJ L 395/70, 31.12.2004.

Council Regulation (EC) No 2252/2004 of 13 December 2004 on standards for security features and biometrics in passports and travel documents issued by Member States, OJ L 385/1, 29.12.2004.

Council Directive 2004/114/EC of 13 December 2004 on the conditions of admission of third-country nationals for the purposes of studies, pupil exchange, unremunerated training or voluntary service, OJ L 375/12, 23.12.2005.

Council Decision 2004/867/EC of 13 December amending Decision 2002/463/EC adopting an action programme for administrative cooperation in the fields of external borders, visas, asylum and immigration (ARGO programme), OJ L 371/48, 18.12.2004.

Council Decision 2004/860/EC of 25 October 2004 on the signing, on behalf of the European Community, and on the provisional application of certain provisions of the Agreement between the European Union, the European Community and the Swiss Confederation's association with the implementation, application and development of the Schengen *acquis*, OJ L 370/78, 17.12.2004.

Treaty establishing a Constitution for Europe, C 310/1, 16.12.2004.

Council Regulation (EC) No 2133/2004 of 13 December 2004 on the requirement for the competent authorities of the Member States to stamp systematically the travel documents of third country nationals when they cross the external borders of the Member States and amending the provisions of the Convention implementing the Schengen agreement and the common manual to this end, OJ L 369/5, 16.12.2004.

Council Decision 2004/849/EC of 25 October 2004 on the signing, on behalf of the European Union, and on the provisional application of certain provisions of the Agreement between the European Union, the European Community and the Swiss Confederation's association with the implementation, application and development of the Schengen *acquis*, OJ L 368/26, 15.12.2004.

Council Decision No 1/2004 of the EU/Switzerland Mixed Committee established by the Agreement concluded by the European Union, the European Community and the Swiss Confederation concerning the latter's association in the implementation, application and development of the Schengen *acquis* of 26 October 2004 adopting its Rules of Procedure, OJ C 308/2, 14.12.2004.

Council Regulation (EC) No 2007/2004 of 26 October 2004 establishing a European Agency for the Management of Operational Cooperation at the External Borders of the Member States of the European Union, OJ L 349/1, 25.11.2004.

Council Decision 2004/581/EC of 29 April 2004 determining the minimum indication to be used on signs at external border crossing points, OJ L 261/119, 6.8.2004.

Council Decision 2004/574/EC of 29 April 2004 amending the Common Manual, OJ L 261/36, 6.8.2004.

Council Decision 2004/573/EC of 29 April 2004 on the organization of joint flights for removals from the territory of two or more Member States, of third country nationals who are subjects of individual removal orders, OJ L 261/28, 6.8.2004.

Council Directive 2004/83/EC of 29 April 2004 on the obligation of carriers to communicate passenger data, OJ L 261/24, 6.8.2004.

Council Directive 2004/81/EC of 29 April 2004 on the residence permit issued to third country nationals who are victims of trafficking in human beings or who have been the subject of an action to facilitate illegal immigration, who cooperate with the competent authorities, OJ L 261/19, 6.8.2004.

Information concerning the entry into force of the Agreement between the European Community and the Macao Special Administrative Region of the People's Republic of China on the readmission of persons residing without authorization, OJ L 285/17, 6.8.2004.

Commission Decision 2004/535/EC of 14 May 2004 on the adequate protection of personal data contained in the Passenger Name Record of air passengers transferred to the United States' Bureau of Customs and Border Protection, OJ L 235/11, 6.7.2004.

Council Decision 2004/512/EC of 8 June 2004 establishing the Visa Information System (VIS), OJ L 213/5, 15.6.2004.

Council Decision 2004/496/EC of 17 May 2004 on the conclusion of an Agreement between the European Community and the United States of America on the processing and transfer of PNR data by Air Carriers to the United States Department of Homeland Security, Bureau of Customs and Border Protection, OJ L 183/83, 20.5.2004.

Council Decision 2004/424/EC of 21 April 2004 concerning the conclusion of the Agreement between the European Community and the Macao Special Administrative Region of the People's Republic of China on the readmission of persons residing without authorization, OJ L143/97, 30.4.2004 and Agreement between the European Community and the Macao Special Administrative Region of the People's Republic of China on the readmission of persons residing without authorization, OJ L143/99, 30.4.2004.

Council Regulation (EC) No 871/2004 of 29 April 2004 concerning the introduction of some new functions for the Schengen Information System, including in the fight against terrorism, L 162/29, 30.4.2004.

Council Decision 2004/338/EC of 22 March 2004 adopting the Council's Rules of Procedure, OJ L 106/22, 15.4.2004.

Information on the entry into force of the Agreement between the European Community and the Government of the Hong Kong Special Administrative Region of the People's Republic of China on the readmission of persons residing without authorization, OJ L 64/38, 2.3.2004.

Council Decision of 8 March 2004 concerning the conclusion of the Memorandum of Understanding between the European Community and the National Tourism Administration of the People's Republic of China on visa and related issues concerning tourist groups form the People's Republic of China (ADS), OJ L 83/12, 20.3.2004 and Memorandum of Understanding between the European Community and the National Tourism Administration of the People's Republic of China on visa and related issues concerning tourist groups form the People's Republic of China (ADS), OJ L 83/14, 20.3.2004.

Regulation (EC) No 491/2004 of the European Parliament and of the Council of 10 March 2004 establishing a programme for financial and technical assistance to third countries in the areas of migration and asylum (AENEAS), OJ L 80/1, 18.3.2004.

Council Regulation (EC) No 378/2004 of 19 February 2004 on procedures amending the Sirene Manual, OJ L 64/5, 2.3.2004.

Council Decision 2004/201/JHA of 19 February 2004 on procedures amending the Sirene Manual, OJ L 64/45, 2.3.2004.

Council Regulation (EC) No 377/2004 of 19 February 2004 on the creation of an immigration liaison officers network, OJ L 64/1, 2.3.2004.

Information on the entry into force of the Agreement between the European Community and the Government of the Hong Kong Special Administrative Region of the People's Republic of China on the readmission of persons residing without authorization, OJ L 64/38, 2.3.2004.

Council Decision 2004/191/EC of 23 February 2004 setting out the criteria and practical arrangements for the compensation of the financial imbalances resulting from the application of Directive 2001/40/EC on the mutual recognition of decisions on the expulsion of third-country nationals, OJ L 60/55, 27.2.2004.

Council Decision 2004/80/EC of 17 December 2003 concerning the inclusion of the Agreement between the European Community and the Government of the Hong Kong Special Administrative Region of the People's Republic of China on the readmission of persons residing without authorization, OJ L 17/23, 24.1.2004.

Agreement between the European Community and the Government of the Hong Kong Special Administrative Region of the People's Republic of China on the readmission of persons residing without authorization, OJ L 17/25, 24.1.2004.

Council Directive 2003/109/EC of 25 November 2003, concerning the status of third-country nationals who are long-term residents, OJ L 16/44, 23.1.2004.

Council Decision 2004/14/EC of 22 December 2003 amending the third subparagraph (Basic criteria for examining applications) of Part V of the Common Consular Instructions, OJ L 5/74, 9.1.2004.

Council Decision 2004/15/EC of 22 December 2003 amending point 1.2 of Part II of the Common Consular Instructions and drawing up a new Annex thereto, OJ L 5/76, 9.1.2004.

Council Decision 2004/16/EC of 22 December 2003 on downgrading Annex 5 to the Common Consular Instructions and the corresponding Annex 14b to the Common Manual and on declassifying Annexes 9 and 10 to the Common Consular Instructions and the corresponding Annexes 6b and 6c to the Common Manual, OJ L 5/78, 9.1.2004.

Council Decision 2004/17/EC of 22 December 2003 amending Part V, point 1.4, of the Common Consular Instructions and Part I, point 4.1.2 of the Common Manual as regards inclusion of the requirements to be in possession of travel medical insurance as one of the supporting documents for the grant of a uniform entry visa, OJ L 5/79, 9.1.2004.

Council Directive 2003/110/EC of 25 November 2003 on assistance in cases of transit for the purposes of removal by air, OJ L 321/26, 6.12.2003.

Council decision 2003/725/JHA of 2 October 2003 amending the provisions of Article 40 (1) and (7) of the Convention implementing the Schengen Agreement of 14 June 1985 on the gradual abolition of checks at common borders, OJ L 260/37, 11.10.2003.

Council Directive 2003/86/EC of 22 September 2003, on the right to family reunification, OJ L 251/12, 3.10.2003.

Council Decision 2003/585/EC of 28 July 2003 amending Annex 2, Schedule A, of the Common Consular Instructions and Annex, Schedule A, of the Common Manual on the visa requirements for holders of Pakistani diplomatic passports, OJ L 198/13, 6.8.2003.

Council Decision 2000/586/EC of 28 July 2003 on amendment of Annex 3, Part I, of the Common Consular Instructions and Annex 5a, Part I of the Common manual on third country nationals subject to airport visa requirements, OJ 198/15, 6.8.2003.

Council Decision 2003/578/EC of 22 July 2003 on guidelines for the employment policies of the Member States, OJ 197/13, 5.8.2003.

Council Regulation (EC) No 1295/2003 of 15 July 2003 relating to measures envisaged to facilitate the procedures for applying for and issuing visas for members of the Olympic family taking part in the 2004 Olympic and Paralympic Games in Athens, OJ L 183/1, 22.7.2003.

Council Decision 2003/454/EC of 13 June 2003 amending Annex 12 of the Common Consular Instructions and Annex 14a of the Common Manual on visa fees, OJ L 152/82, 20.6.2003.

Council Conclusions of 8 May 2003 – Brussels Declaration on Preventing and Combating Trafficking in Human Beings, OJ C 137/1, 12.6.2003.

Council Regulation (EC) No 859/2003 of 14 May 2003 extending the provisions of Regulation (EEC) No 1408/71 and Regulation (EEC) No 574/72 to nationals of third countries who are not already covered by those provisions solely on the ground of their nationality, OJ L 124/1, 20.5.2003.

Council Regulation (EC) No 694/2003 of 14 April 2003 on uniform formats for facilitated Transit Documents (FTD) and Facilitated Rail Transit Documents (FRTD) provided for in Regulation (EC) No 693/2003, OJ L 99/15, 17.4.2003.

Council Regulation (EC) No 693/2003 of 14 April 2003 establishing a specific Facilitated Transit Document (FTD), a Facilitated Rail Transit Document (FRTD) and amending the Common Consular Instructions and the Common Manual, OJ L 99/8, 17.4.2003.

Commission Decision 2003/209/EC of 25 March 2003 setting up a consultative group, to be known as the "Experts Group on Trafficking in Human Beings", OJ L 79/25, 26.3.2003.

Council Regulation (EC) No 453/2003 of 6 March 2003 amending Regulation (EC) No 539/2001 listing third countries whose nationals must be in possession of visas when crossing the external borders of Member States and those whose nationals are exempt from that requirement, OJ L 69/10, 13.3.2003.

Council Decision 2003/170/JHA of 27 February 2003 on the common use of liaison officers posted abroad by the law enforcement agencies of the Member States, OJ L 67/27, 12.3.2003.

Council Regulation (EC) No 415/2003 of 27 February 2003 of 27 February 2003 on the issue of visas at the border, including the issue of such visas to seamen in transit, OJ L 64/1, 7.3.2003.

Council Regulation (EC) No 343/2003 of 18 February 2003 establishing the criteria and mechanisms for determining the Member State responsible for examining an asylum application lodged in one of the Member States by a third-country national, OJ L 50/1, 25.2.2003.

Sirene Manual, OJ C 38/1, 17.2.2003.

Council Directive 2003/9/EC of 27 January 2003 laying down minimum standards for the reception of asylum seekers, OJ L 31/18, 6.2.2003.

Common Consular Instructions on visas for the diplomatic missions and consular posts, OJ C 313/1, 16.12.2002.

Common Manual, OJ C 313/97, 16.12.2002.

Council Directive 2002/90/EC of 28 November 2002 defining the facilitation of unauthorized entry, movement and residence, OJ L 328/17, 5.12.2002.

Council Framework Decision 2002/946/EC of 28 November 2002 on the strengthening of the penal framework to prevent the facilitation of unauthorized entry and residence, OJ L 328/1, 5.12.2002.

Council Framework Decision 2002/629/JHA of 19 July 2002 on combating trafficking in human beings, OJ L 203/1, 1.8.2002.

Council Framework Decision 2002/584/JHA of 13 June 2002 on the European arrest warrant and the surrender procedures between Member States, OJ L 190/1, 18.7.2002.

Council Decision 2002/585/EC of 12 July 2002 on the adaptation of parts III and VIII of the common consular instructions, OJ L 187/44, 16.7.2002.

Council Decision 2002/586/EC of 12 July 2002 on the amendment of part VI of the common consular instructions, OJ L 187/48, 16.7.2002.

Council Decision 2002/587/EC of 12 July 2002 on the revision of the Common Manual, OJ L 187/50, 16.7.2002.

Council Decision 2002/463/EC of 13 June 2002 adopting an Action programme for administrative cooperation in the fields of external borders, visas, asylum and immigration, (ARGO programme), OJ L 161/11, 19.6.2002.

Council Regulation (EC) No 1030/2002 of 13 June 2002 laying down a uniform format for residence permits for third country nationals, OJ L 157/1, 15.6.2002.

Council Decision 2002/352/EC of 25 April 2002 on the revision of the Common Manual, OJ L 123/47, 9.5.2002.

Council Decision 2002/353/EC of 25 April 2002 on declassifying Part of the Common Manual adopted by the Executive Committee established by the Convention implementing the Schengen Agreement of 14 June 1985, OJ L 123/49, 9.5.2002.

Council Decision 2002/354/EC of 25 April 2002 on the adaptation of Part III of, and the creation of an Annex 16 to, the Common Consular Instructions, OJ L 123/50, 9.5.2002.

Council Decision 2002/192/EC of 28 February 2002 concerning Ireland's request to take part in some of the provisions of the Schengen *acquis*, OJ L 64/20, 7.3.2002.

Council Regulation (EC) No 333/2002 of 18 February 2002 on a uniform format for forms for affixing the visa issued by Member States to persons holding travel documents not recognized by the Member State drawing up the form, OJ L 53/4, 23.2.2002.

Council Regulation (EC) No 334/2002 of 18 February 2002 amending Regulation (EC) No 1683/95 laying down a uniform format for visas, OJ L 53/7, 23.2.2002.

Council Decision 2002/44/EC of 20 December 2001 amending Part VII and Annex 12 to the Common Consular Instructions and Annex 14a to the Common Manual, OJ L 20/5 23.1.2002.

Council Decision 2001/886/JHA of 6 December 2001 on the development of the second generation Schengen Information System (SIS II), L 328/1, 13.12.2001.

Council Regulation (EC) 2424/2001 of 6 December 2001 on the development of the second generation Schengen Information System (SIS II), L 328/4, 13.12.2001.

Council Regulation (EC) No 2414/2001 of 7 December 2001 amending Regulation (EC) No 539/2001 listing third countries whose nationals must be in possession of visas when crossing the external borders of Member States and those whose nationals are exempt from that requirement, OJ L 327/1, 12.12.2001.

Council Directive 2001/55/EC of 20 July 2001 on minimum standards for giving temporary protection in the event of influx of displaced persons and on measures promoting a balance of efforts between Member States in receiving such persons and bearing the consequences thereof, OJ L 212/12, 7.8.2001.

Council Directive 2001/51/EC of 28 June 2001 supplementing the provisions of Article 26 of the Convention implementing the Schengen Agreement of 14 June 1985, OJ L 187/45, 10.7.2001.

Council Regulation (EC) No 1091/2001 of 28 May 2001 of freedom of movement with a long-stay visa, OJ L 150/4, 6.6.2001.

Council Decision 2001/420/EC of 28 May 2001 on the adaptation of Parts V and VI and Annex of the Common Consular Instructions on Visas and Annex 6a to the Common Manual with regard to long-stay visas valid concurrently as short-stay visas, OJ L 150/47, 6.6.2001.

Council Directive 2001/40/EC of 28 May 2001 on the mutual recognition of decisions on the expulsion of third country nationals, OJ L 149/34, 2.6.2001.

Council Regulation (EC) No 789/2001 of 24 April 2001 reserving to the Council implementing powers with regard to certain detailed provisions and practical procedures for examining visa applications, OJ L 116/2, 26.4.2001.

Council Regulation (EC) No 790/2001 of 24 April 2001 reserving to the Council implementing powers with regard to certain detailed provisions and practical procedures for carrying out border checks and surveillance, OJ L 116/5, 26.4.2001.

Council Decision 2001/329/EC of 24 April 2001 updating part VI and Annexes 3, 6 and 13 of the Common Consular Instructions and Annexes 5(a), 6(a) and 8 of the Common Manual, OJ L 116/32, 26.4.2001.

Council Regulation (EC) No 539/2001 of 15 March 2001 listing the third countries whose nationals must be in possession of visas when crossing the external borders and those whose nationals are exempt from that requirement, OJ L 81/1, 21.4.2001.

Council Regulation (EC) No 44/2001 of 22 December 2000 on jurisdiction and the recognition and enforcement of judgments in civil and commercial matters, OJ L 12 /1, 15.1.2001.

Council Decision 2000/820/JHA of 22 December 2000 establishing a European Police College (CEPOL), OJ L 336/1, 30.12.2000.

Charter of Fundamental Rights of the European Union, OJ C 364/1, 18.12.2000.

Council Decision 2000/777/EC of 1 December 2000 on the application of the Schengen *acquis* in Denmark, Finland and Sweden and in Iceland and Norway, OJ L 309/24, 9.12.2000.

Council Directive 2000/78/EC establishing a general framework for equal treatment in employment and occupation, OJ L 303/16, 2.12.2000.

Council Decision 2000/750/EC of 27 November 2000 establishing a Community action programme to combat discrimination (2001 to 2006), OJ L 303/23, 2.12.2000.

Council Decision 2000/751/EC of 30 November 2000 on declassifying certain parts of the Common Manual adopted by the Executive Committee established by the Convention implementing the Schengen Agreement of 14 June 1985, OJ L 303/29, 2.12.2000.

The Schengen *acquis* as referred to in Article 1 (2) of Council Decision 1999/435/EC of 20 May 1999, OJ L 239, 22.9.2000.

Decision of the Executive Committee of 28 April 1999 on the definitive versions of the Common Manual and the Common Consular Instructions (SCH/Com-ex (99) 13), OJ L 239/317, 22.9.2000.

Decision of the Executive Committee of 28 April 1999 on the compilation of a manual of documents to which a visa may be affixed (SCH/Com-ex (99) 14), OJ L 239/298, 22.9.2000.

Decision of the Executive Committee of 18 December 1998 concerning the compilation of a manual of documents to which a visa may be affixed (SCH/Com-ex (98) 56), OJ L 239/297, 22.9.2000.

Decision of the Executive Committee of 16 December 1998 on the abolition of the grey list of States whose nationals are subject to the visa requirement by certain Schengen States (SCH/Com-ex (98) 53 rev. 2), OJ L 239/206, 22.9.2000.

Decision of the Executive Committee of 27 October 1998 on the adoption of measures to fight against illegal immigration (SCH/Com-ex (98) 37 def. 2), OJ L 239/203, 22.9.2000.

Decision of the Central Group of 27 October 1998 on the adoption of measures to fight against illegal immigration (SCH/C (98) 117), OJ L 239/205, 22.9.2000.

Decision of the Executive Committee of 16 September 1998 setting up a Standing Committee on the evaluation and implementation of Schengen (SCH/Com-ex (98) 26 def.), OJ L 239/138, 22.9.2000.

Decision of the Executive Committee of 23 June 1998 on measures to be taken in respect of countries posing problems with regard to the issue of documents for expulsion form the Schengen territory, (SCH/Com-ex (98) 18 rev.) OJ L 239/197, 22.9.2000.

Decision of the Executive Committee of 21 April 1998 on cooperation between the Contracting Parties in returning foreign nationals by air (SCH/Com-ex (98) 10) OJ L 239/193, 22.9.2000.

Decision of the Executive Committee of 21 April 1998 on the exchange of statistics on issued visas (SCH/Com-ex (98) 12), OJ L 239/196, 22.9.2000.

Decision of the Executive Committee of 15 December 1997 on the implementation of the Joint Action concerning a uniform format for residence permits (SCH/Com-ex (97) 34 rev.), OJ L 239/187, 22.9.2000.

Decision of the Executive Committee of 15 December 1997 on the guiding principles for means of proof and indicative evidence within the framework of readmission agreements between Schengen States (SCH/Com-ex (97) 39 rev.) OJ L 239/188, 22.9.2000.

Decision of the Executive Committee of 15 December 1997 on the harmonisation of visa policy (SCH/Com-ex (97) 32), OJ 239/186, 22.9.2000.

Declaration of the Executive Committee of 18 April 1996 defining the concept of alien (SCH/Com-ex (96) decl. 5) OJ L 23/458, 22.9.2000.

Decision of 20 December 1995 on the procedure for applying Article 2 (2) of the Convention implementing the Schengen Agreement (SCH/Com-ex (95) 20 rev.2), OJ L 239/133, 22.9.2000.

Decision of the Executive Committee of 20 December 1995 on the swift exchange between the Schengen States of statistical and specific data on possible malfunctions at the external borders (SCH/Com-ex (95) 21), OJ L 239/176, 22.9.2000.

Decision of the Executive Committee of 22 December 1994 on the exchange of statistical information on the issuing of uniform visas (SCH/Com-ex (94) 25), OJ L 239/173, 22.9.2000.

Decision of the Executive Committee of 22 December 1994 introducing and applying the Schengen arrangements in airports and arrangements (SCH/Com-ex (94) 17 rev. 4), OJ L 239/168, 22.9.2000.

Decision of the Executive Committee of 21 November 1994 introducing a computerised procedure for consulting the central authorities referred to in Article 17 (2) of the Convention (SCH/Com-ex (94) 15 rev.), OJ L 239/165, 22.9.2000.

Decision of the Executive Committee of 21 November 1994 on the acquisition of common entry and exit stamps (SCH/Com-ex (94) 16 rev.), OJ L 239/166, 22.9.2000.

Agreement on the Accession of the Hellenic Republic, signed at Madrid on 6 November 1992, OJ L 239/83, 22.9.2000.

Council Directive 2000/43/EC of 29 June 2000 implementing the principle of equal treatment between persons irrespective of racial or ethnic origin, OJ L 180/22, 19.7.2000.

Council Decision 2000/365/EC of 29 May 2000 concerning the request of the United Kingdom to take part in some of the provisions of the Schengen *acquis* OJ L 131/43, 1.6.2000.

Agreement concluded by the Council of the European Union and the Republic of Iceland and the Kingdom of Norway on the establishment of rights and obligations between Ireland and the United Kingdom of Great Britain and Northern Ireland, on the one hand, and the Republic of Iceland and the Kingdom of Norway, on the other, in areas of the Schengen *acquis* which apply to these States, OJ L 15/2, 20.1.2000.

Council Decision 2000/23/EC of 6 December 1999 on the improvement of information on the Council's legislative activities and the public register of Council documents, OJ L 9/22, 13.1.2000.

Council Decision 1999/848/EC of 13 December 1999 on the full application of the Schengen *acquis* in Greece, OJ L 327/58, 21.12.1999.

Council Decision 1999/438/EC of 28 June 1999 laying down the procedures for the exercise of implementing powers conferred on the Commission, OJ L 184/23, 17.7.1999.

Council Decision 1999/435/EC of 20 May 1999 concerning the definition of the Schengen *acquis* for the purpose of determining, in conformity with the relevant provisions of the Treaty establishing the European Community and the Treaty on European Union, the legal basis for each of the provisions or decisions which constitute the *acquis*, OJ L 176/1, 10.7.1999.

Council Decision 1999/436/EC of 20 May 1999 determining, in conformity with the relevant provisions of the Treaty establishing the European Community and the Treaty on European Union, the legal basis for each of the provisions or decisions which constitute the Schengen *acquis,* OJ L 176/17, 10.7.1999.

Council Decision 1999/437/EC of 17 May 1999 on certain arrangements for the application of the Agreement concluded by the Council of the European Union and the Republic of Iceland and the Kingdom of Norway concerning the association of those two States with the implementation, application and development of the Schengen *acquis*, OJ C 176/31, 10.7.1999.

Council Decision 1999/439/EC of 17 May 1999 on the conclusion of the Agreement with the Republic of Iceland and the Kingdom of Norway concerning the latter's association with implementation, application and development of the Schengen acquis, OJ L 176/35, 10.7.1999 and Agreement concluded by the Council of the European Union and the Republic of Iceland and the Kingdom of Norway concerning the latters' association with the implementation, application and development of the Schengen *acquis* OJ C 176/36, 10.7.1999.

Council Decision 1999/438/EC of 20 May 1999 concerning the Joint Supervisory Authority set up under Article 115 of the Convention applying the Schengen Agreement of 14 June 1985, on the gradual abolition of checks at common borders, signed on 19 June 1990, OJ L 176/34, 10.7.1999.

Council Decision 1999/307/EC of 1 May 1999 laying down the detailed arrangements for the integration of the Schengen Secretariat into the General Secretariat of the Council, OJ 117/49, 7.5.1999.

Council Regulation (EC) No 574/1999 of 12 March 1999 determining the third countries whose nationals must be in possession of visas when crossing the external borders of the Member States, OJ L 72/2, 18.3.1999.

Joint Action 98/700/JHA of 3 December 1998 adopted by the Council on the basis of Article K.3 of the Treaty on European Union concerning the setting up of a European Image Archiving System (FADO), OJ L 333/4, 9.12.1998.

Council Decision 98/701/JHA of 3 December 1998 on common standards relating to filling in the uniform format for residence permits, OJ L 333/8, 9.12.1998.

Joint Action 97/11/JHA of 16 December 1996 adopted by the Council on the basis of Article K.3 of the Treaty on European Union concerning a uniform format for residence permits, OJ C 193/1, 16.9.1998.

Council Recommendation of 28 May 1998 on the provision of forgery detection equipment at ports of entry to the European Union, OJ C 189/19, 17.6.1998.

Joint Action 98/304/EC of 27 April 1998 adopted by the Council on the basis of Article K.3 of the Treaty on European Union, concerning the financing of specific projects in favour of displaced persons who have found temporary protection in the Member States and asylum seekers, OJ L 138/6, 9.5.1998.

Joint Action 98/305/EC of 27 April 1998 adopted by the Council on the basis of Article K.4 of the Treaty on European Union, concerning the financing of specific projects in favour of asylum seekers and refugees, OJ L 138/8, 9.5.1998.

Council Decision 98/243/JHA of 19 March 1998 on the sharing of the costs of preparing film masters for the uniform format for residence permits, OJ L 99/1, 31.3.1998.

Joint Action 98/244/JHA of 19 March 1998 adopted by the Council on the basis of Article K.3 of the Treaty on European Union, introducing a programme of training, exchanges and cooperation in the field of asylum, immigration and crossing of external borders (Odysseus-programme), OJ L 99/2, 31.3.1998.

Council Resolution of 4 December 1997 on measures to be adopted on the combating of marriages of convenience, OJ C 382/1, 16.12.1997.

Joint Action 97/477/JHA of 22 July 1997 adopted by the Council on the basis of Article K.3 of the Treaty on European Union, concerning the financing of specific projects in favour of displaced persons who have found temporary protection in the Member States and asylum-seeker, OJ L 205/3, 31.7.1997.

Joint Action 97/478/JHA of 22 July 1997 adopted by the Council on the basis of Article K.3 of the Treaty on European Union, concerning the financing of specific projects in favour of asylum-seekers and refugees, OJ L 205/5, 31.7.1997.

Council Decision 97/340/JHA of 26 May 1997 on the exchange of information concerning assistance for the voluntary repatriation of third-country nationals, OJ L 147/3, 5.6.1997.

Joint Action 97/154/JHA of 24 February 1997 adopted by the Council on the basis of Article K.3 of the Treaty on European Union concerning action to combat trafficking in human beings and sexual exploitation of children, OJ L 63/2, 4.3.1997.

Joint Action 97/11/JHA of December 1996 adopted by the Council on the basis of Article K.3 of the Treaty on European Union concerning a uniform format for residence permits, OJ L 7/1, 10.1.1997.

Joint Action 97/12/JHA of 20 December 1996 adopted by the Council on the basis of Article K.3 of the Treaty on European Union providing a common programme for the exchange and training of, and cooperation between , law enforcement authorities ('Oisin'), OJ L 7/5, 10.1.1997.

Council Decision 1996/749/JHA of 16 December 1996 on monitoring the implementation of instruments adopted by the Council concerning illegal immigration, readmission, the unlawful employment of third country nationals and cooperation in the implementation of expulsion orders, OJ L 342/5, 31.12.1996.

Joint Action 96/700/JHA of 29 November 1996 adopted by the Council on the basis of Article K.3 of the Treaty on European Union, establishing an incentive and exchange programme for persons responsible for combating trade in human beings and the sexual exploitation of children, OJ L 322/7, 10.1.1996.

Joint Action 96/637/JHA of 28 October 1996 adopted by the Council on the basis of Article K.3 of the Treaty on European Union introducing a programme of training, exchanges and cooperation in the field of identity documents ('Sherlock'), OJ L 287/7, 8.11.1996.

Joint Action 96/602/JHA of 14 October 1996 adopted by the Council on the basis of Article K.3 of the Treaty on European Union providing for a common framework for the initiatives of the Member States concerning liaison officers, OJ L 268/2, 19.10.1996.

Council Recommendation of 27 September 1996 on combating the illegal employment of third-country nationals, OJ C 304/1, 14.10.1996.

Council Decision of 23 November 1995 on publication in the Official Journal of the European Communities of acts and other texts adopted by the Council in the field of asylum and immigration, OJ C 274/1, 19.9.1996.

Council Resolution of 20 June 1994 on limitation on admission of third country nationals to the territory of the Member States for employment, OJ C 274/3, 19.9.1996.

Council Resolution of 30 November 1994 relating to the limitations on the admission of third country nationals to the territory of the Member States for the purpose of pursuing activities of self-employed persons, OJ C 274/7, 19.9.1996.

Council Resolution of 30 November 1994 on the admission of third-country nationals to the territory of the Member States for study purposes, OJ C 274/10, 19.9.1996.

Council Recommendation of 30 November 1994 concerning the adoption of a standard travel document for the expulsion of third-country nationals, OJ C 274/18, 19.9.1996.

Council recommendation of 30 November 1994 concerning a specimen bilateral readmission agreement between a Member State and a third country, OJ C 274/20, 19.9.1996.

Council Recommendation of 24 July 1995 on the guiding principles to be followed in drawing up protocols on the implementation of readmission agreements, OJ C 274/25, 19.9.1996.

Council Conclusions of 30 November 1994 on the organization and development of the Centre for Information, Discussion and Exchange on the Crossing of Frontiers and Immigration (Cirefi), OJ C 274/50, 19.9.1996.

Second activity report on the Centre for Information, Discussion and Exchange on Asylum (Cirea) (Text adopted by the Council on 20 June 1994), OJ C 274/55, 19.9.1996.

Honorary consuls already empowered to issue visas who, as a transitional measure, will be allowed to issue uniform visas (Text adopted by the council on 20 June 1994), OJ C 274/58, 19.9.1996.

Council Recommendation of 4 March 1996 relating to local consular cooperation regarding visas, OJ C 80/1, 18.3.1996.

Council Resolution of 4 March 1996 on the status of third-country nationals residing on a long-term basis in the territory of the Member States, OJ C 80/2, 18.3.1996.

Joint Action 96/197/JHA of 4 March 1996 adopted by the Council on the basis of Article K.3 of the Treaty on the European Union on airport transit arrangements, OJ L 63/8, 13.3.1996.

Council Decision 96/198/JHA of 4 March 1996 on an alert and emergency procedure for burden-sharing with regard to the admission and residence of displaced persons on a temporary basis, OJ L 63/10, 13.3.1996.

Council Decision of 22 December 1995 on monitoring the implementation of instruments already adopted concerning admission of third-country nationals, OJ C 11/1, 16.1.1996.

Council Recommendation concerning transit for the purposes of expulsion, OJ C 5/5, 10.1.1996.

Council Recommendation of 22 December 1995 on concerted action and cooperation in carrying out expulsion measures, OJ C 5/3, 10.1.1996.

Council Recommendation of 22 December 1995 on harmonising means of combating illegal immigration and illegal employment and improving the relevant means of control, OJ C 5/1, 10.1.1996.

Council Resolution of 25 September 1995 on burden- sharing with regard to the admission and residence of displaced persons on a temporary basis, OJ C 262/1, 7.10.1995.

Council Regulation (EC) No 2317/95 of 25 September 1995 determining the third countries whose nationals must be in possession of visas when crossing the external borders of the Member States, OJ L 234/1, 3.10.1995.

Council Regulation (EC) No 1683/95 of 29 May 1995 laying down a uniform format for visas, OJ L 164/1, 14.7.1995.

Council Decision 94/795/JHA of 30 November 1994 on a joint action adopted by the Council on the basis of Article K.3.2.b of the Treaty on European Union concerning travel facilities for school pupils from third countries resident in a Member State, OJ L 327/1, 19.12.1994.

Commission Decision 88/384/EEC of 8 June 1988 setting up a prior communication and consultation procedure on migration policies in relation to non-member countries, OJ L 183/35, 14.7.1988.

Council Resolution of 16 July 1985 on guidelines for a Community policy on migration, OJ C 186/3, 26.7.1985.

Commission Decision 85/381/EEC of 8 July 1985 setting up a prior communication and consultation procedure on migration policies in relation to non member countries, OJ L 217/25, 14.8.1985.

Conclusions of the Council of 22 June 1984 concerning a Community medium-term social action programme, OJ C 175/1, 4.7.1984.

Council Resolution of 27 June 1980 on guidelines for a Community labour market policy, OJ C 168/1, 8.7.1980.

Council Directive 77/486/EEC on the education of children of migrant workers, OJ L 199/32, 6.8.1977.

Council Resolution of 9 February 1976 on an action programme for migrant workers and members of their families, OJ C 34/2, 14.2.1976.

Council Resolution of 21 January 1974 concerning a social action programme, OJ C 13/1, 12.2.1974.

Council Directive 73/148/EEC of 21 May 1973 on the abolition of restrictions on movement and residence within the Community for nationals of Members States with regard to establishment and the provision of services, OJ L 172/14, 28.6.1973.

Regulation (EEC) No 1612/68 of the Council of 15 October 1968 on freedom of movement for workers within the Community, OJ L 257/2, 19.10.1968.

Council Directive 68/360/EEC of 15 October 1968 on the abolition of restrictions on movement and residence within the Community for workers of Member States and their families, OJ L 257/13, 19.10.1968.

Council Directive 64/221/EEC of 25 February 1964 on the co-ordination of special measures concerning the movement and residence of foreign nationals which are justified on grounds of public policy, public security or public health, OJ L 56/850, 4.4.1964.

C. Legislative proposals

Proposal for a Council Decision concerning access for consultation of the Visa Information System (VIS) by the authorities of Member States responsible for internal security and by Europol for the purposes of the prevention, detection and investigation of terrorist offences and of other serious criminal offences, COM (2005) 600 final, 24.11.2005.

Proposal for a Council Decision on the establishment of a mutual information procedure concerning Member States' measures in the areas of asylum and immigration, COM (2005) 480 final, 10.10.2005.

Proposal for a Regulation of the European Parliament and of the Council on Community statistics on migration and international protection, COM (2005) 375 final, 14.9.2005.

Proposal for a Regulation of the European Parliament and of the Council relating to measures envisaged to facilitate the procedures for applying for and issuing visas for members of the Olympic family taking part in the 2006 Olympic and /or Paralympic Winter Games in Turin, COM (2005) 412 final, 7.9.2005.

Proposal for a European Parliament and Council directive on common standards on procedures in Member States for returning illegally staying third country nationals, COM (2005) 391 final, 1.9.2005.

Proposal for a Decision of the European Parliament and of the Council introducing a simplified regime for the control of persons at the external borders based on the unilateral recognition by Czech Republic, Estonia, Cyprus, Latvia, Lithuania,

Hungary, Malta, Poland, Slovenia, Slovakia of certain documents as equivalent to their national visas for the purposes of transit through their territories & Proposal for a Decision of the European Parliament and the Council establishing a simplified regime for the control of persons at the external borders based on the unilateral recognition by the Member States of certain residence permits issued by Switzerland and Liechtenstein for the purpose of transit through their territory, COM (2005) 381 final, 22.8.2005.

Council Decision 2005/…/JHA of amending Decision 2003/170/JHA on the common use of liaison officers posted abroad by the law enforcement agencies of the Member States, OJ C 188/19, 2.8.2005

Proposal for a Council Regulation establishing a European Union Agency for Fundamental Rights and Proposal for a Council Decision empowering the European Union Agency for Fundamental Rights to pursue its activities in areas referred to in Title VI of the Treaty on European Union, COM (2005) 280 final, 30.6.2005.

Proposal for a Regulation of the European Parliament and of the Council on the establishment, operation and use of the second generation Schengen information system (SIS II), COM (2005) 236 final, 31.5.2005.

Proposal for a Council Decision on the establishment, operation and use of the second generation Schengen information system (SIS II), COM (2005) 230 final, 31.5.2005.

Communication from the Commission to the Council and the European Parliament establishing a framework programme on Solidarity and the Management of Migration Flows for the period 2007-2013

- Proposal for a Decision of the European Parliament and the Council establishing the European Refugee Fund for the period 2008-2013 as part of the General programme 'Solidarity and Management of Migration Flows'
- Proposal for a Council Decision establishing the European Fund for the Integration of third-country nationals for the period 2007-2013 as part of the General programme 'Solidarity and Management of Migration Flows'
- Proposal for a Decision of the European Parliament and Council establishing the European Return Fund for the period 2007-2013 as part of the General programme 'Solidarity and Management of Migration Flows', COM (2005) 123 final/2, 2.5.2005.

Proposal for a Regulation of the European Parliament and of the Council laying down rules on local border traffic at the external land borders of the Member States and amending the Schengen Convention and the Common Consular Instructions, COM (2005) 56 final, 23.2.2005.

Proposal for a Council Regulation amending Regulation (EC) No 539/2001 as regards the reciprocity mechanism, COM (2004) 437 final/2, 19.7.2004.

Proposal for a Council Regulation establishing a Community Code on the rules governing the movement of persons across borders, COM (2004) 391 final, 26.5.2004.

Proposal for a Council Decision amending Decision No 2002/463/EC adopting an action programme for administrative cooperation in the fields of external borders, visas, asylum and immigration (ARGO programme), COM (2004) 384 final, 19.5.2004.

Proposal for a Council decision authorising the Commission to negotiate a draft European Convention on the fight against trafficking in human beings, SEC (2004) 519 final, 30.4.2004.

Communication from the Commission to the Council and the European Parliament on the presentation of a proposal for a directive and two proposals for recommendations on the admission of third-country nationals to carry out scientific research in the European Community – Proposal for a Council Directive on a specific procedure for admitting third-country nationals to carry out scientific research in the European Community – Proposal for a Council Recommendation to facilitate the admission of third-country nationals to carry out scientific research in the European Community – Proposal for a Council Recommendation to facilitate the issue by the Member States of uniform short-stay visas for researchers from third countries travelling within the European Community for the purpose of carrying out scientific research, COM (2004) 178 final, 16.3.2004.

Proposal for a Council Regulation on standards for security features and biometrics in EU citizens' passports, COM (2004) 116 final, 18.2.2004.

Proposal for a Council Decision concerning the signing of the Agreement between the European Community and the Republic of Albania on the readmission of persons residing without authorization and Proposal for a Council Decision concerning the conclusion of the Agreement between the European Community and the Republic of Albania on the readmission of persons residing without authorization, COM (2004) 92 final, 12.2.2004.

Proposal for a Council Decision establishing a Visa Information System (VIS), COM (2004) 99 final, 12.2.2004.

Proposal for a Directive of the European Parliament and the Council on services in the internal market, COM (2004) 2 final, 5.3.2004.

Proposal for a Council Decision Establishing a secure web-based Information and Co-ordination Network for Member States' Migration Management Services, COM (2003) 727 final, 25.11.2003.

Proposal for a Council Regulation establishing a European Agency for the Management of Operational Cooperation at the External Borders, COM (2003) 687 final, 11.11.2003.

Proposal for a Council Regulation laying down the requirement for the competent authorities of the Member States to stamp systematically the travel documents of third country nationals when they cross the external borders of the Member States and amending the convention implementing the Schengen agreement and the common manual to this end, COM (2003) 664 final, 6.11.2003.

Proposal for a Regulation amending Regulation (EC) 1683/95 laying down a uniform format for visas and proposal for a Council Regulation amending Regulation (EC)

1030/2002 laying down a uniform format for residence permits for third-country nationals, COM (2003) 558 final, 24.9.2003.

Initiative of the Italian Republic with a view to adopting a Council decision on the organisation of joint flights for removals of third country nationals illegally present in the territory of two or more Member States, OJ C 223/3, 19.9.2003.

Proposal for a Council Regulation on the establishment of a regime of local border traffic at the external land borders of the Member States and Proposal for a Council Regulation on the establishment of a regime of local border traffic at the temporary external land borders between Member States, COM (2003) 502 final, 14.8.2003.

Initiative of the Hellenic Republic with a view to adopting a Council Regulation on the creation of an immigration liaison officers network, OJ C 140/12, 14.6.2003.

Initiative of the Federal Republic of Germany with a view to adopting a Council Directive on assistance in cases of transit for the purposes of removal by air, OJ C 4/4, 9.1.2003.

Proposal for a Council Directive on the conditions of entry and residence of third-country nationals for purposes of studies, vocational training or voluntary service, COM (2002) 548 final, 7.10.2002.

Initiative of the Kingdom of Spain with a view to adopting the Council Regulation (EC) No .../2002 concerning the introduction of some new functions for the Schengen information system, in particular in the fight against terrorism, OJ C 160/5, 4.7.2002.

Initiative of the Kingdom of Spain with a view to adopting the Council Decision 2002/.../JHA concerning the introduction of some new functions for the Schengen information system, in particular in the fight against terrorism, OJ C 160/7, 4.7.2002.

Amended proposal for a Council Directive on the right to family reunification, COM (2002) 225, 2.5.2002.

Proposal for a Council Directive on the short-term residence permit issued to victims of action to facilitate illegal immigration or trafficking in human beings who cooperate with the competent authorities, COM (2002) 71 final, 11.2.2002.

Initiative of the Kingdom of Belgium, the Kingdom of Spain and the French Republic with a view to the adoption by the Council of a Decision amending Article 40 (1) and (7) of the Convention implementing the Schengen Agreement of 14 June 1985 on the gradual abolition of checks at the common borders, OJ C 285/3, 11.10.2001.

Proposal for a Council Regulation amending Regulation (EC) No 1683/95 laying down a uniform format for visas, COM (2001) 577 final, 9.10.2001.

Proposal for a Council Directive on the conditions of entry and residence of third-country nationals for the purpose of paid employment and self-employment economic activities, COM (2001) 386 final, 11.7.2001.

Proposal for a Council Directive relating to the conditions in which third-country nationals shall have the freedom to travel in the territory of the Member States for periods not exceeding three months, introducing a specific travel authorization and determining the conditions of entry and movement for periods not exceeding six months, COM (2001) 388 final, 10.7.2001.

Proposal for a Council Regulation amending Regulation 1683/95 laying down a uniform format for visas – Proposal for a Council Regulation on a uniform format for forms affixing the visa issued by Member States to persons holding travel documents which are not recognized by the Member State drawing up the form, COM (2001) 157 final, 23.3.2001.

Proposal for a Council Directive concerning the status of third-country nationals who are long-term residents, COM (2001) 127 final, 13.3.2001.

Initiative of the Portuguese Republic with a view to adopting a Council Regulation reserving to the Council implementing powers with regard to certain detailed provisions and practical procedures for carrying out border checks and surveillance, OJ C 73/8, 6.3.2001.

Proposal for a Council Framework Decision on combating trafficking in human beings – Proposal for a Council Framework Decision on combating the sexual exploitation of children and child pornography, COM (2000) 854 final, 21.12.2000.

Initiative of the French Republic with a view to the adoption of a Council Framework Decision on the strengthening of the penal framework to prevent the facilitation of unauthorised entry and residence, OJ C 253/6, 4.9.2000.

Initiative of the French Republic with a view to the adoption of a Council Directive defining the facilitation of unauthorised entry, movement and residence, OJ C 253/1, 4.9.2000.

Initiative of the Republic of Finland with a view to the adoption of a Regulation reserving to the Council implementing powers with regard to certain detailed provisions and practical procedures for examining visa applications, OJ C 164/7, 14.6.2000.

Initiative of the Portuguese Republic with a view to adopting a Council Regulation on the period during which third country nationals exempt from visa requirements are free to travel within the territory of the Member States, OJ C 164/6, 14.6.2000.

Amended proposal for a Directive of the European Parliament and of the Council on the posting of workers who are third country nationals for the provision of cross-border services, COM (2000) 271 final, 8.5.2000.

Amended proposal for a Council Directive on the right to family reunification, COM (2000) 624 final, 10.10.2000.

Proposal for a Council Regulation determining the list of third countries whose nationals must be in possession of visas when crossing the external borders and those whose nationals are exempt from that requirement, COM (2000) 27 final, 26.1.2000.

Initiative of the Republic of Finland with a view to the adoption of a Council Regulation determining obligations as between the Member States for the readmission of third-country nationals, OJ C 353/6, 7.12.1999.

Proposal for a Council Directive on the right to family reunification, COM (1999) 638, 1.12.1999.

Proposal for a directive of the European Parliament and of the Council on the posting of workers who are third-country nationals for the provision of cross-border services – Proposal for a Council directive extending the freedom to provide cross-border services to third-country nationals established within the Community, COM (1999) 3 final, 26.2.1999.

Proposal for a Council Act establishing the Convention on the rules for the admission of third-country nationals to the Member States, COM (1997) 387 final, 30.7.1997.

Proposal for a Council Directive on the right of third country nationals to travel in the Community, COM (1995) 346 final, 12.7.1995.

Proposal for a Council Directive on the elimination of controls on persons crossing internal borders, COM (95) 347 final, 12.7.1995.

Proposal for a European Parliament and Council Directive amending Directive 68/360/EEC on the abolition of restrictions on movement and residence within the Community for workers of Member States and their families and Directive 73/148/EEC on the abolition of restrictions on movement and residence within the Community for nationals of Member States with regard to establishment and the provision of services, COM (95) 348 final, 12.7.1995.

Proposal for a Decision, based on Article K.3 of the Treaty on European Union establishing the Convention on the crossing of the external frontiers of the Member States and Proposal for a Regulation, based on Article 100 C of the Treaty establishing the European Community, determining the third countries whose nationals must be in possession of visas when crossing the external borders of the Member States, COM (93) 684 final, 10.12.1993.

Amendment to proposal for a Council Directive on the easing of controls and formalities applicable to nationals of the Member States when crossing intra-Community borders, COM (85) 224 final, 7.5.1985.

Proposal for a Council Directive on the easing of controls and formalities applicable to nationals of the Member States when crossing intra-Community borders, COM (84) 749 final, 24.1.1985.

Amended proposal for a Council Directive concerning the approximation of the legislation of the Member States, in order to combat illegal migration and illegal employment, OJ 1978 C 97/9, 22.4.1978.

Proposal for a Council Directive on the harmonization of laws in the Member States to combat illegal migration and illegal employment, OJ C 277/2, 23.11.1976.

Proposal for a Council Directive on the education of the children of migrant workers, OJ C 213/2, 17.9.1975.

D. Official Documents

1. *European Commission Documents*

Report from the Commission to the Council on visa waiver reciprocity with certain third countries in accordance with Article 2 of Council Regulation (EC) 851/2005 of 2 June 2005 amending Regulation (EC) No 539/2001 listing the third countries whose nationals must be in possession of visas when crossing the external borders and those whose nationals are exempt from that requirement as regards the reciprocity mechanism, COM (2006) 3 final, 10.1.2006.

Communication from the Commission Policy Plan on Legal Migration, COM (2005) 669 final, 21.12.2005.

Communication from the Commission to the Council and the European Parliament Priority actions for responding to the challenges of migration: First follow-up to Hampton Court, COM (2005) 621 final, 30.11.2005.

Green Paper on the future of the European Migration Network, COM (2005) 606 final, 28.11.2005.

Communication from the Commission to the Council and the European Parliament on improved effectiveness, enhanced interoperability and synergies among European databases in the area of Justice and Home Affairs, COM (2005) 597 final, 24.11.2005.

Communication from the Commission to the European Parliament and the Council on the implications of the Court's Judgement of 13 September 2005 (Case C-176/03 Commission v. Council), COM (2005) 583 final, 23.11.2005.

Communication from the Commission to the European Parliament, the Council, the European Economic and Social Committee and the Committee of the Regions Unlocking Europe's full potential Commission Legislative and Work Programme 2006, COM (2005) 531 final, 25.10.2005.

Communication from the Commission A Strategy on the External Dimension of the Area of Freedom, Security and Justice, COM (2005) 491 final, 12.10.2005.

Communication from the Commission to the Council, the European Parliament and the European Economic and Social Committee EU Strategy for Africa: Towards a Euro-African pact to accelerate Africa's development, COM (2005) 489 final, 12.10.2005.

Preparatory Actions for return management in the area of migration – Call for proposals 2005, OJ C 224/11, 13.9.2005.

Communication from the Commission to the Council, the European Parliament, the European Economic and Social Committee and the Committee of the Regions Migration and Development: Some concrete orientations, COM (2005) 390 final, 1.9.2005

Communication from the Commission to the Council, the European Parliament, the European Economic and Social Committee and the Committee of the Regions A

Common Agenda for Integration Framework for the Integration of Third-Country Nationals in the European Union, COM (2005) 389 final, 1.9.2005

Communication from the Commission to the Council and the European Parliament – External Actions through Thematic Programmes under the Future Financial Perspectives 2007-2013, COM (2005) 324 final, 3.8.2005.

Communication from the Commission to the Council on the monitoring and evaluation mechanism of the third countries in the field of the fight against illegal immigration, COM (2005) 352 final, 28.7.2005.

Communication from the Commission to the Council and the European Parliament The Hague Programme: Ten priorities for the next five years The Partnership for European renewal in the field of Freedom, Security and Justice, COM (2005) 184 final, 10.5.2005.

Communication from the Commission Green Book on demographic changes A solidarity between generations, COM (2005) 94 final, 16.3.2005.

Commission Staff Working Paper Review of the Afghanistan Return Plan, SEC (2005) 340, 4.3.2005.

Green Paper on an EU approach to managing economic migration (COM (2004) 811 final, 11.1.2005.

Proposal for a Regulation of the European Parliament and of the Council concerning the Visa Information System (VIS) and the exchange of data between Member States on short-stay visas, COM (2004) 835 final, 28.12.2004.

European Commission, DG Justice, Freedom and Security, *Handbook on integration for policy makers and practitioners,* November 2004, written by the Migration Policy Group, Brussels, available at <http://europa.eu.int/comm/justice_home/doc_centre/immigration/integration/doc/handbook_en.pdf>

Communication from the Commission to the Council and to the European Parliament – Report on the priorities for the successful development of a common readmission policy, SEC (2004) 946 final, 19.7.2004.

Communication from the Commission to the Council, the European Parliament, the European Economic and Social Committee and the Committee of the Regions – First Annual Report on Migration and Integration, COM (2004) 508 final, 16.7.2004.

Communication from the Commission to the Council, the European Parliament, the European Economic and Social Committee and the Committee of Regions – Study on the links between legal and illegal migration, COM (2004) 412 final, 4.6.2004.

Commission Staff Working Paper 'The Area of Freedom, Security and Justice: assessment of the Tampere programme and future orientations – List of the most important instruments adopted', SEC (2004) 680, 2.6.2004.

Communication from the Commission to the Council and the European Parliament – Area of Freedom, Security and Justice: Assessment of the Tampere programme and future orientations, COM (2004) 402 final, 2.6.2004.

Communication from the Commission to the Council and the European Parliament on the Development of the Schengen Information System II and possible synergies with a future Visa Information System, COM (2003) 771 final, 11.12.2003.

Commission Staff Working Paper – Intensified cooperation on the management of migration flows with third countries – Report by the Commission's Services on the implementation of the Council conclusions on intensified co-operation on the management of migration flows with third countries of 18 November 2002, SEC (2003) 815, 9.7.2003.

Commission Staff Working Document on the recasting of the Common Manual: towards a "Community Borders Code as regards Movement of Persons"?, SEC (2003) 736, 20.6.2003. [Council doc. 10843/03 FRONT 82 COMIX 405, 24.6.2003]

Communication from the Commission to the Council, the European Parliament, the European Economic and Social Committee and the Committee of the Regions on immigration, integration and employment, COM (2003) 336 final, 3.6.2003.

Communication from the Commission to the European Parliament and the Council in view of the European Council of Thessaloniki on the development of a common policy on illegal immigration, smuggling and trafficking of human beings, external borders and the return of illegal residents, COM (2003) 323 final, 3.6.2003.

Commission Communication on Investing in Research: an Action Plan for Europe, COM (2003) 226 final, 30.4.2003.

Communication from the Commission to the Council and the European Parliament to present an Action Plan for the collection and analysis of Community Statistics in the field of migration, COM (2003) 179 final, 15.4.2003.

Commission Working Document Developing the *acquis* on local border traffic, SEC (2002) 947 final.

Communication from the Commission to the Council and the European Parliament "Integrating migration Issues in the European Union's relations with third countries: I. Migration and Development, II. Report on the effectiveness of financial resources available at Community level for repatriation of immigrants and rejected asylum seekers, for management of external borders and for asylum and migration projects in third countries", COM (2002) 703 final, 3.12.2002.

Communication from the Commission to the Council and the European Parliament on a Community Return Policy on illegal residents, COM (2002) 564 final, 14.10.2002.

Communication from the Commission to the Council "Kaliningrad: Transit", COM (2002) 510 final, 18.9.2002.

Memorandum for the Commission from Mr Vitorino, in agreement with the President, Mr Prodi, Interface between implementation of Title IV of the EC Treaty and the Protocol on the position of Denmark, SEC (2002) 483 final.

Communication from the Commission to the Council and the European Parliament "Towards integrated management of the external borders of the Member States of the European Union", COM (2002) 233 final, 7.5.2002.

Green paper on a Community return policy on illegal residents, COM (2002) 175 final, 10.4.2002.

Commission Working Document "The relationship between safeguarding internal security and complying with international protection obligations and instruments", COM (2001) 743 final, 5.12.2001.

Communication from the Commission to the Council and the European Parliament on a Common Policy on Illegal Immigration, COM (2001) 672 final, 15.11.2001.

Interface entre la mise en oeuvre du Titre IV du TCE et le Protocole sur la position du Danemark: *Est-ce que le Danemark peut participer à la mise en oeuvre des mesures fondées sur le Titr IV du TCE, si oui, sous quelles conditions?*, SEC (2001) 1347, 28.8.2001.

Communication from the Commission to the Council and the European Parliament on an open method of coordination for the Community immigration policy, COM (2001) 387 final, 11.7.2001.

Commission Staff Working Paper – Position concerning the legal base of the French initiative with a view to the adoption of a Council Directive defining the facilitation of unauthorised entry, movement and residence, and the adoption of a Council Framework Decision on the strengthening of the penal framework to prevent the facilitation of unauthorised entry and residence, SEC (2001) 727, 4.5.2001. [Council doc. 8845/01 DROIPEN 45 MIGR 44 COMIX 370, 16.5.2001].

European Commission, Memorandum from the President and Mr Vitorino – Application of the Charter of Fundamental Rights of the European Union, SEC (2001) 380/3, 13.3.2001.

Communication from the Commission to the Council: the EU and Kaliningrad, COM (2001) 26 final, 17.1.2001.

Communication from the Commission to the Council and the European Parliament on a Community Immigration policy, COM (2000) 757 final, 22.11.2000.

Commission Opinion on the request by Ireland to take part in some of the provisions of the Schengen *acquis*, SEC (2000) 1439 final, 14.9.2000.

Commission Opinion on the request by the United Kingdom to take part in some of the provisions of the Schengen *acquis*, SEC (1999) 1198 final.

Commission Communication to the Council and the European Parliament on the special measures concerning the movement and residence of citizens of the Union which are justified on grounds of public policy public security or public health, COM (1999) 372 final, 19.7.1999.

Communication from the Commission Towards an Area of Freedom, Security and Justice, COM (1998) 459 final, 14.7.1998.

Communication from the Commission to the European Parliament and the Council on the possible application of Article K.9 of the Treaty on European Union, COM (95) 566 final, 22.11.1995.

Communication from the Commission to the Council and the European Parliament on Immigration and Asylum policies, COM (94) 23 final, 23.2.1994.

Report on the possibility of applying Article K.9 of the Treaty on the European Union to asylum policy, SEC 1687/4, 3.11.1993.

Commission Communication to the Council and the Parliament on Abolition of Border Controls, SEC (92) 877/5 final, 5.5.1992.

Communication from the Commission to the Council and the Parliament "Abolition of frontier controls", COM (91) 549 final, 18.12.1991.

Commission Communication to the Council and the European Parliament on Migration, SEC (91) 1855 final, 23.10.1991.

Sixth Report of the Commission to the Council and the European Parliament concerning the implementation of the White Paper on the Completion of the Internal Market, COM (91) 237 final, 19.6.1991.

Progress Report required by Article 8b of the Treaty "Completing the Internal Market: an area without internal frontiers", COM (90) final, 23.11.1990.

Policies on Migration and the Social Integration of Migrants in the European Community, SEC (90) 1813 final, 28.9.1990.

Commission Report on the social integration of third country migrants residing on a permanent and lawful basis in the Member States, SEC (89) 924 final, 22.6.1989.

Communication of the Commission on the abolition of controls of persons at intra-Community borders, COM (88) 640 final, 16.1.1989.

White Paper from the Commission to the European Council "Completing the Internal Market", COM (85) 310 final, 14.6.1985.

Commission Guidelines for a Community policy on migration, COM (85) 48 final, 1.3.1985.

Communication of the Commission on Guidelines for a Community labour market policy, COM (79) 115 final, 23.3.1979.

Scoreboard to review progress on the creation of an area of freedom, security and justice

Communication from the Commission to the Council and the European Parliament "Biannual update of the Scoreboard to review progress on the creation of an Area of "Freedom, Security and Justice" in the European Union (second half of 2003) COM (2003) 812 final, 30.12.2003.

Communication from the Commission to the Council and the European Parliament "Biannual update of the Scoreboard to review progress on the creation of an Area of "Freedom, Security and Justice" in the European Union (first half of 2003) COM (2003) 291 final, 22.5.2003.

Communication from the Commission to the Council and the European Parliament "Biannual update of the Scoreboard to review progress on the creation of an Area of "Freedom, Security and Justice" in the European Union (second half of 2002) COM (2002) 738 final, 16.12.2002.

Communication from the Commission to the Council and the European Parliament "Biannual update of the Scoreboard to review progress on the creation of an Area of "Freedom, Security and Justice" in the European Union (first half of 2002) COM (2002) 261 final, 30.5.2002.

Communication from the Commission to the Council and the European Parliament "Biannual update of the Scoreboard to review progress on the creation of an Area of "Freedom, Security and Justice" in the European Union (second half of 2001) COM (2001) 628 final, 30.10.2001.

Communication from the Commission to the Council and the European Parliament "Biannual update of the Scoreboard to review progress on the creation of an Area of "Freedom, Security and Justice" in the European Union (first half of 2001) COM (2001) 278 final, 23.5.2001.

Communication from the Commission to the Council and the European Parliament "Biannual update of the Scoreboard to review progress on the creation of an Area of "Freedom, Security and Justice" in the European Union", (second half of 2000) COM (2000) 782 final, 30.11.2000.

Communication from the Commission to the Council and the European Parliament "Biannual update of the Scoreboard to review progress on the creation of an Area of "Freedom, Security and Justice" in the European Union (first half of 2000), COM (2000) 167 final/2, 13.4.2000.

2. *Council Documents*

JHA External Relations Multi-Presidency Work Programme, Council doc. 5003/06 JAI 1 RELEX 1, 3.1.2006.

Common approach on visa facilitation, Council doc. 16030/05 VISA 328 RELEX 776, 21.12.2005.

European Council, The EU and Africa: Towards a Strategic Partnership, Council doc. 15961/05, 19.12.2005.

Proposal for a Regulation of the European Parliament and of the Council laying down rules on local border traffic at the external land borders of the Member States and amending the Schengen Convention – Approval of the final amendments of compromise, Council doc. 15760/05 FRONT 212 VISA 323 CODEC 1184 COMIX 852, 16.12.2005.

Council Conclusions – Global approach to migration: Priority actions focusing on Africa and the Mediterranean, Council doc. 15744/05 ASIM 66 RELEX 761, 13.12.2005.

EU plan on best practices, standards and procedures for combating and preventing trafficking in human beings, OJ C 311/1, 9.12.2005.

Notification by Iceland concerning visa reciprocity, OJ C 310/1, 8.12.2005.

Notification by the Kingdom of Norway concerning visa reciprocity, OJ C 310/2, 8.12.2005.

Note from the Presidency on a Strategy for the External Dimension of JHA: Global Freedom, Security and Justice, Council doc. 15446/05 JAI 488 RELEX 741, 6.12.2005.

European Parliament and Council Regulation establishing a Community Code on the rules governing the movement of persons across borders (Schengen Borders code), Council doc. PE-CONS 3643/05 FRONT 129 COMIX 495 CODEC 649 OC 566, 28.11.2005.

Council Conclusions on Migration and External Relations, Council doc. 14769/05 ASIM 58 DEVGEN 228 RELEX 674, 21.11.2005.

Draft Conclusions of the Council and the Representatives of the Governments of the Member States on a common agenda for integration, Council doc. 14613/05 MIGR 69, 18.11.2005.

Notification by Denmark concerning visa reciprocity, OJ C 277/1, 10.11.2005.

Notification by Sweden concerning visa reciprocity, OJ C 277/1, 10.11.2005.

Adoption of the Draft Council Decision authorising the Commission to negotiate with Ukraine a Visa Facilitation Agreement between the European Community and Ukraine, Council doc. 13725/05 VISA 268 NIS 147 COEST 180, 27.10.2005.

Summary of discussions of the Ministerial JHA Troika EU/Russia Permanent Partnership Council (PPC) in Luxembourg on 12/13 October 2005, Council doc. 13557/05 JAI 357 RELEX 539 NIS 145, 20.10.2005.

Notification by the Slovak Republic concerning visa reciprocity, OJ C 251/1, 11.10.2005.

Notification by the Republic of Estonia concerning visa reciprocity, OJ C 251/1, 11.10.2005.

Notification by the Republic of Latvia concerning visa reciprocity, OJ C 251/2, 11.10.2005.

Notification by the Republic of Lithuania concerning visa reciprocity, OJ C 251/8, 11.10.2005.

Note from the French Delegation – Proposal to increase the fees to be charged corresponding to the administrative costs of processing visa applications, Council doc. 13111/05 VISA 242 COMIX 648, 10.10.2005.

Note from the Secretariat General of the Council – Contribution to the debate that should lead by the end of 2005 to a Strategy for JHA External Relations, Council doc. 12850/05 JAI 318 RELEX 491, 4.10.2005.

Draft Council Conclusions on voluntary return, Council doc. 12806/05 MIGR 46 COMIX 626, 3.10.2005.

Council and Commission Action Plan implementing the Hague Programme strengthening Freedom, Security and Justice in the European Union, OJ C 198/1, 12.8.2005.

Notifications by the Czech Republic concerning visas reciprocity, OJ C 163/1, 5.7.2005.

JHA External Relations Multi-Presidency Programme, Council doc. 10728/05 JAI 244 RELEX 355, 1.7.2005.

Council Conclusions on initiating dialogue and cooperation with Libya on migration issues, Council doc. 9796/05 ASIM 24 RELEX 291 LIBYE 5, 6.6.2005.

The Hague Programme strengthening Freedom, Security and Justice in the European Union, OJ C 53/1, 3.3.2005.

Draft Council Conclusions on access to the VIS by Member States authorities responsible for internal security, Council doc. 6899/05 VISA 56 CODEC 121 COMIX 150, 1.3.2005.

Integration of biometric identifiers into the uniform format for visa stickers and residence permits for third-country nationals, Council doc. 5748/05 VISA 24 COMIX 62, 1.2.2005.

Adoption of draft Council conclusions on best practice on return with regard to specific countries of third-country nationals illegally staying on the territory of Member States, Council doc. 15122/04 MIGR 107 COMIX 713, 23.11.2004.

Draft Council conclusions evaluating the progress made with regard to the implementation of the programme of measures to combat illegal immigration across the maritime borders of the Member States of the European Union, Council doc. 15087/04 FRONT 201 COMIX 709, 22.11.2004.

Draft Conclusions of the Council and the Representatives of the Governments of the Member States on the establishment of Common Basic Principles for immigrant integration policy in the European Union, Council doc. 14776/04 MIGR 105, 18.11.2004.

Presidency Conclusions on the Integration Policy Conference, 9-11 November 2004, Kroningen, The Netherlands.

Draft Conclusions on the priorities for the successful development of a common readmission policy, Council doc. 13758/04 JAI 389 MIGR 92 RELEX 459, 27.10.2004.

Proposal for a Common Position of the Council, on the basis of Article 34 of the Treaty on European Union, on negotiations relating to the draft European Convention on Action against Trafficking in Human Beings being undertaken in the Council of Europe, Council doc. 12314/04 CRIMORG 78 JUSTCIV 122 MIGR 71, 13.10.2004.

Presidency Note on the Preparation of the political orientations for the multi-annual programme building the area of freedom, security and justice, Council doc. 11122/04 JAI 258, 9.7.2004.

Questionnaire on best practices in EU Member States with regard to the return of illegal residents to specific countries of origin, Council doc. 11223/04 MIGR 61 COMIX 463, 7.7.2004.

Note of the Netherlands Presidency on JHA External Relations Multi-Presidency Programme, Council doc. 11044/04 JAI 255 RELEX 317, 30.6.2004.

Draft Council Conclusions on ways of giving practical effect to the draft Council Decision on shared organisation on joint flights for removals, from the territory of two or more Member States, of third country nationals who are subject of individual removal orders, Council doc. 8540/04 MIGR 30 COMIX 275, approved by Coreper, Part 2, 30.6.2004.

Draft negotiating directives for an agreement between the EC and the Russian Federation on the facilitation of the issuance of short-stay visas to Union and Russian citizens, Council doc. 11071/04 NIS 100 VISA 130, approved by Coreper, Part 2, 30.6.2004.

Communication from the United Kingdom on its intentions to participate in the adoption of the proposal for a Council Regulation establishing a European Agency for the Management of Operational Cooperation at the External Borders, Council doc. 10658/04 FRONT 114 COMIX 413, 17.6.2004.

Council Conclusions on elements for establishing preparatory actions for a financial instrument for return management in the area of migration, Council doc. 10375/04 MIGR 51, 9.6.2004.

EU Plan of Action on Combating Terrorism, Council doc. 10010/2/04 REV 2 JAI 185, 8.6.2004.

Report to the Council on the implementation of the Declaration on combating terrorism, Council doc. 10009/2/04 REV 2 JAI 184, 8.6.2004.

SIS II functions, Council doc. 10125/04 SIRIS 69 COMIX 378, 3.6.2004.

EU-Switzerland Relations, Council doc. 9544/04 AELE 12, 17.5.2004.

Draft Council Conclusions on the re-examination of the legal basis, format and use of the EU Travel Document, Council doc. 9581/04 MIGR 40, 17.5.2004.

Note form the Secretariat on EU commitments vis-à-vis third countries, Council doc. 9166/04 RELEX 169 PESC 337 JAI 140, 4.5.2004.

EU Council Press Release, Joint Statement on EU Enlargement and EU Russia Relations, Luxembourg, 27 April 2004, Council doc. 8664/04 (Press 122), 27.4.2004.

Draft Council Directive on the obligation of carriers to communicate passenger data – Common Guidelines, Council doc. 8842/04 FRONT 77 COMIX 288 OC 450, 26.4.2004.

I/A Item Note on Council Decision on the organisation of joint flights for removals, from the territory of two or more Member States, of third country nationals who are subjects of individual removal orders, Common Guidelines, Consultation deadline: 29.4.2004, Council doc. 8773/04 MIGR 33 COMIX 280 OC 447, 26.4.2004.

Presidency Note on the Proposal for a Council Regulation on the establishment of a regime of local border traffic at the external borders of the Member States and the Proposal for a Council Regulation on the establishment of a regime of local border traffic at the temporary external land borders between Member States, Council doc. 8083/04 VISA 62 COMIX 240, 1.4.2004.

EU Travel document, Council doc. 6445/04 MIGR 9 COMIX 110, 18.2.2004.

Presidency Note – Implementing Decision on the shared organisation of joint flights for removals, from the territory of two or more Member States, of third country nationals who are subject of individual removal orders, Council doc. 6144/04 MIGR 5 COMIX 90, 10.2.2004.

Communication from Denmark concerning implementation in Danish law pursuant to Article 5 of the Protocol on the position of Denmark, Council doc. 5096/04 VISA 4 FRONT 3 COMIX 13, 9.1.2004.

"I/A" Note – Draft Council Conclusions on assistance in cases of short term transit by land or sea through the territory of another Member State in the course of effecting a removal order adopted by a Member State against a third-country national in the framework of the operational cooperation among Member States, Council doc. 15998/1/03 REV 1 MIGR 111 COMIX 757, 12.12.2003.

Note form the Italian Delegation on International Airports Plan – Air Borders Centre project (Italy), Council doc. 13524/1/03 REV 1 FRONT 141 COMIX 612, 1.12.2003.

Programme of measures to combat illegal immigration across the maritime borders of the Member States of the European Union, Council doc. 15445/03 FRONT 172 COMIX 731, 28.11.2003.

Letter from the Irish Permanent Representative to EU Presidency regarding the opting in of Ireland to the Initiative of the Italian Republic with a view to adopting a Council Decision on the organisation of joint flights for removals, from the territory of two or more Member States, of third country nationals who are the subject of individual removal orders and to the Initiative of the Italian Republic with a view to adopting a Council Directive on assistance in cases of transit through the territory of one or more Member States in the context of removal orders taken by Member States against third-country nationals, Council doc. 15325/03 MIGR 105 COMIX 728, 27.11.2003.

Draft Council Conclusions on the establishment of a monitoring and evaluation mechanism of the third countries in the field of the fight against illegal migration, Council doc. 15292/03 ASIM 72 RELEX 447, 25.11.2003.

Communication from Denmark concerning implementation in Danish law pursuant to Article 5 of the Protocol on the position of Denmark, Council doc. 14822/03 FRONT 159 COMIX 693, 14.11.2003.

Communication from Denmark concerning implementation in Danish law pursuant to Article 5 of the Protocol on the position of Denmark, Council doc. 14807/03 VISA 188 COMIX 692, 14.11.2003.

Notification by Denmark concerning implementation in Danish law pursuant to Article 5 of the Protocol on the position of Denmark, Council doc. 14588/03 VISA 183 FRONT 154 COMIX 675, 14.11.2003.

Council Directive concerning the status of third-country nationals who are long-term residents, Common Guidelines, Consultation deadline: 25 November 2003, Council doc. 14679/03 MIGR 96 OC 705, 14.11.2003.

Letter from the UK Permanent Representative to EU Presidency regarding the opting in of the UK to the Initiative of the Italian Republic with a view to adopting a Council Decision on the organisation of joint flights for removals, from the territory of two or more Member States, of third country nationals who are the subject of individual removal orders, Council doc. 14595/03 MIGR 95 COMIX 676, 11.11.2003.

Note of the Spanish and Greek delegations on Sea Borders Centres, Council doc. 13779/1/03, REV 1, FRONT 145 COMIX 628, 29.10.2003.

Addendum to I/A Item Note – Council Directive on the right to family reunification, Council doc. 10755/03 ADD 1 MIGR 58 OC 439, 14.7.2003.

Draft initiative of the Italian Republic for a Council Directive in cases of transit by land in the context of removal measures taken by Member States against third-country nationals, Council doc. 10909/03 MIGR 61 COMIX 412, 3.7.2003.

Multi-Presidency programme on JHA external relations, Council doc. 11091/03, JAI 202 RELEX 269, 2.7.2003.

Council Conclusions on the development of a policy at European Union level on the integration of third country nationals residing in the territory of the European Union, 10622/03 MIGR 52, 17.6.2003.

Presidency Report on the implementation of programmes, ad hoc centres, pilot project and joint operations, Council doc. 10058/1/03 REV 1 FRONT 70 COMIX 354, 11.6.2003.

Presidency Note on Overall state of play of the negotiations with the Swiss Confederation, Council doc. 10240/03 AELE 23, 6.6.2003.

Council Conclusions on more effective management of external borders of EU States, Council doc. 10059/1/03 REV 1 FRONT 71 COMIX 355, 4.6.2003.

Draft Manual of Best Practices on the acquisition of travel documents and the removal of third-country nationals from Member States' territory, Council doc. 8499/3/03 REV 3 MIGR 27 COMIX 246, 26.5.2003.

Council Decision authorizing the Commission to negotiate with Denmark the conclusion of an Agreement concerning the criteria and mechanisms for establishing the state responsible for examining a request for asylum lodged in Denmark or any other EU Member State, and to negotiate with Iceland and Norway the conclusion of a Protocol pursuant to Article 12 of the Agreement between the European Community and the Republic of Iceland and the Kingdom of Norway concerning the criteria and mechanisms for establishing the State responsible for examining a request for asylum lodged in a Member State or in Iceland or Norway, Council doc. 8314/03 ASILE 24, 6.5.2003.

Draft Council Conclusions on migration and development, Council doc. 8927/03 DEVGEN 59 RELEX 160 JAI 123 ASIM 25, 5.5.2003.

Recommendation for a Council Decision authorizing the Commission to open negotiations for the conclusion of two agreements between the European Community and the Kingdom of Denmark, extending to Denmark the provisions of Regulation (EC) No 44/2001 on jurisdiction and the recognition and enforcement of judgments in civil and commercial matters, and the provisions of Regulation (EC) No 1348/2000 concerning the service in the Member States if judicial and extra-judicial documents in civil or commercial matters – Deadline for consultation: Friday, 2 May 2003, Council doc. 8525/03 JUSTCIV 68, 23.4.2003.

Council of the European Union, EU Schengen Catalogue – Issuing of Visa: Recommendations and Best Practices, March 2003.

Presidency Note on the establishment of ILO network in third countries, 7462/03 CIREFI 10 MIGR 20 COMIX 170, 14.3.2003.

Note of the Greek Delegation on a Proposal to establish a Joint Sea Borders Coordination Centre (JSBCC), Council doc. 7491/03 FRONT 27 COMIX 178, 14.3.2003.

Presidency Note, Integrating migration issues in the European Union's relations with third countries, Part II: Report on the effectiveness of financial resources available at Community level for repatriation of immigrants and rejected asylum seekers, for management of external borders and for asylum and migration projects in third countries, Council doc. 6731/03 JAI 55 RELEX 75 ASIM 14 FIN 87, 24.2.2003.

Note of the Spanish Delegation for a Proposal to set up a Cooperation Centre of EU external maritime borders, Council doc. 6445/03 FRONT 14 COMIX 105, 17.2.2003.

Council of the European Union, EU Schengen Catalogue – Schengen Information System SIRENE: Recommendations and Best Practices, December 2002.

Final Report of Working Group X "Freedom, Security and Justice", CONV 426/02.

Operational programme of the Council for 2003 submitted by the Greek and Italian Presidencies, Council doc. 15881/02 POLGEN 83, 20.12.2002.

Appointment of the Migration and Expulsion Working Party as the responsible body for assistance and consultations to the Commission in relation to the negotiation of readmission agreements, Council doc. 15649/02 MIGR 134, 13.12.2002.

Proposal for a Return Action Programme, Council doc. 14673/02 MIGR 125 FRONT 135 VISA 172, 25.11.2002.

Afghanistan return plan, Council doc. 14654/02 MIGR 124 RELEX 248, 25.11.2002.

Council Conclusions on the improvement of the Immigration Liaison Officers Network, Council doc. 14464/02 CIREFI 69 FRONT 134 COMIX 659, 20.11.2002.

Draft Council Conclusions on intensified cooperation on the management of migration flows with third countries, Council doc. 13894/02 ASIM 47 RELEX 227, 14.11.2002.

Outcome of proceedings of the Visa Working Party, Council doc. 13660/02 VISA 157 COMIX 616, 31.10.2002.

Presidency Note on Meetings between Member States' return practitioners, Council doc. 13541/02 MIGR 106, 29.10.2002.

Integration of third country nationals – Draft Council conclusions, Council doc. 12492/02 MIGR 85, 1.10.2002.

Outcome of proceedings of the Visa Working Party, Council doc. 11503/02 VISA 120 COMIX 485, 14.8.2002.

Presidency Note on Road Map for the follow-up to the conclusions of the European Council in Seville – Asylum, Immigration and border control, Council doc. 10525/2/02 REV 2 JAI 152 ASILE 35 MIGR 63 FRONT 64 VISA 107, 31.7.2002.

Presidency Note, Initiation of the creation of network of liaison officers envisaged by the Plan for the management of the external borders of the Member States of the European Union, Council doc. 10917/02, FRONT 69 CIREFI 42 COMIX 452, 11.7.2002.

Communication from Denmark concerning implementation in Danish law pursuant to Article 5 of the Protocol on the position of Denmark, Council doc. 9963/02 VISA 97 FRONT 57 COMIX 397, 20.6.2002.

Plan for the management of the external borders of the Member States of the European Union, Council document 10019/02 FRONT 58 COMIX 398, 14.6.2002.

Proposal for a Comprehensive Plan to combat illegal migration and trafficking of human beings in the European Union, OJ C 142/23, 14.6.2002.

Council Conclusions on measures to be applied to prevent and combat illegal immigration and smuggling and trafficking in human beings by sea and in particular on measures against third countries which refuse to cooperate with the European Union in preventing and combating these phenomena, Council doc. 10017/02 JAI 142 RELEX 122 MIGR 57, 14.6.2002.

Request by Liechtenstein to be "associated with the Schengen acquis and the Dublin Convention, at the same time as Switzerland", Council doc. 10024/02 AELE 14 JAI 145 13.6.2002.

Modification of the terms of reference of the High Level Working Group on Asylum and Migration (HLWG), Council doc. 9433/02 JAI 109AG 20 ASIM 18, 30.5.2002.

Draft Council Conclusions – Criteria for the identification of third countries with which new readmission agreements need to be negotiated, Council doc. 7990/02 COR 1 MIGR 32, 16.4.2002.

Structure and number of JHA working parties and JHA activities other than legislative work (reports, evaluations etc.), Council doc. 6582/1/02 JAI 29 REV 1, 1.3.2002.

Council of the European Union, EU Schengen Catalogue – External border control, Removal and Readmission: Recommendations and Best Practices, February 2002.

Forced repatriation of people who do not fulfil entry or residence conditions – Draft Conclusions, Council doc. 6071/02 MIGR 8, 7.2.2002.

Letter of the Permanent Representative of Ireland to the President of the Council concerning the Irish opt in to the Proposal for a Council Directive on the conditions for entry and residence of third-country nationals for the purpose of paid employment and self-employed economic activities, Council doc. 5084/02 MIGR 1, 8.1.2002.

Article 36 Committee Note on Triggering of checks at internal borders, Council doc. 14181/1/01 ENFOPOL 134, 30.11.2001.

Outcome of proceeding of the Working Party on EFTA – Switzerland – possible association with the Schengen acquis and the Dublin Convention after the model of Iceland and Norway, Council doc. 14637/01 AELE 22 JAI 157 JUR 357, 28.11.2001.

Communication from Denmark concerning implementation in Danish law pursuant to Article 5 of the Protocol on the position of Denmark, Council doc. 14261/01 FRONT 67 COMIX 749, 23.11.2001.

Communication from Denmark concerning implementation in Danish law pursuant to Article 5 of the Protocol on the position of Denmark, Council doc. 14241/01 VISA 136 FRONT 66 COMIX 748, 23.11.2001.

Council preparatory bodies, Council doc. 14132/01 POLGEN 32, 16.11.2001.

Outcome of proceeding of the Visa Group meeting on the Draft Council Regulation on the adaptation of Part VII and Annex 12 of the Common Consular Instructions and Annex 14a of the Common Manual, Council doc. 12796/01 VISA 116 COMIX 673, 16.10.2001.

Working methods in the JHA area, Council doc. 10336/01, JAI 66, 26.6.2001.

EU-Switzerland relations, Council doc. 9524/01 AELE 13 JAI 62 FISC 116 AGRI 137, 18.6.2001.

UK Delegation Note on the Implementation of Schengen in UK, Council doc. 8913/01 SIS 50 COMIX 374, 17.5.2001.

I/A Note – Adoption of Council conclusions concerning the creation of national immigration liaison officers to help control illegal migration flows through the Western Balkan region, Council doc. 8684/01 CIREFI 31 COMIX 344, 10.5.2001.

High Level Working Group on Asylum and Migration – Adoption of the report to the European Council in Nice, Council doc. 13993/00 + ADD 1 JAI 152 AG 76, 29.11.2000.

Adoption of a Council Regulation concerning the establishment of "Eurodac" for the comparison of fingerprints for the effective application of the Dublin Convention, Council doc. 12314/00 ADD 1 COR 1, 6.12.2000.

Guidelines of the Council Legal Service for Member States' initiatives within the framework of Title IV and Part II of the TEC and Title VI of the TEU, SN 3606/2/00, 26.10.2000.

European Union priorities and policy objectives for external relations in the field of Justice and Home Affairs, Council doc. 7653/00 JAI 35, 6.6.2000.

"Recommendations for Council Decisions authorizing the Commission to negotiate re-admission agreements between the European Community and Sri Lanka, Morocco, Pakistan, Russia – 'Schengen relevancy'", 6720/00 MIGR 25, 6.3.2000.

Initiative of the Republic of Finland with a view to the adoption of a Council Regulation determining the obligations as between Member States for the readmission of third-country nationals, Council doc. 5599/00 MIGR 9 COMIX 85, 24.1.2000.

Council decision on the inclusion of model readmission clauses in Community agreements and in agreements between the European Community, its Member States and third countries, Council doc. 13409/99 MIGR 69, 25.11.1999.

Draft initiative of the Republic of Finland with the view to the adoption of a Council Regulation on airport transit arrangements, Council doc. 10867/1/99 REV 1 VISA 61 COMIX 224, 8.10.1999.

Letter to third countries concerning the use of standard travel documents for the expulsion of third country nationals, Council doc. 7665/99 MIGR 27, 26.4.1999.

Responsibilities of Council bodies in the field of justice and home affairs following entry into force of the Treaty of Amsterdam, Council doc. 6166/2/99 CK4 12 REV 2, 16.3.1999.

Action Plan of the Council and the Commission on how best to implement the provisions of the Treaty of Amsterdam on an Area of Freedom, Security and Justice (Vienna Action Plan), OJ C 19/1, 23.1.1999.

Terms of reference of the High Level Working Group on Asylum and Migration, Preparation of Action Plans for the most important countries of origin and transit of asylum seekers and migrants, Council doc. 5264/2/99 REV 2 JAI 1 AG 1, 22.1.1999.

Council Resolution of 18 December 1997 laying down the priorities for cooperation in the field of justice and home affairs for the period from 1 January 1998 to the date of entry into force of the Treaty of Amsterdam, OJ C 11/1, 15.1.1998.

Conclusions of the Council of 22 June 1984 concerning a Community medium-term social action programme, OJ C 175/1, 4.7.1984.

E. Other sources

1. House of Commons Reports

House of Commons, House Affairs Committee, *Identity Cards*, Fourth Report of Session 2003-04, available at http://www.statewatch.org.

2. House of Lords Reports

House of Lords, *Correspondence with Ministers June 2004 to February 2005,* EU Committee 4th Report, 2005-6 Session, London, 6 September 2005.

House of Lords, *Evidence by Commissioner Franco Frattini, Commissioner for Justice, Freedom and Security on Justice and Home Affairs Matters,* EU Committee 1st Report, 2005-6 Session, London, 13 June 2005.

House of Lords, *Proposals for a European Border Guard,* EU Twenty-Ninth Report, 2002-3 Session, London, 10 July 2003.

House of Lords, *Correspondence with the Ministers*, Select Committee on European Union Sixth Report, Session 2000-2001, London, 27 July 2001.

House of Lords, *A Community Immigration Policy,* Thirteenth Report, 1999-2000 Session, London, 3 April 2001.

House of Lords, *UK Participation in the Schengen acquis*, Select Committee on European Union Fifth Report, Session 2000, London, 15 February 2000.

House of Lords, *Schengen and the United Kingdom's Border Controls,* European Communities Select Committee Seventh Report, Session 1998-99, London, 10 March 1999.

House of Lords, *Delegation of powers to the Commission : reforming Comitology*, Select Committee on the European Union Third Report, Session 1998-99, London, 2 February 1999.

House of Lords Report, *Incorporating the Schengen acquis into the EU*, Select Committee on European Union Thirty-First Report, Session 1997-98, London, 28 July 1998.

3. Statewatch Documents

"Biometric ID documents herald a global identification system", *Statewatch*, Vol. 13, No 3/4, May-July 2003, p. 1.

"EU : buffer states & 'processing' centres", *Statewatch,* Vol. 13, No 2, March-April 2003, p. 1-2.

"EU: Mass deportations by Charter flight – enforcement and resistance", *Statewatch,* Vol. 13, No 2, March-April 2003, p. 19-21.

"The birth of the EU's Interior Ministry?", *Statewatch,* Vol. 13, No 1, January-February, 2003, p. 21.

'Schengen: Ireland follows UK opt-in', *Statewatch*, Vol. 10, No 3/4, June-August 2000, p. 3-4.

"Gibraltar: status resolved", *Statewatch*, Vol. 10, No 2, March-May 2000, p. 23.

"Globalising immigration controls", *Statewatch*, Vol. 9, No 5, September-October 1999, p. 29-31.

"The history of Tampere: an undemocratic process excluding civil society", *Statewatch*, Vol. 9, No 5, September-October 1999, p. 1-3.

"Schengen: UK given rough ride", *Statewatch*, Vol. 9, No 5, September-October 1999, p. 25-26.

"Tampere: A victory for "spin" over content?", *Statewatch*, Vol. 9, No 5, September-October 1999, p. 27-29.

"Switzerland: Treaties with Schengen countries", *Statewatch*, Vol 9 no 3 & 4, May-August 1999, p. 29-30.

"Norway joins Schengen", *Statewatch*, Vol. 9, No 2, March-April 1999, p. 7-8.

"Switzerland: Treaties with Schengen countries", *Statewatch*, Vol. 9, No 3 & 4, May-August 1999, p. 29-30.

"Switzerland: Into Schengen by back door?", *Statewatch*, Vol. 8, No 1, January-February 1998, p. 4.

4. Justice reports

"The Schengen Information System – A human rights audit", Justice Report, London, 2000.

"The Jurisdiction of the European Court of Justice in respect of Asylum and Immigration matters, Human Rights and the EU Intergovernmental Conference 1996-7", Justice, London, May 1997.

5. NGO contributions

"Migration and Development: Preliminary observations by NGOs active in the migration, refugee protection and the development field on the European Commission's Communication on "Integrating Migration Issues in the European Union's Relations with Third Countries", COM (2002) 703 final of 3 December 2002 [paper provided by Caritas Europa, Brussels].

6. *News Reports*

(a) EU Institutions

European Commission Press Release, "Policy Plan on Legal Migration", MEMO/05/494, 21.12.2005.

"EU-Switzerland reach number of agreements at first joint summit", Irish Presidency Press Release of 19.5.2004, www.eu2004.ie.

'INTI – Integration of third country nationals', <http://europa.eu.int/comm/justice_home/funding/inti/funding_inti_en.htm>.

"Commission says immigration cannot correct the effects of Europe's ageing population", IP/02/774, 29.5.2002.

'A Network of independent experts to assess the safeguarding of fundamental rights by the European Union Member States', <http://europa.eu.int/comm/justice_home/cfr_cdf/index_en.htm>.

(b) Agence Europe

"EU/JHA/LEGAL IMMIGRATION: Commission unveils "Policy Plan on Legal Migration" with aim of attracting highly qualified workers – Importance of integrating immigrants", *Bulletin Quotidien Europe* No 9095, 22.12.2005.

"EP/JHA/ASYLUM: EP in favour of extending "Dublin II" and "Eurodac" regulations to Denmark and concluding a Protocol with Iceland and Norway", *Bulletin Quotidien Europe* No 9093, 20.12.2005.

"EU/EUROMED: Barcelona Summit adopts code of conduct for fight against terrorism, five year working plan and "declaration of President", *Bulletin Quotidien Europe* No 9077, 29.11.2005.

"EU/INFORMAL SUMMIT/IMMIGRATION: Member States unanimously support Franco-Spanish project at Hampton Court – Franco Frattini continuous tour of Euro-Mediterranean capitals", *Bulletin Quotidien Europe* No 9059, 29.10.2005.

"Special Edition for Nice European Council (7,8 & 9 December 2000)", *Bulletin Quotidien Europe*, No 7860, 12 December 2000.

"EU/Institutional reform: Nice Treaty must respect balance between Member States, says Barnier, hoping Commission would have role to play in enhanced co-operation under second pillar also – Commission willing to contribute with Presidency to "post Nice" debate", *Bulletin Quotidien Europe*, No 7858, 7 December 2000.

"EU/IGC/Germany: Schroeder confirms he is open to restricted Commission and keen on unanimity on asylum issues", *Bulletin Quotidien Europe*, No 7847, 23 November 2000.

"EU/Institutional reform: informal meeting of Vimont group will examine summary document covering all issues from IGC, except those concerning Commission and weighting of votes in Council", *Bulletin Quotidien Europe*, No 7835, 4 November 2000.

"EU/Institutional reform: Luxembourg Memorandum" (Benelux Memorandum), *Bulletin Quotidien Europe*, No 7832, 31 October 2000.

"EU/Institutional reform: Moscovici gives details in France's position", *Bulletin Quotidien Europe*, No 7829, 26 October 2000.

"EU/European Council of Biarritz: Following an initial discussion between Heads of State or Government on institutional reform, Pierre Moscovici hoped that "the Biarritz spirit" was "the will to succeed ambitiously Nice", *Bulletin Quotidien Europe*, No 7820, 14 October 2000.

"EU/Institutional reform: At IGC, still "too much deadlock", says Barnier, announcing that Commission is prepared to play role in preparing post-Nice", *Bulletin Quotidien Europe*, No 7812, 4 October 2000.

(c) Other news reports

"Commission pushes ahead with EU green card scheme", <www.euobserver.com>, 22.12.2005.

"No EU air data to US, says top judge", <www.euobserver.com>, 22.11.2005.

"EU leaders back Franco-Spanish migrant plan", <www.euobserver.com>, 28.10.2005.

"EU asylum policy passed on to Summit", <www.euobserver.com>, 26.10.2005.

"Amnesty criticises Spain over Mellila", <www.euobserver.com>, 7.10.2005.

"Brussels seek to sooth nerves on data exchange", <www.euobserver.com>, 5.10.2005.

"Migrant clashes expose EU shortcomings", <www.euobserver.com>, 4.10.2005.

"Terror at the top of the UK presidency agenda", <www.euobserver.com>, 15.7.2005.

"Malta calls for EU help on illegal migration", <www.euobserver.com>, 11.7.2005.

"Charter flights to deport illegal immigrants", <www.euobserver.com>, 6.7.2005.

"G-5 meeting marked by immigration split", <www.euobserver.com>, 12.5.2005.

"Parlement européen: les convictions morales de Buttiglione", *Figaro*, 6.10.2004.

"Rocco Buttiglione devant le Parlement européen", *La Croix*, 6.10.2004.

"Italian Commissioner struggles to beat off criticism" <www.euobserver.com>, 5.10.2004.

'Amnesty criticizes EU states for violating human rights', <www.euobserver.com>, 25.7.2004.

'German immigration law favours highly skilled foreigners', <www.euobserver.com>, 15.7.2004.

'Big five meet to discuss security issues', <www.euobserver.com>, 6.7.2004.

'Parliament supports legal action over EU-US data deal', <www.euobserver.com>, 20.6.2004.

'Parliament set to challenge EU-US data deal in court', <www.euobserver.com>, 16.6.2004.

'Five EU states move ahead on anti-terror fight', <www.euobserver.com>, 8.6.2004.

"Switzerland inches closer to EU as President hails a 'new era", <www.euobserver.com>, 19.5.2004.

'Russia presses for first moves towards visa free travel', <www.euobserver.com>, 18.5.2004.

'EU agrees fund for return of illegal immigrants', <www.euobserver.com>, 23.1.2004.

'L'elite europea si chiama g5', at invetati.org, 27.10, 2003, <http://www.invetati.org/mailman/publi/borderzerolist/2003-October/000471.html>.

'EU: New 'G-5' group of Interior Ministers meet for second time in France', <http://statewatch.org/news/2003/oct/23g5.htm>.

'Les propositions du G5 à la Baule: pour une meilleure sécurité en Europe', Press Release of the French Ministry of Interior, 22.10.2003, <http://www.interieur.gouv.fr>.

'Les G5 prend des mesures contre le terrorism et l'immigration clandestine', Le Monde.fr, 20.10.2003, <http//www.lemonde.fr>.

'EU's "G5" discuss fight against terrorism, immigration', Euractive.com, 19.10.2003, <http://eubusiness.com/afp/031019103213.px2r95i4>.

'Bilan des actions de coopération internationale', Audition du Ministre devant la Commission des Affaires étrangères de l'Assemblée Nationale sur les actions de cooperation internationale en matière de lutte contre le terrorism et l'immigration illégale, 11.2.2004, available at the website of the French Interior Ministry, <http://www.interieur.gouv.fr>.

"Les Quinze ne sanctionneront pas les pays d'émigration illégale", Le Monde.fr, 22.6.2002.

Index

D

E

F

G

H

I

J

L

M

N

P

Q

R

S

T

Immigration and Asylum Law and Policy in Europe

1. E. Guild and P. Minderhoud (eds.): *Security of Residence and Expulsion.* 2000
ISBN 90-411-1458-0
2. E. Guild: *Immigration Law in the European Community*. 2001
ISBN 90-411-1593-5
3. B. Melis: *Negotiating Europe's Immigration Frontiers*. 2001
ISBN 90-411-1614-1
4. R. Byrne, G. Noll and J. Vedsted-Hansen (eds.): *New Asylum Countries?* Migration Control and Refugee Protection in an Enlarged European Union. 2002
ISBN 90-411-1753-9
5. K. Groenendijk, E. Guild and P. Minderhoud (eds.): *In Search of Europe's Borders*. 2003
ISBN 90-411-1977-9
6. J. Niessen and I. Chopin (eds.): *The Development of Legal Instruments to Combat Racism in a Diverse Europe.* 2004
ISBN 90-04-13686-X
7. B. Bogusz, R. Cholewinski, A. Cygan and E. Szyszczak (eds.): *Irregular Migration and Human Rights: Theoretical, European and International Perspectives.* 2004
ISBN 90-04-14011-5
8. H. Battjes: *European Asylum Law and International Law*. 2006
ISBN 90-04-15087-7
9. Elspeth Guild and Paul Minderhoud (eds.): *Immigration and Criminal Law in the European Union: The Legal Measures and Social Consequences of Criminal Law in Member States on Trafficking and Smuggling in Human Beings*. 2006
ISBN 90-14-15064-1
10. Georgia Papagianni: *Institutional and Policy Dynamics of EU Migration Law.* 2006
ISBN 90-04-15279-2
11. Elspeth Guild and Anneliese Baldaccini (eds.): *Terrorism and the Foreigner: A Decade of Tension around the Rule of Law in Europe*. 2006
ISBN 90-04-015187-7
12. Steve Peers and Nicola Rogers (eds.): *EU Immigration and Asylum Law: Text and Commentary*. 2006
ISBN 90-04-15374-8

Martinus Nijhoff Publishers – Leiden • Boston